THE NEW ZEALAND FAMILY FROM 1840

THE NEW ZEALAND FAMILY FROM 1840

A DEMOGRAPHIC HISTORY

Ian Pool, Arunachalam Dharmalingam and Janet Sceats

AUCKLAND UNIVERSITY PRESS

*This book is dedicated to the late Dr E. G. Jacoby, who in the 1950s
pioneered the cohort analysis of family formation in New Zealand
and contributed significantly to this field internationally, and to
Dr Miriam Vosburgh, whose research in the 1960s opened up the
field of family demographic surveys in New Zealand.*

First published 2007

Auckland University Press
University of Auckland
Private Bag 92019
Auckland
New Zealand
www.auckland.ac.nz/aup

ISBN 978 1 86940 357 7

Publication is assisted by the History Group, Ministry for Culture and Heritage

National Library of New Zealand Cataloguing-in-Publication Data
Pool, D. Ian (David Ian)
The New Zealand family from 1840 : a demographic history / by
Ian Pool, Arunachalam Dharmalingam and Janet Sceats.
Includes bibliographical references and index.
ISBN 978-1-86940-357-7
1. Family demography—New Zealand—History.
I. Dharmalingam, A. II. Sceats, Janet. III. Title.
306.850993—dc 22

Cover image: *The Family: The Beginning of Survival,* by Edward Bullmore,
courtesy of the owners and copyrightholder.
Cover design: Spencer Levine, Base Two

Printed by South Wind Productions, Singapore

CONTENTS

PART THREE: TOWARDS A SYNTHESIS

CHAPTER TEN: CONCLUSION: CONTINUITY AND CHANGE,
PARALLELISM AND POLARISATION

LIST OF TABLES

LIST OF FIGURES

LIST OF ABBREVIATIONS

ARTs	assisted reproductive technologies
CBR	crude birth rate
ECE/FFS	Economic Commission for Europe/Family and Fertility Study
ESCAP	United Nations Economic and Social Commission for Asia and the Pacific
ESCs	English-speaking countries
GAR	general abortion rate
GFR	general fertility rate
GRR	gross reproduction rate
LAT	living apart together
MGFR	marital general fertility rate
MTFR	marital total fertility rate
NZFFS	New Zealand Fertility and Family Survey
NZW:FEE	New Zealand Women: Family, Employment and Education Survey
NRR	net reproduction rate
STDs	sexually transmitted diseases
TAR	total abortion rate
TFR	total fertility rate
WDCs	Western developed countries

PREFACE

Family life is at the core of both personal and societal well-being. We are all part of at least one family, and to that extent everyone is an expert on family life and has their views on what is happening to it. They may or may not agree with our interpretations of changes over time, but we hope that all readers will find, as we did, resonance with their own family histories in the story we have told here.

This book covers a range of years, and many seemingly different situations. But it does so with a particular objective in mind: to see whether or not there are continuities as well as discontinuities in family patterns and behaviours. After all, we cannot argue that a particular period is unique, or without significant antecedents, unless we have eliminated that possibility.

To our surprise, however, echoes of the past are still seen not just in ideologies that make their way into policy, but in family dynamics and morphologies and in value systems. The latter phenomena are not just the enduring, global values that almost all societies apply to their family systems – the bearing and rearing of children, and their role as any society's glue – but also some that are much more culturally specific. This means that, as the story of the New Zealand family unfolds, we must compare and contrast periods in the past with those that are the focus of a particular period, requiring us to repeat seminal points, or to cross-refer to earlier or later sections of the book.

What also shows up in our analysis is that the New Zealand family is far from place bound: historically it consisted of a unit that had been severed from its roots in some other country and then come to rest here. For generations of Pakeha New Zealanders, 'home' for many families was Britain, and this sometimes involved the maintenance of close ties with the 'mother country'. Many New Zealanders will have etched in their minds the memory of food parcels being prepared for distant relatives in war-beleaguered Britain. This link has been more difficult, however, to continue for the minority of long-established Pakeha families from some other 'sources' – for example Huguenot, Jewish, German, Scandinavian, Chinese, Indian and Dalmatian. But this is not just a Pakeha phenomenon: Maori New Zealanders will often cite the places the Pakeha 'side' of their family come from, and, with the benefits of belonging to a society that has a special role for genealogy, sometimes have a more accurate knowledge of their British and other overseas relatives than do some Pakeha.

Today of course this disjunction has been magnified as the linkages now go in two directions. There are the relatives left behind in Britain, or Polynesia and elsewhere in the Pacific, or India, or China, or South Africa, or Canada, or wherever, especially for recent migrant waves. But equally there are connections to be maintained in the opposite direction with the members of the New Zealand diaspora living overseas. To enrich this, often through marriage these expatriates have become members of families in a multitude of other societies that were barely represented, if at all, in the cultural make-up of pre-1980 New Zealand.

This book concentrates on the more manifest aspects of family life, particularly the way in which families are formed and dissolve. We do not deal in depth with more intimate dynamics as these are likely to be time and situation bound, and unique to a particular family unit, whereas we are interested in broad trends followed on average by New Zealand families, or by the 'average' family in various sub-populations. In any case representative data on these inter-personal aspects of family life are not available, and even if they were they are probably reported on better by novelists and dramatists than by academics.

Because of the tremendous interest in the family, we hope that this book reaches a wide audience. But we also want to provide a rigorous scientific analysis of a topic that is often experienced and dealt with subjectively. Thus we have drawn very heavily on demographic methodologies that are used internationally to analyse the morphologies of families, both in their historical and contemporary forms. Our documentation is typically quantitative, presented in tables and graphs, rather than referring to expository and other qualitative evidence. Many of the quantitative data sources are already published and in the public domain, and thus we can follow the normal scholarly conventions simply by referring to these sources so that the interested reader can turn to them. But some sources do not already exist in this form, and thus we are publishing on the web a separate study. It consists in part of detailed tables and time-series computed from official statistics, but typically not assembled previously in published form in this systematic way. Additionally, we publish in the web study data that come from survey analyses, almost all of which are from studies we have directed. These tables are in *A Demographic History of the New Zealand Family From 1840: Tables*, and can be accessed at www.auckland.ac.nz/uoa/ aup/nzfamily/tables.cfm.

Superficially, the family is an institution about which there is shared conventional wisdom – everybody knows what it is, has experienced it and assumes that the concepts they apply are the same as those of most other people. In day-to-day discussions this probably is a fair operating principle, but even then people slip backwards and forwards between using the word to mean a nuclear unit, and their wider family of uncles, aunts, cousins and so on. In New Zealand, moreover, the word whanau may not mean the same as family, yet both are used almost interchangeably. Thus in reality there is no common understanding of what a family and/or household is. This raises problems for the social analyst – and even more for the policy maker – so that some attempt must be made to provide working definitions for the phenomena being studied here.

In this preface and throughout this book, we favour the word 'Pakeha' to describe that majority New Zealand population which is primarily of European origin, but resident in this country. We avoid the the word 'European' as it is inherently ambiguous, conflating both resident New Zealanders of European origin, for whom the term 'European-origin New Zealanders' would be a very clumsy phrase, with people actually living in Europe, some of whom may not be of 'European-ethnicity' (e.g. Bangladeshi minorities in Britain). We also avoid the term 'white' or the pseudo-scientific word 'Caucasian', both of which have racist connotations. For much of the period covered by this book Pakeha were, of course, virtually the only non-Maori population co-residing with Maori, and even today Pakeha constitute the overwhelming majority of non-Maori. Where statistically it is necessary to dichotomise into Maori and non-Maori components we will make that clear, recognising that this latter category includes growing numbers of Asians and Pacific peoples, including Cook Island Maori.

We set the scene for our empirical analysis and lay out our major themes in Chapters One and Two, but, in turn, they are backed up technically by a more academic analysis in another web-based study, *Studying the New Zealand Family: Analytical Frameworks, Concepts, Methodologies, Databases and Knowledge Bases*, by Ian Pool, Arunachalam Dharmalingam, Janet Sceats and Susan Singley, www.auckland.ac.nz/uoa/aup/nzfamily/studyingthenzfamily.cfm. To provide a more theoretical context for the New Zealand analyses reported in this book and to ensure that we are addressing issues that are of significance internationally, this web appendix also makes a detailed cross-comparative study of the results of family demographic and sociological research, and the data sources available to scholars overseas. As in the present book, this web appendix focuses on the more manifest features of family life and not on the social-psychological literature, although in both cases the importance of the roles played by underlying values, norms and mores is implicit in the analysis. Susan Singley, with state-of-the-art knowledge of American family sociology and demography, played an instrumental part in the preparation of Chapter Three in the web-based study. The bibliography in the present book also covers sources referred to in the web-based analysis.

The story of ordinary New Zealanders that unfolds here is one that we found fascinating. We hope that readers join in our enthusiasm. Above all, we came away with a sense of admiration for the way in which families function, adapt and endure. We feel privileged to have been able to record their lives, and the histories of their predecessors in New Zealand.

Ian Pool, Arunachalam Dharmalingam, Janet Sceats
HAMILTON AND MELBOURNE, FEBRUARY 2007

ACKNOWLEDGEMENTS

In writing a book as long as this one and covering such a span of periods it is necessary to consult with many different people and to search for data or references from diverse sources. Inevitably, we will have overlooked thanking someone who helped us in this process, and in some cases the names will be too many to acknowledge – the contacts in various statistical agencies (listed in the bibliography under unpublished sources), or the many historians with whom we have had informal but focused conversations. This is, therefore, firstly a *mea culpa* to those people for not individually acknowledging their support. In the same vein we wish to thank the anonymous peer reviewer of our first draft. Their comments were very helpful and we hope their reward comes in seeing the final product, which often reflects their suggestions. There are other people, however, who have been very gracious towards us and whose support must be acknowledged.

This book grew, many times over like some rapidly expanding bacterium, out of a report on recent family trends commissioned by the Ministry of Social Development and written by Portal Consulting and Associates Ltd. We acknowledge the Ministry's role in initiating this project and in the stimulus this gave us to expand its horizons temporally and hugely in length, in terms of coverage of issues and in the development of a robust evidence base, drawing on both statistical and expository data.

In the preface we have acknowledged the role of Susan Singley, an independent consultant, who is a co-author of the web-published *Studying the New Zealand Family: Analytical Frameworks, Concepts, Methodologies, Data-bases and Knowledge Bases*. Her inputs go far further than this brief comment might suggest, as she was a co-author of the report to the Ministry of Social Development, especially the chapter on New Zealand's knowledge base, and our major knowledge gaps. This chapter was revised and expanded, as were some others, and appear in the web-based study. Susan played a very pro-active role in all of these undertakings, including setting up a framework by which the epistemology of the New Zealand family could be analysed systematically.

Jock Phillips and his colleagues at the Ministry for Culture and Heritage have been extraordinarily generous in sharing data on nineteenth-century migration flows. Sandra Baxendine and Bill Cochrane of the Population Studies Centre at the University of Waikato have given us technical support during the data analysis phases, while Bill Boddington, Robert Didham, who graciously shared results of his ongoing analysis of 2006 census data, and Mansoor Khawaja of Statistics New Zealand have provided us with data and have also made valuable comments on a range of issues relating to data quality. We benefited from discussions on urbanisation and housing issues with David Swain of Waikato University and David Thorns of Canterbury University, who also supplied a cross-national perspective, while Patrick Day, Waikato University, was most informative about colonial welfare regimes. The Population Studies Centre, University of Waikato, funded demographer-historian-sociologist Tahu Kukutai, a doctoral student at Stanford University, to assist us preparing the indexes. William Bolstad of the Statistic Department at the University of Waikato gave us authoritative advice on the advisability of using rank correlations.

Overseas, Tomas Frejka, a United States-based consultant, gave us very useful technical advice on a statistical transformation and Jean-Paul Sardon of the Institut National d'Études Démographiques provided us with data from the Observatoire Démographique Européenne. The Population Activities Unit of the United Nations Economic Commission for Europe accorded the Population Studies Centre associate membership in their Family and Fertility Study, which gave us access to their protocols, instruments and methodologies for our NZW:FEE and NZFFS, and cross-comparative data from Europe and North America. Victor Piché at the Université de Montreal and Rod Beaujot and Kevin McQuillan at the University of Western Ontario provided useful insights into Canadian fertility in general and québécoise in particular. Michael Haines of Colgate University gave us valuable information about American historical demography. Rebecca Kippen of the Australian National University shared with us her knowledge about Australian family demographic history.

The Cambridge Group for the History of Population twice hosted Ian Pool as visiting scholar, invited him to speak in their seminar series and gave him access to the rich resources of Cambridge University's library. This gracious gesture is very much appreciated, as it afforded him the opportunity to discuss many issues of nineteenth-century British demography with Richard Smith, Tony Wrigley, Simon Szreter, Leigh Shaw-Taylor, Eilidh Garrett, Alice Reid and Tom Nutt. Their information on the source populations of the British diaspora and their many authoritative publications have proven invaluable as background material for this book. Jim Oeppen, now at the Max Planck Institute, Rostock, was a mine of information and technical expertise about British demography.

Outside Cambridge, as will become clear from figures we produce later in the book, we drew very much on meetings with Robert Woods, Liverpool University, and on his book on nineteenth-century British demography. We owe a lot to him. Finally, the chance meeting at Cambridge with Stephanie Wyse, a New Zealander pursuing a PhD in London, provided us with as-yet-unpublished information about issues of gender and family wealth.

The Royal Society of New Zealand awarded Ian Pool a James Cook Fellowship during which much of the work that went into this book was carried out. Ian Pool would like to thank the late Michael King for encouraging him to apply for the fellowship and James Belich of the University of Auckland and R. Gerard Ward, an emeritus professor of geography at the Australian National University, who acted as his referees. During his incumbency Ian Pool and Janet Sceats visited centres in Italy and Spain that carry out specialist research on issues of low fertility, the transition towards which is a feature of the New Zealand demographic landscape. We are very grateful to Anna Cabre of the Autonomous University, Barcelona, and the numerous scholars we worked with at the statistics departments of the Universities of Florence and Padua who outlined the fertility regimes seen in Mediterranean countries: Franco Bonarini, Maria Castiglioni, Letizia Mencarini, Faustos Ongaro, Salvina Salvini and Gianpierro Dalla Zuanna. Much of the actual empirical analysis of New Zealand data was supported by grants, notably from the Foundation for Research Science and Technology.

Finally, we also wish to thank Auckland University Press, above all our editor, Anna Hodge, for her unending patience and for gracefully accepting wholesale exposure to demography in its rawer forms. AUP director Elizabeth Caffin first accepted the idea for this book and took it through its early gestational phases.

Ian Pool
Arunachalam Dharmalingam
Janet Sceats
HAMILTON AND MELBOURNE
FEBRUARY 2007

PART ONE: SETTING THE SCENE

CHAPTER ONE

The Ideal Family and its Enemies from 1840

1.1 ROLES, RESPONSIBILITIES AND RESTRAINTS

The historian Miles Fairburn entitled his seminal study on the foundations of modern New Zealand *The Ideal Society and its Enemies* (1989), a play on the title of philosopher Karl Popper's most influential book, *The Open Society and its Enemies.** The 'ideal society's' keystone is the family, as it has responsibilities and performs roles that are essential for the maintenance, cohesion and smooth functioning of any population. It engages in reproduction, the bearing and rearing of children. It is the most basic unit of social organisation, on which the rest of society is built. It is the locus for many economic activities, not only for the consumption and accumulation of assets but also, in more traditional societies, for production. As a result there is a great deal of interest in the family. Too often, however, simple concern turns into anxiety that the family is failing to meet these ideals. Frequently, this is because the family faces material and other restraints, so that its capacities are limited.

Because of its significance for the population, the society and the economy, the family is always a focus for policy debates between the way it fulfils its roles and responsibilities, and the restraints it faces. Such a tension was a central element in the emergence of the welfare state in the Western developed countries (WDCs) over the last 150–200 years, the time-span covered by this book. But during the most recent decades, the welfare state, and particularly family policy, has seen challenges that have arisen for both fiscal and ideological reasons. This has produced academic and popular disputations of a scale and intensity worthy of the Reformation. There have also been calls for the resurrection of Victorian strategies for social service delivery, the last vestiges of which had been discarded after World War II.

---

* Written, incidentally, when Popper was teaching at Canterbury University College, part of the University of New Zealand of that day.

The rationale for invoking the family welfare policies of the past is typically vested in arguments that the family of those days was more self-reliant, supported by community and kin networks, and that it was both more con-tented and more effective in meeting its responsibilities.

Of course, over the same period the family itself has undergone major changes, some of which have gained a very high profile in popular percep-tions, and others of which, regardless of their significance, are more latent. The changes seen in the last few decades may have taken the family into totally uncharted waters. To take the most critical example, childbearing, one can cite Kingsley Davis, among demography's more perceptive think-ers, who was already arguing as far back as 1987 'Never before in recorded history . . . has fertility* been so low for whole societies as it is now in the industrialised world' (1987: 48). Twenty years on the same low levels of fertility are still seen, so that if that situation was deemed a problem, then the crisis has become even more entrenched.

Simultaneously there have been changes in the living arrangements of households and in the ways that family statuses are formalised. Anxieties about the family's capacity to meet its roles and responsibilities are often attributed to these trends, especially to those that are more obvious. In turn trends, particularly those that are seen as family failure or the breakdown of the family and thus threats at least to the well-being of the wider society, are often viewed as deviating from those that are believed to have occurred in the good old days.

The 'good old days' are the central interest of this book, not just because these constitute an inherently fascinating topic of historical research, but also because there is an interest in what they tell us about the present. Much of what occurred in the past has been carried down to today through nos-talgia, and this source of what occurred back then is likely to be highly selective. We cannot even rely on genealogies for they might avoid less palatable facts; many families host and hide secrets, say about abortions or illegitimacy (or ex-nuptial childbearing, as it is correctly called). This extends to whakapapa for, in the view of Sissons, Wi Hongi and Hohepa, they are driven more by political contingencies than by statistical purity (1987: 149–50).

Selectivity may also come in the absence of guile, simply because of more deterministic processes. Nobody alive today comes from a childless union in the past and more people alive today come from the large families of nostalgia than from small families. Moreover, as non-Maori are recent

---

* Throughout this book conventional demographic terminology is used for words such as fertility (= live births). See Grebenik and Hill 1974; also Pool 1991: Glossary. For some curious reasons in English demography fertility and fecundity (innate capacity to reproduce) are the inverse of their use in biology, the health sciences and the Romance languages.

immigrants, unless they are enthusiastic genealogists they will often have gaps in their knowledge about their forebears. We share this deficit with many other neo-Europeans – Australians, Canadians and Americans. French Canadians are somewhat unusual in that the systematic and virtually universal data on baptisms, weddings and funerals in Catholic parish registers, linked by what are termed family reconstitution techniques, provide them with one of the fullest historical records – back to the seventeenth century – for any population anywhere. But no such data source is available to predominantly Protestant New Zealanders.

Beyond that, in many families the experiences in the 'old country' which led to migration were often so painful that they have been suppressed. For others who were semi-literate or illiterate communication with relatives abroad was impossible. In contrast, Maori not only employ whakapapa as an essential constituent of mapping social organisation, but they are like the villagers in 'Old Europe' whose family history is all around them. To add to this the Waitangi Tribunal investigations have performed another latent archival function for Maori: family histories have been documented in detail as a part of the process. A first function, then, of the research here is to document, to the extent that the existing data permit this to be done, what really did occur in the past so as to supplement nostalgic memory with fact, particularly for Pakeha (European-origin) and other more recent migrants.

New Zealanders see their collective identity as a migrant society, subject to population inflows that have determined its patterns of family and social behaviour. Certainly, these had been moulded by the large-scale movements of Pakeha into the country over the first 40 years of colonisation, during which the Maori demographic hegemony at the time of Waitangi (1840) was effectively replaced by a British-origin one. Over the last four decades of the twentieth century the dominance of Pakeha was then challenged by the rapid growth of the Maori population, and, more importantly, by its rapid influx to urban areas. This meant that for the first time since the New Zealand Wars, Maori and Pakeha were brought face to face in a very significant way. Hard on the heels of Maori urbanisation, New Zealand was to draw in arrivals from the Asian and Pasifika diasporas, and these also clustered in the cities, especially Auckland.

Migration then is the more obvious side of the collective memory of the New Zealand experience. But behind the scenes, as it were, other acts have been played out. Once the early influxes of Pakeha settlers had arrived, migration was no longer the prime determinant of population growth. Instead it was the capacity of the colonists and their descendants born in New Zealand to procreate. There was also the minor advantage that, at least for Pakeha (certainly not for Maori), levels of life expectancy were favourable. These two factors gave New Zealand higher levels of natural increase, which is the births minus the deaths, than were seen in most other industrialised countries. Over the twelve full decades from 1880 to 2000, natural increase was not only a more important factor than migration, but it far outstripped it in importance even in those decades when there were spikes of immigration in some years.

There is another aspect to this. From the arrival of Captain Cook in 1769 until the 1890s, Maori succumbed to the diseases introduced by Pakeha, so that their levels of natural increase were negative, a technically exact phrase for what seems a contradiction in terms. But from the early 1890s on, the growth in Maori numbers accelerated, entirely, of course, because of the excess of births over deaths and not through immigration. By the 1950s and 1960s their levels of natural increase, coming from high birth rates and declining death rates, especially from the 1940s to the 1960s, were among the highest seen anywhere and close to biological maxima (Pool 1991).

In sum, then, this book's subject matter, the family, is basic to an understanding of the establishment and maintenance of modern New Zealand society. These processes have been due primarily to fertility, as the main factor, with survivorship patterns (that allowed most Pakeha, and later most Maori, children to survive to parenting ages) in a supporting role, but not to migration. That said, however, a side plot is whether or not the representatives of the different diasporas, who laid down at least the foundations of New Zealand society, have followed the life-ways of their forebears in their countries of origin, or have forged something that is different and uniquely of New Zealand.

A demographic approach has an enormous advantage over most others in this regard, both in terms of research on the more evident family behaviours, such as births and marriages, and also in allowing an insight into some of the major contextual factors, such as migration. This is because the raw materials of population studies are statistics that should be universal in their coverage, and a first analytical step is always to assess how complete each data source is. Moreover, new methodologies developed to study Third World countries with incomplete data, a feature that held true for Maori until World War II, allow indirect estimates for many parameters of importance in this history (e.g. reproduction rates). To add to this, for a very long time, in many cases from before the period covered in this book, the instruments used to enumerate demographic data or to register vital events, such as births, have been standardised in terms of survey methodologies, content and even question design, and the construction of indices. In contrast, many of the normal sources of modern history, beyond the reach of the oral history surveys that are now in vogue, are likely to be selective, as they rely on the available evidence, typically in written form, and thus represent the experiences of the more literate. The use of population data has, however, essentially allowed historians to recreate the century of Mr and Mrs Everyman, and their families. In Europe and elsewhere this has been taken back several centuries. This does not provide in-depth information on social-emotional dynamics, for which traditional sources must be relied on, but it does produce representative results on family formation, forms and structures.

Demographic analytical strategies allow a multi-dimensional perspective on families. Most typically data on households, or family events such as births, will be reviewed at one time point, through cross-sectional analyses, as these are called. Comparisons over time of cross-sectional rates or percentages, between censuses or annually in the case of vital statistics (e.g. birth rates), allow an historical perspective or time-series, to use the technical term for these statistical analyses. To standardise these histories, normally data over time will be referenced to a particular life-cycle stage, such as childhood, youth, the adult ages or old age. In addition, some data collected using life-history approaches permit retrospective glimpses of family events.

Data collected using both cross-sectional and retrospective techniques can also be analysed for cohorts or generations. Cohorts are defined as groups of people who experience the same event at the same time point in the past. Most frequently they refer to people born in the same period, but in this book we also will look at marriage cohorts – people who marry at the same time. Cohorts can be followed over time, and as the members of the cohort pass through different life-cycle stages. This greatly enriches the quality of any analyses. For example, different cohorts of women can be compared so as to determine the ages at which they have their first and subsequent births, and the durations between these events. This information is basic to understanding how couples build their families, showing that these strategies vary over time and between generations. These changes have very significant implications for almost every aspect of social and economic life.

The approaches taken here – cross-sectional, time-series or cohort – provide a documentation of 'the everyday experience of the common people'. But they also allow us to go further than that to address another critical issue: 'the facts do not speak for themselves. To make sense they have to be interpreted; they are intelligible only if they are fitted into a pattern, related to some general principle' (Fairburn 1989: 10). Interpretation and fitting into a pattern is strengthened by the fact that over time, and between countries and regions, standardised and directly cross-comparable statistics are available. Furthermore, the body of analytical literature on the subjects covered in this book, especially in overseas countries, is vast, and thus comparison can be taken beyond statistical analysis and first-order interpretations into more powerful levels of explanation.

1.2 FAMILY VULNERABILITY AND MORAL PANICS

The perception that the family is 'under threat' or 'breaking down' is extremely widespread in New Zealand and in other WDCs. The WDCs are far from uniform in the way that they view the alleged erosion of family life, and thus there are also variations in the policy and regulatory responses to them. But, in all WDCs, concerns about the fate of the family have been driven by an empirically verifiable observation: everywhere there have been rapid changes in the morphology* of families – that is, their dynamics, forms and structures – although the exact mix has varied from WDC to WDC.

Many if not most commentators perceive that these changes in morphology have led to a reduction in the capacities of families to carry out their societal responsibilities. Again, however, there are major differences among WDCs in the mix of functions seen to be under threat. In some countries the focus is on reproduction and thus the maintenance of the population. In others it is the way the family performs its role as the social unit that is fundamental to the cohesion and wellbeing of the entire society. In New Zealand, as in most of the English-speaking countries (ESCs), it is this latter aspect that projects concern about the role of family out on to a much wider screen. In contrast, in Western Europe it is the dimension of childbearing, the replacement of the society, around which deep fears abound.

The depth of concern in New Zealand at the dawn of the new millennium is such that it could be fairly said that we are in the middle of one of the fluxes of 'moral panic' that arrive from time to time. In passing, it should be noted that this is not the first, and probably will not be the last of such anxiety attacks: the dawn of the twentieth century was heralded by one such chorus; the McMillan Committee in the 1930s responded to another; and, stimulated by naughty goings-on in a milk bar in the Hutt Valley, there was yet another commission, perhaps the most publicised, that reported in 1954 (the Mazengarb Commission). The most recent panic has again heralded in a new century. This outburst's most public manifestations have been the establishment of the Families Commission in 2004, and the active entry of diverse religious groups into the political arena in the 2005 election. But in New Zealand, probably more so than in most other WDCs, the recent debate about the family has taken place in a vacuum, in the absence of good evidence.

---

* The word morphology is borrowed from the biological sciences to describe all of dynamics, forms and structures. A distinction between forms and structures outlined below, where these terms are also defined, is essential to the overarching theme of this book.

Family vulnerability is not something that suddenly emerges without any antecedents. Family morphologies evolve over time, and at various periods are subject to different sorts of pressures, whether these are endogenous to the family as an institution, that is, of their own making, or exogenous, because of the effects of trends external to the family. In sum, the family at any time is an outcome of its history, of past patterns of family life and of the social and economic contexts in which they were played out. The prime function of this book is to sketch that story for New Zealand. We use the word 'sketch' advisedly, as we recognise that this book may well raise more questions for future research than it is able to answer definitively.

The wider context in which the family operates at any time may have its more obvious manifestations, such as a war or a depression or economic restructuring. But it may also have more diffused and less evident features that demographers and sociologists must attempt to identify and map, as these too may have major impacts on the family.

Statisticians often embellish their classes in statistics by a piece of seeming hyperbole: that while there is a strong correlation between the decrease in the size of the stork population in Denmark and declines in the British birth rate, this correlation is spurious. But Sir Maurice Kendall, the author of numerous works on multi-variate statistics, used to say (in-house seminars on statistics, World Fertility Survey, London 1975) that perhaps this relationship was not so spurious after all because trends in both were due to 'latent structural factors'. In this case these were the spread of urbanisation and with it a shift to apartment dwellings as the modal form of housing: apartment blocks lack chimneys and thus nesting spaces for storks, and equally they may not provide the type of housing that is conducive to young British couples deciding to go forth and multiply.

Stretching Kendall's argument a little further, one could argue that the destruction of the wetlands that so exacerbated the impact of, say, the 2005 hurricane Katrina in Louisiana, and the real crises hitting the family, may both be because of the massive shifts in patterns of social and economic development and the attendant pressures on the natural environment and on societies over recent decades. As early as 1937, Kingsley Davis was saying 'ultimately the reproduction of the species is not easily compatible with advanced industrial society' (cited in Caldwell and Schindlmayr 2003).

1.3 AN OVERARCHING THEME: FAMILY CHANGE AND FAMILY VULNERABILITY

This book's most important raw materials are those that are drawn on for much of literature, from Shakespeare at one extreme to TV soap operas at the other. The object of our research is also something about which almost every human being has experience and opinions. This makes our task rather daunting as every member of every society can see themselves – justifiably because of their personal histories – as having expertise on the subject this book addresses. The task is doubly daunting because the authors, like all other social scientists, are also members of families, the very same institutions that are the subjects of their scientific investigation. This is a factor that differentiates social researchers from other scientists. However passionate about their research materials, or however much they may show how important they are for human existence, most other scientists, say the vulcanologist or nanotechnologist, are emotionally positioned several standard deviations away from the phenomena they are researching.

To add to this, one can be certain that some commentators will probably disagree with our observations as these may well differ from their own views. But they should not forget that in many instances observed trends do differ from our personal experiences. The job here is not to report every permutation and quirk of family life, however fascinating they might be, for that is the task of the novelist, but simply to record the 'averaged-out' family experiences of members of New Zealand society at different periods. Wherever possible this will be supported with empirical evidence that can be verified by other researchers, and around which they can draw their own interpretations.

The theme this work addresses is how well families have met their responsibilities to the wider society, by propelling it along through the processes of childbearing and -rearing, by providing the glue that allows it to cohere socially, and permitting the economy to operate effectively by being its most basic unit of wealth accumulation and consumption. The flip side to this is whether at different periods the average family, or a substantial minority of families, have been rendered vulnerable, in some way or another, and thus less able to meet their obligations. The function of this book, then, is to analyse the trajectories, the genesis and the determinants of long-term historical changes in the family, looking at factors that might throw light on the functioning of families.

This involves research and not simply description, because it looks for the origins and causes of the patterns of family life and any indicators of vulnerability that may be evident in various eras. This then provides a base from which to identify the consequences for wider aspects of social organisation that may come from changes in the capacities of families. As an end product this process enriches the debates and evidence bases on the role of the family historically, and thus may contribute indirectly to the building of public policy in twenty-first-century New Zealand. In doing this it addresses a number of questions around the functioning and/or vulnerability of the family. The order in which they are approached in any chapter does not, however, necessarily follow that in which they are outlined here, where the basic thesis is being set out.

Nevertheless, before sketching out some questions relating to the book's major theme it is necessary to digress briefly. This is simply to give precision to the later discussions by subdividing the term family morphology into three possible constituents: *dynamics, forms* and *structures*. We recognise that this is a somewhat academic stratagem that flies in the face of everyday language usages where such distinctions are seldom made. Discourse in the 'real world' is in fact rather imprecise when it comes to describing different dimensions of family life. This is not sloppiness but simply because everybody involved probably understands what is being said, as they know the context and the actors concerned. But this imprecision creates semantic and other difficulties for analysts who have to abstract from this, and worse still attempt to measure elements of it, to convey these same things to third very distant parties without losing the true flavour of what they are documenting.

In day-to-day speech the words household and family are used almost interchangeably. Similarly in popular parlance the word home often conflates two concepts: family and house. The words parent and parenting are also employed ambiguously and in quite different contexts: to denote the act of childbearing and to refer to childrearing, when a person/couple is responsible for the material and emotional needs of dependent offspring. This dependence used to disappear in the late teenage years or at the twenty-first birthday party, but in the early 1990s it was extended legally in a number of domains to exact age 25 years. Beyond that, however, once one has children one retains the status parent for the rest of one's life, a status having greater or lesser real significance depending on circumstances. Moreover in common usage the term family itself can cover a range of forms and structures from those that might be subsumed in the wider Maori term whanau, right down to a young person using family to mean his/her parents 'back home', and possibly also their siblings. Researchers must be excused for adopting academic stratagems because they have to attempt to give precision to the imprecise without also destroying its essential character (Cameron 1985a elaborates on epistemological issues affecting the analysis of families and households in New Zealand).

These various terms will be defined in more detail in Chapter Two, but suffice to say here that *dynamics* relate to family interactions and interrelationships, of which the most important for this book is *family formation*, as the family accrues members and conversely as members leave or die. *Family forms* are statuses (e.g. married or cohabiting), the type of household and one's relationship to other members (e.g. child or parent), and *structures* relate to household sizes, when key events occur (e.g. parenting) and the geographical location of the household.

This book will examine the changes in family forms that typically take a high public profile, such as increases in cohabitation, ex-nuptial child-bearing and sole parenting. It should be recognised that these phenomena have often been attributed to mutations in values and norms that come from within, that are endogenous to, the family itself. Where such shifts in values, norms and behaviours are seen in a negative light, the family may be criticised as the architect of its own misfortune. In the policy arena this perspective shades off into ideologies, and often into policy measures that emphasise self-reliance and/or family responsibility rather than community or state support. These are certainly pervasive today, and have had a very long and enduring history in New Zealand, back to the 1840s and before that to the British Poor Laws.

The question to be examined here is whether these shifts in family forms have had more or less impact on family life than have changes in structures, notably the decreases in family size and the delaying of child-bearing. Trends in family structures have a lower public profile and less shock value, say in the media or in political discourse, than do changes in forms. Yet structural shifts may pose more of a threat to the very root stocks of societal maintenance, childbearing and -rearing, than do changes in form. Thus their impacts, one could postulate, are far more fundamental than are the changes in forms.

In their turn, changes in family structures are determined mainly by factors, including values and norms (and their more prescriptive counter-parts: mores and laws), that are external to the household, but typically that affect it by being transmitted through the intermediary processes of family formation. That is, major shifts in the way the society and economy are organised also produce changes in the way family life is ordered, particularly in terms of when and at what ages households engage in childbearing and -rearing (family formation). These dynamics in turn determine the sizes and age distributions, and other features of families.

Exogenous factors also have an impact on forms, but the key argument is that the structures will face the most significant impacts. These come from social and economic transformations, and even 'latent structural' factors, analogous to those that may simultaneously affect the stork population in Denmark and the British birth rate. Parenthetically, it should be noted that these relationships are not uni-directional. Changes in family dynamics, forms and structures in turn have a major impact on the society, and its economy and cultural life, and on both policy and markets.

In the ESCs there is a focus on high-profile changes in forms, by comparison with Western and Northern European countries where, in contrast, structural changes are emphasised (Pool and Sceats 2003). These divergent emphases impose strong and distinctly different imprints on the corpus of policies, laws and regulations in ESCs as against the *corpora* of other WDCs.

For example, in the ESCs there is an almost unhealthy concentration on what are deemed dysfunctional aspects of family life. 'Dysfunctionality' is often ascribed to wider household categories, such as sole-parent or father-less households, or to particular emblematic sub-populations. The wrath of some ESC commentators, and this is certainly the case in New Zealand, descends most forcefully on teenage mothers, who, although not quite an endangered species, face declining numbers, yet who, with the full force of hyperbole, are sometimes seen as among the leading threats to both national morality and fiscality.

In passing, one should note that the dialectic around adolescent pregnancy illustrates a far more important general point that, as noted, debates on the family often employ hyperbole. Those focusing on teenage child-bearing suffer particularly from this ill as they are frequently based on inaccurate, indeed even wildly inexact, statistics and a semantic confusion with ex-nuptial childbearing and sole parenting. For example, commentators will assert that New Zealand's levels for teenage childbearing are 'the highest in the world', although mercifully British Granada TV has pushed us aside and bagged this claim for Britain (programme TVOne, 20 October 2005). Both countries are, in fact, overshadowed by the United States in the WDCs, but in turn that nation falls far below Third World countries such as Malawi (about twice the level of the United States). The sobering truth is that in the area of the marketing of views on the family, and above all those that relate to policy, the rule of *caveat emptor* definitely applies.

Wherever possible a function of this book will be to attempt to divorce perception and hyperbole from reality. An historical perspective is particularly valuable in this regard. For example, to go back to the case in the last paragraph, twenty-first-century observers tend to overlook the fact that levels of teenage pregnancy were extremely high just a few short years ago, in the Baby Boom, but then were often due to pre-marital conceptions, frequently followed by a hasty wedding and thus by a marital birth. Moreover, many of the couples divorcing in the intervening years up to and including the early 2000s, when divorce rates caused much consternation, were people who had married at very young ages in the Baby Boom under those less than propitious circumstances.

This bias in ESC views on the family extends across to policy regimes that are seen to create welfare dependency. The ESCs have also gone further than other WDCs in market liberalisation and the institution of managerialist approaches to the culture of work, both of which have impacts on the family. According to the work of Canadian demographer Anne Gauthier (2002), one of the top scholars in this field, the ESCs are notable for welfare targeting and parsimony and have put in place extraordinary and costly case-management and monitoring systems. In Scandinavia or France, in contrast, benefits are likely to be universal and more realistic in dollar terms.

The analysis of the overarching theme, family change and family vulnerability, requires accepting some working assumptions:

(1)   that the family can be vulnerable, has been so historically and is so today;

(2)   that vulnerability is not just something that occurs in so-called dysfunctional families, whatever they might be, or in families that lack resilience, whatever that other buzzword in debates on the family might mean, but also that 'mainstream' or average New Zealand families, even the financially better off, are often very vulnerable;

(3)   that 'mainstream' families can be vulnerable when they face severe pressures on their capacities to meet their societal responsibilities (working a 70-hour week and frequently missing dinner with your family may affect childrearing as much as being on a benefit and unable to afford school trips for your children); and

(4)   that this vulnerability is determined by factors endogenous to the family itself, such as changes in norms, values, mores and psycho-social dynamics, as well as by those that are exogenous and constituting its milieu, such as the broader society, the culture to which it belongs, the economy and the policy environment.

It will be evident from this brief introduction that the focus of this book is on the family as an institution that performs critical roles and functions for the wider community. Above all, as we will show, it is trends in the function of societal replacement, of fertility, that have gone through wide fluctuations over the period covered here, and it is this aspect that will be emphasised. Before we embark on this analysis, however, it is important to stress the point that we view the family as something far more than a simple instrument that must meet obligations to the society as a whole, important as that may be. We recognise, moreover, that most of its quotidian dynamics are involved with other activities and tasks that revolve around the social and emotional welfare of family members and which are performed for the prime good of family members themselves, in ways that probably vary from household to household, and may well be unique to a particular family. But as collectivities the families of New Zealand, and of its various sub-populations, also on average demonstrate trends that are the raw materials of this book.

Our obligation is to document these macro-level trends which represent merely the more manifest, better recorded and more general aspects of the life of this institution; even if there were data available – and there are few – on the other aspects, on the intra-family dynamics, their analysis is not a central interest here. That said, it must be recalled that the sum of the individual families' behaviours are the trends we are reporting. As the dialect saying goes, 'many a mickle makes a muckle', and as statisticians might mimic this, 'many a micro makes a macro'. The macro-level is something more, however, than merely the sum of the micro-levels: there are also macro-level phenomena in their own rights – the shared values or norms that prescribe the behaviour of individuals across entire societies, and even across generations, is such an example.

1.4 ORIGINS OF NEW ZEALAND FAMILY BEHAVIOURS: OUTSOURCED OR IN-HOUSE?

The rapid and accelerating migration inflows from 1840 until the late 1870s of Pakeha mainly from the British Isles, along with the maintenance of a British Pakeha demographic hegemony from about 1870 until the 1970s, raise questions about the genesis and evolution of New Zealand family behaviours, values and norms. A first question, relating to the period until the 1970s, is: where did these come from? The answer to this would seem fairly obvious: the British Isles in the Victorian era. But this response may well be too simplistic, because the early New Zealand settlers seem to have had patterns of family formation that were different from those of their contemporaries in the 'old country'. Chapter Three will look at this issue in greater detail.

This difference would suggest that Pakeha settlers had either adopted new behaviours, or had adapted British behaviours to meet the new conditions they encountered in New Zealand. But again a seemingly simple answer may not reflect reality. Effectively until the 1970s British-origin Pakeha and Maori were virtually the only inhabitants of the country. From where, therefore, could such behaviours be adopted under the conditions of a British demographic hegemony? Even in the absence of reserve policies of the type seen in the United States or Canada, this hegemony still had the effect of squeezing Maori into the more isolated and rugged northern and eastern parts of the North Island, or into small enclaves elsewhere. It thus seems unlikely that Pakeha norms, values and behaviours would have been taken over from Maori. This is notwithstanding the fact that, even at this early stage, there were no legal barriers to intermarriage, or informal consensual relationships and other interactions, all of which were reasonably common occurrences.

Thus there is a need to look more closely at the sources of British migration. Inflows were highly selective and not representative of the British population at the time (McKinnon *et al.* 1997: 49). The question must be rephrased: were the behaviours, values and norms adopted by the early New Zealand colonists representative instead of the source regions in the British Isles from which migrants were disproportionately drawn?

There is an attendant question that may be more difficult to resolve: what is the degree to which Maori family patterns were affected by inter-marriage? At first this was mainly with Pakeha, but later was increasingly with Pacific peoples and Asians. Underlying this is yet another question, whether or not New Zealand has developed family forms and structures that are unique. Reference has already been made to the ESCs of which New Zealand is a member, in particular to the neo-European ESCs. But the question arises whether New Zealand is merely representative of the ESCs, and whether the norms, values and behaviours seen here are typical of all ESCs, or at least of the neo-European ones.

The question of origins extends across to family policy. As this is normally documented and sometimes enshrined in acts and laws, the trail to sources is reasonably easy to trace. Policy is not, however, something that is formulated in a vacuum. It is contextualised, typically by public discourse that draws on underlying value systems, and these are more diffused and less traceable than formal instruments. Some values, for example the fundamental importance of the family for society, will generate a high degree of consensus and have features that are common to most if not all religions, ideologies and philosophies. But others, such as whether the emphasis in policy should be on individual rights or on equity, be targeted or universal, may result in vigorous debates, and polarised political views.

The formulation of policy through public discourse is itself contextualised because it is an outcome of the history of any society. This is very much the case for a country such as New Zealand that has imported many of its norms and values, been subject to the demographic hegemony of one of its source populations, and then suddenly been exposed to cultural and social diversification. Thus this book will pay attention to identifying, wherever possible, the values and norms that may have been carried along as passive migrants with the early Pakeha settlers, how these differed from or reinforced those of Maori and how they fitted with changes to the family and to the society in more recent periods. Equally, a major issue, at least later in this book, relates to the corpus of laws and regulations, of policies and services formally imported from Britain and implemented here, or modified to meet New Zealand conditions and attitudes. Other measures were of New Zealand origin, including some of the measures passed by the Liberal Government at the dawn of the twentieth century.

1.5 WHERE DO WE GO FROM HERE?

To address the themes outlined here it is necessary to indicate strategies. In this case it will be accomplished primarily by dividing the history into periods representing different stages of what we call a 'family transition'. The definition of key concepts and the identification of the interactions between different aspects of family life and their determinants is a task that plays a role ancillary to the sketching out of a transition model.

There is another attendant question about how well this strategy might allow researchers accurately to document New Zealand family life at any period. This is an important prior step to the substantive analysis because much of the history described here is heavily dependent on official statistical information series. For earlier periods, particularly for Maori, the absence or incompleteness of some official data series (births and deaths) requires the application of what are termed 'indirect estimation techniques', which are very well developed, robust and widely used in demography in historical analyses and above all, as already noted, in building data series in contemporary Third World countries.[*]

The last few chapters turn to survey data, mainly those collected by the Population Studies Centre at the University of Waikato. These enrich the existing sources of information. The question to be raised is whether or not the conventions adopted for the collection of the data used throughout this book, from both official and other sources, their coding and the publication of results are likely to reflect the realities of family life with a reasonable degree of accuracy.

Beyond this it is necessary to ask what is known already about the New Zealand family. This is done by benchmarking the literature on the family in this country to the research findings in comparable WDCs. Chapter Two is devoted to these preparatory questions.

---

[*]   For further detail and explanations on their application to Maori see Pool 1991: *passim.*

CHAPTER TWO

Mapping Changes in the New Zealand Family from 1840*

2.1 THE EVOLUTION OF THE NEW ZEALAND FAMILY

The remaining chapters document the passage of the New Zealand family through what we will call a 'family transition'.† This is a model outlining the various major stages and the periods during which the evolution of the New Zealand family has unfolded. It has shifted from an institution characterised by large structures, the Victorian family/whanau of tradition and memory, to one with small structures. This model provides a framework for the organisation of the rest of the book.

The stages of the transition the model portrays can be crudely delineated for both Pakeha and Maori by using two key indicators of (i) family *structures* (taking family sizes as the measure) and (ii) family *forms* (marital status), both of which indices will be referred to frequently in later chapters. These are the total fertility rate (TFR)‡ and the proportions of women who were 'never married' at 20–24 years, which are graphed in Figures 2.1 and 2.2. The social-demographic processes that these two indices measure do not occur

---

* A detailed, complementary and more technical analysis of the questions discussed in this chapter is in a web-published monograph, *Studying the New Zealand Family: Analytical Frameworks, Concepts, Methodologies, Data-bases and Knowledge Bases* (Pool *et al.* 2007).

† The word 'transition' is used in two very different senses in this book. In this chapter, following demographic convention, it refers to a major societal transformation. A family transition is merely one example of such a set of changes followed at different times by each major New Zealand ethnic group. A second usage will appear in later chapters, following statistical conventions, and relating to changes of individuals or cohorts from one 'state'/status to another. The Canadian demographer Roderic Beaujot (2006), for example, applies it to the study of life-courses, in what he terms 'life-transitions'.

‡ The TFR is a 'measure expressed as births per woman, which shows the average number of children women in a synthetic cohort would bear over their reproductive span if they were to experience the age-specific fertility rates occurring in a particular reference year'. A cohort is a group of people identified by having experienced the same initial event – most commonly a 'birth cohort'. A 'synthetic cohort' is a hypothetical group exposed to rates drawn from the experiences in one specified period (normally a calendar year) of different real cohorts, 'as if this hypothetical cohort were progressing through its life-cycle' (Pool 1991: Glossary).

in isolation but are situated in the wider family and social contexts that will be discussed in detail later.

The juxtaposing of fertility and marriage, as is done here, recognises the central role over most of human history of nuptiality as a means of controlling reproduction. That these controls, and the associated factor of pre-marital chastity, sometimes operated imperfectly is reflected in varying patterns and levels of ex-nuptial conception and childbearing, or illegitimacy, as this used to be called. Ex-nuptial birth can occur only if pre-marital conception is not followed by nuptials and a birth within 'wedlock'. This issue is so fundamental to mapping and explaining patterns and trends in family morphology that it will be raised often in this book.

Across the ESCs the period from the late nineteenth century until today also saw a shift in fertility regulation strategies from those reliant mainly on ages at marriage and proportions marrying, through a number of 'contraceptive revolutions' to those of today involving advanced technologies. During the first such revolution at the end of the nineteenth century, barrier methods improved a little in quality and reliability, and became more widely available and used. At this period there are few data available for New Zealand, and none that have been sifted through systematically in order to eliminate biases inherent in anecdotal accounts. A detailed analysis relevant to the situation in New Zealand has, however, been written by Cambridge demographer Simon Szreter (2002, see esp. Chapt. 8, 'The Culture of Abstinence' ; see also Santow 1993).

A second revolution took place from 1960 with the introduction and rapid uptake of the Pill and a third in the 1970s involved modern technologies for sterilisation. The last was in the 1980s, when a new generation of condoms, improved both technically and aesthetically, was introduced. Consequently, barrier methods once again came back into the picture (Pool *et al.* 1999). The story of these changes in technology and its application is an essential part of the study of family change because contraception, sterilisation and abortion (which will also be covered in this book) are among the most immediate determinants of family formation.

Pakeha fertility was high from the earliest years of colonisation (Figure 2.1) because, for women, marriage was at young ages and almost universal (Figure 2.2). This latter point is clear for Pakeha in Figure 2.2, and, although no rates are available for Maori at that time, the analysis in later chapters will show that it also probably held true for them. For bio-social reasons to be discussed later Maori fertility was high, but not extremely so (Pool 1991: 78–82).

Levels of fertility changed rapidly for Pakeha between the 1870s and 1900, having as an inexorable effect a radical shift in the structures of families, where average sizes decreased and the age- and other aspects of composition changed. As Figure 2.2 shows, a virtual revolution in family structures had occurred by the end of the nineteenth century because of a radical increase over this time in the proportion of women who remained unwed in their twenties. In the 1930s Depression, for Pakeha, marriage rates under 25 years continued to drop, as too did fertility rates, edging down to just under 2.1 births per woman, or less than what is needed for the replacement of the adult population allowing a small margin for infant death. The pattern established then was to continue on until World War II, only to go through a counter-revolution in the 1940s, 1950s and 1960s, before being subject to a counter-counter-revolution in the 1970s.

The counter-revolution during and at the end of World War II saw Pakeha marriage patterns change again very radically. As is seen in Figure 2.2 the percentage never married at 20–24 years dropped to levels that were to go even below those of the 1870s. Pakeha family sizes also rose very significantly (Figure 2.1), although they did not return to the exceptionally high levels seen about a century earlier. The immediate post-war period was, of course, the Baby Boom, which was exceptionally long and intense in New Zealand (Pool and Sceats 2003). In popular imagination, in marketing circles and in urban myth this period has gained a stature that almost no other era seems to have achieved, even the 1970s. The Baby Boom was also the time in which Maori fertility reached, or rather maintained, a peak and then started to come down very rapidly (Figure 2.1).

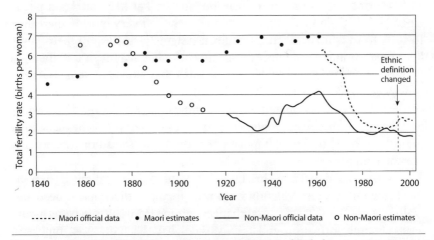

Figure 2.1: Total Fertility Rates, 1840–2002, Maori and Pakeha

Source: Pool *et al.* 1998: Fig. 1; extended to 2002. The baseline data for this and other graphs and text tables are published in Dharmalingam *et al.* (2007).

In the decades following the Baby Boom, Pakeha fertility definitively reached replacement levels, and has continuously remained there or below for the quarter of a century since the late 1970s. At the same time, rates for Maori dropped to unprecedented low levels although remaining on or above replacement. This was associated with a significant increase from 1976 to 1986 in the proportions never married at the reference age-group (Figure 2.2).

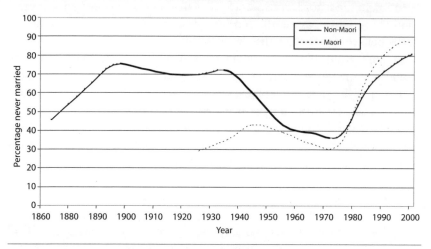

Figure 2.2: Percentage of Women Never Married at Age-group 20–24 Years, Maori and Non-Maori, 1876–2001

Source: Various censuses of population and dwellings. See also the note to Fig. 2.1.

The 1970s also saw a new dimension emerge. Pasifika and Asian populations reached significant numbers and increased very quickly thereafter. In 1976, from which year in this study a systematic analysis of their family life can start, they represented, respectively, only 2% and 0.3% of the total population (*NZOYB* 1992: Table 4.15; see also Krishnan *et al.* 1994; Statistics New Zealand 1995; Vasil and Yoon 1996). By the early twenty-first century, by contrast, they each numbered about 7% of the total population. This diversification will be discussed in later chapters but no attempt will be made to fit these two recent immigrant populations to the family transition model being sketched out below.

There is a need to digress briefly at this point. As can be implied from the preceding outline, reproduction is a central theme of this book. Indeed, our main argument is that structural changes coming from shifts in patterns and levels of family formation, and its co-variates, have been the most important dimensions of family change. That the shifts in family formation also occur co-terminously with other transformations, such as in family forms, in value systems and in the social, economic and policy contexts of family life, will be a theme elaborated in the next section of this chapter. But even there, family formation is a dominant theme.

In this context, it must also be noted that in the substantive chapters the analysis of reproduction will focus on women and, to a lesser degree, couples, while the roles of men as fathers will be a minor theme. This is not a

denigration of the important place of men in the family, but simply a pragmatic recognition of the childbearing role of women: paternal fertility rates
are seldom computed (Shryock and Siegel 1976: 293–94), in part because of
statistical problems such as the fact that details on the biological father may
not be recorded in the vital registers.

2.2 A FAMILY TRANSITION MODEL

In order to analyse changes over time for Maori and Pakeha, the combined
effect of shifts in family formation, structures and forms will be mapped in
later chapters, and an attempt made to interpret and explain changes. In
the different periods covered there the various dimensions of New Zealand
family life coalesce, to a degree, into four stages of a transition, analogous
in form to other transition models used widely in demography. There are
several such frameworks, including the parent model that deals with natural increase, births minus deaths, and thus population growth, and which
is termed 'the demographic transition'. Additionally, there are transition
models on fertility, plus a less formalised one on 'contraceptive revolutions'; mortality and health; migration; nutrition; and sectoral changes in
the industrial labour force. The present authors, to provide a framework
that might be generalised beyond New Zealand but which provides a focus
for this study, have constructed the model outlined here.

Stage One: The Era of Large Families
At this stage patterns of family formation are intense. This is both in
terms of the *tempo* dimension: the timing of marriage and childbearing
(what age the bride or young mother is, and how long after puberty or
marriage that they become parents), and the *quantum* dimension: the
numbers of children couples have.

   This is an era, assuming that pre-marital chastity is a norm, in which
fertility regulation is achieved primarily through marriage patterns: the
age of brides at their weddings, and the proportion of any generation
marrying. For New Zealand, Figure 2.2 graphs one dimension of this,
using the pivotal age-group of 20–24 years. In some societies abortion might play a role, but contraceptive technologies are extremely
primitive, including typically *coitus interruptus* and ineffective barrier
methods. When practised, abstention is, of course, highly effective. In
societies enforcing pre-nuptial chastity, marriage is the sole route to
exposure to intercourse and thus to the risk of conception. Post-partum
abstention, of varying durations, is a norm in every society, while some
couples would also have abstained at other times within marriage, or

had lower levels of coital frequency, whether voluntarily on involuntarily (e.g. because of the prolonged absence of a spouse, or sickness)
(Szreter 2002: Chapt. 8; Santow 1993).

For those who married, especially if they married young, this era
is characterised by large families, frequently with extended multi-generational structures, in which married couples and their children are
often embedded. This is a period also when the extended family plays a
basic role in social organisation. Obviously, by the process of migration,
Pakeha colonists frequently lost easy access to their wider families. In
contrast, Maori social organisation revolved around whanau (families,
especially extended ones) and hapu (sub-tribes). This usage was fundamental to systems of land ownership that the infamous land courts
of the late nineteenth century were established to destroy (Belich 1996:
258). But even in formal policy settings (e.g. the family and youth court
systems), they are still used and carry much the same conceptual weight
today.

Stage Two: The Era of Family Size Decline and Neolocalisation

Wider family structures begin to be eroded through changes in patterns
and levels of family formation, initially driven by shifts in marriage
patterns, producing declines in fertility. During this era, barrier and
other less effective means of fertility regulation and abortion are used
increasingly to regulate fertility, particularly within marriage. Changes
in family size are, however, accompanied by the emergence of reproductive polarisation,* between couples with numerous children and
those with few, and thus many households could still remain quite large.
Polarisation could occur in other ways, most notably between those
women who marry and have children, and those who remain single and
continue their careers. The nuclear family form that emerges in this era
would increasingly take on a neolocal structure. That is, young couples
would move away from the location where their parents lived and 'set
up on their own', as it were, in a new location.

Stage Three: The Era of Family Diversification

While changes in structures, along with shifts in patterns of family formation, continue during this stage, the highest-profile trends relate to
family forms, especially in their status dimensions. Most notably this

---

* The term used throughout this book conforms with the definition provided by the *New Shorter
OED*: the 'accentuation of a difference between two things or groups'. An example of usage that
they give is very apposite here: '*Chinese Economic Studies* The polarisation between rich and poor'.
In this book the term is mainly used in relation to reproduction, but sometimes its use is extended
to other aspects of family life and its contexts.

involves a move from marriage to cohabitation as the preferred form of first union. This shift is accompanied by increases in ex-nuptial child-bearing and is associated in time with increases in divorce rates. These changes spill over into the types of households families live in, as for example sole parent as against two parent.

The changes in family forms and structures (size and *tempo*) are associated with the rapid progression through two stages of the con-traceptive revolution: the introduction and rapid adoption of the Pill, followed shortly thereafter by the growth in use of tubal ligation and vasectomy. A third such shift followed the introduction and use of the new condoms. Even more importantly, although less heralded, have been other historically unprecedented demographic changes that have had significant impacts on household types (increases in single-person and couple-only households). These include the ageing of the popula-tion and delayed childbearing, a factor of family formation.

Stage Four: The Era of Family and Reproductive Polarisation, and Small Families

At the fourth stage the trends that have been emerging at the third stage become more entrenched. Perhaps more critically, levels of family formation reach historic lows over long durations of time. Diversifica-tion takes on new forms because of reproductive polarisation (e.g. by workforce status, such as full-time versus part-time employment) and because of other aspects of family polarisation (e.g. access to the job market and household incomes).

In New Zealand, as in other WDCs especially the other neo-European ESCs, such a transition will not be as neat and tidy as this outline might suggest. In particular, the migration process, an important aspect of demo-graphic replenishment in these countries, often affects family formation and structures. Equally, of course, in multi-cultural societies, such as New Zealand in the twenty-first century, each ethnic group may be at a different stage, while the *tempo* and velocity of transition stages may vary between cultures.

This caveat accepted, the framework is built around the notion of changes over time, and thus provides a set of criteria for the division of the remainder of this book into chapters dealing, albeit imperfectly, with distinct eras. Chapters Three and Four take Pakeha from the era of large families (Stage One) to that of family size decline (Stage Two), and Chapter Four elaborates further on Pakeha at Stage Two.

In contrast, the Maori transition from Stage One to Stage Two is delayed. Thus the era of large families for Maori is covered in Chapters Three and Four. The onset of the shift to family size decline and neolocalisation is dealt with in the latter part of the period discussed in Chapter Five, and completed in the early part of the period covered in Chapters Six and Seven. Although the Maori transition is delayed, it is also accelerated. Consequently, Chapters Six and Seven cover both the transition of Maori into the era of family diversification (Stage Three), but also the evolution of both Pakeha and Maori through that stage. Finally Chapters Eight and Nine take both populations into the era of family and reproductive polarisation and small families (Stage Four) and through at least part of it.

In drawing on the schema just outlined, two major philosophical issues arise; these questions are common to all transition models employed in demography. First, there is the question of whether or not the last observed stage represents the real end of the transition (Demeny 1997; Jones and Douglas 1997). Secondly, related to this is an even more critical issue: if the fourth stage is the last one, or if low fertility, at rates already well below replacement, plummets down even further, then will family structures no longer be able to maintain the populations in which sub-replacement fertility is occurring? This is not some theoretical question but one which is confronting numerous WDCs today, notably the Mediterranean countries.

2.3 INTERPRETING AND EXPLAINING FAMILY CHANGE

The story to be told in later chapters is one fundamental to the future of the society. It describes, above all, a structural shift from large to small families. At the same time there have been changes in ways of prescribing marriage as an almost universal pre-condition of childrearing, to an acceptance of informal unions. At different periods, this latter trend has been confounded by the fact that, from the time of being ceded to the British Crown, at least two perspectives on status definition have co-existed in New Zealand, often rather uncomfortably. Maori and Pakeha each had their own systems for legitimating statuses such as 'being married'. To add to this confusion, however, the enshrining of these mores as laws and regulations drew on only one of the two cultures' systems of norms. Arguably, the laws and regulations as enacted were not representative even of the range of Pakeha mores, but came only from those deemed acceptable by members of the classes from which the administrators and officials were drawn (see below).

The changes in family morphologies did not occur in isolation, but were the product of factors both endogenous and exogenous to the family. In later chapters an attempt is made not only to chart the mutations occurring in the family itself, but also to show how these might have been determined by other transformations. These were unfolding in the wider society and economy, materially and in terms of values and norms, occurring in its different cultures and evolving in the policy environment.

Some of the determinants of shifts in structures and forms are factors that are very closely linked to them. These are 'proximate' determinants, to give them their technical name. Shifts in patterns of family formation, such as employing contraception to delay childbearing, for example, are not only components of family morphology, but also have a direct and immediate impact on both structures and forms. Contracepting in order to put off having a first birth, a very common practice in twenty-first-century New Zealand, means that the size of the family and its age structure will be affected. It might also mean that a couple holds off changing the status (form) of their union from cohabitation to marriage. Formalising a cohabiting relationship by marriage, as a prelude to 'starting a family' (in this case meaning deciding to 'have children'), is an everyday occurrence in present-day ESCs.

In contrast, some determinants have less immediate impacts on family life, and frequently their effects will even be indirect, being transmitted by other factors. These are determinants that are 'causally more remote', again to use the technical term, from shifts in family life. Sometimes, by comparison with the proximate factors, they may even seem, at least at first glance, irrelevant to changes in household forms and structures. An example would be the conflicts that emerge between what happens in the workplace, say working long hours, and family life at home. Another example would be a swing in patterns of religious affiliation and beliefs that might affect some elements of the values system, and be reflected in changes in family behaviours.

It must also be reiterated that these relationships are not uni-directional, because family changes have consequences for the wider society. Most extremely, this applies to family structural changes that have significant impacts on demographic trends such as population growth, and on changes to social, cultural and economic organisation. The determinants and consequences of family change, its so-called co-variates, are frequently constituent elements of broader societal transformations of one sort or another. A number of these have been analysed in the various demographic transition models noted earlier, and thus are reasonably well documented. But others, such as the processes of economic modernisation, are more diffuse and thus less precise models exist.

This becomes particularly true when changes in values and in normative systems are being imputed as explanations of family change. What is an essential element in the analysis of changing family dynamics, forms and structures is typically its weakest link. Attitudinal and other social-psychological surveys yield data on values, although assessing the robustness, validity and longevity of their results is always problematic, as is evident from the debate over the type most widely used, political polls.

Norms are even more problematic phenomena to deal with. This is not the least because there is no clear way of distinguishing between what is done by most people, the norms of family behaviour, and what the society at large or culture deems people 'should do', the underlying attitudinal norms. One has only to think of the two anthropologists, Derek Freeman and Margaret Mead, recording norms and mores surrounding exactly the same behaviour, pre-marital sex among teenage Samoan girls – one scholar from the perspective of the elders, usually older men, the other as reported to the fieldworker by the young female actors themselves – to see how the term 'norms' can carry totally different, sometimes contradictory, philosophical weights. Typically this quandary is resolved by appealing to tautologies: for example, that what people are actually doing, which often can be observed and even measured, represent behaviours that the society or culture deem to be desirable and morally proper.

Unfortunately, the attitudinal norms, values and even mores are tempered further because, although contrary to what is deemed desirable, they may well reflect what is acceptable rather than what is prescribed or if they engender sanctions of some sort, these may be only very modest ones. An example is the tension between mores prescribing pre-marital chastity and the occurrence of ex-nuptial conception. It will be necessary to return to this in later chapters, tracking it down from its British antecedents well before New Zealand was a gleam in the eye of Whitehall, on through to the Baby Boom period here, and the years since. Some behavioural norms may not just be contrary to attitudinal norms, but even opposite to underlying values and precisely spelt out mores. They may even be counter to laws formulated in keeping with social mores. Seeking an abortion when it was a criminal act is an example.

It is in the domain of family life that contradictions between behaviours, norms, values, mores and even laws are likely to be most significant. One has only to think of many of the topics to be covered in later chapters to bring this message home: ex-nuptial pregnancy, cohabitation and divorce are three that leap immediately to mind.

In explaining family change it is necessary to refer to a whole corpus of causally more remote economic, social and cultural contextual factors, and to the values and normative systems just discussed. Sitting alongside all of these is policy, many dimensions of which may be specific to the family, and thus presumed somehow to alter family behaviours. There are others, however, that may have unintended consequences for families, such as the neo-liberal macro-economic measures introduced across the ESCs in the 1980s and 1990s.

Causally more remote determinants may directly determine family forms. For example, shifts in values relating to the importance and social consequences of ex-nuptial childbearing may accompany changes in the rates for this phenomenon, although sometimes in puzzling ways (see Chapter Three). In contrast, the causally more remote factors typically affect family structures less immediately, operating instead, as noted above, through proximate factors, notably patterns of family formation. For example, housing policy, or taxation policy affecting home ownership might have an impact on the capacity of couples setting up neolocal residence and thus the probability that they will start childbearing. This could therefore lead to delayed parenting.

There is less need to dwell on the consequences of family change simply because they are apparent in most of the concerns about the capacity of the family to fulfil its societal responsibilities. That said, there is less precision about how and why this occurs; that is, on what the linkages are between family change and its wider social consequences. This has very significant ramifications because the assertion is often made that the breakdown of the family is destroying the fabric of the society as we know it.[*] Yet robust models that show how these interrelationships might actually be played out are seldom constructed and tested rigorously. Thus the linkages remain diffused, unclear and vague, but at the same time assertions that are not grounded in an evidence base often have resonance for political discourse. Frequently, as in the abortion debate of the 1970s (Sceats 1988: Section 4.3), events overseas and the lobbying organisations that are established to pursue public policy changes generate debate in New Zealand, and even result in copycat organisations and agendas.

2.4 WHAT IS KNOWN ABOUT THE NEW ZEALAND FAMILY?

By comparison with most other WDCs the New Zealand family is insufficiently researched. This is not just a quibble with purely academic implications; it means that the evidence base for policy is very weak and underdeveloped. This can be illustrated by referring to the two major collections of commissioned essays on the family in New Zealand, one published quite recently (Adair and Dixon 1998) and the other twenty years earlier (Koopman-Boyden 1978). They each have only one chapter that covers families in general. While all chapters deal with families in

---

[*]   A recent New Zealand example of this sort of argument comes in *Family Matters: Family Breakdown and its Consequences* (Morgan 2004).

some way or another, most are tangential to questions of dynamics, forms and structures. This is not a critique of the editors concerned but an indication of the lack of research on how mainstream families play out their lives. There has been far more on child development, on family breakdown and on associated legal issues.

A web-published companion study to the present book, *Studying the New Zealand Family: Analytical Frameworks, Concepts, Methodologies, Data-bases and Knowledge Bases* (www.auckland.ac.nz/uoa/aup/nzfamily/studyingthenzfamily.cfm) contains a chapter written mainly by Susan Singley that reviews this question in detail. Working systematically from family formation, through structures and forms to factors related to family change, it adopts the strategy of taking the data- and knowledge bases in other countries as its benchmark, and then rating New Zealand alongside this. The picture it reveals is far from flattering. We summarise it briefly here, but note that Singley's work is essential background reading for any researcher undertaking a serious study of the New Zealand family (see also Pool and Sceats 1981).

First, in all areas of family research relevant to the present book, New Zealand has deficient data sources. There is a lack both of census materials and of surveys on family questions. There are what might be seen to be exceptions to this: census taking, even for Maori, was established from the period of early colonisation, but the range of relevant variables collected was limited until well after World War II. That said, census data on ages and occasionally other data (e.g. the 1911 fertility question) permit indirect estimations of family building (e.g. the TFRs in Figure 2.1) to be undertaken, and thus gives some insight into family structures. The data on marital statuses, graphed here in Figure 2.2, provide a strategically valuable piece of information. For Pakeha vital registration (births, deaths, marriages) was reasonably accurate and long time-series are available. But for Maori the series are shorter, and for both Maori until 1962, and Pakeha until 1913, detailed data are not available (e.g. births by age of mother) (Papps 1985a).

Secondly, and most importantly, unlike other WDCs New Zealand was very late in undertaking national probability sample surveys on families, fertility and related issues such as employment. Sterling efforts locally by Miriam Vosburgh, one of the people to whom this book is dedicated, and other pioneers to whom frequent reference will be made, started to open up this field of inquiry. A regional survey in the Manawatu in the 1970s, directed by Andrew Trlin and Paul Perry (1981), for example, furnished data from which Janet Sceats carried out a pioneer study on the timing and spacing of births that raised some major questions about New Zealand childbearing patterns – the age at which births occurred and the durations between entering a union and the first birth, and between successive births (Sceats 1981). At the end of the Baby Boom, the Society for Research on

Women, who interviewed a sample of urban women (1972), and Gill *et al.*, who surveyed rural women (1975), threw valuable light on topics related to those in this book.

But it was really only the New Zealand Women: Family, Employment and Education (NZW:FEE 1995) survey that allowed New Zealand scholars to enter numerous basic areas of detailed research at a national level on families (e.g. fertility regulation, family formation including timing and spacing, the shift to cohabitation, children in families, etc.) that are commonplace in other WDCs.* The NZW:FEE will be drawn on heavily in later chapters along with two other national probability surveys emanating from the University of Waikato. One was a smaller follow-up to the NZW:FEE, the New Zealand Fertility and Family Survey (NZFFS, 2001), and another, multi-disciplinary study, the first of its kind at the national level in New Zealand, dealt with dynamics, behaviours and networks of family members, titled 'Transactions in the Mid-Life Family'.† Recently, some particular subjects have been addressed in other less ambitious but still innovative surveys, as for example a retrospective, historical analysis of family dynamics 1900–30 by Claire Toynbee (1995), and Mervyl McPherson's (2003) study of the extended family.

Thirdly, an adequate range of census data on household types did not become available until the 1960s. Thus long-term analyses of this aspect of family form are not possible. Prior to the 1966 census, there are at best only fragments of data that generally come from expository analyses rather than quantitative sources. Most of the small sips that can be taken from that research are interesting and nutritious, but they are neither systematic nor necessarily representative and they leave the imbiber unsatisfied and thirsty for more.

Fourthly, some aspects of the research on the family for earlier decades are in better condition than the last paragraph might suggest. In this regard, this book owes a special debt of gratitude to historians. Without their dedication to the documentation of these islands' social story there would be no flesh on the fragmentary statistical skeleton we have dug up. Indeed, historical researchers have served New Zealand exceptionally well. Their work runs from the elegant literary sweep of Michael King (2003) describing the evolution of our identity as a nation and the powerful, encyclopaedic analyses by James Belich (1996, 2001), so reminiscent of the

---

* The Population Studies Centre, University of Waikato, particularly the authors of this book, played instrumental roles in setting up this survey, and have been among the principal authors of analyses of its data in numerous monographs and papers.
† Ian Pool directed the NZW:FEE, Janet Sceats was on the survey's policy and technical committees, and Arunachalam Dharmalingam was involved in sampling and analysis; Dharmalingam directed the NZFFS, and Ian Pool and Janet Sceats were also involved. Dharmalingam was also heavily involved in the 'Transactions in the Mid-Life Family' project, directed by Peggy Koopman-Boyden.

French Annales school, that deal with the development of the country's political economy, through to the more subject-specific, detailed studies, such as the superbly documented work by Charlotte Macdonald (1990), who employed record-linkage across an astounding range of sources to document the statistically significant inflows in earlier years of single women immigrants. There are still gaps, major in some places, but this cannot be blamed on a lack of diligence by the community of historians, but simply that there are limits on how much so few can do.

Fifthly, the basic outlines of Pakeha family formation were laid down by the founding father of New Zealand demography, the late Dr E. G. Jacoby, to whom this book has been dedicated. His work on cohort analyses (1958 and 1961, extended by Mansoor Khawaja 1985, 1986, and others), carried out while on leave at Princeton University, the Mecca for post-war population studies, played a pioneering role that reached far beyond our shores. This aspect of New Zealand demography has also been enriched by the documentation effected by Jain (1972).

Sixthly, a skeleton for the analysis of structures, family sizes and *tempo*, exists way back into the nineteenth century, as should be evident from Figure 2.1. But, as was noted earlier, the data shown there, particularly for Maori, are derived from estimates. With the collection and tabulation of more detailed information on Pakeha (1913) and Maori (1962) the knowledge base on family formation and structures had been extended but still remained very limited. This area, however, was also given a major fillip by the undertaking of the NZW:FEE survey in 1995. As this survey and its successor the NZFFS collected retrospective data, these researchers have been able to project this knowledge back to cohorts of women born from 1936 on, and who were exposed to intercourse, conception and family building from the 1950s on. Thus the coverage over time was also extended.

Seventhly, as just suggested, our knowledge of the finer details of family forms has been extended by the NZW:FEE, whereas some of the broader elements had been previously able to be measured from vital registration – from marriage statistics, and from information on the marital status of the parents on birth registers – from the nineteenth century. But for Maori these data were incomplete until after World War II, and furthermore there must be questions about how applicable some of these statuses are for Maori.

It must be remembered that the vital statuses governing family forms in New Zealand are derived from the civil registration systems introduced in Great Britain in the 1830s. In turn, these entrenched the precepts of legitimacy that had governed ecclesiastical systems for recording baptisms, weddings and burials. In Europe these concepts may have had most relevance for the propertied classes, even those who were highly profligate and immoral, but for whom issues of inheritance were important, or for the less well-off middle classes who sought to maintain the mores and proprieties of genteel society. In the latter category were Jane Austen's flighty Lydia and the bad Mr Wickham who ran off together, but who, it seems, somehow avoided the terrible sin and shame associated with consumated elopement and thus bastardy. In contrast, their aristocratic contemporaries, George III's offspring, including at least one of his daughters, were busy producing illegitimate children, but none of these bastards could inherit the Crown.

These systems and their underlying values were the basis for registration systems in the colonies, and they may have had little relevance for Maori, who already had their own means for the legitimation of conjugal unions and of assigning statuses. The legal academic Nan Seuffert has argued that throughout the early colonial period 'Marriage jurisdiction and law in the creation of public order, including the production of a homogeneous nation . . . and embracing particular notions of gender . . . were increasingly constructed and policed to assimilate . . . Maori' (2003: 186). This conflict of laws became even more problematic with the development of the welfare state, when conjugal and other statuses were used to determine eligibility for benefits or services.

The analysis of forms is further complicated by the lack of data on household types until quite recently. This is a serious lacuna as researchers are unable to assess the impacts of changing patterns of family statuses on the morphology of households. For example, there has been an increase in recent decades in divorce rates. This might seem to correlate with a shift in the percentage of families that are composed of couples without children as against parenting families, and in the proportions of households containing only one person. But this would be a largely spurious relationship, for the growth in non-parenting household numbers turns out instead to be a function of demographic trends, delayed childbearing plus the general ageing of the population, that have little to do with status issues.

Eighthly, a net result of these data lacunae is that there are major gaps even in descriptive analyses in comparison with what is often available overseas. The situation has improved in recent years (e.g. Cameron 1985b; Khawaja 1985; Jackson and Pool 1994; Dickson *et al.* 1997; Statistics New Zealand 2005) but more in terms of cross-sectional reviews – households at one or two periods of time, or time-series analyses of annual rates – than in-depth studies. A more innovative strategy was adopted by the Social Monitoring Group of the New Zealand Planning Council that used a life-cycle approach that covered, *inter alia*, data on families in a series of reports entitled *From Birth to Death* (1985, 1989; continued on by Judith Davey 1993, 1998, 2003).

Ninthly, New Zealand is not well served in terms of the volume of research on the internal dynamics of families, especially their social-emotional and related dimensions. This means that the interpretations to be made here are often speculative, or are drawn from what overseas experience has shown, rather than being hard, empirical findings on New Zealand families. Notable exceptions include the studies by Jan Cameron on couple decision-making about parenting (e.g. 1997); the work of Claire Toynbee, on couple, family and kin interactions, mainly in terms of the work–family life interface (e.g. 1995), and Robin Fleming (1999); the research on intra-family income issues by Robin Fleming and Susan Easting (e.g. 1994); work by Margaret Hope (1997) on kinship support; and a series of papers by Sarah Hillcoat-Nalletamby alone and with others (e.g. 2000 and Hillcoat-Nalletamby *et al.* 1999). Janet Sceats's research on work–life balances was also cross-national (e.g. 2003; Australia and England). A time-use survey in the late 1990s has increased knowledge on that aspect of family dynamics (e.g. Hillcoat-Nalletamby and Dharmalingam 1999).

Finally, the lack of regular New Zealand data series on some variables normally collected systematically in overseas censuses (the fertility question), the short-term runs for other census information (household types), and the absence of national probability surveys all limit the analysis of the co-variates of changes in family morphologies, and thus the explanatory power of any analyses. As a result, New Zealand is behind most WDCs in terms of a knowledge base analysing most aspects of family life and their interrelationships with social, cultural and economic factors. This is less true for that relating to family policy, for which detailed analyses, historical and contemporary, are available, although far less is known about how policy interventions and social services affect family life. A major exception is the very important study in the early 1970s by O'Neill *et al.* (1976) on ex-nuptial children and their parents. Recent research instigated by the Ministry of Social Development, often using data from management information systems, has seen the growth of analyses centred on the problems that family face, on benefits and on interventions by welfare services.

2.5 THE RESULTS OF FAMILY RESEARCH: DO THEY REFLECT FAMILY REALITIES?

This book is a 'macro-level' analysis, looking at the population, or at sub-populations such as ethnic groups. It does draw heavily on micro-level studies, most notably our own NZW:FEE that collected and analysed data on individual women and their family lives, but the focus is on aggregate data analyses. Thus the family that emerges in the substantive chapters is not that of popular-level discussion. Instead, and particularly when we refer to household types, a very significant component of the study, the focus is on categories of families, not on individual households. Instead, reference will typically be to the proportion of all types of families, or individuals, who meet particular criteria, for example being a married, cohabiting, parenting or couple-only household. It must therefore be stressed that the research that has gone into this book does not purport to describe the internal dynamics of families, not least because, as noted above, there are relatively few data on which to base such analyses.

That said, the question arises as to whether or not population-level analyses capture the reality of New Zealand family life, at least its more demographic elements. This concern relates not just to factors such as ethnic or cultural differences, but more fundamental questions about the forms and structures of families and households. Essentially the analysis of family forms and structures, whether involving qualitative or quantitative research, must attempt to put some sort of conceptual order into the complex phenomena being observed. The fear still remains that the resultant 'family' might be more an artefact of the definition employed than of social reality. This is because data collections and analyses of family or household structures usually adopt one or other broad frameworks for their definitions:

- 'Co-residence (same dwelling, or sharing the same eating facilities, or some similar criterion)'; and
- 'Kinship and affinity (here termed kinship)' (ESCAP 1986: 6).

The former tends to be the format used in statistical data collections. The genealogically based construct tends to be more commonly used in qualitative analyses, although the anthropologist Murdock's definition also relates to 'A social group characterised by common residence' (cited in Cameron 1985a).* But both sets of criteria may be exact and reflect reality or, equally, exclude and/or fail to incorporate the essentials of family morphology.

There are two key problems. The co-residence definition excludes persons who are geographically distant, but who may closely interact with other 'family' members. Yet, the definition based on genealogical ties assumes that kinship and affinity also carry with them the fulfilment of family obligations, whereas such a family may include members of the kin-

---

* The tendency is to equate a kinship approach with the anthropology of Third World societies. But a recent study on Pakeha family life from 1900 to 1930, for example, shows the importance of this factor in family dynamics even in the modern era. Indeed, the author extrapolates from her research to muse that the policy and economic shifts of the late twentieth century may have renewed its importance (Toynbee 1995: *passim*).

ship group who do not participate at all in any active way. This becomes critical when there is a shift towards neolocal residence. There is also the major methodological problem of where to set outer parameters for kinship and affinity.

Fortunately, there are New Zealand data available on this issue from a survey* which formed part of a seven-country study carried out by the United Nations Economic and Social Commission for Asia and the Pacific (ESCAP 1986). The study attempted to review whether or not these definitions and other alternatives reflect the complexity of family life. The general lessons to be learnt from this ESCAP study and summarised here are very important for the present book:

- First, and most importantly, family formation, including the size of the family of origin (i.e. how many siblings the parents had) is a critical determinant of other family dynamics (both macro- and micro-level) and family structures. It has even wider implications for the society (see Blum 1984), as it is the basis of population replacement.
- Secondly, kinship approaches may not be as indicative of 'everyday family life' as might be expected. Families are often dispersed, and relationships do not guarantee that obligations will be fulfilled.
- Thirdly, co-residence, the baseline for census data, may not be perfect for defining family structures, but it certainly seems to be the more useful, if only because it determines that some type of contact will occur, however functional or dysfunctional this may be. This is a critical factor for reconciling the complex variety of possible family structures and the data most commonly available to study them.

There is another aspect to this. In practice, the overwhelming majority of New Zealand families have household arrangements that are appropriate for their family life-cycle phase and which are adequately described by census categories. There will, of course, be a minority of units that is difficult to classify. Where data on diverse family forms are collected, typically in non-official data sets, they often relate to living arrangements, or family status categories (for example, cohabitation versus marriage), that are rather significant for the present study. Fortunately, recent national surveys on New Zealand, such as the NZW:FEE, have thrown some light on this beyond what is available through official data sources.

---

* This was directed by one of the co-authors of this book, Ian Pool.

Recently, at a national level, censuses in North America have attempted to obtain more inclusive and less discriminatory data on family statuses around which information was not conventionally collected in the past (e.g. on same-sex unions). In the New Zealand census attention has been given to *de facto* unions; or in national probability surveys (NZW:FEE) to cohabitation and to the common problem of couples 'living apart together' (LATs, as these people are called in Europe). The possibility of reporting same-sex partnerships was first allowed for in both the 1996 New Zealand census and in the NZW:FEE, but was not availed upon by respondents to any degree. Small-scale qualitative or non-probability surveys are more likely to produce satisfactory data on these structures.* Given, then, that there are no systematic data-bases on a diverse range of possible family structures, the data on family statuses in this study are restricted in the main to census categories and those available from large-scale surveys.

2.6 ETHNIC AND CULTURAL DIFFERENCES IN FAMILY LIFE

No serious study of families and households in New Zealand can be undertaken without closely examining ethnic and cultural differences, the analysis of which is fortunately a convention of very long standing here. In contrast, this was a realisation that Britain was only just coming to in the 1990s, when it started to recognise, in more than a superficial way, ethnic differences in family structures (Murphy 1996).

It is also important to approach the study of ethnic differences with a great deal of methodological rigour, for data and analyses in this area really do inform public opinion, yet their underlying premises have not always been clear to casual users.† Moreover, substantive factors may also con-found comparisons. For example, cultural differences in preferred ages for common family-building events have other 'impacts' (as this phenomenon is called, Jackson 2000). To take one case, Maori women, on average, have babies at younger ages than do their Pakeha peers. This affects the average age at which sole parenting may occur and this has other consequences (Jackson and Pool 1996, citing analyses on Maori sole-parent families). Finally, difficulties relating to the classification of ethnicity cross-cut those pertaining to the definition of family morphologies.

---

* E.g. telephone surveys in Auckland on behalf of the NZ AIDS Foundation have been able to get such data (Saxton *et al.* 2002; Reid *et al.* 1998; Worth *et al.* 1997).
† How many users of data appreciate the shifts in tabulation procedures in the public-record data-base from 'prioritisation' of ethnicity to 'total responses'? We will have to inflict this issue on readers in later chapters.

Wherever data are available Maori and non-Maori will be considered separately here. As noted earlier, there will, however, be only a limited review of other ethnic groups for two reasons. First, disaggregated historical secondary data on these ethnic groups typically do not exist. Secondly, where they do exist for recent years, systematic analyses are available for only the three major groups, Maori, Pasifika and Pakeha – or on Maori and non-Maori – but not for Asian and 'Other'. In any case, relatively low proportions of Asians in the nineteenth and early twentieth century had 'normal' family lives because most were men on their own who frequently could not bring their wives to New Zealand (Ip 1990: 14–16). Nevertheless data for recent years will be analysed for Asians and Pacific peoples.

This said, it is important to flag two classificatory problems the solution to which is beyond the scope of this present study.

- First, the category 'Other', used in many earlier published tabulations, is almost meaningless, as it covers Asians, of whom there are several major groups, and numerous minor non-Asian ethnicities.
- Secondly, Pacific peoples, mainly Polynesians, form a far from homogeneous group, yet they are typically bundled together as one category. Few of the secondary analyses on which this study draws disaggregate these, but a separation into major groups can be made for some recent years. This is important because Carmichael (1982; 1996), who did disaggregate this population group, showed that there are major differences in some aspects of family formation (e.g. cohabitation, ex-nuptiality) between eastern and western Polynesians.

The question then arises: how far do census and other official data on family formation and structures reflect the realities of such cultural differences? The ESCAP study of the early 1980s, noted earlier, tested the following point rigorously for Maori and Pakeha: that factors seen as 'familial' might have a wider frame of reference and could be influenced by norms operating across the family's broader cultural milieu. This postulate recognises that the family is the agent that, through socialisation and acculturation, transmits these cultural norms, and its own internal working principles, to each new generation.

To analyse these effects, the ESCAP study in New Zealand was divided into two sub-surveys: Pakeha and Maori. The Maori survey was further subdivided so that it covered two randomly selected, interpenetrating subsamples. One of these was interviewed using a core instrument designed by an ESCAP expert committee, used in six Asian countries and in the Pakeha segment of the study, the other with a survey instrument (termed whanaungatanga, family dynamics) developed by Edward Douglas,[*] 'in collaboration with Maori social scientists, Maori elders and other Maori . . . to conform closer to Maori cultural values relating to reproduction and the family' (ESCAP 1986; Douglas 1981).

This test concluded that there were few differences between the two approaches in the Maori survey, either in terms of the results relating to family structures and forms, or in relation to whanau interventions towards couples on issues involving family structures and forms. Nevertheless,

> A broad understanding of the Maori world view as it relates to the family [i.e. perceptions about values relating to formation processes and to structures] and socialisation of children could be gained from the whanaungatanga questionnaire (ESCAP 1986: 10).

This last point has two implications for the present study. First, this book will not be dealing with socialisation *per se*, as it is outside its scope. Secondly, and in contrast, 'an understanding of the Maori world view' is extremely important for the central concerns of this study relating to family formation, structures and forms. For example, at a population or macro-level, value systems are manifested by the ways in which the patterns of registered marriage and family formation in general, and the structures of Maori and Pasifika families, are different from those of Pakeha or Asians (Pool and Sceats 1981: 52; Pool 1991: Chapt. 2; Jackson and Pool 1996; Pool *et al.* 1998; Kukutai 2003).

2.7 KEY CONCEPTS

KEY TERMS
In setting out the themes to be developed in this book reference was made to four terms: family dynamics, family formation, family forms and family structures. It is necessary now to define them in some degree of detail, as they are critical for the rest of this book.

> *Dynamics* are ongoing processes, such as the evolving inter-relationships and interactions within families, and how family life unfolds. One dimension of dynamics involves many different *social transactions* and *psycho-emotional interactions* and these play a major role in determining the way families evolve. Unfortunately, in

---

[*] A senior member of the New Zealand ESCAP survey team.

New Zealand, there are few studies on these aspects of average family life. In contrast, we have far more on the effects of family breakdown and related psycho-legal issues.

Perhaps the most important, or at least the most evident, set of dynamics are those processes comprising *family formation* or *family building* (entering a marriage, or commencing cohabitation; the birth of successive children) and, somewhat counter-intuitively, family dissolution and decrement (terminating a union through divorce or death; children leaving home). These will be the aspects of dynamics covered most exhaustively in this book.

Family formation is the immediate determinant of family structures and family forms, although its effects are mediated by shifts in norms and values (e.g. from marriage to cohabitation as the preferred first union). The patterns of causality are multi-directional because family formation is, in turn, determined by family forms and structures. To cite the most obvious example, a celibate person must form a relationship before becoming a parent, and in this process they will pass through different family forms and structures.

Family forms are statuses and situations. These are the markers that permit us to describe types of families and households as entire units, for example a sole-parent, two-parent, childless-couple or single-person household or a household composed of unrelated persons.

As the word 'form' suggests, this is where formalisation of statuses through laws and regulations are most directly applicable to the family. Thus the term 'family form' relates to the type of union the family is built around, sometimes called living arrangements, such as formal marriage or cohabitation.

In the past 'legitimacy' and 'illegitimacy' were important family statuses that further defined relationships. The same was true for adoption, as against biological descent, and this continues to be the case today.

Family forms also cover relationships within families, such as the categories used in the census that describe members by their relationship to the 'occupier', the person who fills in the household questionnaire, and who historically was called the household head. Thus, for example, in parenting households there will be dependent children and their parent(s) and, less frequently, dependent parents.

Other dimensions of form can be defined in terms of differences between nuclear and extended and/or multi-generational families. The latter may well include kin, affines or even unrelated people among their number.

Family structures are the patterns and trends in family sizes, including the timing of family events, such as whether a woman has a first baby as a teenager or in her thirties. These patterns and trends also comprise related factors, such as the age-, generational, ethnic and socio-economic composition of households.

Family structures can involve differences in characteristics among family members, such as whether anyone is on a benefit or jobless. Equally these features can comprise, at a macro-level, the distribution of households by these and other attributes (e.g. income differentials). In this case, unless custom-designed tabulations are available, the categorisation of the household will often have to be based on the reported characteristics of the occupier. In heterogeneous families, or those with marked status or other differences between spouses and/or other members, the resultant data may not be representative of the household. It thus creates major problems for analysts, a point to which we return in later chapters.

Further, we include the location of a family or household in relation to other dwellings of family members under the rubric of family structures. The issue of location is expanded below.

FAMILIES AND HOUSEHOLDS

Social analyses often distinguish between a family and a household, but in common usage such distinctions are seldom maintained. These concepts, fundamental to this book, are normally seen as dimensions of family forms, but there is a need to discuss some related issues that arise from a discussion of these terms.

For statistical purposes the convention is that a household may comprise one or more families, and in any dwelling there may be more than one household. Following popular parlance, this book will use the words family and household interchangeably, but, in analyses carried out by the Population Studies Centre, household rather than family data are normally used, and thus for tabulations and graphs presented here this convention will generally be followed.

The reason for this strategy is simply that in statistical usage a family is a more narrowly defined unit that excludes some normal living arrangements at various life-cycle stages, such as a widow living alone in a single-person household. By using the wider term one can document better the changes in living arrangements. Another advantage is that the wider definition gives a more accurate portrait of sole parenting. Many sole-parent families (typically a mother and her child/children) are in reality embedded in wider households, frequently the home of the parents of the sole parent. This is particularly the case for Maori and Pasifika, and for teenage mothers. As a result, sole parents are often not the isolates of popular perception, as implied, for example, somewhat ambiguously in the term 'lone parent' widely used in North America.

It is important also to recognise that sole parenting is a situation not a state. It may be due to a change in status, such as divorce, but does not last permanently or even necessarily for the long term. By definition, once the children leave home sole parents are no longer parents in the sense that they have children materially dependent on them. More importantly, a high proportion of sole parents form new relationships relatively soon: the NZW:FEE showed that half to two-thirds of female parents who separate have re-partnered by five years after the split-up. This was true, however, only for a third of those with four or more children or whose youngest child was aged fifteen years or above at the separation. Thus many sole parents will re-partner, and, conversely, many people who are currently in unions may become sole parents.

This book is a history covering periods in which longevity was well below the levels now enjoyed in the early twenty-first century. While today sole parenting is seen very much as an outcome of disharmony in a conjugal union, traditionally this situation was one faced by widows and widowers. Of course, some women reporting themselves in censuses as widows or as currently married may have been deserted wives, particularly at times of economic depression. It was not until the first Labour Government that their plight was recognised, but until then these women would have been largely dependent on charity (Sutch 1966: 61, 177–78). In World Wars I and II separations because the husband was overseas at war forced many women to become *de facto* sole parents during their husbands' absences, but, of course, they did not face the opprobrium that such women (and men) often face today.

The distribution of household types is affected by changes in family status, such as when a couple first marry and move into their own home as a childless couple, whether they decide to cohabit rather than marry or what their marital status is when a baby is born. More importantly, the household type also reflects normal processes of family formation and demographic change.

Delayed childbearing has meant there are now many households composed of young childless couples, 20–29 years old, by which age in the Baby Boom they would already have been parents. But their own parents probably were the early starters of the Baby Boom, and may now be empty-nester couples at pre-retirement or early retirement ages, and who are also childless in terms of living arrangements. The category 'childless couple' is the most rapidly growing type of household followed by the single-person household. The increase in the latter category is driven primarily by population ageing, which sees many older persons becoming widows or widowers. Thus shift-shares, as economists call these processes, in household types are not so much a function of family breakdown – a conclusion some commentators draw from the decline in the proportion of households that are composed of two parents and their dependent children – but a result of changes in the balances because of 'natural' processes.

LOCATION OF HOUSEHOLDS IN RELATION TO OTHER FAMILY MEMBERS
Structures are primarily a function of the processes of family formation defined above, although there is also a dimension relating to where a family is located geographically in relation to other kin and affines, and particularly where a newly formed family settles. In New Zealand most young couples used to take up neolocal residence apart from their parents in a separate dwelling, one they would probably be buying on a mortgage. This was the quintessential type of household structure in the Baby Boom. The first baby would come home from the hospital to this house – in contrast to much of urban Europe where the first baby will come back to a rented apartment. Today in New Zealand neolocal residence of this sort is a dream slipping away from many young couples.

Cross-cutting these family structures and forms is the LAT phenomenon, young couples 'living apart together' in different flats or in their own parents' houses, and consummating the relationship from time to time, typically in the parental home; the parental generation of today seems tolerant by comparison with its predecessors. This household form, which also has structural ramifications (e.g. the size of a parental household), has appeared here in New Zealand as overseas: in 1995, 20% of young women aged 20–24 years were in LAT relationships.

The LAT phenomenon is not restricted to the young. Anecdotal evidence suggests that it also occurs among older persons, particularly those who have ended a long-term relationship but who, for whatever reason, do not wish to co-reside with a new partner. Research in European countries directed by Jenny Gierveld, Emeritus Professor at Amsterdam Vrije Universiteit, sheds light on this. Her survey data show that there unmarried retired couples may also remain LATs for a wide range of reasons: pension scheme conditions; tax; a desire to maintain independence yet also have an intimate relationship; or a need to remain near other family such as children or grandchildren (2005).

COMPARTMENTALISING FAMILY FORMS AND STRUCTURES
For the sake of simplicity, family structures and forms have been described here as watertight categories, but in reality they are not mutually exclusive. For example, in societies in which procreation can occur only within

formal marriage this affects both the forms and structures of families. To take another case, the neolocal New Zealand household consists typically of one nuclear family.

Moreover, the tidy picture of yesteryear composed of the prototypical neolocal Naenae couple in their early twenties, who had moved away from mum and dad in Ngaio has inexorably altered. This is not just because of the emergence of the LAT phenomenon as a significant trend, but also because of the rapid cultural diversification of New Zealand over the last three decades that has seen the arrival of structures and forms different from those of Pakeha that had dominated so long. One can add to this mix the shifts to later childbearing and the co-terminous changes in laws and policies, such as those relating to civil unions, or the Domestic Purposes Benefit.

2.8 CONCLUSION

The following chapters document the New Zealand family, as it changes over time, in its Maori, Pakeha, Pasifika and Asian components. These various mutations frequently move family morphologies away from those that were accepted and that were the orthodox behaviours of earlier generations. That past, however, often remains to the fore in popular memory, and aspects of family life recalled from history are often the central stories passed on by the process of socialisation. It is, after all, the family, perhaps reinforced by the school system, that is the vehicle charged with the responsibility of conveying to a new generation what happened in the past or what is thought to have happened. Such nostalgia may often form the model not only for subsequent normative structures and values systems, but as the baseline for policy formulation.

We can never be certain, however, that nostalgia has provided a statistically exact glimpse into the past. An attempt to throw some light on this is a by-line for the major themes being explored in this book. But whether memories are accurate or not, changes to what is familiar, to the family forms that people were accustomed to in childhood or early in their lives, may disconcert some observers and thus be translated into wider concerns about the capacities of families.

On migrating to New Zealand, the 'familiar' for the colonists would have been what had occurred customarily in the 'old country', and may have differed from the new things confronting them in the colonies: Maori cultural patterns that were very different from their own. Not only were these unfamiliar to them, but, to judge by the writings of nineteenth-century settlers, bolstered by the very Victorian belief in the superiority of British customs and mores, they were often disturbing or were considered to be inferior to those imported by the settlers (Pool 1991: *passim*). But Pakeha quickly constituted the demographic, and probably cultural, hegemon in New Zealand, and thus the antecedents for their behaviours, norms and values may have been those of the old country, regardless of whether or not these were remembered accurately or filtered through migration. Albert Wendt's *Sons for the Return Home* portrays the gap between the Samoa as remembered by a more recent wave of migrants to New Zealand, especially as they expound on these to their New Zealand-born or -raised offspring, and the reality of those norms and mores back in the islands.

These are potent themes, but as shown in this chapter their exploration is impeded by the absence of adequate information and knowledge bases. The present authors can only produce a skeleton that, hopefully, will be fleshed out by other researchers.

With these caveats in mind we now turn to the start of the New Zealand story, when Maori families came into increasing contact with Pakeha. This interface was not, however, one of equality because not only did Pakeha soon outnumber Maori, but the legal and policy instruments that came to assist, direct and rule family life were those of the colonial administrators. In turn, these were derived from the family values and norms of the British society from which the administrators were drawn, even though they were not necessarily representative of the Pakeha immigrants whose household forms and structures were to become the most common denominator for New Zealand family life.

PART TWO: TRENDS IN THE NEW ZEALAND FAMILY

CHAPTER THREE

The Large Family of Yesteryear, Trends 1840–1945

3.1 THE GENESIS OF NOSTALGIA ABOUT THE LARGE FAMILIES OF YESTERYEAR

THE PARAMETERS OF FAMILY CHANGE

In some ways this chapter and the next are the most important in the book. They attempt to analyse systematically what actually happened to New Zealand family life over the period 1840 to 1945, compared to what remains in popular memory. This period set the scene for popular perceptions about the New Zealand family, or at least about its two principal variants, Maori and Pakeha. The family of yesteryear is frequently cited as a sort of benchmark against which contemporary family life might be assessed.

These two chapters thus identify the emergence over the period from 1840 to 1945 of attitudes and norms that provided the rationale for the fundamental tenets for what, in the public policy discourse of the twenty-first century, are called 'family values'. These tenets, reinforced by reference to what are seen as 'traditional structures and forms', continued to be adhered to throughout the era discussed in these chapters and were evident even after World War II. Arguably, they still underlie much of the debate about the family in the twenty-first century, a point to be revisited in later chapters. From a twenty-first-century vantage point, family structures and forms seem to have remained intact over the period from the debut of Victoria's reign until at least World War II.

For example, the popular perception remains that, even as recently as World War II, families were far larger than they are today. It may be that this perception arose in part from a confusion between the size of the family of procreation: the couple and their children, and the numbers in co-resident families (often grandparents or other relatives lived in the household). But even with such caveats put to one side, most people believe that in the past families of procreation *per se*, excluding other relatives or non-related persons, were larger than they are today, and for some observers this merges into nostalgia about the 'good old days'.

But when a demographer takes a closer look at the data on families some rather awkward questions about this cosy picture emerge. Most crucially, over this period a critical dimension of Pakeha family life, patterns of family formation, went through a series of radical changes, although this was not the case for Maori. While Maori family life will be looked at in detail in this chapter and the next, far more emphasis will be given to Pakeha. There are two simple reasons for this: (i) after about the 1890s Maori family morphologies did not change* – this was to occur after World War II – and (ii) Pakeha were the demographically hegemonic group from 1870 to 1970, and controlled the country's political and economic life. Thus we can assume that their value system was also dominant, not just in the nation's social life but also in moulding the policy environment.

These chapters start in the nineteenth century, between 1840 and the 1870s, when Pakeha average family sizes, as measured by the number of births per woman, were certainly large:† in fact, we will show that hyperfertility reigned at that time. But over the next thirty years, from the 1870s, Pakeha families went through a major decline in size, at least as indicated by falling fertility rates for women of all marital statuses combined (see Figure 2.1). This reached a nadir in the 1930s when levels of reproduction fell slightly below the level needed to replace the adult population. Surely then, one could argue, the data show that, at least for the first four decades of the twentieth century and certainly during the Great Depression of the 1930s, the families of yesteryear were not large.

---

* We must make it very clear that the relative weights assigned to Maori and Pakeha are not an indication of the importance we allot to the problems Maori families faced, but more a factor of the rapidity of Pakeha demographic change in this era – later, in Chapters Five to Seven, a great deal of attention will be paid to the emergence of the Maori family of today. Moreover we recognise, as will be documented later, that colonisation was not some benign process. Instead, the New Zealand Wars, land confiscation and resource alienation through so-called legal means had major, disruptive impacts on Maori family life. But from about 1890–1900 a gradual recuperation was under way for most Maori. As a result, continuing resource loss in the twentieth century had more nuanced effects, and, in any case, Maori had developed mechanisms allowing them to deflect many of the more negative ones.

† The Pakeha crude birth rates (CBRs) of this period – equal to or above the highest rates seen in any British Isles county at that time – were high: 43 per 1000 total population (i.e. men, women and children) in 1866; 41 in 1871; and 42 in 1876, but dropped to 38 (still high by British standards) in 1881 (Khawaja 1985: Table 73). But these crude rates are not extraordinarily high (compare 46 for Maori after World War II, or over 50 in Kenya from the 1950s to 1980s), even though the fertility levels (as against the crude rate) achieved by the colonial Pakeha women of those times (see later in this chapter) exceeded those for post-World War II Maori, and were not too far short of those for Kenyans in the 1950s. The reason is that the Pakeha CBRs were dampened down because they were subject to age-compositional and gender effects that inflated their denominators at the expense of the numerators – a common problem with crude rates. This point can be simply illustrated: in 1878, for example, when there was almost sex parity in the births (101 male births to 100 female, which fits the norm for those times) the gender-specific birth rates were 38 boy babies per 1000 *males of all ages*, but 47 girl babies per 1000 *females*. In this case, the large number of single men is a critical factor. They may well have participated in sexual relations, perhaps with great gusto (Eldred-Grigg 1984; Levesque 1986), but were not actively engaged in reproduction *per se*.

For the older generations of early twenty-first-century Pakeha New Zealanders, the parents of the early Baby Boom, the family life of the inter-war period is their comparative framework and the basis for the common perception that the families of their parents' and grandparents' generations were 'large'. In fact, many will have genealogical evidence drawn from their own family that demonstrates this.

This apparent paradox will be resolved later in the chapter. But we must signal at this point that differences in perceptions can even result from the type of index of fertility employed: for example, crude rates using the total population as the denominator (see footnote, p. 47); rates based on *all* births to women of *all* marital statuses; or rates based on nuptial births to married women.

A clear contrast does exist between Maori and Pakeha. For bio-social reasons that will be discussed later, Maori fertility rates were only mid-dling to high in the late nineteenth century, and then their rates gradually increased to very high by World War II and after. So, in terms of averages, one can be very clear about Maori: their family sizes were indeed large for the entire period covered by this chapter and the next.

To tease out this apparent paradox for Pakeha, we have to turn from considering *all* women (as for the general fertility rates, GFRs, and the total fertility rates, TFRs, used later in this chapter and elsewhere in this book) to focusing on *married* women (as for marital general fertility rates, MGFRs, and marital total fertility rates, MTFRs). Here fact seems to fit better with perception. To support this argument it is necessary to point out that, in the era 1840 to 1945, most Pakeha came into the world as the offspring of a married couple. Furthermore, the case is strengthened by the fact that, even after average fertility rates for all women declined in the late nineteenth century, those for married women, essentially families of procreation (overwhelmingly married couples and their children), were typically large although, on average, not of the 'cheaper by the dozen' genre. Nevertheless, sufficient proportions were large and thus for perceptions of ample-sized families in past eras to be an accurate memory for many persons looking back on their predecessors. Moreover, they are almost certainly descended from 'married' recent ancestors – less likely if they go back to the pre-Victorian period, but that is another story. There is thus a conflation of marital status with ample family size, which again is a perception that has informed the tenets that have become the bases for the family values of many twenty-first-century observers.

There is another twist to this story. By the late nineteenth century, various forms of what we will term 'reproductive polarisation' (the conventional phrase in the literature) had emerged, a point we will elaborate later in this chapter and the next. In terms of the prevailing reproductive regime of the era between 1840 and 1945, the key to this, and perhaps the resolution of much of the seeming paradox outlined above, was *who* got to marry, and thus who was likely to produce offspring and then a line of descendants.

Post-1945 values relating to aspects of family life, such as desired family size and marital status, have often owed their genesis to nostalgic notions about households in the past, notions that are sometimes based more on myth than reality. In fact, as will be investigated here, some extant values, at least for Pakeha, could have had their antecedents in British normative systems existing before or at the time of the British diaspora. Thus this chapter may cover questions of more than merely academic and historical interest; it may throw some light on the current public discourse on families.

THE NORMS OF FAMILY LIFE AND THEIR DETERMINANTS

The early and most rapid decline in family size, between the late 1870s and 1900, had been produced, in the absence of effective means of contraception, by a very significant shift in conjugal patterns from universal and early marriage, in the 1870s, to delayed entry into unions and spinsterhood for a significant minority of women by the 1900s (Sceats and Pool 1985). Marriage was the normal route to parenthood and was to remain so across this era. Because the migration process was weighted towards young families or single people, households were typically neolocal in residence, but sometimes were also extended in structure, not uncommonly including grandparents and other adults. Throughout this period and until the 1960s, Maori family sizes were large because marriage was universal and the age at entry into marriage was young.

The early period (up to probably the 1880s) set in place some norms relating to family structure antecedent to what occurred after World War II in the Baby Boom, and even after. Some latent normative structures may still persist as ideals, seldom realised in the low-fertility period of the early twenty-first century, that have their roots back in the years of early settlement. Interestingly, the declines in fertility from 1880 on also presaged shifts in reproductive patterns (albeit different in quantum terms) almost a century later.

Thus the reproductive norms of this period, even in later years when fertility overall was low, remained centred on large families. But it will have been noted that reference has been made here to 'average' family sizes for Pakeha. This is a term that obscures the reproductive polarisation of this period. From the earliest years until the 1940s, some women had numerous children, while others had very few. In the last decade or so of the nineteenth century and in the first half of the twentieth a significant minority of women had none, often because they were spinsters.

As will become evident, throughout the period covered here marriage was the factor that determined family size. It was the key Malthusian 'preventive check',* and its efficacy as a mechanism for fertility regulation persisted, as we will show, even after barrier methods of contraception and other techniques of fertility regulation became more prevalent (Sceats and Pool 1985a; Pool *et al.* 1999). Limitation of family size through marriage has two dimensions: delayed marriage and permanent celibacy. Engelen and Kok (2003) show that these two factors may act independently despite seeming to be deterministically interlinked. Thus, over the next two chapters, it will be necessary to attempt to disaggregate their effects.

The early part of the history described here, certainly until the early 1900s, deals with populations, Maori and Pakeha, which bore most of their children within marriage, and did not have access to effective contraception. These two characteristics render the interpretation of data much easier than for societies, such as the New Zealanders to be encountered later in the book, who adopted more complex modes of fertility regulation. Above all, analysis can focus on two key determinants identified by Engelen and Kok (2003): who married (here the index proportion still never married by a given age is used) and the age at which they married. Thus data relating only to married women, as in the censuses of 1911, 1916 and 1921, or an index such as mean age at marriage computed only for those who marry in a given year, allow only part of the story to be told. They cannot throw light on the proportions of any cohort marrying, yet this is a very important element of the history here. One of the so-called Princeton indices, *Im*, that will be defined and used below, especially in Chapter Four, advances the cause to a degree as it combines age at marriage with proportions celibate (Woods 2000: 86–87).

The three Princeton indices,† used throughout Chapters Three and Four, are not straight conventional rates, but are ratios that allow the population in which one is interested, the numerator statistic, to be compared to the denominator that uses as a benchmark the well-documented reproductive regime of the Hutterites, an Anabaptist religious group. The indices cover three dimensions of family formation: proportions married, *Im*, to which reference was made in the last paragraph; marital fertility, *Ig*; and ex-nuptial or illegitimate fertility, *Ih*. Historical demographer Simon Szreter explains these indices 'take the form of decimal fractions [that are] calibrated against a notional "standard" of "absolute" or "natural" fertility recorded by the Hutterite Anabaptist community of North America in the 1920s'.

---

* According to Robert Woods (2000: 10), in the schema developed by the Thomas Malthus, *An Essay on the Principle of Population* (1798), 'the effect of falling real incomes will be to reduce nuptiality which will consequently lead to lower fertility'.
† Or Coale indices, after Ansley Coale of Princeton University who developed them.

Szreter expresses many misgivings about these indices (1999: 160–61). We share his concerns, especially of the appropriateness of the denominator, a so-called 'natural fertility' regime that procreates under very carefully controlled circumstances. It is this element of 'un-naturally' controlled circumstances that is the problem: Hutterite fertility is almost entirely legitimate; marriage occurs within a narrow and prescribed range of ages: between 19 and 21 years, that are neither too early (in the biomedically risky early to mid-teen ages); nor too late; and they had access to good general and obstetrical health services. Nevertheless, the Princeton methods have been very widely used, and thus New Zealand researchers have available to them good comparative analyses. New Zealand and Australia were the subjects of Elsie Jones's (1971) important study based on these indices.

This chapter and the next also raise two issues of significance for later chapters. The first derives from a general perception, on which Chapters Five to Eight will focus, that family life has changed radically and immutably since 1945; that until then the morphologies of the traditional family had remained more or less intact only to undergo radical shifts in the Baby Boom and thereafter. The second is whether or not trends evident prior to 1945 were precedents for some of the changes that have occurred since. We will look at both of these questions.

Beyond this, there are two other key points that are almost self-evident but which are important to recognise. What happened to families before 1945 will have played an important role in what has occurred since. In this regard, it is a truism, but useful, to say that the size of the households of the forebears of any kin-group will be among the major determinants of the size of today's families, extended families and whanau, and thus of their networks. This is a more manifest example of the effects of the past on the present and future, but there may also be continuities coming from less tangible aspects of family life such as with normative structures.

A corollary to the last point is that many, albeit now a minority, of the people in families today will have been born before 1945, a tiny number even in the early 1900s, and thus will have experienced family life of a prior era, which sets antecedents and benchmarks for what has occurred since World War II. A very few of those born before 1945 will not only be experiencing family life, but could still even be involved as parents of very young children, often as a result of a second or subsequent union with a much younger partner.

With these issues in mind, the rest of the chapter analyses in further detail the period prior to 1945 as interesting in its own right. But it will also, as a sub-theme, assess the degree to which the years 1840 to 1945 constitute a period from which post-war society has drawn behaviours, norms and values relating to family dynamics, structures and forms.

DATA SOURCES AND LITERATURE ON NEW ZEALAND

Data sources for the period are rather limited. The censuses, which will be a major source for later chapters, had few questions on the family in this period. There were none on family and household structures equivalent to those data that have been collected in recent enumerations. The fertility question addressed to married women in 1911, 1916, 1921 (Pakeha only) and 1945 (Maori only) is an invaluable source of information. The most useful systematic data set on family forms is that on marital status. There were no national sample surveys on families as this development was essentially a post-World War II phenomenon even in the United States (Pool *et al.* 2007: Chapt. 3).

The family formation dimension of family structure is far better served, at least for Pakeha, because vital and marriage registers enrich the database. However, for Maori even basic parameters, such as crude birth rates (CBRs) and family size, can only be estimated until after 1945 (Pool 1991: Chapt. 6). A major gap for Maori is the absence of age-specific fertility data until 1962. Pool (1977) has demonstrated, however, that over much of the period covered here, the Maori population's age structure was 'quasi-stable', a technical construct allowing the analyst to infer that fertility levels have remained relatively unchanged. Khawaja (1986), as part of a wider study on national cohort fertility, used this finding to estimate age-specific rates back to the 1930s.

A reasonably detailed picture can be built up for Pakeha nuptiality and fertility trends drawing on the work of a number of authors, most importantly on what are New Zealand classics: Jacoby (1958–59 and 1961), Gibson (1971), Jones (1971), Jain (1972) and Vosburgh (1978), and the more recent but also authoritative studies by O'Neill (1979, 1985) and Khawaja (1985). Far more speculative is the analysis of fertility regulation over the period (Sceats and Pool 1985). Even more difficult to chart is the normative and attitudinal context for changes in family structure, although, fortunately, we have available to us the work of several social historians (e.g. Olssen and Levesque 1978; Macdonald 1990; Toynbee 1995). For Maori, Pool's analysis is the major source. It also synthesises other more specific studies, including ethnographic. Recently, Pool, in collaboration with Kukutai and Sceats, has detailed for the Waitangi Tribunal some aspects studied earlier by Pool in a more general way (Kukutai *et al.* 2002; see also Pool 1991).

There is only a limited amount of time-series information from historical studies and literature. Much of historiography has been highly focused on particular demographic and social themes, or has been on particular regions (e.g. Eldred-Grigg 1980), so that we lack wider-sweeping historical studies on the family *per se*, except for those noted in the last paragraph. But broad, provocative analyses, synthesising a wider range of studies, are found in James Belich's books (1996: 391–97, and 2001: 181–88). Michael King's elegantly woven story of New Zealand (2003) provides an essential social and cultural backdrop to our account.

A general, wide-ranging and rather provocative paper on the Pakeha family in early colonial New Zealand by the historian David Thomson was published recently (2006). It raised numerous major issues and challenged many conventional views on the colonial Pakeha family. This literature review would be incomplete were it not to pay special attention to his arguments.

HISTORIOGRAPHY OF THE COLONIAL PAKEHA FAMILY: A DIFFERENT PERSPECTIVE

David Thomson's central thesis provides a very useful working hypothesis for this part of our book. His paper postulates that, in contrast to what numbers of other scholars have argued, both historians and the authors of the present book (in this very chapter we have already talked about hyper-fertility), the early colonial (pre-1880) Pakeha family was not 'exceptional', certainly not by comparison with those in other neo-Europes, and perhaps not even by comparison with those in the 'home country' (Thomson 2006). The emphasis in his paper was on the families of married women, so that perhaps this argument should be refined to read, the early colonial family of a married Pakeha woman was not exceptional by the standards of British married women. But this does not take the analysis very far because marriage is the very mechanism by which fertility was controlled: for the colonial family and its British counterpart. The most important proximate determinants of fertility were *who among the women became married and at what age*. Thus a major factor to be looked at is whether or not colonial Pakeha and British women shared similar patterns of nuptiality.

Thomson's central argument also has a number of important sub-texts that serve as foci for key issues the importance of which were reinforced by his paper. First, he critically analyses arguments favouring what he terms a 'frontier demographic effect'. He asks, 'Did "the wilderness master the [Pakeha] colonist" on the New Zealand frontier, as Turner put it so colourfully of the American West, or did the imported culture here prove the more powerful? . . . will "the frontier" bear the freight of explanation that we often load upon it, in demography or in social and political history more broadly?' At different times in the twentieth century the frontier was a major interest not only of historians but also of geographers, and, although this intellectual movement was primarily American in genesis and focus, comparative studies were carried out in Australia and, to a lesser degree, New Zealand. Thomson's review shows that it has been an important theme in New Zealand history, but he also questions whether or not New Zealand had a real frontier of the Australian or North American type (2006: *passim*, 127).

The 'demographic effect' of the prototypical frontier of history and of fiction came about, it is normally postulated, because of high masculinity ratios (males to 100 females), although Thomson argues there is a need to adopt 'caution about the force of an unbalanced sex ratio in New Zealand's history'. The surplus of men theoretically allows universal and early marriage for the women colonists. He employs data from New Zealand from the 1850s to 1870s, drawn from regional studies by Pickens (1980), Macdonald (1990) and that by Maureen Molloy on Waipu (Northland), to conclude that 'New Zealand's figures fall unobtrusively within the British range at mid-century'.

Then, employing both marriage data and those on fertility, he argues that a key factor might have been selectivity in the migration streams; that Pakeha could have been drawn from early-marrying populations with higher fertility. This is a question that is addressed in detail later in this chapter including by means of a systematic coverage of all British Isles regions for which data are available (for some parameters, data are available only for England and Wales).

Another point Thomson raises is that family size is a function not just of fertility but also the survival of children to adulthood. He argues that in this respect Pakeha colonists were privileged by comparison with their British peers, a point that we develop later in the present chapter. We also show, however, that low levels of infant and childhood survivorship definitely had a major negative effect on the sizes of Maori families at this time.

After reviewing a range of indices, Thomson uses the fertility data in the 1916 New Zealand census and comparable data from 1911 in the British and Australian censuses, relating to women who had married in the 1860s, as his prime evidence base. From these he concludes that the 'spreads' of family sizes were similar. As these data figure so largely in Thomson's analysis it is necessary to discuss them a little further. He presents some conventional caveats about them as sources, of which an important one is differential survival (for example, was it the more fecund or less fecund who survived to old age, a classical problem with these data? What about those who died in childbirth and who are thus not represented among the mothers being studied?). These women had married on average 50 years earlier, and thus would have been about 70 years of age or older at these censuses.

However, Thomson does not seem to raise what may be an even more important caveat relating to the respondents in these censuses (Thomson 2006: 125–26; 131–36; *passim*): that by comparison with the British women enumerated in 1911, most of whom spent their lives in Britain, the New Zealanders would have represented a population among whom a significant proportion could have borne their children outside New Zealand, presumably following the norms of British society. In short, the New Zealand data will be severely contaminated by a British experience (a less likely situation with the Australian simply because they had been colonised longer and thus their 1911 data were more likely to include Australian-born), whereas the British would not be contaminated by experiences in New Zealand.

The most important family-style migrations to New Zealand were in the 1870s under the Vogel scheme (to be discussed below), whereas inflows of the 1860s had been more weighted towards unaccompanied men; this is clear from the sex-ratio data by age (Neville 1985: Tables 22 and 23). Thus, these inflows would have included women who had married in Britain in the 1860s, thereby likely to follow British conjugal and reproductive norms, and would already have completed some of their fertile, probably their most fecund, years there. One can add to these women an unknown number, who, having married in Britain in the 1850s or 1860s, entered New Zealand during the decades between the peak years for migration inflows (1860s and 1870s) and the 1916 census, when they were enumerated in New Zealand. In sum, the census data for 1911 and 1916 on cohorts married in the mid-nineteenth century represent very different populations from those who were living in New Zealand and having children in the 1860s and 1870s.

It is for this very critical methodological reason that, while some illustrative use is made of the valuable 1911 and subsequent censuses' data, the analysis in this book has instead focused primarily on the behaviours of Pakeha women actually living in New Zealand during the period of early colonisation, who would have followed the norms prevailing here. Then comparisons are made with their contemporaries living and childbearing at the same time in the British Isles. For these purposes a mix of census and vital data are used in this book. This information base is more extensive and analysed in more detail than Thomson suggests in his paper. Not only are there data at a national level, but for both New Zealand and the British Isles there are also relatively detailed regional sets that will be drawn on (see also Dharmalingam *et al.* 2007). This means that this book has used sub-national data sets that systematically cover every region of New Zealand and the British Isles (for which data are available), and thus allow valid comparisons to be made between New Zealand and Britain on nuptiality and fertility, and at the same time to look into the issue of migration selectivity.

3.2 CHANGES IN FAMILY MORPHOLOGIES UNTIL 1945

As was shown in Chapter Two (Figs 2.1 and 2.2), our period begins in the 1840s, with very large Pakeha families and very early and almost universal marriage. In this pioneer period women married young but men did not – in 1876, for example, 38% of Pakeha women aged 20–24 were married compared with only 10% of men of the same age. This pattern changed quickly in the last quarter of the nineteenth century to one of later marriage for women,

with a decline in the gap between men and women in the proportions married in their twenties, and with a significant minority of women remaining
single. By 1900, family sizes were smaller and New Zealand had gone from
having one of the highest fertility rates in industrialised countries to one of
the lowest (Gibson 1971). Beyond this, the age-structural and prevalence
patterns for marriage had become entrenched and would remain so until
World War II. In contrast, in terms of fertility, Maori families remained
large throughout the entire period until the 1960s. But, as we will show, the
Maori family of the early part of this era was beset by other problems, most
notably low levels of infant and childhood survivorship that affected its size
and even threatened Maori with extinction.

It is worth noting that from the 1860s, when Maori and Pakeha numbers had been on par for the last time, the majority, indeed most, New
Zealanders were Pakeha of British origin. This produced the British Pakeha
demographic hegemony already referred to, a dominance that lasted until
the 1970s, well beyond the end of the period covered in this chapter. This
probably had a major impact on New Zealand normative structures. A
function of this chapter and the next is to attempt to assess if that assertion is true and, if so, how far it were true, and how and why New Zealand
norms and behaviours were affected. To do so these chapters pay attention to the family lives of the early Pakeha settlers, comparing them to,
and looking for antecedents in, the household structures and forms in the
mother country.

The change in ethnic distribution was very rapid. At the time of the
Treaty of Waitangi in 1840, Maori had outnumbered Pakeha by the order
of 40 or 50 to one. From 1858/59, when about half the population had been
Maori, the proportion dropped radically until by 1874 they comprised only
14%, and by 1878 and 1881 merely 9% (Papps 1985b: Table 9). This continued
to be their contribution to the total population until 1976 when fewer than
8% of the total population were Maori. Asians and Pacific peoples became
important minorities only from the 1970s on. Chinese had come in small
numbers from the time of the gold-rushes (the 1850s and 1860s), but they
were mainly single men who faced major problems in seeking wives (Ip
1990: 14–16). In sum, except for isolated rural areas mainly in the north,
centre and east of the North Island, for a whole century this was largely a
Pakeha country, and for most of the twentieth century fitted happily into
the appellation 'white' Dominion.

3.3 MAORI FAMILY MORPHOLOGIES

Much of the rest of this chapter will look at Pakeha families, as this is
where very significant changes were evident. In contrast, Maori family

morphologies were to undergo a fundamental change only during and after World War II. At this point it is necessary therefore merely to summarise some key features known about the period 1840–1945.

This was an era in which Maori life was forever altered by contact with Pakeha, by the New Zealand Wars, and by huge migration inflows of Pakeha settlers. Above all, Maori were affected by both confiscation of land at the time of the wars and, arguably more importantly, the application of so-called 'legal' processes of land purchase and other methods of alienation before and after those wars. But, despite that severe impact, Maori cultural values surrounding the whanau seem to have endured robustly and did not change until during and after World War II (see Chapter Five; Pool 1991: Chapts 4 and 5, and pp. 171–75; see also Kukutai *et al.* 2002 for the impacts of land alienation).

Throughout much of the period covered by this chapter Maori were a minority, and generally a small minority. But in a sense the proportion of the total population who were Maori at this time is less important than the fact that, until the 1960s, Maori had very different patterns of family formation from Pakeha. There are few data on most aspects of Maori family structures at this time, but those available show that at least from the 1880s their family sizes were relatively large, and, unlike those of Pakeha, continued to be. The estimated total fertility rates (TFR) were above 5.5 births per woman from 1886 and were between six and seven from 1921 until the 1960s (Figure 2.1). The gradual increases from 1844 to 1920 were due to bio-social factors outside this study's area of interest and discussed in detail elsewhere (Pool 1991: *passim*, plus glossary, Fig. 4.1 and Table 6.2). Suffice to say here that conception rates were probably high, while fetal loss would also have been high, especially following the introduction of gonorrhoea and other venereal and non-venereal disorders (e.g. pelvic tuberculosis). These were diseases that Maori had never experienced before and to which they had no immunity. In the case of syphilis, Maori had not been subject to a related disease that was widespread in the tropical Pacific, yaws, exposure to which gives some immunity against syphilis: a sort of cowpox–smallpox relationship.[*] Moreover, elevated levels of fetal loss are normal concomitants of very high levels of general mortality, which Maori experienced over the early years of colonisation. Nevertheless, this was also a population with 'natural fertility' (no recourse to artificial means of fertility regulation), and probably early and almost universal marriage (at least judging from census data available since 1926, see Figure 2.2).

Until legal marital status became linked to welfare measures after

---

[*] The empirical evidence on the epidemiologic situation of Maori and other Polynesians, and other immunologically virgin populations, is reported from the literature by Pool 1991: 78–82.

World War II, unions tended to be legitimised by the gaining of community approval rather than by registration. 'As Maori already had a culturally acceptable and perfectly viable system for the legitimation of marriages, state-enforced registration was not appealing, unless there were other benefits, like social security eligibility' (Pool 1991: 109, drawing on Douglas 1977: 267–79).*

From the time when the first census data on Maori marital statuses became available (1926), all but a minority of Maori men and women at 25–34 years reported that they were married. For Maori women, moreover, marriage was at young ages (high proportions married at 20–24 years). Although the Depression of the 1930s and the absence of men still overseas on war service in 1945 occasioned slight delays in getting married, there was nothing akin to what was seen for Pakeha women at the end of the period covered in this chapter (Dharmalingam *et al.* 2007: Table 3.1, Maori; Table 3.2, Pakeha). The decreases in early marriage for Maori in recent years has been due not so much to a change in the propensity to enter unions (a structural factor), as to the change in the form such unions take.

The large Maori family sizes of this period came, then, from early and universal marriage and no systematic attempt to practise fertility regulation. According to Douglas (1977), these levels were maintained by a series of cultural props, such as the adoption of children into the lineage and thus the wider whanau, which was of major significance. Beyond this, the very low survivorship rates of children born alive, compared to Pakeha at that time, was a major factor producing strongly pro-natalist norms. When Dame Whina Cooper, the renowned Maori leader who herself was to become a nonagenarian, was born in the early 1890s, 40% of the Maori girls born at the same time failed to reach their first birthday, and only a minority their seventh birthday; this great kuia (old lady) was thus equally a great survivor. Between the time of her birth and about 1910 the infant and early childhood mortality rates had dropped rapidly, largely because of the health campaigns launched by the Department of Health and Maori medical practitioners such as Pomare and Te Rangihiroa, so that by then 74% were reaching age one and 53% age 20 years (Pool 1991: 77–78, 118–19). As is the norm in populations with low levels of life expectancy undergoing declines in mortality, the force of the changes fell on the youngest ages, not on the elderly, increasing the proportions of infants and young children. This illustrates the great importance of survivorship effects on family structures, especially the proportions at childhood ages, in high-mortality populations.

---

* Only from 1938 on.

Results of a question put to Maori only at the 1945 census show very low levels of either childlessness or sub-fertility. At ages 25–34 years fewer than 10% of women had never had a child (Pool 1991: 110–13). As the national Maori TFR was 6.5 births per woman in 1945 (Pool 1991: 6.2), there was little room for marked socio-economic and regional differences within Maori society. Nevertheless, some did occur, and thus the small minorities living in the South Island, and in and around Auckland and Wellington cities, had smaller family sizes than other regions in both 1926 and 1945. At the end of the period, in 1945, the estimated rural fertility rate was extremely high (7.1 births per woman), more than double the rate for urban areas (3.1), where, however, only 26% of Maori were living at that time (Pool 1991: 126–27).

In the period after colonisation, the land wars and land loss forced the local movement and resettlement of Maori. This affected whanau structures. From the late nineteenth century another factor entered into this equation: Maori men undertook circular mobility to engage in casual or seasonal work (Kukutai *et al.* 2002; Bedford and Pool 2004). Again whanau structures become strained as a result.

3.4 PAKEHA FAMILY MORPHOLOGIES: BRITISH ANTECEDENTS

GENERAL ISSUES
One of the curiosities of New Zealand family sociology is the fact that there are two conflicting views of the pioneer Pakeha family. It is often treated as something like Topsy: an entity that had a unique, unheralded and unanticipated nascency, almost independent of its British roots. Alternatively, it is seen as simply an antipodean version of the Victorian family (the major thesis of Thomson 2006). Neither perspective is correct: the Pakeha family of the late nineteenth century deviated markedly from its British counterpart. For a start, and most importantly, marriage patterns were very different, fertility levels were higher and nuclear families were more likely to be neolocal. Yet, if one reviews the literature on the antecedents to the late Victorian Pakeha family, say by going back 40–50 years earlier to the first decades of the nineteenth, or even into the eighteenth, century some interesting points emerge. As there are fewer data on other countries within the British Isles many of the remarks apply primarily to England and Wales, but, in any case, the largest single birthplace group of colonists, a bare majority, came from there.

An interest in early Pakeha family and social life has been a relatively recent historiographical trend. The development of a strong stream of social history has had to await a shift in interest away from the traditional concerns, say, of Maori–Pakeha conflict or legislative and political history.

Today historians, such as Charlotte Macdonald (1990), are filling some of the critical gaps, while James Belich (1996) incorporated social and demographic patterns into the broad sweeps his approach demands. Yet, the impression remains that probably we know far more about the ethno-history of Maori, albeit sometimes through badly distorted prisms, than we do about Pakeha. Links to the socio-cultural root stocks of the British diaspora are even rarer, although some historians are now starting to map this (e.g. McLean 1990; or Toynbee 2000, although in her case for a more recent flow).

To look for the antecedents for Pakeha reproductive behaviours we can refer to the entire three-century span – the seventeenth, eighteenth and nineteenth centuries – before the colonisation of New Zealand. Fascinatingly, reproductive rates increased during the latter part of the eighteenth century in England and Wales, to peak during and just after the Napoleonic Wars, but before Victoria became queen. Levels had even been lower in the Restoration period, renowned for its libertine lifestyles, than when Jane Austen was writing. There was a gross reproduction rate (GRR)[*] of 2.91 female births per woman for England and Wales in 1801–25, as against 2.57 in 1826–50; 2.49 in 1851–75, (when large flows of immigrants were entering New Zealand); and 2.01 for 1876–1901 (Woods 1996: 305–06).

Even the rates for the peak years of reproduction, 1801–25, for England and Wales cannot rival what Pakeha in New Zealand achieved in the 1870s. The Anglo-Welsh GRR for 1801–25 is roughly equivalent to a TFR of 5.8 births per woman and had dropped to about 5.0 by the period New Zealand was being colonised, whereas Pakeha TFRs in the 1870s and 1880s almost reached 7.0. The first registration records for Scotland show that rates there were even lower: a TFR of 4.1 in 1855. For Ross Shire in the north, where levels had been among the highest in the late eighteenth century, the TFR was only 3.5 in the mid- to late nineteenth century (Flinn *et al.* 1977: Table 5.3.5). This means, moreover, that British peak rates of 1801–25 had been reached and surpassed at least fifteen to twenty years before New Zealand was made a colony.

It also seems that Pakeha fertility patterns in the 1870s were representative of the rates across the period of early settlement prior to that date. Estimates show that Pakeha colonists already had high rates in the 1840s (approx. 6.5 births per woman) and maintained these levels until the

---

[*] The GRR should not be confused with the GFR used frequently in this and the next chapter and defined here. The former is derived from the TFR, also defined below, and represents the female births per woman, and is thus a measure of replacement of the female population. The net reproductive rate (NRR) referred to in the next chapter is a derivative of the GRR, refining it by controlling for survivorship of the female births to the age their mothers were at when these girl-children were born.

beginning of the 1880s (see Figure 2.1). Rates may actually have edged up slightly closer to 7.0 in the 1870s, but this difference would have been very slight.

In the late nineteenth century there were declines in marital fertility across the British Isles, and even in rural Ireland by the end of that period. There is also strong, albeit indirect, evidence of fertility limitation using a range of traditional barrier methods and abstention, and this seems to have extended to women with older ages at marriage, especially in England and Wales (Anderson 1998; see also Szreter 2002: Chapt. 8).

The British peak in fertility came at the end of a period starting in the mid-eighteenth century and following an era in which rates had been lower. The determinant of the trend is simple to identify: a shift to a younger age at marriage and more universal entry into unions (Wrigley 1981: *passim* and esp. Table III), the very feature that was to characterise the Pakeha family of the 1870s when the first detailed data become available. In the case of Pakeha at first settlement, however, age at marriage was even younger and nuptiality virtually universal, and thus fertility that much higher.

From the start of the Victorian period British ages at marriage went up and remained this way at least until World War II. In England and Wales, for example, the mean age of marriage for women in 1826–50 was low by comparison either with the ages recorded before the late eighteenth century or in the second half of the nineteenth century, but was still over 25 years, and had edged up to 26 by 1851, to remain at that age or higher throughout the rest of the period covered by this chapter (Woods 2000: Fig. 3.5). In Scotland from 1861 to 1931 the mean followed more or less the same pattern, but the median ranged around 24 years (Flinn *et al.* 1977: Table 5.2.8). In 1876 the Pakeha median was below 23 years, but had reached the Scottish level by 1896 (see below). In the Depression of the 1930s the non-Maori mean exceeded 26 years of age (O'Neill 1985: Table 106).

Early and almost universal marriage for women should, in theory, also be associated with low levels of ex-nuptial conception and childbearing, or 'illegitimacy' or 'bastardy' as the British historical demographers say; a function of the diminution of 'vice' when the perverse effects of the Malthusian preventive checks are reduced. In a perfect Malthusian world, sex would only occur between married consenting adults, but in a less-than-perfect one delaying marriage might lead to men seeking solace through the sex industry. Robert Woods has posited a hypothetical relationship between proportions of married women and illegitimacy. He points out that in a society like China in the 1930s, almost all women married and illegitimacy was all but absent (Woods 2000: 102). At the opposite pole would be societies that have few taboos relating to intercourse and ex-nuptial childbearing. British populations certainly did not fit the 'no taboos' model, but historically they (and others) have also not fitted the high proportions marrying early/low levels of illegitimacy hypothesis.

In this regard, 'In most, if not all, traditional societies other than Western Europe women married very young and few remained single'. Britain in particular, and early modern Western Europe in general, seems to be a deviant case (Wrigley 1981: 143). Instead illegitimacy has been a feature especially, and in contradiction to the hypothesis, when ages at marriage are young and marriage rates are high. The resolution of this paradox is that bridal pregnancy was widely accepted, and this held true even when marriage took place after a birth had occurred. In fact, 'the Church [of England] held that children born to couples who married were legitimate whether or not their birth took place after their parents' marriage' (Wrigley 1981: 161). In a sense this compromise would itself have been a determinant of early marriage. 'The most likely reason for this peculiarity is the widespread acceptance of bridal pregnancy as a means of legitimising the illegitimate. Disregard for virginity [in some periods] should not be confused with acceptance of bastardy' (Woods 2000: 106).

BRITISH ANTECEDENTS: REGIONAL DIMENSIONS

In general, then, it seems that, by comparison with what was seen in the British Isles, the Pakeha colonists had established different overall patterns and levels of reproduction. Nevertheless, a nagging concern is whether Pakeha immigrants, especially in the two decades around the key period of 1870, were representative of the British population or if instead, because of selective migration, they were very different. The detailed work carried out by Jock Phillips, Terry Hearn and their colleagues at the Ministry for Culture and Heritage shows that the migrants were not only selective by country (within the British Isles) and county of origin, but also in terms of occupation.[*] We draw on their evidence, and also on vital data for the four different countries of the British Isles around 1870, plus British census data for these dates.

If the date 1871 is taken as an approximate reference point, Scots were significantly over-represented among Pakeha colonists (27% of Pakeha, as against only 11% of the British population), and Irish slightly so (21% as against 20%). By contrast, English were significantly under-represented – they made up only 50% of the colonists from the British Isles, but 65% of the British home population – and Welsh were barely represented at all (1% as against almost 5% of the people of the British Isles).

*   Grateful acknowledgement is made to Jock Phillips for furnishing us with these painstakingly assembled data.

The Highlands and Far North, including the Shetland and Orkney islands, seem over-represented among the Scots, and the central part of the country under-represented. But, as was true for the Scottish population as a whole, the majority (about 60%) of the immigrants coming from Scotland came from the Scottish Midlands and Lowlands regions (74% of Scotland's population). Around 40% of the Irish migrants in these key decades came from Ulster, whereas this held true for under a third of the population of Ireland. The major sources of English migration proportionately were London, the Home Counties and the South West. Curiously, persons from the Channel Islands and the Isle of Man were over-represented (1% versus 0.4%); so too were Shetland and Orkney islanders, but sheep-farming links there seem more natural.

When the regions that were the favoured sources of migration to New Zealand are examined it seems that, broadly speaking, settlers came from areas that had middling (e.g. around 35 per 1000 population) to lower (<33) CBRs, and proportionately fewer came from those areas where rates were elevated (38+). Of course, age-compositional effects may account for some of these differences (see second footnote, p. 47), but the age and gender distributions in most British Isles regions at that time would have been less distorted than those in New Zealand, where denominators for crude rates were inflated artefactually and thus rates were deflated (see footnote). The data on birth rates and on marriage patterns in the British Isles and its regions in the late 1860s/1870s cited here are available elsewhere (Dharmalingam *et al.* 2007: Table 3.3).

Circa 1871, the English counties overall had middling birth rates. London, first equal among sources of New Zealand migration at this time, was close to the countrywide level, whereas the other lead source area, the South West, had low rates, as did the South East, the next most favoured place of origin. Of the remaining regions, taking those which were more important in that they each contributed around 5–7% of the English inflows:

- the West Midlands (with the sole exception of Staffordshire, comprising the Black Country coal-mining area, that had a rate of 42) had low to middling rates;
- the South Midlands (including Oxfordshire, where rural unrest that spread to other counties led to emigration) again had low to middling rates;
- the remainder of the Midlands and the East (Essex, Suffolk and Norfolk) all had low to middling levels;
- Lancashire–Cheshire was split between Cheshire, which was middling, and Lancashire (again comprising a coal-mining area), which was higher (38); and
- finally, the West Riding of Yorkshire was higher (38), but the East

and North Ridings were middling (Registrar-General, England and Wales 1878).

In the case of Scotland, the second most important source of immigrants to New Zealand, estimates show that even in the late eighteenth century Scottish CBRs had not been extremely high, only at the level they were to be at in the 1850s to 1870s, around 34 to 35 per 1000 population. Of interest, however, is that in the 1790s, rates in the Highlands and Hebrides were much higher, at 40 per 1000, than those for the rest of country, yet by the 1850s and thereafter they were the lowest in Scotland (Flinn *et al.* 1977: Tables 4.4.5 and 5.3.2). In Scotland in the 1870s, the North and Border regions had notably low rates, Edinburgh and its environs and most of the Midlands and Lowlands low to middling rates, and only the area around Glasgow had rates that approximated those for Pakeha. Interestingly, higher rates were characteristic of urban areas and lower rates of rural Scotland, but despite this, overall levels in that country fell well below those in New Zealand (Registrar-General, Scotland, 1868).

Ireland had had somewhat higher fertility, associated with early marriage, before the potato famine of the late 1840s than thereafter. In the 1830s the CBRs were around 33 per 1000 and in 1840 the GFRs were around 130, a level that would be low by Pakeha settler standards. At that time there was little difference between regions (Connell 1975: App. II, Table e). In Ireland in the 1870s, the range was still modest but the CBRs were low: 25–27 per 1000. In the 1870s, Ulster and Leinster (the area north, south, inland from and including Dublin) had slightly lower rates; Munster and Connaught (from which fewer migrants came) had higher rates. In the 1860s, however, the order had been slightly different, with the area corresponding to Ulster having a rate of 33 per 1000 population, that area approximating south-western Munster 32, and the remaining regions below 30, giving a rate of only 26 for Ireland as a whole (Registrar-General, Ireland, 1878, 1870).

In sharp contrast, when one turns to Irish marital fertility, as against levels of reproduction for women of all conjugal statuses, then one starts to see fertility patterns that resemble those among early colonists in New Zealand. The Irish marital general fertility rate (MGFR) of 307 in the 1870s was equivalent in level, but probably not in pattern, to those of the New Zealand regions with higher rates at that time (Kennedy 1975: Table 59).[*]

---

[*] The major difference was that, on average, Irish women married later. This would mean that age-specific rates, were these available for Pakeha, would probably show that the Irish outran their Pakeha peers, a differential that is opposite to those for the overall fertility patterns. Thus Pakeha women had very high fertility, but they were not emulating their Irish counterparts. At younger ages Pakeha would have had much higher fertility, as against at older married ages where Pakeha levels were probably lower. MGFRs = births within marriage per 1000 married women at the reproductive ages.

BRITISH ANTECEDENTS: OCCUPATIONAL DIFFERENCES

A further element of selectivity is that of occupation. Certainly rural populations seem to have been well represented in these pivotal decades, particularly among assisted-passage immigrants. A farming background was most marked for Irish colonists. For Scotland, data on the population in rural districts suggests that farmers and agricultural labourers coming to New Zealand were proportional to their contribution to Scottish population numbers.

Data on the British Isles relating to fertility by occupation point to high levels among agricultural workers and among builders and labourers, two groups well represented among migrants to New Zealand (Szreter 2002: Fig. 7.1). To the extent that one can assign the same categories to the data available for Pakeha and those in Szreter's figure, it seems that, apart from these two categories, other occupations that were reasonably well represented in New Zealand had lower fertility. In any case his rates relate to marital fertility and, as will become clearer below, are well below the levels of nuptial fertility computed for Pakeha: 7.5 births in Britain per married woman who had a coal-mining husband – the most fertile of Szreter's categories – as against around 9.0 for New Zealand Pakeha of all occupations combined, a level close to biological maxima. But miners of any sort constituted only about 4% of the inflows to New Zealand, and some of them may have been from tin-mining areas in the South West of England, and thus were not coal miners, who had the highest fertility of any occupational grouping in Britain.[*]

BRITISH ANTECEDENTS: ILLEGITIMACY AND MARRIAGE

Levels of illegitimacy were generally low in the British Isles around 1870, notably so across Ireland. Its region with the highest rates, Ulster (3.9% of all births were illegitimate, as against 2.3% for the country as a whole), which contributed disproportionately to the Irish diaspora to New Zealand, was below the level for every English, Welsh and Scottish county except Surrey

---

[*]   A caveat should be mentioned here: Szreter's data are from the 1911 census of England and Wales, relating retrospectively to children ever born alive, whereas ours are indirect estimates from MGFRs, a method described below in footnote 12. His data are thus subject to some of the problems noted earlier in the chapter when discussing the New Zealand censuses of 1911 and 1916. The MGFRs yield estimates of MTFRs. The TFRs (but not the MTFRs) from 1913 on can be compared to, and are very close to, TFRs that are directly computed from statistics only becoming available then and thus seem reasonably robust (see below). But this may be somewhat academic as Pakeha married women *as a whole* had MTFRs that were 1.5 births higher than the rate seen for the wives of British coal miners. The Pakeha MTFR was, moreover, 2–3 births above the rates seen in Britain among those groups who were well represented among colonists. These differences are so significant that the effects of different sources and methods of computation are probably limited.

(3.9%) and Middlesex (3.8%). The Anglo-Welsh rate was 5.6%, reaching its highest in Cumberland on the Scottish border (9.7%).

It was the Scots (10.2%) who excelled in this regard, with a countrywide rate almost five times that of Ireland, and almost twice that of England. Very high rates were seen in the North East, around Aberdeen (15.8%), and the Border region (14.1%) (see Dharmalingam *et al.* 2007: Table 3.3). At the same time there were wide differences in Scotland, with the rates for the Shetlands below those for the lowest English county, but still above most Irish counties except around Belfast. As will be shown later in this chapter, Pakeha levels of ex-nuptial fertility in the late Victorian period resembled those of Ireland rather than Britain.

With the rather significant exception of Scotland, it can be argued that almost all reproduction would have taken place within marriage – more than four-fifths even in Scotland. Thus at the time of the pivotal migration flows to New Zealand around 1870, entry into marriage was still a major regulating factor for exposure to both intercourse and to conception. As Robert Woods has argued, 'The preventive check . . . was still working well, although perhaps more geographically diverse, towards the middle of Victoria's reign [i.e. around 1870] when fertility began to be controlled directly within marriage' (Woods 2000: 109).

By comparison with the British Isles, marriage at a young age was certainly in vogue among Pakeha settlers. In New Zealand at the 1874 census, a minority (46%) of women aged 20–24 years had never been married. But in England the rate was 66% and in Scotland 74%. In England, London and the Home Counties, which contributed most heavily to migration to New Zealand, were above the countrywide level, and the South West well above (73%). In Scotland most of the major source areas – the North, North East, the Midlands and the area around Edinburgh – were all above the total Scottish level. The area around Glasgow was well below (66%), but above the rate for England and well above New Zealand's (Dharmalingam *et al.* 2007: Table 3.3).

THE EFFECTS OF THE SELECTIVITY OF EMIGRATION FLOWS TO NEW ZEALAND

Looking at this evidence it is hard to draw absolute conclusions. Nevertheless, the selectivity of the migration appears not to have played the instrumental role that one might have expected in shaping reproductive behaviours among the settlers who came to New Zealand. Migrants did not come disproportionately from areas with high fertility: they were, in fact, more likely to come from areas with middling or lower levels of natality. Moreover, 'high' birth rates in the British context merely meant a level about or slightly below that of Pakeha around 1870. While farmers and farm workers, who in Britain had higher fertility, were well represented among the colonists, they still constituted only a minority of the migrants, and their marital fertility in Britain seems to have been below levels observed here. Even if one takes the rates of marital fertility for Pakeha as a whole recorded in 1896, when fertility had already entered a decline, so as to make sure that they correspond more closely to those represented in the British 1911 census, the New Zealand rates were higher than for the British occupational group with the most elevated fertility. This occurred even though the Pakeha data are an average across all regions and occupations combined.

If one had to make a 'guesstimate' of the impact of migrants from British regions and occupations with higher fertility, the combined effect of their contribution would probably amount to no more than 25–30% of the fertility patterns in New Zealand. It would be impossible to argue that selective migration to New Zealand from British regions of elevated fertility had much impact on the overall New Zealand rates. Against this, about the same proportion (25–30%) of Pakeha settlers coming from low fertility areas and occupations would have changed their reproductive behaviours on immigration to New Zealand, and adopted a much higher fertility regime than they had left behind in the British Isles; and about 50% would have come from counties with middling regimes by British standards (say 34–36 per 1000), but significantly below the overall level in New Zealand (41–43 per 1000, but this was an artefactually deflated rate; see footnote p. 47).

Later in the next chapter we will look at regional differences within New Zealand. These strengthen the argument put forward here because in the 1870s inter-regional variance was limited, again a contrast with the British Isles where county levels for birth rates varied between the mid-20s and the low 40s. Taking all of this together, it implies a significant level of adaptation: a major shift in both normative and behavioural systems.

Of course, there might possibly have been more micro-level dimensions of selectivity – perhaps commentators from the wilder shores of evolutionary psychology could hypothesise that the more adventuresome, virile and fecund were those most likely to have migrated. But with mass assisted-passage migrations, as in the Vogel period, which would surely have subverted any possibility of abnormally virile people being the modal class of settlers, this hypothesis would seem wildly far-fetched, even if one had the data to test it. Moreover, as variance in patterns and levels (everywhere very high) of reproduction was minimal once they arrived in New Zealand, any such speculation would have to assume that hyper-fecundity was not merely the mode, but characterised most settlers.

It seems highly unlikely, then, that biological selection provides an explanation of fertility levels in New Zealand, beyond the obvious point that the more adventuresome were likely to migrate. Even this may not have held as, in some cases, so-called 'push' factors were operating at the point of origin. Rollo Arnold's research has shown that turmoil in agricultural England at around 1870 might have been a factor producing some of the migration in the Vogel period (1980: Epilogue). The Irish famine of the late 1840s had been a prototypical push factor that might have been expected to affect emigration in the period covered in this chapter, and thus the sources on which New Zealand drew. Yet, somewhat surprisingly, the Irish were not over-represented: their flows were more or less proportionate to their population in the British Isles and the famine did not produce a surge in the direction of New Zealand.

The family formation patterns of Pakeha New Zealanders were certainly different from those occurring among the different populations in Britain around 1870. British precursors for some settler behaviours and norms at that time can be found over the decades before the large migration inflows of the 1860s to the late 1870s. Among the attitudes and behaviours that might have shaped New Zealand norms and their underlying values, and may have given them an enduring conservative flavour, were those in the British Isles surrounding ex-nuptial conception followed by marital birth and ex-nuptial childbearing, in relation to marriage patterns and family building in general. Periodically, these values re-manifest themselves in policy and other debates in Pakeha New Zealand society. At times their reappearance is associated with high rates of ex-nuptial conception, and on these and other occasions concerns over ex-nuptiality may be of sufficient magnitude to generate calls for sanctions against unmarried mothers, and drive moral panics and/or policy formulation, a point discussed in later chapters. The key issue here is that the same antecedents, both the patterns of behaviour and the same responses, were also reported for the source populations in what one would assume to be the more conservative cultural groups in the British Isles. It may be significant that these streams were disproportionately represented among the outflows from the British Isles to New Zealand.

The largest single migration flow in this period, indeed one of the largest ever, the Vogel schemes of the early 1870s, had brought in, so Rollo Arnold has argued, disproportionate numbers of 'village labourers' from England who were skilled or semi-skilled, and who were overwhelmingly literate. Not only did they make an important contribution to the colony's agrarian life and development, as Arnold asserts, and as was Vogel's aim, but probably imported with them more conservative norms reflecting the underlying value systems of the stable, rural English life-ways of that time and from which they were drawn. It is true that the English countryside was temporarily in turmoil because of calls for agrarian reform. But to seek opportunities to maintain and improve their lifestyles was the very reason many abandoned the mother country and set out courageously to make a 'Better Britain' (James Belich's term) in the Antipodes and elsewhere (e.g. South America, Arnold 1980: Epilogue). Their attitudes would have differed from those of the British urban under classes of the 1870s.

3.5 EARLY COLONIAL PAKEHA FAMILY MORPHOLOGIES: TRENDS

MARRIAGE, MIGRATION, MASCULINITY, MOTHERHOOD

Turning now to the Pakeha who had arrived and were resident in New Zealand, we look first at marriage patterns, then at aspects of family morphologies other than fertility. Then we turn to reproduction itself, and follow this by attempting to make first-order explanations of trends, mainly at a national level – we leave higher-order interpretations and the in-depth analysis of regional and other differentials to Chapter Four. This part of Chapter Three focuses on the period up until the start of the twentieth century. We then finish this chapter by following the patterns and trends through to World War II.

The trends in the following analysis must be seen in the context in which they were played out, and thus a brief parenthetic comment must be made at this point. Levels of ex-nuptial fertility were very low until the 1960s (<5.2% of total births except for 1944, when it reached 6%, Jain 1972: v.3, 81; Sceats and Pool 1985; Zodgekar 1980; and Levesque 1986: 4, who notes that 'New Zealand Europeans had the second lowest rate of illegitimacy throughout the Australasian colonies'). Moreover, in contrast perhaps with the last few decades of the twentieth century, the period prior to 1945 is one in which most Pakeha unions were formalised as marriages, and separation and divorce were relatively rare. Nevertheless, this does not cover all aspects of nuptiality and ex-nuptiality. As E. G. Jacoby first showed (1961), for Pakeha New Zealand, particularly during the Baby Boom, a 'culturally acceptable norm has been for ex-nuptial conception to be followed by a precipitated marriage and nuptial live birth' (Pool and Crawford 1980: 25; see also Trlin and Ruzicka 1977; and Carmichael 1982).

As can be seen in Figures 2.1 and 2.2, during the pioneer period up to the end of the 1870s, family sizes were large and parenting started at very young ages. For women aged 20–24 years in 1876 marital fertility probably approached what would be expected for a population with 'natural fertility' – that is, where no attempt is made to control reproduction. Even at 35–39 years rates were 90% of these biological maxima (Sceats and Pool 1985: Fig. 26) and, as just noted, most childbearing was within marriage.

Pioneer Pakeha women married at young ages, so that by the time they reached their early thirties most women had been married at least once.

Very early marriage rates were lower for men than for women in the pioneer period, but this was a function of the gender balance in the colony (Neville 1985). It was so extreme at that time that there would have been a large surplus of potential grooms. Thus the gap between the sexes in terms of the proportions never married was not only very marked, but this continued on at least into the 30–34 year age-group (Dharmalingam *et al.* 2007: Tables 3.2 and 3.4). But what has been described here for marital patterns turned out to be an historically aberrant situation (although it was to be repeated in the Baby Boom) that was righting itself by the end of the nineteenth century: in part because of a change in the masculinity ratio of the population; in part because of increases in the age of marriage for women.

The surplus of males is a manifest but insufficient explanation for high rates of nuptiality at young ages. It is insufficient because the male surplus at marriageable ages had not disappeared when marriage rates dropped in later years of the nineteenth century, although the changes at the dawn of the twentieth century can be partly explained by other demographic determinants that affected the 'marriage market' and that will be discussed below. The high masculinity ratios argument can also be shown to be insufficient because of a later event: very young ages at marriage for women, but also for men, were to recur in the Baby Boom (see Chapter Five) when high masculinity ratios were not at all in evidence.

This view conforms to the arguments of David Thomson (2006: 126–27). That said, his analysis is somewhat selective as he tends to compare New Zealand with societies that were penal colonies (e.g. Tasmania) or, at the stages for which he provides figures, had mixed agrarian and primary exploitative economies (e.g. mining, trapping and hunting, and data for Michigan 1810, Washington and Oregon in the mid-nineteenth century), when not unexpectedly their sex ratios were of the order of 150–200 males per 100 females. But fairer comparison with those jurisdictions would be with New Zealand regions that had primary-sector exploitative industrial bases. For example, at the 1878 census the South Island goldfields had a sex ratio of 197 males per 100 females; in Wakatipu County in 1871 it had been 418, and at 21–39 years it was 750. These statistics support the argument that New Zealand also had frontiers where males dominated, but this is of little import in assessing the role of masculinity in determining nuptiality and fertility trends. High levels of masculinity may have played a role in that more men were available to choose from, were colonial women hard up for spouses, but it was far from being an important factor in shaping fertility. The reason why this is so is simple – women have babies, not men, so no matter how many surplus males there were, the key factor was what women did.

To confirm this argument further, as a part of the analysis of provincial differentials in levels of reproduction and some demographic co-variates to be presented in Chapter Four, correlations between masculinity ratios (males per 100 females) and a range of variables were computed (Dharmalingam *et al.* 2007: Table 3.5).* The results of these computations show that masculinity levels, coming from much higher male than female migratory inflows, had very weak correlations in any direction (mainly negative in fact) with marriage patterns, fertility rates (GFR and MGFR) and the percentages of the population who were New Zealand born – masculinity levels were normal in the child population, a significant proportion of which was New Zealand born, but not at reproductive ages where, at least in 1878, a high percentage of the age-group were overseas born. Thus high levels of marriage in the late 1870s among Pakeha women settlers, overseas or New Zealand born, seem to be more a function of norms than of quirks in the bio-demography, such as the presence of large numbers of unattached males in the population. This latter trend points away from structural explanations and towards values and attitudes as drivers of demographic behaviours. Regardless, the patterns of family formation of Pakeha settlers, at least until the 1890s, were certainly very different from what was occurring at that time in the British Isles populations from which they were drawn (Macdonald 1990: 138–39).

In 1876 the marriage registers show that less than 1% of men married as teenagers, as against 21% of the women that year, but 43% of new husbands were over 30 as against only 13% of wives (many of whom would have been widows). The median ages for marriage had a gap of 6.1 years (28.8 years for men, 22.7 years for women). To show how extreme the gender difference in the pattern of nuptiality in the 1870s was, one can usefully compare this situation with what occurred exactly 100 years later, just after the end of the Baby Boom. In the 1970s, men, whether widowed, divorced, or single, married at a median age of 24.4 years; women were only 2.6 years younger (21.8). A mere 22% of men and 15% of women marrying that year were aged 30 years and over (and by 1976 many of these were divorcees). But, in 1976, 27% of the brides and 6% of the grooms were teenagers, above the levels of 1876.

Thus demographic determinants of the narrow range of ages at which women married, such as high masculinity rates, were mediated by ideational and economic factors. These may have included changes in the value system coming from settlement of a new country. For example, one could cite freedom from the constraints imposed by the rules of primogeniture, where

---

* As there are no individual-level data the analysis had to be made at this level of aggregation. As the number of observations was limited (N = 9 provinces), on the advice of William Bolstad, Department of Statistics, Waikato University, to whom grateful acknowledgement is made, we used Spearman's rank order method. In a purist sense the results must still be treated with caution as, statistically speaking, they are not extremely robust. That said, we can have some degree of confidence in some correlations that are very strong (>.80), and we were heartened by the systematic nature of the results, always a good omen in statistics. We are thus not quoting some maverick result.

these were significant (see below), and the fact that a newly married couple had better economic prospects generally than had their contemporaries in the home country.

Why a shift was then to occur to an older age at marriage and to decreases in the proportions ever marrying is perhaps less clear, particularly as a marked surplus of men at marriageable ages was to be perpetuated until World War I (Neville 1985: Table 23). This surplus, however, would have been moving to older and older ages, a function of the heavy inflows earlier, especially of men to the goldfields, in the 1860s and 1870s, and thus perhaps including many permanent bachelors set in their ways. Migration had dropped off drastically during the long depression of the 1880s, and to add to that the high fertility of the early years of settlement meant that behind the 'balding bachelor bulge' were large cohorts moving through adolescence towards parenting ages. Their sex-ratios, coming from natural increase, were far more balanced. In 1878, notwithstanding the presence in Macdonald's sample of some very young girls who had travelled alone, most teenagers had come to the colony as 'passive' migrants as part of a family, or had been born in New Zealand. Thus the masculinity ratio for adolescents was around normal for that period: 98 males per 100 females. In contrast, at 45–49 years it was markedly unbalanced, and this continued for the rest of the century: 199 males per 100 females in 1878; 174 males per 100 females in 1886; and 132 males per 100 females in 1896.

The men from the first really large colonial birth cohorts (born in the late 1870s, 1880s) would still have been below marrying ages in the 1890s, whereas their potential brides, say five years younger, would have been on average more marriageable. The net result meant that, disproportionately, the available men on the colony's marriage market could well have been either 'past it', or not yet ready. This composition effect could explain in part the decreases in crude marriage rates in the 1880s and 1890s. This trend, termed a 'marriage squeeze' in the literature, was first reported, it seems, as early as 1911 by James McIlraith (cited in Roth 1980: 104–05).

This provides an explanation of underlying factors that may also have caused the shift by brides to older ages at marriage and in the proportions of women marrying – recalling that the male levels barely changed. Both these patterns themselves would have reduced crude rates in the period in which the shifts were occurring by producing a hiatus as those women, who would in earlier decades have married at young ages, would have delayed or would not have married at all. Two determinants of these shifts could be cited here: cultural-ideational and economic. The former, the more plausible, as the same trends in family formation were seen in Anglo-America and Australia, would see the colony maturing and with this a reprise of norms that were operating in much of the old country.

An 'economic-deterministic' argument, proposed by McIlraith in 1911, was that marriage rates were linked to New Zealand's levels of prosperity as measured by prices for farm products. As he shows, in the depression of the 1880s marriage rates were low, while they rose in the 'land boom' of the early 1900s (cited Roth 1980: 104–05; McIlraith 1911). Unfortunately as yet no definitive studies exist that disaggregate cultural, demographic and economic factors, but there are probably more plausible, less economic-deterministic reasons that revolve around marriage-squeeze effects. The massive migration inflows of the 1870s had dried up by the 1880s, meaning that any new entrants to the marriage market would increasingly have to be locally born and raised, and as noted above they were not yet at conjugal ages, but would certainly be by the early 1900s (earlier for women). Only detailed research on age/gender/ marital-status-specific nuptiality rates, which are available, would be able to confirm this alternative hypothesis.

Regardless, however, by 1896 the gender age gap at the time of marriage had narrowed to 3.8 years as the female median age at marriage increased (to 24.0 years) and the male dropped a little (to 27.8). The proportion of grooms who were teenagers was still below 1%, but for brides this had dropped to 12%, while only a third of men and only 14% of women marrying in the 1890s were aged over 30.

The high masculinity ratios in this early period, however, had other effects on family life, especially structures. The Pakeha population included many men who had never married or formed families: 'in 1881, for instance 30 per cent of men in their 40s and a quarter in their 50s were still single' (Thomson 1998: 150–51). Thus the sex-ratios for marital statuses at older ages were different from what would be expected today, as is shown in Table 3.1. This had other impacts, such as on gender differences in death rates for accidents at older ages (see below), and, as just noted, also affected family networks. The old 'codger' living in a hut on his own, often in an isolated locality, was a feature of colonial life and was even around in the 1940s. Thus there would also have been many 'quasi-families' of older bachelors, widowers or men living alone, separated from their families. Because migration of Chinese women was so highly controlled, an aspect of racist anti-Asian policies, Chinese men were perhaps the most extreme example of what was obviously a not uncommon phenomenon even among those populations not subject to such active discrimination.

There is a bizarre side-effect of the phenomenon of the male living alone evident in the mortality statistics for 1876 and 1896. Normally, the incidence of accidental death at older ages is higher among women than men, simply because a widow living alone who falls may not be rescued in sufficient time to avoid death from secondary causes if no one is alerted to her plight. But in late Victorian New Zealand the statistics were reversed, with the rate per 10,000 at ages 65 years and over being 28 for males (many of whom would have been living alone) and nine for females (Pool 1985: Table 123).

Table 3.1: Sex Ratios (Males/100 Females) by Marital Status at Ages 65+, 1886
and 1986

Year	Total population	Never married	Currently married	Widowed	Divorced or separated
1886	103	532	188	64	None reported
1986	71	58	133	23	89

OTHER EFFECTS OF MIGRATION ON FAMILY LIFE

The influence of migration in this early period cannot be overstated. The inflows in the late 1860s, driven in particular by gold-rushes, and in the early 1870s, because of assisted-passage migration of settlers, often families, were massive relative to the small base (59,000 Pakeha in 1858), with gains by 1874 from immigration, entirely Pakeha, of 219,000, as against 96,278 natural increase (Maori and Pakeha) by 1875. By 1901 there were 816,000 people in the colony. From 1875 to 1885 the net migration inflows diminished, but were still high (83,700 persons). By then, however, natural increase had become the dominant contribution to population numbers (130,000) (Papps 1985b: Table 7). Then in the late 1880s during the long depression the flows became negative, whereas natural increase levels remained very high. This meant that by the 1890s the Pakeha population and most Pakeha families were bifurcated by age. Those over 20 or 30 years of age were likely to have been born overseas, most commonly in the British Isles, while those below these ages were likely to have been born in New Zealand.

Beyond this, and over and above the surplus of males noted above, there were other impacts on family and household structures. The colonial settler family was neolocal. Typically young couples left their extended families and migrated alone to New Zealand, or met and married there, often unaccompanied by elderly family members. This meant that households lacked the wider family networks often found in the British Isles: Pakeha New Zealand thus has 'relatively shallow kinship structures' (Thorns 1992: 254). This would have differentiated many Pakeha families from their Maori counterparts with their deeper kinship structures.

Neolocal residence may have involved more than a simple separation from kin. The historian Miles Fairburn paints a picture that is rather different from that of nostalgia. The family may not have had the community support networks that are often believed to have been the mark of more traditional societies. His sketch is one of 'atomisation', of a

> minimally organised society. Although some people lived close to others
> and interacted with them, social isolation was the prevailing tendency. The
> primary cause arose during the period between the 1850s and the 1880s, when

the population was swamped by a tide of . . . people who had been severed from their associations in metropolitan society and had not dwelt long enough in the colony to replace those that had been lost.

He also quotes numerous geography theses that show that Pakeha New Zealand society at that time was at least as transient as that of North America. In the late Victorian period, on average, mobility was 'high being at the top end of the North American scale' (Fairburn 1989: 191, 130–31).

Nevertheless, Fairburn also reminds us that 'the slump [of the 1880s] allowed the natural agencies of birth, death, and ageing to yield an increasingly normal demographic structure. This in turn expanded the network of kinship ties, as former immigrants and their offspring aged and bore children, so producing cousins, nephews, aunts and grandparents' (Fairburn 1989: 251). Thus, it was probable, because of the very high fertility of the early colonial period, 'that substantial fractions of the end-of-century elderly [Pakeha] had extended pools of surviving kin, both lateral and linear'.

REPRODUCTION IN VICTORIAN PAKEHA NEW ZEALAND: MEASURING THE LEVELS

The levels of fertility achieved in early colonial Pakeha society can be shown using observed rates, general fertility rates (GFRs) and marital general fertility rates (MGFRs), drawn from a thesis by Fred Tiong (1988). The GFR is simply the births divided by *all* women at reproductive ages (15–44 years) and cited per 1000 women; and the MGFR is computed from the legitimate births per 1000 *married* women at these ages. By comparing the two indices the effects of the 'preventive check' of marriage as a type of fertility regulation can be gauged. Where the GFR and the MGFR are close, most fertility falls within marriage, most women are married and this occurs at young ages. The converse holds true when the GFR falls well below the MGFR.

A major problem with these rates is that they cover the entire age span, including both the ages at which, for bio-social reasons, probabilities of conceiving are highest (say 20–29 years), and those either side (15–19 and 30+) when probabilities are lower. To illustrate the composition effects that might ensue from age-specific differences in fertility, one could envisage two regions: A, in which all or most women are married and aged 20–29 years, and another, B, in which most women are at older reproductive ages. Even though age-group by age-group their childbearing rates could be the same, region A would have more babies and higher GFRs than B. If the researcher is interested in comparing fertility patterns, it is necessary to find a strategy to overcome these effects. This was an issue that Tiong addressed by carefully age-standardising the rates using a conventional demographic technique that reduces or eliminates them. The application of this method allows us to be reasonably confident that comparisons over time and between regions in New Zealand are robust and not an artefact of age-compositional differences. Tiong's study also rendered a second important service: he checked the quality of the registration data from 1878 to 1921 by comparing observed rates with estimated rates. The estimates had been calculated by computing 'expected births' in the five-year period leading up to a census through 'reverse survival' from the census population aged 0–4 years (again a conventional technique).

But there is yet another difficulty that must be overcome: some of the children aged 0–4 years may not have been born in a particular area, and those enumerated at this age are the children who, having been born alive, have also survived until the time of the census enumeration. Thus Tiong adjusted for passive migration effects (children who had accompanied migrant parents rather than being born in New Zealand, or in any region) and for differences in survivorship. His results show that the vital registration data were reasonably accurate, at least from 1880 onwards. The differences between observed and estimated in 1878 may, however, have been a function of over-estimating passive migration effects. Tiong points out that 'the early British Settlers were from a country that had an efficient registration system, and compulsory birth registration in New Zealand was effected as early as 1855'. Robert Woods's detailed analysis in England and Wales confirms this – by the time that most settlers would have been departing for New Zealand, under-reporting of births in the home country would have been as low as 4%, and by the '1880s the accuracy of civil registration was acceptable' (2000: 69, Fig. 2.2).

In this regard, Tiong also notes that compulsory education was introduced in 1877. Thus a need for birth certificates for enrolment would have reinforced the completeness of birth registration, as did labour legislation requiring birth certificates before permits could be issued allowing children to be employed (Tiong 1988: 71–72). That vital registration was reasonably accurate for Pakeha at that time is also confirmed for death registration, especially for infant and childhood mortality. Concerned that an earlier analysis by Sceats and Pool (1985b) indicated that there might have been under-registration, especially of neonatal deaths, Pool and Cheung did an exhaustive re-analysis and concluded that if under-registration had occurred in the 1880s and 1890s it would have been very slight (2005).

REPRODUCTION IN VICTORIAN PAKEHA NEW ZEALAND: THE EMPIRICAL EVIDENCE

We can now turn back to substantive issues and do so with a reasonable degree of confidence in the statistical data at our disposal, starting with the earliest years of the colony. David Thomson argues with a great deal of feeling and a lot of justification that most studies ignore the early colonial period (prior to the 1880s) because there are few available data (2006: 120). The 1870s are less bare of data so that some indices are available, and there are the local area analyses noted earlier (Pickens 1980; Macdonald 1990). Nor is there a total absence of data prior to this, thanks to what are termed indirect estimation techniques, a body of methods widely and successfully used in demography. Ironically perhaps, estimates of Maori fertility can be made from the 1840s, while for Pakeha are only available from the 1858 census, and the 1870s (Figure 2.1).

The evidence that the 1858 figure provides is very clear. It shows that fertility then, as measured by the TFR for that year,[*] was high, and that it differed little from the levels computed both through indirect estimates for the 1870s made from census age distributions, and independently by extrapolation from GFRs. The figure for *circa* 1860 is 6.5 live births per woman, very significantly above the rate of about 5.0 for England and Wales in either of the two overlapping periods 1826–50 and 1851–75 (Woods 1996: 305–06), and even further above that for Scotland in 1855 (4.1, Flinn *et al.* 1977: Table 3.5.5). If the two countries are weighted to allow for their contribution to migration inflows to New Zealand, their combined figure is about 4.7. Thus, contrary to Thomson's argument, fertility in early colonial New Zealand, around 1860 and in the 1870s, was well above that of the two major migrant source populations from the mother country.

In 1878 the GFR was 227 per 1000 women, a very high rate. A GFR of this level implies a TFR well in excess of 6.5 births per woman. Moreover, it infers that one in every 4.4 women in the entire age-range, regardless of marital status, whether married, single or widowed, would have had a birth each year. The significance of this is even greater as, first, denominators include women who had never married and thus in those days likely never to have been exposed to intercourse; secondly, they also comprise both

---

[*]   This approximation is rather crude: TFR = (GFR x 30)/1000. That is, the central rate for one calendar year across all reproductive ages is converted into a TFR. TFRs use age-specific rates for one calendar year as if it were a true cohort surviving over 30 years of its life, from age fifteen to age 45 years; by multiplying the GFR by 30 one attempts to obtain an approximation of the more refined TFR. As the TFR uses the age-specific rates for what is a hypothetical cohort, as opposed to following a real cohort over time, it is termed a 'synthetic' rate. A TFR differs from a GFR not only in this regard, but it also is free of age-composition effects. A well-documented analogous form of estimation of a total rate from a general rate is sometimes used in abortion research when age-specific data are not available (e.g. Tietze 1981, 4 and elsewhere; Frejka 1983, 498; Atkin and Frejka 1990; we thank Tomas Frejka for his comments on this issue – he used this technique on advice from Christopher Tietze who was an expert on abortion statistical methodologies). We have followed the same technique to estimate MTFRs that are analogous to TFRs, but for nuptial births and married women. Estimates of MTFRs from MGFRs are likely to be less robust than in the case for the GFR–TFR transformation, because the underlying assumptions of stability are less likely to be sustained. Stability is a very important concept in demographic theory, and has extremely wide applications empirically (see Chapt. 4, 150n; also Pool 1991: Glossary).

those women who were teenagers and those who were nearing menopause, both of whom had lower levels of fecundability (that is, the capacity to conceive in any inter-menstrum); and, thirdly, denominators also cover those women who were pregnant but would deliver the next year, plus those who had delivered last year and were breastfeeding, abstaining or still amenorrhoeic (subject to frequent anovulatory periods).

It is essential at this juncture briefly to raise another point that reinforces the validity of the methodology we have just outlined. The reason this is so critical is that the power of much of the analysis in this chapter and the next, and more particularly the interpretation of patterns of replacement and fertility for Pakeha over the period prior to 1913, depends on the validity of this transformation of GFRs into TFRs. Fortunately, we can make tests for robustness, and these show that crude approximations of the TFR from the GFR yield far from wild estimates. The estimated TFR for 1911 (3.4 births per woman) is almost the same as the fertility rate of 3.2 in 1913 computed directly from the age-specific data that became available for the first time that year; the estimate of a TFR of 3.2 derived from a GFR of 108 in 1921 is very close to the TFR directly calculated for 1920 (Khawaja 1985: Fig. 21).

As one would expect, the MGFR for Pakeha in 1878 was even higher than the GFR: 299 nuptial births/1000 married women. While we must recognise that transformations between the MGFR and the MTFR are likely to be less robust than between GFRs and TFRs, this technique, described above, does provide some indicative results that are fascinating. One can infer from such a MGFR that the marital TFR in 1878 would have been almost nine births per married woman. In any calendar year one in three married women would have given birth to a child. Later in the next chapter it will be shown that some provinces surpassed even these levels of hyperfertility, and it must be reiterated that these are results that are relatively free of age-composition effects.

The dramatic drop in fertility between 1878 and the end of the nineteenth century can be explained with a considerable degree of confidence. Rates then declined far more slowly between that time and the post-World War I period. Further gradual but systematic decreases continued until the end of the 1930s Depression.

Thus by 1896 the GFR, at 126, was 44% below its level a mere eighteen years earlier, implying a TFR of only 3.7 births per woman. In contrast the MGFR had dropped by only 16% to 241, still implying 7.2 births per married woman. In 1878 the GFR had been close to the MGFR (a ratio of 76%), whereas by 1896 this ratio had dropped down to only 52%. By the end of Queen Victoria's reign the marriage 'preventive check' was operating in two ways: both by delaying and by restricting marriage. Sceats and Pool estimated that almost two-thirds of the rapid decline in fertility from 1878 to 1901 came from the shifts in the proportions marrying and by increases in the age at which this occurred (1985: Table 92).

In 1878, therefore, relatively few women at reproductive ages were not being exposed to intercourse and conception, and one in three to one in four could expect to bear a child in any year. These are levels of reproduction that really do approach bio-social maxima. In contrast, by 1896 many were avoiding exposure to intercourse, and thus the risk of conception, by not marrying, and only one in eight would become a mother in any twelve-month period. Yet, among those married, the odds of having a baby in any year were still 1:4. This underlines the significance of changes in marriage patterns for fertility regulation. In contrast, the impacts of birth control within marriage were relatively limited as marital fertility rates changed very little. The TFR obtained from the GFR for 1896 implies that the rate of replacement had dropped to about 3.5–4.0 births per woman, and had crept down a little more to 3.4 around 1911, about half of where it had been in the 1870s. To put the rates around 1900 into context, although they had fallen so far they were still only slightly below the levels that were to be seen at the height of the Baby Boom in 1960, our reference point today for high fertility.

The effects of the extremely high fertility of the colonial period on family structures can be evaluated by referring to one of the few other pieces of direct statistical information on the late Victorian period. It comes from a question on children ever born alive to married women in the 1911 census. Data from this enumeration are presented in Table 3.2, that also allows a comparison to be made with the 1981 census. The rates at that latter date would have reflected the fertility patterns of the Baby Boom that had finished a few short years before, representing the only period of higher fertility in the twentieth century.

The larger family sizes of the 1870s and 1880s, by comparison even with Baby Boom families, are indicated in 1911 by the higher averages at the older age-groups (40 years and over), by the percentage of women at those ages who had had six or more live births, and by the very high proportion of children belonging to large families. Thus in 1911 the pattern at older ages is very different from what is seen in 1981, both for average family sizes and the distribution of women by family size. At younger ages (30–34 and 35–39 years), in contrast, the overall levels and profiles are much closer.

Although the overall picture in 1911 is of much larger family sizes than in the Baby Boom, the data for the earlier year also show larger proportions at the two extremes, zero children, and six or more. By contrast, the Baby Boom family sizes are less dispersed but cluster around one to five children, with few women having either zero or more than six. At the end of the reproductive span 86% of the Baby Boom parents (women aged 45–49 years, who would have been in their early thirties around 1960) had borne one to five children. For the 1911 census respondents who were having children prior to 1890 (i.e. aged 50 years or older) only 32% were in the middle cluster, half had large families, but one in six had no children despite this being a cohort composed of married women. On the other hand there was less reproductive polarisation in 1981 than in 1911, a point to which we will return later. When the children rather than the mothers are looked at (row iii) it can be seen that a child born in the late Victorian period was far more likely to be a member of a large family than was a Baby Boom infant.

Table 3.2: Two Non-Maori Family Structural Profiles, 1911 and 1981, Married Women only: (i) Average Number of Children; (ii) Distribution of Married* Women by Family Sizes; and (iii) Proportion of Children Born into Families with 6+ Children

	1911				
	30–34 years	35–39 years	40–44 years	45–49 years	50+ years
i) Average no. of live births/woman	2.5	3.3	4.1	4.8	5.8
ii) Percentage of women					
With zero births	16	14	14	14	16
With 1–2 births	40	28	22	16	10
with 3–5 births	36	39	36	31	22
With 6+ births	8	18	27	38	52
Total	100	99	99	99	100
iii) Percentage of children born into families with 6+ children	23	41	51	67	81
	1981				
i) Average no. of live births/woman	2.2	2.8	3.2	3.0	2.8
ii) Percentage of women					
With zero births	9	6	5	6	11
With 1–2 births	53	42	33	29	36
With 3–5 births	37	49	56	57	44
With 6+ births	1	2	5	8	9
Total	100	99	99	100	100
iii) Percentage of children born into families with 6+ children	2	7	11	18	25

*Married 1911; Ever married 1981.
Source: Censuses of New Zealand, 1911 and 1981.
Note: Thomson argues that the census of 1916 produced more accurate fertility data than that of 1911, because the latter had higher levels 'not stated' for numbers of children. As the heading of the 1911 table notes, 'In the column "not stated" are entered all married women who apparently had no children, but omitted to state so in the schedule' (*Census 1911*, 'Conjugal Condition of the People': Table XIII). Here 1911 is used simply because it is closer to the nineteenth century and thus has more respondents who would have survived from that era, so is more representative of nineteenth-century populations. In any case, the combined percentage of women with zero children (not stated plus zero, 1911) remains the same across two censuses for the cohort at the end of its reproductive span, aged 40–44 (1911) and 45–49 (1916). Moreover, the average number of children counted as born alive to this same cohort was virtually the same at the two censuses (*Census 1916*, 'Detailed tables with Govt Statistician's Report Thereon': 97). Thus the 1911 census may not be any more inaccurate than that of 1916.

3.6 EARLY COLONIAL PAKEHA FAMILY MORPHOLOGIES: SIGNIFICANCE

The very early period until the 1880s or 1890s is important for the rest of this book as it seems to have entrenched Pakeha values relating to family structures that have determined trends until the present. This is reinforced by the fact that this era also saw Pakeha assume a demographic hegemony that was to last 100 years, and thus was a period in which both their demographic behaviours and probably their value system were to become virtually the only high-profile model. Above all, New Zealand had then, and probably still has, value structures that favour having children (Sceats 1988b; 2003). Yet by the end of the nineteenth century reproductive behavioural regimes were departing from what was prescribed by these values, setting in place a basic contradiction between 'should do' norms and 'what people actually do' in terms of family sizes. This conflict between behaviours and values was to cause concern at the dawn of the twentieth century (see Chapter Four), a source of tension that was to continue for a long time, even perhaps to the present.

There were other tensions at this time. The first involved the belief that women should not bear children outside marriage, typically seeing this as linked to adolescent promiscuity. Yet this seems to have sat alongside the ready acceptance in the 1870s of very early and universal marriage, with parenting confined within it, seemingly ignoring the risks of conception at young ages. These were patterns of behaviour and attendant strains that were to reappear in their most extreme form in the Baby Boom and will be detailed in Chapter Five. In the meantime, between the pioneer period and World War I, European norms of later marriage had become the modal behavioural pattern, and economic modernisation, urbanisation and female employment also created tensions (see later chapters).

Another pervasive norm, first manifesting itself in the 1880s and 1890s, was the capacity for Pakeha at a population level to make sudden, radical shifts in family formation, even in the absence of efficient means of contraception, that have major impacts on family structures (Pool 1992). This parallels, although at a greatly accelerated pace, what had occurred in eighteenth-century England and Wales (Wrigley 1981), which was also an era in which marriage rather than contraception played the key role in fertility regulation. The key point here is not just the velocity of change, but the fact that the ruptures this produced in family structures could be very significant; a drop from a family size of 7.0 to one of 3.5 totally changes the morphologies of households (Sceats and Pool 1985: 183–86; see also Pickens 1980). But, of course, the implications of the family size shifts were obscured by the fact that for married couples the structures were less radically re-ordered, just modestly downsized. This was a transformation achieved by altering the dynamics of the marriage market and thus excluding many women, or allowing many to 'choose' to exclude themselves, from marriage and consequently parenting.

Thus from the 1880s and 1890s there was a rapid increase in the proportion of women at young ages who had never married. In 1878, 81% of women aged 25–29 were married, but by 1901 this had dropped to 54% (see also Dharmalingam *et al.* 2007: Table 3.2). It was the adoption of this pattern of later marriage, coupled with higher levels of spinsterhood, that brought Pakeha New Zealanders closer to the family structural patterns seen among their British cousins, and produced the radical decline in fertility.

FIRST-ORDER EXPLANATIONS OF THE HIGH LEVELS OF FERTILITY IN THE 1870S: WHAT DID THE COLONISTS DO?

A picture has emerged of hyper-fertility in the early period of Pakeha settlement, followed by a rather spectacular 'baby bust'. Spectacular is a relative term, but certainly it was impressive in an era in which fertility regulation was brought about mainly by changing marriage patterns or, less successfully, by resort to primitive contraceptive technologies and abortion. The importance of the 'nuptiality valve' (changes in ages at marriage and in the proportion married), as Engelen and Kok (2003) call the Malthusian check, is shown by the provincial-level correlations to which we referred earlier (see footnote 10; also Dharmalingam *et al.* 2007: Table 3.5). In both 1878 and 1896 there was a strong negative correlation (>-0.85) between the proportions of women still single at 20–24 years and the GFR. In 1878 there had been a very strong positive correlation between the GFR and the MGFR, but this had dropped to a weak and probably not significant relationship by 1896 (0.67). The correlation between the proportions still single and the MGFR was never significant. It went from weak and negative in 1878 (-0.60) to positive but even less significant in 1896 (0.38).

We have also shown that the reproductive regime of the early colonists was very different from those of their peers in the British Isles, but by 1900 it had turned to echo what was occurring there. This needs explanation, although it must be acknowledged that the explorations below will not provide definitive answers to the issues we are examining. It is hoped, however, that they will spur historians and others to evaluate, and perhaps to rebut what we are putting forward.

As a prelude to this explanation it is necessary, however, to revisit a point documented earlier in this chapter. In the 1870s the differences between marital and overall fertility rates had been limited, whereas, in total contrast, just two decades later at the very end of the nineteenth century high levels of marital fertility coexisted with lower overall fertility. Pakeha never went as far along this track as the regimes seen in late Victorian and early twentieth-century Ireland. The latter represents an extreme example of such a regime, but in that country it was achieved in part by massive levels of migration. Paddy Murphy went off for twenty years to dig gold in far-off Westland, New Zealand, or to build railways in Canada, or to fight for the Queen in the India of the Raj, or to run a revolution in Latin America, returning, if at all, in his forties to marry 38-year-old Mary Malone, his sweetheart of yore who had waited patiently for him. In New Zealand in the latter half of Victoria's reign the flows would, of course, mainly have been inward, although migration research shows that any inflow is likely to produce some backflow. Normally the net flow was strongly positive (inflows far exceeded outflows), but in the long depression of the 1880s the reverse effect was seen for a short period.

To explain hyper-fertility among the colonists, by comparison with their British peers, it is necessary to return to Malthus' check, marriage, the nuptiality valve. This section concentrates on the 1870s when the valve was opened, very wide by British standards, although not perhaps by the standards of the New Zealand Baby Boom 70–90 years later. But, by deduction, this check applies in reverse to the turn of the nineteenth century, by which time the valve had been partially closed.

No British region had the high levels of early marriage seen among the New Zealand settlers. To reiterate, the effects of nuptiality on fertility in a non-contracepting society with almost no ex-nuptial childbearing operate through age at marriage plus the proportions marrying. In the early colonial period, as illustrated here mainly by data from the 1870s, New Zealand Pakeha stood out from their British counterparts – data presented earlier show that ages at marriage were lower among Pakeha, and proportions ever marrying, typically at these young ages, were higher. Moreover, in 1861 very few districts in England and Wales had Princeton index *Im* values (referred to earlier) anywhere as high as the national Pakeha level in New Zealand. Moreover, the districts from which Pakeha migrants had disproportionately come were significantly lower, or much lower (Woods 2000: Fig. 3.8; compare Figure 4.1 in this book, even for 1801–25, a peak period for fertility in England and Wales). It is a simple bio-social fact that if women in their twenties, the peak ages of reproduction, living in these sorts of societies are to achieve very high levels of fertility, they must marry in their early twenties as Pakeha did, and not in their mid- to late twenties as the English and Scots did.

This might lead some observers to suggest that, if the colonists had had the same marriage patterns as their British peers, their 'fertilities' (to use Szreter's 2002 term) would have been similar, and thus that there was nothing really distinctive about the colonial reproductive regimes. This, however, is a spurious argument as the real issue is that marriage was the way in which populations at this time, consciously or unconsciously, controlled their fertility. Thus the fact that marital patterns were different was the self-evident reason why 'fertilities' were different. Regardless, this case is blown further out of the water when one turns to data that control for the effects of the nuptiality valve by using MGFRs and their derived estimates of MTFRs, as we did earlier in this chapter. We have shown that, across the board, Pakeha had higher marital fertility than did the British, and also had nuptial reproductive rates close to natural fertility (uncontrolled) models. Thus not only did they marry at younger ages and in greater numbers, but once married they also reproduced more (Sceats and Pool 1985a: Section D).

This difference might be explained by Robert Woods's (2000: 109) quote cited earlier: that at the midpoint of Victoria's reign British women had started to regulate fertility within marriage by such techniques as abstention, *coitus interruptus* and abortion (see also Anderson 1998). A lag effect, to be discussed in Chapter Four, could have meant that this knowledge found its way to the colonies later.

The surplus of men is another argument that is often suggested. It was discussed earlier and shown to have been a transitory phenomenon, and a rather simple but weak explanation. To elaborate, for example, the Pakeha population of Westland had far higher masculinity ratios than much of the colony, but did not have either notably high fertility, or high proportions of women married at 20–24 years. High masculinity ratios simply mean that there is a mechanism by which women can secure advantage on a marriage market, if they so choose or if pressured by family; obviously in the 1870s Westland women had not chosen to do so to the same extent as their compatriots in most other provinces.

However, Macdonald notes another side to this: 'Given the excess of men and the younger age-profile of the female population in New Zealand [1850s–1870s] it is surprising that the age at which women married for a first time was not lower and the proportion of young marriages was not higher than it was' (1990: 138–39). Her observation is particularly acute given the seeming pressures of such a marriage market – not just an abundance of eligible men but a climate in which families had a say in getting their daughters into secure and prosperous unions. But it should be remembered that 46% of women were still unmarried at 20–24 in 1878, and that that proportion had grown to 62% at these ages a decade later. Indeed, the percentage celibate in 1878 at this age was higher than would be seen in the Baby Boom almost a century later when the sex ratio was very different (Dharmalingam *et al.* 2007: Table 3.2). But marriage was obviously still the favoured option, for in 1878 the level of celibacy by 25–29 years was down to 17%.

A comparison provides a benchmark for us and suggests that a lower-than-expected early marriage rate was not unique to Pakeha settlers. About the same percentage of women among the first generation of women born in seventeenth-century Quebec, where the disequilibrium between the sexes was also very marked, were unmarried at 20–24 years. Yet young women in Quebec had an 'out' not available to Pakeha Protestant New Zealanders: disproportionately they examined the available surplus of male talent and fled off to join celibate orders, including undertaking mission work at what was a very dangerous frontier. In those early days in Quebec, so Hubert Charbonneau tells us, when masculinity ratios were very high, contrary to expectations, 'the religious market had priority over the matrimonial market', yet its power diminished as imbalances between the sexes decreased (1975: 156; Ian Pool's translation).

One suspects that New Zealand Pakeha families may have encouraged their daughters, at ages 20–24 years in the majority of cases and certainly before they were 30, to marry older and more financially established men. On average, this was at younger ages than in the old country. Moreover, many of Charlotte Macdonald's newly arrived young, single migrant women quickly broke with British custom and married (1990: 49, 147). In Britain domestic service had been one major occupational opening for young single women, a job that required celibacy and often involved long hours of work and unpleasant conditions of employment. Perhaps marriage to a settler who was older but had his own land in Canterbury may have seemed a better deal for young single women escaping domestic service and coming to New Zealand.

But the nuptiality valve seems to have been controlled by two seemingly contradictory factors. On one hand, and this was the more important trend, by comparison with the British model marriage for Pakeha women was almost universal and early – well below age 25 years. On the other hand, this did not signify extreme precocity, for colonist girls were not marrying in huge numbers at teen ages. Thus it did not seem that female settlers were being pushed into marriage, or throwing themselves into unions, at adolescence – perhaps they and/or their parents took some time to check out the field (and the prospects of any groom) and to observe proprieties. It was this incipient pattern of behaviour, a period of delaying – albeit of a short duration in New Zealand (say marrying at 22 years rather than eighteen years) – for those who had some resources to bring to the marriage market, that most reflected contemporary patterns in Britain, where the delay was longer, until age 25 years was passed. This may have set the tone for the minority, and, as we will show below, became the dominant trend among Pakeha a decade or so later.

WHY DID NEWLY ARRIVED PAKEHA SETTLERS ADOPT A VERY HIGH FERTILITY REGIME?

Unfortunately, the argument still cannot be finally signed off. Pakeha women did not just re-adopt some earlier pre-Victorian British pattern of family life. Instead they launched from that model to create a more extreme version of it. Thus the real problem is to explain why Pakeha women and couples had gone further than the antecedents from early nineteenth-century Britain and taken childrearing within marriage almost to its biological limits, well beyond what had been seen in Jane Austen's Britain. But in turn, this may have been possible because of the improvements in standards of living to which they had been exposed as migrant settlers. It can be argued that the superior living conditions encountered in the colony, even in its early days, gave them significant bio-social advantages over their British forebears.

First, Pakeha had a comfortable economic environment. By world standards at that time, New Zealand was wealthy and this was conducive to family formation – for example in the bio-social dimensions such as maternal nutrition, to which further reference will be made later. Despite the long depression from the late 1870s to the early 1890s, the economy 'started from a high level relative to other countries, and maintained a high level' (Hawke 1985: 77). Moreover, incomes and wealth were better distributed than in the old country or in other colonies: 'material life was not bleak, and did not engender a demeaning paternalism in which the many depended on and were beholden to the few' (Fairburn 1989: 114). New Zealand's early economic wealth and modernisation is an issue that will be returned to in more detail in Chapter Four, as it forms a component of a more general analysis of the socio-economic context for family changes from 1840 to 1945.

Secondly, and a major cause of this wealth and modernisation, was the wresting of land from Maori. Initially this was in the South Island and later in the North. A key mechanism enabling the rapid exploitation of this land was generous government assistance for land settlement under the Vogel schemes of the 1870s, and this meant that colonists could hope to have their own land, something that was only a dream in Britain (Pool 2002). Land development was facilitated by the family system emerging in the colonies. As Miles Fairburn (1989: 113) has argued, the land was abundant, 'there was no development of a strong social organisation based on client–patron relationships' and this fitted well with 'the flexibility of the family structure'.

New Zealand thus differed from Britain. The British Isles land-tenure system, from which the colonists had emigrated, was very complex, varying from district to district. It encompassed not only huge landed estates, but also small free-holdings; it included share farming and tenant farming, and elsewhere the employment of labour both on a short- and long-term basis; and, as the Fairburn citation above argues, was often associated with other long-standing factors of social structure, typically hierarchical in nature.

Cutting across this is a useful distinction between 'capitalist' and 'family' farms. In a review of English counties using the 1851 census Leigh Shaw-

Taylor employs data both on patterns of employment and farm sizes. Large capitalist farms were likely to be engaged in cropping, particularly grain, rather than grazing. Shaw-Taylor makes a distinction between the interests of 'social historians [who] are prone to count the actual number of small farms . . . while economic historians tend to focus on the amount of land in those farms' and concludes that 'the family farm was a very unimportant feature of both the social and economic landscape in Southeastern England by the mid-nineteenth century. By contrast in the Pennine region small family farms continued to outnumber capitalist farms in the mid-nineteenth century and were far from insignificant in an economic sense' (Shaw-Taylor 2005: 189). With the exception of the South West, which on Shaw-Taylor's maps fits somewhere between South East and Pennine England, the major inflows of rural population to New Zealand came from South East England, and thus from a zone of large-scale capitalist farming; that is, many if not most emigrant family heads will have been employees rather than landholders.

The situation in New Zealand was not only simpler, but was linked more to who had access at a given moment to farmable land than to some entrenched social order. Of overarching importance was the fact that, unlike England at least, whether family or capitalist in scope, farming in New Zealand was focused on grazing. In the south-east of the North Island and in the eastern South Island the dominating issues were how to purchase a large block or get control over an extensive lease in order to set up a sheep station, the latter endeavour in much of the South Island bringing run-holders into conflict with provincial legislatures. In much of the North Island, by contrast, the over-riding concern of many settlers was how land could be wrested from Maori control and sold to Pakeha farmers. In some areas with extensive pastoralism or large grain farms there were more complex employer–employee relationships, but often the farm was owner-operated (dependent on the family workforce), yet relatively large by British standards for such units. Where there were grazing leases, as in Canterbury, these were often turned into *de facto* ownership. Wealthy farmers and merchants constituted the 'gentry' of the colony, although in some less frequent cases, such as people like the famous 'Lady Barker', they did come from genuinely genteel backgrounds (Belich 1995: 342–45, 363–67, 401–03).[*]

The dominance of the family farm, emerging in the period of early settlement, was subsequently ensured in New Zealand by technology

---

[*] Lady Barker is known in New Zealand by the name of her first husband, but was in fact a widow who was remarried to Frederick Broome while she was briefly here, before leaving with him in 1869. He then engaged in services to the empire in Australia and elsewhere. She wrote *Station Life in New Zealand* and *Station Amusements in New Zealand*.

(refrigeration of pastoral products; machine milking, 1880s) allowing capital-intensive methods to be applied to owner-operated units of a viable size. This was reinforced by policies introduced by the Liberal Government (1890s; early 1900s): graduated land tax; land reform; and the 'compulsory acquisition clause' of the Land Settlements Act 1894, which allowed large estates to be broken up. This latter measure was further enhanced by 'private subdivision [that] exceeded state subdivision by at least a factor of five. But the Liberals also introduced a system of Advances to Settlers, supplying cheap credit to buy and develop farms' (Belich 2001: 44).

To conclude, using Shaw-Taylor's capitalist/family farm dichotomy, New Zealand definitely became a land of family farms and thus very different from much of the British Isles. That said, there had been an attempt to establish capitalist farming here, but, except for the South Island's brief period of investment in 'bonanza wheat farms', a trend that reached its peak in the early 1880s (Sinclair 1959: 154), these enterprises were largely directed to extensive pastoralism rather than cropping, and flourished most in periods when wool prices were high.

In Britain, even those who came from landholding families were able to inherit only if they were the eldest son, so younger sons had to move away from the land. Access to land and other capital assets was also affected by rules of inheritance, especially in rural areas. Primogeniture is one such practice that is often cited as a major factor affecting access to farmholdings and thus to marriage. Certainly its ascendancy is well documented for 'the aristocracy and gentry'. According to Mary Murray, 'By the end of the 13th century, primogeniture had become the law of England for free tenures'. But there is less evidence that it spread to other social groups. Moreover, in the English family reconstitution data there is little evidence of any of the effects of primogeniture that might be expected: that older sons would marry earlier, for example (Murray 2004: 124; Wrigley *et al.* 1997: 167–71).* Murray also sees primogeniture as a factor sustaining both patrilineages and patriarchy (Murray 2004: *passim*).

Whatever the exact situation in Britain, in New Zealand bequests of land and other capital assets do not seem to have been gender bound: according to Jim McAloon, who studied the wealthy in Canterbury and Otago, 1840–1914, 'daughters were likely to inherit equally and without restriction'. He does note, however, that 'The legal forms and customs of the day reinforced the husband's dominant role in the family economy' (McAloon

---

* Acknowledgement is made to E. Anthony Wrigley of the Cambridge Group for the History of Population, who drew to Ian Pool's attention the fact that in actual practice the principle of primogeniture may be implemented unsystematically: for example, it may not be followed at all in bequests; siblings might buy others out; and siblings may share among them regardless of the terms of a bequest.

2002: 92–93). Ongoing doctoral research by Stephanie Wyse on urban probate records, 1890–1950, confirm McAloon's conclusion.* Notwithstanding
McAloon's caveat noted above, this equality in bequests surely gave Pakeha
women some degree of control over family and life decisions, such as
whether or not, and whom, to marry, a factor that may explain to some
degree, for example, the trends in the late nineteenth century when levels
of spinsterhood and rates of delayed marriage rose radically.

While systems of primogeniture, bequests and land tenure were complex in Britain, it seems that involvement in farming and landholding was
likely to put some sort of brake on commencing conjugal life. In England
and Wales in 1884–85, the mean ages for marriage for spinsters were highest for those marrying farmers or farmers' sons (28.9 years). Turning to
bachelors, it was the farmers and farmers' sons who had the second-highest
ages for marriage (29.2), just below those in professional or 'independent'
classes (31.2) (Woods 2000: Table 3.1, drawing on a study in the *Journal of
the Royal Statistical Society*, 1890, by William Ogle). A variant of this was
the Irish stem family system, 'the practice of allowing only one child in
each generation to inherit the family holding, marry and produce the next
generation' (Kennedy 1973: 151–63).

The only other systematic evidence that is available on marriage differentials in the old country that might have had an impact on New Zealand
settlers' conjugal patterns is Robert Woods's analyses of *Im*, one of the so-
called Princeton indices discussed above, a measure of the propensity to
marry. This index, Woods argues, 'may be accused of concealing as much
as it reveals since age at marriage and the extent of celibacy are expressed
by a single number'. Nevertheless, one can take some consolation from the
apparently limited variance, implying a high degree of stability in the relationship, of these factors for the whole of England and Wales: proportions
of women ever married at ages 40–44 years (indicating levels of celibacy)
over the period 1851 to 1901 barely changed from close to 87%, while the
mean age at marriage fluctuated only between 25 and 26 years. The same
stability seems to have occurred in regional patterns. In 1861, 1891 and 1911,
'In rural England and Wales, the further one moved towards the west and
north the lower *Im* [and thus the propensity to marry] was likely to be,
while among urban districts low levels were found towards the south and
east away from the urban-industrial centres of the North' (Woods 2000:
85–87, Fig. 3.5).

---

* Personal communication from a thesis nearing completion, Kings College, London: 'Gender,
  Wealth and Margins of Empire: The Economic Participation of Urban New Zealand Women,
  c.1890–1950'. The authors thank her for permission to quote from her findings.

For the New Zealand analyst this provides a complex picture. Overall among Pakeha, levels of marriage were very high at age-group 20–24 years, which differs markedly from the global experience of England and Wales. The English immigrants sourced from rural areas came disproportionately from regions with higher *Im*s by British standards, but, as will be seen in Figure 4.1, the levels were still much lower in England, even in districts where marriage by British standards was earlier and more common, than among the Pakeha colonists (<0.6 in 'high' rural districts in South East England in 1861; as against 0.7 for Pakeha as a whole in 1874). Moreover, the higher *Im*s of rural immigrants to New Zealands were counterbalanced by the fact that the English coming to the colony also included in their number very significant proportions from London and other south-eastern urban areas with notably low *Im*s (Woods 2000: Fig. 3.8 and *passim*).

Thus unlike many of their peers in Britain, Pakeha colonists could gain access more easily to a family farm, allowing women colonists to marry earlier while lower proportions of them remained celibate. This might seem to give vague support to the notion that the 'open frontier' had in fact led to high fertility produced by the nuptiality valve being flung open fully. But this viewpoint cannot be sustained once one considers some other factors documented earlier and elaborated further in Chapter Four. These include the lack of regional variance in fertility in the 1870s between more developed and less developed regions, and the rapid declines in rates in the late Victorian period which took New Zealand down from the top of the industrialised country league to levels that were almost at the bottom. In addition there was lower fertility at a time when land was still being 'opened up' at the dawn of the twentieth century, and when the large estates were being redistributed to families whose breadwinners became self-employed farmers. The 'frontier' as an environment may have had social, economic and cultural implications for its populations, a point some twentieth-century environmental determinist geographers took to an extreme. But this raises questions outside the scope of this book: were there major qualitative differences between frontier geographies? And was the frontier a 'transitory' phenomenon, that moved on as more intensive forms of farming and other forms of production replaced ranching and exploitative primary industries?

Few Pakeha families in the 1870s would have faced an unfenced frontier of the lawless form where primary exploitative industries held sway, or open-range pastoralism of the American ranch or the Australian 'Man from Snowy River'. But this need not imply that New Zealand family lifestyles were an exact replica of what they left behind in Britain. Their age structures were different (they married and were parents younger) and they had more children. Furthermore, Miles Fairburn's seminal study (1989) has suggested that there were many other differences, such as a degree of isolation both from other settlers and from their relatives back in Britain.

Also, turning to more specifically bio-social factors, both levels of nutrition, especially because of cheaply available meat proteins, and living conditions, two factors affecting the biological and the attitudinal aspects of childbearing, were undoubtedly better in New Zealand. Not only was this related to the greater wealth and economic modernisation seen in New Zealand, but there were other factors determined by the environment to which colonists were exposed. Almost every family, even in central urban areas, had access to a garden plot, and the temperate climate ensured that in most areas fresh vegetables and fruit could be grown all year round. Moreover, there were no tenements, virtually no apartments, and thus almost all families, urban as well as rural, lived in dwellings set apart from others. Sanitation, water and sewage systems were certainly primitive – the main street of Auckland had open drains, and animals grazed around the city's water catchment – but the low population densities meant that the diffusion of germs was that much more difficult (Pool 1994).

These advantages were reflected in the relatively good health of the settlers, as Pakeha women were the first national-level population in the world to reach 55 years (1870s) then 60 years (1901) life expectation. Not only, then, were the colonists exposed to higher levels of longevity at the peak period for migrant inflows, but the improvements by the end of the nineteenth century were rapid and remarkable in a society in which, as was true everywhere then, public health, preventive and curative medicine and the health system in general were primitive (Pool and Cheung 2005).

This last point has major ramifications for childbearing and is a partial explanation for the exceptionally high levels in what was a natural fertility regime (no conscious effort to limit by contraception, abortion or abstention). Pakeha women in the 1870s were in a reproductive climate which brought them close to the fertility of the Hutterites, with traits associated with the bio-social maxima for reproduction. Adherents of this religion marry early, but not too early (pre-nubile pregnancy carries greater risks than that in late adolescence); they have good levels of nutrition; they have high levels of longevity and thus good health; and they have good obstetric care (Eaton and Mayer 1954).

For Pakeha the fit with this model was not perfect in that they married in their early twenties rather than in late adolescence. While their longevity and health were superb by the standards of the day, they were below those for twentieth-century Hutterites, and medical and obstetric care were dangerous to health (the well-off kept away from hospitals for birthing). Good health, it should be added, has several advantages: it may well be related to coital frequency; it certainly reduced the risks of fetal loss; it meant that babies had higher probabilities of surviving the high-risk infant and childhood ages; and the chances of women themselves surviving the reproductive ages, and thus having a higher completed family size, were enhanced.

This brief digression into the dimensions of morbidity and mortality has raised issues of direct significance for the analysis of Pakeha families at this time. Households would have grown in size because in what were already conditions of hyper-fertility, more babies and more mothers survived. Furthermore, by the 1870s the majority of girls born alive could expect to become adults, thus swelling household sizes. Most women married, and married women on average had almost nine live births; some more and some fewer than this. That said, however, the fact that more children were surviving to adulthood meant that there might have been an incentive to reduce fertility, by whatever means possible. This cannot be directly proven, but the fact that fertility declined so rapidly in the late nineteenth century when life expectancy reached exceptionally 'high' levels by the standards of those times fits well with demographic theory (Borrie 1970: 149–51). The factors that favoured hyper-fertility, high levels of maternal, fetal, infant and childhood health, also sowed the seeds for attitudinal changes conducive to declines in fertility, and these, in turn, affected survivorship at all these ages, the multiplier effects of which were further decreases in levels of reproduction.

These changes affected family morphologies in two opposite ways: fewer births but more surviving offspring. Moreover, the subsequent declines in fertility (1876–1901) were closely related to the rapid decreases in infant and childhood mortality occurring in the late nineteenth century that had flow-on effects for cohort survival at older ages well into the twentieth century (Pool and Cheung 2003, 2005). This shows, incidentally, that a demographic change at one moment may have effects that last a very long time.

A further side-effect on family dynamics was that declines occurred also for most major causes of death among children. Notable among these were decreases in 'accidental' deaths, one of the few for which diagnosis and certification would not differ too far from present standards (Pool 1985). The decrease in this cause of death can be explained in two ways: (i) that supervision of children improved, as family sizes decreased and increasingly as parents could take on this task themselves rather than assigning it to older children; and (ii) that the stresses caused by looking after numerous offspring dropped off, and with them family violence and death. Neither of these explanations fits the image of an idyllic family life as sometimes portrayed in nostalgia – perhaps family life was not like that of the Waltons, but was a little more Hobbesian, although, by the standards of the Victorian era, undoubtedly better than in many environments in the British Isles.

There was another interesting side to this: the health of mothers also improved. During the fertility decline mortality rates for females at parenting ages decreased significantly, not just from maternal causes, but, again, right across the board. Most notably this occurred for tuberculosis, again one of the few causes of death for which nineteenth-century certification practices would not have been too far distant from those today (Pool 1985). Along with this there was a crossover from higher male rates of survivorship through these ages to higher female levels (Pool and Cheung 2003, 2005).

WHY DID THIS CHANGE BETWEEN THE 1870S AND THE EARLY 1900S? THE EFFECTS OF THE VOGEL SCHEMES AND ALTERNATIVE HYPOTHESES

With such a high level of fertility and a seemingly entrenched locally developed regime, it seems surprising that levels of reproduction then decreased rapidly in the last decades of Victoria's reign. Of course, similar changes were occurring across the ESCs, including the British Isles themselves (Festy 1979; Szreter 2002; Garrett *et al.* 2001; Woods 2000). Indeed, one of the more interesting findings of demography is that societies that are widely different in all sorts of ways may follow similar general population trends. This empirically demonstrable simultaneity of major demographic shifts is puzzling, as it stands apart from normal explanatory frameworks that look for factors that immediately affect individual couples within particular societies. There may be a macro-level explanation: of some sort of widespread normative shift that might be as vague and as ill-defined as 'modernisation'. For the moment we will merely flag this as a possibility, and turn and search for more immediate local factors, but this idea will be resurrected in later chapters. In the late nineteenth century the local aspect was the speed and intensity of the changes from the very top of the fertility league to near the bottom that set New Zealand Pakeha apart.

We have argued that many dimensions of the reproductive regime seen in the 1870s were, in essence, locally generated. They represented a significant departure from what was seen at that time in Britain, although probably deriving major features from some aspects of pre-Victorian Britain. Thus the question arises as to whether the decline from that period until the end of the century was merely concomitant with a more general trend sweeping the ESCs, or whether it had some features that were unique to Pakeha society.

Perhaps an explanation for this is purely demographic in that it lies in two totally different migration streams. Over the six decades from 1840 to 1900, 32% of all net arrivals came in the decade of the 1860s and 38% in the 1870s. The early 1860s saw gold-rushes and inflows of unaccompanied males. As the gold petered out in Otago the miners often stayed in the South Island, but some moved north to join in the 1867 rush to Thames. This early migration trend affected national sex ratios: in 1867 at ages 15–64 years there were 190 men to every 100 women. In the 1870s, in contrast, the Vogel schemes brought in rather more gender- and age-balanced flows, so that by the 1886 census the sex ratio at working ages was down to 121 (Papps 1985b: Fig. 1; Neville 1985: Table 23). From 1876, natural increase outran migration as the source of growth in the Pakeha population in every five-year period; by then family building was clearly the dominant factor in the family and social life of the colony, and the Pakeha demographic hegemony also held sway.

It is necessary to entertain another hypothesis: that the huge inflows of the Vogel period altered the colony's social fabric and normative systems by the wholesale infusion of new ideas reflective of the changes occurring in the British Isles at that time or immediately before. At the 1867 census 68% of the Pakeha population at age group 21–40 years had been male, and almost 50% of all males fell into this age-range, critical for setting up households and becoming a parent. By 1878 at ages 21–40 years 60% were male, but only 33% of all males were in this key family-building age-group. In 1886 the figures had dropped to 55% for masculinity at those ages, but only 28% of all males were in the critical age-range – the percentages who were children or older adults had increased; and by 1896 the sex ratio at these ages was almost equal, while the proportion of all males who were in this age-group was the same as in 1886 (*Census 1896*, 'Ages of the People': Tables II and III). The major changeover seems to have occurred between 1876 and 1886. Many of those couples or families who entered New Zealand at that time would have imported the emerging family values of their peers in Britain. The decade 1876–86 could thus have been a watershed for the transmission of norms from the metropole to the colony.

To look at possible 'Vogel scheme' age-gender effects on reproduction one has to turn back to the two indices, GFRs and MGFRs, that were differentially affected by both migration and patterns of reproduction. The key factor affecting fertility was nuptiality – the so-called 'check' or 'valve'. This shows in Table 3.3 in the trend figures indexed to 1878 (= 1.00). Caution must be shown in inferring temporal patterns from this table – 1878–81 is only a three-year period whereas all other intervals are quinquennia.

The index trends for GFRs and MGFRs are rather different. The falloff for the index for the MGFR is slower than that for the GFR. Beyond this, the same table permits some degree of disaggregation of the effects not only of the links between marriage and fertility, but also of the changing age structures that arose from the switch from massive migratory inflows in the Vogel period to a virtual cessation of migration for a decade or so thereafter. It also allows some insights into the pattern of change.

Table 3.3: General Fertility Rates and Marital General Fertility Rates, 1878–1901

Year	General fertility rate				Marital general fertility rate			
	Ob. Rate	Index	Stand. Rate	Index	Ob. Rate	Index	Stand. Rate	Index
1878	221	1.00	227	1.00	341	1.00	299	1.00
1881	192	0.87	206	0.91	318	0.93	286	0.95
1886	164	0.74	179	0.79	293	0.86	271	0.91
1891	139	0.63	148	0.65	279	0.82	260	0.87
1896	118	0.53	126	0.56	255	0.75	241	0.80
1901	112	0.51	117	0.51	246	0.72	233	0.78

Source: Tiong 1988: 122.
Note: GFR = births per 1000 women aged 15–44 years; MGFR = nuptial births per 1000 married women 15–44 years; Ob. = observed; Stand. = age-standardised rate; Index, where 1878 = 1.00.

Taking this last point, the Vogel schemes had peaked in the mid-1870s and then dropped off very quickly. The effects of migration and through it the importation of new ideas on reproduction would surely then have been felt before 1878, and certainly by 1881. By 1886 one could have expected a significantly altered pattern of fertility in the colony, one much closer to that in the British Isles. But, looking at the GFRs, such a trend starts to become apparent only from 1886 to 1896, then slows. A comparison of the observed GFRs with the age-standardised GFRs shows the impacts of migration on the age structure, as reflected by the wider gap between the two rates in 1881 and 1886 than had been true in 1878, or was true thereafter. The age-standardised GFRs give a more robust indication of changes that were most accelerated from 1881 and, especially, from 1886 to 1891.

For married women (MGFRs) little change is apparent until 1896 or 1901, and even then, as the indexed results show, the rate still represents as much as four-fifths of that seen at the peak period in the 1870s. While age-standardisation has some effect on the rates it is rather limited.

These data suggest then that two somewhat paradoxical things were happening. First, by the mid- to late 1880s Pakeha were joining in the general trend in the ESCs, both the neo-Europes and the old country itself. But, secondly, they did this in a New Zealand-ish way. They still used marriage as the 'valve', although by 1896 or 1901 birth control within marriage was probably coming into use more and more. Against this, despite the huge migration inflows of the early to mid-1870s, an infusion of modified norms (the favouring of distinctly lower levels of childbearing) into the colonial value system seems to have taken about a decade or so to have had an impact on colonial values.

Perhaps, in fact, the reverse occurred, with many of the Vogel-period migrants adopting the prevailing colonial norms to replace what had driven their reproductive behaviours in the British Isles. There is a smidgen of available evidence in support of this hypothesis. In the correlations noted earlier, the proportions of New Zealand-born per province in 1878 had a weak and undoubtedly insignificant relationship with other factors cor-related there, and by 1896 this was even weaker. To take some illustrative cases, in 1878 Marlborough and Hawke's Bay both had very high GFRs and MGFRs, yet had widely different proportions of New Zealand-born: 54% in Marlborough as against 36% in Hawke's Bay. Nelson and Taranaki had similar percentages of New Zealand-born (48%) but widely different fertilities (Taranaki highest, but Nelson lowest for the GFR and second to lowest for the MGFR). If the Vogel effect had been marked then one would have expected stronger correlations: the higher the proportion of New Zealand-born, the higher the fertility level.

Unfortunately, we cannot give a definitive verdict on this. The jury must remain out until genealogical evidence comparing the behaviours and attitudes of segments of the same families in Britain and New Zealand is available. To be more conclusive additional expository research will also be needed. We can be definitive about one point, however: simple cultural transmission does not seem to have been the sole determinant of changes in the sizes of colonial Pakeha families, and thus other factors – social and economic change, and policies – may also have been involved. Policy questions mainly revolved around welfare, an issue that will be discussed in the next chapter. Here, though, we must address a simple question: if proportionately fewer women were marrying, and those who did were doing so later, then there had to have been some alternatives available to them.

Thus perhaps there were economic factors, 'causally more remote determinants' as we defined this term in Chapter Two, underlying the changes in marriage patterns documented here that so clearly drove the fertility decline. Above all we can point to transformations in the industrial labour force, and particularly the part played by women, that might provide a clue. The painstaking reconstructions by Brendan Thompson, who drew on the work of economic historian Gary Hawke, certainly provide some insight on this.

Participation of men and women in the primary sector peaked in the gold-rush and Vogel periods (56% in 1871), then dropped off to around 40% by 1896, and down to 29% in 1926. This was compensated for by the growth of the secondary (manufacturing) sector, from 13% in 1871 to 25% by 1896, and up to 30% by the 1930s. Much of this was the production of goods for the local market and was not the large-scale, heavy manufacturing seen overseas, as near at hand as New South Wales. The tertiary sector grew gradually until 1896 (35%), and further in the early twentieth century (Thompson 1985: Table 257). More importantly, numerical changes show major shift-shares occurring, and to a significant degree these reflected movements of women in and out of the workforce. Between 1871 and 1896 the labour force grew 2.4 times, the primary sector only twice, but the secondary sector 5.4 times and the tertiary 3.1 times.

For women a first opportunity arose in work in the secondary sector, especially the manufacture of textiles and clothing, in its most rapid growth period, with major increases in the post-Vogel period. Then, ironically for women, participation in the

> primary industry grew faster. Refrigeration created a primary-industry job that was considered suitable for women, that is, milking cows. The number of women in farming more than trebled between 1886 and 1891. For the next 30 years the female work force involved in the primary sector expanded whenever dairying was growing rapidly and male labour was in short supply. Female labour seems to have been particularly important when a dairy farm was being established (Thompson 1985: 123).

Importantly, the women in the primary sector were not just farm-wives but single women. When the establishment phase was over and men took over milking (also with machines replacing hand milking) the surplus women, the 'milkmaids', moved into the secondary sector. While the tertiary sector appeared relatively stable, in fact for women workers there were all sorts of changes. Domestic service peaked in 1881 at 48% of the female workforce, but was surpassed by the other service industries, and thus by the early 1900s a major shift-share was occurring in the Pakeha female workforce (Thompson 1985: Fig. 48, 123).

In short, it is clear that the women operating the nuptiality valve were not remaining idle, although this may have been the case for the better-off. Instead, the expanding gap between nubility and marriage, and for some the decision not to marry – recalling that there were still male surpluses – could be filled by paid employment. In the 1870s there had been only one option – marry and procreate – but by the 1890s a number of others had opened up. Call this modernisation, call it the adoption of norms in common with women in other ESCs, call it whatever you like, the argument is fairly clear: at a proximate level of explanation many women were choosing not to marry or to delay marrying; the more causally remote explanation can be found in the labour-force shifts occurring at that time. This much can be documented. There may have been other more causally remote normative changes shared with women in other ESCs, but this becomes a speculative argument proved only by the fact that co-terminous shifts were occurring in the Americas and in the Australian colonies.

3.7 PAKEHA FAMILY MORPHOLOGIES, 1900S–1940S

PATTERNS AND TRENDS OF FAMILY FORMATION
A great deal of attention has been given here to the Victorian era simply because it appears to have been fundamental in laying down future behaviours and norms. Over the next four decades the more manifest aspects of family structures – sizes, and proportions of women marrying, becoming mothers and delaying childbearing – were to change only modestly. But other more nuanced structural transformations did occur, and were then to set antecedents for reproductive regimes that re-emerged only at the end of the twentieth century.

From 1900 to 1945, and in contrast with the pioneer period, Pakeha patterns of family formation reached almost an opposite extreme to what had been seen in the 1870s. This was a period of reproductive conservatism: late marriage, a significant minority of celibate women, and small family sizes. The 'advent of the small family system' (Gibson 1971: Chapt. VII) was accomplished by 1901 and it became entrenched between then and the end of the Great Depression of the 1930s. A minor exception was the brief set of fluctuations between 1915 and 1920. In 1916 the TFR had been 3.1; it crashed to 2.6 in 1919 at the time of the 'flu pandemic; and then there was reproductive reprise to 3.2 in 1921 through the combined effects of recuperation from the 'flu and the fact that the troops were now home from World War I (Khawaja 1985: Fig. 22, 154). By 1929 at the eve of the Great Depression it was already down to 2.9, and continued down to reach just below replacement in the mid-1930s. This brief interlude of sub-replacement fertility has greater import than its short duration might imply as it occurred before the advent of modern, efficient contraception and was a trend shared with other WDCs, especially in Europe (van de Kaa 2004). There was then an upsurge in the TFR around the outbreak of World War II, to which attention will be drawn below (and then again in Chapter Eight in relation to the specific issue of multiple births).

Until the late 1930s marriage was increasingly delayed (Vosburgh 1978: Table 8.1). By the time of the Depression 27% of women and 38% of men under age 30 had never married, whereas a decade later this figure had dropped to 13% and 25% respectively. The shift to later ages at marriage had been accompanied by an increase in celibacy among women (Dharmalingam *et al.* 2007: Table 3.6 uses cohort data to illustrate this point). If we take women at marriageable ages in the period from the 1890s to World War I (i.e. women born 1872 to 1896) and compare these women with cohorts born before and after, not only were they more likely to postpone marriage, but a sizeable minority would never marry. This shift in marital patterns represents more than merely a change in forms – it produced other significant but less obvious shifts in family structures.

First, the childless, spinster 'maiden aunt' of Victorian British fiction and fact also became a feature of New Zealand family life, either living alone, caring for elderly parents or living with other married relatives. Frequently the maiden aunt worked and if living with a nuclear family or an elderly parent often would have contributed to the household's income. Some married women with children, particularly widows or those in lower socio-economic groupings, did work – often as domestic staff or in factories while 'Women with dead, absent or incapable husbands could run small businesses [including farms]' (Belich 1996: 392). Many currently married women with children were the buttresses or even the mainstays of family businesses, most notably the family farm. Unfortunately, this can be recorded only through anecdote or family history – it was not to be recorded in systems of national accounts, and thus in censuses and surveys, until well after World War II – and the suspicion remains that the contribution of many wives will have been played down or relegated purely to the kitchen. But this was an era in which for women in the more formal salaried sectors, the choice was either to work (and to remain childless) or to marry (and have a family), the latter situation often involving forced retirement. Even highly qualified women who were in cohabiting relationships might have difficulty finding employment, as James McNeish documents occurring in Otago-Southland in the case of Winnie Gonley MA, the lover, later wife, of renowned scholar and author Dan Davin (2003: 164). According to the historian Melanie Nolan, 'From 1913 women civil servants had to resign on marriage'. This lasted until 1947 (Nolan 2000: 27, 65, 218).

To add to this, ex-nuptial childbearing was very uncommon. By the early twentieth century, therefore, there was a lack of 'reproductive choice', a situation that was to manifest itself again at the other end of the twentieth century. In this period the 'drive to control and discipline [Pakeha] motherhood, and to discourage illicit motherhood, [was also] a drive to encourage legitimate maternity' (Belich 2001: 181).

The workforce trends for women that underlay the marriage patterns noted earlier were reinforced especially in the 1920s, thus providing increasing alternatives to marriage and motherhood; of course, 'women without a male breadwinner were more likely to be in paid employment than the women with one.' But for single women work opportunities also increased: 'In 1891 about 39% of women aged 15–24, most of whom were single, were in paid employment. By 1921 the proportion had grown to over half, and had reached 60% by World War II' (Nolan 2000: 33, 65, 69, see also Chapt. 3, fn. 1). As milking machines that farm owners could use to replace hand labour pushed single women off farms in the 1920s, their numbers in the secondary sector grew, especially in the clothing industry. The surplus of women workers, often no longer employed on farms, saw an upsurge in domestic job numbers in the 1920s and especially in the Depression (Thompson 1985:

123). By 1906 tertiary sector jobs in industries other than domestic service had exceeded domestic service, 'the proportion of office workers who were women rose from 2% in 1891 to 40% in 1921, and then stabilised until the late 1930s'. In contrast, the 'proportion of women public servants peaked during World War I at one-third of permanent staff, dropped considerably in the interwar period, and rose to about one-quarter of all staff by 1945' (Nolan 2000: 65).

Secondly, as has just been implied, the shifts in marriage patterns had a major impact on fertility, but in a direction that was contrary to the desire to increase 'legitimate motherhood'. In fact, nuptial family sizes dropped significantly albeit slowly over the 1900s to late 1930s (again it must be stressed that most births occurred within marriage). At first, in the virtual absence of effective contraception, and with limited resort to abortion, the changes in marriage patterns had acted as a very effective means of fertility regulation. The 1870s had been one of the great eras of precocious child-bearing in New Zealand; the Baby Boom, especially around 1970, almost a century later, was to see a reprise of this norm. By 1901, in contrast, the delayed childbearing of Great Britain had became the norm in Pakeha New Zealand, again a trend that was to reappear a century later at the dawn of the twenty-first century.

Thirdly, by the early decades of the twentieth century, childbearing was occurring at later and later ages. But alongside that, fewer and fewer married women were bearing children in their thirties and early forties, and an analogous but less marked decline in marital fertility was seen even among women in their twenties (Khawaja 1985: Fig. 22).

Finally, family sizes declined: a TFR of 2.9 children per woman in 1921 (all marital statuses), dropped to 2.4 in 1931, and down to slightly below replacement during 1934–36. By 1939–41, however, rates had risen significantly.

REPRODUCTIVE REGIMES, 1900–1945
At various times, notably in the 1920s, the New Zealand family size profile showed a far greater variation than was seen after World War II and up until the end of the 1980s. This variance would have long-term implications for the structures of families much later in the century, especially for kin networks and particularly sibling support among the elderly (McPherson 1991 *passim* and Table 6.7). This is illustrated here in Tables 3.4a and 3.4b (see also Dharmalingam *et al.* 2007: Tables 3.7 and 3.8). A comparison between the 1920s and 1930s and the Baby Boom years (discussed in Chapter Five) shows that distribution was far more evenly spread across the reproductive ages in the 1920s and 1930s than was the case for any of the other periods covered there. But as the data for 1911 analysed above show, this belies other important factors.

Table 3.4a: Patterns of Reproduction for Non-Maori, 1921–2001

Year	TFR	Percentage of TFR at ages		
		<25 years	25–34 years	35+ years
1921	2.9	23	53	24
1931	2.4	24	53	23
1951	3.4	32	54	15
1971	3.0	43	49	11
1991	2.2	29	61	11
2001	1.8	22	61	17

Table 3.4b: Force of Reproduction for Non-Maori, 1921–2001: (i) Births Indexed to 1921 (= 100); (ii) Modal Age-group; (iii) Percentage Occurring at 30+ years; and (iv) Ratios

Year	Index (1921 = 100)	Modal age-group	Percentage of births 30+ years	Ratios	
				20–24/ 35–39	25–29/ 30–34
1921	100	25–29	46	1.4	1.2
1931	93	25–29	41	1.8	1.4
1951	156	25–29	35	2.5	1.6
1971	196	20–24	19	8.4	2.3
1991	186	25–29	37	2.5	1.3
2001	151	30–34	54	0.8	0.8

Sources: Dharmalingam *et al.* 2007: Table 3.8.

In the early twentieth century a significant minority of women did not marry at all (Dharmalingam *et al.* 2007: Table 3.2), and because of the conventions of those days, the overwhelming majority of them remained childless. The effects of this can be evaluated by looking at the census data for 1911, 1916 and 1921 on births to 'married women'. Let us assume that very few births occurred to single women. This assumption is not unrealistic, as 'illegitimate' birth rates, derived from vital registration, a juridical and thus one assumes a closely monitored process, were likely to be accurate and were at very low levels. The census data, both on birth and marital status were, by contrast, obtained through self-reporting, allowing 'single' women in consensual unions, or not in a union, with or without children, to report themselves as 'married'. This analysis cannot be taken to higher ages than those reported below in Table 3.5, as some of the women 'not married' at a census will have been widows, and thus the data presented here are only for women nearing the end of their reproductive spans.

Table 3.5 draws on fertility data collected at three censuses, for two of them reported in a somewhat unconventional way, and it differs from Table 3.2 as it includes two more censuses and adds in columns for all women. The data in this table show that the effects of not marrying were very marked. Nearing the end of their reproductive spans fully one-third or more of all women had had no children, and had been effectively excluded from childbearing. A benchmark against which to compare these data comes from the Pakeha Baby Boom, an era which taught us a lot about the bio-social aspects of parenting. It showed that, given the opportunity of being exposed to risk of conception, more than 90% of women would bear a child (Sceats 1981).

The average levels of childlessness among *all* women (ever married plus never married) in the first quarter of the twentieth century were thus three times what might have been expected naturally for populations with reasonable health standards. The proportionate impact of celibacy on levels of reproduction was to reduce it by between a quarter and almost two-fifths. At the opposite extreme, for example, more than two-fifths of *married* women in 1921 in their early forties had borne four or more children (not shown on table), while this was true for only one-third of *all* women.

Table 3.5: Married and All Women Aged 35–39 and 40–44 Years, 1911, 1916 and 1921: Average Number of Children Ever Born and Percentage Childless

| | Age Group | | | |
| | 35–39 years | | 40–44 years | |
	Married	All	Married	All
Children ever born:				
1911	3.3	2.4	4.1	3.0
1916	3.1	2.4	3.6	2.8
1921	3.0	2.3	3.4	2.7
Percentage childless:				
1911	14	37	14	36
1916	14	33	14	33
1921	13	33	14	33

Source: Censuses.

Therefore, Table 3.5 provides evidence of reproductive polarisation, determined to a significant degree at that time by whether or not a woman opted to marry. This topic will be returned to in Chapter Four, but it does suggest that 'reproductive choice' – a concept that from the 1970s centred on whether or not younger women, say below 25 years, can choose to remain childless – may have other dimensions. In contrast, for generations living in the early years of the twentieth century, 'reproductive choice' was really a 'Hobson's Choice', as it was between whether or not a woman would enter a union over her family-building ages and thus could become a mother, or would remain single and childless. The latter was typically the only option for women who wished to pursue a career in many occupations that today employ both single and married women as a matter of course. For example, the traditional female occupations of teaching, into which the hapless Winnie Gonley wanted to enter, and nursing were structured so that working and being married were seen as incompatible; the Matron was unlikely to have been a matron.

The more conventional meaning of reproductive choice relating to younger women and to issues surrounding methods of fertility regulation would remain an important consideration even in the twenty-first century. Yet an echo of what had been the prime criteria in the first half of the twentieth century was to re-emerge at the dawn of the new millennium to produce forms of reproductive polarisation that were reminiscent in some ways of what had occurred much earlier. Although the patterns of exposure to intercourse and the mechanisms for fertility regulation were vastly different at the start of the twenty-first century, the dichotomy among women at older reproductive ages into childbearers and childless was to reappear. As had been the case early in the twentieth century, labour-market factors once again were to play an important part in this equation. As we will show, the job market again became the most extreme element in what is now called the 'work–life balance', played out this time in terms not of marital status but of the incompatibility of full-time employment and motherhood.

A further issue is that for married women levels of childlessness, shown in Table 3.5, were just above 10% (see also Dharmalingam *et al.* 2007: Table 3.9). These were above the levels in the Baby Boom, but they were not too far above what would be expected from what is known of the bio-social aspects of reproduction in societies in which levels of life expectancy were still not as high as they would become, for example, by the 1980s, and when obstetrical and gynaecological care were below contemporary standards. Nevertheless, some important breakthroughs in maternity care and peri-natal survivorship were achieved in the 1920s and 1930s (Sceats and Pool 1985b: 247).

The family size declines over this period around World War I are, then, an indication of increasing fertility regulation within marriage. Normally, how-ever, this practice would not have been adopted until after a first pregnancy (Sceats and Pool 1985: 187–88). This is confirmed by the fact that in the 1920s and the Depression 40–50% of first births occurred within the first twelve months of marriage, and half of these were within the first eight months (i.e. ex-nuptially conceived, Jacoby 1961). This corresponds to what happened in late eighteenth-century England (Wrigley 1981: 162). Within marriage, couples would have used inefficient barrier and rhythm methods, absten-tion, withdrawal and abortion; outside marriage these were employed but, of course, avoidance of exposure to risk was achieved by not marrying at all and thus not being exposed to intercourse (Sceats and Pool 1985: 187). Condoms and other barrier methods were far less effective, even in the 1950s and 1960s, than they are today (Pool *et al.* 1999: 86, citing Dr Margaret Sparrow, a pio-neer of modern family planning in New Zealand).

In this era, sole parenting was less common than it was to become at the end of the twentieth century, at least as far as one can estimate from census marital status data. Nevertheless, it was still an important factor in days when welfare state protection was only in its infancy. More commonly, however, this status was far more likely to be because of widowhood than divorce. In 1936, the 3000 or more widowed women at a pivotal parenting age (45–49 years) outnumbered divorcees by 3.2 to 1.0.

In 1926 divorce and separation were uncommon (data on divorce, separation and widow(er)hood by age are shown in Dharmalingam *et al.* 2007: Table 3.10), whereas widowhood was far more frequent than it is today. By 1956 in the Baby Boom, the combined figures for these two marital statuses were actually slightly lower than they had been in 1926. But, by the Baby Boom, at younger ages there had been a shift-share in categories from widow(er)hood to divorce and separation, whereas for women at older ages widowhood was still the more important factor. By 1986 the situation had changed very significantly, to what we know today, when widowhood at reproductive ages is very rare.

The impact on 'family' structures of a 'sole adult', often with dependent children, cannot be underestimated. The fact that widow(er)hood rather than divorce or separation is the determinant is immaterial. But in 1926 a fifth of families in which there was a woman aged 50–54 years were composed of a 'sole adult', a higher level than in 1956, and this held true for almost every age-group (see Dharmalingam *et al.* 2007: Table 3.11). Thus the widely held view in the new millennium that sole parenting is a recent phenomenon is far from exact. Structurally, it was always important; it is the form that has changed. Moreover, families of currently married women bringing up children on their own were not unusual in the Depression and war years when husbands and fathers were away from their families for prolonged periods, in the armed forces or seeking relief work. Mothers with absent husbands were often sole parents for very long periods, often as long as the duration of the Second World War.

Yet another major change in Pakeha family life was also occurring at this time, particularly in the 1920s. A shift to a neolocally focused nuclear-family lifestyle was starting to occur in the new suburbs that began to spread out beyond the central cities. Electric trams, buses, ferries and cars for the well-off made it possible to commute to places like Three Kings, Takapuna or Mt Albert in Auckland, where California-style bungalows, as they were called, were sprouting up, providing 'happy homes' for couples. That said, however, grandparents and other relatives (often unmarried siblings of parenting couples) were frequently housed within the family, and this gave the illusion, noted earlier, of the maintenance of extended family structures into this period. This movement out to commuting zones and the cultural changes that accompanied it were to have long consequences, not just for the morphologies of families but also for their underlying values and norms. The new suburbs and their happy homes became the models for New Zealand family lifestyles, in reality as in nostalgia, reaching a zenith in the Baby Boom but still around in the new millennium. This regime is so important in the pattern of New Zealand social life to the end of the twentieth century and into the twenty-first that it will be returned to in later chapters.

THE PAKEHA FAMILY: PRELUDE TO THE BABY BOOM

By the late 1930s, the story outlined above was starting to change, however, as births to mothers at all ages up to 40 years increased. 'By the end of the 1930s both birth intervals and mean ages of achieving lower parities had begun to decline . . . [heralding] the key characteristics of marital fertility patterns of the Baby-Boom' (Sceats and Pool 1985: 188). But at that point came World War II, and with it a brief surge of fertility at its outbreak, in part a natural recovery from the Depression years, and in part the result of intimate farewells as troops left for the war (see also Chapter Eight, in reference to multiple births). Against this, the war caused many couples who had intended marrying, or having a first or next child, to delay doing so, and thus fertility dropped again: the 'war served to "suspend" the demographic experience of those involved' (Fletcher 1979). But perhaps by way of compensation there were slightly elevated levels of ex-nuptial childbearing in 1944 during the war; or this slight upsurge may have been a side-product of the presence of large numbers of American soldiers based in New Zealand from about 1942 (the nature and demographic impacts of which are summarised well in Belich 2001: 287–92).

Moreover, many women, who would otherwise have been married and settled in suburbia outside the labour force, instead volunteered for, or were conscripted into, employment for the duration of the war. At the end of hostilities most were 'cajoled or pushed out of jobs that returned servicemen could fill' (Olssen and Levesque 1978: 18). But the seeds of a mutation and a mutiny in values and behaviours had been sown, and these were to have major implications in the Baby Boom of the 1940s and later (see Chapter Five, citing Belich 2001).

The 1930s Depression and the war had the effect of bottling up the processes of family formation and of postponing radical changes in family structures. The scene was set for the Baby Boom, but it took the end of the war to release these pent-up forces. In this context, it is worth recalling, however, that many of those who had married in the 1930s 'were still reproducing into the 1950s' (O'Neill 1979: 133).

Thus the prelude to the Baby Boom came somewhere near the end of the period discussed in the present chapter, but when exactly is open to debate. The precise date is less relevant than the trend line and its characteristics: we know for sure that sometime in the early 1940s fertility rates started to increase rapidly, yet, in one sense, this upsurge can be seen as merely a continuation of existing trends evident at the very end of the inter-war period. Yet if one looks behind this trend to its particular attributes, notably ages of childbearing, then the pre-war reproductive regimes were still operating immediately after the war, albeit, for historically unique reasons, producing higher rates and birth numbers than had been seen in the Depression. But any residual pre-war patterns quickly gave way to new and totally different regimes, which for Pakeha were reminiscent not of the recent twentieth-century model but of that model last seen in the 1870s.

3.8 SUMMARY AND CONCLUSION: NEW ZEALAND FAMILIES UNTIL 1945

This chapter has examined behavioural changes in patterns of family building and has outlined some of the contextual factors that accompanied these changes. The next chapter will look briefly at the impact of fertility regulation, and then in more depth at the norms and values surrounding not only birth control, but legitimacy and illegitimacy, the family itself and reproduction. To this end it will also review in further depth another factor: the emergence of reproductive polarisation and related questions of reproductive choice. These throw further light on norms and values but also raise questions that have long-term implications and an impact on policy.

The present chapter has dealt with a so-called era of large families, a situation that remained more or less constant for Maori, although their reproduction rates never reached the truly hyper-levels described for Pakeha pioneer women prior to the 1880s. Indeed, because of bio-social factors, primarily to do with poor health and nutrition, and disruption due to the wholesale loss of their land resources, Maori rates were not extremely high in the 1870s. They gradually shed these constraints, so that by the end of the period covered in this chapter Maori women were reaching the high levels of fertility that they were to achieve during the Baby Boom.

Pakeha had very large families only in the earlier pioneer years covered here – say until the 1880s. It is clear that, prior to the last years of Victoria's reign, of those women who married – and most did – the majority had super-large families. But we must not forget that there was an increasing minority, even among those marrying, who had zero or few offspring. There is no clear social reason for this phenomenon, and one must turn to theory relating to the bio-social aspects of reproduction to explain it. These revolve around two sorts of maternal risks: obstetrical and general ill-health. These risk factors were comparable to those for Maori but far less severe: Pakeha, by world standards of the day, were already very privileged in terms of health.

The early Pakeha women colonists had remarkable levels of reproduction, both in terms of the proportions marrying and having children and the lack of limitation at older ages. Yet, in spite of hyper-fertility in the early years of settlement, they did not quite achieve one reproductive record realised 80–100 years later by their granddaughters and great-granddaughters: the virtually universal childbearing of the Baby Boom of 1943–73. From what we know about Hutterites and similar populations (e.g. eighteenth-century Quebec women), the age at childbearing in the Baby Boom was almost perfectly structured to maximise the chances of pregnancy. At older ages, however, barrier methods and later the Pill allowed birth control for Baby Boom couples at higher parities. Of course, neither of these options had been available to their forebears, and thus women in late Victorian New Zealand started at young ages with high fertility but continued on until they died, became widows or reached menopause.

To return to the hypothesis suggested by David Thomson's work (2006) and outlined at the beginning of the chapter, and to some of its sub-texts, the early colonial family was not a minor variant of the contemporary British model. In fact Pakeha patterns of nuptiality and fertility in the 1870s and earlier were markedly different even from those recorded in peak periods of reproduction in Britain, notably 1801–25. The implications of this will be further explored in the next chapter. What is clear, however, is that the Pakeha family had a morphology far more akin to those in early settlements in the Americas* or Australia, and thus it fitted well with the neo-European model. Not only was fertility higher than in the mother country, a consequence of early marriage and lower levels of celibacy, but marital fertility was also at higher levels.

It is when one turns, however, to explanations that some of Thomson's arguments have resonance, notably that neither the surplus of males, nor the frontier provide sufficient explanations for these patterns. But an alternative hypothesis – that the settler inflows were selected from high-fertility and high-nuptiality sub-populations in the British Isles – has not been supported by the data presented here on those countries. While the British sources for migration flows were highly selective by region and occupation, our evidence has shown that, on balance, the Pakeha immigrants were not representative, disproportionately, of higher fertility British sub-populations; if anything, migrant selectivity leaned towards regions with lower fertility, lower nuptiality rates and later marriage. In any case, sub-populations with high fertility in Britain still had levels that fell below those estimated for the Pakeha population as a whole.

---

* Michael Haines, a leading American historical demographer, notes that some data on very early American settlements relate to small, isolated communities and may be subject to random and other statistical errors, and thus should be treated with caution (personal communication).

These comments apply, however, to the early colonial period. Starting about 1880, and by the late nineteenth century, the situation changed dramatically for Pakeha, setting in train a trend that continued until the late 1930s. By the 1890s the New Zealand family had indeed become a colonial variant of the model seen in the British Isles. James Belich's apt term 'recolonisation' is not just applicable to the political economy and popular culture as these unfolded from about the 1880s (2001: 27–31), but also describes the reproductive patterns of Pakeha colonists from that time.

From the 1890s on, the large family became a somewhat illusory phenomenon. It is true that well into the twentieth century many couples did continue to have the large families of memory, but increasing proportions had fewer children, and a significant minority were childless, most frequently because they had not married at all. Along with this, the locus of family life shifted from the pioneer farm or the central part of the urban area to suburbia, a new adjunct to the city. In Auckland this was a move from Freeman's Bay, Ponsonby, Grey Lynn, Parnell or Grafton to Mt Eden, Mt Albert, Sandringham, Epsom or Remuera. The onset of World War II and the Baby Boom and Baby Bust that quickly followed the end of hostilities were to change New Zealand family life forever.

CHAPTER FOUR

The Large Family of Yesteryear:
Factors Underlying Change

4.1 CHANGES OVER THE PERIOD 1840–1945

MAJOR THEMES

The major trends experienced by the New Zealand family between 1840 and 1945 are documented in the last chapter. The main conclusions presented there can be summarised briefly. For Maori there was extreme disruption of family life through war, confiscation, land court processes and the attendant loss of resources, then gradual change dedicated to societal maintenance and recuperation; for Pakeha there was a shift from colonial hyper-fertility to reproductive polarisation, which became more obvious in the Dominion period after 1906. Pakeha family life was to be increasingly centred on suburbia, and this was linked to the establishment of marked patterns of polarisation of fertility patterns.

For Pakeha in the late Victorian period, the impact of these trends on the colonial psyche was so strong that around 1900 there was a moral panic, to be described later in this chapter. Concern focused on the mechanisms by which the declines had been brought about, with most publicly stated opinion blaming 'birth control', by which was meant contraception and abortion. This perception contrasted with the reality, described in Chapter Three; the preventive check of marriage was the more important factor.

But Chapter Three left hanging a more fundamental question: what were the determinants of the adoption of various means of fertility regulation? By drawing on relevant demographic data and the rather restricted literature on family dynamics in this period, the aim is to see if a coherent picture emerges of the underlying value systems of colonial and then early Dominion New Zealand. Thus Chapter Four is concerned with a higher level of explanation than was the case in Chapter Three; we will draw on some of the same material but look at it from a different perspective. This analysis is then extended to a review of the more macro-social and economic contexts in which were situated both the value system and the behavioural elements of the familial and reproductive regimes.

The second component of the Pakeha trends from 1900, reproductive polarisation, a factor noted in Chapter Three, will then be examined in further detail. The substantive issue already raised is that the fertility decline involved not merely a shift from almost universal childbearing to lower levels overall, but also the emergence of sometimes marked differentials: between those groups who had babies and those who did not. Obviously in this situation perceptions may be as important as reality but, regardless, public attitudes may be influenced either way. Thus Chapter Four will review different patterns of variance, regional, socio-economic and socio-cultural, and build on analyses presented in Chapter Three.

Reproductive polarisation is of inherent interest in its own right, but by parsing it in more detail it is possible to throw further light on the links between aspects of socio-economic and socio-cultural segmentation and family trends. But this is not the end of the affair for this line of analysis. It also raises another issue, alluded to in the last paragraph: the embedding in New Zealand society of norms and attitudes, which are often redolent of prejudices relating to the differences families face in reproducing themselves and thus in maintaining their 'line'. The issue of who has and who does not have babies is fraught, going well beyond twenty-first-century notions of children as a type of conspicuous consumption or consumer durable and touching the most sensitive and fundamental roots of being for couples and their wider families. The period 1900–40 is important in this regard as the first in which Pakeha society and other WDCs, with the possible exception of France, had to face low fertility and develop attitudes to deal with it. The overture to what unfolded during the first forty years of the twentieth century had already been played out in the late nineteenth, when pioneer patterns of hyper fertility had suddenly evaporated. This set an antecedent to the Baby Bust that was to occur about a century later and on into the twenty-first. Thus part of the agenda here is to find synergies between what is happening in the new millennium and what happened in the first four decades of the twentieth century.

Finally, this chapter considers the policy context and the way it responded to family needs. It starts by looking at how society handled the most basic needs surrounding poverty and welfare, and then sees how responses in this area went beyond mere sustenance to provide a better environment in which to raise a family. This takes the chapter back to its starting point, the impact of declines in fertility on social attitudes and thus on policy formulation.

TRENDS AND DIFFERENTIALS

The Pakeha household is the focus of the present chapter, although the dynamics of Maori whanau will not be ignored as they are an important part of the story of the evolution of the New Zealand family (see below). For Maori, sheer societal maintenance was the critical element of family life over much of the period 1840–1945, and this chapter will address the determinants and effects of what was, eventually, a highly successful recovery. In contrast, the Pakeha family was wrested from its original social and economic environment and adapted to a new one. It then passed through further societal changes of a very significant sort; for example, new morphologies evolved with industrial labour-force transformation and accompanying urbanisation. Family transition in the period was accompanied by *angst* of various kinds, and thus moral panics. Despite the seemingly inexorable growth of the Pakeha population, concern even extended, as was the case for Maori, to anxiety about societal survival.

If we take the whole period from 1840 until 1945, the most rapid shifts in Pakeha family structures in terms of sizes – a transition from hyper-fertility to restrained reproduction – had occurred before 1900 (see Figure 2.1). This is arguably the most interesting aspect of the history of the New Zealand family before World War II. Certainly, as will be shown, it had an impact on broader society-wide attitudes about demographic maintenance. British-origin Pakeha had quickly become by far the largest population group. They had only recently arrived in significant numbers, probably carrying with them norms and values from the 'old country', yet, as was shown in Chapter Three, their reproductive regime differed in important ways from British patterns at that time, particularly in terms of family sizes. How, then, did all these various trends meld together to form a Pakeha New Zealand model? And, perhaps more importantly, did Pakeha families of the last years of the Victorian period build a legacy to be handed down to future generations?

From about 1900 to 1943 changes in family formation were modest, and thus, in looking at causes and consequences of different fertility trends, focusing on the period prior to the Edwardian years is crucial. Nevertheless, there are other very critical questions to be asked about families in the first four decades of the twentieth century. The pioneer era had been one in which 'everyone was doing it' (to misquote the inter-war 'rag' song); almost every woman who could was having children. But over the first four decades of the twentieth century the reproductive regime diversified and new questions must be addressed: who was 'doing it', where, in what sort of familial context and why?

THE DIVERSIFICATION OF PAKEHA FAMILY MORPHOLOGIES
Fertility rates were not the only aspect of the morphology and function of the Pakeha family to change in the century following Waitangi. While declines in the levels of fertility had decelerated from the 1890s on, other fundamen-

tal changes to family life and functions were occurring. As was noted last chapter, the locus of family life in the inter-war years increasingly centred on suburbia. Also complex patterns of reproductive polarisation – largely a dichotomy between those women who were married and had children and those who remained single and childless – became apparent. There was also an increase in the spread of family sizes among those who were married. The issue here is whether this phenomenon was strictly determined or delineated by demographic factors, as in the case of the availability of marriage partners and thus exposure to conception, or whether differentials were starting to be moulded by the social and economic factors that provide a context to norms and behaviours relating to family sizes.

In Chapter Three differentials were analysed in terms of the spread of 'fertilities' (to use Simon Szreter's term to denote patterns as well as levels), mainly determined in the late nineteenth century by marriage or celibacy. But Szreter's data on Britain at the 1911 census (2002: Fig. 7.1), reflecting patterns of reproduction in the late Victorian and the Edwardian periods, identify another dimension. At least by that date, the ranges of British fertilities by social status and occupation were very wide. Taking 'sources of male employment' as his indicator of class, and completed family sizes at menopause as his measure of reproduction, his data are evidence of relatively lower rates of reproduction, around three to four births per woman, among those with husbands in professions, retired from business or with private means, all seemingly better-off groups. But these were also the levels seen among some of the less well-off, such as tobacconists, domestic, college and club servants, lodging-house keepers and those in Poor Law service. At the opposite extreme, with double the fertility or more (7.0–7.5 births), were British labourers of different sorts, and coal miners.

Clearly in the mother country there were significant differentials by social circumstance, and it can be fairly assumed that these patterns were exported to the colonies. Thus, there is a need to look for signs of such socio-economic and other patterns of variance in family regimes in New Zealand for the period 1840–1945.

4.2 THE IMPACTS OF FAMILY SIZE CHANGES ON SOCIETAL ATTITUDES

THE END OF PAKEHA HYPER-FERTILITY

In the late Victorian period the Maori population fought for its very survival, whereas Pakeha went through a period of extraordinary growth, from a mere 2000 in 1840 to almost half a million in 1881, to a million in 1911, to 1.5 million in 1936. The early years in particular, especially from 1860 to 1880, had been supercharged both by massive migration inflows and hyper-fertility. As a result Pakeha had become habituated to very high growth, so much so that rapid population increase became one of the society's most basic cultural tenets. This ethos still exists in the Pakeha psyche of today. It is composed of a self-image revolving around virility,* as seen in the larger family sizes than those in the metropole, and a cargo-cult attitude that saw migration as the key to economic growth, provided, of course, that the migrants were of the right sort. But in reality, from the late 1870s migration dropped off dramatically and average family sizes started to decline. These events had an impact on public attitudes because they ran contrary to perceptions about growth.

As was shown in Chapter Three, prior to 1900 changes in Pakeha family sizes had gone through an accelerated decrease because of a major shift upward in the age of first parenting, and from a change in the marital status distribution of the female population. It is worth stressing that the quantum and velocity of family structural change in the late nineteenth century as measured by fertility trends were remarkable. The drop, from a TFR of almost 7.0 births per woman down to 50% of that rate, was very significant. In fact, it was even greater than what occurred at this time in the neighbouring Australian colonies. In an era in which contraceptive technology was still primitive, the velocity of change achieved through adjusting the nuptiality valve was also astonishing.

To understand the social and policy significance of the speed of this shift and the impact it was to have on norms and values then and in later periods, even in the years after World War II, it is useful to look briefly across the Tasman at the birth of the new Commonwealth of Australia. In the colony of New South Wales, right on the eve of federation, concerns about seemingly rapid declines in fertility and, as in other Australasian colonies, unprecedented population changes led to a major statistical enquiry (see Coghlan 1903, who undertook analyses of a high quality).

This enquiry was a component of the Royal Commission on the Decline of the Birth Rate and on the Mortality of Infants in New South Wales, 1903–04. According to the New Zealand historian Philippa Mein Smith, who details the context for the hearings themselves and then the attendant panic, the processes and the report of this commission sparked a great deal of interest in New Zealand. This reached right up to Premier Richard Seddon himself, who responded specifically to the issue of societal demographic maintenance. Smith notes that Seddon, 'impressed by the

---

* This is not unique to New Zealand. In 1982 Ian Pool was interviewed on New Caledonian radio over the TFRs that had just been published showing that levels were higher in that Territoire Outre-Mer than in metropolitan France. The first question was rhetorical, expressing with glee: '*Donc, nous sommes plus viriles que la métropole?*'

Commission's report, adapted its findings in his own memorandum on child life preservation in 1904; "reproduction is essential for the continuation of the human race", Seddon told Parliament' (Smith 2002: 309–10). Anything that reduced levels of reproduction – be it contraception, abortion or entry of women into the labour force in such a way as to lead to birth limitation – was deemed undesirable. This theme was reiterated during the course of the following decades. Interwoven with this *angst* was another population question that appeared to echo emerging orthodox scientific thought and gave greater credence to the panics. The advent in the late nineteenth and early twentieth centuries of the new disciplines of genetics and psychiatry, in an era in which social Darwinism also flourished, had added a new condiment to the mix: eugenics concerns. These started with Francis Galton's observations, built on notions of class differentials in fertility which saw the 'professional class as the most evolved', with inherited ability but low fertility. When compulsory education was introduced in Britain in the late Victorian period, it was often observed that the poorest and most deprived 'could not keep up academically', and this quickly developed into arguments that linked 'pauperism' with 'feeble-mindedness'. The fledgling Eugenics Education Society (founded 1907) 'focused on the elevated fecundity of the pauper class, in which, it alleged, every family, in their terms, was studded with paupers, the impoverished, inebriates, criminals and the feeble-minded' (Mazumdar 2003: 319–20; see also her description of German eugenics).

Thus the moral panic in the early 1900s also ushered in another sub-theme inherent in the eugenics argument and that was to repeat itself through the entire twentieth century in New Zealand: that the 'wrong people were having babies'. Initially eugenicist arguments had revolved around the physically and mentally handicapped, although there was always a tendency to see these malfunctions in social Darwinian terms, as something likely to be more prevalent among the lower social orders. Later, especially near the end of the twentieth century when it was no longer considered appropriate to single out the disabled, the focus turned increasingly towards social handicaps, and became directed more and more at beneficiaries and low-income families.

The eugenicist attitudes emerging at the dawn of the twentieth century fitted comfortably with some views on family policy and service delivery that seem to have been imported from the old country, and that will be discussed later in this chapter. But as was often, but not always, the case for New Zealand panics, rhetoric of this sort was translated into a rather pragmatic outcome. Seddon's concerns 'generated a legislative response in the form of the Midwives Act 1904, intended to reduce infant and maternal mortality among respectable working-class mothers who were potentially eugenically desirable' (Smith 2002: 309–10).

The societal-maintenance theme had another dimension to it, shared with Australia: that a decline in the birth rate had wider population and geo-strategic (defence) implications for the 'racially defined polities' of 'White Australia and New Zealand'. There was a need to fill up our empty spaces either by births and fewer deaths (Smith 2002: 309), or by migration. Dr Morton Anderson, in his 1906 presidential address to the annual meeting of the New Zealand branch of the British Medical Association, expressed concern over the 'Declining birth rate in "the Britain of the South"', contrasting this with the 'much greater ratio' in 'Germany, and our ally Japan'. He commented favourably on the colony's human capital, or at least on its Pakeha settlers:

> the physique of the colonists is on the whole exceptionally good I think few will deny, nor can they be regarded otherwise than favourably from the intellectual or educational standpoint . . . Our population therefore should increase rapidly, not simply by immigration, but the natural increase should be high. But this is just where the expectations raised by our favourable conditions are not fulfilled . . . .

'If the Empire is to be maintained', he concluded in ringing patriotic tones, 'we must rely not simply on our navy or army, or on both, nor yet upon physique, but on numbers also' (Anderson 1906, reprinted in 2006).

This theme, and racist, eugenicist accompaniments, has re-emerged from time to time in New Zealand, sometimes blatantly, sometimes subtly, as in the migration policies urged by the Dominion Population Committee established in December 1945. As the geographer Ruth Farmer has noted, 'the opinion was clearly expressed that immigrants of British stock from the British Isles would be most satisfactory in New Zealand' (Farmer 1985: 64). This balance between migration and family formation as a means of stocking New Zealand has been a continuing counterpoint in public policy debates.

Historically, the declines in the late nineteenth century represented the greatest *quantum* change ever in Pakeha levels of reproduction. The Maori fertility decline in the 1960s and 1970s, to be discussed in Chapters Five and Six, produced a shift that exceeded that of Pakeha in the late nineteenth century (Pool 1991: 170), but the efficient contraception and sterilisation available from about 1960 had provided a vastly different array of proximate factors producing change. The *velocity* of the declines in the late nineteenth century was certainly rapid, but fluctuations in rates of reproduction either side of the Baby Boom, for Pakeha before and after, and for Maori in the 1970s, were to produce more accelerated short-term changes.

THE MAORI FAMILY: FROM MERE SURVIVAL TO CERTAIN RECUPERATION

Over much of the period (1870s to 1945) covered in this chapter, 'mainstream' New Zealand was dominated by Pakeha family and social institutions, but another powerful although essentially latent drama was being played out among Maori, albeit largely ignored by the Pakeha majority. After an initial period of the negative impacts of colonialism, prior to the early 1900s, Maori family life changed relatively slowly and there were few family size differentials. 'High fertility was maintained by a series of cultural props, such as the adoption into the kin-group of "excessive children"'(Douglas 1977).

While family formation strategies remained more or less unchanged, other aspects went through major shifts. Maori family life had been subject to extreme disruption because of the New Zealand Wars, particularly those of the 1860s, and associated land confiscation, and Maori were assailed further by the brutal loss of land through the land courts. Data on the very low levels of infant and childhood survivorship in the late Victorian period provide the starkest witness to the effects of these events on the Maori family and its size and age distribution, as does evidence on local migratory movements and the clustering of dispossessed whanau in different kainga, or small villages. There is very strong evidence, for example, that survivorship rates decreased – that infant and childhood mortality rates went up – in direct response to the onset and implementation of land and resource alienation. This occurred at different periods by region and iwi (tribe), between the 1840s and 1850s (e.g. Ngapuhi) through to the early 1900s (e.g. Tuhoe and Ngati Maniapoto). Some iwi such as Tuhoe and others of the Mataatua canoe saw survivorship rates decline, then improve and then decline again as two separate onslaughts were made on their resources. For others, most extremely the Taranaki tribes, the loss of resources was repeated a number of times, so that the negative effects were more or less continuous (Pool 1991: Chapts 4 and 5).

From the early 1900s the most severe effects on Maori families had already been felt, however, and from then on patterns of whanau organisation remained largely unchanged. That said, their living standards were precarious and dependent on a semi-subsistence economy. They lived in isolated rural areas, mainly in the North Island (Kukutai *et al.* 2002; Pool 1991: 88–100; Chapt. 6).

It was not just the alienation of resources that had manifest impacts on families. Even more severe effects may have come from the introduction through contact with communicable diseases against which Maori often had no immunity. The twin effects of loss of resources, as an indirect cause of high rates of mortality, and the direct impacts of disease show up in the population's age structures and undoubtedly there were analogues to this in family structures. It is often forgotten that, even in situations of high fertility, high-mortality regimes have lower proportions of their totals at younger ages, simply because the force of low levels of survivorship falls on infants and children. By contrast high-fertility, low-mortality regimes, as Maori were to experience by 1960, have very high proportions at young ages. In 1857 only 29% of female Maori and 27% of males were at childhood ages; by 1901 the respective figures were 38% and 36%. In 1857 for every 100 Maori women there were only 87 dependent children; by 1874 this was 116; and by 1901 it was 127. One must stress that the figures on dependent children do not point to a lack of births but primarily to the deaths of children born alive (Pool 1991: 68–73, 91–102).

Eventually life expectation and survivorship levels for infants and children did improve, above all during the primary health-care campaigns of the first decade of the twentieth century, so that more and more children reached parenting ages (Pool and Cheung 2004, 2005), and thus population growth accelerated. Maori life expectation at birth, in years, had increased from the low twenties to the low thirties between the 1890s and about 1910. Around 1890 only 42% of Maori girls would survive to age 20 years; by 1910 this had risen to 53% (Pool 1991: Chapt. 6, esp. 77–78).

These comments on life expectation are important, not just because Maori life chances were starting to improve but, far more critically in the present context, because these shifts in patterns of survivorship affected Maori family structures. Maori were not only developing mechanisms by which to respond to the loss of resources – the substitution of cultivation, hunting and gathering, and fishing, all of which were no longer possible, with the earning of cash from wage employment when available – but, because of more specific health reasons, they had growing immunity to introduced diseases.

Four consequences of this can be identified. First, more and more children passed through the most risky period of their lives, infancy and early childhood, and survived into adolescence. Secondly, more Maori were reaching parenting ages. Thirdly, as a consequence, with more mothers at childbearing ages, the number of babies born would have risen even if fertility rates had remained unchanged. Finally, decreasing general mortality would have been accompanied by declines in fetal loss so that more pregnancies would have survived through to birth. These trends were due, of course, entirely to reproduction and replacement, not to migration, and thus they were very much family centred.

Until the 1890s it had been generally assumed that Maori were a 'disappearing race'. The perceptive Maori Cabinet minister, Sir James Carroll, argued against that view, by being the first prominent New Zealander to discern a turnaround in trends (AJHR 1891, G-1: xxix). The impact of improving survivorship became increasingly obvious over the period, with

Te Rangihiroa stating 'the quick and easy death prescribed in 1881 by Dr Newman has not been availed of as he led us to expect' (1924: 362–63).[*]

By World War II the recuperation of the Maori was not only assured but apparently was giving local eugenicists pause for thought. In 1944, H. I. Sinclair showed that the 1942 Maori CBR was more than double that of 'Pakeha',[†] then stated, 'If the white people of New Zealand do not awaken to their responsibilities and if the present trend of Maori population continues this country will be populated by a coloured race'. He went on to describe Maori in favourable, although to our ears patronising, terms ('lovable, loyal, industrious, thrifty and enterprising'), then finishes, 'but it is for us to determine by our own actions whether the Pakeha or Maori shall predominate numerically' (Sinclair 1944: 91). In a far less ambivalent way, without eugenicist overtones, and looking with pleasure on the demographic renaissance of the Maori at the time of the New Zealand Centenary (1940), the anthropologist I. L. G Sutherland pointed out, with a degree of prescience, that this recovery would generate challenges for the entire society (1940: 441). Later chapters will pick up this theme, a twenty-first-century manifestation of which is the oft-stated comment – generally in approbation – that New Zealand, and especially its stock of children, is 'browning'.

4.3 FACTORS HAVING AN IMPACT ON FAMILY SIZES, 1840–1945

INTERMEDIATE OR PROXIMATE VARIABLES

For both Maori and Pakeha, as noted already, the key driver of reproduction through this period was the nuptiality valve, affected by adjusting marital patterns, of which the most important were shifts in the age at marriage and in the proportions of women who remained celibate. In the early colonial period, marriage had been the route to hyper-fertility for most women, but this quickly changed and more complex questions arose: who could marry and at what age this might occur. There was little control of fertility outside marriage. If ex-nuptial relations took place and led to a conception, the options were almost always illegal abortion, an accelerated wedding date or adoption, all of which involved some element of shame and often sanctions. And, until the 1960s and the advent of the Pill, control over family size within marriage could be achieved only through the use of less efficient barrier and traditional means of birth control, plus induced abortion.

---

[*] A. K. Newman (1881: 77) in 'A Study of the Causes leading to the Extinction of the Maori'. Newman was a social Darwinian and anti-Maori.
[†] 'Paheka' is his word.

The technical reality of fertility regulation in this era seems not to have been widely understood by the commentators of the period. Instead of blaming the late Victorian declines in fertility on a very transparent shift, from colonial to metropolitan marriage regimes, the villain of the piece was typically seen as birth control, although this phrase remained ill-defined in the popular discourse – and there was little distinction between contraception and abortion. This section of the chapter turns to these methods of fertility control, assessing their technical significance and evaluating attitudes towards their adoption. From the research on Britain it seems that, despite the inefficiency of the available contraceptive methods other than abstention, by the late Victorian period they were being resorted to along with abortion. We must therefore review the evidence for New Zealand, such as it is, to look for evidence here of these trends. There is also a need to look at contextual factors shaping norms and values.

There may have been a distinct cultural factor that shaped norms in the colonial and early Dominion days, perhaps derived from those that had previously driven attitudes favouring hyper-fertility. We have already made reference to the way fertility declines were seen by the New South Wales commission and their impacts on Australasia-wide views. Above all contraception was rated as something inherently undesirable, but why and from where had such attitudes come?

Some of the evidence from Britain suggests that, by the late nineteenth and early twentieth century, 'fertility limitation' within marriage was occurring. Because of a lack of systematic evidence on this point it is necessary to draw on macro-level demographic data and to attempt to interpret these. These were the sources used by Michael Anderson (1988), who drew from an analysis of 1911 census data to argue that women and couples were resorting to birth control. But, through the 'tyranny of distance', New Zealand may have been less advanced, although news of the high-profile court trials of early family planners would have circulated to the colony and, according to James O'Neill (1979), some information on barrier techniques seems to have been available. A similar situation seems to have been evident in the Australian colonies, as Lado Ruzicka and John Caldwell have argued (1977).

Overall, however, the effects of contraception must have been limited. While GFRs dropped very significantly in the late Victorian period, among late nineteenth-century Pakeha fertility was very high among married women and marriage was the only route to childbearing on any extensive scale. Moreover, while MTFRs did decrease, this was from almost nine births per married woman down to a very high seven. This certainly infers that even in the early 1900s family limitation among married couples was not widely used, and there was certainly no full-scale trend under way. Sceats and Pool (1985) also used maternal mortality data to look at the possible resort to abortion in this period and could find little evidence for its use in any demographically significant way.* There is little doubt that some abortions occurred, but for us the real issue is the impact of these interventions on family morphologies. In this regard anecdotal data are of limited use, unless one can point to widespread and systematic reports.

It is necessary, then, to ask why Pakeha might have had more conservative attitudes than Anderson has suggested the British had. To do so is to turn from behaviours and to attempt to assess norms and values. At this juncture we encounter a major constraint. Anderson's conclusions came from analysing macro-level demographic patterns, interpreting trends he observed in 1911 census data. But more qualitative data on Britain may give a different, even seemingly contradictory, picture. It fits with the idea of late Victorian Britain as a period in which moral rectitude was reinforced with a culture of fear about the medical and social repercussions of sex outside marriage.

The colonial value system, which was ignorant about or even hostile to the use of birth-control techniques, may have come from late nineteenth-century British Victorian attitudes, summarised by Simon Szreter. He refers to England and Lowland Scotland, which he compares with France:

> There is plenty of corroboration for the proposition that late 19th- and early
> 20th-century English society was a society with little knowledge of the
> more effective methods of birth control within marriage, while even basic
> knowledge of sexual anatomy was commonly withheld from the premarital,
> young adult generation wherever possible, especially among young women.
> Parental and institutional community control over courtship was tightening
> among both middle and working classes. The markedly falling illegitimate
> birth rate throughout the period [late Victorian] is consistent with a culture
> of abstinence and prudence among young adults coming to be increasingly
> embraced by the populace at this time. There is also a range of cultural
> evidence to support this thesis of increasing preoccupation with sexual
> restraint and its psychological implications [. . . including] the considerable
> upsurge in popular anxiety, to a great extent orchestrated by the increasingly
> vigorous feminist movement and by some within the medical profession, over
> the dangers and degrading nature of venereal disease (Szreter 1999: 167).

Szreter paints a picture of 'a discourse of fear expressing anxiety over lack of control in the sexual domain and an uncomfortable relationship towards sexuality' (167–68). Cobbled together were sexuality *per se*, venereal disease and

---

* As these data comprise 'post-abortal sepsis', changes in those trends, expected during a period of rapid declines in fertility in the absence of efficient contraception, the pattern in the late nineteenth century, are a widely used indirect indicator of shifts in the levels of induced abortion.

the fear that it would be spread by prostitution. Also common was the view, still echoed today in a muted form by some conservatives, that contraception would unleash (male) lust and thus spread sexually transmitted diseases (STDs).

The pre-conditions for this mix, adopted from Britain as the prevailing set of norms dictating patterns of sexuality even in the post-1900 period, especially the control of sex outside marriage, were even stronger in 'the Britain of the South' than in the metropole. Early marriage and childbearing by young women in colonial Pakeha New Zealand meant that there was little freedom for rampant extra-marital sexual congress, at least for the women if not the men in the colony. Moreover, illegitimacy rates were very low. But there was another contextual factor that was very powerful and very heady, at least in fomenting policy debates.

At the turn of the twentieth century, opposition to contraception had come from the 'first-wave' feminist movement, to use the term employed by Philippa Mein Smith (2002). This may at first glance seem counter-intuitive: this was the very generation that had fought for suffrage, more successfully than had their counterparts in the old country. During World War I the same movements came within a hair's breadth of triumphing over the 'demon drink' and turning New Zealand into a prohibitionist state. According to Smith they wanted

> chaste men as the key to new sexual – and – moral order. Most in the WCTU [Women's Christian Temperance Union] and NCW [National Council of Women] opposed birth control measures that would have made women more sexually accessible to men. Women's sexuality was for reproduction, and to argue 'otherwise was to debase women to a level of sensuality from which they had hoped to raise men' (Smith 2002: 310).

Despite such constraints, birth control within marriage must have become gradually more and more prevalent. Certainly, family sizes continued to go down, albeit with decelerated pace, until the 1930s, when reproductive levels became very low, just at replacement. This was a pattern driven in the Depression of the 1930s by the need for women and couples to reduce family sizes by applying the old and established preventive check, avoiding marriage or, if married, limiting family sizes. The latter objective was achieved by a growing use of barrier methods of contraception, and perhaps by increasing resort to abortion, particularly in the Depression (Sceats and Pool 1985). Once again, though, contraception was blamed for evolving trends:

> As a result of the adoption of these less efficient means of contraception and declines to sub-replacement fertility, there was a panic about societal

regeneration, to such an extent that conservative and eugenics groups saw barrier contraceptive devices as inherently evil (Johns, cited in Sceats and Pool 1985: 186).

Even quite early on New Zealand was not immune to the wider eugenics movement, as Mein Smith documents (2002). A stimulus in the inter-war years came from the application of a new demographic methodology, the net reproduction rate (see Chapt. Three, 60n), which implied that European populations were not replacing themselves. This led to concerns about the future and survival of the 'white races'. A home-grown, perhaps more ambivalent, argument compared Maori and Pakeha rates and looked internationally at trends (Sinclair 1944).

In a more measured way, observations about declines in fertility, and the purported role of abortion in these trends, led to the establishment in the 1930s of a government committee on abortion (the McMillan Committee of 1937). In retrospect, their report seems to have confused abortion with contraception. Nevertheless, and somewhat paradoxically given the level of panic, the McMillan Committee came up with a compassionate response to what they perceived to be the prevalence of abortion as a major means of family limitation, especially within marriage: the provision of family benefits as an incentive to couples to take conceptions through to parturition. Whether or not the levels of abortion were notably high is open to question (Sceats and Pool 1985: 187–88) – they seem to have been at about the levels for England and Wales in the early 1980s, and far below recent United States levels – but the suggestions of the commission were to have a positive impact on policy. They appear to have fed into the debates surrounding the introduction of the 1938 Social Security Act that introduced comprehensive family support packages, which were then upgraded in 1946 to universal benefits (see Nolan 2000: Chapt. 5, for a history of these policies). Speaking on the eve of the Baby Boom, H. I. Sinclair also came out in favour of family allowances as a means of increasing family sizes: 'the sooner we face the necessity of arranging family allowances and place some worthwhile plan in action the sooner we shall correct our ominous population drift'. But then, citing the international eugenicist literature about class and fertility, he goes on to say: 'If family allowances are established they should be directed as far as possible towards increasing the birth rate on a qualitative basis . . . [the authorities] should grant bonuses on an increasing scale in line with academic status of parents or on some other qualitative basis' (Sinclair 1944: 119–20). Nevertheless, for reasons outlined in Chapter Three, this Act did not have an immediate pro-natalist effect desired by its sponsors: the rise in fertility rates around 1939–40 probably had more to do with expanding employment and the advent of military recruitment, final leaves and sad goodbyes. This issue will be returned to when we review the

Baby Boom (Chapter Five), a period in which meaningful and universal family allowances were introduced.

CROSS-CUTTING FACTORS: MARRIAGE, EX-NUPTIAL CONCEPTION AND EX-NUPTIAL BIRTH

The diverse factors reviewed in this section of the chapter coalesce, it seems, around the interface of marriage, conception and ex-nuptial birth. By looking at the available empirical data on these factors it is possible to speculate about the normative structures that appear to have arrived with Pakeha settlers on their migration. In the period covered in this chapter ex-nuptial conception and birth carried with them far higher levels of stigma than is the case today in twenty-first-century New Zealand.

In the last chapter, reference was made to British antecedents for Pakeha New Zealand's patterns of family formation and reproductive behaviour. To study British fertility patterns, marriage and ex-nuptial childbearing and to explore some of the issues we noted earlier it is useful to return to macro-level quantitative analyses that derive from the research drawn on in Chapter Three. The British historical population geographer Robert Woods (2000) has linked the various factors together in an interesting study that can be applied to Pakeha New Zealand. It draws on some widely used techniques that Woods also employed, the so-called Princeton/Coale indices of reproduction relating to (i) marital fertility, (ii) proportions married and (iii) illegitimate fertility, first introduced and discussed last chapter.

Woods (2000) extended this type of analysis by employing another technique that allowed him to look at interactions between these different factors as measured by the Coale indices. He graphed one index against another, in what are called bi-variate scattergrams, plotting points at which values for two variables, that should in theory be interrelated, intersect on the graph. He did this not just for one point in time, but followed the inter-sects over many decades in what he called 'time-paths'. We have graphed in Figures 4.1 and 4.2 intersects for Pakeha alongside those for England and Wales. Tracking these two sets of bi-variate trends over time enhances the narrative, for they provide an analysis not only of patterns, by comparison with British populations, but also of similarities and differences in timing of trends in New Zealand and in Britain.

Figure 4.1 traces the intersects for marital fertility and proportions married. New Zealand and England and Wales are graphed on the same figure, England and Wales from 1801–25 to the Baby Boom, and Pakeha from 1874, when the first relatively comprehensive data become available, until the Baby Boom. The broad pattern for England and Wales is more or less followed by Pakeha in New Zealand, but two differences emerge. First, at the extreme points (1874, 1901 and 1961), Pakeha intersects are more strongly influenced by proportions married than is true for England and Wales: well above Britain in 1874 and 1961, but well below in 1901. Secondly, and more importantly, there seems to be a time-lag in the graph's trajectories: what was happening in England and Wales in 1801–25 was repeated, albeit more extremely, by Pakeha in 1874. By that stage, while the mass migration from Britain to New Zealand was taking place, the English and Welsh had moved a significant distance from their patterns of 1801–25.

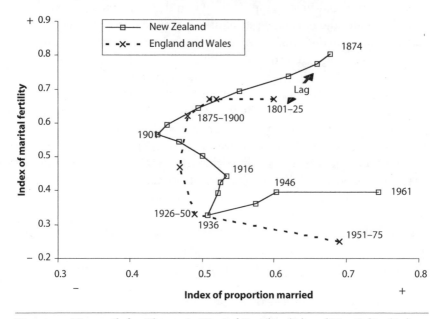

Figure 4.1: Timepath for Change in Marital Fertility (*Ig*) and Nuptiality (*Im*), Pakeha Census Dates 1874–1961, and England and Wales 25-year Ranges, 1801–25 to 1951–75

Note: The indices Marital fertility (taking the notation *Ig* in the international literature), Proportions married (*Im*) and Illegitimate fertility (*Ih*) (see Fig. 4.2) are the Coale indices (1969), discussed in the text, and developed for a large Princeton University study on European historical demography.
Sources: (1) For Coale Indices for NZ, 1874–1936, Jones 1971: Appendix; and 1941–61, O'Neill 1979: Table 6.1. He published a ratio between the indices for those years and for 1921–26 (= 1000). These were then converted back to indices by taking the average of Jones's results for 1921–26 and multiplying it by O'Neill's ratio for year t, divided by 1000. (2) The inspiration for Figures 4.1 and 4.2 comes from Woods (2000: Chapt. 3). His indices are the averages for 25-year periods: 1801–25, 1826–50, ... 1951–75. For reasons of space only selected intersects have been graphed and selected dates given. Moreover, while intersects are available for England and Wales before 1801, they are not graphed here.

From this graph combined with snippets of information presented in the last chapter, it seems probable that the results for Pakeha in 1874 were broadly representative of earlier decades of colonisation. Moreover, the last chapter's analysis suggests that Pakeha patterns were not strongly reflective of selective migration streams (by occupation, rurality, county or religion).

Instead they differed both from England and Wales overall, and from those extant in the leading places of origin of New Zealand settlers.

Figure 4.2 takes this analysis further, exploring another important issue. The bi-variate time-path for illegitimate fertility and proportions married is plotted as well as a hypothetical line, A–B, showing the theoretical relationship between marriage patterns and legitimacy. 'A' is probably the common case where entry into marriage, and thus exposure to intercourse and fertility, are controlled, and where women marry young and marriage is universal. Thus, at least theoretically, the risks of ex-nuptial conception are limited; though of course ex-nuptial pregnancies are often a trigger for early marriage. At the other extreme, 'B' relates to societies where pre- and extra-marital sexual taboos are virtually absent.

Figure 4.2: Timepath for Change in Nuptiality (*Im*) and Illegitimate Fertility (*Ih*), Pakeha, Exact Years 1874–1961, and England and Wales 25-year Ranges, 1801–25 to 1951–75, Compared to a Hypothetical Relationship Between Illegitimate Fertility and Nuptiality (Line A–B)

Note: For indices, see note to Figure 4.1. Woods's intersects are averages over 25 years.
Line A–B: In Figure 3.2 the line A–B is a hypothetical relationship between illegitimate fertility and nuptiality, elaborated by Woods (2000: Fig. 3.14, 101–6).
Scale: For A–B this is notional, and is not based on actual values.

Populations that fall into the quadrant in the top-right area of the graph would deviate markedly from the hypothesised relationship in that levels of both marriage and illegitimacy would be high. This is the situation recorded for England and Wales in the late eighteenth and early nineteenth centuries, represented by 1801–25 on the graph. The bottom-left quadrant also denotes populations that deviate from the hypothesised relationship between marriage and ex-nuptial reproduction. For societies in this category not only is marriage strictly controlled, late and not universal, but illegitimacy rates are low. This was exactly the sort of society that prim and proper late Victorian middle-class England perceived itself to be.

In Figure 4.2, Pakeha New Zealand differs from England and Wales in a number of ways. First, until the Baby Boom (1961 in this graph), levels for both the bottom-left and top-right quadrants are more extreme in England and Wales than for Pakeha. Secondly, in the years covered in this chapter (to 1945), illegitimacy levels are generally lower in New Zealand than in Britain and they force the intersects to remain systematically, and with little variance, in the lowest third of the graph (as calibrated from the vertical axis). Rates for ex-nuptial childbirth, however, were to become much higher for both populations, but especially New Zealand in the period discussed in later chapters (e.g. 1961). Levels for New Zealand in the early years were very low but, significantly, by the late Victorian era this was also the case for the British ratios (see plot for 1901–25, England and Wales; 1901, New Zealand). In contrast, for England and Wales, the effects of proportions married on the trajectory of the intersects is very limited, and they cluster just below 0.5 (as noted in Figure 4.1 the British intersects are for 25-year periods). Finally, in the Baby Boom the intersects for both populations, driven by high levels for the indices represented on both axes – the vertical and horizontal, leap up into the top-right quadrant, but far more so in the case of Pakeha. For both populations, then, the Baby Boom saw a marked departure from the hypothesised relationship between ex-nuptial fertility and the proportions married.

Unfortunately, unlike British researchers, who use individual record linkage of data in parish and civil registers for earlier periods, until the 1920s and 1930s we cannot take this further as we do not have data allowing us to analyse ex-nuptial conception and marital birth against illegitimate birth. But when this information does become available it shows that bridal pregnancy was a significant factor, quite in keeping with antecedents set in the old country. That is, from when the first data become available, a significant minority of babies were being born in the first few months of their parents' marriages (Jacoby 1961).

Finally, if a comparison is made of the trend lines (not the levels), from 1878 to the 1900s for Pakeha, and from 1801–25 to the 1900s for England and Wales, there is a time-lag. That is, to a degree the two lines are parallel: both start in the top right quadrant above the line A–B, then shift towards the lower left. In contrast to the patterns for the trend lines, the levels do not show the same lag but are rather different. In the mid-Victorian period (1826–50, 1851–75, England and Wales; 1874 and 1878, New Zealand) both populations cluster around the hypothetical line, but by 1901 they are well in the lower left quadrant, with low marriage indices and low illegitimacy indices, and they stayed there until the end of World War II. At that stage, to be discussed in later chapters, Pakeha departed from the British model and shot off on their own trajectory.

FROM A COLONIAL TO A DOMINION REPRODUCTIVE REGIME

These graphs throw light on an interesting mix of reproductive regimes. First, as is clear in Figure 4.1, the links between marriage and marital fertility in early Pakeha colonial New Zealand, in the 1870s, resemble to a degree antecedents set in Britain around the time of Waterloo. Thus there is a time-lag but, driven by the rates of marital fertility, the Pakeha intersects are significantly higher. By the 1890s, however, the results for the two poulations had merged, and from then on patterns remained similar, although the levels for the plots differ. The comparison of the levels shows that for most time periods or dates the couples of 'Better Britain' were more fertile than those of England and Wales, and, except briefly at the very end of the Victorian period when the nuptiality valve was being manipulated to reduce reproduction rates, the proportions married were higher.

Secondly, Figure 4.2 suggests far more complex and different trajectories were being followed. At the time that the first data become available, the Pakeha trend lines, that is the *patterns*, for the relationship between marriage and illegitimacy also have a time-lag by comparison with the British. But thirdly, and in contrast with what is seen in Figure 4.1, once this lag pattern is taken into account, Pakeha *levels* for these intersects for the period of early settlement do not at all resemble those for England and Wales. The intersects for Pakeha were lower, both by comparison with Britain in the early nineteenth century and at the time of mass colonisation to New Zealand. Then briefly in the first quarter of the twentieth century the intersects on this graph resemble those of the mother country – levels and patterns merge. Thereafter patterns are similar, but levels are not.

This analysis suggests that the pro-natalist norms carried to New Zealand by the pioneers were very strong, favouring high fertility within marriage. But it also shows that these attitudes may have been grounded in value systems that had become outdated in Britain (going back, instead, to those extant in the first quarter of the nineteenth century). In contrast, the behaviours of Pakeha relating to illegitimacy seem more in accord with norms starting to be observed in England and Wales at the time of the large-scale inflows of migrants of the 1870s (compare the intersects in Figure 4.2 for Pakeha in 1874, and for England and Wales 1851–75 and 1876–1900), and not with what had been occurring earlier in Britain. That is, in the 1870s, both colony and metropole had relatively low levels of ex-nuptial fertility.

By the end of the nineteenth century both populations not only had low levels of ex-nuptial fertility but also low marriage indices, taking them deep into the bottom-left quadrant (compare Pakeha in 1901, and England and Wales in 1876–1900 and 1901–25). Thus by the 1900s, in terms both of marriage patterns and levels of illegitimacy, the colony resembled the metropole. This also applied to marital fertility for a brief period. Jacoby's analyses (1961) were able to take this issue further. He showed that, at least in the 1920s, ex-nuptial fertility may have been uncommon, but ex-nuptial conception was not, implying that this was a pattern of behaviour that was acceptable provided that the 'decencies were observed': these would be a hasty white wedding followed by a birth publicised among friends and family as 'premature'.

There is no obvious reason why the regime of the 1870s was not a con-tinuation of what had occurred prior to the 1870s in very early colonial New Zealand. It might have been expected to have been imported, along with pro-natalism, from the value systems operating in pre-Victorian Britain. The snippets of information (only estimated TFRs) presented in the last chapter for the earliest colonial period certainly show that overall fertility levels were almost as high as in the 1870s; we do not have details as to the legitimacy of the births then. But the mechanics of reproduction in the 1870s were such – early marriage and hyper-fertility within marriage – that by then ex-nuptial childbearing was a far from frequent event, and it would seem logical that this was also true in the earliest colonial period.

There may be another interesting side to this. In the last three decades of the nineteenth century, the higher prevalence of illegitimacy in the Presbyterian areas in Scotland, or in Ulster – but there only relative to the more Catholic provinces of Ireland and not by comparison with their Scottish Protestant cousins – suggests another hypothesis: that some British sub-societies had less flexible, perhaps more punitive or, one might say, Calvinistic attitudes to ex-nuptiality in its various forms. In North East Scotland, the young women concerned were forced to enter single moth-ers' units in parish poorhouses, where they were condemned to ex-nuptial childbearing and became marginalised (Blaikie 1993).

Presbyterians from Scotland and Ulster were over-represented among early settlers. Moreover, as Rosalind McLean (1990) reports, the tensions between the more and less extreme Presbyterian factions in Scotland were mirrored in early New Zealand in Dunedin, manifesting themselves not just over family values but even for issues seemingly far from the quotid-ian life of the city, such as debates on Darwin's theories (Stenhouse 2005). This might explain the persistence in Pakeha society of values that saw pre-marital sex and especially ex-nuptial childbearing as highly undesirable.

This set of values runs counter to some of the more flexible attitudes that were prevalent, at least in England and Wales in the pre-Victorian period and which seem to have played some role in forming colonial attitudes. Yet the over-representation in the settler populations of Presbyterians and other nonconformists from areas in which illegitimacy rates were high seems to contradict the fact that when fertility was exceptionally high in the late nineteenth century, illegitimacy rates were low. But, equally, almost three-quarters of the settlers came from Ireland, England and Wales, where rates were low at the time. The answers to this conundrum may come from the fact that Presbyterian colonists appear to have adopted very different patterns of reproductive behaviour from their British counterparts, but ones that closely resembled those of their Pakeha compatriots. If the critical indices, proportions of women still unmarried at ages 20–24 years, the proportions never married at 45–49 (only 4%), the GFR (all women) and the marital GFR, are looked at, Otago, the most Presbyterian province, is very close to Canterbury and to New Zealand as a whole (Dharmalingam *et al.* 2007: Tables 4.1a, b). Like their counterparts elsewhere in the colony, Otago women married at young ages, they had very high levels of both marital and overall fertility, and the marital and overall fertility rates were close. Instead, the real significance of Scottish flows in the migration streams and their impact on New Zealand fertility regimes could be the impact of Scottish norms on the development of the colonial welfare system. Like the Scottish charity model, it was miserly and fragmented.

Whatever the role of different value systems, British norms of one sort and another, sometimes contradictory, seem to have been installed well and truly by the time of the death of Queen Victoria and the inception of the fledgling nation-state, the Dominion of New Zealand (1906). In retrospect, the early colonial period's lack of fit with some aspects of the British model, say in the four decades up to 1880, seems a little aberrant; but the rapid changeover by 1900 brought Pakeha closer to what might have been expected for a loyal, white offspring of 'mother England', and certainly for a 'Better Britain'. As shown in Chapter Three, however, the two major migratory streams, those of the gold-rushes and those of the Vogel schemes that together brought in a high proportion of all net arrivals over the six decades between 1840 and 1900, had a limited effect in producing either the high fertility of the early colonial period, or the rapid declines between the end of the 1870s and 1900. Indeed, if anything the evidence points in the opposite direction.

4.4 THE SOCIO-ECONOMIC CONTEXT OF FAMILY LIFE, 1840–1945

FROM FIRST-ORDER TO HIGHER-ORDER ANALYSIS
The analyses so far have been of a first order, and their results beg two more critical underlying questions. (1) Why in the early and mid-Victorian

periods did Pakeha women adopt rather different norms from those prevalent in the old country, opting to behave differently from their British peers by marrying at young ages and, once married, reproducing almost to capacity? (2) And why, from about 1880 on, did they then rein back their colonially generated norms and patterns of behaviour and shift their reproductive regimes closer to those in Britain?

Perhaps the clues to the first of these questions rest in deep-seated normative and behavioural antecedents in eighteenth- and early nineteenth-century Britain, which were then imported to New Zealand. Importantly, normative structures governing attitudes to sex, reproduction and family size are as much a part of the reproductive regime as the resultant fertility patterns. In looking for explanations for the latter Woods has noted, 'It was [the] unique combination of high and rising urbanisation, accelerating industrialisation and commercialisation, and the reorganisation of agricultural labour which so quickly, substantially and generally reduced the mean age at marriage in the late 18th and early 19th centuries'. But this regime had started to turn around in the period 1825–50, as a range of factors, economic and social, including the problems of urban life and employment conditions, effected a rapid and relatively significant reversal of the earlier trend in age at marriage. This also ushered in a desire to seek some alternative means of controlling fertility within marriage (Woods 2000: 88ff, 109, Fig. 3.18, *passim*; see also Szreter 2002: *passim*).

The process of migration to New Zealand, and the freedom from the constraints operating in Britain, perhaps allowed women and couples in the early decades of settlement to resume the patterns seen in the British Isles prior to the start of Victoria's reign, options that had closed off for couples remaining in the old country. This points less to the impact of a 'free frontier' on the establishment of totally new reproductive norms, and more to the possibility that the colonists had been provided with the opportunity to revisit British normative and behavioural antecedents. In the early years of settlement Pakeha formed families that in terms of sizes were larger than, but resembled, those of late eighteenth-century and pre-Victorian nineteenth-century Britain. Moving to New Zealand afforded the settlers not only material improvements but the opportunity to entertain a family life that accorded with traditions of recent memory that had become decreasingly possible in Britain by the middle years of the nineteenth century. This was perhaps the ancestor of several waves of nostalgia for an earlier and seemingly idyllic pattern of family life that were to re-emerge at various times, often in association with a burst of moral panic, and to shape perceptions about the family, typically at odds with reality, across the twentieth and into the early twenty-first centuries.

In Chapter Three it was noted that, virtually from the earliest days, New Zealanders had been the beneficiaries of high per capita incomes. This advantage was maintained well into the twentieth century, to the end of the period covered in this chapter. Moreover, in common with other English-speaking WDCs, especially the neo-Europes, New Zealand, at least its Pakeha component, had gone through economic modernisation at a very early stage (Pool and Sceats 2003, citing the international public policy literature). The term modernisation is loosely defined here as a diffused set of social changes in a context of more objectively delineated economic transformations and policy shifts (e.g., for New Zealand, high per capita income; the growth of export industries; sectoral labour-force transformations; and policy initiatives of the Liberal Government at the dawn of the twentieth century).

In this regard a conceptual model is available. The historical links between macro-economic change and the family have been usefully summarised by Tony Wrigley (1971: 183), who differentiates the English from the French and Swedish variants, calling the former a 'wage variant' and the latter a 'peasant variant'. It is a useful guide for the New Zealand situation, but it is necessary to re-categorise these relationships as a 'mixed wage and self-employed variant'. The ready availability of land in the 1860s to 1890s meant that pioneer farmers typically became self-employed, owning relatively large units of land that, in general, were economically viable, export oriented and managed using what was high technology. New Zealand thus became the small-business society that it was to continue to be – dominated by the self-employed or small-scale employers in both urban and rural enterprises. This produced a curious hybrid: in the formal sector the application of technologies that by international standards were advanced for their time alongside dependence on the family as the unit of production as well as the unit of reproduction, like a peasant economy. In some senses the New Zealand dairy-farming family functioned like a Scottish crofting family, yet was a production unit that might use an Alfa-Laval milking machine to strip the milk from cows in what in Britain would have been a large dairy herd for an owner-operated farm.

As noted earlier, in the late nineteenth century Pakeha New Zealand had high per capita incomes, perhaps the highest anywhere. Once the 1880s depression was over most economic indicators were very positive. Technological changes (e.g. the freezing of primary produce), land reform and major social policy initiatives in the 1890s and early 1900s were key factors that reinforced the development of an economy that had been strong in the 1870s. In terms of income generation and distribution, the underlying economic structures favoured a highly advantaged quality of life.[*]

---

[*] The last two paragraphs are drawn from a summary in Pool and Cheung (2005) and Pool (2002) that cite inter alia the major economic histories, especially Hawke (1985); see also Gibson (1971: Chapt. 7) and O'Neill (1979).

Moreover, this was reinforced by a peculiar and less well-recognised dimension of the late nineteenth-century Pakeha economy. The historian David Thomson (1998: 81) has pointed to the way that the colonists addressed questions of thrift and saving: 'At its root was a very large supply of cheap land that could be given away only once to the early-comers. This was a special colonial form of thrift, which did not fit readily into either economists' theories of saving, or the approved savings patterns brought from Home'. One might note that this tension, between the patterns of thrift and investment in property adopted by the wider public and the paradigms of economists, has been a continuing theme in New Zealand and is still seen today.

In the late nineteenth century, then, not only did New Zealand modernise, but many of the conditions that are now seen in the international literature as determining low fertility – high levels of infant and childhood survivorship; high incomes; lower income inequalities; free, compulsory primary education – were already in place or were being generated in the 1870s, 1880s and 1890s. The ideational determinants, such as knowledge about the emergence of decreasing fertility regimes in Britain, were being diffused to Pakeha by each new group of migrants and by the arrival of British newspapers. Even urbanisation, a factor seen as related to the onset of fertility declines, was increasing rapidly. Had fertility levels not dropped, Pakeha would have been a deviant population out of kilter with international experience (for a review of fertility-decline theories see Freedman 1982; for the role of ideational factors see Cleland and Wilson 1987).

But in late Victorian New Zealand there was still one critical factor missing that we would expect today: accessibility to reliable and efficient means of contraception. A substitute, changes in marital patterns, could exist in a population that closely monitored the nuptiality valve, and that had shown itself in the 1870s to be very adept at opening it wide, although keeping in place a few pre-conditions (e.g. limiting teenage marriage). Now in the late nineteenth century, the valve was tightened, as it had been in the mid-nineteenth century in the mother country. That said, around 1900 those who made it through the valve and married still had high levels of marital fertility. The next section of this chapter seeks to identify whether this valve operated uniformly; particularly, whether or not there were differentials in the rates of marriage and childbearing that might have linked variance in patterns of reproduction to the socio-economic determinants outlined in the last paragraph.

The social and economic conditions in the New Zealand colony were not unique, being very similar to those in Australia. These were the coincidence of the introduction of compulsory education (1877 in New Zealand, implemented fully by 1900), with a transformation of pioneer, rural life, when 'children were no great economic problem', to an industrialised and urbanised society in which children (especially while at school) became 'dependent' (Ruzicka and Caldwell 1977: Chapt. 1; see also Pool and Tiong 1989; Gibson 1971; and O'Neill 1979). The 'peasant' or 'rural-labourer' farming family structure that was to perpetuate itself until after World War II (for example in France) had largely disappeared in New Zealand by the early twentieth century; and, although there were extensive sheep and cattle stations and 'bonanza' wheat farms that were affected by the land reforms of the 1890s, New Zealand never really had *latifundia* or similar rural institutions.

URBANISATION IN A PASTORAL DEMOCRACY

Instead, and underlying the declines in Pakeha fertility, New Zealand was an urbanised society even by the end of the nineteenth century, in spite of its image as a pastoral democracy and its dependence on the export of primary products (Pool and Bedford 1997; Pool 2002). In the twentieth century this intensified to become in the inter-war years by far the most dominant way of life, at least for Pakeha. This fits with the experiences of other English-speaking WDCs (Pool and Sceats 2003). By 1911, three-quarters of the British and half of the New Zealand population were urban and by 1936 this was true for 60% of New Zealanders; by 1920 this also applied to more than 50% of Americans (Coleman and Salt 1992: 86; Pool and Bedford 1996: 14; National Commission on Urban Problems, US, 1969: 40). Within Europe in the 1930s, the percentage of the United Kingdom's population that was urban (76%) was only exceeded by the proportions for Belgium and the Netherlands; the rate for England and Wales (excluding the other countries in the UK) equalled those in the Low Countries. In contrast, in the 1930s most European countries were still below 50%, the exceptions being Austria (61%), France (52%) and Italy (52%), with Germany alone (70%) resembling but not equalling the United Kingdom (see Pool and Sceats 2003: Table 10; also Lampard 1967: Table 3; Kirk 1946, reprinted 1968).

Early urbanisation in New Zealand and other ESCs tended to take a different form from that found elsewhere in the WDCs. Low-density housing, terraced/row houses, semi-detached or fully detached dwellings became the mode in the ESCs in the late nineteenth or early twentieth centuries, whereas multi-storey apartments were more common in the big cities on the continent of Europe.* This was particularly true for the neo-Europes, except, say, in the large eastern-seaboard cities of North America that were the normal ports of entry for immigrants, but it even held true in

---

* These comments on housing are based on personal observations plus very useful discussions with David Thorns, an urban sociologist at Canterbury University, and David Swain, a Waikato University family sociologist whose current research on genealogical data in the UK, NZ and other WDCs has confirmed many of these points.

the United Kingdom. The ESCs led the early developments in commuter transport, most notably the automobile that spawned the suburbia of the neo-Europes. The ESCs also led the way in the shift to owner-occupied housing, and this led to differences in provision for the less well-off, in rental housing estates that were publicly funded versus the institution of rent-controls on private-sector rental housing (Barlow and Duncan 1994: Figs 2.1 and 2.2; Harloe 1995: Chapt. 1). From the 1920s in the United Kingdom and in other ESCs, building societies and similar mutual benefit associations were helping couples to finance dwellings.

The first available data confirm that for Pakeha this pattern of home ownership had indeed become prevalent in New Zealand at a very early date, even in urban areas, as is seen in Table 4.1. The 1916 New Zealand census had reported that 52% of dwellings lived in by Pakeha were owner occupied (typically, of course, bought with a mortgage or by time payment). By 1926, levels were just below post-World War II rates, but obviously financial constraints during the Depression led to a turndown during that period.

Table 4.1: Dwelling Tenure: Non-Maori, Percentage of Dwellings Owned With/ Without a Mortgage, 1916–1966*

	Urban	Rural	Total
1916	47	58	52
1926	62	60	61
1936	49	51	50
1945	56	58	57
1956	69	64	67
1966	71	67	70

* From this date on separate data by ethnicity are not published.
Source: Censuses.

In turn, the housing patterns in the neo-European ESCs, and even Great Britain, meant that household morphologies were somewhat different from those typical in the cities of the other WDCs. The fact that family formation was likely to be neolocal, at least in Australasia and North America and especially in pioneer areas, has already been commented on. In rural areas this meant that the settler family typically lived in a dwelling they owned, as against a tithe-cottage or a dwelling held through some other form of tenancy, or by grace and favour. In urban areas, other than large metropolitan ports, such as on the east coast of North America, the typical neo-European household lived in an owned detached or semi-detached dwelling. In most WDCs in 'old Europe', urban life was played out in rented apartments. In New Zealand even in the late nineteenth-century home ownership was already entrenched as the prime route towards saving for old age. Thomson (1998:

154) has argued that 'A substantial majority of ageing colonists probably owned their own homes, often with some land as well, and probate records suggest that many had other assets in addition'.

Therefore, in New Zealand, as in the other neo-Europes, a different type of city life was being fashioned. By the 1920s, ownership of a detached dwelling, as against renting an apartment, had become an essential part of urban Pakeha family life. Neolocal residence could be sustained only in this way, and thus the boom periods saw the early development of suburbia, consisting of clusters of such dwellings along tram, ferry, bus and train lines. The importance of the inner city–suburban balance, both for the strategies of economic modernisation and for the family, has been documented by the geographer Mary Watson. Writing in 1985, she argued that this was a process 'largely complete by the mid 1920s . . . the inner city areas have lost population since 1921' (Watson 1985: 126).[*] The owner-occupied dwelling also became the locus for parenting and particularly for the nuclear family structures and forms that emerged at that time. This 'family-scape' was to become the overwhelmingly dominant form in the Baby Boom and had important ramifications for family life into the twenty-first century.

Thus the importance of a synergy between dwelling type and family structures and forms in the New Zealand context, particularly in urban areas, cannot be overstressed. This relationship underlies national social and economic development and demographic change. Housing is a somewhat unusual issue; buying a house will typically be the most important single investment a family will make, and is thus a critical factor, and a key indicator, for all components of the market dimensions of economic growth. In this context it involves issues of demand and of discretionary expenditure on the part of families. But that is not the end of the story, for housing is not a simple consumer item or market good: for many individual households lacking financial resources the issue is not one of demand but of the basic need for shelter. While in a country such as New Zealand this may in extreme cases involve homelessness, a far more common problem for low-income families is affordability. When there are disjunctions between supply and market demand for dwellings – and this is an area in which markets often fail – then what should merely be market demand translates into a basic need, and becomes a central issue of public policy (Pool 1959, 1986). Not surprisingly, therefore, housing was and still is a major issue for the social welfare system.

Housing was not the only social and economic policy issue. For the colonists economic conditions were to vary: there were depressions in the

---

[*]   This last comment no longer holds true; a return movement is under way.

1880s and in the 1930s, a recession in the early 1920s and growth in the early 1900s. But the economy was essentially based on a marked gender division of labour. For Pakeha women, labour-force participation increased until 1921 to reach 27% in 1926, then declined, only to increase once again during World War II.

A factor of greater importance than the rate of labour-force participation by women was the profile of female employment. Essentially, for most women it was a transitory passage between school and marriage. Davies (1993) describes the age pattern at this time as a 'reverse J-shaped curve', to contrast with later patterns during and after the Baby Boom that were 'M-shaped' – higher levels of participation for women just out of school, a deep trough during the childbearing and -rearing years, and then for many a return as the children left home.

This section of the chapter has focused on Pakeha, but throughout the period covered in this chapter New Zealand was a country with a dual economy: Pakeha overwhelmingly participated in the formal sector, and Maori engaged in semi-subsistence activities, supported monetarily with casual work. Equally, New Zealand's society was profoundly segmented. Maori were deeply disadvantaged and often suffered poverty and high levels of malnutrition. They were not deemed to be economically active (Pool 1991: 120–22; Kukutai *et al.* 2002) and, thus, at first in the Great Depression 'were not eligible for employment on public work schemes' (Thompson 1985: 124; see also Condliffe 1959: 95–96). The labour-force participation of Maori women had actually declined from when records first became available (1926), but increased significantly in the 1940s when they were drafted into war industries (Davies 1993: 27; Pool 1991: 122).

For Maori the driving factor to maintain family size was very basic – the need for the society to survive – and this had to be achieved within the constraints imposed by the rural semi-subsistence life of most Maori. As was noted above, the possibility of cultural survival seemed uncertain until the 1890s when the turnaround was first noted by Sir James Carroll. From then until World War II, whanau structures continued to meet many of the basic needs of most Maori, with production centred there, and access to the formal economy limited to casual or seasonal work. The cash gained by these means was then used for a limited range of market goods (Pool 1991; Kukutai *et al.* 2002).

Maori at this time were not only rural, but typically lived in whare or huts around kainga, or pa, as these were often called in popular parlance. In-depth documentation presented to the Waitangi Tribunal (e.g. Kukutai *et al.* 2002, relating to the central North Island) shows that while housing was 'owner occupied', standards were very poor, and that this situation still held true in the 1930s when housing was analysed as a key determinant of the high levels of tuberculosis Maori suffered at that time. An impressive epidemiologic study of East Coast Maori carried out by Dr H. B. Turbott produced shocking but robustly documented results, which probably held true across much of New Zealand (Turbott 1935; Pool 1991: 120). The housing, nutritional and other conditions quantified by this research team were appalling for a country that, overall, had among the highest living standards in the world at that time.

4.5 THE FAMILY SIZE TRANSITION: DECREASING LEVELS, INCREASING VARIANCE

THE DIVERSIFICATION OF FAMILY MORPHOLOGIES

Throughout this era, from 1840 to World War II, both Maori and Pakeha maintained what could be called conservative family structures and forms. Although for Pakeha there had been dramatic declines in fertility in the late Victorian period and modest decreases thereafter, in the 1930s many married women were still having large families and following a household model that fits with what many modern-day commentators see as traditional: parents, children and a clear gender-differentiation, for household tasks, in the wider working world and in terms of legal rights and responsibilities. More importantly, in public perception it was the married couple and their dependent children that became *the* family. The 'spinster' aunt, the grandparent or the lodger were peripheral to these units as elaborated in the popular mind, although frequently a feature of family morphologies and often an essential element for financial reasons or, conversely, because the nuclear family provided welfare that was not available in the public policy domain.

The nuclear family was suited, at least manifestly, to performing the functions of replacement, nurturing, socialisation and the care of children. Additionally the family might care for those extended family members who, in the absence of a well-developed welfare state, had no other social institution to provide for their sustenance, but this was not a primary function. Whether the family really performed these parenting or non-parenting functions effectively is not at all clear from the evidence available, but it is evident that the nuclear unit, often neolocal in residence, was now increasingly being seen as something separate from the wider family. This paved the way for it to become the major type, certainly in the Baby Boom, but also something that was relatively distinct from other types of household, including those in which several generations shared a dwelling. Along with this distinction came a growing trend towards the separation of functions, between, on the one hand, the replacement and the socialisation of children, which was the role the nuclear family played and, on the other, cohesion in the wider family. This functional dichotomisation was to become more marked in the Baby Boom.

Initially the replacement function had been a central feature of national social life. The achievement of high levels of nuptial Pakeha fertility in the Victorian era was far more than the establishment of a reproductive regime. It was a key development strategy for nation building and a mechanism, along with migration, by which Maori would be 'swamped', the dream of some Pakeha politicians. Both these population trends were dependent on the rapid alienation of land from Maori, and then settlement by young Pakeha couples not just in coastal areas but far into the hinterland (Belich 1996: 242 and *passim*; see also Hawke 1985: Fig. 43, 69–73; Farmer 1985: Fig. 14; Pool 2002). These produced large Pakeha families initially and systematically across much of the country. Over the longer term, as Pakeha fertility declined, this replacement function and with it the attendant wider effect as a stimulant for growth became threatened, with the nadir reached, at least for the period covered by this chapter, in the 1930s. Less manifestly, this change did not take place evenly over every region or uniformly across all social groups.

As overall levels of fertility *per se* decreased for Pakeha, diverse forms of reproductive polarisation, as far as one can measure them, began to be evident. In one sense this had always been true as far back as there are data – even in the 1870s there had been regional differences, but they had occurred within the narrow parameters of what was everywhere a regime of very high fertility. By the late nineteenth and early twentieth centuries, however, as average family sizes decreased, more complex and more significant forms of variance were emerging. The evidence for this is primarily geographic but fragments of other data can be drawn on to round out the picture.

It is the diversification of Pakeha family morphologies that will be of prime interest to this section of the chapter. For Maori there was very little variance and one has to search carefully to find much of any significance. Nevertheless, as reported in the last chapter, while most Maori lived in the rural North Island and had uniformly high rates of fertility, a small minority in North Island urban areas and in the South Island had lower levels.

Over the first four decades of colonisation Maori fertility rates had been below the exceptionally high levels registered for Pakeha (Figure 2.1), but the pattern then reversed. High Maori and low, or relatively lower, but fluctuating levels of Pakeha fertility were the patterns that persisted until the 1970s. Even at the height of the Baby Boom, when Pakeha couples responded with great gusto to the task of childbearing, their rates only reached upper-middle ranges (just over 4.0 births per woman), not the high levels of their predecessors in the 1870s. In the Baby Boom the ethnic reproductive gap was to exceed two live births per woman. It is not widely recognised that there is much less absolute ethnic difference today, but the history of an ethnic gap in levels of fertility favouring Maori, at least since the 1880s, seems to have been the source for persisting eugenics concerns already expressed by Sinclair (1944) for the period covered by this chapter. Moreover, ethnic polarisation of another sort persisted over much of the early twentieth century, disappeared largely in the Baby Boom, but reappeared and continued to this day: from the late nineteenth century on, except for the Baby Boom, the Pakeha force of reproduction fell on older mothers, while for Maori it was centred on younger ages.

PROVINCIAL DIFFERENCES IN PAKEHA NUPTIALITY AND FERTILITY, 1878–1896

An analysis of provincial-level data allows an assessment of the way in which Pakeha family size declines occurred in relation to differences in patterns of nuptiality. A useful starting point is British antecedents. The research cited in Chapter Three on nineteenth-century Britain has pointed out how important regional differences were in family patterns at this time, not only between the countries of the British Isles (e.g. England as against Ireland), but between districts within each country. Given that migration to various parts of New Zealand often drew selectively from particular regions in the British Isles and produced different mixes of British settlers – for example, the Scots are associated with the southern regions in New Zealand, the English with Canterbury – and that stages of economic development varied across New Zealand, it would be expected that historically there would have been regional differences here at that time.

In the 1870s and again in the 1890s there was a point of similarity: the relative ranges between the highest and lowest GFRs were marked, both in the British Isles and in New Zealand. Beyond this the comparison is weak because levels were far higher in New Zealand in 1878, the first year for which observations are available, than they were in Britain at a comparable time. By 1896, in contrast, colonial rates were starting to resemble more closely the British ones, yet varying ranges were still evident.

For example, one can compare the regional differences in Scotland and Pakeha New Zealand. In 1871, the Scottish GFR (births per 1000 women aged 15–49 years) was 136; the New Zealand Pakeha level for 1878 was much higher, 227 per 1000 women aged 15–44 years.[*] In that same year the highest GFR for a Scottish region was 155 (Western Lowlands); the second highest was for the settlement category termed 'Towns'. In contrast, levels far below this were seen in the Far North and the Highlands (102 and 104, 52% lower than the Western Lowlands). But in New Zealand the lowest level was for Nelson (193), far above the highest Scottish rate, while the highest Pakeha rate for 1878 was in Taranaki, 47% above the lowest New Zealand rate. By 1891 the

---

[*]   The slight difference in the computational details of these indices – the age-range employed – has little effect on this comparison.

range in Scotland was from 89 (the North and Highlands) to 136 (Western Lowlands), again a 52% range. By 1896 the New Zealand national level (126) had dipped much more closely towards that of Scotland as a whole (120), but the highest New Zealand rate (Taranaki, 162) was still 48% above the lowest (Westland, 109) (For Scotland, Flinn *et al.* 1977: Table 5.3.3; data for New Zealand in this and the following paragraphs are drawn from Dharmalingam *et al.* 2007: Tables 4.1a and 4.1b; and from Tiong 1988: Table E.2).

In following this issue for New Zealand, not only are both nuptiality and fertility data available at a provincial level but, by subtraction, the total provincial data minus comparable data on boroughs, it is possible to make a direct estimate of the rural GFRs, and thus to undertake a crude urban–rural intra-provincial analysis. Moreover, marriage rates at key ages are available for the provincial levels of aggregation. This section of the chapter is based on directly computed rates; a later section that provides measures relating to more refined geographical units will be based on indirect estimates. All are derived from the work of Fred Tiong (1988).[*]

Changes in patterns of marriage for Pakeha started in the 1880s, but shifts in family size due to this factor at the end of the nineteenth century were not evenly spread. This experience fits with what was happening in Australia (Ruzicka and Caldwell 1977: Chapt. 1) and indeed differentials occurred at this time across the developed countries (Festy 1979: 106–8). The driver thus appears to be general social and economic development that also brought Pakeha New Zealand closer to the pattern seen in other WDCs. This section looks for geographic differences that might throw further light on underlying determinants of trends.

Shifts in patterns of nuptiality were, as noted already, the major drivers of fertility changes. Not surprisingly, therefore, there were also provincial differences in marital status patterns at successive censuses, 1878, 1886 and 1896. In 1878, the proportions of teenage Pakeha women who were married were relatively high, but varied from 6% (Nelson, an early settled and urbanised region) to 13% in next-door pastoral Marlborough; by 1886 and 1896 levels had become so low that in absolute terms differences were minimal.

Far more importantly, nationally in 1878 the percentage of women still celibate at 20–24 years was low. This is a very important piece of information. In a society with almost no ex-nuptial childbearing that employs the nuptiality valve as virtually its only means of fertility regulation, the proportion already married at age-group 20–24 years becomes the key discriminating factor between different fertilities. In 1878 there were already suggestions of some geographical variance in this critical indicator. Rates varied, with levels

---

[*] · The details of his methodology and research have been discussed in Chapter Three. See also Pool and Tiong 1991. The results are in Dharmalingam *et al.* 2007: Tables 4.1a and 4.1b.

lowest (i.e. most married early) in rural regions (e.g. 38% in Hawke's Bay; 36% Marlborough), but highest in Auckland (still then a province that was mainly urban; see below in the discussion on GFRs) and in the South Island regions except for Marlborough. By 1886 levels of spinsterhood at 20–24 years had increased in every province, but the gap had widened between a low of 48% unmarried at this age (Marlborough), and 52% in Hawke's Bay and Taranaki, to 66% (Otago). At the 1896 census, proportions single were higher again but still varied between 65% still single (Hawke's Bay) and 81% (Otago). Between 1878 and 1896 the Auckland province had been the scene of large-scale land loss for Maori and inflows of farmer settlers, and thus it was by then affected by rural patterns within the province. The inter-provincial ranges in the proportions single increased between fifteen percentage points (1876) and eighteen in 1886, but had dropped to sixteeen in 1896.

Throughout the entire eighteen-year period 1878–1896, across all regions, males at 20–24 years were overwhelmingly bachelors (around 90%). At older ages more than a quarter were still unmarried, a reflection of the shortage of women. This was most extreme in gold-mining areas (e.g. Westland 53%) but, not surprisingly, the sex-ratios there were also often badly distorted (Westland, 1878 at 45–49 years, 470 males per 100 females).

The effects of changes in the nuptiality valve on fertility can be better shown by comparing the GFRs and MGFRs for provinces (drawn from Dharmalingam *et al.* 2007: Tables 4.1a and 4.1b). These results parallel conclusions advanced in Chapter Three from correlations between GFRs and MGFRs (drawing on Dharmalingam *et al.* 2007: Table 3.5), and illustrate how effectively the nuptiality valve was operating. One further statistic can be quoted in support of this: there is a positive Spearman's ranked correlation between the GFR and the percentage of women married at 20–24 years, and it was very high in both 1878 and 1896 (>0.85).

In 1878 Pakeha GFRs had been high for most provinces, with two exceptions: Nelson and Westland. These two areas still had significant mining communities (*NZ Historical Atlas* 1997: 55–56) and thus had somewhat different family structures. They were, it was alleged, societies driven by 'vice and wickedness' (Levesque 1986, citing Alfred Saunders: 2). For the remaining provinces, levels were at least 214 births (Auckland) or higher per 1000 women at childbearing ages, reaching an exceptionally high rate of 284 births per 1000 women in Taranaki. To restate what was noted last chapter, rates of this magnitude imply very elevated levels of reproduction and replacement, between 6.4 and 8.5 live births per woman whether married or single; even the deviant cases of Nelson and Westland had rates that were just below six. That said, however, there were also differences, but, again with the exceptions of Nelson and Westland, these were between high and extremely high levels, and some extreme values may be a function of small numbers and thus random statistical errors. These errors are probably not critical; the two uppermost provinces, Taranaki and Marlborough, systematically maintained their top ranking, and were joined by another pastoral developing province, Hawke's Bay. By 1886 not only had levels dropped but so too had the range. In 1896 levels still varied, but were everywhere lower, implying reproduction falling to a range between less than five live births per woman (Taranaki), down to around 3.3 (Westland).

Rates for marital fertility were exceptionally elevated in 1878, and the inter-provincial range ran from very high to extremely high, particularly if viewed alongside British fertilities of that time. This shows that, regardless of where they lived, most colonial women were marrying and reproducing almost to biological limits. Unfortunately MGFRs cannot be estimated for the sub-provincial regions referred to in this section of the chapter, but one can say with some degree of confidence that in some areas the rates could have been above nine live births per married woman. While small numbers may result in errors, statistical interpretation is enhanced by systematic 'runs': the rank orders, remained similar, with the mainly pastoral provinces Taranaki, Hawke's Bay and Marlborough at the top in both 1878 and 1896. That said, rural Canterbury, the first and prototypical sheep-farming region, was very high in 1878 (second in rank) but had dropped to fourth by 1896.

In 1878, in the urban areas of the day, GFRs fell below the levels of their entire provinces (Tiong 1988: Table 6.8; see also Jones 1971). Tiong provides data on the Auckland, Wellington and Otago provinces, each of which had large boroughs. Auckland, the urban area with the lowest rates (180), saw levels of fertility at around 5.4 births per woman, whereas the rest of the province was well above this, at between 6.5 and seven. The urban areas at this time for which one can directly compute rates were also major ports and thus the denominators for these indices were probably inflated by the presence of newly arrived immigrant spinsters, who often soon became married (Belich 1996: Chapts 13 and 15). In contrast, the rural parts of these provinces had even higher fertility, around seven live births per woman, 20% above the urban areas (Tiong 1988: Table 6.8). Unfortunately one cannot verify this rural–urban difference by directly computed *marital* GFRs.

That said, we do have some indirect insights on this question. Charlotte Macdonald's valuable study of single migrant women arriving in New Zealand in the years of hyper-fertility, based on an exhaustive analysis of linked individual records, argues that 'It cannot be said that women came to New Zealand to marry'. Nevertheless, the intervals between their median and modal ages at the time of embarkation for the colony (20.4 and 20 years) and at first marriage (22.7 and 22) were rather short, particularly if one allows several months for the voyage itself. Of course, as Macdonald emphasises, the modal age for migration is also one at which women often married; and they were at a life-cycle stage characterised by what the American demographer Ronald Rindfuss (1991) has called a high 'demographic density' (the clustering of life-cycle demographic events, among them marriage and first childbirth). The ages at which the single women migrants married were similar to those at which New Zealand-born women did, as her comparisons with Pickens's Canterbury data show. But it must also be noted that they were marrying at ages well below those of their British counterparts (Macdonald 1990: 67, Chapt. 5). Whether or not they set out to New Zealand with the intention of marrying is perhaps not the point; what is germane to our study is that, by the time they had been in the colony for a short period, their conjugal norms differed little from those of other colonial women. Independent they may have been, as Macdonald argues, but this did not preclude marriage at an early age.[*]

By 1896 fertility levels had dropped everywhere, by 51% in urban New Zealand (from a lower starting point) and 45% in rural New Zealand. But fertility in the rural parts of the provinces was 34% higher than in the urban. Between 1896 and 1921 urban fertility decreased by a further 24%, taking the GFR down to 78. This level was roughly equivalent to only 2.0–2.5 births per woman, or just above replacement. In contrast, rural rates went down by only 7%, and were by then 55% higher than urban (Tiong 1988: Table 6.8), or about what the national GFR had been in 1896 (126 per 1000).

SUB-PROVINCIAL, REGIONAL DIFFERENCES IN FERTILITY, 1878–1916[†]

Data on GFRs for more refined geographical units, based on groupings of contiguous counties or boroughs that have similar socio-economic features (N = 23) are available from Tiong's research (1988: Table E.2; his earlier appendices define the groupings), and confirm the results presented above. This analysis is also extended to 1916, and additionally allows comparisons within as well as between provinces. By way of background, it is useful to provide a benchmark for the Pakeha population as a whole: in 1878 their

---

[*]   On a related issue, Belich (1996: 393) has contested Macdonald's argument that 'The evidence does not show that this group of women married men of significantly higher social status'. He argues that her conclusion does not seem to be supported by her data. Indeed, most of the women for whom she has data, 72%, were in 'unskilled' occupations prior to migration and 82% were unskilled at the time of marriage, whereas this held true for only 19% of their spouses. Of the 12.5% for whom there are no data, some will have been teenagers – women came out as young as twelve years of age – who might not have been previously employed before embarkation (Macdonald 1990: 49, 147).

[†]   The method Fred Tiong (1988) used for estimating regional GFRs is noted in our Table 4.2. His data go up to 1921, but both numerators and denominators at that date had been affected by events just before – the 1918 influenza pandemic that resulted not only in direct mortality but also in marital dissolution by the deaths of husbands, wives or both spouses, thus reducing the births and the population (P) aged 0–4 years in 1921 (Tiong's starting point for estimating births in the previous five years). The 1916 census was affected to a degree by the absence of troops, but P (0–4) included children born before the war, and obviously few women (P 15–44) were absent. Thus 1916 seemed a better end point than 1921 for an analysis based around estimates derived from child survivorship to a census, as against births registered in a calendar year.

national age-standardised GFR was 227; by 1896 it had dropped radically to 126; but in 1916 it was still at 112, only a little below the level for 1896.

The most important finding is that, once rates declined, differentials opened up. Thus the absolute range between the highest and lowest sub-provincial regions for the GFRs was significantly wider in 1896 than it had been in 1878 – 107 versus 73 – and remained wide (103) in 1916. In the two latter years, the directly computed, age-standardised national rate barely exceeded the range between the highest rate per region and the lowest rate, and the ranges in 1896 and 1916 significantly exceeded the rates observed for the lowest regions; in 1878, in contrast, the range (73) had fallen far below the lowest rate (193).

The regions can be broadly classed in various ways according to their level of urbanisation and their more important economic characteristics. This allows some degree of experimentation to tease out possible determinants of levels and trends, to review factors that might have had an indirect effect on various reproductive regimes occurring in the colony and Dominion at this time (1878–1916). It should be signalled that while these are indirect estimates (see Table 4.2), a comparison between directly observed and indirectly estimated GFRs suggests that error levels are reasonably low (Tiong 1988: Table 6.5). No estimates of marital fertility are available for these regional groupings. Some key results are presented below in Tables 4.2 and 4.3.

Table 4.2: Pakeha, Estimated General Fertility Rates (Age-standardised, per 1000 Women Aged 15–44), Means and Ranges, Urban–Rural Continuum, 1878, 1896 and 1916

Class of urbanisation	1878		1896		1916		Decrease (%)	
	GFR	range	GFR	range	GFR	range	1878–96	1896–1916
Urban	209	37	107	32	77	15	48	28
Peri-urban	224	66	133	83	93	15	41	30
Rural:								
North Island	223	57	163	58	143	51	27	12
South Island	213	56	159	23	143	53	25	10

Source: Tiong 1988: Table E.2, and *passim* in his text.
Note: Fred Tiong's birth estimates were derived by reverse survival techniques, allowing for regional differentials in infant and early childhood survivorship, from the census populations aged 0–4 years, and were adjusted to eliminate the effects of the passive migration of children. By also age-standardising, he thus attempted to eliminate all compositional factors that could have produced artefactual differences. He could not, however, control for differential marriage rates. As the raw data were not available, we have computed simple means for each class. Tiong's different geographical groupings are delineated in his Appendix A. The urban areas include all interior boroughs. The Wellington peri-urban fringe was Hutt County (1878 and 1896) and Hutt plus Makara (1916). Its rate was very high in 1896, thus increasing the mean and range for this entire category in that year.

In Table 4.2 the regions are classified along an urban–rural continuum and by island, North and South. Huge South Island land tracts, mainly taken by government agents, were most widely exploited first, particularly for extensive pastoralism. That pattern of development was extended to the north as blocks of land were taken progressively from various iwi. This started with large-scale land purchase or confiscations of the areas most suited for immediate extensive pastoral farming (such as Hawke's Bay) or that were the most productive (the Waikato and the Bay of Plenty littoral). It moved then into the Rotorua Lakes area that would become developed for tourism; and, finally, in the 1890s and early 1900s took over the hill country and south-central North Island regions (e.g. the Ngati Tuwharetoa, Ngati Maniapoto and Tuhoe territories), typically areas with intense local relief. Land alienation continued after 1906, but in a more localised way, as by then Maori had already lost much of the North Island (Pool 1991: 88–100).

In 1878 urban–rural differences in Pakeha fertility were minimal, and no distinct continuum is evident. The range between classes of regions was also minimal. In short, fertility rates were either very high or extremely high.

In contrast, by 1896 and again in 1916 the range of rates had opened up and there was a distinct gradient between the most urban and most rural. In both inter-censal periods (which vary in duration, eighteen years, 1878–96, versus twenty years, 1896–1916) declines were more marked in the urban and peri-urban zones than in the rural areas. In general the ranges, in contrast to the levels, show no meaningful pattern until 1916. But by then the ranges were systematically higher in rural areas than in the more urban. In sum, this table points to a distinct urban–rural variance once fertility rates declined, but not in the years of hyper-fertility. It suggests that in later years inter-class differentials were more important than variance within the same group of regions.

Table 4.3 refines the analysis. It is based on the years after rates of reproduction had fallen significantly at a national level. Its main aim is to look at the rural regions to assess whether differences in the pattern of development had a uniform effect on their fertility levels. The classifications used here cut across one another, so that an early settled region such as the Coromandel falls into three different categories: in panel A of the table it is seen as long established; in B it is seen as mixed; and in C it is rated as given over primarily to exploitive industries (notably mining, timber-milling). Similarly, Westland is counterpointed against the remaining more developed regions of the South Island in panel A; mixed in B; and an exploitive primary economy in C. Allocation by region has had to be subjective and thus any results must be accepted with some degree of caution.

Table 4.3: Pakeha, Estimated General Fertility Rates (Age-standardised, per 1000 Women Aged 15–44), Means and Ranges, Rural Regions Classified by their Prime Economic Characteristics, 1896 and 1916

	1896		1916	
	GFR	Range	GFR	Range
A. DURATION OF SETTLEMENT				
North Island				
Long established	165	58	143	28
Pioneer	130	39	153	51
South Island				
Long established	150	23	142	35
Westland	154	–	178	–
B. PRIMARY ECONOMIC FUNCTION				
Extensive pastoralism	161	55	138	29
Dairying	171	53	148	20
Mixed, including mining, timber	155	41	144	35
C. MIXED-ECONOMY REGIONS				
Mining and timber-milling dominant	150	3	169	19
Mixed farming, mining, timber	144	7	135	19

Source: See Table 4.2. As raw data were not available the results are based on means for each grouping.

Nevertheless, and all caveats aside, these data provide some interesting results. In 1896 there were few strong and systematic differences, no matter how the cake is cut. It does seem, however, that the more mature regions, those with extensive pastoralism and dairying, had higher fertility. In particular, dairy regions stand out as still having relatively high fertility, the equivalent of just over 5.1 births per woman. In one sense this result seems counter-intuitive, at least for the dairying areas that had modernised economies. In the 1890s, the New Zealand family-owned dairy farm was probably among the most efficient and modern forms of farming anywhere in the world. But the clue to why they had higher fertility is that they were 'family owned' and, as a corollary, 'family operated'. The Taranaki dairy farm of this era was a family business that depended on its own members for labour. For this reason dairy farmers had been vociferous in opposition to compulsory schooling, particularly in the milking season (Pool and Tiong: 1991). One is tempted here to call in the big guns and to cite John Caldwell, the Australian demographer and leading fertility theorist: the case of dairying in Pakeha New Zealand in the 1890s seems to support his hypotheses of inter-generational wealth transfers. In this example, despite being a high-tech process, at least for those days, the transfers were what one would expect in more traditional peasant farming contexts: from children (farm workforce) to parents, and thus higher fertility levels were maintained. But this was in conflict with compulsory education, where the costs of having children absent, not working on the farm and thus not contributing to the household's income, would be borne by the parents and the direction of the transfers was from the parents to the children (Caldwell 1982). Of course, this neat hypothesis is muddled by the fact that farm children probably milked cows before and after school.

By 1916 the last residuals of higher but not hyper-fertility for Pakeha, although still well in excess of four births per woman, were seen in the more pioneer, later-settled areas, and in regions where economies were driven by exploitive industries. It will be recalled from the last chapter that coal miners were the occupational group with the highest fertility in Britain but in New Zealand mining regions had not had extremely high fertility in the 1890s. They not only had switched rank by 1916 to be lead areas, but even seem to have gone through an increase in rates in the early years of the century. It must be reiterated that controls for most composition effects have been built into these data, but one important one remains – the effects of marriage patterns. One suspects that in the late nineteenth century the marital distribution of the female population had been skewed by the presence of numbers of unattached women in the hospitality industries, but that by 1916 these former mining regions were increasingly developing more mixed economies and were composed of pioneer farming families, couples and their children.

SUMMARY: GEOGRAPHIC DIFFERENTIALS

The provincial-level and sub-provincial regional data analysed here have produced some interesting results. First, they show that the hyper-fertility of the early period of settlement was a colony-wide phenomenon – in the 1870s there were almost no regional differences of any magnitude.

But, secondly, this situation had changed by 1896. By that stage, patterns of development, particularly urbanisation, were related to both fertility levels and patterns of decline. By the 1890s larger families continued to typify the backblocks, whereas smaller families had become the modal form in the nascent colonial cities – say just over three births per woman in urban areas as against almost five in rural New Zealand. This urban–rural difference was still marked in 1916. Parenthetically, it is worth noting here that 100 years later the same geographical areas, the urban areas that had led the nineteenth-century fertility decline, once again had the lowest fertility (Pool *et al.* 2005a).

Thirdly, these data reinforce the point that differential marriage patterns were a critical factor in the varying patterns of fertility decline between regions. Fourthly, in 1916 really high fertility continued in the remaining pioneer areas, although earlier they had relatively lower levels because of their unusual – at least for the colony – marriage patterns.

Finally, and most importantly, these results allow a firm conclusion to be drawn. In the era of very high fertility, back in the 1870s, any observed differentials were within a high range, between elevated and extremely elevated. Only Auckland City seems to have put a slight damper on the colony's rampant reproduction during the Vogel era.

But once fertility levels declined, regional differences opened up. Here we must move from measurement to speculation. What we cannot say with any degree of certainty is what this situation represented. Was it due, for example, to the effects of new ideas about marriage, as a factor alone or in combination with the related questions of sexuality and reproduction? In the early years of the twentieth century these could have been imported into the country by newly arrived immigrants, whether British or Australian. Alternatively, was it because new norms had been generated in New Zealand cities and from there diffused to the backblocks?

We now look at other factors that may have produced differentials. But to do so, we must leave behind the nineteenth century and move fully into the twentieth, when new but fragmentary sources of data first become available.

4.6 PAKEHA, OTHER DIFFERENTIALS

DEMOGRAPHICALLY DEFINED DIFFERENCES

Within the Pakeha population reproductive polarisation in the early twentieth century took a form that has echoes today in the early twenty-first century (see Pool and Sceats 2003). At the turn of both centuries marriage was delayed. Moreover, age-specific fertility rates and the percentage of the TFR falling into the early and late (as against middle) years of the reproductive span were more evenly spread than they were to become in the intervening period of the Baby Boom. The similarities end there, for the entirely new factor at the end of the twentieth century was access to modern, efficient means of fertility regulation, which was not available to couples at the end of the Victorian era.

In the period prior to the Baby Boom, delayed marriage was the mechanism by which Pakeha women postponed first exposure to intercourse and the risk of conception (see Dharmalingam *et al.* 2007: Tables 3.4); by the 1980s, in contrast, control was through access to efficient means of contraception. But at both times – in the twentieth-century decades prior to the Baby Boom and after the Baby Boom at the turn of the twentieth century – this age-specific control was also linked to lower overall levels of fertility. Thus prior to 1945 the two phenomena, levels of fertility and reproductive polarisation, were primarily a function of marriage because it determined exposure to intercourse: those who were able to marry or who chose to do so could become parents. As was shown earlier, in the decades prior to 1945 those who chose not to marry were unlikely ever to become parents. This, then, was the clearest form of reproductive polarisation.

Nevertheless, once the fertility decline of the late nineteenth century had occurred, even among the married women there was greater diversity in the patterns of reproduction. Around the 1926 census, about 50% of married women aged younger than 20 years had a birth in any given calendar year; this was true for around a third of those aged 20–24 years,* and a quarter of those aged 25–29 years (Dharmalingam *et al.* 2007: Table 4.2). For those who married, this constituted fairly intensive reproductive regimes, although, to a certain extent, the not uncommon occurrence of pre-marital pregnancy followed by a nuptial birth reinforced this effect. Thus this squares with the point raised earlier that brides may have been pregnant, or became so soon thereafter because there was little attempt in the first years of marital life to avoid conception. In any case the means available for doing this, other than through systematic abstention, were still rather inefficient. So, although TFRs had declined significantly and by then were at quite low levels, for the recently married they were up towards bio-social limits.

The force of reproduction was, however, also spread right across the age-groups, so that 46% of births to married women were at age 30 years and over in 1926. If 1946 is excluded because of the aberrant returned-soldier effect noted earlier, nuptial fertility rates were higher in 1926 than at later dates. Against this, at that census one-fifth of women aged 30–34 reported that they had never married, the effects of which were outlined earlier. From the 1926 census data are available on Pakeha for a rather non-conventional statistical category: 'family heads', comprising married men, widows and widowers. If one takes the key childrearing reference age, 40–44 years, which gives a good estimate of completed family sizes, these family heads had on average 2.22 dependent children, a figure that was to be exceeded in the Baby Boom. But fully one-fifth of these families with an ever-married head had no dependent children, a figure that, in contrast, was well above the levels seen in the Baby Boom (the data in this paragraph are drawn from Dharmalingam *et al.* 2007: Tables 3.2, 4.2 and 4.3).

---

* To interpret this, it is necessary to recognise that over the five-year period in which married women were in the age-group 20–24 years, one-third of them would have a baby each year. For those who were fecund (in demography defined as the capacity to reproduce), one-third could have had a baby in the previous year and be abstaining from intercourse and/or breastfeeding, one-third might have a baby in the following year, but some of these women will already be pregnant in the reference year and will deliver in the next.

SOCIO-CULTURAL AND SOCIO-ECONOMIC DIFFERENCES

Fragmentary data, but in a time-series running from 1916 until 1986, show that there was also relatively systematic socio-cultural polarisation over a long period, for which we use religion as a proxy. Estimates made by Joanne Young (1997; tabulated in Dharmalingam *et al.* 2007: Table 4.4), based on what is termed Rele's technique,* show that families belonging to the mainstream Protestant churches (Anglican and Presbyterian) had fertility around or slightly below the national level. This is not entirely surprising as together they comprised almost 60% of the population through this period (Young 1997: Fig. 5.2). Nonconformist groups (Methodists, Baptists and Brethren), generally had lower fertility rates, and Catholics and Salvation Army adherents trended above the national level at this time. Curiously, those with no religion or 'Object to state' (those who refused to answer) are also above. Taken together for adherents to a religion, it does seem that there were differences, but not as marked as might be expected.

Yet another set of fragmentary data, presented in Table 4.4, permits a brief glimpse at socio-economic polarisation. Once again, however, imperfections in the baseline data-source place constraints on the analysis. As age-specific data are not available this affects the results especially for householders with zero children. This is because both family building and career paths are heavily age dependent. A further problem is that the data set relates only to wage and salary earners. In the rural sector a significant component of the labour force, the self-employed, are excluded. This issue is less important in the urban sector, although the family business sector will be under-represented. In the raw data the income categories were reasonably, if somewhat idiosyncratically, calibrated, except for the modal

---

* This technique, developed by the distinguished, now deceased, Indian demographer J. R. Rele, has been used by Pool on Maori (1991: Chapt. 4) and in work he carried out in West Africa (Courel and Pool 1973; Dankossou *et al.* 1973). It allows estimates of different vital rates (e.g. GRR) to be made from child–women ratios (e.g. children aged 0–4/women aged 15–44), a widely available, simply calculated statistic. The West African work and Rele's own experiments, even with populations that are far from stable, show that it is a very robust technique. To be classified as stable, a population's age-structures must remain unchanged because they have been generated by fertility and mortality rates that have remained constant over a long period of time, or forever. Clearly this theoretical condition is never seen in real populations, but a great deal of experimentation has shown that 'stable' population techniques are extremely practical in providing estimates for populations that lack reliable vital statistics. They work well for populations that have merely 'quasi-stable' structures, that do not meet the most rigorous definitions. Rele's contribution was to be able to demonstrate that this was true even when instability was marked (e.g. the rapidly changing birth rates of post-war Western European countries). Nevertheless, because the age-structures of the populations Young dealt with are likely to be highly destabilised as people move in and out of religious faiths, these results must be treated with some degree of caution. The comments here serve also to reinforce the argument made in Chapt 3, 78n relating to the transformation from GFRs to TFRs. These technical terms are defined in Pool 1991: Glossary.

category that included about half of the urban workers and just under a third of their rural counterparts.*

Table 4.4: Annual Income Levels: Pakeha 1926, Number of Dependent Children, Households of which Heads were Wage and Salary Earners (Percentage)

Number of children	Urban				Rural			
	Below mode	Mode	Above mode	Total	Below mode	Mode	Above mode	Total
0	34	47	18	100	61	30	9	100
1	24	55	21	99	47	41	11	99
2	22	55	23	100	46	41	13	100
3	24	55	22	100	46	42	12	100
4	26	54	20	100	46	42	12	100
5	28	55	18	100	48	42	10	100
6+	31	54	15	99	50	42	7	99
Total	28	52	20	100	52	37	11	100

Mode: L208–311; urban: median L241; rural: L194. Percentage of households that are urban, 74%.
Source: Census 1926.

These caveats acccepted, the results in Table 4.4 are rather interesting. First, there is a marked rural–urban difference, with much higher proportions, around half of the rural households, being below the mode, as against about a quarter in the urban areas. In part this is a function of the rural population, mainly wage earners rather than self-employed farmers, represented in the data set. Secondly, higher incomes characterise the middle family sizes, while both smaller and larger sizes are more characteristic of lower-income households. The results for low-income families with smaller sizes are probably because the wage or salary earner concerned was younger, commencing their career and at a low salary levels, and just starting family building. But larger family sizes could have been achieved only by older persons whose career paths were more advanced and thus their promotion chances potentially higher; yet their incomes were lower. Thus these data indicate an economic dimension to reproductive polarisation. This almost certainly had policy implications.

---

* The categories are (L = pound): no income; under L52; L52 to L155; L156 to L207; L208 to L311 (mode); L312 to L363; and L364 plus. With a half to a third of the cases in the modal category and with such a peculiar distribution, standard income measures (quartiles, medians, etc.) could be computed but had limited discriminatory value. Thus a decision was made to split the households into three categories: below the modal group, the mode, and above the mode.

4.7 POLICY RESPONSES TO FAMILY CHANGE AND FAMILY NEEDS

Given these effects of economic polarisation, if the family were to meet its responsibilities a policy environment would be needed that protected and enhanced family life, either through government intervention, as in modern welfare states, community institutions, the British Poor Laws, charity or family self-reliance. The neolocal Pakeha household with its shallow kinship structures noted earlier could not rely on wide family networks for support and thus there was a need for other forms of policy intervention.

Claire Toynbee's New Zealand-born Pakeha respondents, most born before 1912,

> showed little evidence of ... close and important ties with kin .... [Moreover] as a result of the acceleration of industrial capitalism in New Zealand, men became divorced from economic relationships with kin, leaving kinship as largely the concern of women .... By the turn of the [ninteenth] century it was clear that many people could not provide food, clothing and shelter for themselves in the ways they did under pre-industrial conditions (Toynbee 1995: 108, 133, 204).

To respond to this situation and others, innovative and radical legislation was introduced at the end of the nineteenth century and the beginning of the twentieth. The haphazard and rather punitive regimes that had existed prior to that in the early colonial period, to which we will now turn, had clearly become insufficient.

The changes introduced at the end of the nineteenth century started to reform earlier structures for the delivery of welfare that had in part owed their genesis to the systems operating in the old country. But they also had their origin in experiments that took the corpus of British welfare systems and selectively tampered with them. The historian David Thomson has argued that, 'while much of English law was brought to colonial New Zealand, the Poor Laws were not. Instead, the colonists separated out the various objectives and mechanisms that were woven into the Poor Laws, and implemented a piecemeal selection of them to reflect their own new priorities' (1998: 22). In particular, New Zealand settler governments were strongly influenced by a major ideological shift and associated structural changes in Britain that had taken place during the Victorian period:

> a marked decline in public income support for the needy, and a determined push to replace this with individual and family responsibility, supplemented by private charity. This was true particularly in England, where most of New Zealand's [Pakeha] settlers came from, and it may well have been part of a longer historical cycle of alternation between personal and public responsibilities in welfare matters (Thomson 1998: 9).

The British welfare system in inherited from the Poor Laws and stretch-ing back centuries placed an emphasis on local (typically parochial) provision to meet local needs. Staffing, infrastructure and provisions varied from place to place, particularly in Scotland, where the 'parochial system was ill-designed to cope with the worst features of poverty . . . , [which] for the remoter Highlands and the city slums strained it to breaking point' (Crowther 1990: 277 and *passim*, esp. 270–72). In England and Wales in the early nineteenth century, prior to and about the time of early New Zealand colonisation, the prevailing ideology was increasingly in favour of self- or family-reliance, especially for the 'able-bodied' (Thomson 1998: 9–17), 'but in Scotland this seemed irrelevant since the able-bodied had no right to relief' (Crowther 1990: 271).

New Zealand early on, in the Destitute Persons Ordinance 1846, 'placed responsibility firmly with the "near relatives" of the needy'. This took the notions of self-reliance and family responsibility prevalent in the old country further, and, according to Thomson, this legal position persisted through various amendments to this ordinance until its residuals were finally repealed more than a century later, in 1968 (Domestic Proceedings Act). But simply legislating against need does not drive it away, and thus a more comprehensive set of welfare measures, however parsimonious and fragmentary, had to be introduced. As Thomson notes, 'The counterpart to the laws on individual and family responsibility was a "system" of public welfare provision, though there was little systematic about it' (Thomson 1998: 22 and 28).

This situation has been described succinctly by historian W. H. Oliver for the 1988 Royal Commission on Social Policy: 'The 19th-century label for welfare was "charitable aid". Too various to be called a system, it was a complex mixture of locality, region and centre, and of public, corporate and individual agency. In effect it was a colonial Poor Law'. The 1852 constitution allocated this function to the provinces, and they subsidised voluntary institutions,

> channelling through them a modest amount of money for the relief of
> indigence among the elderly, deserted women and families and children in
> need of care. In principle it was laid down by the Destitute Persons Act of
> 1877, that responsibility lay with the near relatives of the indigent. In practice,
> many families were absentee, broken or otherwise incapable . . . The extent
> to which Maori shared in the welfare and pension provision of the later 19th
> century has not been investigated.

When the provinces were abolished in 1885, Charitable Aid Boards, 'in most cases identical with Hospital Boards', were set up (Oliver 1988: 14, 17).

It should be stressed that the early colonial governments were not ideo-logically averse to government intervention. Rather the contrary, in fact, for they were proactive in development, notably through immigration and public works, rather than social welfare (see Thomson 1998: Chapt. 3; see also Pool 2002). The first advanced welfare state structures were laid down by the colony at the turn of the twentieth century, especially by the Liberal Government of 1891–1911 (Oliver 1988; Sinclair 1959: Part 2, Chapt. II; Sutch 1966: Chapts 5 and 6; Nolan 2000 Chapts 1–5). Interestingly, among the first functions of these policies was to give support to one family form: the widow and her dependent children. This period also saw the development of voluntary agencies which aimed at supporting aspects of family life. The creation of the Plunket Society in 1908 was one such case. Its founder, Sir Truby King, had been a psychiatrist and had eugenicist views. He was in favour of segregation and sterilisation, arguing 'obviously unfit and bad strains should be got rid of' (Smith 2002: 306, citing King).

It would be comforting to believe that these measures were legislated by politicians advised by policy makers who were driven by a set of ideals of justice and social equity; regretfully, at least in the family policy arena, these were often simply pragmatic responses to a moral panic. To give this period a context, as Margaret Tennant has reminded us, 'There has probably never been a time in New Zealand's history since colonisation when one group or another has not perceived the home and family life to be under threat, but in the late nineteenth and early twentieth centuries alarm about the issues seems to have been especially intense' (2000: 24). Indeed, national anxiety about fertility, virility and seeming class differentials in fertility led Britain, and the two Australasian Dominions (New Zealand in 1911) to include fertility questions in their censuses (Garrett *et al.* 2001: 4–6; Mazumdar 2003: 319).

Much of the policy directed at the family in this period, but not all (Nolan 2000: *passim*), related to the function of 'legitimate maternity', Belich's summary phrase cited earlier. It focused on issues such as abortion or aspects of maternal and child health. Earlier in this chapter it was noted that these concerns were the catalysts for family benefits and similar welfare and family support instruments, both to meet the narrower objectives of limiting demands for abortion and the wider goal of increasing fertility. Some authors, such as H. I. Sinclair who held eugenicist views, also expressed opinions that have a surprising resonance for public policy debates today, albeit written in what now seems a quaint style, about other aspects of family support that might stem declining fertility. Sinclair said, for example, 'Unless some special provision is made to enable women in industry to have babies conveniently and have them cared for in nurseries or crèches whilst they are at work, women of childbearing age in industrial employment are a positive drain on fertility' (1944: 136–37).

There was another policy issue that assumed major importance for much of the twentieth century; and, arguably, as will be discussed in later chapters, it may have been the most critical family support and thus prop for child-bearing and childrearing. The family dwelling became an issue of policy concern from the dawn of the twentieth century, again with the Housing Act in 1919, and above all with the legislation and initiatives following the election of the Labour Government in 1935. The financing and building of the family home was a central policy intervention by the public sector, and by 1944 the state was constructing 5000 houses per year (*NZOYB* 1990: 517–18). In New Zealand, for more than a century the supply of housing has been a function both of the market, which catered for demand and discretionary expenditure, and public policy, which responded to the basic need for adequate shelter. There has always been a tension between these support systems. The fully detached family home, 'owned' with or without a mortgage, was the site for neolocal residence and became a stereotypical place, the home for bringing up children. Well before 1916 this had been the established pattern in rural New Zealand, where settlement was dispersed (Thomson 1998: 67–68) and, by 1926, even in urban New Zealand (see Table 3.5). This set New Zealand and the other neo-Europes apart from continental Europe, and even from Great Britain, where semi-detached and row houses were the modal urban type even in neighbourhoods peopled by professionals (Pool and Sceats 2003). This aspect of family life remained constant until the late twentieth century. By then, as we will discuss in later chapters, financial and other constraints were reducing the capacities of young New Zealanders to achieve this cultural norm.

For the average New Zealand family, house ownership is a social and cultural expectation, seen as a means of accumulating wealth, and this has affected public policy (Easton 1980). Recently neo-liberal economists (e.g. Reserve Bank governors) have criticised this pattern of behaviour, very much as if it were simply economic in nature and, at least in their view, not a rational choice. Yet, at a practical level, much of the stock of housing in the country is of this type and there are virtually no alternatives for the couple starting to form a family. In any case, as suggested, it is a deeply instilled norm, and one that was central to social policy for much of the twentieth century, stretching back to the Workers' Dwellings Act 1905, and the Advance to Workers Act 1906 (mortgage finance, for urban housing). The principle that government should support house purchases, as well as rental housing, was reinforced by the establishment of the State Advances Corporation in 1936 (Oliver 1988).

The most comprehensive body of welfare legislation having an impact on families came with the 1938 Social Security Act. Income support had been directed earlier to widows (1911) and some families (1926). But the 1938 Act went far beyond this, notably by extending family benefits both in scope and in the population groups that were covered. It extended previous welfare provisions by including aliens, 'Asiatics', illegitimate children and, explicitly, Maori (*NZOYB* 1990: 204–5; Nolan 2000: Chapt. 5 details the history of family allowances).

From the Liberal Government reforms of the 1890s, the central premise of family policy revolved around the notion of a social or family wage. This was to provide income support to a married man and his family at a level which allowed a basic standard of living for a family, or to replace his wage-earning capacity if his wife were widowed (Shirley *et al.* 2000; Nolan 2000: *passim*). In the international literature on family policy this model, called eponymously by Australian political scientist Francis Castles the 'antipodean' model, is seen as unique to Australia and New Zealand. In New Zealand's case, the 1938 manifestation of the social-wage approach involved a comprehensive welfare state of Scandinavian dimensions (e.g. Castles 1993a, 1998; Esping-Andersen 1999; summarised in Pool and Sceats 2003).

In a sense, the evolving colonial family structure described in this chapter was the cornerstone of national development. Through technological change, agricultural tenure systems and the land reforms of the Liberal Government at the turn of the twentieth century, the rural sector essentially became dependent upon the owner-operated, yet highly scientific, New Zealand family farm, a unique phenomenon (*NZOYB* 1990: 37). Even in the nearby Australian colonies, this link between the family, as a highly efficient social and economic unit, and cash-sector farming was not as well developed. Moreover, because of questions of scale, in New Zealand the typical manufacturing and tertiary-sector business also remained small. Here, too, the family business dominated. Thus New Zealand became a family business society, with neither the large landed estates nor the large-scale industrial plants found elsewhere. This was to continue until well after World War II.

There was an analogue to this in Maori society, which more explicitly forged links between the family and development. The movement towards consolidation and amalgamation developed by Sir Apirana Ngata in the 1920s essentially built up corporations based on genealogy and whanau membership (Hunn 1961).

4.8 CONCLUSION: THE ROOTS OF THE CONTEMPORARY NEW ZEALAND FAMILY

TRENDS AND IMPLICATIONS

This conclusion synthesises and highlights major issues relating to the period spanned in both Chapters Three and Four. The period 1840–1945 is not simply one of historical interest to contemporary New Zealanders or the starting point for an analysis spanning the years until the present. The story that has been recounted here is also inherently fascinating in its own right:

how a society (Pakeha) could swing from hyper-fertility to reproductive polarisation and then down to sub-replacement. It was also an era that saw the development of behaviours, value systems and policy frameworks that have had major implications beyond World War II and even for family life in the twenty-first century. This became increasingly clear to the authors as they started to synthesise what they had previously viewed as primarily an empirical exercise setting the scene for the most modern period.

The demographic trends of this period can also be viewed as the most publicly evident and systematically recorded manifestation of wider trans-formations across many dimensions of social life. Most specifically, Melanie Nolan has commented that 'New Zealand women have been portrayed as being markedly domestic' (2000: 15). Arguably, this 'cult of domesticity' is revealed most strikingly in the reproductive patterns of married Pakeha women. Each of the dramatic changes reported in the last two chapters were related to shifts in many different aspects of society, families and domesticity, from gender relations to residential patterns, from the work-place to the policy environment..

In some ways the era 1840–1945 is distant from our lives now, yet in that period the behaviours and norms that are apposite for family life today were established for Pakeha, by importing these from Europe or by moulding them to create new structures and forms. It is also an era in which Maori were con-fronted not just with a colonial regime but also with different family systems, especially their more formal and legal elements. These were alien to what existed here at the time of Waitangi. The problem arose when the dominant Pakeha prescribed their family system, especially in its more formal guise, as the only way to do things. Yet for Maori families the key issues were very different from Pakeha needs and were very basic: demographic maintenance and the protection of the way they had always done things.

Demographically, this era was characterised by very significant transfor-mations in the *structures* of Pakeha families, but this must be set alongside very limited changes in Pakeha family *forms*. In contrast, the period saw few shifts in either family structures or forms for Maori; arguably the most important came from the rapid improvements at infant and childhood ages that had the effect of making the structures of Maori families younger. Other aspects of the morphologies of Maori whanau (e.g. early marriage) and, for both Maori and Pakeha, the formal dimensions of the family (e.g. marital statuses) remained very stable right through this period. Throughout this era, moreover, family formation occurred almost entirely within marriage, as defined by each culture. Maori maintained through this period a distinct system of legitimating unions, and these have been considered here as formal marriages. Sometimes this process was reinforced by a religious ceremony and/or by formal registration but, whichever form was taken, these were legitimate marriages.

Nevertheless, forms and structures for both Maori and Pakeha interacted to an overwhelming degree earlier in the period, and even significantly later on. It is impossible to say whether young women or couples of that period deliberately chose to marry and procreate or to remain celibate, or were driven in either direction by pressures emanating from the wider family. These could include concerns about the possible future faced by members who were spinsters,* by community sanctions, by subtle family approval or disapproval (such as by perceiving some bachelor as a 'good catch') or by the fears associated with ex-nuptial childbearing or disease. But, regardless, the instruments that manipulated the nuptiality valve were the adoption of family forms that could be cemented by legal marriage or, conversely, the acceptance of permanent celibacy and childlessness. The manipulation of this valve had flow-on effects that produced major shifts in Pakeha family structures over this era. For Maori the valve remained more or less in the same position throughout the period, and is thus the reason why this chapter and the last have focused heavily on Pakeha, who were going through major shifts. For them, early and universal marriage gave way to delayed marriage and relatively high levels of celibacy. In turn, this directly affected levels of reproduction and thus both family sizes and their structures.

Of course, looking back from the safe distance of today these might seem not only a purely rational set of choices, considered like the moves in a chess game, but also that couples consciously and deliberately linked marriage to childbearing, whereas, as just noted, they probably had a plethora of personal reasons for marrying. Yet it is remarkable how strongly people follow trends and hold to the modal patterns of their era; in this sense, many norms that can be assessed by observing mass behaviours may also parallel prescriptive norms (what people should do).

It is tempting but simplistic to attribute the very high fertility and its associated marriage patterns in early Pakeha colonial society up to the 1880s or 1890s to a surplus of males and/or to wide open frontiers and thus an expansiveness and optimism that carried across to reproduction. Further analysis shows that fertility levels became much lower at a time when relatively high rates of masculinity still persisted (well into the twentieth century). Indeed, taking this further, in the Baby Boom (Chapter Five) early and universal marriage, and a return to high fertility rates, especially at young ages, were to occur in a period when neither pre-condition – high masculinity ratios nor an open frontier – was evident. High masculinity ratios are, at most, an enabling

---

* Jane Austen's much maligned Mrs Bennet was unconsciously attempting to operate the nuptiality valve, with good intentions and in the best interests, as she saw them, of her spinster daughters' futures. To the extent that her behaviour was representative of early nineteenth-century customs and that it was reflected in non-fictional family life, it might have been the sort of model that Pakeha colonists imported with them.

mechanism for, not a determinant of, universal marriage, and by 1900 this was no longer a factor once norms relating to nuptiality had changed.

Nor is a rural existence, however idyllic, a sufficient explanation of levels – in the late nineteenth century, for example, Highland Scotland had far lower GFRs than urban Scotland. The broader economic conditions such as enclosures and clearances in the Highlands compared to more positive developments in much of rural Lowland Scotland might provide some clues, but the 'pestilential' conditions of, say, Glasgow hardly provided a favourable urban environment (Campbell and Levine 1990; Morris 1990). In New Zealand, Pakeha levels of reproduction in the 1870s were uniformly high for almost every sort of geographical area: rural or urban; long established or pioneer; economies that were mixed, or based on extensive pastoralism or dairying. But at that stage, areas in which mining and other exploitive industries were significant seemed to have had lower fertility. Nevertheless, it is possible to exaggerate the range of fertilities in the colony in the 1870s, for the differentials ranged from hyper-fertility down to merely very high.

Once family size changes got under way in the late nineteenth century, these shifts do seem to have disseminated from the major cities, which were also ports, and were thus the routes by which new ideas entered the colony. In contrast, while regions of a pioneer sort, New Zealand's equivalent to the frontier, had relatively lower fertility rates in the period of early settlement, by the 1920s these were the only regions with higher regimes. But by then their functions had shifted from mining and timber milling increasingly to farming, and it is likely that the age or marital status distributions of their female populations were weighted towards younger married women. While age-composition has been controlled for, unfortunately we cannot do the same for marital distributions and thus have not been able to come to firm conclusions on this point.

By the end of the nineteenth century the Pakeha reproductive regime was starting to resemble that of Britain at the time, although fertility was still higher. Moreover, the rates for married women had not declined to the same degree as those for women of all marital statuses. This shows that the nuptiality valve rather than contraception within marriage was a key factor. But gradually during the course of the first half of the twentieth century family planning within marriage, including traditional means such as abstention, seem to have become more widespread, thus moving Pakeha couples towards trends that had become more widely extant in earlier decades in Britain.

These material contexts of nineteenth- and early twentieth-century Pakeha family life only yield limited and rather superficial clues as to why trends occurred. Instead, in seeking underlying determinants for Pakeha family patterns, one must appeal to the roles of value systems, and perhaps most importantly those imported from the British Isles. The problem is that the patterns of the family formation, and thus presumably their underlying values in the early years of colonisation, did not accord closely with those in Britain at the time but seem to have harked back to Britain in the pre-Victorian era. Moreover, we cannot really offer this as an explanation, merely an explicandum. Thus we cannot solve this question; we merely pose it as a challenge to historians and other scholars.

THE IMPLICATIONS OF THE DIVERSIFICATION OF REPRODUCTIVE PATTERNS

The shifts in Pakeha marriage patterns and the attendant family size revolutions at the end of the nineteenth century did not occur uniformly or affect all population groups evenly and simultaneously. As fertility declined, differentials increased. The magnitude of polarisation even between aggregates, such as regions, became marked; by 1896 the range for fertility rates between the highest and lowest regions (Hawkes Bay, 190, minus Dunedin, 89, equals 101) was a figure that almost equalled the values reported for all urban areas combined (107) (Tiong 1988: Table e.2). Thus this period was marked by geographically defined reproductive polarisation. Data available to this historical review only for the twentieth-century decades show that this also held true for religion and socio-economic status. But the most important distinction was whether or not one married, and, if married, the family that was produced.

Pakeha reproductive polarisation in this era had a concomitant factor: a lack of reproductive choice. As noted earlier, in the first half of the twentieth century this was determined to a large degree by whether or not a woman married, not whether the couple used contraception. In the pioneer period around 1876 there had apparently been little choice about marriage, as most women wed at young ages. As this was essentially a Protestant population, there was not even the option of entering a celibate order of nuns. The result was a high level of fertility at and from the early adult ages. It must be reiterated that relatively few women married as teenagers, and that ex-nuptial childbearing rates were very low. This means that the analyst must see family building in the early colonial period in very deterministic terms: to reach a TFR of more than 6.0 live births, it would have been a bio-social necessity for most women to have married in their early twenties, soon thereafter to have had a first birth, and then to have borne offspring throughout their reproductive span. Thus the Pakeha population in 1876 was essentially one with natural fertility (defined earlier), the same reproductive strategy that Maori also followed, not only then but until after World War II. For married Pakeha women this pattern continued for a number of decades into the early twentieth century

In today's international community, experts concerned with issues of fertility would consider rates of the magnitude observed for Pakeha in the 1870s, remembering that they are averages, as indicators of a lack of reproductive choice, and this fertility pattern would be linked to economic under-development. It still occurs today only in some of the least developed countries, and one or two places in the Middle East (e.g. Palestine). Yet, at that time, say the 1870s, this was a rich population living in a developed country with one of the highest incomes per capita anywhere.

By the end of the nineteenth century, faced with a buyers' market, Pakeha women were making a choice in a rather more instrumental way by not marrying at all or by delaying marriage. Efficient contraception, the mechanism by which 'choice' is implemented today, was not available to them, although in all probability less efficient means were starting to be used within marriage.

What does seem clear, however, was that by the end of the nineteenth century the nuptiality valve was being controlled, because for women there were viable alternatives to the sole pioneer option of marriage and child-bearing. In the early pioneer period virtually the only work opportunity available for single women had been domestic service, from which many escaped by marrying their employer. But from the 1880s women could enter employment in other sectors, and thus had a choice, albeit a stark one: marry and have children but give up paid employment, or remain in the remunerated workforce and remain spinsters. Thus by the early twentieth century women were clearly postponing this decision and marrying later, as reflected in relatively high levels of marital fertility at older ages and the higher percentage of births later in the reproductive span. This occurred despite an increasing propensity to use fertility regulation within marriage, at older ages and higher parities.

In the 1870s relatively high fertility, albeit not quite as elevated as rates seen in New Zealand, was seen across the neo-Europes, so Pakeha were not unique. There was another similarity: as economic modernisation occurred in this group of countries so too were there declines in average fertility rates, although once again it was Pakeha who went through the most rapid drop.

The simultaneity of the shift from high to low across the WDCs, especially the neo-Europes, is a sub-theme of wider theoretical interest that has emerged in this chapter and the last. What has been documented here is the occurrence in New Zealand of a national trend, occurring across much of the country during a relatively compressed period, but this trend was a microcosm of an even vaster mega-trend. Thus beyond looking for explanations in terms of factors that might have immediately influenced the behaviour of any woman or couple, it is also necessary to seek reasons in the wider processes of settlement and then modernisation.

THE LARGE FAMILY OF NOSTALGIA

This period also saw patterns of family life that would enter the cultural memory of both Maori and Pakeha. Over time, whether based on myth, reality or a composite of the two, these memories became the original benchmarks around which family values and norms in later decades were constructed. The collective recent and seemingly more reliable memory, based mainly on the inter-war years, is selective, based not on modal or average families of the time, but on the minority of families that had numerous children and thus probably many descendants. This is in part a legitimate type of selectivity, due to an empirically verifiable fact about not the parents but their offspring: four-fifths of children recorded in the 1911 census had been born into large families. The corollary to this is tautological: few people alive today are descended from the small families of the inter-war years. Yet at that time small families would not have been uncommon: indeed many, albeit a minority, of married couples had only one child or no children. In reality the large family that remains in collective memory was not the universal or overwhelmingly prevalent structure. What has been passed down to the present is the memory of the family the *majority* of us are descended from, the family with six or more children. But such large households represented only a *minority* of all family units.

Along with this, it was almost always married couples that parented large families, although a minority of these people would become widows or widowers while the process of family formation was unfolding. But it is the coincidence of an apparently large family produced by a married couple that has become the family of yesteryear in later generations' collective memory. All the other permutations discussed here, such as the minority of sole-adult families, are pushed into the back of our memories. For example, cohabitation may well have occurred to a limited degree, even outside bohemian circles, and this marital status may well have been reported in the census as 'married'. But what is far more certain is that the offspring were overwhelmingly legitimate. Today of course we know from DNA testing that some children are not the biological offspring of the parent(s) reported on the birth certificate. Moreover, long-held family secrets about in-family adoption sometimes come to light through intra-family gossip. But the fact that registration is a legal process ensured that the overwhelming majority of children reported as legitimate were in fact born in wedlock, even if by some chance one of the named parents was not really the biological parent.

Moreover, along with the large family of nuptially born offspring headed by a married couple, there is nostalgia for social-emotional qualities that are often attributed to the family of yesteryear. These frequently include factors such as firm discipline and cohesion, but also reputed warmth, trusting relationships and a supportive environment. Whether or not those families were more or less likely than the family of today to have displayed such characteristics will never be known in a quantitative way. The analysing of diaries and of the fiction of the period is the closest researchers can come to finding a source from which this might be ascertained, but novels and diaries are seldom a representative data source.

IS THE PAST CONSTRUCTED FROM SELECTIVE NOSTALGIA OR DOES HISTORY REPEAT ITSELF?

This period also has another lesson for us. It saw the initiation of what were to become recurring features of New Zealand family life. It is helpful to remember this when one is being exposed to some of the more strident discourses on modern household trends and contemporary family breakdown.

Some family formation patterns have passed through repeated cycles with waves that are strangely uniform, spaced out at almost hundred-year intervals. During the Baby Boom, not quite a century out from the period of the 1860s–70s, family sizes were large, a factor once again of early and universal marriage, as in the pioneer period, although the Baby Boom parents did not precisely mimic the pioneers. The Baby Boom was followed by the Baby Bust, a trend that echoed what had occurred in the 1880s–90s, when there were fertility declines. Thus almost a century later, in the late 1970s and the 1980s, Pakeha went through a Baby Bust and, in pursuing this trend, re-adopted the strategies of the colonial period right down to employing the mechanism of delayed childbearing. Of course, this comparison cannot be taken too far because in the Baby Bust the patterns of union formation and fertility regulation were very different from what had been seen in the late nineteenth century. Yet, interestingly, following each of these two Baby Busts there were moral panics about reproduction. New Zealand, and particularly Pakeha society, seems to be remarkably subject to, or subjects itself to, waves of panic coupled with nostalgia, typically co-terminous with, or following, the initiation of a new pattern of family life.

It is not just in terms of morphologies that the pioneer family laid down norms that were to be perpetuated. The exceptionally young age for marriage and the early childbearing that characterised the Baby Boom may have had their roots in early colonial family life when family formation occurred at young ages, although not as early on average as in the Baby Boom. But it is not too speculative to posit that norms favouring early pregnancy could have filtered down to Baby Boom descendants from Pakeha colonial society. In turn, at least for some aspects of Pakeha family life, especially early and universal marriage, observed behaviours seem often to have harked back to models that came from pre-Victorian Britain. In contrast, there seem to have been clear differences in the family formation patterns of the 1870s between late Victorian New Zealand Pakeha and their British cousins.

Not only were structural changes in the colonial and early Dominion family to be replicated, albeit in a somewhat mutated form, by later generations in the twentieth and early twenty-first centuries, this seems to hold true for value systems. In later chapters dealing with these periods, echoes of early colonial norms and their British antecedents will be heard. Many of the values contextualising much of the debate about family policy in the early twenty-first century, in what are turbulent times, do not constitute modern responses to contemporary issues, but instead are strangely reminiscent of what was said in the late colonial period. As Thomson (1998: 165) argues, 'The "new" ideas advanced, solutions proposed and procedures put in place are mostly re-runs of earlier forgotten ones, with the very words and phrases of a past age undergoing an uncanny and often unwitting revival'.

RADICAL FLUCTUATIONS IN PATTERNS OF PAKEHA FAMILY
FORMATION

Finally, this period saw significant and often rapid fluctuations in structures, above all in family sizes. To a degree this aspect of family formation also reflected cultural norms imported from the mother country – the changes in late eighteenth-century England for example, as family sizes rose, and then at the start of Victoria's reign when they decreased. But Pakeha went through fluctuations more quickly and more extremely. In the space of less than a quarter of a century, 1878–1900, TFRs for Pakeha New Zealanders plummeted from 7.0 births per woman to 3.5, then fell further to exact replacement, yet rose rapidly again at the end of this period with the onset of the Baby Boom. Stage One and the first part of Stage Two of Pakeha New Zealand's family transition, outlined earlier in this book, left behind a particular heritage, just as the delayed Maori family transition occurring in the 1970s was to do for Maori society.

These sudden fluctuations induced by radical shifts in patterns of childbearing affect every aspect of population change, because births of cohorts of very different sizes, and thus of generations, have long-term implications for the entire society, not just through the replacement of the adult population. This is because the consequent disordered cohort-flows produce turbulence in New Zealand's age structures, one of the most extreme in WDCs, and this, in turn, affects every aspect of social life, of the economy and of social policy. One only has to think of the effects of fluctuations in birth rates on primary-school class sizes five years on to recognise the impacts of cohort-flows. Moreover, they also affect the sizes of future parental cohorts, and thus the potential for variations in birth cohort sizes in years to come (Pool 2003).

It is to the early part (1876–1900) of the period covered in this chapter that we owe the genesis of the propensity for destabilised family transitions, the very behaviour that has characterised New Zealand society since World War II. But equally the survivors of the births in the second part of the era spanned here, 1900–45, are still with us and these cohorts are still moving inexorably up the age pyramid, having an impact on New Zealand's society, economy and polity.

THE MAORI FAMILY, 1840–1945

To conclude this part of the book, it must not be forgotten that two totally different demographic and family transitions were being played out in this period. For Maori the most turbulent period had occurred by the 1880s or 1890s during which period their numbers continued to drop off, finally reaching a nadir in the 1890s, when the population was only half the size it had been in 1840 at the time of the Treaty of Waitangi. With this went massive disruptions to family life and morphologies; above all, mortality had exerted disproportionate force on the child population, and by extension had significantly affected not only the sizes but the structures of families.

But by the turn of the twentieth century, a definite recuperation was under way. The remainder of this period, until World War II, saw this accelerate, reaching a peak after the war. But all this was occurring in isolated rural areas of New Zealand outside a mainstream whose family norms were very much dictated by the Pakeha majority. Again, as has been the case for Pakeha, for Maori the past has moulded much of the present and will affect the future. While the problem of demographic maintenance, the most basic of all family issues, is now no longer dependent on the birth and survivorship to adulthood of Maori cohorts, what happened in the nineteenth and early twentieth centuries is such a powerful memory for some Maori that it still is raised at times in the public policy discourse of the twenty-first.

CHAPTER FIVE

The Baby Boom Era, 1945–1973

5.1. DELINEATING AND DOCUMENTING THE NEW ZEALAND BABY BOOM

THE BABY BOOM ERA

The history of the Baby Boom, starting nominally in 1945, is described in this chapter. This year provides a convenient break, although in 1943 hints of an impending major shift started to emerge and in 1947 the real 'classical' Baby Boom, with all its enduring features, began. The chapter ends in 1973 although use is made of data from the 1976 census, which covered structures and forms that had mainly been set in place over the period 1943–73.

In popular discourse and in the media the Baby Boom is often seen as an emblematic era, certainly in terms of nostalgia. The term Baby Boom carries with it a whole range of meanings: it is a set of demographic trends, but also a wider phenomenon than that would imply, and is an era that has developed its own mystique and mythology. It was probably the period in which were fashioned some of the cardinal norms and values that still have resonance for New Zealand society in the twenty-first century, and that, in turn, came down from the decades covered in the last two chapters – above all the inter-war years. The two and a half decades after the Baby Boom were to see these norms and values, and their associated behaviours, challenged. Certainly, no other generation has gained quite the same cachet as the 'Baby Boomers', as these birth cohorts have forced a passage across the social, political and economic landscape, indelibly marking out their territory.

The fact that this generation was so large by comparison with those before it, and even with those of the Baby Bust following it, has added to its disproportionate position in the cultural history of New Zealand and most other WDCs. This chapter looks in detail at the origins of this generation and, because of its significant social demographic implications, discusses what happened over the spread of years during which the Baby Boom children were born. In passing, the question will be raised whether the term Baby Boom really applies to this era in all WDCs, or just a sub-set of them.

The Baby Boom has become something more than a population trend played out over a specified period. It represents an era in which particular family and other social behaviours, attitudes, norms and values were dominant; the generation born at that time has gained almost the aura and legitimacy of a culture. Certainly, the cohorts born at that time are viewed as a body of people having shared values, for example by marketeers or by policy makers looking at ageing, and thus as more than just a group of people born in the same period. In the same vein, the Baby Boom period itself has captured the popular imagination, at least in retrospect. Often it is the manifest forms, the living arrangements, marital statuses or nuptial births of Baby Boom families, that are constructed socially as a 'golden era' of family life; 'our country's golden age', in the words of one leading politician (Sir John Marshall, quoted by Belich 2001: 307). For some observers this period is taken, consciously or unconsciously, as a benchmark era from which recent parenting generations have shifted, to the detriment of family values and the viability of the family (Morgan 2004); to posit a deterioration in aspects of social life it is necessary to have a comparison that is deemed more favourable.

The task here is not to endorse these perceptions uncritically, but to pose some trenchant questions. One can begin with the issue of parameter setting. In this regard, for example, one problem for the New Zealand observer is that local media, marketing people and others derive many of their ideas from overseas. They typically copy articles appearing there in the press or in magazines setting the 1960s as the termination point of the Baby Boom, without recognising, as we will show, that the New Zealand Baby Boom was rather different. Again, in marketing and popular perceptions the Baby Boomers are seen almost as a homogeneous wave, as a collectivity, as a singulate generation. But a generation born over almost 30 years, a period that was longer than the inter-war years, will itself be composed of different cohorts and this must be looked at. This issue would be less critical if the Boom had spanned only, say, twenty years, 1946–1966, but becomes more problematic for something that might have run from 1943 to 1973, as will be argued here. If the modalities of family formation are looked at (timing and spacing of births, and above all the number of children born), New Zealand's Baby Boom not only spread out across a 30-year span, but in the process produced large but different sized cohorts, with two very important peaks, one in 1960 and the other in 1970.*

---

* The *size* of the birth cohorts is a far more important defining characteristic than the *rate*, because the Baby Boomers are seen as a 'generation'; that is, a number of birth cohorts forming a group of people born in the same era who then proceed through their life-cycles. Fluctuations in birth cohort sizes create major problems for policy (Pool 2003).

THE PARAMETERS OF THE BABY BOOM AND THEIR IMPLICATIONS
It is a moot point as to when the Baby Boom actually started, but from about 1943 an upswing in fertility and marriage was evident, following the return from overseas of the First Military Echelon, and this may be considered the onset of the Baby Boom. In the case of New Zealand this phenomenon was to continue for a long time, until about 1973, longer than in other developed countries.

In other senses 1946 can really be seen as the changeover year because, not surprisingly with the troops arriving home, the TFR went up suddenly to 3.3 live births per woman, a level not seen since around 1900. But the age-specific pattern in 1946 differed from that occurring thereafter. The rates being reported by the end of the 1940s rather than the patterns seen briefly in 1946 were to become the norms for the rest of the Baby Boom. For example, in 1946 the percentage of births to women over 30 years went up to the highest level it had been at since 1931, but then by 1951 had quickly dropped back down, to reach an all-time low by the end of the Baby Boom in the early 1970s (Dharmalingam *et al.* 2007: Table 3.8). The year 1946, then, could be seen as a sort of false beginning, a bit like the 'phoney war' of 1939–40, before the real Baby Boom set in.

The most important questions for this chapter go far beyond these measurement and definitional concerns. They are, in fact, fundamental to the family regimes that are now in place in the twenty-first century and that will be covered in later chapters. The Baby Boom produced very different family morphologies from those seen since and indeed from what were seen between the 1880s and the end of World War II. The question that must be posed, therefore, is whether the conditions that provoked and facilitated the Baby Boom could ever be recaptured. Put another way, was the Baby Boom a once-off, never to be repeated? A corollary to this is whether the Baby Boom, at least in its New Zealand manifestation, was an unconscious attempt to re-create earlier New Zealand family-building patterns, as we have implied in the conclusion to Chapter Four. Was the Baby Boom a last dying gasp of traditional fertilities (Szreter 2002) or might it recur some time in decades to come, with all its positive and negative connotations?

Related to this is another question from the analyses in Chapters Three and Four. They showed that from about 1880 a fertility decline got under way, culminating in sub-replacement reproduction during the Depression of the 1930s; later chapters will show that sub-replacement fertility has become the demographic norm since the late 1970s. It must be asked: was the Baby Boom an aberrant period in what is really a long-term trend towards a failure of the population to replace itself, and ultimately for it to decline in natural increase, as seems to be the case for some Mediterranean countries? To answer this question it is incumbent on demographers and policy makers to understand the morphologies and dynamics of this era.

The key parameters of the period covered in this chapter are determined by the Baby Boom itself, as we define it. Strictly speaking, it was almost entirely a Pakeha phenomenon, but constituted far more than simply a change in family sizes, and these aspects of family life affected Pakeha and Maori alike. Thus as a follow-up to the more narrowly delineated, but very important, demographic questions raised above, there is a need to parse the Baby Boom itself, asking if family life then was quite as idyllic as is portrayed in TV series or by those commentators who take the era as a model of traditional household morphologies and behaviours. Its power as a model is enhanced for us because it is so recent; no other earlier era was captured *in situ*, as it were, as non-fiction on film and by the new medium of TV – there are fragmentary glimpses of the inter-war years but a detailed record of the Baby Boom. The task here is to see whether that record is as selective as are memories of the large families of the pre-war generations.

In this regard the policy context of the Baby Boom is also important. Historian Bronwyn Labrum has argued that it was a 'golden age' for welfare: 'Good times were buttressed by the extensive social security system'. She adds an important qualification that serves to introduce two other features of the Baby Boom:

> not everyone benefited. . . . Urbanisation and suburbanisation produced raw monotonous and sprawling instant communities in areas such as the Hutt Valley. Social problems persisted to the perplexity of many community leaders and politicians and appeared to symbolise underlying difficulties in family and community life (Labrum 2004: 163).

Perhaps the Baby Boom was not as unrelentlessly 'golden' as its boosters then and since have suggested, but it did see the reification of a way of life: neolocal suburban residence.

For Pakeha this was the dominance of neolocal, nuclear, two-parent family structures and forms: a married couple and their children, who typically moved away from their parents' household to a newly established suburb and formed their own independent family unit. Maori and Pakeha were to share this aspect of the Baby Boom. This period also saw, for Pakeha, a return to larger nuclear family sizes, resulting from very early marriage, and rapid childbearing. It is this last aspect of the Baby Boom, along with the birth of large cohorts, rather than the fertility rates of the period that are the unifying feature across its 30-year span.

MAORI IN THE BABY BOOM: PARTICIPANTS IN, OR OBSERVERS OF, A SEMINAL PAKEHA EVENT?

As a demographic phenomenon the Baby Boom in the strict sense of the term was not a phase passed through by Maori. But, given that the Baby Boom is a clearly defined period (1943–73), the term can be used to time-reference events occurring to Maori simultaneously and to their generations born then. The determinants, the patterns and the consequences of Maori trends in family life at this time were very different from those for Pakeha.

What sets Maori apart is that their family sizes had continued to be large since the nineteenth century and until at least the 1960s. Yet a transition in their whanau structures and forms was already under way from the 1940s. It resulted not from shifts in patterns of family formation, but from the emergence of neolocalisation of the parenting couple, and thus a related rapid change in social organisation. This produced shifts that were fundamental to the underpinnings of Maori culture and created a severe dislocation that Maori society attempted to grapple with. The 'new Maori Migration' (Metge 1964) was to have 'major implications for social organisation, iwi cohesion, kinship' (Hopa 1996: 54), and in the process changed the very nature of whanau (Metge 1995). By the end of the period another marker of transition was seen – a shift in family sizes in terms of numbers of children had commenced, but was to be most rapid in the period covered in Chapters Six and Seven.

Superficially, documenting the implications of the Baby Boom seems a remarkably straightforward exercise: birth numbers increased significantly, precipitating a population wave, and then went down. But any retrospective assessment of the Pakeha Baby Boom must deal with a period and with a major set of social phenomena that, in addition to being reconstructed after the fact through nostalgia in the popular imagination, are in reality very complex. In one sense, the era can be seen as pivotal for those that followed it, because some of the values, norms and even behaviours that have since driven family life were laid down at that time. While the period up until 1945 created the foundations of New Zealand family life, as was stressed in earlier chapters, many aspects were to be continued, even reinforced, during the Baby Boom. Yet viewed over the New Zealand family's long-term history, other trends in this era were major diversions that led to a cul-de-sac. Patterns that might have seemed at the time to point a clear route to the future, to presage or even prescribe what would follow, turned out to be ephemerae. Most notable of these was the very factor that gave the Baby Boom its name: rates of parenting. The years from the 1880s to World War II had seen a long-term trend towards low fertility, a movement from which the Baby Boom departed rather dramatically, turning some aspects of family life on their head. But after this spectacular deviation from the previous reproductive regimes, the post-Baby Boom saw an almost total rejection of the patterns characterising the Boom, and the re-adoption of other childbearing patterns of the inter-war years that had been briefly flung to one side.

The Baby Boom certainly made a large imprint on New Zealand society and culture, for it was an era of major and fundamental changes in the residential pattern of families and thus of their structures. These coincided with huge shifts up and then down in Pakeha family sizes, and in the 1960s – and more so in the 1970s – leading to the Baby Bust, the subject of Chapters Six and Seven. The changes in Pakeha family size were accompanied, and some would say were led by, shifts in patterns of nuptiality. Crude marriage rates rose in 1936–40 and 'again in 1945–48, the latter being the primary cause of the so-called "Baby Boom"' of the early post-war period' (O'Neill 1985: 197). James O'Neill's argument is that the Baby Boom could almost as equally have been called a 'Marriage Boom' (see also Zodgekar 1980), because it saw a return not only to younger ages for childbearing but, closely linked to this, a reprise of the pattern of almost universal marriage at younger ages, last seen in the 1870s.

The post-war story had its immediate genesis in the Great Depression of the 1930s. As was noted in Chapters Three and Four, the Depression and the war bottled up the processes of family formation and radical changes in family structures. From about 1943 an upswing in fertility and marriage was evident, and can thus be considered the onset of the Baby Boom. But 1946 was the hinge year for the Baby Boom proper as it combined pre-Baby Boom and Baby Boom effects, composed of this bottling-up factor plus a shift in the force of reproduction to younger ages.

This era was notable not just because it saw the unfolding of a series of demographic events. Of great interest for the present exercise are its qualitative dimensions; the term Baby Boom is much more than a descriptor for a fertility trend. It denotes all dimensions of the family structure, life-ways surrounding family formation and the world in which those cohorts, the Boomers – born over a 20-year period in Europe and North America and over 30 years in New Zealand – were raised. It is this wider Baby Boom, the age-structural, residential, family status and living arrangement dimensions, and their social and economic co-variates, that are addressed in this chapter as well as the question of reproduction *per se*. Increased fertility was the determinant of larger birth cohort sizes and thus it is crucial that this aspect of the Baby Boom is properly documented, but it was the consequences of reproduction, the nurturing of this generation and the impact of their childhood and passage through adulthood, that was to be the more critical story.

As we have stressed already, within New Zealand the Baby Boom was a Pakeha phenomenon, although it was one Pakeha shared with their counterparts in Australia, North America and, perhaps, with Western Europe.[*]

---

[*] It will be argued in this chapter that the Baby Boom, as strictly defined, was a neo-European occurrence, not experienced by Western Europe.

In this period Maori were undergoing a different and in many ways an even more radical family restructuring that will be described below. But Maori and Pakeha share one major point in common: that the family demographic change during the three decades covered in this chapter saw ruptures with the family structures prevalent in the past, and the new structures were different from what was to follow.

Maori society was subject to a more extreme transformation at this time. The typical, rural-resident whanau of 1936 or 1945, in which family sizes even of the component units were large, had by the 1970s given way to the smaller, neolocal, nuclear Maori family of urban New Zealand. This benign-sounding description of a process that occurred over a very short period, from the 1940s to the 1960s, belies the significance of the radical changes this effected on every aspect of Maori society. Underlying their neolocalisation was a rural exodus, discussed here in terms of its the socio-economic context.

The Maori rural exodus and the Pakeha Baby Boom together determined all other aspects of their respective family and social lives in this period. In the long term they also constituted revolutions that made an impact on New Zealand society for the rest of the twentieth century and into the twenty-first.

Finally, the Baby Boom was not a uniquely New Zealand phenomenon but occurred in all WDCs, including Japan. Later in this chapter we question whether this term is appropriate for all populations to which it is often applied, using Pakeha New Zealand as our poster-child of a true Baby Boom. But, such caveats aside, something happened to increase fertility rates more or less simultaneously across the WDCs in the early post-World War II period. Thus here is another example of a co-terminous, transnational demographic mega-trend, the first case of which we drew attention to in Chapter Three in relation to the fertility decline at the end of the nineteenth century.

DATA SOURCES AND METHODS

The analyses in this chapter are derived from a richer data-base than that available for Chapters Three and Four. As was the case for those chapters, the separate web publication *A Demographic History of the New Zealand Family From 1840: Tables* provides detailed tables, in the main not previously published, and not included here in the text (Dharmalingam *et al.* 2007). Nevertheless, as is discussed elsewhere (Pool *et al.* 2007), by comparison with their peers overseas, New Zealand researchers face severe limitations, particularly for data relating to living arrangements. These data first became available from the census only in 1966, near the end of the period covered in this chapter. For that period they have been most systematically analysed by Cameron (1985b) and Pool (1986). But even data such as those on household incomes do not become available until after the Baby Boom. At least for Pakeha, however, given the maintenance of a gender division of labour within the family – the wife staying at home and the husband being the wage earner – individual incomes give some general notions of household levels and patterns.

The best and most consistently available data sources are still censuses and vital statistics that relate largely to aspects of family formation: essentially fertility and nuptiality.* For the Baby Boom, these sources include both census marital status data and information coming from birth and marriage (and divorce) registrations. Beyond these official sources there are also data coming from surveys, which provide wider perspectives on union formation, and on the timing and spacing of pregnancies. In general the Baby Boom period was not well documented by field research. But in 1967 there was a survey of women in a number of Wellington suburbs (N = 942, all Pakeha) with its sample drawn from women marrying as early as the 1920s. Its emphasis was on the timing and spacing of births rather than on other aspects of family structures and forms (Vosburgh 1978; a small-scale survey was also done in Auckland, see Keys 1969).

Vosburgh's pioneer study was subsequently elaborated by a detailed analysis of the timing and spacing of pregnancies (Sceats 1981), using retrospective data from a regional study in the Manawatu (Trlin and Perry 1981). This covered the Baby Boom period and she was also able to make a direct and methodologically robust cross-comparison with a Canadian regional study (Sceats-Pool 1976). That research has since been confirmed by retrospective data coming from the survey New Zealand Women: Family, Employment, Education (NZW:FEE), reaching back to the cohorts born from 1936 on, and composed of women who thus were parenting in the Baby Boom. In addition there have been two direct cross-comparisons relating to fertility, first with the United States (Morgan *et al.* 1998) and then with a range of other WDCs (Sceats 1999). A further cross-comparative (with Canada) study of marriage and cohabitation also touches on this period (Lapierre-Adamcyk *et al.* 1997).

The NZW:FEE and the follow-up New Zealand Family Formation Survey (NZFFS) (2001) have a wide range of data on Baby Boom family formation and other factors (see Pool *et al.* 2007). Moreover, both these studies (the 2001 sample to a lesser degree) have data on aspects of living arrangements, not just formal marriage but also cohabitation.† This chapter

---

* The latter variable, covering marriage and its dissolution (e.g. divorce), is complex both to measure and to interpret (see Pool *et al.* 2007).

† Both survey and census data record 'marriage' as reported by the respondent, and thus subject to either conscious or unconscious misreporting. In contrast, vital registration is a legal process and misreporting may be judged to be a misdemeanour, or even worse.

and those following draw on these surveys, which have already produced four monographs, numerous papers and a number of theses. The fourth monograph has seen these two data sets further exploited (Dharmalingam *et al.* 2004). Results presented here include a synthesis of aspects of the family size, age-structural and status dimensions and their determinants that can be analysed from NZW:FEE and NZFFS data, and cover the period from the late 1950s on (see Pool *et al.* 1999). In this chapter and in the following ones we also have included results from the two surveys not published elsewhere (see also Dharmalingam *et al.* 2007).

The analysis of retrospective survey data permits the researcher to follow the family history or 'career', as it is sometimes called, of an individual respondent whose data file has been 'anonymised' to protect confidentiality. This significantly increases the power of analyses by allowing a wide range of innovative statistical techniques to be applied. Two must be mentioned here in passing as they are frequently employed in this book, and are important as they provide robust results on family formation and other aspects. First, results from what are called life-table techniques will be cited for they produce results in the form of probabilities that are free from the statistical biases termed 'censoring'. These occur because the interview itself intervenes, as it were, in an ongoing family career and thus the survey censors out any event which might occur after the research is finished. This means that data on respondents from different cohorts that are part way through their family career (or any other pattern of behaviour that unfolds over time) can be included up until the time when the data were captured.*

Secondly, at times in this chapter and those that follow the source research on which we draw will have employed analyses using 'proportional hazards models'. These are conventional statistical techniques that take life-table probabilities and apply a variant of regression techniques to them to allow a multi-variate analysis of the determinants of trends.

It must be stressed that these methods provide results that are free of age-compositional effects. As age is a prime determinant of most family career events, this is critical. Often we will merely quote results from research, allowing the reader to go back to the original source to look at the data in detail (some previously unpublished are in Dharmalingam *et al.* 2007).

---

* An alternative strategy is sometimes used here: it 'truncates' data, comparing like with like (e.g. women having a birth before 30 years for all cohorts aged 30 years and over). This technique is simpler to carry out but is wasteful as it cannot include those respondents who are only part way through a particular stage in their life-cycle path.

The published literature on this period is rather limited and the most systematic deals with the size, age and status aspects of structure, but there is little on living arrangements. Once again, as for the previous period, for Pakeha this study draws primarily on the works of Jacoby (1958, 1961), Gibson (1971), Jones (1971), Jain (1972), Vosburgh (1978), O'Neill (1985), Khawaja (1985) and Sceats and Pool (1985). For Maori, the most systematic national source is by Pool (1991). May's (1992) study gives us an insight into post-war Pakeha family dynamics, and surveys on urban (Society for Research on Women 1972) and rural women (Gill *et al.* 1976) provide some insights on women at the very end of the Baby Boom period. We have also drawn on the work of historians (e.g. Labrum 2004, Nolan 2000) as they throw light on important contextual factors.

From the late Baby Boom, cross-national data become more readily available, both through the auspices of the United Nations Population Division's publications and from various national statistical offices (UN various years; see unpublished sources at the end of the bibliography). More recently the United Nations Economic Commission for Europe's Family and Fertility Study (ECE/FFS), of which the NZW:FEE is an associate member, has published standard country reports that for a number of countries give data stretching back to the Baby Boom years (see ECE/FFS in the bibliography, for details; NZ's monograph in this series is listed under Johnstone *et al.* 2001).

5.2 CHANGES IN FAMILY MORPHOLOGIES, 1945–1973

OVERALL CHANGES

This period was dominated by the Pakeha Baby Boom that first saw family sizes increase and with them birth cohort numbers. Birth cohort numbers peaked twice and decreased twice, the second time definitively. Along with this, the age at which the formation of conjugal union takes place, in this case marriage and not consensual union, shifted to very young ages, and thus had the effect of significantly changing the age-structural dimension of families. Beyond this, the Baby Boom was the era, *par excellence*, of the neolocal nuclear family. Both Maori and Pakeha followed this broad trend, but, as will be shown, there were also major differences.

In one sense there were two phases to the Pakeha Baby Boom. The first, in 1945 and especially in 1946, was really a family size catch-up, following the periods of low fertility in the Depression and war. The other, from then until the 1970s, was one in which large family sizes (relative, at least, with what went before and came after) became the norm. The Pakeha Baby Boom is such a defining feature of the twentieth-century family-scape that it is easy to overlook what was happening for Maori at this time.

As narrowly defined for technical demographic purposes, the Baby Boom was a Pakeha phenomenon; Maori fertility rates remained at the high levels they had been at prior to World War II (see Figure 2.1; also Pool 1991: Tables 6.2, 7.1 and 7.2). But in 1945–46 the return of Maori troops from the war produced its own brief peak. The published CBR for this period and an adjusted rate for 1946 are presented in Table 5.1.

Table 5.1 illustrates several important general points. First, Maori rates were very high by international standards, and remained at the level shown here until the early 1960s. Secondly, the sudden peak in 1946 was in part due to the registration of births that had occurred as far back as the 1930s – the figure in parentheses adjusts for that – but shows that a 'returning-troops effect' was not restricted to Pakeha alone in 1946 and 1947. The reason for retrospective registration was so that Maori could obtain birth certificates and Maori children and their parents could receive welfare payments.* An echo of this effect will be seen later in relation to marriage registration.

Table 5.1: Maori Crude Birth Rates (per 1000 people), 1943–49, and the Adjusted Rate for 1946 (in parentheses)

Year	Rate
1943	46
1944	45
1945	46
1946	57 (49)
1947	48
1948	46
1949	45

Source: Pool 1977: Table 4.2.

In addition to the high fertility of this period, a rapid and co-terminous mortality decline from 1945 to 1961 saw Maori death rates tumble and fertility reach high levels. It will be recalled from Chapters Three and Four that 90–100 years earlier Pakeha population had also had very elevated levels of fertility that can be compared to benchmarks set by the Hutterites; after World War II it was the turn of Maori to reach towards the levels of hyper-fertility estimated for pioneer Pakeha women.

But it was the decrease in mortality in the early Baby Boom period that had the most impact on Maori family structures. As is normal when a high-

---

* The problem is that the CBR (57 per 1000 of the population) for that year was grossly exaggerated because the universal family benefit had just been introduced, replacing a means-tested measure that many eligible Maori had found difficult to access. For the new benefit, proof of birth was required, and thus Maori births previously unregistered from as far back as the 1930s were reported. Adjusting for this effect gives a rate of 49, which is still above the mean at that time (42–46 per 1000).

mortality population goes through a decline in death rates, the effects of mortality declines were most marked at younger ages, so that the Maori age and family structures took on the youthful shape that was their key feature over the succeeding decades. Because of improved survivorship, and that factor alone, the size of the age-group 0–4 years increased by 16% (for boys) and 20% (girls) between 1945 and 1961, thereby rapidly altering family age structures.

Thus birth rates were high, death rates (especially crude rates that were affected by age-compositional factors) were low and Maori rates of natural increase approached the 'biological maxima recently achieved by some of the fastest growing national populations, which have exceptionally high rates of fertility' (Pool 1991: 141, Tables 6.2 and 7.6; e.g. Kenya). For Maori by the 1960s mere demographic survival was no longer a high-priority family function.

At the very first stage of the Baby Boom, the age structures of New Zealand families were still undergoing change. While a size catch-up was occurring in 1946–47, the age patterns of Pakeha parenting families remained as in the pre-war period, Pakeha mothers and fathers often being the older parents pictured in Plunket handbook photos of the immediate post-war period. In contrast, Maori continued a long-standing cultural tradition of marrying early and having children at young ages. Nevertheless, for Pakeha, another pattern was starting to emerge around 1946 and was to produce the dramatic revolution of the rest of the Baby Boom. Increasingly, teenage and young-adult Pakeha were returning to the family formation patterns last seen in the pioneer period of the 1870s, so that, in a sense, the timing of Pakeha first births moved towards the pattern seen for Maori. From this baseline, the Baby Boom proper got under way.

This post-war period was one in which, despite high levels of inter-marriage, the two major ethnic groups pursued largely independent existences, and thus they will be considered separately in this chapter. As will be shown, however, this period laid down the basis for increasing interaction.

NEOLOCAL NUCLEAR PAKEHA FAMILIES: FAMILY SIZES AND AGE STRUCTURES

The initial phase of the Pakeha Baby Boom saw radical family size changes occur. Fertility rates went up at every single age-group (Khawaja 1985: Fig. 22), but shortly after this they declined again at older ages (compare the indices for 1946 and 1951 in Dharmalingam *et al.* 2007: Tables 3.7 and 3.8). If one scans the entire Baby Boom until 1973, the peak rates were reached at older reproductive ages at the very beginning, about 1945–46. In contrast, for what was the real Baby Boom and not merely a returning-troops effect, rates increased steadily at younger ages: until around 1960 for women aged 20–24 years, and until as late as 1970 for teenagers. At ages 25 and over the rates that had peaked around 1945–46 dropped back a bit and then plateaued until about 1960, only to decline significantly in the 1960s.

The early Baby Boom was thus still showing residual effects of the regime that had endured from about the 1880s, when conceptions later in the reproductive span, often unwanted, were commonplace simply because adequate means of *limitation* were not available once desired family sizes had been reached. But in the later Baby Boom this was dramatically dispensed with, and reproductive strategies favouring early to very early *timing* of first childbearing, and limitation thereafter, were to dominate. It is not clear whether this involved a shift in norms and values, or simply that the availability for the first time ever, especially to married couples, of a truly effective means of contraception, the Pill, allowed more certainty in terminating childbearing once two to three children had been born. This point will be picked up in detail later, but the impression remains that, in New Zealand more than elsewhere, the drive in the Baby Boom and into the Baby Bust, at least as indicated by life-table probabilities by age of mother and by order of birth (*parity*) of the babies born to them, and the intervals between births (*spacing*), was to get childbearing over and out of the way quickly (Sceats 1981, where Canada and New Zealand are compared using regional studies, Ottawa and the Manawatu; also 1988, which looks at contextual values). This norm may even have continued into the twenty-first century because in New Zealand birth intervals, controlling for the age of the woman and her parity, are still shorter than in other WDCs for which there are comparable data (Sceats 1999; Morgan *et al.* 2001; both use NZW: FEE national data to confirm Sceats's earlier work).

The force of early reproduction in this period cannot be exaggerated: it was more extreme than for any period for which age-specific rates can be computed. In 1971 the ratio of the number of births at 20–24 years to those at 35–39 years reached 8.4 times (21, 124: 2, 510). By contrast, before and since the ratios have been much lower (e.g. 1.8 times in 1931 and even less than that, at 0.8, in 2001) (see Table 3.4b).

The nuptiality valve was still operating in the Baby Boom: early marriage was linked to pre-nuptial conception, or was followed quickly by conception, but in this the precocious childbearing of Baby Boom parents even surpassed that of the pioneers. Recalling that almost all births in the nineteenth century were nuptial, precocity can be judged by comparing data on ages at marriage for the period 1870s to 1945 with those for the Baby Boom.

The dynamics producing early reproduction among Pakeha can be further detailed from survey data (see Dharmalingam *et al.* 2007: Table 5.1; in this chapter and those that follow we present data from survey analyses, some of which results were computed specially for this book). Life-table probabilities of having a first birth by ages 20–25 years were high for the cohorts born in 1936–49 and 1950–59. These cohorts comprised women who would have been teenagers in the late 1960s and early 1970s, and thus at the upper margins of the Baby Boom parenting generation.

In the Baby Boom proper, the proportions of Pakeha women who had married at young ages was very high (Dharmalingam *et al.* 2007: Tables 3.2, 5.3). But it is also important to note that the proportions of each female cohort who remained never married at age-group 30–44 years had also dropped radically. This provides very strong documentation of the effects of early and near universal marriage.

Beyond this, the levels for those already married at young ages were high by international standards, so that the reality for Pakeha youth almost matched the themes of pubescent love portrayed in the 'high-school sweet-hearts/only sixteen/teenage queen' popular songs of the 1950s and 1960s. Recalling that most New Zealand school pupils of the day left school soon after they turned fifteen, many a girl had started a first job, dated, frequently become pregnant and married, or married and become pregnant, all before she received the prototypical twenty-first-birthday present of the day, a key to the front door of her parents' home.

The rush to marriage was not just restricted to the very young; one's heart goes out to the fathers of Baby Boom brides for often they paid in rapid succession for the weddings of both their older daughters and their own adolescent younger sisters. Earlier on, in particular, weddings had to be furnished both for older cohorts of women who had postponed marriage in their early twenties (e.g. those born 1912–16 who were aged 20–24 in the 1930s), as well as those who reached early adult ages in the Baby Boom and who married at younger and younger ages (Dharmalingam *et al.* 2007: Tables 3.2 and 3.6). As James O'Neill has documented so vividly, 'Between 1945 and 1971 the proportion of ever-married females aged 15–19 more than doubled, those aged 20–24 increased by 73%, and those 25–29 by 17%' (O'Neill 1979: 132; also 1985; see also Olsen and Levesque 1978: 8).

These nuptiality rates surpassed even those of the pioneer period, as comparisons made between 1876 and 1976 in Chapter Three showed. Despite almost universal secondary-school attendance in the Baby Boom, teen-age marriage rates exceeded those seen in the pioneer period in 1876 when compulsory schooling had not yet been introduced,* yet Baby Boom women

---

* A whole genre of North American literature on the family written around the 1960s and 1970s focused on homogamy (e.g. by social status of the brides' and grooms' parents/religion/ethnic origin), and saw high schools and colleges/universities, and associated activities like dating and high-school balls, as a means of ensuring that this occurred. In this context, much of the mainstream family sociology of that day seems quaint from today's perspective. The widening of entry intakes into expensive and/or prestigious United States universities has increased the probability of exogamous marriages, although measured by educational status they may still be endogamous.

were marrying men just a year or two older than they were (2.6 years), not men significantly older (6.1) as had been the case in the pioneer period. Moreover, this pressure on the marriage market occurred despite the fact that any surplus of marriageable males had virtually disappeared by the Baby Boom (Neville 1985; Table 23). This situation points to the importance of latent forces, probably the existence of norms and values that were profound and that went back to the pioneer period, and quite possibly through the early colonial period further back to pre-Victorian Britain norms described in Chapter Three.

Nevertheless, the end of the Baby Boom was also to mark the terminal point for the transmission of some conjugal norms and values, and their associated behaviours. It was the last period in which the family forms that had come down from the nineteenth century were not merely the modal type of conjugal union, but almost the only sort. As was detailed in Chapters Three and Four, in the 1870s, and this was also was the case in the Baby Boom, early and virtually universal registered marriage for women had been the norm. Moreover, at the end of both these eras there was then a shift to a later age for the onset of formal marriages. But at that point the similarities cease. If the term nuptiality valve is restricted to legal marriage, as this status was defined in the nineteenth and twentieth centuries, then in the 1880s and 1890s and continuously thereafter until World War II, the nuptiality valve had operated only in two ways. These were a shift to later marriage, with almost all unions formally registered, and a significant minority of women not marrying at all, with most of them probably not forming unions of any sort, formal or consensual – we know this because of the low level of ex-nuptial childbearing in an era in which contraception was imperfect. At the end of the Baby Boom there was also a shift to later registered marriage, but, in contrast, participation at young ages in a union of whatever type did not suddenly cease. Instead the type of first union favoured at young ages moved from formal marriage to consensual cohabitation. This can be illustrated and contextualised more exactly from NZW:FEE data, which also permit the examination of another key point: entry into any form of union, marriage or cohabitation.

For women aged younger than 20 years, the probabilities of commencing any form of first union were actually *lower* in the Baby Boom than would be the case in the Baby Bust that followed it, but were as high or higher by age 25 (this issue will be discussed further in Chapter Six, see Figures 6.1 and 6.2). But the difference between the Baby Boom and its successor the Baby Bust was that, in the period 1946–73, formation of the first union essentially took the form of marriage. The probabilities of becoming married at young ages peaked in the periods 1960–69 and 1970–79 and then dropped off (Dharmalingam *et al.* 2004: Table 2.4). During the Baby Boom, levels of cohabitation had been low by comparison with what occurred later, although rates were starting to edge up in the 1960s (Dharmalingam *et al.* 2004: Table 2.7). When cohabitation properly speaking did occur in the Baby Boom (defined in NZW:FEE as a consensual union lasting for three months or more, as against pre-marital encounters), it typically led to marriage with the same partner after a relatively short duration (see Carmichael 1984). Dissolution of a consensual union, as against conversion to marriage, was less common at that time, but was to become more frequent later (see Dharmalingam *et al.* 2004: Table 2.8). In sum, marriage was by far the preferred form of first union for the cohort of 1936–49, who were the Baby Boom couples, but for that of 1950–59, the cohorts born in the early Baby Boom who comprised the late Baby Boom/early Baby Bust couples, cohabitation was of equal significance for a first union, and thereafter, for the true Baby Bust couples, cohabitation far outran marriage (drawn from Dharmalingam *et al.* 2007: Tables 5.2, 5.3, 5.4, 5.5 and 5.6).

In terms of Pakeha patterns of nuptiality, therefore, the Baby Boom represents a critical turning point. As had been true in pre-war decades, in the Baby Boom marriage and marital status were still factors critical to family structures and forms. Exposure to intercourse, the probability of conception and thus family sizes were determined to a significant degree by marital status. While this held true in the Baby Boom, the decline in the age at marriage and the increases in the proportions marrying produced the 'Marriage Boom' that drove the Baby Boom. But, as just discussed, a new factor was emerging. This was the shift to cohabitation as a preferred form of first union, the age-specific probabilities of which later, at least until the 1990s (see later chapters), were to rival the first-marriage rates for teenagers and young adults recorded in the Baby Boom.

This changeover in Pakeha marriage patterns in the late 1960s and into the 1970s, from registered to consensual forms for first union, represented, therefore, a revolutionary shift in the determinants of reproduction. Prior to this time, risks of conception had depended on being married (or marrying quickly in the case of a pre-nuptial pregnancy) plus fertility regulation within marriage using techniques of limited efficacy.[*] In the 1970s, contraception, sterilisation and, to a lesser degree, abortion were to replace these two strategies as the means of birth control, regardless of the marital status of the woman or couple. This shift from Stage Two to Stage Three of the family transition is very important and will be returned to later. Nevertheless, one key point needs to be stressed here: marital status, which in the

---

[*] In demographic dictionaries (e.g. Grebenik and Hill 1974) 'efficacy' is defined as the probability of conception in any inter-menstrum, *when contraception is being employed*. Thus it is the inverse of 'fecundability', defined earlier to mean the probability of conception when no conscious effort is being made to control births.

past and over much of the Baby Boom was a factor of critical importance for both structures and forms, became from the 1970s on predominantly a determinant of family forms in terms of statuses. From the dying days of the Baby Boom it would no longer be the driver of family structures nor a pre-determinant of family formation.

SETTING UP THE BABY BOOM NEST

This was also a period during which younger and younger Pakeha couples in registered marriages took up neolocal residence, filling the rapidly developing new suburbs that were largely dependent for commuting on the internal combustion engine (car or bus). This took them out beyond the prototypes of suburbs developed in the inter-war years, when the tram or ferry was the more likely form of transport, into the new suburbia such as those, for example, edging up the Hutt Valley, Wellington, or beyond Mt Albert Rd in Auckland's Mt Roskill. The geographical setting of these new commuting zones constituted the theatre in which was played out the rest of the Pakeha Baby Boom, involving the increase and then the decrease of family sizes; as early as the 1956 census, for example, there was a distinct difference in Auckland between the commuting zones with higher female child/woman ratios, and the long-established areas with low ratios (Pool 1959a: Vol. 2, 23). This occurred, as noted already, through younger and younger parenting, yet was achieved by couples who throughout the period, although very young in age, lived independently away from their own parents, in neolocal nuclear families. Because most of the newly married adolescent or young-adult couples of the period were separated residentially from their families, home ownership levels (with or without mortgages) were extremely high, as is seen in Table 4.1 (see also Cameron 1985b). This issue is returned to later in this chapter.

It is the image of this neolocally resident, young married Pakeha couple that has been passed down as the quintessential Baby Boom family, and which has fashioned popular attitudes on what family structures should look like. This image combines all dimensions of Pakeha family structures and forms at that time: size, age structures, statuses and living arrangements. Thus,

> We tend to reconstruct [the Baby Boom] in a somewhat idealised form: a happily married [Pakeha] couple in their early to mid-twenties, with two well-adjusted offspring. Somewhat unexpectedly several years later they will conceive a third child, who will become the darling of its older siblings. This Baby Boom couple may have lived in a three-bedroom house, say in Te Atatu or Stokes Valley [i.e. in neolocal residence in the new, automobile-era commuting zones], and there performed their parenting with mother a leading light in Plunket or the local kindy association, and father away as the

breadwinner. Of course such a retrospective picture selectively overlooks the moral panics of yesteryear which produced inter alia, the Mazengarb Commission of the early Baby Boom [on juvenile delinquency in the Hutt Valley, a quintessential Baby Boom suburban development] (Pool 1996: 12).

As May shows us, however, the seeds of later radical changes were being laid down even in the early days of the Baby Boom; the ideal may not always have been the reality. 'The exaggerated emphasis on family life in the post war period [was] a legacy of contradictory experiences [during the war] . . . a new political and personal consciousness of women's abilities generated by the war existed alongside the support for separate spheres for men and women' (May 1992: 43).

Moreover, the clear gendered division of labour essential for this reconstructed model to work may have been less perfectly delineated in practice. The historian Melanie Nolan has pointed to a contradiction: 'The state's [and the society's] emphasis on women's domesticity in the post-war period is legendary . . . [Yet its] post-war labour market policy encouraged women into paid employment and, in doing so, further undermined the male breadwinner wage and modified idealised concepts of motherhood'. She notes that the proportion of women in paid employment declined in the early Baby Boom. This is hardly surprising, given the rapid shift to a much younger age for marriage and pregnancy – women essentially shifted from productive to reproductive activities. Against this, however, is an interesting counterpoint: 'the participation rates of married women and of Maori women were rising steadily [in this same period] . . . the most striking change for both Maori and Pakeha women was the steady post-war rise in the participation rate of married women, especially in part-time work . . . From 1951 two groups in particular entered paid employment: younger wives (aged under 25) and older married women' (Nolan 2000: 192, 205–6, Table 220). These latter trends do provide a hint of what was to come in the later Baby Boom and beyond, yet perhaps they do not represent as radical a break with domesticity as they might first seem: these were women who had not yet started, or had finished, childbearing, a function that terminated at a very early age during the peak Baby Boom years. The growth of paid employment among Maori women is also not so surprising: in 1936, when rates were very low, they had resided mainly in rural communities away from significant labour markets. Rapid post-war urbanisation dramatically improved their access to far wider range of sectors and workplaces (Pool 1991: 151–53; see also Davies 1993).

Family sizes not only increased in this period, as was shown in Figure 2.1, reaching a peak TFR of 4.15 births per woman in 1961 (Khawaja 1985: Fig. 21), but childbearing was compressed into the youngest age-groups, and fewer families had no dependent children by comparison with the pre-war period (O'Neill 1979: 133; also see Dharmalingam *et al.* 2007: Tables 3.7, 3.8, 4.2 and 4.3). Parenting became almost universal, timing early and birth intervals short, closer than for Canada (Sceats 1981) or for the United States (Morgan *et al.* 2001). This established a pattern that was to continue into the 1990s. A detailed analysis of these cohorts shows that in this regard New Zealand differed from every other WDC in the United Nations ECE/FFS survey for which there were comparable data (Sceats 1999: 32).

This point can be illustrated by reference to Table 5.2, showing data on the timing of the first birth, and highlighting the weighting towards the early reproductive ages. Typically, Pakeha births were nuptially born, but often in the Baby Boom they had also been ex-nuptially conceived, especially in the case of teenage nuptial births. For the Pakeha birth cohort of 1936–49, more than three-quarters of all teen first births were ex-nuptially conceived, and only 23% were conceived after marriage. But pre-marital conception most commonly resulted in a birth within marriage: 48% of all babies to teenage mothers were born 'maritally', after a marriage had legitimated the pregnancy. In contrast, 83% of births to women over age 20 were conceived and born after marriage. For the next cohort, that of 1950–59, the odds had changed for teenage conceptions: only 22% of such first births were conceived after marriage, but the proportion legitimated by marriage had dropped to 33%. At 20 years and over, however, their odds were similar to those for the preceding cohort of women. For later cohorts, to be considered in the next two chapters, percentages of births to teenage women who were cohabiting, or outside a union, comprised 80–90% of all births to women in this age-group. Even after age 20 years, this proportion had reached 25% for the birth cohort of 1960–69 (the most recent available data) (Dharmalingam *et al.* 2004: Table 4.3).

Table 5.2: Life-table Estimates of the Cumulative Proportion of Women Having a First Birth Before a Given Age

| Birth cohort of | Before age | | |
	20 years	25 years	30 years
1936–49	0.15	0.60	0.84
1950–59	0.18	0.52	0.75
1960–69	0.14	0.42	–
1970–79	0.14	–	–

Note: These data relate to both Maori and Pakeha.
Source: Dharmalingam *et al.* 2007: Table 5.1, from Dharmalingam *et al.* 2004: Table 4.1.

Not only did the timing of Pakeha births move to young ages, but spacing, the interval between births, shortened (see Dharmalingam *et al.* 2007: Table 5.7). At the peak of the Baby Boom 57% of women who had delivered a first live birth would have had a second birth within two years, and most (80%) by three years. In later periods these percentages dropped markedly: 25% in the late 1980s had a second birth within two years and only 54% within 36 months. As was the case with timing, New Zealand families stand out in these cross-cultural analyses for their short birth intervals (Sceats 1981, 1999; Morgan *et al.* 2001).

The net result also was a shift downward in the age of parenting families. This downwardly weighted age structure of family life was very frequently a function of the early timing of births within marriage because of ex-nuptial conception, or by conception very soon thereafter (Dharmalingam *et al.* 1996, 1997, 2004; Morgan *et al.* 2001).

Much of the Pakeha ex-nuptial conception occurred in adolescence. To a large degree it was this factor that made this, in fact, the great era of teenage childbearing, the rates for which increased to reach a peak near the end of the Baby Boom, at least for the twentieth century and probably ever, in Pakeha New Zealand. In the highest year (1971) the level was 0.305 births per woman under age 20 (Pool and Crawford 1980). That is, there was a 30% likelihood that during her adolescence a woman would have a baby. By the end of the Baby Boom (1976) there were still over 8000 births a year to adolescent women, half of them nuptially born, many of whom had been ex-nuptially conceived, about one-seventh of all births that year. But by 1994 this had dropped to only 4822 births to teenage mothers, only one twelfth of the total born (Pool *et al.* 1998: Table 3).

DIVERGENT EX-NUPTIAL OUTCOMES; CONVERGENT COMPLETED
FAMILY SIZES

Of course, not all ex-nuptially pregnant young women rushed into marriage. But in this era the most typical alternative was adoption (Sceats 1988b: *passim*). Belich reports that over the short span of the 36 years from 1944 to 1980 (during and immediately after the Baby Boom) 87,000 adoptions occurred, on average 2416 per year; in contrast, over the much longer period of 63 years, from 1881 to 1944, only 16,000 were placed in this way, the number per year, 254, a tenth of the Baby Boom average (Belich 2001: 505). Most of these children would have been born ex-nuptially, and most going through legal adoption would have been Pakeha. While adoptions did occur for Maori, most were within families, often of births conceived by single women who were living away from home in larger urban areas.

In making this comparison, there is clearly a need to control for the size of the birth cohort into which the adopted baby was born, but even then the Baby Boom stands out. Taking birth numbers from tables and graphs in Mansoor Khawaja's paper on trends (1985: Table 73, Fig. 21) it is possible to get a rough estimate of cohort sizes. What is surprising is how these numbers remained relatively stable within each of the two periods 1880–1944 and the Baby Boom, but differed between them: a guess would put the numbers around 22,000 on average from 1881 to 1944, and about 48,000 between 1944 and 1980. Prior to the Baby Boom, then, about 1% of the annual stock of babies would have been adopted out; but in the Baby Boom this had shot up fivefold to one in every twenty babies.*

In 1970, at the end of this era, a team of officials in the Department of Social Welfare headed by David O'Neill wrote a very competent, detailed review entitled *Ex-Nuptial Children and Their Parents* based on research relating to the 8332 ex-nuptial births occurring that year. This remarkable study covered a very wide range of variables. As just noted, this was still an era in which adoption was common, so 30% of the ex-nuptial births, 2499, just above the average figure for that time estimated in the last paragraph, were 'placed' (as the parlance of the day has it) in good homes. About the same proportion were living with a mother who was a sole parent, and one-quarter with both parents, who were mainly cohabiting couples, plus a small percentage who were married parents. Cohabiting parents of ex-nuptial children were likely to be older than those parents who did not cohabit. The cohabiting relationships were likely to be less stable than legal marriages, but to some degree this was because one of the partners 'had experienced a prior legal marriage' (O'Neill *et al.* 1976: 324 and *passim*). This finding equates with the experience, for example, in the United States (e.g. Rindfuss and Van den Heuvel 1990; Cherlin 1990; Bumpass *et al.* 1991).

The end of the Baby Boom saw a very significant change in this pattern, a point that will be discussed in later chapters. Suffice to say here that the point of inflection at which this occurred was so important that it could be taken as one of the key markers of the closure of the Baby Boom. It could be identified by a radical shift towards women keeping their babies, yet not marrying hastily between the infant's conception and its birth.

Seemingly paradoxical is another, more important trend: a convergence in family formation patterns. This made the Baby Boom qualitatively different from the period that preceded it, when reproductive polarisation was marked, and from the decades since when differences have reappeared. The Baby Boom saw the virtual elimination of the major demographically determined differentials: family sizes and by age. Of course, a significant ethnic difference (Maori/Pakeha) continued. This remained at two to three

---

* In the earlier Baby Boom the proportions of ex-nuptial births adopted out were probably much higher. If we accept the figure of 5% of all births, and that adoptees were mainly ex-nuptially born, then, in 1962, for example, about 50% of children born outside marriage would have been adopted. Many of the remaining ex-nuptial births would have been Maori, often to unions that were sanctioned in the community but that had not been formalised through registered marriage (Pool 1977: 87–88, drawing in particular on the work of anthropologist Joan Metge).

births per woman even at the peak of the Pakeha Baby Boom, when Pakeha TFRs briefly touched four, but Maori rates were 6.2, and possibly higher (cf. Khawaja 1985: Table 77; Pool 1991: Table 6.2). In passing it is worth noting that for Maori not only were fertility rates high, but, not surprisingly, differentials were limited. These were to open up only in the 1970s (Pool 1991: Chapt. 8).

As shown in earlier chapters, there had been rural–urban differences in Pakeha fertility in the period between the 1880s and World War II. A survey of rural women at the end of the Baby Boom showed that mean ages at first marriage and at first birth had been lower for rural women than for all women in the early decades of the twentieth century, and that this continued for patterns of marriage in the Depression years. But in the Baby Boom these differences all but disappeared (Gill *et al.* 1976: 43–44).

The Manawatu survey executed in 1978, but relating mainly to patterns built up cumulatively in the Baby Boom, showed limited differentials. Most commonly these were Maori/Pakeha but even this was not systematic. In fact, Maori and Pakeha levels were similar for some key reproductive variables: sterilisation and desired family size (Trlin and Perry 1981: Appendices).

Within urban areas at the height of the Baby Boom there were some geographical differences in marital and overall fertility, as might be expected. But in Auckland, for example, these were largely a function of the clustering of younger Maori and Pasifika families in the central areas adjacent to the CBD (e.g. Freeman's Bay), and Maori, Pasifika and Pakeha families in the new rapidly growing suburban areas. Survey data show that, once marital duration was controlled for, socio-economic and socio-cultural differences were rather limited, with the exception of those between Pakeha and ethnic minorities (Keys 1969: *passim*). The differences in child/woman ratios between the central city and the new suburbs noted earlier for Auckland was a function not of fertility *per se*, but that families at reproductive ages had located themselves in the commuter zones.

This allows a very important conclusion to be made. Putting aside differences between, on the one hand, Pakeha and, on the other, Maori and Pacific peoples, it seems that the reproductive polarisation that occurred earlier in the century, and that was to occur later, was not a major feature of the Baby Boom years. This lack of reproductive polarisation for Pakeha was associated with a return to higher fertility, largely determined by operating the nuptiality valve to produce early and almost universal marriage.

A new feature was that, in contrast with the 1870s, fewer couples chose to have a birth in the later part of their reproductive spans and thus the Baby Boom did not result in the hyper-fertility of the pioneer period. In this dimension of family life, as in some others, the Baby Boom started off almost as a replay of the pioneer period, then lost the plot part way through and thus did not perfectly imitate what had occurred for early colonial Pakeha. The major difference came from the increasing availability of more efficient means of family limitation, a point to be picked up later in this chapter. But first a further look at the family forms of the Baby Boom is necessary.

NEOLOCAL NUCLEAR PAKEHA FAMILIES: FAMILY STATUSES

As noted earlier, detailed census data on some aspects of family forms are not available prior to the 1960s, but census marital status data in conjunction with vital registrations can be used to speculate about the missing pieces. They show that in the Baby Boom few women were divorced or separated, although a small but a visible minority of sole parents were widows. But this was the exception, for the Baby Boom neolocal family was very much one composed of a married couple and their children.

To take a pivotal age-group for family statuses, 45–49 years, in 1936, 1956 and 1976 the number of widows remained relatively similar: 3200–3500. In the same age-group there were 1160 divorced or separated women in 1936, 1951 in 1956, and still only 4187 in 1976, after the Baby Boom. In 1936, widows in this age-group had outnumbered divorced and separated women by 3.2 to one, in 1956 by 1.5 to one, and in 1976 there were still 78 widows for every 100 divorced and separated women at this age.

Registration data support this. Divorce rates remained low for much of the Baby Boom, starting to increase only at the end of the 1960s (McPherson 1995: Fig. 1; also McLuskey 1999; O'Neill 1985). In part this was because of a law change: the Matrimonial Proceedings Amendment Act of 1968. Major increases in levels of divorce came in the period to be covered in the next chapter.

Thus divorce levels were low *during* the Baby Boom, but this did not mean that the couples marrying then escaped marital breakdown and dissolution. Rather, 20% of all women belonging to the cohorts married prior to 1970 had been separated before fifteen years of marriage, and one-quarter by their twentieth anniversary. But for most this meant divorce *after* the Baby Boom had come to an end and, typically, when the couple was at later parenting ages (Dharmalingam *et al.* 2007: Table 5.8). The Baby Boom was remarkably successful in covering over its cracks. These often appeared only in subsequent years when they were frequently attributed to events, 'family breakdown', occurring at the time rather than to the true underlying causes.

Among the most critical determinants of an eventual divorce were whether women had married at a young age, and were pregnant at the time of marriage or very shortly thereafter (Dharmalingam *et al.* 1998a; see also 2007: Table 5.8). Thus the upsurge of divorces over the last two and a half decades of the twentieth century was determined in part by patterns of family building that had typified the golden era of family life, the Baby Boom.

A high percentage of women who separated did re-partner, especially those who had separated at younger ages. Sole parenting was more likely among more recent birth cohorts of women, and when it did occur it was most likely among those who had their births during adolescence. These women were not, however, likely to remain sole parents for more than three years. It is important to note an oft-forgotten truth, that sole parenting is a fluid situation, not some status set in stone (Pool and Moore 1986), and in most cases it certainly is not a lifetime status. Many currently married persons become sole parents, many sole parents may form other unions and, as the task of sole parenting infers the nurturing of dependent offspring, most sole parents will eventually see their children leave the nest. In terms of re-partnering, there is little difference between Baby Boom and later cohorts in the propensity to form blended families after separation (Dharmalingam *et al.* 2004: Tables 3.4, 5.1, 5.2, 5.3 and Chapt. 6).

In some ways, during the Pakeha Baby Boom separated or divorced sole parents were the trend-setters of that era. The situation had been rarer, at least as reported, in the pre-war period – in earlier chapters we did note the fact that some women who reported themselves as married may have been abandoned temporarily or permanently, while in both wars many women saw their soldier-spouses depart for spells of varying length. But in minor ways Baby Boom sole parents were a little different from those who were to follow them. They were more likely to be in professional or semi-professional occupations, and they were often older than was true later (Dharmalingam *et al.* 2004: Tables 5.5 and 5.9).

Ex-nuptiality as a family status has already been covered when looking at family formation. In the Baby Boom the status 'ex-nuptial birth' or 'ex-nuptial mothering' was less frequent for Pakeha than it was to become, but this apparently low rate obscured the reality of what was actually happening. The high incidence of pre-marital conception followed by a precipitated rush to gain 'married' status, typically in a church service, and thus to ensure that the child was 'legitimate' was a remarkable re-run of patterns long established in Pakeha society. For Maori the counterpoint between nuptial and ex-nuptial was dictated by a different set of circumstances that will be discussed later in this chapter.

NEOLOCAL NUCLEAR PAKEHA FAMILIES: LIVING ARRANGEMENTS AND RESIDENTIAL PATTERNS

In terms of the effects of family formation on wider family structures, the early marriages and parenting of the Baby Boom also involved newly-weds quitting their families of origin at a very young age. They purchased detached houses and set up neolocal residence as largely independent nuclear families. Thus the extended Pakeha family of the pre-war period, with its adult offspring members, gave way to two nuclear parenting families: the older generation with its remaining dependent children, plus the neolocal couple and their young children. That said, in a Christchurch study in the 1970s carried out by the sociologist Peggy Koopman-Boyden, some 24% of the elderly were living with others, usually family. Moreover, this same study showed that 43% had siblings in the urban area and 72% had children. In short, neolocality did not eliminate intergenerational contacts (Koopman-Boyden 1978: 58). Furthermore, kinship still served many functions. Toynbee (2000) shows, for example, that between 1947 and 1974 economic factors were a prime consideration for Scots deciding to migrate to New Zealand, but their decision was mediated by kinship links.

Until the early to mid-1970s single offspring usually stayed at home until they married, while those forced by jobs to live away from home boarded or stayed in hostels. But by the end of this period the expansion of tertiary education meant that increasing numbers were leaving the family nest and living in households of non-related people, as had always been the case for a small minority of people at university. A further erosion of the large pre-war family structure saw households less likely to include among their members kin or lodgers (Olssen and Levesque 1978: 19).*

The first glimpses of what living arrangements were like in the Baby Boom come from censuses at the end of the era, in 1966, 1971 and 1976 (Cameron 1985b; Pool 1986; Jackson and Pool 1994; Dickson *et al.* 1997; summary data on the living arrangements of households at this time are presented in Dharmalingam *et al.* 2007: Tables 5.9 and 5.10). Moreover, these data are probably representative of much of the early Baby Boom. This can be inferred from the fact that, by comparison with the period following 1976, there were minimal changes to household arrangements between 1966 and 1976. In 1966, 64% of households were parenting (i.e. they had a dependent child aged sixteen years or younger), but this had decreased to 58% by 1976. The number of households of all forms increased more than those that were parenting families (by 28%, as against 18%). This trend was a prelude to what was to become a major set of shift-shares from 1976 on.

This was, however, still the great era of neolocal parenting in nuclear families. Over the entire decade 1966 to 1976 the proportion of all households that were two-parent families was very high, at just under half of the total, although there is a three-percentage point decrease in this category over

---

* It will be recalled that Toynbee's (1995) research documented the shallowness of kinship roots in Pakeha society. But adversity seems to have forced some re-assessment and thus a resort to kin. The intergenerational, grandparent–parent link is a special case of kin contact, as is that of siblings.

that decade. The only other change of such magnitude was a decrease in the 'family plus others' households, a form of household that will be discussed in later chapters. In contrast, as a prelude to the Baby Bust period from the 1970s to the late 1980s, couple-only households increased by two percentage points, as did one-person households. Sole-parent households remained at 5–6% of the total in the period 1966–76 but, as was noted above, these would have been as much a reflection of widowhood as of divorce and separation.

These data show, however, that there have always been Pakeha sole-parent households. Moreover their contribution to the total did not become dramatically higher in the period after the Baby Boom – it grew by only three to four percentage points over the entire period from 1966–71 to 2001 (Dharmalingam *et al.* 2007: Table 5.9). Thus the statistical evidence does not fit comfortably with popular perceptions of a blow-out in sole-parent numbers that is often cited as an indicator of the breakdown of the family. This politically sensitive topic will be returned to in later chapters covering periods when it was central to the public policy discourse.

There were other minor changes in this period. A modest drop in the two-parent household category that came at the end of the Baby Boom was expected as an accompaniment of the declines in fertility occurring in the 1960s and 1970s, while an increase in proportions of couple-only families was the inverse trend. The decrease in the family-plus-others category was probably the end of the residual effects of the inter-war pattern of in having kin or lodgers in households (Olssen and Levesque 1978: 19).

The distribution of living arrangements then and since is due as much or more to a mix of demographic factors – family size, the timing of family formation, the age structure of parenting households in relation to the population's overall age structure, and the ethnic distribution of households – as it is a function of the way families choose to organise their living arrangements. In the Baby Boom period, for which there are data available only at a point just after it ended, New Zealand households were overwhelmingly Pakeha: 88%. Almost two-thirds of these Pakeha family units were parenting households and 84% of the parenting households were the nuclear family units today viewed as the classic Baby Boom Pakeha family. Pakeha families were proportionately represented or over-represented in most other household types, except for extended families (Dharmalingam *et al.* 2007: Tables 5.10 and 5.11, which tabulate 1976 data).

From 1976 on, however, all this changed. Through immigration (Asian and Pacific peoples) and through further fertility declines, the contribution of Pakeha decreased (Dharmalingam *et al.* 2007: Table 5.11). The shift-shares from then on, and the ethnic and age-structural drivers of these, will be discussed in later chapters.

MAORI AND PASIFIKA FAMILY MORPHOLOGIES

This part of the chapter focuses on Maori, but Pacific peoples began to make an appearance in New Zealand in significant numbers at the end of the Baby Boom and the first data available on them will be reviewed at the end of this section. Over the earlier part of the period 1943–73 Maori family sizes were very high – over six births per woman. From the early 1960s Maori fertility rates began to decline but were still around five at the end of the period reviewed in this chapter (Pool 1991: Chapts 7 and 8). But, as was noted earlier in the chapter, another factor played a significant role in shaping Maori family sizes and structures and in making them even younger. This was improved survivorship, the greatest force of which benefited infants and children. In 1945 of 100 Maori boys born alive only 81% would reach age fifteen years, and this was so for only 83% of Maori girls. In the entire Maori epidemiologic transition this was the period in which the most rapid improvements were made at the youngest ages (a normal attribute of the early stages of transition). Thus by 1966, 95% of boys and 96% of girls were reaching age fifteen (Pool 1991: 145; Pool 1994).

Levels of teenage fertility were very high in this period; 1962 had the highest rate for any year for which there are data. Since then Maori adolescent childbearing rates have gradually declined (Pool *et al.* 1998: Table 3). Methods of fertility regulation were becoming more efficient, especially with the widespread introduction of the Pill in the later years of the Baby Boom. For Maori, however, there was a lag, so that high uptake of more efficient techniques (the Pill, sterilisation, IUD) was held over until the 1970s. Thus for much of the Baby Boom period, for Maori of all ages, use of contraception remained very limited (Pool *et al.* 1999: especially Chapts 7 and 8).

Although differentials were lower in 1966 than they became in the 1970s, in the 1960s Maori family sizes as measured by age-standardised GFRs had been higher among rural than urban populations, an intuitively expected result. But by 1971 and 1976 the situation had reversed and urban family sizes were larger than rural. There were differences, however, within the Auckland and Wellington urban areas. The highest age-standardised rates anywhere were in surburban South Auckland, a pattern that was to persist until the 1990s and beyond (Pool 1991: Table 8.12, Fig. 9.2).

Census data show that Maori women married at a young age (Dharmalingam *et al.* 2007: Table 3.1). But Maori marital status data must be interpreted with some degree of caution because the processes by which marriages are sanctioned by family and the community differ between Maori and non-Maori. As noted in Chapters Three and Four, the process of registration was imported and grounded in one sub-culture, the British middle and administrative classes, who in turn essentially turned long-standing ecclesiastical procedures into civil law (Pool *et al.* 2007: Chapt. 2). Consequently, the 'formalisation of marriage through registration is often less immediately relevant to other [non-British ethnic] groups which have their own valid prescriptions for legitimating unions' (Pool and Sceats 1981: 52).

All this would be of little matter except that a difficulty arises when vital registration becomes embedded in the entire corpus of social policy, laws and regulations. This may have significant flow-on effects for individuals and couples, such as predetermining access to welfare state provisions. Many of these prerequisites have been gradually eliminated from welfare regulations, but some were still operating in the period after World War II. Thus the NZW:FEE data show that registered marriage for Maori peaked among the cohorts of women entering unions at that time, especially the late 1960s, being higher than for both earlier and more recent marriage cohorts (Lapierre-Adamcyk *et al.* 1997).

Not surprisingly, therefore, Maori who had ex-nuptial births, in the survey of ex-nuptial children and their parents noted earlier, were more likely to cohabit than were their Pakeha peers. Over 40% of ex-nuptial birth parents who cohabited were Maori, whereas fewer than 20% of non-cohabiting parents were (O'Neill *et al.* 1976: 294). In general in this period, Maori levels of cohabitation were higher than for Pakeha (Carmichael 1984).

For Maori the patterns of early marriage and childbearing and large family sizes were to continue until the late 1960s. From these years on, however, other changes were evident and involved major shifts in residential patterns. These movements were driven by the socio-economic contexts of Maori family life and will be returned to in a later section of this chapter. The shift created the severe fragmentation within whanau, hapu and iwi, between iwi and between different components of Maori society (especially the rift between urban and iwi Maori, termed the 'Torn Whariki', Hopa 1996) that endure today.

Finally, the living arrangements for Maori at this time can be inferred from census data (Dharmalingam *et al.* 2007: Tables 5.10 and 5.11) – at this point we will not cover Asians and Pacific peoples in detail because their proportionate contribution to the total of households was very low (2% each, but for Pacific peoples see below). In terms of living arrangements Maori households at the end of the Baby Boom period were different from Pakeha. Maori had much lower levels in the couple-only household category, a function of their higher fertility. In contrast, however, they had high proportions of households that fitted the classical nuclear model of parents and children, but also higher proportions of extended family households. Because of their young age structure, single-person households were not common.

These statistics do not really reveal the macro-structural changes affecting Maori society, shifts that had an analogous impact at the micro-level on every aspect of Maori family structure and organisation. Most important was the move noted above to neolocal residence accompanying the massive rural exodus occurring at this time. The underlying causes and effects will be covered below, but the impact of this migration on family structures and Maori society as a whole has been described by the anthropologist Ngapare Hopa: 'Among other things, this has had major implications for social organisation, iwi cohesion, kinship, depth of knowledge about tikanga, and identity' (Hopa 1996: 54).

Most Pacific peoples at this stage and in the future chose to live in the Auckland urban area. This concentration was less marked for earlier Asian groups, who had lived in rural as well as urban areas and some of whom had settled in New Zealand as far back as the gold-rush period of the 1860s, but by the end of the twentieth century Asians were clustered in Auckland. Their numbers were small, however, and thus more detailed comments on Pacific peoples and Asians will be held over until the next chapter. Nevertheless, it is worth noting in passing that a pioneer anthropological analysis of Cook Islanders in Auckland was carried out in the late 1980s by the anthropologist Antony Hooper. He showed that this group clustered in inner areas of Auckland city surrounding the CBD. In fact most were concentrated – in a few streets in Parnell, to the east of the central city, where 'the great majority prefer[red] to remain within a close circle of kin and neighbourhood associations' (Hooper 1958: 18–19). This probably summarises the life of the early Pasifika migrant families. A survey by John McCreary of 305 Pasifika households in 1963 gives an insight into their family structures at this period. Of the households he surveyed, 50% were nuclear, 44% had an extended structure, and 6% some other sort (McCreary 1966, cited in Cameron 1985b). Cluny Macpherson reported similar patterns for Samoan households in the early 1970s (1978: 122). Thus the patterns of extended families and of living in close contact with kin and persons from their own ethnic group that were to characterise Pasifika families in later periods, to be covered in later chapters, were already evident among early migrant group in the Baby Boom period.

5.3 FACTORS DRIVING CHANGE

COMPARATIVE SPEED OF CHANGE IN THE PERIOD 1945–1973

The period covered in this chapter was one of very rapid change. In the next chapter, on the shift from Baby Boom to Baby Bust, it will be shown that the most rapid period of change in Pakeha family structures and forms occurred at the end of and immediately after the Baby Boom, between 1973 and 1976. But the onset of the Baby Boom had also seen an accelerated transformation in structures (Pool *et al.* 2000; see also Figure 2.1).

For Maori the last years of the period reviewed in this chapter saw the onset of a transition in family sizes. This was to reach its most accelerated speed, to be discussed in the next chapter, in the radical Baby Bust from

1972 to 1978, exactly co-terminous with the Pakeha shift from Baby Boom to Baby Bust.

This part of the chapter reviews how these rapid changes occurred. It focuses on the end of the Baby Boom when first one new element entered the equation and then a second hard on its heels: the first and far more important was the Pill; the second was the application of micro-surgical techniques to sterilisation – in particular tubal ligation, but also vasectomy. The whole new package of contraceptive methods altered forever the biomedical aspects of fertility regulation. For the first time in human history there were efficient means of controlling the timing, spacing and limitation of parenting, and this permitted couples not only power over their own life-cycles, but control over the processes of family formation.

But the story does not end here, because, particularly in the case of the Pill, these were something more than simple biomedical techniques. Contraception went beyond the bedroom, the pharmacy and the doctor's clinic. It came out of the shadows to become a central component of almost every aspect of the cultural, economic, social and family life of WDCs, and by the last years of the Baby Boom the Pill had become a quotidian part of the standard diet of the mass media.

CONTRACEPTION AND FAMILY FORMATION

We have described earlier (in Chapter Two) the roles played by the so-called proximate variables. These have a direct role in governing family formation by driving the processes of family formation and through them the size and age dimensions of family structure. What is documented in the present chapter is a major transition in the determinants of fertility regulation. The roles of the nuptiality valve, less efficient means of contraception and the resort to abortion within marriage for reasons of birth limitation that had dominated family formation in the inter-war years and in the early years of the Baby Boom gave way to the new technologies for fertility regulation. By the later years of the Baby Boom a revolution had taken place.

The data on marriage and childbearing presented earlier, and references above to the short inter-birth intervals that characterised New Zealand patterns of reproduction, indicate that during the first part of the Pakeha Baby Boom, and this held true for Maori, fertility regulation by any means was not widely used at younger ages and over the early years of marriage. But increasingly the adoption of birth limitation at older ages and for couples at later durations of marriage became a factor that dominated fertility regulation. The role of the nuptiality valve, the proximate determinant that till then had been the major driver of patterns of reproduction, was virtually eliminated by the end of the Baby Boom.

For both Maori and Pakeha the post-war period was one of early and almost universal marriage. For Pakeha this factor distinguishes this era from all decades from the 1880s until the 1940s, as well as those since the early 1970s. For Maori, by contrast, this pattern was merely a continuation of past trends, but with an increasing amount of family building and whanau life taking place in a new location, urban areas rather than in rural northern and eastern New Zealand.

Moreover for both populations, as had been true in the past, union formation – registered marriage for Pakeha and both legal marriage and unions sanctioned and thus legitimated by the community for Maori – was directly linked to conception. Normally, pregnancy followed closely on commencement of a union, but for a significant minority of couples pre-marital conception precipitated marriage (Morgan *et al.* 2001; Carmichael 1982).

The Baby Boom, or at least its early part, was the last period in New Zealand's family history when there was such a close link between marriage and childbearing. The reason was simple: the available means of fertility regulation, other than permanent celibacy or delayed marriage, were not very effective until late in the Baby Boom. By the end of this period, however, the situation had changed completely and inexorably.

The NZW:FEE throws some light on the situation for Pakeha women commencing family formation in the early to mid-Baby Boom: they were far less likely than their equivalents in cohorts who followed them to use contraception at first intercourse and, even if it were employed, it was likely to be a less efficient method (Pool *et al.* 1999: 38–42). The situation was even more problematic than this comment might suggest. Condoms are included under efficient methods but at this period they 'were of inferior quality, and, as they were imported from the United Kingdom, frequently perished during the sea passage' (Pool *et al.* 1999: 86, citing Dr Margaret Sparrow, a pioneer family-planning physician).

From 1962 on, however, this changed as New Zealand women, particularly Pakeha in the early stages, went through their second and third 'contraceptive revolutions'. The first revolution had been the shifts, recorded in the last two chapters, occurring earlier in the century from traditional to barrier methods (e.g. condoms, diaphragms). The second revolution came in the early 1960s, during the Baby Boom, when New Zealand women enthusiastically adopted the Pill (Trlin and Perry 1981; Pool *et al.* 1999: Chapt. 9). The Pill was to become the preferred method for the timing (of first birth), for spacing (intervals between births) and for the limitation of births (the termination of reproduction). Initially there were restrictions on Pill use by the unmarried or the young, but by the end of the Baby Boom these were disappearing or had already disappeared (Pool *et al.* 1999: 110). Thus, by the last stages of the Baby Boom, the Pill had become the preferred method for timing and spacing of pregnancies for women of all ages and marital statuses. Maori adoption of the Pill was delayed by comparison with Pakeha but by the early 1970s this got under way with tremendous speed. A third contraceptive revolution, the rapid adoption of sterilisation by women and couples, was to follow hard on the heels of the second, spanning the last phase of the Baby Boom and into the Baby Bust. Thus by the end of the Baby Boom, the Pill was being displaced by sterilisation as a means of limitation by older women and by couples who had several children – multiparous couples, as they are termed.

Fertility regulation, it must be stressed, is merely a mechanism not a determinant of family structures; it is the outcome of decisions to use a particular technique, an attitude affected not only by ease of access to the method and by its media profile, but by values and norms relating to reproduction and the wider family environment. In turn these may be affected by a wide range of cultural, social and economic contextual factors which will be discussed later in this chapter. The Pill was the prime mechanism for the contraceptive revolution at the end of the period, with the new methods of sterilisation carried along a few years later on its coat-tails. But this revolution for both Maori and Pakeha brought with it enormous and historically unique changes in normative structures and other attitudes relating not just to contraception *per se* but to all aspects of family structure. The Pill, contraception in general and other aspects of fertility regulation, above all abortion, frequently became the subjects of controversy, typically revolving around questions of access to, availability of and the legal status of birth control (Sceats 1988b: Chapts 4 and 11).

The debates on birth control merged into those on gender and became important elements in the campaigns of the feminist movement in the 1970s and 1980s. A central plank both of this movement and of family-planning advocates was that of 'reproductive choice', and its links to issues such as equal access for girls and young women to education and careers. It also overlapped with the noisy and divisive debates about abortion that exploded in New Zealand and elsewhere in the 1970s (Sceats 1988b: Chapt. 4). This is somewhat ironic, for, as was noted in Chapters Three and Four, the early or first-wave feminists had doggedly opposed contraception at the dawn of the twentieth century because they thought it would liberate men's lusts and in the process degrade women. Yet 60-odd years on, for their granddaughters, efficient contraception was to be a key determinant of the liberation and empowerment of women.

There do not seem to be New Zealand data on the micro-level dimensions of this societal transformation and the effects of the debates surrounding it, but in all probability many of the changes occurring in New Zealand parallel what was taking place in Canada at that time. A large multi-disciplinary, multi-level (demographic, sociological, social psychological, social psychiatric) random-sample survey on contraceptive practice among female university students was directed by two of the authors of the present book at two Ottawa universities, Carleton and Université d'Ottawa (a bilingual institution). It showed that by the early 1970s the use of family planning was no longer constrained by questions of access or knowledge – although the students had a surprisingly poor understanding of reproductive biology – but primarily was determined by social psychological traits such as achievement motivation or by socio-economic background, for example rural/urban, anglophone/francophone or parents' social class (Sceats and Pool 1978).

Thus the second contraceptive revolution was more than merely the adoption of a new technology. It also produced a cultural and social revolution in what the British demographer Murphy has called 'macro-contraception' (1993: fn. 49; Pool et al. 1999: 110–11; Edmeades 1999). This term comprises changes in the entire nexus of a range of factors, including family formation, structures and fertility regulation, the development of more transparent views and public discourse about sexuality and contraception, changes in values relating to many aspects of family life and shifts in societal normative contexts. Most important of these was that women and couples could control to a considerable degree the processes of reproduction without having to limit exposure to intercourse. Reproductive choice became not just a catch-cry of family-planning agencies and feminist groups but, as will be shown in the next chapter, a reality for many women and couples. Issues of fertility regulation and family formation as a normative behaviour pattern could thus be divorced, to a considerable degree, from the institution of marriage. As will be considered in later chapters, however, by the late 1990s this apparent freedom to choose was itself subject to new challenges for many couples and women.

The technological innovations had impacts that went far beyond the simple control of reproduction. It has been argued elsewhere, for example, that the ease with which sterilisation was accepted in the 1970s would not have been possible without the changes in attitudes wrought by the rapid acceptance and use of the Pill (Pool et al. 1999: 110–11). Much more broadly, and as an issue of critical importance here, it can be argued that the ready availability of reasonably efficient means of conception control (but not necessarily of the capacity to conceive) meant for the first time a technological change could be used to influence the patterns of family formation. This was to affect two key dimensions of family structure: family sizes and ages at parenting (Pool et al. 1999: Chapt. 11, esp. 11.2). As was shown in Chapters Three and Four, there was nothing new in the notions of delaying childbearing and spacing: these had been attempted prior to 1945 but, in the absence of efficient means of contraception other than total abstention, had far less sure outcomes. Not surprisingly, therefore, at the end of the twentieth century the contraceptive Pill was rated among the great social and biomedical changes of the century, and even of the millennium. In addition, the apparent mastery of reproduction spread to a desire to control other aspects of family life and thus family structures. Most notably, by the end of the Baby Boom there was a decrease in the tendency for pre-marital pregnancy to be followed by nuptial birth; increasingly an ex-nuptial birth was the outcome and, with it, the decision for a woman or couple to keep the child rather than adopting it out (Pool and Crawford 1980; Carmichael 1982). Secondly, the last days of the Baby Boom saw many of the features of the Baby Bust laid down, not least among them the onset from the early 1960s of a Maori fertility decline, which in the Baby Bust period was to reach its highest rate of acceleration and involved not only the Pill but also other contraceptive methods that were now acceptable and efficient (e.g. sterilisation, IUD).

In sum, then, the advent of the Pill provided the technology for fertility regulation to become a major proximate determinant of family structure. By the end of this period contraception was having a major impact on family size, but only minor effects on family age structures (its effects on age, however, became more evident in the period discussed in the next chapter). The Pill went far beyond being a mere technical innovation: it produced normative changes in the entire value system of New Zealand and other WDCs.

THE SOCIO-ECONOMIC CONTEXTS OF FAMILY LIFE: PAKEHA FAMILIES

This section first considers why Pakeha might have adopted the family structures of this period. Of critical importance is the wider context for the emergence of the large post-war Pakeha family, as measured by numbers of children and households with younger age structures, and in most cases involving families consisting of married parenting couples, residing in a neolocal location. Rural–urban migration was a factor for a minority of Pakeha, but was far less significant than for Maori simply because most Pakeha already lived in cities and other urban centres, and had done so for much of the twentieth century. Migration for Pakeha was more likely to be inter-urban or intra-urban.

In general in this period, the socio-economic context was family friendly, particularly for Pakeha who, on average, did not have to struggle to escape the extreme rural poverty and the quasi-subsistence economy that still typified Maori society. During the Baby Boom there was overall prosperity, economic expansion and labour shortages. Throughout the period until the mid-1970s, real incomes, inflation adjusted, increased, while inequalities decreased (Martin 1998: *passim*). For Pakeha, female labour-force participation increased, especially from 1961, when the fall-off in family sizes achieved through childbearing started (Davies 1993: 27).

When discussing contexts it is necessary to start with the dwelling in which the Baby Boom couple lived. It was the neolocal residence in suburbia that provided the essential setting for the Pakeha Baby Boom and even for the Maori influx of this time (see below). The 'Great Suburban Building Era', mainly comprising the Baby Boom and Baby Bust years, was to a large degree the child of the welfare state (for levels of home ownership see Table 4.1). Describing this era, Mary Watson argues that:

> Central and local government bodies . . . played a key role in suburban
> development, efficiently creating inexpensive sections (or single dwelling
> lots) and cheap substantial housing. Through the intervention of the
> Welfare State New Zealand [in the Baby Boom had] no slums, no shortage
> of accommodation and very high rates of home ownership . . . [It] has been
> regarded almost as a right of citizenship, in contrast to the United States
> where suburban property is a measure of worth, a reward for achievement.
> The difference in philosophy shows most clearly in public housing: in the
> United States only small amounts of public housing are provided, and
> these tend to be high-rise units in the inner city; in New Zealand the state
> provided suburban life-styles for low income families, accommodated
> mostly in single-family dwelling units until the late 1950s. The Government
> also provide[d] a large pool of housing finance to ensure that most low
> income households [were] able to realise their goals of homeownership
> (Watson 1985: 145).

So-called state housing estates mushroomed first in areas such as Three Kings, Orakei or Owairaka in Auckland, or Ngaio in Wellington. By the 1950s really large blocks such as Glen Innes and Point England in Auckland were being established. Already these estates were typified by a degree of population homogeneity in terms of socio-economic status and family life-cycle stage (young parents and their children) (Pool 1959b). The same was true for some private housing estates built with government support (see below). The homogeneity of suburbia, especially on public housing estates, by ethnicity in addition to socio-economic status and family life-cycle stage, was to become far more marked in the period to be covered in the next chapter. The housing estates were to become much larger and were to take on, to a degree, the features of slums or ghettos.

The government also intervened in mortgage markets, thereby assisting middle-income families. Moreover, 'Those with dependent children [were] further aided as their family benefits [could] be capitalised by receiving a lump sum which can be applied to the [home purchase] deposit' (Watson 1985: 145).

The historian Belich summarises this synergy between housing, suburbia and the Baby Boom:

The wedding of romantic domesticity and massive state aid goes quite a way towards explaining the Baby Boom. Another boom booster may have been an element of female populism, a mothers' mutiny in reverse whereby young women sought greater freedom and adulthood in marriage and motherhood … A 'home of her own' was not only a escape from rental housing but from parental housing. There might be a sense in which the mass entry into 'Nappy Valley' was a search for independence rather than a turning away from it (Belich 2001: 493).

These patterns of family building translated into policy: 'The nuclear family, consisting of mum and the children at home and dad out at work, was the focus of much government policy of that period, including family benefits, wage policy, free maternity care and housing. Central to the ideology was the existence of a woman in the home providing care and nurture, "the housewife"' (Shaw 2000: 165). Thus, in post-war suburbia, where most Pakeha New Zealanders lived, the wife was at home with the children and the other young mothers; the father at a job he had typically started straight out of school. This 'was consistent with a new [child-centred] approach to motherhood in which women saw their primary role as servicing the developmental needs of their children in a more intense way than before' (May 1992: 146 and *passim*).

A new factor, however, was starting to enter the equation: perhaps buoyed by the experiences gained in World War II, some mothers began to enter the workforce (Olssen and Levesque 1978: 18–19). Nevertheless, female labour-force participation was encouraged only to a point. Marriage, and certainly pregnancy, meant that most women left the labour force and age-specific participation rates resembled an 'L-shaped' curve, with its peak at school-leaving ages and a sharp drop-off by 25 years. In the 1940s and 1950s this was in part a matter of decorum and 'in part a recognition that, once the "bulge" showed, a woman was expected to resign her job' (May 1992: 133). But the demographer Lisa Davies showed that by the early 1970s, an 'M-shaped' curve for female labour-force participation was emerging as more and more women started to return to work when their children were older and after they left home. For Maori women in this period neither pattern was as marked, being more in the form of a gradual decrease from a peak at the school-leaving ages (Davies 1993: 68–71)

A generally buoyant economic context was reinforced for Pakeha by the whole complex nexus of factors embodied in the welfare state, in the broadest sense of the term. This extended beyond the question of housing, noted above, to health, education, employment and income support. Social policy for both Maori and Pakeha, for all were equally eligible, was directed to a family wage that enabled a man (for it was very gender specific) to maintain adequately a wife and three children. In this 'the family was narrowly conceived as a nuclear household with clearly defined domestic and employment responsibilities. It is doubtful whether this approach was ever entirely appropriate to the needs of Maori' (Shirley *et al.* 1997: 214 and 300). It also privileged registered marriage for couples, and widowhood. Nevertheless, policy changes introduced late in the Baby Boom started to shift the system away from this emphasis, at least in a formal legislative sense, to extend coverage to all sole mothers, including the never married (Goodger 1998).

It will be recalled from earlier discussion that the Baby Boom was triggered by the intersection of two factors: (i) the reprise of marriages and parenting delayed by the Depression and the Second World War, for older women; and (ii) the sudden shift to early and universal marriage for younger women. A prelude to this increase had occurred at the end of the 1930s at a time when the first effective, but not universal, child-support payments were introduced. Then in 1946 these benefits were made universal, and at a level that made a real impact on family budgets. It is tempting, therefore, to suggest causality, but a macro-economic study comparing the Netherlands and New Zealand shows that the effect was to enhance fertility, but not necessarily to determine trends: 'The regression models suggest that the introduction of a substantial subsidy to families just after World War II boosted fertility greatly. This was occurring at a time when fertility was increasing in any case'. But the authors, Poot and Siegers, add that their results suggest that 'the complete absence of social security payments to children would have reduced fertility in New Zealand by 28%' (Poot and Siegers 2001: 24–25). Arguments about the pro-natalist effects of family benefits cannot be taken too far. The capitalisation of the family benefit (the Family Benefit Home Ownership Act 1964), surely one of the most pro-natalist measures ever promulgated in any social democracy (Pool *et al.* 1998: 121), was correlated in time, paradoxically, with the onset of a fertility decline.

MAORI FAMILIES: SOCIO-ECONOMIC CONTEXT

Many of the factors identified as contexts for the Pakeha Baby Boom also apply to Maori, although there are also some significant differences. For Maori up until and probably into the Baby Boom, ethnic survival, through the maintenance of large family sizes, was still an issue; Maori life expectancy remained not only well below that for Pakeha, but was low until after World War II. Then events caught up with Maori: survivorship probabilities, in particular for children, as was noted earlier, increased dramatically between 1945 and 1961. Pool has borrowed the Quebec demographer Mathew's term 'demographic shock' to describe this, the first of four such effects which were to have a very significant impact on Maori in the post-war period. These were: (i) improved survivorship; (ii) urbanisation; (iii) fertility decline; and (iv) the onset of the Maori diaspora, especially to Australia.

A consequence of the first shock was that the need to have a large family simply to ensure replacement was no longer as imperative. This was undoubtedly the major determinant of the declines in Maori fertility that commenced in the 1960s (Pool 1991: Chapts 7 and 8). Co-terminous with the trend of improving survivorship was the urban influx (see below), whereas the Maori diaspora overseas was to start in earnest only in the 1980s, although it can be seen as a natural extension of the rapid urbanisation of the immediate post-war period (Bedford and Pool 2004). As the major impact of fertility decreases on Maori family sizes came only at the very end of the period being discussed in this chapter and in the early part of the years covered in the next, they are discussed in further detail in later chapters, as is the overseas diaspora.

Although not unique to Maori, the cardinal feature of their life in the Baby Boom years was rural–urban migration, a sort of diaspora from the north and east of the rural North Island. This migration was a radical change, involving a move from what was frequently an isolated community (kainga) dominated by a few extensive whanau to a provincial centre or a big city and, with this, neolocalisation. It could involve either a couple or young people severed from their family networks relocating to a central-city slum area, especially at first (Pool 1959a), or to a suburb where they would be surrounded by Pakeha, Maori from other iwi or, increasingly as the Baby Boom progressed, Pacific peoples. This family structural change was really a component of a far more significant 'demographic shock' that radically changed the whole face of Maori society. The anthropologist Joan Metge called this massive exodus from the isolated rural heartlands of Maoridom in Northland, the Waikato, Bay of Plenty, Tairawhiti and Hawke's Bay the 'New Maori Migration' (1964, see also Metge 1976; Bedford and Pool 2004).

Starting during the war and in part fuelled by conscription of younger people, especially women, for war industries, this movement became far more rapid thereafter. This was especially true for the period 1961–66 when there was a rise from 46% to 62% of Maori living in urban areas, and a numerical loss of 77,000 in the Maori rural population. This was a very rapid rate of urbanisation, perhaps the most accelerated anywhere for a national population prior to the 1970s (Pool 1991: 152–59, Gibson 1973, who drew on a University of California, Berkeley, study). Initially a movement of young single people, by the late 1950s this had become a family migration stream. In part, this was because of 'policy interventions, notably the provision of low interest loans for housing in areas deemed to have potential for economic development' (Pool 1991: 154, citing Poulsen *et al.* 1975: 323).

Whatever the cause, this urban influx shaped both urban family structures and the wider whanau still living in rural areas. Moreover, from the mid-Baby Boom era the typical Maori family was no longer found in the Hokianga or in Te Kaha, but was at least urban resident if not urban born. At an early stage in the influx Maori were clustered in the central-city districts, but by the late 1950s, and certainly beyond that date, they were moving to the new housing estates described earlier. These estates, while not ghettos, saw concentrations of low-income families among which Maori, at first, then Pacific peoples were heavily over-represented (Pool 1961; Rowland 1971, 1973).

In the international literature, historically urban fertility rates are lower than rural, and certainly in the early post-war period this held true for Maori, at a stage when national Maori rates were still very high. The rapid urbanisation just described was one of the factors that combined to cause 'a decrease in fertility [that] seems inevitable once a certain threshold . . . has been passed'. The statistics are astounding: a TFR of 5.5 births per woman in 1966, 5.1 in 1971, down to 3.1 by 1976 and 2.5 in 1981 (Pool 1991: Table 8.2, 172–73).

An unusual trend, however, was that patterns of Maori family formation and thus family sizes changed not only in urban areas, but also in rural areas (using age-standardised measures), consequently minimising rural–urban differentials in levels. Normally, one expects rural levels to exceed urban. In 1966 the Maori urban GFR had been only 61% of the rural level, but by 1971 it was 11% higher; and 31% higher in 1976. In 1966 the urban GFR had been 187, as against 250 for the rural; by 1976 the rates were 113 (urban), as against 90 (rural) (Pool 1991: Table 8.12).* By the 1970s reductions in family size were being achieved through the very rapid uptake of the Pill by Maori women across the country, the diffusion of which was achieved by the active encouragement of Maori women's organisations arguing for family size changes (Pool 1991: 185–87; 201–3). Thus for Maori, as for Pakeha in this period, both the more strictly biomedical and the wider contextual elements of the adoption of the Pill were in evidence.

The shift of Maori to urban areas was associated with a mutation in whanaungatanga which sometimes strained traditional whanau structures and even the descent lines recorded in whakapapa, and led to the development of new entities. For the anthropologist Ngapare Hopa these are 'variations on a "familial" theme that are emerging in response to the interplay of cultural, demographic and market-based processes or compulsions' (1996: 56). This geographical redistribution had its greatest impact on family formation in the period up to the start of the Pakeha Baby Bust, but the structural changes discussed here and in the next chapter were to be felt long after this. By the 1990s, so it was estimated, 'more than three-quarters of the membership of

---

* These data are age-standardised. This strategy is essential because, as the urban influxes were concentrated at young adult ages, the reproductive potential of Maori society had shifted to urban areas.

most tribes now live outside their tribal boundaries' (Hopa 1996: 54, citing Douglas 1994: 91).

Urban living brought Maori into more everyday contact with Pakeha life-ways and value systems. Moreover, it also seems to have accelerated inter-marriage, although this had always occurred in New Zealand. Anthropologist John Harre's detailed manual examination of marriage registry records indicated that almost half of the marriages made by Maori in Auckland in 1960 were to Pakeha (Harre 1966 and 1972).* This would have involved further changes to whanau structures, embedding some Pakeha value systems but also taking Maori norms into Pakeha families.

Alongside this, Maori urbanisation was accompanied by a huge shift-share in their industrial labour force, particularly for men, from the primary to the secondary sector. For Maori women, growth in the dominance of the tertiary sector, mainly in less skilled service jobs, was accelerated at this time (Pool 1991: Chapt. 7), ensuring rapid increases in Maori female labour-force participation from about 1951 on (Davies 1993: 27). This in turn had an impact on Maori family structures.

One normal co-variate of family-size changes – universal education – does not seem to have played a major part in the Maori fertility decline. Theoretically, its role is to affect values and attitudes, and to alter the patterns of economic support between generations (school children can no longer contribute to family household economic activities and, even in a free system, some costs are entailed). But for Maori a question remains; 'given a century of universal literacy through a school system which is culturally Pakeha, [one must ask] why Maori fertility did not decline earlier' (Pool 1991: 171). The answer rests with the fact that other factors counteracted this one. Above all, as noted earlier, these were the impacts of low levels of childhood survival until the post-war period and the effects of strong pro-natalist norms and cultural props (Douglas 1977).

5.4 IMPACT ON FAMILY FUNCTIONING

Retrospectively, the Baby Boom is often seen as an era in which families functioned well. This is because in the popular view the neolocal two-parent family of the Pakeha Baby Boom is today the model for old-fashioned family values. It is seen as the natural heir to the family types of the inter-war period and before, and thus has become very much the symbol of family nostalgia

---

* He also presents trends from 1890 on. Ethnicity was determined from first and family names.

(Pool *et al.* 1998: 88–92). In this it has often been conflated inaccurately with its predecessors for, as has been shown earlier in this chapter, the Baby Boom family was not an exact copy of those of the inter-war years. To add to this problem, as differentials in family formation patterns were minimal in this period, the same nostalgic vision is probably shared across most socio-economic status groups: it is not middle class, upper class or working class, but a collective Pakeha-wide cultural memory. Thus there is a latent notion of equality of experience. Maori have a somewhat different collective memory of very large whanau.

Consciously or unconsciously, the Baby Boom family is seen retrospectively as some sort of ideal, focused around the notion that it provided a cohesive environment for the nurturing of children and mutually supportive spouse relationships. The era is attractive to some commentators as it was the last one in which a larger family size was the norm, and in which, seemingly, there were low levels of marital disruption, at least as evidenced from divorce statistics. It is not the intention here to judge the Baby Boom family as better or worse than those that preceded or followed it, but it is necessary to point out that family life in that period was certainly not free from problems, as has been shown earlier and will be further discussed below, while many of its potential shortfalls, notably family breakdown and ultimately divorce, remained latent, only to appear after the Baby Boom had given way to the Baby Bust. To take another example, the high levels of adoption point to dysfunctionality in some aspects of family life. This is not to make a blanket criticism of adoption, whether formal or informal, because often it benefits all parties involved, but simply to say that the high prevalence noted earlier point to major problems surrounding the very function in which the Baby Boom had undoubted success: producing babies.

In the past this ideal family epitomised by the Baby Boom was even accorded academic credence. The functionalist sociologists of that period turned this viewpoint into models, arguing that it fitted 'the needs of industrialism' and was the form towards which 'all social systems are moving fast' (Goode 1965: 108). For these sociologists the 'small democratic family' and the 'Companionship family system towards which the American Family is moving' would privilege 'affection', 'mutual acceptance of procedures in decision-making' and 'common interests' (Burgess Locke and Thomes 1971: 8–9).

New Zealand's Baby Boom family had advantageous props that have virtually disappeared since. Above all, this was the emblematic period of the comprehensive welfare state, of a Nordic type albeit differing in some important 'antipodean' ways. Its wide scope extended not only to the more universal measures of social security (e.g. family benefits and health care), but also to discretionary welfare. It became more fully integrated into the wider system, 'a means of topping up'. Moreover, detailed micro-level historical analyses, such as that by Bronwyn Labrum (2004: 163, 158), suggest that rather than eroding the family, the basic axiom of neo-liberal economists and policy writers (these issues will be taken further in Chapter Seven), the welfare state 'reconstituted and preserved it'.

In reality the functioning of the neolocal, nuclear New Zealand Pakeha family, or its counterpart in the United States and elsewhere in the neo-Europes, was not as smooth as nostalgia might suggest, at least not as viewed retrospectively from today, but looking at how it was perceived at that time. 'Anxious perceptions of "juvenile delinquency", especially in urban areas and the new suburbs, more unmarried mothers [although this was more common in the 1960s and 1970s], and ongoing revelations of inadequate family life, suggested that all was not well' (Labrum 2004: 163). This is clear, for example, from the fact that there was a major panic about the behaviour of teenagers highlighted in the Mazengarb Commission, noted earlier. Presided over by Dr Oswald Mazengarb QC, it produced a report sent to every household, thereby introducing them to terms like teenager and juvenile delinquency, which became almost conflated in the public's mind, and frightening the wits out of an entire generation of parents.

The factor that triggered the panic had its origins in a purely demographic phenomenon: the appearance of a seemingly large group with a high profile, the Hutt Valley teenagers. But their prominence came not from the size nationwide of the birth cohort from which they came, but from the peculiar circumstances surrounding the development of Wellington's Hutt Valley suburbs. The Mazengarb Report was published just before the height of the Baby Boom, but it related to inflated cohorts that had not come from the Baby Boom itself, as the oldest Baby Boomers of that day would have been only nine to eleven years of age. The Hutt teenagers were born around fifteen years earlier, at the end of the Depression or the start of World War II. The inflated size of the cohort at adolescence was a result of families with similar age structures clustering in the Hutt Valley housing estates of the day.

Other seeds had been sown for what would come to be seen, logically or not, as indicators of dysfunctionality: increases in divorce rates. This trend was to manifest itself in later periods, after the Baby Boom was over, but among couples who had married in that epoch. Levels of divorce and separation increased and were highest among the most proto-typical Baby Boom families: those marrying at a young age, particularly when this was associated with early and pre-marital conception (Dharmalingam *et al.* 1998a).

For Maori, the shift to neolocal residence in the post-war period affected every aspect of the functioning of the whanau (Hopa 1996). The severing of the young couple from their whanau roots affected the functioning of the Maori nuclear family. At the very least it cut them off from immediate day-to-day contact with the events occurring on their home marae.

The family policy framework for this period for Maori and Pakeha had been laid down in the 1938 Act referred to last chapter. This set out the welfare state *par excellence* in New Zealand. Writing in 1988 the historian W. H. Oliver could say 'By the early 1940s "social security" was in place. For more than 40 years it has stayed there, often questioned, sometimes examined, but only marginally altered' (Oliver 1988: 25). In Chapters Six to Nine we will discuss the radical changes introduced since then, in the 1980s and 1990s, that saw an end to much of the welfare state. In retrospect the policies of the 1950s and 1960s seem almost quaint and certainly patronising, paternalistic and patricentric. But they did provide a comprehensive and significant support package for most families, not only in terms of income but for many other aspects of their lives, for exmaple housing.

5.5 IMPACT OF CHANGES IN FAMILY MORPHOLOGIES ON THE WIDER SOCIETY

Perhaps no other period – at least not since the land wars of the 1860s and the Vogel migration schemes of the 1870s – has had a greater impact on wider New Zealand society both collectively for Maori and Pakeha, and separately for each of them, than the Baby Boom. For both ethnic groups a key factor was the shift to, and embedding of, the neolocal family unit as the basic organising block for society. The Baby Boom built successfully on what had gone before, taking the values and norms imported into New Zealand by Pakeha in the colonial period, but by focusing these around the neolocal nuclear family it put its own very particular stamp on them. The problem was that if this entity came under strain socially, as happened in the 1970s, or economically, as occurred in the late 1980s and 1990s, the resultant vulnerability would have an impact across the entire society and economy.

For Maori, the shift from whanau located in kainga to families taking up neolocal residence and its driver, the rural exodus, were to permeate every aspect of their social life. It was also the trigger that led to their most recent migration overseas, and especially to Australia. There is a more latent effect arising from the large Maori family sizes of this period. The people born then will produce a rapid numerical ageing of the Maori population over the first decades of the twenty-first century: the size of the Maori elderly population will increase fourfold from the 1990s to the 2020s, as against only 2.5 times for the population as a whole. The Baby Boom not only produced birth cohorts with inflated sizes, but was notable for the marked fluctuations in cohort structures, both of which factors have made, and will continue to make, a marked impact on our national life. Figure 5.1 shows how the Pakeha Baby Boom (total used here as a proxy for Pakeha) distorted what had been a simple exponential growth in the numbers of births. Moreover, because it went through two separate waves this distortion was increased. Each wave and each trough developed a momentum that has carried across into each life-cycle phase, an effect that will continue until the last Baby Boomer passes away.

This has meant that the Baby Boom not only brought pressures on to both the policy and market sectors, but did so in a rather turbulent way, producing on- and off-again effects as waves were succeeded by troughs. That was not the end of the story, for secondary momentum effects have also been felt, most notably in the way that a large Baby Boom cohort born around 1960, and reaching parenting ages around 1990 (the Baby Blip) at a time when childbearing on average had been delayed, produced large birth cohorts even though rates had dropped: more parents having fewer births per couple still can have more births. The Maori data in Figure 5.2 show a marked wave effect, but in their case it was only one wave.

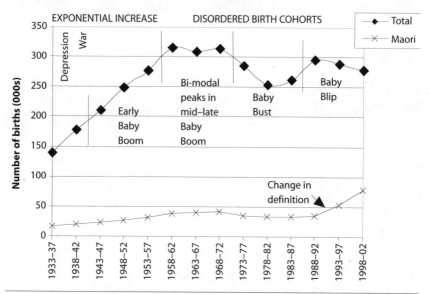

Figure 5.1: Births per Quinquennium, New Zealand Total and Maori

Source: Pool 2003. For total data and Maori 1963 to present: Statistics New Zealand, Vital Statistics; Maori before 1962: estimates derived from Pool 1964: Table 12.1, which adjusts for under-registration.

From the moment the Pakeha Boomers were conceived, they required many different policy initiatives to meet their needs and, as they pass through their life-cycles, these inflated cohorts will affect all aspects of service industries and consumption as they pass through their life-cycles. To take a few examples, they put pressures on obstetric, paediatric, adolescent and then adult health services and on pre-school, school and tertiary education. At first their pasage had positive effects on labour markets, as the early Baby Boomers, born in the 1950s, were the beneficiaries of the rapid expansion of tertiary education in the 1970s, and in turn brought their skills to the labour market. But by the late 1980s these effects became negative (Honey and Lindop 1997).

Moreover, the Baby Boomers have dominated different segments of consumer demand across every part of the market from the media to clothing and leisure. Today, of course, the first Boomer cohorts are reaching late middle age, and again these waves are having an impact in services and markets directed to these age-groups (Pool 2003). Thus the inflated Baby Boom generation, comprising the children born from 1943 to 1973, have had a significant impact on every aspect of our economy, public policy, social life and the market, and will continue to do so until about the mid-twenty-first century.

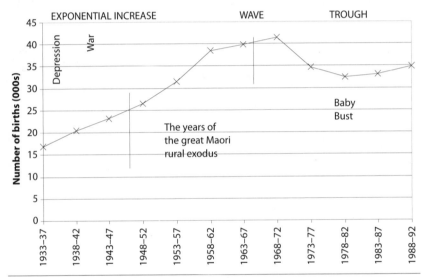

Figure 5.2: Maori Births per Quinquennium

Source: As for Figure 5.1.

The other form of ageing – structural ageing, or the percentage of the population at older ages – is also due to these waves and troughs. Society would not be structurally ageing over the next decade were it not for the two waves created by the Baby Boom peaks and the declines in fertility in the Baby Bust (Pool 2000b; Pool 2003; see also Pool *et al.* 2005: and Pool and Wong 2006). The waves (and troughs) have what are termed 'echo effects'. The early Baby Boom around 1945–50 had such an effect around 1970. This reintroduced renewed pressures on maternity and paediatric health, and on schooling services, that had been evident in the early Baby Boom. Moreover, the second wave, born around 1965–73, reached the labour market in the late 1980s at exactly the point at which radical restructuring of the economy took place. These 'reforms of the late 1980s took no visible account of human capital issues. Above all they seem to have ignored the arrival at the labour market of the inflated birth cohorts born 1966–75, at the second peak of the Baby Boom'. This echo reverberated in the 1990s, while further echoes to this latter echo will be seen around 2016, and so on. The inflated Maori and Pasifika cohorts born in the Baby Boom era and reaching the workforce at this time were even more disadvantaged, and this had a negative impact on these ethnic groups and their families that will endure into the 2020s (Honey and Lindop 1997; Pool 1999: 76 and *passim*; 2003).

These figures, especially 5.1, illustrate a major point in this chapter. The Baby Boom is primarily notable for the *size* of the birth cohorts it produced rather than the fertility rates reached at that time. This is important not only for pragmatic reasons related to both the market and to policy, but also more theoretically, in defining baby booms.

Finally, the Baby Boom saw a return to early childbearing. A curious delayed echo of the most extreme form of this was to occur later: in 1990, the daughters of mothers who had had a baby as an adolescent in 1970 were more likely than others to have a baby themselves at an age below twenty years (Dharmalingam *et al.* 2004: Table 4.4).

In sum, the family structural changes – in family sizes, in neolocation, in age structures, and in living arrangements and marital statuses – occurring in the period reviewed in this chapter had impacts on New Zealand society at that time. But beyond that, the impacts of the way families were built and structured in those decades and the forms they took will last a very long time into the future. Thus there is a need to know far more than is currently understood about the dynamics of what was occurring then.

5.6. CONCLUSION

THE BABY BOOM: ALONGSIDE LONG-TERM NEW ZEALAND TRENDS

The period covered in this chapter relates perhaps to the most important stages (outlined in Chapter Two) in both the Maori and Pakeha family transitions – the last part of the second stage for Pakeha, and the onset of the first part of the second stage in the case of Maori. It formed a bridge between the past, which although often traumatic had produced changes for which there were antecedents, and the period since then, which has deviated markedly from what had been known historically. As the family is undoubtedly the basis of much social organisation and change, these three bridging decades represent among the most significant epochs in the building of New Zealand society. Not only are they a passage, a transition between two worlds, but they have many features that are unique.

For Maori the most significant change, and one that was in many ways extremely traumatic, involved the shift from a marae lifestyle – not necessarily of a traditional nucleated settlement type, but at least one in which kin and affines lived in relatively close proximity – to neolocal nuclear family life in urban areas. At first this was in central-city areas, but soon thereafter the locus of Maori urban life was the suburbs and their lifestyle was little different in essence from that of their Pakeha neighbours. By the end of the period covered here, the quotidian aspects of Maori family life were primarily being enacted in suburbia, not in marae-centred rural communities. Maori had to respond to these radical changes which ruptured family life and all that this entailed. By the 1970s, Maori society and Maori family life had changed inexorably, and this set the scene for the next three decades.

Pakeha society too went through radical changes, not the least of which was the neolocalisation and suburbanisation of family life. In this environment were played out most aspects of what are associated with the Baby Boom. Although arguably not as traumatically as for Maori, Pakeha family life, nevertheless, was mutated in a way not seen ever before, or for some aspects not since the 1870s, nor seen since. It then 'counter-mutated', in ways that were reminiscent of what had happened 100 years before, by going through a decline in family sizes.

But the main axis of the Baby Boom was, of course, reproduction, marked by high rates of fertility and precocious ages of childbearing, around which everything else clustered. In contrast with the periods before and since it was not really about differentials in levels of reproduction except between Maori and Pakeha; in this regard the Baby Boom was a throwback to the pioneer period. Not unexpectedly there was a difference between Pakeha and Maori rates, but not in terms of the rhythms of family building as far as timing and spacing were concerned. Family limitation and thus family size was a different matter, although even here Pakeha rates reached very high levels for a European-origin population in a WDC. Within each ethnic group, however, there were only minor differences in patterns of family formation and outcomes, as measured by family sizes. Homogeneity was the prevailing feature, so that the reproductive polarisation of the pre-war years had largely disappeared in response to the Baby Boom's crowning glory, early and almost universal exposure to intercourse and risk of conception within registered marriage (at least for Pakeha, who constituted the vast majority of the population at that time, over 90% in 1961).

Even more complex forms of reproductive polarisation than had been seen in the inter-war years were to emerge after the Baby Boom, but there were few hints of this even in the dying days of the Baby Boom. In one sense, the Pakeha Baby Boom can be seen as aberrant, as something that was a counter-factual trend in a long-term shift in family structures and forms (Demeny 2005; Vallin 2002). Ultimately, in fact, this may be its most defining feature, but at present, as we are still sitting under its shadow, its long-term significance is more difficult to assess. In future we may see it as a phenomenon that comprised a peculiar set of temporally bound circumstances that were to be eventually superseded by a reprise of some of the reproductive values and behaviours that were widespread between the 1890s and World War II. This reprise coincided with the introduction of a totally new technology for fertility regulation, erupting in the 1960s and 1970s in the second and third contraceptive revolutions, which introduced an entirely new dimension into the picture.

Together the changes of the late 1960s and early 1970s ushered in not just a return to a long-term downwards trend in fertility levels, but, paradoxically, what was also to be three decades of change across uncharted territory. While there were echoes in the Baby Bust of many of the purely demographic features of earlier days – lower TFRs and delayed childbearing – there were no precedents for other aspects of family life that were to follow the Baby Boom. But it must be stressed that some of the seeds for what was to follow were laid in the Baby Boom.

An issue arising here was identified by Janet Sceats two decades ago: the *speed* of diffusion and uptake by New Zealand women of the Pill in the 1960s and then of the new techniques of sterilisation in the 1970s. She cites evidence that New Zealand saw one of the most rapid diffusions of the Pill of any WDC. By 1975, prevalence rates were higher only in the Netherlands, but by then tubal ligation and vasectomies were mounting very strong challenges to the Pill in New Zealand (Sceats 1988: Chapt. 11; see also Pool *et al.* 1999, which used newly available data that fully confirmed Sceats's earlier argument). Her observations, especially about the Pill, raise some interesting questions about the speed of diffusion of ideas and knowledge, both to and within the country, in an era in which, at least in New Zealand, mass media and communications were far less developed and immediate in impact than today. When the rush to the Pill started, TV was only just being introduced on any scale, and international telephone contacts were still by wireless not cable.

The Pakeha Baby Boom and the same period for Maori whanau can be seen in another light, in which the playing out of many of the old verities going back at least to both eighteenth-century England and pre-colonial Aotearoa reached a crescendo and finale. The next concert in the same setting, the Baby Bust, was quickly to take us into the unknown. The Baby Boom has the orchestration of Strauss, who 'sometimes went to excess in the violent expression of passionate emotion', but who, through Wagner and Liszt, was in line with classical traditions. In contrast, in later chapters we will be describing the Baby Bust, which was more in line with the compositions of Stravinsky, who 'ignored existing conventions' (OCM 1978: 985–86).

Up to and including the Baby Boom, the story of the New Zealand family has primarily been an account of changes in family formation and structures, especially declines in average family sizes. These then increased significantly in the Baby Boom, but by the 1970s indices relating to the most critical structural element, family size, had witnessed a return to the lower levels recorded prior to the Baby Boom. This thereby ended, *grosso modo*, what had been a period of deviant trends. But what followed the Baby Boom, as will be reported in the few next chapters, is unprecedented, as we have stressed, in that much of the more manifest story relates to family forms, not to their structures. Nevertheless, when looked at in detail, nuanced but significant structural changes can also be seen. A key point here is that some of the shifts in family morphologies since the early 1970s had their genesis in patterns of family behaviour seen in the Baby Boom, but were not to become evident until later.

THE NEW ZEALAND BABY BOOM AND THE BOOM INTERNATIONALLY
Aberrant or not, seedbed of later changes or not, the Pakeha Baby Boom remains, in nostalgia, perhaps the most emblematic epoch in the history of the New Zealand family. This retrospective picture may conceal more about the period 1943–73 than it reveals. The Baby Boom was very complex and, for Pakeha, set down structures that were to have long-term consequences, including the genesis of later changes in family forms, such as increases in rates of divorce and separation. This chapter has shown, for example, that the Baby Boom was not a homogeneous period. It had two and possibly three distinct phases: a sort of phoney war as the Second World War ended and troops returned; an early phase up to the early 1960s; and a final phase from then until the early 1970s. The first of these saw pre-war family patterns reinforced; the second was the quintessential Baby Boom; the last of the phases saw ex-nuptial conception and early childbearing reach a crescendo, while the other aspects of the proto-typical Baby Boom began to recede in the background.

Alongside the more manifest aspects of the Pakeha Baby Boom that remain in popular memory, even more radical changes in Maori family life and society were being, or were about to be, played out. These trends, neolocalisation and the onset of the Maori fertility transition, were to hold extremely significant portents for Maori society, but were rendered latent, almost out of sight, as it were.

There is one other matter, of wider international theoretical interest, that has implications for the way in which one can interpret trends that have emerged since the 1970s. The term Baby Boom is widely used to describe upsurges in fertility across the WDCs, including Japan, in the post-war period. The New Zealand Baby Boom is a poster-child for this phenomenon. But in New Zealand it was, as has been stated, a Pakeha trend, not a Maori one, and involved several key features:

1. TFRs went up from about 2.1 (1936) to 4.2 in 1961, a major increase in family size.
2. Conjugal patterns changed dramatically from a later age at marriage and significant levels of celibacy, to very early and almost universal marriage.
3. The force of reproduction moved to very young ages.

The New Zealand post-Baby Boom bust was very severe, only surpassed in the ESCs by Canada (Henripin 1968; Legare 2003: Fig. 5.2).*

As Pool and Sceats (2003: 10) note, though, using the data for WDCs reported there (see Dharmalingam *et al.* 2007: Table 5.12) as evidence for their argument:

> In these senses [the Pakeha model] a Baby Boom, properly speaking is really a neo-European [Australasia, North America] phenomenon, because the United Kingdom looks more like its continental European counterparts, and Ireland was following a different path from other WDCs, with a long-term decline. On the continent Austria meets the criterion of higher levels of force at younger ages, but not that of level. For the TFR, in contrast, the Netherlands certainly meets the criterion of level but does not experience elevated early force. On both these criteria it is perhaps Norway that comes closest to the neo-European ESCs yet its TFR is still well below theirs. The decline after the boom was also more marked in the ESCs than in the remaining WDCs with the exception of the Netherlands, while among the ESCs the UK has a lower decrease.

This raises a major question as to whether or not Europe went through a Baby Boom. Australia, Canada, New Zealand and the United States certainly did. What is interesting is that at the onset of the Baby Boom these four countries all shared something else that was lacking in Western European countries except the United Kingdom: high levels of urbanisation and high levels of urban home ownership that in the neo-Europes took the form of detached dwellings in suburbia – a seemingly ideal setting for parenting in a modern, urban, industrial world. This may have provided a solution, at least temporarily, to the seeming conflict between such a social

---

* But Canada was confounded by the totally different trend in Quebec, which in the inter-war period and right through the Baby Boom years was undergoing a fertility decline resembling that of Mediterranean countries rather than ESCs.

and economic environment and reproduction (Caldwell and Schindlmayr 2003), allowing couples to have quasi-rural lifestyles, yet to participate in the urban economy and benefit from access to urban facilities and institutions. But, as will be shown in later chapters, this tidy solution, perhaps only achieved in the Baby Boom and in the immediately post-Baby Boom years, does not seem to have been sustained.

There was also a negative aspect to this form of urban life. Even when this suburban lifestyle reached its apotheosis at the peak of the Baby Boom it may have been far from perfect: the marked gender-division of family functions and of the labour force, and reputed syndromes such as suburban neurosis may bear witness to the hidden down-side of Baby Boom family life. Certainly the wedded bliss of the Baby Boom parents often turned to separation and divorce much later, while the rapid post-Boom increases in female labour-force participation, even for women with young babies (something that would have been virtually unheard of in the Baby Boom), is also an indicator that the Baby Boom model was not necessarily ideal. Perhaps, therefore, the neolocal nuclear suburban family of the Baby Boom was as aberrant a phenomenon as the higher fertility and earlier childbearing of that era.

Finally, reference to international trends takes one back to the question raised earlier in this conclusion about the diffusion of the Pill. Regardless of whether or not old Europe went through a real Baby Boom, there is still the fascinating question as to why countries spaced out across the globe, with inadequate communications – most arrivals in New Zealand from overseas came by a ship journey that took a minimum of several days from Australia, to six weeks from Europe – saw the same phenomenon start more or less simultaneously at the end of the war. New Zealand is one country that broke the mould in terms of a finishing date for the Baby Boom, but that had adopted the Pill in almost perfect unison with other WDCs.

The fact that New Zealand was out of kilter for the end of the Baby Boom, at least as measured by some key indicators of behavioural norms, may point to the deep imprinting of value systems carried forward into the Baby Boom from the pre-war period and early colonial era. This may be because of the way that the Baby Boom was played out in New Zealand, especially the way in which the state and families themselves privileged the suburban, neolocal, nuclear family lifestyle that was the signature tune of the Baby Boom in this country. The question then arises, did these traits became imprinted in the New Zealand collective psyche in such a fashion as to affect post-Baby Boom family life?

Underlying all of these issues is one of the fundamental questions of demography to which we return in the last chapter: could a baby boom occur again? Or, more realistically, could a baby boom of a modified sort occur again? And, if so, what might those modified circumstances be?

CHAPTER SIX

Redefinition of the Nuclear Family, 1970s to the 1990s: Trends

6.1 THE END OF OUR GOLDEN AGE

CHANGES IN STRUCTURES AND FORMS

The story of the New Zealand family presented in the last three chapters, covering the period until the 1970s, has seen major shifts in household structures – size, age structures within households, neolocal suburban residence – but all this took place within a framework defined by one family form: a married couple and their offspring, and perhaps other close relatives. This chapter and the next see the accent shift, however, to high-profile changes in family forms, as living arrangements and marital status go through radical mutations and diversify. The family structural elements, by contrast, do not change in as manifest a way, although, in part, the redefinition of forms has also had an effect on structures. Moreover, the lower-profile structural changes themselves have major ramifications.

The last chapter covered a period that ended on a fulcrum: it could have tipped in either direction – more of the Baby Boom patterns, as seemed to be appearing around 1970 when teenage fertility reached a peak for Pakeha, or a reprise of the pre-war patterns abandoned in the headlong rush into the Baby Boom with its elevated fertility rates and early childbearing. Instead, the 1970s saw a sort of hybrid regime emerge: a period of low fertility, called the Baby Bust, comprising a radical shift back to the late childbearing of the inter-war years. Fertility below replacement, normally taken as 2.1 births per woman (i.e., a child each for the husband and the wife, plus a small allowance for failure to survive among a tiny minority of babies), was conditioned not by the nuptiality valve, the key factor in earlier years, but sat alongside, and seemingly despite, an early initiation of intercourse and the continuing exposure to it thereafter through consensual or more casual unions. This hybrid creature so strongly mutated and fused different elements of the past that it really constituted a new departure and one without precedents. Moreover, through the three decades since the onset of the Baby Bust this regime has become more and more entrenched.

This period not only witnessed changes in family forms, but saw family sizes drop in the 1970s and 1980s to levels below what had been seen at the depths of the Great Depression. There was a struggle to get back, momentarily, to exact replacement, before the population seemingly gave up and saw its levels of fertility fall below the magic level of 2.1 births per couple. Thus these two chapters cover a very important period in the history of the New Zealand family. Chapter Six describes the trends; Chapter Seven then attempts to analyse the co-variates and determinants of these trends, and their consequences. That story describes structural changes over the decades following the Baby Boom, changes that in the long run could seal the fate of the New Zealand population in the very long run, even to whether it survives or not.

There is yet another dimension to these changes in the family. Once again the New Zealand trends focused on here, including the associated panics and genuine *angst* they have engendered and that we will describe, are not unique to us, but in one form or another have occurred across all of the WDCs. Indeed, analogous changes are also taking place across the former Soviet Bloc countries in Europe, across East Asia and South-east Asia, and even in South India (Caldwell and Schindlmayr 2003). In the Soviet countries, the Mediterranean and in some parts of East Asia the Baby Bust has even seen some societies face levels of sub-replacement, 1.1–1.3 births per couple, that are historically unprecedented at a national level in normal times at least for as long a period. The dual themes of this commonality of experience and the continuity of low levels of replacement will be returned to in later chapters, but suffice to note here that the Baby Bust is yet another example of a megatrend, similar to those noted earlier for the Baby Boom and the end of the nineteenth century, occurring simultaneously in a number of countries.

At the same time there were other things occurring that were far more manifest, at least in the eyes of the media and public, and these were the changes occurring to other dimensions of family morphologies. This period saw a shift away from the neolocal nuclear family to, for the first time in this history since 1840, an increasingly wide range of family forms. The appearance of these forms, or more strictly speaking the increased prevalence that therefore gave these behaviours a higher profile, was blamed for other wider social transformations and even the breakdown of society itself. If a link was made to the structural changes, such as falling family sizes, it was also to blame this on shifts in family forms.

This seemed to take the society into new and troubling situations, although none of the family forms that emerged in the 1970s and 1980s were totally unheard of: each one had some sort of antecedent. Take, for example, cohabitation: there had always been a small number of couples who cohabited. In some social circles, such as the aristocracy, adultery and other forms of extra-marital sex were frowned upon and gossiped about yet were also not uncommon events. But it was the increasing prevalence rather than the novelty of such morphologies, reinforced by the fact that they were now coming out in the open, along with an almost bewilderingly wide range of other moral and legislative changes,* that gave them their high profile. The proportional contribution of these different approaches to sexual and family life increased dramatically, or else their prevalence became more widely reported and more publicly evident, and transformed the overall architecture of family forms during the period from 1973 to the 1990s. Moreover, this transformation took place very quickly – of the entire story written about in this book, covering 165 years, this revolution took place over only ten to twenty years (only 6–12% of the entire span). One can sympathise to some degree with socially conservative observers who have looked on these rapid changes with feelings of deep concern about the future of the society; certainly, one cannot dismiss their fears as baseless.

An increasing democratisation of the transgression of sexual taboos had been seen in the Baby Boom, with the so-called dating patterns of that era occurring among at least a significant minority of teenagers and starting at high school – the American family sociology textbooks of the era were replete with chapters on dating and related behaviours. But in that pre-Pill era the pregnancies that often followed were seen as something shameful, to be cloaked by rapid marriage or by adoption. The Baby Bust, however, was to see transparency taken to its logical conclusion, the more hypocritical elements dispensed with, perhaps for ever, and for dating ('going steady') to become cohabiting and associated relationships. Above all pre-marital sex was no longer a transgression but a prevalent social behaviour out in the open under unabashed public gaze, as was evident a decade ago in this 1995 engagement notice in the *New Zealand Herald*:

Jocelyn and Shane announce with glee, We're engaged to be married and about to become three.

A SEARCH FOR UNDERLYING CAUSES
In part, the range of morphologies seen in the early twenty-first century is a function of inexorable demographic changes of two sorts. One has its genesis within the family itself, a result of what is termed 'a demographic squeeze'. But secondly, alongside that were shifts in the wider society because of age-structural transitions, including ageing (Pool 2003), and other factors such as

---

* For example, moral and legislative changes relating to authority and power relations within marriages, the rights of married women, divorce, civil marriage, easy access to contraception, especially the Pill, lifting of interdictions against abortion, decriminalisation of homosexuality, recognition of the rights of natural children, replacement of paternal authority with parental and the disjunction between marriage and family building (listed by Peron 2003: 122).

migration. These changes have been driven by, or co-varied with, transformations in societal value systems.

The squeeze compressed the childbearing and parenting span, not for all women but certainly for a significant proportion. It came about because younger cohorts (<30 years) were delaying parenting, while the older cohorts of Baby Boom parents who had had their children at young ages were often 'empty nesters'. But the compression of childbearing, concentrated among couples in their late twenties and at ages 30–39 years, that emerged in this period happened to occur when the age-structural transition delivered inflated cohorts, born during the first peak of the Baby Boom around 1960, into these strategically important childbearing ages. This was essentially the genesis of the Baby Blip regime of the years around 1990. This echo-effect was then to be repeated around 2000 when generations born during the second peak of the Baby Boom, around 1970, reached their late twenties and thirties. But there was also a difference between the events of 1990 and those of 2000: around 1990, there was a sudden and short-lived return to very early childbearing that occurred among women born around 1970, women who themselves had been born to very young mothers. This perhaps was the one-off factor that ever so briefly carried the TFR across the line into replacement. These largely demographic phenomena affected other morphologies. Increases in the proportions of non-related, couple-only and single-person families, documented in the Baby Bust, were of this provenance. These changes then produced transformations in living arrangements.

Turning to other wider demographic trends, age-structural changes came from what are termed disordered cohort-flows,* and their resultant momentum effects. These have played a significant role in population change nationally and regionally (Pool 2003; Lepina and Pool 2000; Pool *et al.* 2005a-e), and in dictating the sizes of cohorts at various life-cycle stages, including, most importantly for our purposes, the parenting ages. Overall population growth slowed despite very large migration inflows, especially in the early 1970s and in the early and late 1990s, and again in the early 2000s. Yet, despite immigration and despite decreases in fertility during the Baby Bust, from 1971 to 2001 natural increase was still overwhelmingly the most important contributor to overall growth. For example, from 1971 to 1996, the period covered in Chapters Six and Seven, migration only contributed 11% of the total population growth (Pool and Bedford 1997). Nevertheless, because of its age and ethnic specificity, its regional impacts (especially in Auckland) and its

---

* Disordered cohort-flows come about through the birth, at irregular intervals, of cohorts of significantly varying sizes. These effects may be further mediated by mortality (but only in high-mortality regimes), and by migration inflows and outflows, but birth cohort sizes remain the over-riding factor (Pool 2003).

effects on the ethnic distribution of New Zealand-born offspring, especially in the case of Pacific peoples, migration added to factors transforming New Zealand's family morphologies in this period.

Beyond these demographically driven changes there was an increased prevalence of forms and other structural factors, such as sole parenting, which were due more to lifestyle and values transformations than to endogenous family demographic changes. Above all, there was a shift in the family statuses of all household actors, of children, families, couples and individuals, from formal to more informal forms. Examples are the move to cohabitation rather than marriage as a preferred form of first union, and, as a concomitant shift, increases in the rates of ex-nuptial birth (albeit often to couples in stable unions) and changes in living arrangements (such as more adult children residing with their parents and more couple-only households, in part attendant upon increases in the prevalence of 'cohabiting unions', involving both co-residence of the couple and when they do not co-reside). Although the high-profile changes discussed in this chapter revolve around forms, all dimensions of family life went through shifts in this period: there were size changes and, as noted above, because of the squeeze family age-structure profiles were transformed.

Taking the history of New Zealand family morphologies documented in this book, one of the periods with the greatest short-term changes, as measured by velocity, occurred at the beginning of the two and a half decades covered in this chapter – the other had been at the onset of the Baby Boom. In the 1970s, change was both rapid and consistent for Maori and Pakeha, but was extremely accelerated for Maori. In the 1940s it had been more turbulent, dictated by the troop flows in and out of New Zealand, and thus the speed of trends at that time is more difficult to gauge (see Khawaja 1985).

There were also incipient signs of what might be a new, historically unique, set of transformations emerging by the early 1990s. These intensified over that decade and into the twenty-first century, and will be the subject of later chapters. The outline above relates to the population as a whole. But beneath this averaged-out set of changes the story was far more complex. The patterns of family change varied between ethnic groups, and, in turn, were also affected by wider macro-demographic changes. These had a differential impact on the distribution and trends of the population across various ethnic groups and between New Zealand's regions. Such mutations and transformations meant that family life in New Zealand was becoming more diversified, a trend that strengthened in the period to be covered in later chapters.

Despite the relative insignificance of net migration, New Zealand diversified ethnically in this period; the new arrivals were often replacing departing New Zealanders. First this was because of inflows from the Pacific in addition to immigration from traditional sources; then secondly and more recently through rapid inflows from Asia which added to the traditional flows; and, thirdly, from new sources such as South Africa and a wide range of other countries. Today higher and higher proportions of Pacific peoples are born in New Zealand, and the major movements to and from Pacific countries are likely to be short term as New Zealand-born or -resident Pacific peoples travel to visit these source countries. The impacts of this diversification were mainly felt, however, in Auckland, as migrants clustered there, and to a lesser degree in Wellington. These are the only two regions in the country in which more than 10% of the population comes from ethnic groups other than Pakeha or Maori (Pool *et al.* 2005e).

The period from 1971 was notable for the high level of inter-regional mobility and for marked patterns of regional redistribution. This contrasted with the previous decades, from about 1920 to 1970, during which a sort of regional equilibrium had been maintained (Pool 2002). The mobility over the 1980s and 1990s was linked to a major industrial labour-force transformation, involving a shift to both the highly skilled and the less skilled tertiary-sector jobs. As a result there was a dichotomisation into regions with demographic and job growth and regions where growth was slow or even negative. This, in turn, was related to individual and household incomes (Pool *et al.* 2005c; Cochrane *et al.* 2007).

DATA SOURCES AND METHODS

Of all the periods discussed in this book those covered in Chapters Six to Nine have at their disposal the best documentation. While this is hardly surprising, there must be concern that, despite some recent catch-up, New Zealand's evidence base in this area still falls well behind those of many other developed countries (see Pool *et al.* 2007).

More specifically, problems abound for the analysis of nuptiality. Except briefly from 1948–52, no separate data on registered marriage have been collected by ethnicity and thus any rates relate to the total population. Even for the census marital status data there are problems, as Maori data were available by broad age-groups only in 1976, 1981 and 1996. Thus, generally speaking, the nuptiality analysis here for the family statuses dimension, and in relation to research on marriage, divorce and remarriage using registration data, involves no disaggregation by ethnicity (see Jackson and Pool 1994: 45 and 73–74). In contrast the NZW:FEE data do permit such a breakdown, but are based on self-declaration not on a registered procedure.

Nevertheless, compared to previous eras, the period since the mid-1970s has seen major advances in the range and quality of data sources and thus in the studies available:

- Census data on living arrangements are available from 1976 in computer-readable format (prior to 1976 one is dependent on published tabulations). The adequacy of these data as indicators of everyday life and the structures they describe has been examined already in the introductory chapters (see also Pool *et al.* 2007). This analysis concluded that the census data do generally reflect the family forms experienced by most New Zealanders. The census collected data on children ever born alive at the 1971, 1976, 1981, 1996 and 2006 enumerations (Heenan 1977; Hockey and Khawaja 1982; Khawaja 1985; Khawaja and Hockey 1979; Maclennan 1981; Statistics New Zealand 2001, 2004). In writing this book in late 2005 and early 2006, we could not avail ourselves of data from the March 2006 census.

- From the 1980s onwards, regular Household Labour Force and Household Economic surveys have been conducted.
- The NZW:FEE survey gives retrospective data on dynamics and structures relating to cohorts born from 1936 to 1975. The 2001 NZFFS survey reinforces this.
- There has been a range of other more highly focused surveys on aspects of structures and dynamics (e.g. Fleming and Easting 1994; Koopman-Boyden *et al.* 2000).
- There have been two large, long-running longitudinal surveys of children born in Dunedin (1972) and in Christchurch (1977), of which the latter provides a more varied insight into family dynamics (Fergusson 1998).
- There is a more recent longitudinal analysis of Maori families and households (Fitzgerald *et al.* 2000; Durie *et al.* 2003).
- Recently there have been childcare and time-use surveys (Ministry of Women's Affairs and Statistics New Zealand 2001).

There are also some systematic substantive studies, several of which should be mentioned. The Social Monitoring Group (SMG) of the New Zealand Planning Council initiated a cross-sectional stock-taking of New Zealanders at various life-cycle stages using the 1981 census as a data-base. This was repeated for the 1986 census (SMG 1985, 1989) and one member of the group, Judith Davey, has continued this through to the 1991, 1996 and 2001 censuses. Davey's 2001 report not only provides a snapshot for this period, but compares across all five censuses (Davey 1993, 1998, 2003). Jackson and Pool prepared a comprehensive report for the New Zealand Institute of Social Research and Development. This brought together data on family formation over a very long time span, marital registrations and statuses over a very long period, and family structures from 1976 on (Jackson and Pool 1994: detailed data tabulated in appendices). Janet Dickson and others (1997) updated this. Pool (1991) analysed changes in Maori society in the 1970s and 1980s. Ian Shirley, Peggy Koopman-Boyden, Ian Pool and Susan St John carried out a

comprehensive analysis of family policy in relation to formation and structures, as part of a cross-national study (Shirley *et al.* 1997).

Finally, Johnstone and Pool (1996b) identified links between labour-force
participation by family members, family size and household incomes. This
area has been expanded by a number of studies which are more relevant to
Chapters Eight and Nine and will be discussed there (e.g. see Callister 1998).

6.2. OVERALL CHANGES IN FAMILY MORPHOLOGIES

This period has seen high-profile changes in family structures and forms
for all major ethnic groups in New Zealand. Because the patterns of change
differed, separate attention will be paid to them below. Together, however,
for all the dimensions identified in Chapter Two, the changes created a very
different family-scape from that which had pertained in the early 1970s:

- family sizes changed within both nuclear and extended families;
- following a Baby Bust to below-replacement levels of fertility
  around 1990, in the Baby Blip, Pakeha rates of reproduction
  returned to replacement and continued drifting slowly down until
  the end of the period covered here;
- Maori fertility decreased very rapidly and then increased
  modestly, a trend that may well have been confounded by changes
  in the reporting of ethnicity on birth certificates and in censuses;
- family age structures changed very significantly;
- the patterns of family statuses changed radically;
- the profile of living arrangements also changed; and
- the trend towards dispersed, neolocal nuclear residence was a
  dominant feature but took on a variety of forms.

The changes involved are a curious mix. In terms of family size and age
structures, there was a reprise of the conservative family types, particularly
the delayed marriage and childbearing, of the inter-war years (Pool *et al.*
1998). Yet, along with that, there was a shift to informal statuses and living
arrangements that had no significant precedents in New Zealand family
history. Such forms had existed in the past, but only among marginal
groups or small minorities; it was the high prevalence of consensual unions
that was a new factor.[*]

---

[*] The term 'consensual' is used here as in Roman law to mean that only the consent of the partners
is necessary, whereas a registered union is one requiring the witness and consent of third
parties, notably of course the state, plus for religious weddings the publication of banns, a public
announcement in church and the consent of the preacher.

Beyond this, and underlying the other major changes, was a driver also without antecedents. For the first time in history contraceptive technology was so effective that, for the vast majority of women and couples, the direct links between first regular exposure to intercourse, entry into unions and parenting were broken (Santow 1989). Nevertheless,

> There is still not perfect control of reproduction. Some women will become pregnant when very young and face the burden of being a young parent, often requiring welfare support, yet, unlike what happened in the Baby Boom, not putting up their babies for adoption. There is a minority of others who delay childbearing and who are very effective contraceptors, but for whom difficulties may be encountered conceiving when they finally decide to have children. They may also not find babies available for adoption (Pool *et al.* 1999: 155; see also Ball 1999a, b).

A change related to this was a shift in patterns and levels of nuptial and ex-nuptial childbearing. It will be recalled from the last three chapters that both Pakeha and Maori New Zealand had a long-standing tradition of ex-nuptial conception, typically followed by marriage and nuptial parturition. This trend reached its peak in the mid-Baby Boom years, as can be implied from the data in Table 6.1. But over the next 30 years the situation changed, so that by 1992 a significant minority of children were born ex-nuptially, but lower percentages of the ex-nuptially conceived were born within marriage.

Table 6.1: New Zealand, Total, Nuptial, Ex-nuptial and Ex-nuptially Conceived Births, 1962, 1972, 1982, 1992 and 2002 (Percentage of Total), All Ethnic Groups Combined

Year	Total born	Total nuptially born		Nuptially born within one year of marriage*		Ex-nuptially born		Total ex-nuptially conceived	
	No.	No.	%	No.	%	No.	%	No.	%
1962	65,014	59,787	91	8356	13	5227	8	13,598	21
1972	63,215	53,821	85	7689	12	9394	15	17,034	27
1982	49,938	38,552	77	3512	7	11,386	23	14,800	30
1992	59,165	37,474	64	2891	5	21,742	36	24,079	41
2002	54,021	30,473	56	2471	5	23,548	44	26,019	48

* Most of these would be within the first nine months, see Pool and Crawford (1980); Morgan *et al.* (2001)

Sources: Department of Statistics (various years), Vital Statistics; Department of Statistics (1982), Demographic Trends.

Unfortunately public discourse in this area is coloured by the fact that there is a great deal of confounding of ex-nuptial childbearing with (i) ex-nuptial conception but marital birth, (ii) adolescent fertility and (iii) sole parenting. As was shown in Chapter Five and will be discussed further here, adolescent birth rates peaked in the Baby Boom then plummeted during the Baby Bust. But this peak was associated with early marriage precipitated by pregnancy, a trend that affected couples married during the Baby Boom but who often divorced thereafter, in the periods covered in this chapter and the next two. In contrast, ex-nuptial fertility properly speaking increased, as is shown in Table 6.1, but the age of childbearing outside marriage also went up (Dharmalingam *et al.* 2007: Table 6.1). Finally, it must be stressed that sole-parenting rates are highest at the middle reproductive ages (Dickson *et al.* 1997); again, an important truism that is often overlooked. To be a sole parent one must first become a parent. If on average parenting is delayed, then so too will be sole parenting.

6.3 CHANGES IN FAMILY FORMS: THE SHIFT FROM MARRIAGE TO COHABITATION

ISSUES

One of the clearest revolutions occurring in the post-Baby Boom period took place over a few years in the 1970s. At that time, both Maori and Pakeha went through a major change in family forms, indicated by a radical shift away from formal marriage as a preferred first union to informal cohabitation, a movement to a type of union not nearly as prevalent, at least in New Zealand, in any earlier period for which there are data. This very significant crossover shows up in Figures 6.1 and 6.2. What is evident in these figures is the rapidity of the shift from marriage to cohabitation. But the net result was that the propensity to enter into unions of any form did not change very much. Entry into unions, then, was not declining, but the form they were taking was. In multi-variate hazards models the most powerful co-variates of the propensity of women to cohabit were: the cohort to which they belonged (the younger the cohort, the higher the level); the period (higher propensity more recently); and whether they were working (higher), regardless of their occupation (Dharmalingam *et al.* 2004: Table 2.7; for definitions see also Chapter Five, the section on data sources).

The shift in status from marriage to cohabitation did not mean that there had been a decrease in union formation. In fact, until very recently (see below) the combined total of first marriages and consensual unions has been similar to those for marriage alone in the Baby Boom. Moreover, entry into a first union was at a young age, again until very recently. But the availability of efficient contraception meant that for many couples, whether living together or married, parenting was being delayed. This had the same net effect, but for a very different reason, as the delays in marriage which were common before the Baby Boom (Dharmalingam *et al.* 2007: Tables 5.2–5.4 and 5.6).

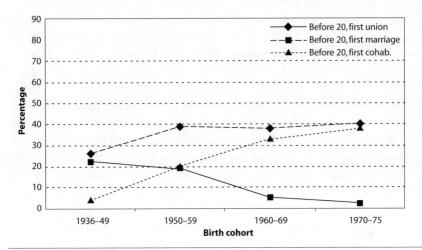

Figure 6.1: Percentage of Women in Each Cohort who by Age 20 had: (1) Entered a First Union, of Whatever Type; and (2) Married or Cohabited

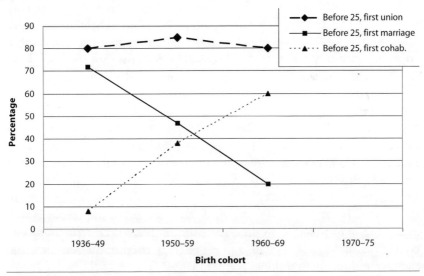

Figure 6.2: Percentage of Women in Each Cohort who by Age 25 had: (1) Entered a First Union, of Whatever Type; and (2) Married or Cohabited

Note: Marriage + cohabitation = entering a first union of whatever type.

For Maori, as concepts of legitimacy and illegitimacy were challenged in legislation, some of the shifts in the proportions of unions that were consensual were a function of the declining need to register marriages in order to be eligible for social benefits. For them this often represented, however, a return to community-sanctioned unions.

Data coming from directly comparable studies show that cohabitation is now widespread not only in New Zealand but in other Anglo-Saxon countries such as Canada, Australia, the United States and Britain. This has been analysed exhaustively for Canada (e.g. Lapierre-Adamcyk and Charvet 1999: 5–6; Peron 2003; Beaujot and Muhammad 2006: 28–30). New Zealand's levels, for both Maori and Pakeha, are at the higher end of those in Western developed and Eastern European countries (Klijzing and Macura 1997). They are also higher than those for English Canadians, but near those for French Canadians (Lapierre-Adamcyk *et al.* 1997). There is, moreover, what Michael Murphy has called a 'qualitative' change in cohabiting (for example, average length). He reports that while cohabitation may be seen as a prelude to marriage and therefore as having a positive impact, but it may also have 'negative effects', in that it may delay marriage or become an alternative to it (Murphy 2000: 53–54).

Furthermore, there is the vexed question of the stability of cohabitation (Beaujot and Muhammad 2006: 28) and the way in which such unions are becoming a prevalent form for families of origin for children. More and more, some commentators say, American 'families with children are very much affected by the increased time spent in cohabitation rather than marriage' (Bumpass and Liu 2000: 39), but this presupposes that cohabiting unions are not only less stable, but also are likely to have negative consequences for the children, a point under constant debate.

Even taking the simple formal dimensions alone, putting to one side the structural aspects, this raises a fundamental set of questions that have legal as well as social policy implications, particularly in the light of initiatives aimed at reforming laws relating to issues such as 'matrimonial property'. In 1998 Pool had already noted that in New Zealand 'a problem of defining cohabitation may arise', when we compare census data on *de facto* unions and survey data on cohabitation with *de jure* unions as reported in the census. The number of reported *de facto* unions in the census is well below the percentage of women reporting in NZW:FEE that they were cohabiting. In 1991, 16% of 20–24 year olds reported in the censuses that they were in *de facto* unions; NZW:FEE gave a level at the same age of 28%. He concluded that 'we now may be seeing three sorts of conjugal union: *de jure* – that is registered marriages; *de facto* – implying greater durability and public commitment; [and] other forms of cohabiting' (Pool

1998: 325–26).* Burch and Belanger (1999) have argued that this question is far more complex than such a simple trichotomy (or now quartet, see footnote) might suggest.† It also involves complex processes that such categorisations obscure. For example, a 'committed union' could involve either of co-residence or LAT status (see below).

Finally, not only have recent decades witnessed the separation of the links between union formation and reproduction referred to above (Santow 1989) – essentially, the ending of the nuptiality valve effects – but a clear division has emerged between union formation *per se* and household formation. The Quebec demographer Yves Peron has set out very clearly the Baby Boom pattern that was the norm prior to this disjunction that now affects every aspect of family morphologies (Peron 2003: 111 and 125, translation present authors):

> Before the 1970s it had been hardly ever accepted that a young couple could set up a household before they became formally married. Young people would normally 'go around' together [date] for some time in order to get to know one another better and to become better acquainted with their future in-laws, then, after the marriage proposal had been made, they would eventually become engaged and following that would marry before cohabiting; if a pregnancy ensued when they were going out together, they would marry before parturition occurred, and if not they were separated and, in many cases, the young woman was placed in an institution to bear the child and leave it there. The children born or conceived within marriage were the only ones to enjoy full family rights . . .
>
> [By the 1990s] it was not only at the start of conjugal life that marriage was deemed less and less necessary, but also for the other steps of conjugal life, including the birth of a first child.

Thus there were massive shifts in the value systems relating not only to union formation but also to households and wider family relationships. Legal systems in jurisdictions such as New Zealand have had to legislate to accord rights to the immediate partners involved in cohabiting relation-

---

* There is also a problem with the reporting of a *de jure* unions in the census. Pool estimated that 7% of women claiming to be 'married' in the 1986 census were in fact cohabiting (1992). Recent legislation has delineated the legal rights of couples in 'civil unions' and allowed their registration. This adds a fourth, more formally recognised type of union falling between *de jure* and *de facto*.

† Indeed, just in terms of that dimension, and according to Villeneuve-Gokalp (1990), there are five forms of cohabitation alone: (i) 'prelude to marriage'; (ii) 'a test before marriage'; (iii) an 'ephemeral union lasting less than a year'; (iv) 'a stable union without commitment (implying neither marriage nor children, but prolonged)'; and (v) 'a consensual union' ('union libre' in French; consensual is not an exact translation), 'a couple with one or more children, but not married' (translation Ian Pool, from Burch and Belanger 1999: 34).

ships of given durations and their natural offspring. But increasingly these trends may involve less and less often issues of laws and mores between individuals, and more and more the socio-legal organisation of family structures.

In this way the law has struggled to keep up with social custom. For Pakeha, unions increasingly became 'formalised' not by some legal process but by their mere endurance and, through that, by community acceptance (as had long been the practice for Maori) but until recently such a sanction had no legal underpinnings. In a chapter written in the mid-1980s for a book on New Zealand population issues, the lawyer, later judge and governor-general Sylvia Cartwright noted that 'Although *de facto* relationships are rapidly becoming acceptable to the community, except in some legal circumstances or where there is a child in the relationship, the *de facto* husband or wife has little or none of the statutory protection afforded to their married counterparts' (1985: 187). In the Civil Union Act 2004, however, Parliament attempted to overcome most aspects of this lack of 'statutory protection', and also extended this to same-sex couples. Legislation was simply trying to catch up with societal practice.

In contrast, the reconciliation between law and social practice for the rights of children had been established much earlier, in the later Baby Boom, by the Status of Children Act 1969, passed well before Cartwright wrote her paper. She noted:

> This piece of legislation although largely unnoticed at its inception has had a profound effect on the rights of children in New Zealand. Essentially the Act was introduced to remove all discrimination between children born in or out of marriage, and as a consequence even the term 'illegitimate' is no longer used in legislation or in judicial decisions . . . A child born during marriage or ex-nuptially now has the right to be treated equally with any child of either parent's marriage under his or her will (1985: 188).

EMPIRICAL EVIDENCE

The only data allowing a review of these issues over time and on a national scale come from the NZW:FEE and NZFFS (Dharmalingam *et al.* 1996; Lapierre-Adamcyk *et al.* 1997; see also Marsault *et al.* 1997). Analyses of this survey, as noted already, show that at a more general level the rise and spread of cohabitation coincided with the decline of marriage as the preferred first union. Among both Maori and Pakeha women born after 1951 and who had not entered into marriage as a first union, about 75–85% entered first cohabitation by age 29 years. There were, however, some ethnic differentials in the cumulative proportions cohabiting by age 21 years. While about 70% of Maori women born during 1971–75 (and who had not entered marriage as first union) were cohabiting by age 21, the corresponding figure for Pakeha was 44%. A difference of this magnitude between Maori and Pakeha is noticeable for all birth cohorts, including the oldest (Dharmalingam *et al.* 2004). The pattern of union status by age at the time of survey is consistent with the 1991 census results (Carmichael 1996), although, as we have just remarked, the census figures are under-counts. In the NZW:FEE age-specific cohabitation rates decrease from a high of about 27% for 20–24 to 9% for the 35–39 age-group.

Results of a multi-variate analysis of NZW:FEE data confirm that those born after 1955 were more likely to have entered cohabitation as a first union than those born before 1955, and Maori had higher rates than Pakeha. It is also clear that having an educational qualification decreases the propensity for first cohabitation compared to those with no qualification, and the university educated have the lowest likelihood of entering consensual unions (Dharmalingam *et al.* 2004: Table 2.7). While the entire period after 1970 has experienced increased probabilities compared to the pre-1970 period, there seems to have been a relative decrease in the likelihood for the most recent period for which data are available, 1991–95. This is an interesting result which fits with what is being reported, for example, for Sweden and Canada (Lapierre-Adamcyk *et al.* 1997).

Thus, by the early 1990s, levels of cohabitation among women in their early twenties were dropping. This seems to have been because of the increased enrolment in tertiary education institutions, and the growth of attend-ant costs since the late 1980s, making living in an independent union less desired or feasible (Jan Hoem, formerly Stockholm University, now at Max Planck Institute, Germany, personal communication in response to Dharma-lingam *et al.* 1996). This explains the overall lower rates, noted above, for the university educated, because, in contrast, the probability of having cohabited by age 25 or 30 years shows no such difference by education (Dharmalingam *et al.* 2004: Tables 2.5).

Supporting this is the fact that a new living arrangement was emerging by the last decade of the millennium, especially for Pakeha women aged 20–24 years (Pool 1998; Pool *et al.* 1999). This was a pattern whereby couples lived separately but in an intimate relationship – LATs, living apart together, as the Europeans term these conjugal unions. In 1995 in the NZW:FEE, 20% of women at this age were in this sort of union, as against 27% cohabiting and 37% in no union of any sort (Pool 1998: 320).* This was simply an indication

---

* In Europe the LAT phenomenon has a further dimension not yet reported for New Zealand: older couples (widows, widowers or divorcees) who form this type of relationship. For many older people there may be advantages to do with pensions in remaining legally widowed or divorced while seeking the companionship of a relationship (Gierveld 2005).

of another trend, that the young were now quitting the family nest at older and older ages; North Americans call this trend the 'cluttered nest' (Boyd and Pryor 1989; discussed further in later chapters). Indeed, the 1991 New Zealand Budget had formalised aspects of this by making families responsible for 'dependent' children in their late teens, and, unless the family had a low income, for unmarried offspring until they were 25 years old (Jackson 1994a, b, c).

The international literature has suggested that cohabitation or involvement in a *de facto* union can reduce the likelihood of marriage but, conversely, increase the rates of separation for those marriages that do occur (Cherlin 1981; Sarantalos 1984; Spanier 1983 and 1985; Khoo 1985; Bennet *et al.* 1988; Rindfuss and VandenHeuvel 1990; Teachman *et al.* 1991). The longitudinal study of children in Christchurch showed that cohabitation converted into marriage was associated with an increased likelihood of separation; this result was also supported by multi-variate analyses of the NZW:FEE data (Dharmalingam *et al.* 2004; Fergusson 1987).

Not surprisingly, formal marriage rates, both crude and age-specific, have also declined in New Zealand, especially at ages below 25 years. Moreover, the highest proportion of marriages at each age switched dramatically in this period from 20–24 years (men) and 16–24 years (women) to 25–34 years for both sexes. In part, this shift was a component of the reprise noted earlier, but it was also a function of the shift from marriage to cohabitation as a preferred form of first union (Jackson and Pool 1994: Chapt. 5; O'Neill 1985). The NZW:FEE data showed that the experience of cohabitation increased the likelihood of first marriage, but having a birth before marriage decreased this probability (Dharmalingam *et al.* 2004: 2.5). There thus seems to be another dimension: 'if cohabitation precedes most marriages, and is also gradually replacing marriage, then only those that are committed to the "traditional values" (e.g. the desirability of having children in a legal conjugal union) will [enter a first union as a] marriage and thus [incidentally, also be] exposed to the risk of legal divorce' (Dharmalingam *et al.* 1998a).

It appears that at the macro-level (national) there is a positive correlation between the level of cohabitation and childbearing in this status (Klijzing and Macura 1997). In general, countries with a high level of cohabitation overall have a high level of childbearing in cohabitation. In New Zealand, about 15% of mothers aged 30–34 at the time of survey in 1995 were cohabiting when they had their first child; in Canada (in 1990), with very low levels, it was only 2%, whereas it was 48% in Sweden, the highest of all countries (Klijzing and Macura 1997). According to Klijzing and Macura, New Zealand is in the group of countries with higher levels.

These comments should not be read as suggesting that a propensity to form unions of any sort at all has declined significantly; the rates for all forms of unions in Figures 6.1 and 6.2 should dispel this notion. Thus in New Zealand, as in Canada, 'there is a strong preference for living in unions' (Beaujot and Muhammad 2006: 28, referring to Canada). Instead, the drop-off in marriage rates has been offset to a considerable degree by the increases in cohabitation.

In this period cohabitation frequently became a step towards marriage with the same partner, and this seems to be true for a wide range of social groups (e.g. there are few differences by ethnicity or education, see Dharmalingam *et al.* 2007: Table 5.5). For the cohort born in 1950–59 and for more recent generations, the overwhelming majority of women, more than four-fifths, had formed a union by age 25 years, but this was likely to be a cohabiting union rather than a marriage. In this regard there is a clear-cut difference between women born before 1950, who were the Baby Boom parents, and who formed their first union as a marriage, and those born since then, who became the Baby Bust and Baby Blip parents and whose first unions typically took the form of cohabitation; those born 1950–59 represent the cohorts in transition. But of those women who had cohabited in a first union, most converted it to a marriage. Data from NZW:FEE show that this occurred within five years in the case of the 92% of such women who first cohabited at eighteen years or older, and within ten years for those who first cohabited at ages below eighteen years. As is shown in Table 6.2, the younger the birth cohort, the greater the proportion of women who were likely to enter into cohabitation as their first union. For instance, among those born in the 1960s who had entered into a first union, 60% had cohabitated compared to 38% among those born during the 1950s and only 8% among those born before 1950.

Nevertheless, there may well be increases in the numbers of people, even at prime reproductive ages who, although perhaps sexually active, are choosing to live alone, neither marrying nor cohabiting. Again, this is not a new phenomenon: the ageing bachelor or the working spinster who boarded with a widowed landlady or in a 'boarding house' was certainly a tradition of the inter-war years, but this type of arrangement was less evident in the Baby Boom except for younger students, apprentices or workers. Today this has taken a different form as, rather than board, such people tend, literally, to live alone. This has the effect of increasing the numbers of one-person households whose occupier is aged younger than 45 years. In 1976, this figure stood at 5% of all households with occupiers aged 30–44 years; by 2001 this had grown to 14% (Dharmalingam *et al.* 2007: Table 5.11).

If the analysis is restricted to registered marriages, it appears that the age-differentials between partners of all statuses at the time of the wedding for first marriages were limited (around two years) and did not change much in this period: the age-gap for first marriages actually rose more quickly than that for remarriages. The narrow gap followed the pattern in the Baby Boom but contrasts markedly with what had occurred in the pioneer period when, typically, grooms had been significantly older than brides (five or six years). Moreover, in the Baby Bust this relatively narrow gap even carried across to the remarriage of divorcees (3.5 to 3.9 years), whereas for widowed persons the gap was much larger (7.1 to 8.9 years). What is perhaps more important is that, over the period, there was a systematic increase in the median age of marriage for each gender of three years for first marriages and four years for divorcees. The median age for first marriages remained in the twenties; for remarriage of divorcees the range was in the thirties, but reached 40.7 years for males in 1991; and for widowed of both genders it was older, varying between 50.4 and 61.8 years for men, and 52.61 and 53.4 for women. The proportion of marriages involving at least one divorcee rose from 12% of all marriages in 1976 to 22% in 1991 (Jackson and Pool 1994: Table 5.10 and 73).*

A related and interesting but less frequently studied issue is the entry of men into unions: the focus is normally on women because of the flow-on effects to family formation. In one of the rare New Zealand studies on this issue the social economist Callister (2000a: 19) looked at men and showed that there were declines between 1986 and 1995 in the proportions living in couples. Among the co-variates he studied was employment and he concluded that 'men who have poor prospects in the labour market also have poor prospects in the marriage market'.

Women who first cohabited at older ages (25 years and over) were likely to convert these unions into marriage with the same partner after a short duration. Thus it is only partially correct to see cohabitation as a substitute for marriage. Typically it had become a family formation sub-phase: from celibacy one entered a first cohabiting union, and then converted this into marriage. In this regard, the term celibacy here does not imply the total absence of exposure to intercourse, but simply not being in a longer-lasting relationship (in the NZW:FEE the question on cohabiting/marriage excluded relationships of less than three months), and thus took a different form from that earlier in the twentieth century.

It is interesting that the proportion of Pakeha women who had had two or more unions increased, but was still a minority: 6% before age 20, and 21% before 25 years. For Maori the proportion having one partner or two or more before these ages was much higher. But as was true for Pakeha, there were some indications over the early 1990s of a downturn in this

---

* We computed medians for populations of each gender and status. Strictly speaking, this is not an exact measure as a man of one status may marry a woman of a different status. But getting a more exact measure involves far more complex computations.

phenomenon (Pool *et al.* 1999: Table 2.3). Data on the number of cohabiting unions entered into by a woman show that about one-third of those who had cohabited by the time of the survey in 1995 had done so more than once. There do not seem to be ethnic differentials in the proportion of women having cohabited more than once.

Table 6.2: Type of First Union, of Any Sort, Entered Before a Given Age, by Birth Cohort, NZW:FEE

Characteristics		Cumulative proportion entering any first union, by type, before age:				
		20 years	25 years	30 years	30+ years	Number of women
Birth cohort	Union type					
1936–49	Marriage	.22	.72	.81	.84	685
	Cohabitation	.04	.08	.11	.14	109
	Not yet entered	–	–	–	–	12
	All unions	.26	.80	.92	.98	815
1950–59	Marriage	.19	.47	.51		430
	Cohabitation	.20	.38	.43		379
	Not yet entered					18
	All unions	.39	.85	.94		827
1960–69	Marriage	.05	.20			213
	Cohabitation	.33	.60			592
	Not yet entered					82
	All unions	.35	.80			887
1970–75	Marriage	.02				34
	Cohabitation	.38				282
	Not yet entered					171
	All unions	.40				487

Source: Dharmalingam *et al.* 2007: Table 5.6. Note the 'not yet entered a union' is purely a detail as obviously the younger the cohort the greater the number.

6.4 CHANGES IN FORMS: DIVORCE, UNION DISSOLUTION, REMARRIAGE

Given the shift-shares between marriage and cohabitation that we have shown above, it is not surprising that patterns of union disruption and reconstitution have gone through significant changes as well. Divorce rates, which, it must be stressed, denote only the formal termination of unions, also increased in this period, going through their most rapid increases in the 1980s. There was an acceleration at two points when new legislation increased the support women would get following a dissolution: the Social Security Amendment Act (1973), which brought in the Domestic Purposes Benefit, and the Matrimonial Property Act (1976), which attempted to provide for an equitable distribution of property after separation or divorce. Rates that had been climbing monotonically were then interrupted by a spike, an almost doubling of the rate, attendant upon the Family Proceedings

Act (1980) which further liberalised grounds for divorce (cf. Canada, Peron 2003: 125–29) (O'Neill 1985; Cartwright 1985). From then on rates increased, but at a decelerated speed (McPherson 1995: esp. 7; see also her bibliography) particularly when age-specific rates are examined. Moreover, as fewer people were marrying, even when age-specific marriage rates went up a little (for example, at 25–29 years, see Jackson and Pool, 1994: 63–66), the number of divorces dropped overall (Pool *et al.* 1998: 111). The NZW:FEE confirms this, showing a 35% decline in the likelihood of divorce between the 1980s and 1990s (Dharmalingam *et al.* 1998a), thus supporting McPherson's argument (1995) that the trend had peaked. This is similar to the trend observed in the United States as well (Goldstein 1999). In this context, it must be stressed that the individual-level data from NZW:FEE are the only robust series on divorce. It is the only set in which links at the individual level between a marriage and a divorce from that marriage can be established.[*]

The NZW:FEE also throws light on differentials of divorce. It gives broad support to two earlier multi-variate analyses (Patterson 1976; Carmichael 1982; Carmichael 1988b). Using unit record data, these studies showed that most of the differentials are between birth cohorts. For example, one out of every ten marriages for the birth cohort of 1966–75 had been dissolved by two years' duration, while only 3% of the 1936–50 cohort had been. There were also two socio-economic differentials of interest coming out of the NZW: FEE multi-variate models, results of which are broadly consistent with those from the longitudinal study of children in Christchurch (Fergusson 1987). First, controlling for all other factors, Maori divorce levels were higher than non-Maori, and the highly educated were less likely to be divorced than the less well educated. The women and men marrying in the 1970s, as against cohabiting, were exceptionally young, so much so (27% of brides were teenagers) that prolonged schooling would have been impossible, although later in their lives some women may have taken advantage of opportunities for second-chance education. This latter result is different from what is shown in some, but not all, overseas studies, yet fits with the literature on the effects of education on the economic resources couples bring to marriages (e.g. Scanzoni 1972: Chapt. 4).

Secondly, the NZW:FEE data lend support to the general observation that the younger cohorts have a higher rate of divorce than the older cohorts (see Dharmalingam *et al.* 2007: Table 5.8; see also Dharmalingam *et al.* 1998a; McCluskey 1999). For instance, within the first two years of

---

[*] While vital registration of divorces collects data on duration of marriage, those data are confounded by changes to the original marriage cohort by immigration and emigration, and by the fact that no control can be made for conditional probabilities. The only way to analyse divorce for any marriage cohort is if one can analyse the joint probabilities that any individual who is still married at duration 't' of a particular union gets divorced at duration 't+n' of the same union.

marriage, about 11% of non-Maori born during 1966–75 had been divorced, compared with 3% among the 1936–50 cohort. The ethnic differentials are interesting: except for the oldest cohorts (born during 1936–50) and the youngest (born during 1966–75), the level of separation among Maori, particularly in the first few years of married life, was much higher than for non-Maori. The younger birth cohorts had a higher likelihood of divorce than older cohorts, and the chances of divorce did almost double from the 1960s. Increased divorce risks were associated with teenage marriage, premarital intercourse and premarital conception, all of which were more likely to pertain to Maori.

Table 6.3: The Status of First Cohabiting Unions at the End of Four Years' Duration, NZW:FEE

	Cohabiting union status			
	Converted into marriage (%)	Dissolved (%)	Still intact at survey (%)	All (N)
Year entered into cohabitation				
Before 1970	75	14	11	100 (83)
1970–79	54	33	13	100 (393)
1980–89	41	45	14	100 (596)
Ethnicity				
Maori	36	42	22	100 (247)
Non-Maori	44	39	17	100 (1107)
All	43	40	17	100 (1355)

Results from the NZW:FEE in Table 6.3 show that the levels of stability for first consensual unions have undergone major changes. Among those who entered into their first cohabitations before 1970, about 75% converted this status into marriage within five years and 14% broke up. But the corresponding percentages for those who entered into a first cohabitation during 1970–79 were 54% and 33%, and for the period 1980–89 the percentages were 41% and 45%. Thus it is clear that from the 1970s cohabiting unions were more likely to break up than to be converted into marriages. At the same time, the proportion of cohabiting unions that were likely still to be intact at the beginning of five years also increased – this fits with the argument that enduring cohabiting unions were increasingly likely to be acceptable to the wider community and in that sense 'formalised'. The ethnic differential is again interesting: first cohabiting unions were more likely to break up among Maori women than among non-Maori; conversely such unions were less likely to be converted into a marriage, yet more likely to be still intact as a cohabiting union among Maori compared to non-Maori. Perhaps the reasons for this were similar to those noted above for divorce.

Both bi-variate and multi-variate analyses showed that premarital cohabitation increased the risk of divorce by about 30% (McCluskey 1999: 73–74; Dharmalingam *et al.* 2004). An exception to this was that the likelihood of separation for those women who had not cohabited with the man to whom they were currently married, but who had cohabited before with someone else, was little different from those who had never cohabited with any other person at all before marriage (unpublished tabulation prepared for the present study; see also Dharmalingam *et al.* 2004: Chapt. 3). Controlling for other factors, the effect of education plays some role, as the highly educated were less likely to dissolve their marriage than those with lower levels or no qualifications at all. Having many children also reduced the risks of divorce.

Remarriage is another important proximate determinant of family sizes, age structures, statuses and living arrangements. As was shown above, the age differences between the spouses at the time of remarriage is likely to be a little wider for divorcees, but much wider for widowed persons. Divorce and reconstitution influence the prevalence of blended families. But the literature on remarriage in New Zealand is limited (Fleming 1999 looked at the different needs of such families). Cross-sectional census data show that remarriage following divorce doubled from about 12.5% in 1976 to 21.7% in 1991. While females were more likely to enter first marriage than males, it is the reverse for remarriage: females are less likely than males to remarry following divorce. However, this gap narrowed between 1986 and 1991 (Jackson and Pool 1994: 66–72; also see Carmichael 1985). Divorcees are more likely to opt for cohabitation or singlehood than legal marriage (Carmichael 1996; McPherson 1995).

Analysis of the NZW:FEE data suggests that one in five separated women re-partnered (cohabitation or marriage) in the first year of separation; by that time levels of re-partnering involved three out of five separated women (Dharmalingam *et al.* 2004: Table 3.4). A vast majority of separated women (about 80%) who re-partnered within five years of separation entered into cohabiting unions rather than into married unions. Maori are marginally more likely to have re-partnered than their non-Maori counterparts: by the end of four years of separation, 59% of Maori women as against 51% of non-Maori women had re-partnered; for higher durations of separation the ethnic differences in re-partnering have narrowed.

Those women whose first cohabitations broke up were likely to enter another consensual union within five years: 61% formed another cohabiting union over this duration; another 6% moved into a first marriage; and about 33% remained single at the end of four years from the break up. There was no ethnic differential in the levels of entering into another union after the break up of the first cohabiting unions.

People whose separations from first marriage took place after 1975 were more likely to re-partner in the first three years of separation than those whose separations had occurred before 1975. This may be an indication that a significant change in patterns of conjugal mobility had occurred during the Baby Bust. But this must be qualified because, in the post-1975 period, re-partnering in the first three years was the highest for the period 1976–85, perhaps in part a function of divorce law changes at that time and the attendant damming up prior to this, spilling out as *de facto* separations that were subsequently translated into *de jure* ones. In contrast, the subsequent decade, 1986–1995, experienced a decline in this probability. These data relate only to rapid remarriage, but another factor related to re-partnering is that for durations of separation beyond three years, the cumulative proportion eventually re-partnering does not seem to have varied much by period.

Remarriage produces reconstituted and blended families and other complex morphologies. These have always been a feature of New Zealand families. Most people have merely to track back through their own genealogy or whakapapa to confirm this, by finding a sole parent, widow or widower who remarried or decided to co-share parenting. That said, some genealogical lines may have been broken in the Baby Boom when another factor operated: the tendency to adopt out ex-nuptially conceived babies.

But by the 1980s and 1990s reconstituted and blended families had became far more common and seem to have been, at least in their manifest dimensions, one of the more important of the changes to the nuclear family occurring in this period. In the Baby Boom and prior to that period, nuclear families seem almost to have been sealed units, inviolate until death did them part. Of course, we do not have reliable data on the patterns of conjugal mobility in these earlier eras, but anecdotally and from divorce records it seems that families endured together even if the partners had lost all close emotional bonds and to all intents and purposes lived apart even if sharing the same dwelling. In the Baby Bust, in contrast, the nuclear family became an amoeba-like form, with parts sometimes breaking off on their own for whatever reason, and then reconstituting as new and separate entities.

Associated with this, the Baby Boom patterns of neolocalisation from the time of the wedding, constituting a young couple leaving their own parents and family home once and forever, also broke down. They were replaced by a far more fluid situation: mobility between cohabitation, marriage or LAT unions; to say nothing of phenomena such as the cluttered-nest syndrome with its dependent or boomerang (adult) kids. Thus neolocalisation has taken on a totally different meaning, if indeed it is still of any analytical use at all. The couple staying together in an intimate way in his/her parents' home are certainly not forming a neolocal household of the sort that was the norm for conjugal relations in the Baby Boom. Yet they are displaying a degree of independence that would have been unheard of then, and Baby

Boom parents probably would not have accepted this situation, at least not publicly. This is a high-profile issue today and will be returned to in later chapters.

6.5 CHANGES IN FAMILY FORMATION, FAMILY SIZES AND THE AGE-PROFILES OF 'NUCLEAR' FAMILIES

FAMILY SIZES, FAMILY FORMATION STRATEGIES, MARITAL STATUSES OF MOTHERS

The family-size dimension of structure is affected, of course, by the ways in which the statuses, noted above, translate into living arrangements. But there are other arguably more important elements to this: family sizes, in terms of the numbers and ages of the children in a household, simultaneously have both immediate and less immediate implications for family structures. As two Canadian authors note, 'One of the most significant family changes is in terms of the numbers of children' (Beaujot and Muhammad 2006: 15). For example, this factor determines the number of dependants living at home: the greater the number of children the more likely it is that dependent offspring will still be at home, although this effect will be mediated to a degree by the ages at which childbearing occurs.

In the long term family size is a key determinant of the the maintenance of the line. Thus at its most poignant, the absence of children or grandchildren or rapidly diminishing family sizes, as Maori have recently seen occur in their whanau, may strike at the heart of family cohesion and of familism or whanaungatanga: whether or not the lineage will continue.

The age structure of the family is also affected by reproduction and dependency, and by the timing and spacing of births in the family life-cycle. In this last regard, as will be seen, a major shift to later childbearing has occurred, but, paradoxically, the New Zealand pattern of early childbearing, for Pakeha as well as Maori and Pacific peoples, has persisted. For Pakeha it declined in importance, but, relative to most other WDCs except the United States (and today England and Wales), early childbearing rates remained high, and were a factor driving increasing reproductive polarisation by age. This trend became more marked in the 1990s and will be discussed in later chapters.

Family sizes declined significantly in this period as both Maori and non-Maori went through a Baby Bust (see Figure 2.1, Table 5.2; Dharmalingam *et al.* 2007: Tables 5.1 and 5.7; Dayal and Lovell 1994; see also Romaniuc 1984 for a comparative view of this trend in Canada). It involved a mix of delaying first births (tempo) and the lengthening of intervals between subsequent births (spacing). The Maori fertility decline was so massive that it will be detailed separately below. Nevertheless, it is important to note here that the decreases in fertility they went through involved a simple limitation in family size, whereas the Pakeha Bust was due in part to this, but was also the result of a major shift to later and later childbearing, the particular characteristics of which will be dealt with later in this chapter. The Pakeha change was, however, also very rapid, and occurred at the same time as a related shift was occurring across all WDCs (Jackson and Pool 1994: Chapt. 1; Pool 1992; Pool and Sceats 2003). The Europeans have called this period of transformation the 'second demographic transition', a term which has become very widely used (e.g. van de Kaa 1987, 1988, 2003; Lesthaeghe 1991).

As a result of the two different Baby Bust trajectories in this period, overall New Zealand fertility patterns dichotomised into a peak at ages 20–24 for Maori and at 25–29 for non-Maori. For the cohorts born 1960–64, there was a difference, for example, of eight years in the timing of the peak age of childbearing (20 years for Maori, 28 years for non-Maori) (Jackson and Pool 1996: 159–63). In the Baby Boom a significant proportion of all births for both Maori and non-Maori had occurred before age 25 years; by 1993, the early childbearing level for non-Maori was only a quarter of all births, whereas for Maori it had actually increased to almost 50% (mainly a factor of decreases at older ages that were reminiscent of what happened to Pakeha around 1973) (Dharmalingam *et al.* 2007: Table 3.7).

Unlike the transition a century earlier, delayed exposure to intercourse and thus to the risk of pregnancy was not a cause of the upward shift of Pakeha childbearing. In fact, rather the opposite was true, for ages at first intercourse have become younger and younger, although this started to change slightly in the 1990s. By then, conception rates at young ages had decreased because of the use of very efficient contraception. The likelihood of using effective birth-control methods, even at first intercourse, was high for Pakeha and almost half of young Maori women. Moreover, even if not used at first intercourse, these methods were employed soon thereafter. This propensity was far higher, as one might expect, when sex was initiated at older adolescent ages than at ages below sixteen years (Pool *et al.* 1999: Chapt.2; Dharmalingam *et al.* 1996, 1997). The net result was that the interval between the initiation of sex and first birth has become longer and longer, a key element in timing and spacing today (Sceats 1999; Morgan *et al.* 2001).

The trend towards later childbearing (noted above) also paralleled what was happening for Pakeha nuptiality. For those who chose to form a union or to marry, an increase in the age at which this took place continued.

One of the striking features of family formation trends in the Western world in the post-war period is the increasing proportion of children being born outside traditional marriage. This contrasted with what had been seen at the peak of the Baby Boom, when many marriages were precipitated by pregnancy with couples entering into marriage to legitimise the birth. This was particularly the case among those who became pregnant in their teens.

The distribution of marital status at the time of first birth by ethnicity, birth cohort and age at first birth (below 20 and 20 years and over) is given in Table 6.4. Maori women were more likely to have their first child outside marriage than were their non-Maori counterparts. Among those who had their first birth before reaching 20 years of age, about one-third of both Maori and non-Maori women did so outside any union. However, more Maori women had their first births while cohabiting (35%) than did non-Maori women (21%). On the other hand, non-Maori women had a greater tendency to legitimise their first births by marrying than Maori.

The data in Table 6.4 establish the strong correlation between early first birth and non-marital birth status. This is most marked among non-Maori women: 56% of those who had their first birth as teenagers did so outside of marriage, compared with only 17% of women who had their first birth from 20 years on. Among Maori a similar, although weaker, pattern was evident: 69% of Maori women who had their first birth before the age of 20 did so outside of marriage, compared with 53% of those who had their first birth after age nineteen. The association between early birth and non-marital status at first birth has grown stronger across successive birth cohorts. For instance, among women who were born in the 1960s and who had their first birth in the 1980s and 1990s before age 20, only 14% (of both Maori and non-Maori women) had such a birth within marriage. This was down from the rates for nuptial births among their predecessors born in the 1950s: 54% for non-Maori women and 37% for Maori.

Although the data for the 1970–75 birth cohort, reaching parenting ages in the 1990s, are incomplete and sparse, it appears that the trend of having first births (and probably subsequent births) in cohabitation is gaining momentum. For instance, among non-Maori women born in the period 1960–69, 15% of those who had their first birth after nineteen years of age did so in cohabitation (compared to 9% born outside any union); this figure was up from 9% for those born during 1950–59. The corresponding figures for Maori women were 45% (for the 1960–69 birth cohort) and 22% (for the 1950–59 birth cohort).

Thus it is evident that women of more recent birth cohorts have a greater likelihood of having their first births (and possibly higher-order births; that is births that are second, third or above in parity)* in cohabi-

---

* In demography, 'order' refers to the place of a new child in the order of siblings already born; in obstetrics this may be the order of the pregnancy, although gravida is the exact term for the pregnancy order for someone who is 'gravid'. We have purposely avoided using most compound descriptors stemming from these, such as nulliparous, as they are not in everyday use.

tation or outside any union. This likelihood is higher for Maori than for non-Maori. It is also clear that if the first birth is in the teenage years, then it is several times more likely to be outside marriage. In fact, for the youngest birth cohort (born 1970–75), around nine out of ten non-Maori women who gave birth in their teenage years were either cohabiting or not in any union. For Maori, the pattern was even more striking: around nineteen out of twenty Maori women who gave birth in their teenage years were either cohabiting or not in any union. It must be reiterated, however, that the propensity to have a teenage birth, nuptial or ex-nuptial, had become much lower for earlier birth-cohort decades.

Table 6.4: Percentage Distribution of First Births, by Mother's Marital Status and Age at that Event, by the Ethnicity and Birth Cohort of the Mother, NZW:FEE

	Birth cohort				
	1936–49	1950–59	1960–69	1970–75	All
NON-MAORI					
Age at first birth <20 years					
Post-maritally conceived	22.5	21.8	3.9	4.5	15.7
Legitimated by marriage	48.0	32.7	10.5	4.5	28.6
Born in cohabitation	5.9	10.0	39.5	50.0	20.8
Born outside any union	23.5	35.5	46.1	40.9	34.9
Total % (Ns = mothers)	100 (102)	100 (110)	100 (76)	100 (44)	100 (332)
Age at first birth ≥20 years					
Post-maritally conceived	83.2	78.0	65.7		74.4
Legitimated by marriage	8.4	7.9	9.8		8.4
Born in cohabitation	1.9	9.0	15.4		9.4
Born outside any union	6.5	5.1	9.1		7.8
Total % (Ns = mothers)	100 (583)	100 (533)	100 (449)	–	100 (1565)
MAORI					
Age at first birth <20 years					
Post-maritally conceived	22.7	12.5	6.1	4.2	10.4
Legitimated by marriage	63.6	25.0	8.2	0.0	20.7
Born in cohabitation	0.0	27.5	44.9	58.3	34.8
Born outside any union	13.6	35.0	40.8	37.5	34.0
Total % (Ns = mothers)	100 (22)	100 (40)	100 (49)	100 (24)	100 (135)
Age at first birth ≥20 years					
Post-maritally conceived	60.9	51.0	20.0		37.3
Legitimated by marriage	10.9	12.2	9.2		10.2
Born in cohabitation	8.7	22.4	44.6		31.1
Born outside any union	19.6	14.3	26.1		21.5
Total % (Ns = mothers)	100 (46)	100 (49)	100 (65)	–	100 (177)

The effects of the growth in cohabitation and of the likelihood of bearing a child ex-nuptially even at older reproductive ages, typically in a long-lasting consensual union, shows up in the data on the percentage distributions by age of ex-nuptial births (Dharmalingam *et al.* 2007: Table 6.1). In the Baby Boom ex-nuptial childbearing had been concentrated at young ages. But this was true, of course, for all childbearing in that era. Thus this fact simply reinforces conclusions about family formation for England, reported earlier, relating to the eighteenth and nineteenth century (Wrigley 1981; Woods 2000: Chapts 3 and 4): that high levels of ex-nuptial childbearing can correlate with early marriage and childbearing. It also fits with what is known about abortion (Sceats and Parr 1995; see Chapts Seven and Eight).

In 1962, 67% of ex-nuptial births were to women aged younger than 25 years, and 77% in 1972. In fact, in that latter year, the peak period for Pakeha teenage childbearing, the modal age (43% for ex-nuptial childbearing) was less than 20 years. This statistic is breathtaking; it could be achieved only in the face of two bio-social factors: the lower fecundability at nubile ages and the high level of ex-nuptial conceptions that ended in marital births for teenagers at that time. By 1992, 61% of ex-nuptial births were at 20–29 years, as against only 47% in 1972 and by 1992 the percentage contribution of women aged 25–29 years to all ex-nuptial births exceeded the contribution of teenagers. By 2002, this gap had extended and the percentage at 30–34 years even exceeded the contribution made by teenagers.

By the 1990s, for New Zealand women as a whole, the rate of childbearing at 25–29 years was barely exceeding that at 30–34 years. This changing age structure for parenting was all the more remarkable because the late 1980s and early 1990s also saw a resurgence in family sizes, albeit a very modest one. Around 1990, fertility rates increased overall almost to replacement levels (2.1 live births per woman), and this occurred for both Maori and Pakeha, constituting a blip but not a boom (TFRs would have been much higher in a true baby boom). Rates edged downwards during the early 1990s for non-Maori, for example to 1.80 in 1996, but not for Maori (Dharmalingam *et al.* 2007: Table 2.1). It is not clear whether this is because of a real trend or an ethnic classification effect whereby babies who were partly of Maori identity and previously reported as non-Maori were now coded as Maori.

In the Baby Boom ex-nuptial and early conception and childbearing were almost inseparable trends but, as the analysis above shows, in the Baby Bust and into the Baby Blip this no longer held true. Indeed, the whole tempo and spacing of childbearing changed very significantly during the Baby Bust to later and later childbearing. Moreover, the Baby Blip, that upsurge of births around 1990, occurred because of the changes in timing rather than in spite of it. Those who had delayed their births were now in their late twenties and thirties and having babies. This effect was reinforced by the fact that the cohorts at the key Baby Blip parenting ages were larger than those ahead and behind them.

THE TIMING OF FIRST BIRTHS AND THE SPACING OF SUBSEQUENT BIRTHS

Life-table estimates of the cumulative proportions of women having their first births before a given age (before 20, 25, 30, 35 and 40 years) are available (Dharmalingam *et al.* 2007: Table 5.1). They show that close to 90% of New Zealand women born 1936–59, the only cohorts for whom we have cumulative proportions at ages 35 years and above (that is for women near the end of their reproductive spans), had had a child before 35 or 40 years of age. However, this will not necessarily be the case for the youngest cohorts of women covered in the NZW:FEE and NZFFS surveys. For instance, while 60% of those born before 1950 had had their first child before they turned 25 years of age, only 52% of those born in the 1950s and 42% of those born during the 1960s had done so. Similarly, there are differences between older birth cohorts in the proportion of women having a child before reaching 30 and 35 years of age, although the differences narrow as the age of the women increases. A pertinent question here is whether the lower rates of birth at younger ages are simply a reflection of delays in childbearing or whether they presage a reduction in the total proportion of women who will ever eventually give birth. These data do not allow us to answer this question in a definitive way. Nevertheless, this question will be picked up again in later chapters.

For all cohorts of women born 1936 to 1975 combined, Maori and non-Maori women differed significantly in the timing of first births.[*] While about 72% of Maori women had had their first births before age 25, only 46% of non-Maori women did so. Similarly, a higher proportion of Maori women had their first child in their teenage years (around one in three), compared to non-Maori women (around one in eight). However, the higher rates of earlier childbirth among Maori were almost counterbalanced by higher rates of later childbirth among non-Maori, leaving only a small residual difference in the proportions of women who had given birth by age 40.

There were clear educational differences in the proportions reaching parenthood at younger ages, again for all cohorts combined. Before reaching age 25, 70% of those with no qualification had had their first child, compared to only 47% among those with secondary qualifications and 17% of those with university qualifications. The differentials persisted, although they narrowed, as the age of the women rose (before 30, 35 and 40 years).

To complement the data on the cumulative proportions of women attaining parenthood presented earlier (Table 5.2; see also Dharmalingam *et al.* 2007: Table 5.1), we provide in Table 6.5 the rates of reaching

---

[*]   Because of small numbers, in looking at ethnic and educational differentials we have had to combine all cohorts. It must be stressed, however, that these are life-table estimates, a technique that permits one to eliminate both censoring biases and age-composition effects.

parenthood while passing through different age-groups by selected socio-demographic characteristics. It is clear from this table that for all women the likelihood of having a first child was greatest at the 25–29 age-group; the chances of having a first birth were more or less equal at ages 20–24 and 30–34 years. If a woman were childless at age 25 she had a 52% chance of having a child in the next five years, whereas at age 20 she had a 40% chance, and at age 30 she had a 41% chance (see also Dharmalingam *et al.* 2004: Chapt. 4).

The birth cohort and ethnic differentials in first-birth probabilities are of particular interest. The younger their birth cohort, the less likely women were to have their first child before 25 years of age and, correspondingly, the more likely they were to have their first child after the age of 29. This resulted in a shift in women's relative odds of having their first child in their early twenties compared with their early thirties, and can be seen by comparing the rates of first births for women born before 1950 with those born in the 1950s. While the probability of first births peaked in the 25–29 age-group for both cohorts, those born in the 1950s had a higher probability of having their first birth after age 29 than before age 25; in contrast those born before 1950 had a higher probability of having their first birth before age 25 than after age 29. The further reduction in the probability of a first birth before age 25 for the cohort of women born in the 1960s suggests that this trend is likely to intensify in the future.

For all cohorts combined, for Maori the probability of first birth peaked at ages 20–24 (58%) followed by ages 25–29 (37%). But for non-Maori, the peak rate was at ages 25–29 (53%) followed by ages 30–34 (42%). An interesting comparison can be made here: for Maori women, the chances of having a first birth in their teenage years were very similar to the probability of having a first birth in their early thirties; but for non-Maori women the likelihoods of teenage parenthood were less than one-third of the chances of having a first birth in their early thirties.

It is clear from the first-birth rates for various educational groups (Table 6.5), once more for all cohorts combined, that those with higher levels of education were more likely to have their first births in their late twenties and in their thirties. Women with a university qualification had lower probabilities of having a first birth before 35 years of age than did the rest, but such women had a higher probability in the 35–39 age-group (34%) than the rest (e.g. 9% among those with no qualification).

A modest reprise in teenage childbearing, the exact determinants of which are unclear, accompanied the Baby Blip. Nevertheless, data from NZFFS (not reproduced here) indicate that, by comparison with all other parenting cohorts, the teenage mothers of the Baby Blip were most likely themselves to be the children of adolescent mothers. These were women born at the peak period for adolescent fertility, around 1971, referred to already in earlier chapters (Dharmalingam *et al.* 2004: Table 4.4). This trend, however, was very short lived; today adolescent childbearing rates are half the levels they were at the end of the Baby Boom (Pool *et al.* 1998: Table 3; see also Dharmalingam *et al.* 1996, 1997; Dickson *et al.* 2000).

Table 6.5: Rates of First Childbearing: Births at Various Ages by Selected Socio-demographic Characteristics, NZW:FEE

Characteristics	Age-specific rate of first birth					
	15–19	20–24	25–29	30–34	35–39	Number of women
Birth cohort						
1936–49	0.15	0.53	0.61	0.38	0.21	803
1950–59	0.18	0.41	0.47	0.45		934
1960–69	0.14	0.33				860
1970–75	0.14					420
Ethnicity						
Maori	0.34	0.58	0.37	0.33		513
Non-Maori	0.12	0.39	0.53	0.42	0.19	2504
Education						
No qualifications	0.28	0.58	0.57	0.41	0.09	787
Secondary qualifications	0.12	0.40	0.57	0.41	0.26	765
Other tertiary qualifications	0.11	0.36	0.48	0.44	0.14	1163
University qualifications	0.03	0.14	0.40	0.37	0.34	302
Overall	**0.15**	**0.40**	**0.52**	**0.41**	**0.19**	**3017**

By the period covered in this chapter, the spacing of births had also changed dramatically, although intervals were still shorter than they were in the United States (Morgan *et al.* 1998). In 1976, 72% of women had not only had one birth by 25 years, but 48% had had a second birth by the same age. In 1991, however, the proportion having a first birth by 25 years had almost halved, but an even more marked trend was that the proportion going on to a second birth by age 25 years was less than a quarter of what it had been in 1976 (Pool *et al.* 2000). In the 1950s, 45% of American women, as against a higher level of New Zealanders (57%), had had a second baby within 24 months of bearing their first child, and 66% and 80% respectively by 36 months. During the Baby Bust (1975–89), for United States women the proportions were 26% by two years and 47% by three years; for New Zealand they were still higher than American levels, at 27% and 56% respectively, but were much lower than had been the case in the 1950s. While the proportions having a second child by 24 months in 1990–94 were similar to levels seen in the United States, at 30 months there was a difference, with Americans having lower percentages. New Zealand spacing was also shorter than for other WDCs (Sceats 1999).

An analysis of changes in the timing and spacing of births by different birth cohorts of New Zealand women shows clearly the movement towards later commencement of childbearing, in spite of earlier ages for the onset of sexual activity. This increase in control of the timing of the first birth reflects the widespread adoption of efficient means of contraception, particularly among women born after 1950. Indeed, the 1950–60 cohort may have been the pivotal generation for the dramatic changes in family formation patterns, between the early and rapid childbearing of the early Baby Boom mother born 1936 to 1950, and the later onset and increasing birth intervals of the younger cohorts born since 1960 (Sceats 1999).

Finally, delayed first childbearing has also had an impact on the later reproductive period. The NZW:FEE shows that the population childless at age 30 had increased from 17% for the Pakeha cohort of 1936–55 to 28% for the cohort of 1956–65, while for Maori the increase was more modest but did rise from 11% to 15% (Ball 1999a: Table 6.1; see also Ball 1999b). The increased force of reproduction at 30–34 years, and even at 35–39 and 40–44 years, was *not* merely due to declines at younger ages but from increased rates at older ages. Absolute changes between 1981 and 1991 produced increases of 37% at ages 30–34 years, 19% at 35–39 years and 2% at 40–44 years (Pool and Jackson 1994: Table 2.10). These continued in the 1990s, but did not offset declines at 20–29 years. At the dawn of the millennium this trend was still continuing and strengthening (see later chapters).

6.6 CHANGES IN LIVING ARRANGEMENTS: SHIFT-SHARES IN HOUSEHOLD FORMS

The living arrangements of households underwent significant shift-shares in this period. In part this was because of the family formation trends of the sort just noted above. But in part it was because of changes in lifestyles and thus family forms, and there were variations in this between ethnic groups. The shift-shares in household types also took place in a context of an overall increase in household numbers of 36% between 1976 and 1996 (Dharmalingam *et al.* 2007: Tables 5.9–5.11, which update to 2001 earlier studies noted in the table sources).

The number of two-parent households decreased over this period by 5%, whereas, numerically, sole-parent households increased by 138%. This figure is somewhat misleading, however, as the shift-shares were much more modest: the contribution of two-parent households to the total decreased by thirteen percentage points, while the percentage of the total that were sole-parent households went up by only four percentage points. The number of extended families, the other form of parenting household, increased modestly by 19%, but their contribution to the total actually declined slightly. Overall, parenting households increased numerically by 12%, but their share of the total dropped by eleven percentage points. In percentage-point terms the greatest increase in contribution came from one-person households, six percentage points. Numerically they grew by 92% (see Davey 1999), while couple-only households increased in number by 66%, yet the change in their share (4%) only equalled that for sole parents (Dharmalingam *et al.* 2007: Table 5.10).

Behind these overall changes in numbers and shift-shares are complex interactions and differences between the profiles of household forms, ethnic groups, age-groups and cohorts. The latter is important because, by following them, one can describe and start to explain how changes in the timing of family formation affect family statuses and living arrangements differentially at each stage of the family life-cycle. Detailed analyses of the interaction between all of these have been elaborated elsewhere (Jackson and Pool 1994; Dickson *et al.* 1997; for each stage of the life-cycle see Davey 1998) and thus need only be summarised here.

The decline of the two-parent family over the period from the 1970s to the Baby Blip was an artefact, first, of the overall decline in fertility and thus a decrease in total parenting at that time. But secondly, and as a consequence of decreases in family sizes, it resulted from a 'demographic squeeze' coming from the sudden age-shift, particularly by the Pakeha population in the late 1970s, to later parenting. The squeeze, producing a deficit of parenting families and increases in the couple-only category, was evident in the 1990s as

> Couples composed of persons aged 45–54 in the 1990s had often begun parenting in their early adult or even adolescent years in the 1960s/70s. Today they are 'childless' as their children have often left home. In comparison, younger people today spend longer periods in 'non-related' (for example, student flats), young single-person and couple-only households. Normally they delay parenting to their late 20s or early 30s. This produces a 'demographic squeeze' in particular on the two-parent family (Johnstone and Pool 1996a: 299; see also Dickson *et al.* 1997: Figs 6.1 and 6.2).

It is interesting to note that the highest-profile family type, the sole-parent unit, did not play a significant role in this set of shift-shares (Dickson *et al.* 1997: 24) except in one regard: as the modal age for sole parenting was at 30–49 years of age (see below), a lower proportion of parenting families at the ages at which the squeeze operated would have been two parent, but the level was still high. In 1991, 77% of Pakeha parenting households whose occupier was aged 30–49 years were two parent, 15% were sole parent and the rest were extended family in form (Jackson and Pool 1996: Appendix

C.1). Overall this change was driven by Pakeha trends simply because most households whose occupiers were aged 30–49 in 1991 were Pakeha (89%). That said, there are differences between ethnic groups. For Maori and Pacific Islanders the two-parent family at this age-group was still the majority type of parenting household (53% in each case). But, for Maori, the number of sole-parent households numerically exceeded the extended-family category, although the difference was not great. For Pacific peoples, extended families significantly exceeded sole-parent ones (Jackson and Pool 1994: Appendix C1). The issue of extended families will be picked up again in later chapters.

Alongside this, and as a secondary and minor effect coming in part from the status changes noted earlier (e.g. divorce), was the shift to one-person households, especially for occupiers at 40–59 years – the key parenting ages – when such a status would be unexpected. The proportion of single-person households at older ages (60 years and over) increased for males, but decreased slightly for females at ages 60–74 years (a function of increases in male longevity and thus the maintenance of couple families). At 75 years and over there was an increase until 1991 and then a slight decrease (Davey 1999: 83). Moreover, as was noted earlier, there has also been an increase in one-person households whose occupiers are at prime reproductive ages. Taken together, perhaps these data signify a latent trend towards an increase in the proportion of people who will never enter a conjugal union.

6.7 CHANGES IN LIVING ARRANGEMENTS: SOLE-PARENT HOUSEHOLDS

Sole parenting is largely independent of the squeeze effect discussed above, although demographic factors do play a role: the younger the average age at which parenting unions are formed, or at which pre-marital conception occurs, the earlier the risk of being in a sole-parent union. In this regard there are major differences between Maori and Pakeha and these have important implications (Jackson and Pool 1996; for an overview see also Pool and Johnstone 1996; Mowbray and Khan 1984; Dharmalingam *et al.* 2004: Chapt. 5).

The proportion of households that are sole parent increased over the period 1976–2001, as is seen in Table 6.6. At the beginning of this period there was a steady increase, from 5.1% in 1976 to 9.3% in 1991, but the rate of change then slowed, so that in 2001 still only 9.5% of all households were sole parent (Dickson *et al.* 1997, updated to 2001 in Dharmalingam *et al.* 2007: Tables 5.9–5.11). In 1976 there had not been a great range of difference between ethnic groups, but by 2001 this had opened up. Levels then were highest among Maori and Pacific peoples. For Pakeha, the trend in the growth of sole parenting in the last quinquennium resembled that occurring for households overall, but the percentage of Maori households that were sole parent actually decreased slightly.

Table 6.6: Sole-parent Households, 1976 and 2001, as a Percentage of All Households, by Ethnicity*

	1976	2001
Pakeha	5.0	8.1
Maori	7.4	19.1
Pacific peoples	4.8	14.4
Asian/Other	5.0	10.0
Total	5.1	9.5

Source: Appendix Table 5.11, drawn from censuses.
* 100% = the total households lived in by a given ethnic group.

Moreover, a different picture emerges if, instead of families, the proportion of adult women or men who were in such households is taken as a measure – that is, if the impact of this phenomenon on the population is analysed. Janet Dickson and her collaborators followed these trends from 1976 to 1996. For men there was an increase in the percentage until 1991, from 0.9% to 1.6%, but since then the rates have remained stationary; for women there was also an increase, a doubling, until 1991 from 3.3% to 6.6%, but from then on a decrease, to 6.3%. But even at the peak age of 35–39 years only 11% of women at the 1996 census were sole mothers and at most age-groups the figure was 8% or less. This was more than merely the effect on this phenomenon of a restructuring by age of households for, as will be discussed below, it occurred across most age-groups and for both genders (Dickson *et al.* 1997: 74 and Table 6.7; reproduced in Dharmalingam *et al.* 2007: Table 6.2).

The stereotypical sole-parent household is seen as a sort of social isolate headed by a very young woman, but in the 1990s the reality was rather different. First, in 1976 one-quarter and in 1996 approximately one-third of all sole-parent families were embedded in other households. This proportion had grown between 1976 and 1991, and at a more accelerated rate between 1991 and 1996. But both the proportion and this increment varied between ethnic groups. In 1976, 22% of Pakeha sole parents had been in extended families, and this level was still only 23% in 1996. At the opposite extreme, the proportion of Maori and Pasifika sole-parent families embedded in this way grew significantly, although the most rapid increase was in the Asian/Other category. There were also age differences in levels of embeddedness, with rates being highest among the youngest female sole parents and, to a lesser degree, the oldest (Pool *et al.* 1998: Fig. 8).

Secondly, and contrary to what is often assumed, the highest proportions of men and women who are sole parents are not found at the youngest ages.

For all women the mode is at ages 25–44 years (see Dharmalingam *et al.*
2007: Table 6.2, drawn from Dickson *et al.* 1997). This phenomenon is most
prevalent at ages 30–49 years for Pakeha sole mothers, and 35–59 years for
Pakeha sole fathers, peaking in the late thirties and late forties respectively.
For Maori, the distribution for sole mothers is younger, with the mode falling
between ages 25 and 29 and peaking in the early thirties, whereas the pattern
for Maori sole fathers resembles that for Pakeha.

The misleading impression that sole parenting is most prevalent among
young women is because the figures quoted often relate to sole-parent families or households, not to the percentage of the population. At younger ages
few people are in independent families or households of any sort – one has
only to think of the 20% of women aged 20–24 years who were in LATs at that
time – but those who are in households will typically be sole parents. Just to
show how insignificant this high-profile category really is, the percentage of
women aged 15–19 years in sole-parent households varied between 1–2% of
each ethnic group. Even if family data are used the percentage of women is
still small, varying between 2% (Pakeha) and 8% (Maori) (Pool *et al.* 1998: Fig.
8 and Dickson *et al.* 1997: Fig. 4.1 and Table 6.8).

About 80% of sole-parent households are headed by women. The proportion of all women who were in sole-parent households increased rapidly from
1976 to 1991 and then decreased at every age-group except 35–39 years, where
a very slight rise (only 0.04 percentage points) was seen. To compare this, it
is worth noting that for men a decrease occurred at every age-group from
25 years on. At the key ages of sole parenting, decreases in the proportion
who were sole parents occurred for Pakeha women between 1991 and 1996
at every age except 35–39 years. For Maori the changes were less systematic:
decreases at 20–34 years; increases at 35–44 years; decreases at all older ages.
The Pasifika rates also showed decreases over this period for all age-groups
except 15–19 and 35–39 years. The Asian/Other trends are confounded by
problems of classification (Pool *et al.* 2007: Chapt. 1).

6.8 ETHNIC DIFFERENTIALS IN FAMILY MORPHOLOGIES IN THE BABY BUST PERIOD

So far in this chapter an overall picture relating to changes in family structures
has been presented. But, as holds true across all areas of social organisation,
the effects of cultural difference are marked for many aspects of family life,
and thus we turn to each major ethnic group.

Many of the differences between ethnic groups have been covered
already. At this point the agenda is to identify and elaborate on some particular distinguishing characteristics for the four main ethnic groupings:

Pakeha, Maori, Pacific Island and Asian. It is recognised that several of these groupings are statistical categories encompassing a number of different real ethnic groups. Beyond this, the hierarchical system of assigning ethnicity since 1986 has normally prioritised Maori (Pool *et al.* 2007: Chapt. 1), but following procedures introduced recently by Statistics New Zealand, the data relating to Pacific peoples and Asians have often been reclassified into what are termed 'total response' categories.* By this methodology, persons who are Maori-Pasifika, Maori-Asian, Pasifika-Asian or Maori-Pasifika-Asian, and Pakeha and any/some/all of these, could, in effect, be included two or three times. The numbers involved are not inconsiderable, so the resulting figures are biased for this reason. Moreover, the data on each group include some bi-/multi-cultural persons whose prime cultural preference may or may not be the ethnic group of reference in the analysis.

PAKEHA FAMILIES
In this period, Pakeha formal marriage occurred at later and later ages. In this regard, and in terms of their delayed childbearing to be discussed below, the behaviour of these cohorts was very conservative, for this represented a reprise of family formation strategies last seen in the 1920s and 1930s. Alongside this, the shift to cohabitation, increases in divorce and separation and the decline in the strength of norms that traditionally had led to premarital conception being followed by nuptial birth produced a rapid increase in the proportion of births which were ex-nuptial. The number of births to adolescent mothers had almost halved between 1976 and 1994/5, but those that were ex-nuptial increased slightly, while the percentage of teenage births that were ex-nuptial rose dramatically from 46% to 86%. Against this, however, the stereotype of ex-nuptial fertility, as something that occurred just to teenage women, no longer fitted but was widened to include the whole gamut of age-ranges. In 1976, 42% of ex-nuptial births had been to adolescents and 30% to women aged 25 years and over, but by 1994/5 only 18% were to teenagers and 48% to women aged 25 and over (Pool *et al.* 1998; for all women see Dharmalingam *et al.* 2007: Table 6.1).

The Pakeha Baby Bust saw two trends occur. In common with other populations in WDCs, they went through a decline in fertility. By 1978, the TFR had fallen below the low rate reached in the 1930s Depression, the lowest

---

* This change has no effect on the continuity of Maori data sets as all persons reporting as Maori, solely or in combination with another category, had been previously 'prioritised' into the classification Maori. But it does mean that persons of mixed-ethnicity are counted more than once.

level ever until then, and it declined further to reach 1.87 births per woman in 1983–84. Pakeha thus participated in the second demographic transition, when WDCs, regardless of their politico-religious and economic norms and structures, almost simultaneously went through a fertility decline (see Pool and Sceats 2003; Lesthaeghe 1977, 1983, 1991; van de Kaa 1987, 1988, 2003; Pool 1992; Jackson and Pool 1994: Chapt. 1).

Secondly, around 1990 Pakeha fertility rates then increased slightly. Briefly there was a modest reprise of adolescent childbearing, but the dominant trend was one of changes in the age structure of parenting. This is reflected in associated changes in marriage patterns (Dharmalingam *et al.* 2007: Table 2.1): if 2001 is compared with, say, 1956 and 1936, then the most recent data (for the period covered in the present chapter), stand out as very different from those for the Baby Boom (1956), instead showing a strong return to the late age at marriage of the inter-war years (represented in this comparison by 1936). The only difference was that, by the 1990s, there were similar proportions of each gender married by key ages;* this was a histori-cally unique phenomenon.

Between 1976 and 1996 Pakeha living arrangements shifted, mainly be-cause of the changes in size and age structure noted earlier. Thus two-parent families decreased as a proportion of all households, while the percentage in couple-only and single-person households increased to counter-balance this. There were far more modest increases in the percentage of sole-parent house-holds and decreases in extended and non-related households (Dharmalingam *et al.* 2007: Table 5.10). Pakeha levels of cohabitation increased to rates that differed little from those of Maori. The cumulative proportion by a given age in this type of first conjugal union increased very rapidly in the 1970s and has been at high levels since (Lapierre-Adamcyk *et al.* 1997).

A new element of neolocal residence also became evident. The young adults of the Baby Boom had shifted to new suburbs in outer Auckland or the Hutt Valley and begun their childrearing. But their equivalent in the 1980s and 1990s were often living in Australia (Carmichael 1993), or London, or wherever. They were working and travelling, 'doing their OE', and often cohabiting or marrying, perhaps to settle permanently in an overseas neolo-cal residence, or returning to New Zealand to start a family.

Data on the percentages of each household type belonging to various eth-nicities (Dharmalingam *et al.* 2007: Tables 5.10 and 5.11) show that the Pakeha contribution to the stock of all types of parenting families has declined by twelve percentage points. This is higher than the drop in their contribution to all forms of households (eight percentage points).

---

* To a large degree New Zealand national rates for statuses such as marriage and divorce reflect Pakeha trends.

MAORI FAMILIES

In the 1970s, Maori went through a spectacular Baby Bust, seeing their TFR drop from 5.0 per woman in 1973 to 2.8 in 1978, seemingly the most rapid fertility decline anywhere. These shifts took place, moreover, in both rural and urban New Zealand (Pool 1991: 170). This decline had a very significant effect on all aspects of the structure and organisation of whanau, but the implications are not yet perhaps fully appreciated. It is clear, however, that defining whanau is far more complex today than in the past. For example, as Metge notes, 'Where formerly I identified rural whanau as the primary whanau and regarded urban whanau as a departure from it, I now prefer to place rural and urban whanau with a descent groups core on an equal footing, regarding them as variations on a common theme' (Metge 1995: 78).

Most of the key determinants of these changes in fertility came from within family structures themselves. These were, above all, the radical improvements in survivorship over the preceding period, from 1945 to 1961, plus factors such as rapid urbanisation and all that this entailed. This coincided with the rapid diffusion of TV. Education was probably not a particularly significant factor simply because free compulsory schooling had been a policy formulated for Maori and Pakeha since 1877, and had been effective since the early 1900s. Moreover, while there were what were called 'native', or later Maori, schools, there were no constraints on Maori attending general schools or to Pakeha going to Maori schools. In all these schools the curriculum and the teaching materials were weighted towards majority Pakeha cultural models, although some Maori legends and other stories were contained in the *School Journals* of the 1940s.

For Maori reproduction, the mechanism for change was efficient fertility regulation: first the very rapid adoption of the Pill, in tandem with what was occurring for Pakeha, and then sterilisation (Pool 1991: 166–75, and 185–87; Pool *et al.* 1999). It is worth noting that the sheer velocity of this reproductive revolution is all the more remarkable because family planning is very much a private concern in New Zealand, not coming from public policy initiatives or government intervention in large-scale programmes (Pool 1991: 166–75 and 185–87).

Maori family sizes tumbled, converging towards those for Pakeha. Nevertheless, the processes of Maori family formation remained unchanged in one major respect. This was the early force of reproduction (especially at ages 20–24 years), accentuated by the rapid declines in the 1960s and 1970s in fertility at older ages. 'These patterns are very clearly affected by a cultural difference in approaches to creating families, not in the overall dimensions of a family' (Pool 1991: 167).

This process of Maori family formation and its structural correlates have continued unchanged to the end of the twentieth century, although by the 1990s a slight shift between younger and later childbearing had appeared. The factor of reproductive force, producing significantly higher levels of fertility for Maori 15–24 year olds than is the case for non-Maori, has highly deterministic effects. Early childbearing affects all aspects of later family and social life (Howard 1999a, b), and thus has major implications for Maori family structures and for policy (Jackson and Pool 1996: 163; see also Jackson *et al.* 1994). For example, reference has been made earlier to the higher levels of conjugal instability for Maori and the fact that this seems related to childbearing at younger ages. But there may well be other factors operating independently or as co-variates (e.g. labour-force participation and income levels); this seems to be an area requiring further research. By comparison, fertility at older ages has declined massively, so much so that by the 1980s Maori age-specific rates at 25–39 years had fallen well below those for Pakeha.

While Maori and Pakeha had similar patterns of marriage and cohabitation, living arrangements varied. Above all Maori were far more likely to be in sole-parent (as was discussed earlier) or extended families. The number of sole-parent households has increased over the period under review. Moreover, Maori were significantly over-represented among both sole-parent and extended families, and to a lesser degree among all parenting families, and under-represented in two-parent, couple-only and one-person households (Dharmalingam *et al.* 2007: Tables 5.10 and 5.11). In part these reflect the age-dimensions of family structures, but this profile also indicates that there were major life-cycle shifts. As families get older on average, and differing proportions enter various family life-cycle stages at later ages, then changes in profiles may be due more to these compositional factors than to real changes in the probabilities of entering sole-parent unions.

As was true for Pakeha, Maori neolocal residence also became more dispersed in this period. Alongside this there was the rapid growth of an Australian Maori population (Pool 1991: 193–95). While there were attempts to replicate whanau, hapu and iwi life through the formation of new 'tribal' entities (for example Ngati Ranana in London), and marae, this still entailed a further wrenching of family support systems.

In earlier periods, because Maori and Pakeha comprised almost the whole population of New Zealand, the structures of their households had dictated the overall family patterns in New Zealand. That said, between the 1880s and the 1970s, because of the Pakeha demographic hegemony, to a large degree the public image of the characteristics of the 'ordinary' New Zealand family was a Pakeha one. But over the last three decades this picture changed, first as family forms went through radical realignments, with an increasing impact on the architecture of the New Zealand family in general, and secondly as Maori population numbers have rapidly increased. The image we have of today's New Zealand family primarily owes its features to the emerging family patterns of these two major ethnic groups. Indeed, the Maori word whanau has firmly entered the public discourse and is often used to refer to Pakeha families, particularly extended ones. So too have associated terms, such as mokopuna and its abbreviation 'moko' (used to mean biological grandchildren), slipped into everyday English speech.

But the dominance of Maori and Pakeha, both demographically and in the public image of the New Zealand family, is being challenged today. No study of New Zealand family structures and forms covering the last few decades can ignore Pasifika and Asian families, to which we now turn. By the time of the Baby Bust, the Maori and Pakeha trajectories were joined by that of a rapidly growing immigrant group, the Pacific peoples. Beyond these groups, mainly Polynesians and Fijians, there were always small minorities of Asians and others, but their numbers were to become much more significant in the late 1980s and 1990s (see Pool *et al.* 2007: Chapt. 1, for problems of definition).

PASIFIKA FAMILIES

Pacific peoples in this section of the chapter are persons reporting sole Pasifika ethnicity, or Pasifika and any other; that is we use data based on 'total responses'. The problems this creates were mentioned earlier.

As Gordon Carmichael has shown, Pasifika family structures are not homogeneous, for there is a marked difference, at the very least, between those from eastern and western Polynesia (Carmichael 1982, 1996; see also Pool and Jackson 1994: 19–21; Bedford and Pool 1985, which summarised the then existing knowledge on Pasifika demography). In 1985–87, for example, TFRs for Polynesian Pacific peoples resident in New Zealand varied significantly: 2.9 for Cook Islanders and Niueans; 3.5 for Samoans; and 6.0 for Tongans (Jackson and Pool 1994: 20). In this book, however, for reasons of data availability, we are generally forced to combine these groups. Their major points of similarity are in terms of a common Polynesian origin (mainly, but there are also 'Fijians', some of whom may also be of Indian ethnicity, see Pool *et al.* 2007: Chapt. 1), their date of arrival in New Zealand, the pace of that movement, and their concentrated residence, mainly in the Auckland and Wellington urban areas although this is not uniform across all groups.

At the 1981 census, family sizes measured by the average number of children ever born to Pacific peoples were higher than for Pakeha but lower at every age than for Maori (Khawaja 1985: 171). This was because census data reflect the past – the high fertility of Maori in the 1950s and 1960s, and the migratory history of Pacific peoples, often involving temporary disruptions to family life and thus decreases in exposure to intercourse, meant that Pasifika family formation had often been less intense than for Maori up until the 1970s.

By the 1990s, while Maori and Pakeha family sizes converged towards 2.1 births per woman, the normally accepted cut-off point for replacement,

Pasifika levels were still higher (a TFR of 3.4 in 1991), slightly above that for 1983. This slight increase over the 1980s could have been due more to a shift in the ethnic composition of the Pasifika population, an increase in the proportion of Pacific peoples who were from Tonga and Samoa (Krishnan *et al.* 1994: 30–31), than to a real increment in Pasifika fertility. This change in the ethnic distribution of Pacific peoples came both from migration and from natural increase – levels of reproduction among western Polynesians were higher than among eastern, both in their home countries and in New Zealand.

Cross-comparative data from the NZW:FEE, relating to the mid-1990s (Ball *et al.* 1999),* show that age at first intercourse, current union status (married, cohabiting, living together apart, no relationship), and the number of unions before age 20 years for Pacific peoples were similar to those for women of all New Zealand ethnic groups combined. Against that, Pacific peoples had on average more live births and had a higher probability of having a first live birth at a young age than was true for New Zealand women as a whole (at less than 20 years, 21% versus 15%). This is not surprising as age-standardised rates relating to ever use of contraception by Pacific peoples were below those for New Zealand women as a whole, and their levels of use at first intercourse even in 1995 were very low (19% versus 56% for all women). Age-standardised rates of ever use of contraception show that proportions using any efficient method of fertility regulation were much lower for the most important methods (the Pill, sterilisation, condom), marginally lower for the IUD, but higher for hormonal injections than held true for the total population. Significantly, the last method does not require constant motivation and its use may not necessarily be evident to a spouse, which may explain its appeal.

Related to their lower age-standardised ever-use rates of contraception, Pasifika women at this time had significantly higher levels of induced abortion than did Maori or Pakeha (almost double), and disproportionately it was older Pasifika women at higher parities who sought abortions. This pattern is consistent with experience overseas for populations at a similar stage of demographic transition as the Pasifika population in New Zealand. At that point for such populations fertility is falling, but abortion is often employed as a means of limitation, particularly by older married women who are at higher parities (Sceats and Parr 1995; Sceats 1988b; see also later chapters).

The living arrangements of Pacific peoples are very different from Pakeha and even from Maori. When considering the stock of New Zealand families, Pasifika households are heavily over-represented

---

* Cross-comparative data from the NZW:FEE, relating to the mid-1990s, can be used to study Pasifika fertility, but as their numbers in that sample were small one can only employ totals for all ages and Pasifika ethnic groups combined. Age-standardisation does, however, allow one to control for composition effects.

among extended family households, in which are sometimes embedded sole-parent families, as noted above. They are also more likely to be in sole-parent households, and in all forms of parenting families combined. In contrast, they are under-represented among two-parent, couple-only, non-related and one-person households (see Dharmalingam *et al.* 2007: Tables 5.10 and 5.11).

Eighty-two per cent of all Pasifika families consist of parenting families, a far higher proportion than for any other group, even Asians (see below). The percentage of their households that are sole parent is exceeded only by the rate for Maori. The Pasifika two-parent household has a lower frequency than might be expected given the high overall level of parenting, but it is the extended family that often performs this function. Thus at recent censuses the number of extended Pacific Island families has approximated that for two-parent families. To make a comparison, there are five times as many two-parent Pakeha families as there are extended families. For Asians, the ratio is 2.4, for Maori 1.6, but for Pacific peoples it is 1.2, so that the two rates are almost at par (see Dharmalingam *et al.* 2007: Table 5.11).

The role of the extended family is far more comprehensive than this might suggest. As was noted earlier, Pasifika sole parents and their children are most frequently nested into extended family households. These households also often play a role in assimilating and acculturating new arrivals.

ASIAN FAMILIES

In the past most analyses categorised 'Asian' as a residual category of ethnicity normally classified along with 'Other' (mainly Africans). Moreover, Asians from various cultures and countries of origin are combined together, even though there are vast differences between the various groups.

A study based on the 1991 census, however, when 'eight out of 10 adult Asians living in New Zealand . . . were born overseas', does extend our knowledge of this group (Statistics New Zealand 1995: 33). It should be noted that the data covered in this section of the chapter are total responses that relate to those people who reported Asian sole ethnicity, or Asian and anything else (Statistics New Zealand 1995: 99)

These data show for Asians in general and for different major groups (for example, Chinese, Indian, etc.) that 'there was a lower proportion of unmarried people in every age-group than among New Zealanders as a whole' (Statistics New Zealand 1995: 34). A distinction must be made, however, between those born in New Zealand, who were less likely to be married at ages 20–24 and 25–29 years, and those born overseas. The proportions of Indian teenage women born overseas, mainly in India and Fiji, who were ever married was particularly high by contemporary New

Zealand standards (a third of the India-born and a fifth of the Fiji-born). Patterns for New Zealand-born Asians were much closer to those for the total population (i.e. Pakeha plus Asian and other plus Maori plus Pacific peoples). This is also true for the marital statuses of the New Zealand-born Asians. But overall Asian New Zealanders had far lower proportions divorced and separated, and were 'considerably less likely' to be living in a *de facto* relationship (Carmichael 1996).

Because the sub-sample was so small the NZW:FEE did not analyse Asians in the same detail as Maori or Pakeha. Nevertheless, where there were results they point to small family sizes, delayed childbearing and the use of efficient methods of contraception.

The data in the 1995 Statistics New Zealand report covered families not households, and thus the real richness of Asian family structures is not addressed there. Among parenting families those of Asians are more likely to be two parent and less likely to be one parent. Data on housing show that Asians are more likely than New Zealanders as a whole to share accommodation (Statistics New Zealand 1995: 45). But with respect to older Asians the results of this study are fascinating. Far higher proportions of Asians 65 years and over live in 'one family plus others' and 'two or more families' than is true for New Zealanders as a whole (Statistics New Zealand 1995: 49).

This analysis by Statistics New Zealand can be extended by other data relating to households not families (Dharmalingam *et al.* 2007: Tables 5.10 and 5.11). By comparison with the population as a whole, Asians have high proportions in two-parent families. Only Pacific peoples have higher levels in the category 'parent plus'. As the large-scale Asian migrations were at the end of the period 1973–90, and above all in the 1990s, this issue will be returned to in later chapters. But it should be noted here that, because the majority of Asians are recent immigrants, Asians in New Zealand typically have taken up neolocal residence. Nevertheless, through family reunion migration and the living arrangements noted above, they then created structures that partially replicate extended family systems in their countries of origin.

Traditionally, migration has created household structures in which working-age males, in particular, are the 'active' migrants, who have come to New Zealand in search of work, and wives, children and relatives are 'passive' migrants. But by the 1990s Asian migration to New Zealand, Canada and Australia had taken a different form: the active migrant was often engaged instead in 'circular mobility'. The men, or the couple, would be absent overseas, typically maintaining business interests in their home countries. These were the so-called 'astronaut families' composed of 'children living in New Zealand while both of their parents are absent . . . [and] referred to as the "parachute" children'. Using complex re-tabulations of census data, this issue has been investigated by Ho *et al.* (2000: 3; see also Bedford *et al.* 1997). Their results (unlike those in overseas studies) for the first time permit estimates to be made of the numbers and proportions of astronaut families and parachute children among north-east Asian migrant groups arriving between 1991 and 1996. Their research found that this phenomenon was common 'among recent Chinese immigrants from Taiwan and Hong Kong, but low among those migrants from China and Korea' (Ho *et al.* 2000: 35).

6.9 SOCIO-ECONOMIC DIFFERENCES IN TRENDS

The analysis of the relationships between family morphologies and socio-economic factors in New Zealand has typically focused on three issues: poverty; income, in general; and, of course, ethnicity, which has already been considered in detail above. The question of poverty is critical, but is outside the scope of this study and is the subject of detailed analyses and also debates (see, for example, Stephens *et al.* 1995). Likewise, neither factors underlying family income generation (e.g. Callister 1998) nor factors of intra-family income distribution (e.g. Fleming and Easting 1994) will be discussed in detail here, but some of these will be addressed in later chapters. The issue of income in relation to family size, age structures, statuses and living arrangements will, however, be considered. It should be noted that in this case most of the available studies are based around families rather than households. Davey (1998) does use household data but did not apply equivalence scales that take account of the number and ages of persons sharing incomes, and for that reason her work will not be referred to here.

A critical issue is the structure of the family in terms of size and the ages at which family formation occurs, including the timing of the first birth. In turn this is affected by socio-economic factors such as education and occupation. The existing studies show, for example, that there is an inverse relationship between the level of education of women and family size, with weaker relationships with other economic factors (Khawaja 1985). Recent analyses using NZW:FEE data have reviewed socio-economic differentials for a wide range of factors relating to family size. Generally speaking the relationships are weak, even with education, and are overshadowed by cohort, period and ethnic differences (e.g. Dharmalingam *et al.* 1996, 1997, 1998b).

If instead one turns to patterns of family formation, then education definitely is a factor affecting rates, as was shown earlier in this chapter (see also Dharmalingam *et al.* 2007: Tables 5.1–5.4). But the role of education is in the incremental phases of family formation – prolonged education delays the formation of parenting unions and child-bearing – but not in the decremental phase. This issue has become even more critical at the turn of the twenty-first century and thus will be discussed further in later chapters.

When the focus moves from family formation to structures, the interactions between socio-economic context and family life become rather stronger. An important contribution to this area came in the pioneering analyses of the income–family size relationship by Wolfgang Rosenberg (1958), a topic later elaborated by Brian Easton (1977, 1978, 1979). The relationships they identified have, however, become rather more complex over recent years. Increasingly they are related to living arrangements, life-cycle stage, and the labour-force statuses of each of the adults in a couple or household (Callister 1998), and in turn interrelated with ethnicity. This is because of a wide range of factors, notably increases in income inequality and a decline in the real value of individual incomes from 1976 to 1996 (Martin 1998).*

Overall, household incomes barely changed during the period reviewed in this chapter. Age-standardised, equivalised (for family structures), inflation-adjusted median incomes increased by just $73 between 1986 and 2001, after dropping dramatically between 1986 and 1991, picking up significantly by 1996, and again but less sharply to 2001, as is seen in Table 6.7. Pakeha levels were always above Maori, but the gap increased markedly during the period, from $4,416 (1986) to $9,358 (1991), reflecting the effects of the economic restructuring of that time on Maori families. It expanded a little by 1996 ($9,546), and persisted thereafter ($9,426 in 2001). Whereas Pakeha incomes had increased by $2,014 over the fifteen-year period, by contrast Maori levels in 2001 were still well below what they had been in 1986 ($3,000, or 11% below). Thus the apparent lack of change overall was the result of markedly different patterns by ethnicity that increased and then entrenched household inequality, an aspect of the structural polarisation that became a feature in New Zealand family life and persisted into the twenty-first century.

---

* The work of Johnstone and Pool on households (1996b) and Martin on families (1998) cited here uses equivalence scales in all family income computations, and also real income dollars adjusted to a reference year. These studies use the census not Household Economic Survey data: cell sizes are far larger, allowing detailed disaggregation and there is a longer-running time-series. But the problem is that they cover income from all sources combined, as distinct from earnings. It is recognised that income is one of the more sensitive issues asked about in the census and the absolute values in income recorded may not necessarily reflect the true situation for some families. Under-estimates of real income are possible for a variety of reasons, including remuneration in kind rather than in cash.

Table 6.7: Age-standardised, Equivalised Median Household Incomes, Maori, Pakeha and Total, Consumer Price Index-adjusted to 1996 Dollars

	1986	1991	1996	2001
Maori	28,509	21,852	24,364	25,513
Pakeha	32,925	31,210	33,910	34,939
Total	32,830	30,095	32,984	33,003

Source: Cochrane *et al*. 2007; computed from census data.

The persistence of ethnic inequalities has had the effect of privileging two-income families, especially childless couples, most typically Pakeha, and disadvantaging one-income and benefit-dependent families, especially sole parents (Stephens 2000). In turn, this is influenced strongly by their stage in the family life-cycle. Young parents are individually more likely to be on lower salaries than older parents or couples, and more likely to have only one member working full time, simply because of the competing demands of work and childraising. Older couples will be at the empty-nest stage, and are more likely to consist of two full-time workers, who for reasons of seniority may also be in higher earning categories. Because of a combination of age and living arrangements, and the high levels of unemployment in the period 1986 to 1991, young Maori families were the most likely to be in the lowest income group. But because of the restructuring of the late 1980s, this became also true for Pakeha two-parent, middle-aged and older families where there was also unemployment or only part-time work (Johnstone and Pool 1996b: Table 8; for the effects of unemployment on families see Eckert-Jaffe and Solaz 2000). These issues will come up again in later chapters.

Barry Martin, employing decomposition analysis, shows similar results that again set an agenda for later chapters. His conclusions raise a

> general concern: that increasing amounts of participation in the labour market are required to maintain family incomes. Between 1976 and 1996 the average wage has increased, but only by 2.7% in real terms between these two dates. For much of this period, between 1982 and 1993, earnings have been declining or constant in real value. Incomes of two-parent families with dependent children have increased in real terms (by 20% between 1976 and 1996), but this has been achieved by increasing the amount of paid work . . . even where there is full participation in remunerated employment, the gap between low- and high-earning families is growing . . .

In the 1991–96 period 'there was employment growth, but despite the fall in unemployment, the growth in family income inequalities has not diminished. On the contrary, family income inequality was higher in 1996 than it was in either 1991 or 1976' (Martin 1998: 267).

Inequality had been exacerbated by the growth in what Callister calls work-rich, as against work-poor, families. Much of the increase in 'participation in paid work of prime-age women' came 'amongst those couples in which their partner was in paid work. This has led to an increase in work-rich families'. He goes on to note that 'work-rich' does not automatically equate with high income, and he distinguishes between 'dual career families' and 'dual job families often struggling under a double burden of paid and unpaid work' (1998: 118).

Entry or re-entry into the labour force after a birth is highly dependent on support resources, formal and informal, inside and outside the family (Hope 1997). The first, involving pre-school services and/or maternity leave, has the stronger effect, but may be more readily available to the two-career rather than the two-job work-rich families identified by Callister (1998). Informal support comes more typically from partners or other co-resident adults. For Pakeha this was often an individual other than a partner, whereas for Maori it was likely to be a partner. The life-table cumulative probabilities of entry or re-entry were higher for those who had a birth at a young age, but cutting across this was past work experience (Hillcoat-Nalletamby *et al.* 1999).

The increase in the numbers of two-earner (often couple-only) families along with

> sole-parent families (of all labour force statuses) and unemployed families has contributed to the increased inequality of family incomes. Sole-parents have been the group with the single biggest influence upon the distribution . . . the effect of change in composition by family type [to sole parent and couple only from two parent] outweighs the effect of changing composition by labour force status (Martin 1998: 266; for households see Johnstone and Pool 1996b).

Finally, reconstituted families may have particular problems. They have different needs and interrelationships because of their complex lateral and vertical linkages (Fleming 1999; see also Villeneuve-Gokalp 1999).

These results raise issues of major importance for this book. The analysis of family incomes (a micro-level factor) allows the identification of what is perhaps the most critical linkage between the external socio-economic context (macro-level, to be discussed in the next chapter) and the family. At a micro-level, by the 1990s the maintenance of an adequate or above-average family income could normally be achieved only through both partners working, at least one full time. Unlike 1976, therefore, by the 1990s the quality and quantum of family life was more dependent on both partners juggling the demands of both the workforce and family life. Under these circumstances, support networks were clearly of major importance. Despite the increased access of partners to the labour market in the 1990s, family incomes of two-parent families ('the stereotypical "stable" form much favoured by the moralists', Pool 1996: 28) were maintained only by increasing the amount of (and one can assume the duration spent in) paid work. The economic environment had made life increasingly difficult for the two-parent family; it produced even more severe pressures for other forms of parenting families.

These particular sets of relationships became more critical during the economic restructuring of the late 1980s and 1990s. By the turn of the twenty-first century they had become high-profile policy questions; a more detailed discussion of this will be deferred until later chapters, which deals more specifically with the period of the late 1990s.

6.10 SUMMARY: A PERIOD OF RADICAL CHANGE

AN UNPRECEDENTED 'MUTATION' OF FAMILY LIFE?
The concluding comments to this chapter really revolve around one major point. That is, in the entire post-war era, indeed since earliest records permit reasonable analyses, the most rapid changes ever in family life, not just in family formation and related structures but also in family forms, occurred in the bridging period in the 1970s as the Baby Boom came to an end and the Baby Bust started. Numerous examples can be cited to support this statement: family sizes changed very significantly for both Maori and Pakeha and family age structures were transformed, with a seismic shift from early to late parenting (and all that this entails). For both major populations there was a radical change from marriage to cohabitation as the preferred form of first union, and there were rapid shifts in patterns of living arrangements. All of these put together, as well as the accelerated Pakeha decline in fertility and the co-terminous Maori reproductive revolution, give a picture of an unprecedented mutation of family life, affecting both its forms and its structures.

Moreover, not only was this transition short and brutish, but many features have produced negative feelings among a great number of observers and commentators, analogous in a way to the reactions of the first performance of Stravinsky's *Rite of Spring* (1913). But whereas first responses – frequently horror – gave way to admiration for Stravinsky's artistry, there is little admiring acceptance of the family structures and forms that emerged in the 1970s and that have become almost normative today. Concerns about family breakdown typically revolve around the more demographic aspects of family life, the changes in formation, structures and forms recorded here (Morgan 2004). This issue will be returned to in later chapters, but suffice to say here that these shifts are seen by some as having dire consequences.

By the middle of the Baby Bust, Pakeha TFRs were less than half the rates at the peak of the Baby Boom, and Maori rates a third of those at their peak around 1960. From a trough in the Baby Bust, Pakeha levels then went up to replacement, but in the 1990s dropped gradually away to historically low levels, discussed in later chapters. Maori rates have fluctuated, in part as an consequence of changes in definitions of ethnicity in vital registration.

For New Zealand, and indeed internationally, these were very significant changes. Nevertheless, in common with other ESCs, especially the United States, levels of fertility were still 'high' relative to those seen in some other WDCs. According to United Nations time-series data (*Population Estimates and Projections* 2000), New Zealand had the highest TFR in the WDCs in 1955–60 during the Baby Boom, with Canada second. In 1985–90, the rank orders for TFRs in the WDCs were Ireland top at 2.3 births per woman, New Zealand at 2.1 and then the United States at 1.9. By 1995–2000, it was the US at 2.04, NZ at 1.97 and Ireland at 1.9. Australia and Norway were next at 1.8 (Pool and Sceats 2003: esp. Appendix; see also Dharmalingam *et al.* 2007: Table 5.12). France stood steady at around 1.85–1.92 throughout these years. Thus New Zealand featured in the high-fertility WDC group throughout the period covered in Chapters Six to Nine. One should note in passing that the absolute (versus ordinal) inter-country ranges in recent years were far narrower than in the Baby Boom. But it is necessary to put that into perspective: as Francesco Billari (2004) has commented, for regimes with sub-replacement fertility an absolute difference of only 0.2 births per woman can be seen as a wide gap in relative terms. A TFR of 1.4 is 17% higher than one of 1.2; we have become accustomed to wider absolute gaps – a TFR of 7.0 is a whole birth higher than 6.0, yet only 17% greater.

The decreases in TFRs are a result of a shift to delayed childbearing across the WDCs and in New Zealand. There were ethnic differences in rhythms of parenting and by period and cohort, whereas cumulative fertility by the end of the reproductive span varied little by educational level. In contrast, the tempo of family formation producing the cumulative probabilities varied markedly by education. This has had ramifications for family life that are now so important that they will be among the foci of later chapters. As will be shown there, however, the differences in family formation strategies reflect more than a simple difference by educational level or any other measure of socio-economic status; more importantly they correlate with workforce participation status (full or part time).

Despite the overall trend to delayed childbearing, paradoxically New Zealand also maintained relatively high levels of early childbearing (at younger than 25 years) throughout the period covered in this chapter. In the late 1960s to the 1980s, New Zealand had the highest rates of early childbearing among the WDCs (Dharmalingam *et al.* 2007: Table 5.12), but otherwise generally fell a little below the United States, and by the 1990s was well below. By the late 1990s, it was also marginally below Austria, Ireland and the United Kingdom, and equal to Canada. But all except Austria are ESCs, which were well above the remaining WDCs in Europe and Japan (Pool and Sceats 2003: Table 3).

NEW ZEALAND AND THE OTHER ENGLISH-SPEAKING AND WESTERN DEVELOPED COUNTRIES

The question that must be posed is why the ESCs were so different in terms of early childbearing, and how New Zealand differs from other ESCs. In the Baby Boom, particularly in its later phases, early childbearing was the dominant regime in New Zealand and delayed parenting was uncommon. But now in New Zealand and the ESCs, parenting at young ages is also associated with a growing trend in delayed childbearing, whereas in the other WDCs it is the middle part of the reproductive ages (25–34 years) in which parenting is overwhelmingly concentrated. These differences are of significance not only in their own right in charting New Zealand's cultural path, but have a wider interest across the WDCs, some of which are very concerned about extremely low fertility. This theme will be picked up in later chapters.

It might be assumed that an explanation of the higher fertility of the ESCs, especially the United States and New Zealand, could lie in their ethnic distributions: the presence of relatively large cultural minorities who have higher fertility (Maori, Pacific peoples, African-Americans, Hispanic-Americans). This hypothesis has been examined in detail by Chandola *et al.* (2002), and by Pool and Sceats (2003: Table 5). These researchers came to similar conclusions: that while the minority fertility levels overall and at younger reproductive ages were certainly higher than for the majority European-origin populations, the combined impacts of minority fertility were very limited – for the United States, Frejka (2004) concludes that the effect is only about 6–7%. In New Zealand at the start of the period covered in this chapter, the TFR of non-Maori was above 3.0 births per woman, for Maori 5.0, but for the total population only 3.2; in 1990 the TFRs for all ethnic groups were all around or above 2.0. By 2001, although Maori rates were at 2.6, and the non-Maori down to 1.8, the total at 2.0 was still marginally above that for the majority population.

Of all the changes over the period, the rapid shift in family status profiles, both in terms of the propensity to be married and the likelihood of becoming divorced, was the prime topic in the media and popular discourse. Associated with these shifts was the degree to which family living arrangements went through a major change, in part because of lifestyle changes, but also in part because of the effects of family and general demographic transitions. Except perhaps for the issue of teenage childbearing, family status profile changes overshadowed interest in trends in family sizes and structures in New Zealand, the factors that in the longer run are going to have the most impact on family life and the society in general.

Above all, there was a focus in public discussions on sole-parent families. But, as this chapter has shown, in terms of the proportion of the population as against the households, or in other words the impact of this phenomenon on the society, a different picture emerges. Even as sole parenting is normally analysed, most of its growth had finished by the late 1980s and increases in the 1990s were minimal.

The other various shifts described in this chapter often started in the 1960s and continued into the 1980s, but they clustered temporally around the 1970s. Moreover, they were driven by changes in both the proximate factors and the socio-economic context (to be discussed in Chapter Seven).

The transition in New Zealand paralleled, in time and directions, transitions occurring across the WDCs for which there are directly comparable data (e.g. Austria, Canada, France, Netherlands, Norway, Sweden) (Pool *et al.* 2000; Pool and Sceats 2003; see also Lesthaeghe 1991). This factor of co-variance in time across similar developed countries is valuable for the present analysis. Often the socio-economic context of family structural change is better charted overseas, and thus we can draw on their analyses to attempt to explain what happened in New Zealand.

The changes, both the radical ones in the 1970s and those later, seem to have been associated with broader socio-economic changes in the society and above all in value systems. Major policy initiatives in the late 1980s and again in the 1990s turned the society in yet another direction, towards a polarisation in various aspects of national, regional and family life. Some of the family demographic changes in the late 1980s and early 1990s have been referred to already and will be analysed further in Chapter Seven. In Chapters Eight and Nine it will then be shown how these aspects of family transition, already evident in the period covered in this chapter and the next, became entrenched and by the dawn of the twenty-first century had taken the New Zealand family along previously uncharted paths.

Redefinition of the Nuclear Family, 1970s to the 1990s: Explanations

7.1 FACTORS DRIVING FAMILY CHANGE

This chapter analyses the factors producing the radical changes reviewed in the last chapter. To do so, it moves out from the proximate factors to the causally more remote determinants, and also assesses the impacts of the trends on the wider society. Changes across a whole range of bio-social and socio-cultural factors were so marked in the 1970s that special attention was drawn to them in Chapter Six; so distinctive was that decade that in a paper they wrote the authors of this book felt compelled to pose the question, 'What happened in the 1970s, Mummy . . . ?' (Pool *et al.* 2000).

The contextual changes include not only economic factors, particularly those relating to the labour market, but also the broader sweeps of modernisation, urbanisation and the policy context. In order to site and attempt to understand New Zealand's corpus of policy and the ideational factors that shape it, an analysis is also made of the different policy regimes in the WDCs.

7.2 PROXIMATE FACTORS DRIVING CHANGE

Looking at first-order explanations for shifts in family age structures, statuses and living arrangements, one must turn to complex interactions between changes in patterns of fertility regulation, and the other processes of family formation: first intercourse, union formation, whether this was marriage and/or cohabitation, then separation and other forms of dissolution. The key issue here is that easy access to efficient contraceptive technology had produced by the early years of the Baby Bust an unprecedented transformation in the control of family size, and in the timing and the spacing of births. This revolution underlay almost all the other changes in family structures, and therefore requires further analysis here. The context for the remarks that follow is thus that during the Baby Bust the nuptiality valve, that powerful first-order explanation of trends discussed in earlier chapters, all but disappeared as a determinant of family formation and thus of attendant family morphologies. For many people marriage had become a major social ritual signalling public commitment and the bond between two people; it was no longer an essential pre-requisite of family building.

FERTILITY REGULATION

A first aspect of family formation that changed in this period was the mechanism by which it was achieved through fertility regulation. The decrease in family size and the move to delayed childbearing in the face of a shift to younger ages at first intercourse, came about because of major changes in patterns of contraception use, the details of which were outlined earlier in Chapter Five. Suffice to say that in the Baby Bust use of two methods dominated: the Pill for timing (less so for Maori) and spacing, and sterilisation for limitation.

Trends for sterilisation intensified in the 1970s. Because of the downward force of reproduction in the late Baby Boom, childbearing was often completed at very young ages and limitation through sterilisation then followed at an early stage in the reproductive span. Twenty per cent of women born in the quinquennium 1946–50, Maori and Pakeha, were sterilised, or their partner had had a vasectomy by 30 years of age (Pool *et al.* 1999: 89 and *passim*).

These patterns, produced by the contraceptive revolution of the 1960s and 1970s, remained more or less in place until the end of the period covered in Chapters Six and Seven. Above all, use of the Pill, the modal method, stabilised from the early 1980s (Pool *et al.* 1999). Discontinuation of use, when it occurred, was typically because of a desire to become pregnant or the shift to sterilisation (Dharmalingam *et al.* 2000). A search for longer-lasting methods not requiring daily motivation or use each time intercourse occurred led many women, especially Maori, in the 1970s and 1980s to turn to injections (e.g. Depo-Provera), a method that subsequently lost popularity. But more typically if women had the number of children they desired the preference was for sterilisation for them or their partner. New Zealand rates of sterilisation, as well as Pill use, rivalled those in North America. But the relatively high proportion of couples where the man had a vasectomy was an unusual feature of fertility regulation in New Zealand (Dickson 1997; Pool *et al.* 1999: 89 and *passim*).

Three changes in the profile of contraception emerged over this period. First, very high levels of sterilisation at young ages, as seen in the 1970s, could occur only in a period in which childbearing had been completed at young ages. With the shift to delayed childbearing there came delays in proceeding to sterilisation and eventually this led to significant decreases in the overall rate. If childbearing were still occurring when they were in their late thirties and forties, couples might decide to continue with hormonal or other methods until the woman reached menopause rather than one or either partner being sterilised for contraceptive purposes (Dickson 1997; Pool *et al.* 1999 Chapt. 8; for hysterectomy see Dharmalingam *et al.* 2000; also Dharmalingam *et al.* 2007: Tables 7.1 and 7.2).

Secondly, Pill use (and other hormonal methods) dropped off. Rates peaked in the 1970s and then were slightly lower at each age in the 1980s and early 1990s. Since then they have fallen to levels below what was observed in the late 1960s and 1970s.

Thirdly, especially among younger women, Pill use was increasingly being replaced or complemented by a return to condom use, particularly by those women and men having intercourse only intermittently. In part this was to protect against STDs, and in part because the newly available condoms were technically and aesthetically much better than those available earlier. By this time, the condom also was frequently being used at first or early intercourse when recourse to efficient methods is now the norm, as noted earlier.

By 1995, 35% of Pakeha women at ages 20–24 were using condoms alone or with the Pill – one-fifth the condom alone. This was also true for one-quarter of Maori women. At older ages for both Maori and Pakeha the choice seemed to be between the condom and the Pill, presumably depending on whether the relationship in which women found themselves was of longer duration or more casual, From age 30 years on, sterilisation increased in prevalence (Pool *et al.* 1999: Tables 4.1 and 4.2; Dharmalingam *et al.* 2007: Tables 7.1 and 7.2).

INDUCED ABORTION

It has already been stressed that abortions had never been a major factor of fertility control in New Zealand. In the 1930s there had been alarm about estimated rates; these Depression levels were double those for New Zealand in the Baby Bust period, an abortion ratio of perhaps 20 per 100 live births,[*] according to the Committee of Inquiry, 'a level one and one-half times that in the late 1970s' (Sceats and Pool 1985: 187–88). Nevertheless, they were still around those seen in the 1980s in, say, England and Wales (1979: 16)

---

[*] Today a statistically more robust index, the total abortion rate (TAR), is usually the preferred measure – see Table 7.1. Abortion ratios, the abortions to live births (or, ideally, 'known conceptions'), are a far less stable measure. They do not accurately measure abortion trends *per se* as they are dependent statistically on changes in the denominator ('fertility levels which may be independent of the incidence of induced abortion', Sceats 1988: 411) as much as those in the numerator (the abortions).

or some of the Nordic countries, whose levels were in the modal range for WDCs at that time, but below those for the United States (1980: 30) (Sceats 1988: Table 13.2). In the Baby Boom, levels must have been low to sustain the high TFRs of that period. More tellingly perhaps, with the exception of Pacific peoples, New Zealanders typically turn to abortion at a young age for an unwanted first pregnancy; to have achieved the very high age-specific fertility rates at young ages in the Baby Boom there simply could not have been much resort to abortion. This argument is further verified by the various estimates Janet Sceats gives for the very end period of the Baby Boom. She evaluated available clinic admissions data, factored in the possible movement of women to Australian clinics and came up with levels lower than those reported in the period from 1973 to the 1990s, as is shown in Table 7.1. (Sceats 1988: Tables 6.2 and 6.3, 159–170).

The increased rates in the period covered by the present chapter resulted in a wide belief in the 1970s and 1980s that, in the words of Carmichael (1983, cited in Sceats 1988: 432), 'the supply of ex-nuptial children for adoption almost certainly dropped, primarily because pregnancies which formerly yielded such children were increasingly terminated by abortion'. This is yet another popular belief that does not stand up to detailed and careful evaluation. Instead, as Sceats shows, the real factor was a major shift by women, documented last chapter, to have an ex-nuptial birth (rather than marrying to have a nuptial birth or adopting out their child, the alternative of last resort in the Baby Boom) and to raise the child themselves, alone or with a cohabiting partner.* Underlying this change was the Domestic Purposes Benefit (DPB), which became statutory in 1973, entitling any parent to support for themselves and their dependent children. Moreover, 'improved administration gave eligible solo mothers better access to the benefit'. Uptake rates for the DPB increased by 38% per annum from 1969

---

* Sceats used 1970 adoption patterns applied to 1976 and 1982 ex-nuptial births. As subsequent reports have shown, closed adoption, where the links between the baby and its biological parents were severed, often after coercion had been exerted on the young mother, was often an extremely gruelling experience for her and often later for her biological offspring. Equally, the adoptive parents also sometimes faced emotional problems, even under the most ideal and loving circumstances. Complex ripple effects may even spread out to subsequent generations and to many persons other than the immediate actors involved: for example, Baby Boom adoptees are typically parents themselves now. These impacts can be captured in works of fiction, and perhaps by biography, but almost certainly not by the methods we have used here. Yet, as the data quoted in Chapter Five showed, adoption was a common and sanctioned event, the consequences of which are still unfolding in many families today, and the number of New Zealand families to which these ripple effects have spread must be considerable. Interestingly, the fathers were almost totally disregarded – they were seen as profligate seducers, wicked if married or irresponsible if young and single. The media is only now starting to discover the stories of the Baby Boom fathers of adopted-out children. This comment is not a criticism of adoption, but simply a recognition that, like abortion, it is a reproductive strategy that is often fraught with ethical and socio-psychological issues that are not always easily resolved. It is also an aspect of the Baby Boom that is studiously put out of mind by those who see that era as the golden age for family values.

to 1973 (Easton 1981: 41, cited by Sceats 1988: 454; see also Sceats 1988: Table 14.6 and 451–55; and Oliver 1988: 37, who underlines the significance of this legislation). The rates for induced abortion (excluding spontaneous fetal loss, see Pool 1991: Glossary) presented in Table 7.1 show a rapid increase in the early 1970s, something that was reported for a number of countries undergoing legislative and other changes in abortion practices at this time. In the 1980s, New Zealand had had among the lowest rates on record (at that time), but since then has seen fairly systematic rises (Table 7.1), and now, among the WDCs, has one of the higher rates (Table 7.2).

Table 7.1: New Zealand Total Abortion Rate,* Selected Years 1971–2001

	Total abortion rate (abortions per woman)	Rate of change (%) per quinquennium
1971	0.02	–
1976	0.19	–†
1981	0.27	39
1986	0.30	13
1991	0.41	36
1996	0.52	28
2001	0.60	15

Sources: Sceats 1988: Table 6.7; Sceats and Parr 1995: Figure 3; *Demographic Trends* 2003: Table 4.
* Computed as for TFRs used throughout this study: thus the TAR = 5 x sum age-specific abortion rates, completed for five-year age-groups. This computation eliminates composition effects, measures levels of abortion *per se* (see 271n) and provides a measure that is easily comprehended as it has the same rationale as the TFR.
† Incomplete data, Sceats (1988): Chapt. 5.

Table 7.2: General Abortion Rates* (per 1000 Women 15–44 Years), Low Fertility English-speaking Countries

	Circa 1981	*Circa* 2000
Australia	[Data available only for South Australia]	1996: 22
Canada	1981: 11	2000: 15
England and Wales	1983: 12	2001: 16
United States	1982: 29	1997: 22
New Zealand	1981: 10	2002: 20

Sources: Sceats 1988: Tables 6.5 and 6.6; *Demographic Trends* 2003: Table 7.02.
*Computed as for GFRs used in Chapter 4. GAR = abortions/1000 women aged 15–44.

Table 7.3: Total Abortion Rate* per Woman by Ethnicity

	Pakeha	Maori	Pasifika	Asian
1982	0.25	0.33	0.65	N/D
1991	0.42	0.51	1.02	N/D
2002	0.48	0.80	0.93	1.01

Sources: Sceats 1988: Table 7.12; Sceats and Parr 1995: Fig. 5; *Demographic Trends* 2003: Table 7.7.
*See notes to Table 7.1.

A number of factors appear to have produced this change. There seems to have been a catch-up effect, noted above. That said, unlike some of the other countries New Zealand has not been able to turn its rates down, although it is not unique in this (for France see Bajos *et al.* 2004). A key to this might be the relatively low availability of family planning services (Sceats and Parr 1995: 20).

Table 7.1 also shows that there were fluctuations in the growth in levels. It is difficult to know what has caused these. It is tempting to link them to underlying economic conditions and to the family policy environment. Thus, after the initial catch-up, an increase occurred coinciding with the radical economic restructuring in the late 1980s, and this slowed as the economic situation improved in the 1990s. Janet Sceats and Angelique Parr (1995) also show, however, a link between abortion and the 'total known conception rates'; as the latter go up, so too does abortion, and the inverse was also true until about the mid-1990s (Sceats and Parr 1995: 11; see also Johnstone 1996). In the late 1990s as fertility levels continued to decline abortion rates increased but at a lower velocity; as the TFR has edged up again in since 2000, so too have abortion rates. This possible temporal link between fertility trends and abortion fits with the trends for nuptiality and ex-nuptial fertility in the period prior to the end of the Baby Boom, and historically in England and Wales, as discussed in earlier chapters.

Cutting across this, however, is the ethnic profile of women having abortions. Earlier on, as can be seen in Table 7.3, Pasifika rates were well above those for Maori and Pakeha. If Pasifika rates had approximated those of the total population, the GAR for New Zealand for 1983 would have decreased from 9.7 per 1000 to 9.2, a not insignificant drop given that only 3% of all women aged 15–44 years were Pacific peoples (computed from Sceats 1988: Appendix 1, Table 4 and Table 7.11); if Asians had had Pakeha rates in 2001, the GAR would have been about nineteen per 1000, below the American rate, and not too far above the United Kingdom level (this issue is developed further in later chapters).

While Pakeha women had their abortions at young ages, for Maori, and especially for Pacific peoples, this was more evenly spread across age-groups and parities. A national survey of abortion patients Sceats conducted (1983) 'suggests that family planning services are not as successful at reaching Maori and Pacific Island women as they might be'. Citing the classical text by Malcolm Potts *et al.* (1977: 147) she argued that 'in populations that are beginning their fertility decline "induced abortion plays a relatively more important role in fertility control than it does later . . . with the passage of time contraceptive practices improve and the resort to abortion is reduced but never eliminated"' (Sceats 1988: 266 and *passim*).

The most recent data suggest that New Zealand has not been particularly successful in reaching these groups, although a slight downturn in

Pasifika rates can be seen. The recent inflow of permanent and short-term Asian residents has been accompanied by an increase in the rates for abortions. Their contribution, infinitesimal in the 1980s, had risen above that of Pacific peoples to 16% of the total in 2002, when their TAR was above one (Table 7.3). This issue will be returned to later, but it must be stressed that in the new millennium the Asian female population, especially at 15–24 years, was inflated by the presence of large numbers of short-term (less than one year) visitors on student visas.

Essentially, then, the decades from the 1970s to 1990s saw the functional separation of what had historically been inseparable factors: the commencement of sexual relations and/or conjugal unions, and the risk of conception. This separation of procreation and marriage is observed across the WDCs (Santow 1989), and applies as much to the parenting generation as to the majority of their adolescent or young-adult offspring, who are typically initiating intercourse at young ages. The key to this separation sits mainly with one factor: better-quality contraception. The ramifications of this have been very wide. They include increases in the prevalence of LAT-relationships, cohabitation and couple-only households, even for couples in their late twenties and early thirties. Co-varying with these have been values-driven shifts relating to marital statuses: *de facto*, formally married, divorced and other morphologies, all discussed in Chapter Six.

But contraception is merely a proximate determinant, a mechanism by which these changes could be implemented. This leaves still open the more profound question of why, in this era, new attitudes could have been so easily assimilated as norms and effective contraception quickly adopted.

7.3 CAUSALLY MORE REMOTE FACTORS DRIVING CHANGE: THE MACRO-LEVEL SOCIAL AND ECONOMIC CONTEXTS OF FAMILY PATTERNS AND TRENDS

The macro-societal context of the family trends that were outlined in Chapter Six revolve around society-wide changes that have been occurring across a large range of sectors (Pool *et al.* 2000). What will be termed here 'policy' (the public policy environment and system, and the legislative framework) was also reformulated radically in this period, often in ways that undermined the welfare state system built up from the 1930s and even before, discussed in earlier chapters. The economy, which, as was argued earlier, has an impact on the family through the household's material well-being, was also restructured very significantly in the period. This was a time when social factors, including cultural ones (e.g. see Young 1997 on patterns of religious affiliation), were also going through major transformations affecting values and normative systems. Some of this was a result of macro-demographic shifts.

When one turns to this task, identifying very broadly the factors that may be involved is the easy part; analysing and measuring them and their impacts in a more specific way is a problem of a very different order. Not least, this is because there are very few data, particularly on attitudes and normative systems. It is here that we must rely heavily on cross-comparative analysis (see Pool *et al.* 2007: esp. Chapt. 3).

UNDERLYING VALUES AND NORMATIVE SYSTEMS

Over the two and a half decades covered in this chapter, values and normative systems appear to have changed. In some ways the argument is almost tautological: one can state that attitudinal norms (meaning the values guiding what one should do) have changed because behavioural norms (what people actually do most commonly) have been shown to change. Cases in point are the acceptance of cohabitation as a status even for couples with children, or to the 'social acceptability' of divorce or separation (Phillips 1981). The acceptance of these has occurred somewhat paradoxically in a society that was organised around the principle of the male breadwinner (Easting 1992, this has implications for policy, see below; see also Sommestad 1998), and which favoured what has been described as a 'cult of motherhood and domesticity' (Sceats 1988).

Underlying these changes have been other meta-attitudinal shifts that have interlinked value systems relating to the family with wider political-economic ideologies. Thus

> in Europe and North America representative samples indicate changes between Baby Boom and post Baby Boom cohorts in terms of the way the actors in families are viewed: from child centered to seeing the parents' needs as also of importance.
>
> This shift has been accompanied by changes from more egalitarian community-oriented values to New Right neo-liberal attitudes privileging individual freedom. At the same time, the most recent European data suggest an allied increase in conservative political attitudes favouring 'authoritarian . . . top-down management principles' but these are not associated with a return to the old style of family (Pool 1996: 15, quoting Lesthaeghe 1991, and Lesthaeghe and Moors 1995).

This raises some fundamental questions about meta-values. Notably, there is confusion between ideologies relating to the state and governance, and real concerns about the moral stature of the family *per se* (Pool 1996: 15). Typically it has been conservative commentators who see wider family values eroded by the changes in forms, such as in living arrangements, documented last chapter, and by the social policies of the 'Nanny State', which has, so they argue, encouraged attendant patterns of welfare dependency. Yet through trenchant critiques of the welfare system leading to its radical restructuring, values, norms and attendant behaviours as well as material supports that advantaged families have also been eroded. Challenges to the viability of the family have thus come as much from conservative, so-called neo-liberal, quarters, because of the reformulation of the legislation and the cutting of benefits – such as the changes introduced in the 1991 Budget – as from the old-style liberalism which drove changes such as divorce and abortion reform or the 'hippy revolution' (Pool 1996). Typically these realignments of values and norms, of whatever provenance, have been temporal and cyclical.

There is, however, a more fundamental, long-lasting, perhaps even permanent factor underpinning, if not driving, some of the shifts in values just noted: the effects of 'macro-contraception' (Murphy 1993), to which we have referred earlier. Michael Murphy infers that the Pill was more than a mere mechanism, but gave women a degree of reproductive choice and thus was a factor empowering them. It also removed the spectre of unpredictable and inevitable reproduction that had been the justification for excluding women from access to higher education and participation in many sectors of the remunerated labour force. Beyond that, and probably more importantly, it realigned value systems. Its dramatic debut completely, and radically, changed the whole nature of social discourse on family issues, whether informal, in the media or in public policy fora.

The changes in Pakeha values and norms occurring over the last few decades, though, may have also been in conflict not just with Baby Boom attitudes and behaviours around the cult of domesticity, noted above, but with the broader ideational system that had its genesis in the patterns of modernisation experienced in New Zealand and other ESCs, especially the neo-Europes. To an extent Maori shared these, at least as behavioural patterns if not cultural norms, simply because of the changes wrought on family life by the urban migration discussed in Chapter Five.

One must turn, therefore, to some set of underlying values and norms that shape New Zealand family forms and structures and that may also predispose it, and some other ESCs, to higher fertility, achieved – among other ways – through the greater force of reproduction at earlier ages. This has been a behaviour pattern not only among ethnic minorities but also by European-origin majority populations such as Pakeha. While rates at younger ages changed dramatically over the period covered in this chapter, relative to most WDCs New Zealand's reproduction was more concentrated at younger ages, was far less clustered at ages 25–34 years, but, by comparison, came up again towards WDC levels at the older reproductive ages. This issue will be returned to in later chapters.

The value system in New Zealand and the other neo-European ESCs, especially for the majority populations of European origin, comes from a shared experience of being 'British', mainly as colonies but also as independent countries that maintain close links with the United Kingdom, as most public policy analysts argue (see below). But there may be something more fundamental than this common origin and language. There are some differences between the neo-Europes and their former metropole (e.g. TFRs in the Baby Boom, Dharmalingam *et al.* 2007: Table 5.12), even though socio-political interactions are often close: as recently as the late 1960s New Zealand was still intimately interwoven with Britain economically and in many other ways (Belich 2001: *passim*). As was discussed earlier, the processes of migration and colonisation have meant that, for example, 'Australia and NZ, unlike Britain, have relatively shallow kinship structures' (Thorns 1992: 254). For many New Zealand families, kinsfolk and affines, the people from whom a great deal of support will come, resided back in the mother country. This is clearly a factor of importance in the area of family policy.

The net result of the migrations from Europe is that the ESCs as a block became rather different from all other WDCs. This is because most ESCs are outside Europe: 84% of the ESCs' population live in neo-Europes and, of course, the United States alone accounts for 71% of the total. This is important for New Zealand in that, in the WDCs, we share not only a common English-speaking heritage but one that is essentially neo-European.

The ESCs do have a common history that extends, however, beyond the simple links of colonisation and migration.* They share a distinct set of cultural traditions, especially those relating to family formation, as was described in earlier chapters. But the similarities go far beyond what are normally seen as cultural factors, say ethnicity, language, religion, family ties of kith and kin, norms and mores. Rather, the factors that comprise this shared culture, in a broader sense of the word, are also sited in the macro-economic, macro-social and macro-cultural spheres of life, and accompanying these some micro-social norms and expectations. The

---

* Ireland does not fit as clearly to the ESC model. It was a colony, but unlike North America and Australasia, that were to be colonised by settlers, the Irish were 'subject people', colonised 'to enhance military and political control and to exploit economic resources' (Castles 1993a: xxii). Also, unlike other ESCs, it did not join in the radical policy restructuring of the 1980s and 1990s (Castles 1993b: 5). Kamerman and Kahn, in setting up their cross-cultural studies, the first of which deals with English-speaking countries (including Canada, although its linguistic status is less clear), excluded Ireland, classifying it as part of a peripheral Catholic European grouping (informal meeting, Oxford University, early 1995).

important issue for this chapter is that this aspect of our history may explain what has happened in recent decades.

To support this point it is necessary to return to New Zealand's family history outlined in Chapters Three and Four. By setting our history into a broader cross-national context it is possible to show that many of the patterns reported there were shared with other ESCs. In common with the other neo-European ESCs, New Zealand seems to have followed a peculiar cultural tradition that has driven trends in reproduction, and this may well affect contemporary patterns. At early settlement, CBRs were often higher for European-origin neo-Europeans than for metropolitan European populations, even England and Wales and Scotland, and were driven by early and almost universal childbearing.

Nevertheless, there were other significant aspects of family formation that, with a lag effect, resembled the earlier patterns of nineteenth-century England. As was demonstrated in previous chapters, New Zealand differed from the metropole of 1870, but may have carried forward norms from pre- and early Victorian Britain. A key point emerging from British historical analyses is that, in the early modern era, even before methods of contraception improved, there were still fluctuations in patterns of family formation.

The New Zealand and other neo-European ESC rates then declined significantly to around those in Europe. An exception was Canada, whose levels declined in most provinces, even pioneer Manitoba, but nationally were maintained at relatively higher levels (in 1921, 4.0 births per woman, versus 2.9 for Pakeha in NZ) because of higher levels of fertility in Quebec. Neo-European rates then decreased further, so that by the Depression – again with the exception of Canada because of the higher rates in Quebec at all ages 20 years and over, and especially 25 and over – levels were barely at replacement, resembling North-western Europe. Most importantly they fell well below those of Catholic Southern Europe (Henripin 1968: 25, 30; see also Romaniuc 1984: 14–16; Sceats and Pool 1985: Fig. 25; Festy 1979: 241–97). For Pakeha New Zealand, they dropped below replacement in every year from 1932 to 1937 (Khawaja 1985: Fig. 21, Table 73, 154), a trend seen in several neo-Europes in the Depression (e.g. British Columbia in 1937, Henripin 1968: 30).

Of more than passing interest is the rapid decline in fertility in the neo-Europes in the late nineteenth century, and their lower levels relative to much of North-western Europe and the Mediterranean over the first few decades of the twentieth century, even in pioneer zones like Manitoba (see above), or, by 1901, in the newly settled interior North Island of New Zealand (Pool and Tiong 1989). Parenthetically, this means that arguments about inherent higher fertility arising from a 'frontier spirit' and the 'optimistic expectations' this might engender are not particularly persuasive. Instead, as has just been argued, they are probably underlain by norms stretching back to Britain, and even to a Britain prior to Pakeha settlement of New Zealand.

Below it will be argued that there is recent memory of high fertility by WDC standards in New Zealand and other ESCs, a function in part of the way economic modernisation evolved here; but this brief history of the culture of reproduction also implies that two other factors may be of significance. Moreover, there is a long history in New Zealand not only of exceptionally high fertility by any standards in the pioneer period, but since then of a series of rapid ebbs, then waves (Baby Boom), then ebbs again, that by WDC standards have been radical, even in recent memory. But against this, we should not entirely dismiss the possibility of a longer-term residual memory of sub-replacement fertility, carrying over from the Depression of the 1930s, an issue to be discussed further in later chapters.

These patterns could be compared with the more or less continuous decreases – with much less marked fluctuations – in fertility over several decades seen in, say, Japan or Southern Europe. This could mean that New Zealanders, especially Pakeha, and the populations in other ESCs have somehow developed strategies for fitting fertility trends to macro-social and economic circumstances, something that other WDCs are still coming to terms with. It is instructive that the countries that had lower fertility during the Depression (TFR at replacement or below) typically had higher fertility in the 1990s (1.7+ births/woman) (e.g. ESCs, except Canada, and elsewhere in the WDCs, France) and vice versa (e.g. Italy, Spain, Netherlands; cf. Festy 1979: 241–97; Rindfuss and Brewster 1996: Table 1; Pool and Sceats 2003: Appendix).

In sum, then, in the area of family patterns New Zealand has a shared history with the other neo-European ESCs. To explain why this may have come about, it is useful to look at the way in which the ESCs, especially those that are neo-European, have developed economically and socially.

ECONOMIC MODERNISATION

The demographic transition may have been related to another trans-formation. The ESCs were the first WDCs to go through economic modernisation, to 'become richest earliest subsequently grow more slowly and [to be] gradually overtaken' (Castles 1993b: 28), and this was to shape their social morphology and value systems as much as their economic structures. For example, some neo-Europes had exceptionally high levels of life expectation in the latter years of the nineteenth century, with New Zealand arguably the highest (Pool and Cheung 2002, 2004). This early modernisation also affected expectations about wealth and generated the complacent view that the path to development followed by the ESC societies was the ideal model for others to follow.*

Early modernisation was accompanied, at least in Australia, New Zealand, the United Kingdom and, to a lesser degree, Canada, by legislation laying down the bases of welfare states. In Australasia, these privileged the stereotypical family through emphasising the 'social wage', so that the widow and family of a working man who had fallen on hard times would be maintained at a level of well-being not far below that of the average working man's family. As historian Melanie Nolan has noted, 'The state, by granting the [family] allowance [to the woman herself], helped struggling breadwinners to keep their families in food and their wives at home' (2000: 137 and Chapts 3 and 5). But Nolan goes on to qualify this, showing that this model was eroded over time. Then in the dying decades of the twentieth century it was radically restructured into targeted forms of social assistance, as will be discussed below. These latter-day reforms represent in some ways attempts to reincarnate pre-welfare state systems of social security, 'a past age undergoing an uncanny and often unwitting revival' (Thomson (1998: 165). Unexpectedly, however, this reincarnation may have been positively associated with fertility, rather than being anti-natalist. It is the less well off with higher cumulative fertility by, say, 30 years who were most likely to seek such benefits; the better off achieved this privileged status frequently because they stayed childless as long as possible as they laid down their careers and equity (Johnstone and Pool 1996b).

Of course, the paths of causality are far from uni-directional: early childbearing by accident or by design, recalling that this is a culture that still has a strong memory of such patterns, places many couples in a vulnerable situation so that they must seek targeted assistance. Typically, however, this is so parsimonious that, contrary to what neo-conservatives argue about 'sending out the wrong messages' (e.g. Richardson 1995), the availability of targeted benefits is not itself a sufficient reason for early childbearing.

THE EFFECTS OF ECONOMIC MODERNISATION ON URBANISATION AND HOUSING
Economic modernisation in the ESCs had come, in the main, first from the manufacturing and associated exploitative industries (e.g. coal mining) and from the trading sectors, and later from growth in the service industries. The development of these sectors naturally led these

---

* This is implicit in the vast literature on modernisation emanating primarily from the United States in the era of functionalist sociology; more recently the Anglo-Saxon Reagan/Thatcher model of economic restructuring was widely applied by Bretton Woods agencies.

countries into early urbanisation. It is less evident why those neo-Europes dependent on the export of primary commodities – New Zealand is the extreme example – also urbanised at an early stage, as was discussed earlier. Regardless, with the exception of Ireland, the ESCs still figured among the more urbanised WDCs through the entire post-war period (see Pool and Sceats 2003: Table 10).

It was also argued in previous chapters that early urbanisation in New Zealand and other ESCs tended to take a different form from that found elsewhere in the WDCs. Low-density housing, terraced or row houses, semi-detached or detached dwellings had become the mode in the ESCs in the late nineteenth or early twentieth centuries, whereas multi-storey apartments were more common in the big cities on the continent of Europe.* The ESCs had also led the way in the shift to owner-occupied housing: in 1971 only Iceland in the Western countries had higher levels than Australia (69%), NZ (68%), the US (63%), Canada (56%), Belgium (56%) and, lowest among ESCs, Britain (50%). Other WDCs for which data are available were below 50%. In Australia and New Zealand the level was already at 50–60% in 1945 (Kilmartin and Thorns 1978: 22, 104).

The argument here is that early modernisation, urbanisation and their accompaniments (particularly neolocalisation in individually owned separate dwellings) plus the introduction of welfare state measures, starting in New Zealand in the late 1890s, together created a distinctive value system that still existed in the 1970s and 1980s. At an early stage, ESC populations developed lifestyles allowing them to accommodate family formation to urban living and even, as was implied earlier, patterns of reproduction were adapted to meet economic changes (e.g. during the 1930s Depression).

The Baby Boom reproductive regimes associated with suburban family life in a detached house set the values for later generations, at least in the neo-Europes. These Baby Boom regimes involved *inter alia* a return to marked levels of early reproductive force that, in Pakeha New Zealand and elsewhere, had also characterised the pioneer period. It may have been easier for very young parents to raise a family in a detached suburban house than in an apartment, provided they had the means to buy a home. This varied across the neo-Europes, but frequently involved some form of family support.

Moreover, over recent decades there has been increasing demand for larger houses, not just as a form of conspicuous consumption but also for other reasons to do with norms and mores. For example, with changing

---

* These comments on housing are based on personal observations plus very useful discussions with David Thorns, an urban sociologist at Canterbury University, and David Swain, a Waikato University family sociologist.

values about the 'quality' of childrearing there was increasing opposition to the notion of children, particularly of different ages or genders, sharing bedrooms, the norm earlier in the twentieth century. This left, as it were, a recent residual memory, particularly centred on the Baby Boom, of fertility levels that were high by WDC standards, even Mediterranean European, yet achieved in a peculiar urbanised environment of owner-occupied, detached dwellings. As has been frequently demonstrated overseas, this residual memory, or nostalgia, may persist for some time, and could do so indefinitely, producing ideal family-size levels that are above achieved family sizes. Even the intended family sizes of women and couples themselves may exceed those for their completed families. As Kellie Hagewegen and Philip Morgan argue in an analysis of American data employing a detailed review of the international literature, 'women and couples act in accordance with contemporary anti-natalist constraints [i.e. socio-economic and bio-social factors that limit their opportunities to become parents] and have few children, but continue for a period (a time-lag) to express the prevailing cultural imperatives to be parents and to have at least two children' (Hagewegen and Morgan 2005: 507–8).

The realisation of the material contexts of family behaviour continued over the period of the Baby Bust and into the Baby Blip. But by the end of the period covered in this chapter the residual memory of this aspect of New Zealand family life was increasingly becoming just that: a dream. Above all, by the early 1990s owner occupation was becoming difficult for young couples. In a long and detailed report on housing tenure and aspirations prepared for the Centre for Housing Research, Aotearoa New Zealand, and Building Research, and drawing on a report by the geographer Philip Morrison, DTZ New Zealand showed that 'family circumstances' and age are the key factors in determining aspirations to own a house. But between 1991 and 2001 the percentages of owner-occupied dwellings declined both systematically and significantly at the key childbearing ages: from 69% to 56% for occupiers aged 30–34 years; from 76% to 66% at 35–39; and from 81% to 72% at 40–44. (DTZ 2005: 56, 98, Appendix p. 22). A recent housing boom seems not to have been because of budding parents seeking a first home but instead because of people seeking a second home, often as an investment for rental purposes. Effectively, this cut many young would-be-house-owning couples out of the market, or, if they bought, presented them with crippling mortgages.

Thus over recent decades one of the most important material props for family building – the ownership, typically with a mortgage, of a family home – has started to become unattainable, and increasingly endures only in nostalgia. This slippage has not gone unnoticed by the populace at large and by the media: it has manifested itself in popular culture, as exemplified by TV. The family sitcom of the 1970s to 1990s, with its suburban house, attached two-car garage and family of cute children has yielded place to childless and cohabiting couples, LATs and singles. *The Brady Bunch* had been replaced by *Sex and the City*.

7.4 POLICY FACTORS DRIVING CHANGE:* THE WELFARE STATE AND ITS DECLINE

In earlier chapters the evolution of the welfare state was described. This institution provided props for – although it was not a determinant of trends in – family formation and structures and thus the maintenance of the family. This was particularly true in the Baby Boom. But in the last decades of the twentieth century the welfare state came under threat and many of its instruments were dispensed with. David Thomson, with the resignation of the historian who has seen it all before, argues that reforms such as those over the last twenty years are cyclical 'through the history of Anglo-Saxon societies with turns every 100 or so years' (1998: 165). Whether or not they represent a reprise or the application of new ideas, there is a need to review these changes as they have evolved recently as well as the ethos that drove their formulation/reformulation.

In this endeavour we are relatively fortunate, for this period and that covered in the next chapter have seen an extraordinary growth in the literature on aspects of family policy and family welfare, much of it emanating from neo-liberal critiques of the role of the state and some questioning the very existence of most state functions. One would welcome these concerns and the upsurge of interest in family welfare, were it not for their focus on family breakdown, not as an issue in its own right – assuming that the changes in forms and structures we have recorded here were indeed to represent this – but as a symbol, even a determinant, of the failure of the welfare state. The solo mother, especially if a teenager, is conflated into the prime cause of both moral and fiscal national decay. There is an interplay between two seemingly different if not contradictory philosophical traditions, of the moral right, which is prescriptive and regulatory in inclination, and the fiscal right, that emphasises 'liberal' values for individuals and for economic undertakings. It has become a peculiar aspect, although perhaps not without historical antecedents, of the late twentieth-century social and political-economic dialectic, especially in the United States. An asyndetic,

---

* We are indebted to Tom Nutt of the Cambridge University Group on the History of Population and Social Structure for leading Ian Pool through the complexities of British family policy in the eighteenth and nineteenth centuries.

opportunistic alliance between moral and fiscal conservative ideologies also loomed large in the New Zealand policy arena, as was true across the ESCs (Pool 1996).

How a nation-state views family policy is a result of its own social and cultural development. Thus the policy context for the family varies greatly from society to society. In peasant and pre-modern societies the family and/or the community might play a key support role. Industrialisation and attendant changes saw this formalised through parishes in pre-modern Britain and consolidated in 1601. Then came the poorhouses of the nineteenth century under the 1834 Poor Law Amendment Act, underwritten philosophically by calls for self-reliance and family responsibility that were the inspiration for a particularly punitive form of welfare in New Zealand. Underlying these were value systems that almost saw the poor as profligate: it was their own fault that they were poor, as they had failed to provide for themselves and their families were too large. The 'propertied class effectively enshrined the concept of ['too many children'] in the philosophy underpinning the New Poor Law of 1834, in order to impress it on the labouring poor' (Garrett *et al.* 2001: 430).

These philosophical positions, including the view that the 'Poor should stop breeding' (Bassett 2003a), made a reappearance in the 1980s and 1990s in some welfare debates, in the guise of minimising welfare dependency, and thus meeting two objectives: enhancing public-sector accountability and, as in Victorian Britain, ensuring rectitude on the part of charity recipients. Among the measures in the new Poor Laws implemented in many counties in the British Isles during the Victorian era was the condition that the mothers of bastards were supposed to work to meet their costs, an idea that has also resurfaced in some late twentieth- and early twenty-first-century policy commentaries, albeit in a more nuanced form – that sole parents, most of whom are mothers, should work or lose eligibility for welfare. This was deemed necessary to assist, or coerce, them to escape the welfare dependency trap.

THE IMPACTS OF THE DECLINE OF NEW ZEALAND'S WELFARE STATE

Policy, at least as manifested in legislation and regulations, is sometimes less a driver than a consequence of society-wide shifts in values and behaviours. Around 80% of the young are likely to cohabit as a first union, and this has remained the proportion since the early 1980s (Pool *et al.* 1998: 112). Yet it is only now that laws relating to the contractual aspects of such unions are being addressed. There are, however, emerging issues that have major policy implications, including the definition of cohabitation and of LATs (Pool 1998). The status of cohabitation has now in part been formalised through legislation on civil unions (2005) and some earlier acts (e.g.

the Property Relationships Act 2001). In contrast, the roles, obligations and rights of couples' parents and grandparents, as when children are fostered by them, is an under-developed legislative area. This becomes more complicated when children are born to LATs or when boomerang kids come back home, particularly if they are accompanied by their offspring (Pool 2005). Moreover, policies that are drafted to meet the needs of some, or most, families may not suit others. A case in point is the reconstituted family; policy inconsistencies often place them in a disadvantaged position (Fleming 1999).

Nevertheless, policy and legal changes have often accommodated changes in statuses (e.g. divorce) and living arrangements (e.g. sole parents; see Goodger 1998). This is different, however, from arguing that policies have produced the changes, for much policy formulation is after the fact, reactive rather than proactive.

In contrast, there are other policies that have been proactive and may have had negative effects on families. In this regard some recent initiatives have all the hallmarks of a colonial version of British nineteenth-century Poor Law legislation and of New Zealand's own Destitute Persons Ordinance of 1846 (Thomson 1998: Chapt. 1): sole-parent beneficiaries should work; ex-nuptial births should be adopted out. The sudden and virtually unannounced cuts in benefits in New Zealand's 1990 December mini-budget are perhaps the most glaring recent example, but there are many others that are as important: the redefinition of family responsibilities (e.g. extending their obligations to dependent children out to 25 years) as implemented in the 1991 Budget and its aftermath put significant burdens on families (Jackson 1994a, b, c); and the student loan scheme may place constraints on family building for many members of an entire generation of New Zealanders (Pool 2000a). Among other consequences this may have an effect on the capacities of young couples to raise mortgages and set up a family home.

The revolutionary changes in the policy paradigm at this time had an immediate impact on services. Historian Bronwyn Labrum, in a study that provides a longer-term historical perspective, notes the paradigm shift and its attendant implication for family welfare services:

> The state took a back seat in social policy and the 'family' was trumpeted as the nexus of care and assistance. Two measures in particular were emblematic of this shift. The Children, Young Persons and their Families Act 1989 encapsulated the notion of 'family solutions to family problems' and asserted 'the primacy of families, whanau and family groups in having and taking the responsibility for the welfare of their members' .... Almost a decade later the 1997 Code of Social and Family Responsibility attempted to strengthen still further the responsibilities of families and communities to meet their members' needs (Labrum 2004: 157).

The policy initiatives that ultimately may have had the most impact on families were, however, exogenous to the family itself as, in principle at least, they were directed at fiscal, financial and economic sectors and not at social policy. The restructuring in the 1980s and 1990s, above all through changes in access to and need for employment, has very significantly affected families (Martin 1998; Callister 1998). The negative impacts of macro-policy (the implementation of economic restructuring and the way it was done, Pool 1999) have probably been greater than the positive effects of particular measures (listed in Hillcoat-Nalletamby *et al.* 1999: 600), a point that will be considered by reviewing micro-economic factors below. Thus some aspects of what seem exogenous macro-economic policy changes appear to have effected micro-economic changes on family life and, it must be noted, on the workplace. By the last decade of the twentieth century changes in families and the labour market were interacting and for many households, even perhaps the majority, were also having undesirable consequences for family life.

The net effect is that families are attempting to carry out their functions in a climate in which income inequalities have increased. This has caused them stress as they attempt 'to reconcile the conflicting requirements of "public" employment and "private" domestic spheres' (Hillcoat-Nalletamby *et al.* 1999: 595). For the 'dual-job' families, identified by Callister, 'the "double burden" of paid work and unpaid work is exacerbated by the lack of "'family friendly" supports both in their workplaces and in their communities' (Callister 1998: 118).

Nevertheless, props such as paid maternity leave and family benefits may themselves be insufficient, at least to maintain levels of fertility close to replacement. This is best illustrated by looking at international analyses. For example, for a long period Italian family sizes have been far below that level, 1.3 births per woman, and with a potential to drop further (Livi Bacci 2004a). Yet they

> still follow traditional marriage customs of a form, and with a prevalence (almost all first unions) which would bring cheers from most New Zealand conservative commentators. In contrast, take the Swedes, cohabiting away through their dark winter nights, the very examples of the breakdown of family life feared by the moral right, but with total fertility rates which are far closer to replacement (Pool 2000b).

The difference is the availability in Sweden of comprehensive family-friendly policies, above all those mediating the interface between work and the family (Pinelli *et al.* 2000; Corman 2000; Oláh 2001). As John Hobcraft argues, 'what matters is the reality of practical support to ease parenthood in Northwestern Europe, rather than the rhetoric of pro-natalism in

Southern Europe . . . [the] enabling [of] the combination of motherhood and work, although leading to foregone leisure, was much more acceptable than the starker choice between work and motherhood' (Hobcraft 2004: 82, citing research with Katherine Kiernan). One could add France to this example; it has comprehensive welfare state policies and higher fertility (Letablier 2002).

The importance of this broader policy context for the functioning of the household, not just for family building but more importantly for the general well-being of households, cannot be overstressed. In particular, as Janet Gornick and Marcia Meyers outline, family policies mediate the 'conflicts between earning and caring'. Many of the key parameters for social policy, essential for family well-being as much in New Zealand as in other WDCs, are set out in their comparison between Europe and the United States (Gornick and Meyers 2003: 1):

> Imagine a world in which mothers could take a few months away from their jobs following the birth or adoption of a child, without sacrificing either job security or their paychecks. Imagine a world in which both mothers and fathers could spend substantial time at home during their child's first year, while receiving nearly all their wages. Imagine a world in which mothers and fathers could choose to work part-time until their children are in primary school without changing employers or losing their health benefits. Imagine a world in which the normal workweek was 37 or even 35 hours, and parents had the right to take occasional days off, with pay, to attend to unexpected family needs. Imagine a world in which all parents had the right to place their children in high-quality child care provided by well-educated professionals. Imagine a world in which this child care was provided at no cost or very low cost to parents.
>
> A world such as this, indeed, can only be imagined by American parents. It is a reality, however, for parents in several countries in Europe.

As this quotation infers, the discussion here is not about a given policy measure but the wider environment; it is about providing a sympathetic environment in which family values and life-ways can flourish. Their comments only refer to a segment of family life – the early years of parenting (and, normally, also of earning), but still involve a wide range of measures.

THE FAMILY POLICY ENVIRONMENT: NEW ZEALAND IN A COMPARATIVE CONTEXT

The reformulation of social policy around 1990 produced a radical shift from the antipodean model of a welfare state, an indigenous version of the social-democratic regimes of the Nordic countries, to an extreme version of a neo-liberal regime (Pool and Sceats 2003). These measures, introduced brutally and without prior warning in the 1980s and 1990, were replete with features, for example an emphasis on targeting and the paring down of the monetary value of benefits, that have become the dominant axes of family policy.*

To put New Zealand in context in the period covered in this chapter and the next it is necessary to see it alongside other countries. The so-called 'worlds' constituting policy environments had been classified by Gosta Esping-Andersen (1990) as "'social-democratic" (basically the Nordic countries), "conservative" ([the Gemanic-, Dutch- and French-speaking northern] Continental Europe), and "liberal" (the Anglo-Saxon Nations)'[†] (cited in Esping-Andersen 1999: 12). He argues that *liberal* policy is essentially 'residual' in that 'social guarantees are restricted to "bad risks" . . . it adheres to a narrow conception of what risks should be considered "social" [and of] its encouragement of the market . . . . Besides universalism the *social democratic* welfare state is particularly committed to comprehensive risk coverage, generous benefit levels, and egalitarianism . . . . The essence of a *conservative* regime lies in its blend of status segmentation and familialism' (Esping-Andersen 1999: Chapt. 5 *passim*). Janet Gornick and Marcia Meyers summarise Esping-Andersen by seeing the Nordic regime as one where 'entitlements [are] linked to social rights'; the continental model links benefits to 'earnings and occupation, and public provisions tend to replicate generated distributional outcomes'. There, 'social policy is also shaped by the principle of "subsidiarity", which stresses the primacy of the family and community for providing dependent care and other social supports. Social benefits in the ESCs are usually organised to reflect and preserve consumer and employer markets, and most entitlements derive from need [i.e. not social right]' (2003: 23).

Clearly, gender is a major determinant of the need for adults to seek many entitlements: for example, most sole parents are women; there are more geriatric widows than widowers. In this regard, Gornick and Meyers (2003: 23) make a very critical observation:

In the 1990s many critics (including [Gornick and Meyers themselves]) charged Esping-Andersen with ignoring gender issues . . . . Yet subsequent

---

* These reforms came in two waves: one was more macro-economic (around 1988), involving such measures as the elimination of tariffs and the sale of state assets, both of which immediately affected families through high levels of unemployment; the second, mainly introduced in the 1991 Budget and written into law that same day, was more micro-economic, affecting every single welfare sector.

† ESCs are used here instead of Anglo-Saxon.

empirical efforts to establish welfare-state typologies that incorporate gender have largely confirmed Esping-Andersen's classification . . . . In the Nordic countries, the social-democratic principles that guide policy design are generally paired with a commitment to gender equality; the market replicating principles in the Continental countries are often embedded in socially conservative ideas about family and gender roles; in the English-speaking countries the principles of the market nearly always take precedence.

Canadian sociologist John Myles in a paper entitled 'When Markets Fail' (1996: 118) takes these points further by comparing the residual 'social assistance' model, implemented under these circumstances, with the 'industrial achievement model' based around 'labour market performance' and the 'citizenship model' of 'universal social benefits'. The Nordic states have been the prototypes of the third model, but one would have to add France to this list for, if anything, its family policies are more comprehensive than the Northern European and seemingly rather effective (Letablier 2002). Among European countries France has been most successful in keeping levels of reproduction up, only just below replacement, consistently since the late 1970s.

In his most recent book, however, Esping-Andersen has added three different new models, possibly together constituting, as he puts it, a 'fourth world'. First among these, as noted above, there was the Antipodean model (Australia and New Zealand) in which what seem modest, typically needs-tested, benefits were coupled, however, with 'functionally equivalent welfare guarantees that were implanted in the labour market via the wage arbitration system'. It is important for the present study to note that New Zealand was to become a pioneer welfare state through its Industrial Conciliation and Arbitration Act, 1894, and the underlying ideology of a 'social wage' sufficient to sustain a working man and his family. These, and full employment in many years, were to underpin the maintenance of social equality until, it could be argued, the radical shift to an extreme liberal regime in the late 1980s–early 1990s (Shirley *et al.* 1997, esp. Chapt. 2).* An interesting comparison can be made here with the very different philosophy underlying Swedish social policy. The Antipodean model privileged the 'male breadwinner family', whereas Swedish policy pivoted on 'citizen-based entitlements [serving] to underline the basic similarity

---

* See also Kamerman and Kahn 1997a, who give a very succinct analysis of the similarities and differences in family changes and family policies in four of the ESCs; besides Shirley *et al.* 1997 on New Zealand, see also essays on Great Britain by Ringen (ed.) 1997, Canada by Baker and Phipps 1997 and the US by Kamerman and Kahn 1997b.

between married and unmarried women, and between women and men'
(Sommestad 1997: 174).

A second is the Mediterranean model that perhaps differs from the Continental European (Esping-Andersen debates this point, but it certainly
seems to contrast with what is seen in the ESCs) by 'the use of social benefits
... for purposes of political clientelism' and its emphasis on 'familialism'.
For example, 'In Italy, even in the industrialised north, the accepted meaning of family remains encompassing. It is a solidarity network consisting
not only of a couple and their children, but also of grandparents, uncles,
aunts, cousins and even more distant relatives' (Chesnais 1996; 735).

As the Mediterranean experience provides a counterpoint to that of the
ESCs or the Nordic countries, or indeed France, it is worth looking at in
more detail. Livi-Bacci and Salvini define the Italian model as 'too much
family and too few children', citing a key mechanism:

> Prolonged co-residence of young adults with their parents is a central aspect
> of the Italian situation; [it is] directly associated with the postponing of
> marriage and childbearing, and relatively low rate of nuptiality, and without
> doubt it counts among the principal causes of the growing gap between
> expected and achieved family size (Livi-Bacci and Salvini 2000: 231–32;
> translation by present authors).

But this must be seen in context, so they argue: that social transfers for
young adults fall below those in much of Europe.[*] Yet from eighteen to 60
years tax burdens are relatively high, whereas comparatively low percentages of GDP are spent on education. Moreover, deposits for purchasing
dwellings are high. Thus in a sense Italian familialism is not a return to
the traditional parent-child household and moral values. Instead, it is a
familialism that maximises the utility of the family as a sort of policy/
service delivery instrument. Italy is not unique in this; Livi-Bacci and Salvini also identify this factor in Spain and Japan (2000: 252). The key point
here is that a system that maximises what might be called 'family values'
does not seem to have found the magic formula by which families can
prosper and reproduce in a way that also assures societal maintenance.
Among Italian scholars and the wider public this has produced a level of
angst that goes beyond moral panic (see the special issue of *Genus* 2004,
LX, 1).

---

[*] 'Social transfer' may be defined as the 'conveyance' (to use the legal term applied in the private
sector to refer to properties and equities) of income supports and other social benefits from the
state or other public or non-profit agency to those in need, or in a 'universal' system to defined
eligible recipients (e.g. all citizen and long-term residents over 65 years in the case of New Zealand
national superannuation).

The East Asian model, notably including Japan, is the third and in many senses a hybrid. It depends on high levels of targeting, and is one in which the family still plays a major role in family welfare, particularly in caring for the elderly (Esping-Andersen 1999: 88–92).*

In their cross-comparative research on WDCs, Australian researchers Castles and Mitchell (1993: 117–19) take this further. They analyse a range of political and public policy variables, from which they derive a set of propositions allowing them to classify nations into 'families'. The ESCs, including New Zealand, are all countries in which, since World War II, 'the political right has enjoyed long periods of political office', but there is variation between the political strength of their labour movements, the level of public policy expenditures and their use of 'equalising instruments'. Those ESCs low on two or three of these factors are Canada and Ireland,† while the United States is low on all. They conclude that 'the impression is of an extraordinarily close fit between political structure and the character of welfare provision . . . . Three of the six [ESCs], Australia, New Zealand and the United Kingdom have an historical legacy of [radical egalitarianism, as distinct from neo-liberal]. Two others have characteristics which cross-cut the Radical and Liberal worlds. The United States alone is clearly an inhabitant of the Liberal world' (123–24). Elsewhere Castles (1998: 8–9) sets out what he calls 'families of nations', comprising the ESCs and others (Continental West European, composed of France and the German- and Dutch-speaking countries), with 'a historical legacy of dynastic links, cultural (particularly religious) similarities and policy diffusion'; Nordic; and Southern European; while Switzerland and Japan were difficult to classify.

The recent reputation of ESCs as 'liberal', low-social-spending states that rely on targeting (Kamerman and Kahn 1997a: 10) is belied by history. '[T]he case for an English-speaking family of nations united by a common "status" of welfare state laggards sits very uneasily with the historical record . . . . The New Zealand Social Security Act of 1938 was regarded by the ILO as having "more than any other law, determined the practical meaning of social security"' (Castles and Mitchell, 1993: 93–94). Within the ESCs, the United States is different in this regard in that many components of welfare programmes vary from state to state, and thus historically some have been highly innovative in diverse areas, but this may not show up at the national level. Some uniformity is achieved, as in the New Deal, by federal interventions to pressure or support individual states (Kamerman and Kahn 1997b:

---

*   John Campbell notes a special case that he terms the Japanese model, 'a full-employment policy powered by the private sector' (cited in 'The Japanese Model: Past, Present and Future', *Asahi Shimbun*, 12–13 Oct 2002: 25).

†   In Canada's case federal–provincial trade-offs produce more equitable policy than would otherwise be the case (Castles and Mitchell 1993: *passim*).

passim). In Canada, as already noted, federal–provincial trade-offs affect family policy formulation and implementation.

To Castles the ESCs are different, a point that is critical for our case here. The ESCs share

> a link [that] can be traced to the timing of sequences of historical development that differentiate the experiences of the ESCs from other nations of advanced capitalism. The argument is simply that slow economic growth, policy ineffectiveness and high threshold electoral systems [in the 1970s and1980s] are all, in some degree, consequences of the relative earliness of economic, social and political modernisation in Britain and in the countries largely settled by British migration (Castles 1993b: 28).

The ESCs have another feature in common: a '1980s shift to anti-statism' (Castles 1993a: xviii). Under Reagan and Thatcher, liberal welfare policies were extended in the United States and United Kingdom (Castles 1993b: 6–7), while in the antipodes the supports of the 'social wage' and full employment virtually disappeared. These guarantees were eroded by the shift to liberalism in Australia in the 1980s. In Esping-Andersen's words, 'they were effectively eliminated in NZ' (1999: 89; see also Castles *et al.* 1996). What is surprising about the antipodean changes was that they were initiated by a Labour (left-incumbency) government, although then carried further, especially in New Zealand, by right-incumbency cabinets.

FROM THE UNIVERSALISTIC WELFARE-STATE MODEL TO TARGETED FAMILY POLICY

Much of the public policy literature deals with the family and its interface with the labour market, a theme that will be picked up in the next part of this chapter. But it is also the case that a considerable degree of attention is paid to family formation and structures, and, because rates are so low in many WDCs, to levels of fertility *per se* (Castles 1999: Chapt. 7; Esping-Andersen 1999: Chapt. 4; Kamerman and Kahn 1997; Day 1992: his Chapt. 5 looks at policy alternatives in low fertility societies; the official positions for all ECE countries, including Canada and the United States, are reported in UN(ECE)/Council of Europe 1994).

In the ESCs there is a focus, almost an unhealthy concern, in both policy research and formulation in political circles on what might be seen as the non-traditional family forms which are often viewed as dysfunctional: cohabitation, ex-nuptial childbearing and sole parenting (Kamerman and Kahn 1997a). These concerns in research and policy turn attention from more normative family issues and more universalistic family policies to those relating, say, to the narrower questions of poverty and the supports for childrearing by families. 'The fiscal malaise of [ESCs], and thus calls to demolish the welfare state, is often attributed to family dysfunction, and particularly to the sole-parent, which is usually female-headed' (Pool 1996: 12). One recent study of this genre argues that New Zealand is an extreme case not only in terms of its family demographic trends, but also its policy support for solo parents and ex-nuptial childbearing (Morgan 2004: *passim*).*

The recent trend towards ageing and low fertility across the WDCs has, however, revived interest in factors that might lead to higher fertility, particularly in the WDCs that are not ESCs. In their study, already cited, a macro-economic, cross-comparative (Netherlands–NZ), time-series analysis, Poot and Siegers argue that fertility levels are influenced by economic factors. In the case of factors that might affect real costs of childbearing these causal links were, however, 'fragile' and 'suggested that the causality runs from fertility to real interest rates rather than vice-versa'. In contrast, there were stronger effects coming from policy interventions, notably the 'impact of social security payments on fertility . . . the introduction of a substantial subsidy to families just after World War II boosted fertility' (2001: 96).

A comprehensive review of a wide variety of family policies is found in Anne Gauthier's work. Of particular interest to the present study is her work on cash benefits to families and other interventions that might be seen to have pro-natalist impacts, such as maternity leave. She summarises the effects of these in a figure (Gauthier 1996: 189) that trichotomises support into high, medium and low categories. The ESCs, except for the United Kingdom, and the Southern European countries are in the low grouping. At the time she wrote New Zealand was at the bottom of the WDCs.

In her most recent paper Gauthier fits family policies into the Esping-Andersen country clusters. She shows that state support for parents has not converged in response to the fact that countries face some common problems, but have actually diverged. In this regard the liberal cluster, including all the ESCs except Ireland, plus Japan and Switzerland 'has been increasingly marginalised' (Gauthier 2002: 467). Among these states, New Zealand is the most extreme.[†]

---

* 'War has been declared on the family' by an 'Unholy Alliance of Feminism, Marxism and Sexual Liberation' (Morgan 2004: 68). See also some of the Maxim Institute web publications (www.maxim.org.nz), such as 'The Costs of Killing the Family' (Winter 2002) or 'Power Feminism failing NZ Women, Children and Society' (August 2003).
† At a seminar at Victoria University (Institute of Policy Studies) in April 2006 on 'Reconciling Work and Family', in the discussion of her paper, Janet Gornick suggested that the recent legislative changes such as parenting-leave provisions lifted New Zealand a little, from the very bottom into the bottom grouping.

In another paper Gauthier and Hatzius restrict their analysis to the links between benefits and fertility, for a period (1970–90) that post-dates the post-war decades when social security may have acted as a positive incentive (see above Poot and Siegers 2001). Gauthier and Hatzius's (1997: 302) results show that cash benefits did not affect fertility in the ESCs, but had a marked impact in Scandinavia, and that the Continental and Southern European countries fell in between, varying according to the parity order of the child for whom the benefit was received. Where the value of the benefit also increases by birth order this effect is maximised. They conclude, however, that 'The potential effects of benefits should also be investigated. These include means-tested benefits and benefits in the fields of day-care, housing, health care and education' (Gauthier 2002).

Thus New Zealand and the other ESCs have different fertility and policy regimes from the rest of the WDCs. Their focus on residual and targeted assistance means that today the ESCs fall not only behind some other groupings of WDCs, but that cash incentives for fertility have minimal impact in these countries. Against this the ESCs, particularly the United States and New Zealand, have higher fertility than most other WDCs, and this is marked at younger ages at which it could be assumed the need for supports and family-friendly policies would be greatest. This summary thus leaves a number of unresolved questions: Are there are other demographic factors that might explain this paradox? Are there cultural factors in New Zealand, relating to values around childbearing, family formation and household structures? It may be that there are more muted aspects of the policy environment, or rather that it is the way the populace responds to it that affect fertility trends and patterns. Indeed, as Gauthier and Hatzius remind us, family-friendly and potentially pro-natalist policies may relate to many aspects of well-being and not just comprise family benefits (see also Letablier 2002, reporting on France; for a New Zealand and cross-comparative study see Callister 2002; see also Callister 2000b). In the Baby Boom, as was noted in Chapter Five, support for housing seems to have been a crucial factor, perhaps as important or more important than family benefits. And in the assault on the welfare state in recent decades it has not just been direct assistance to families that has been minimised or eliminated, but also indirect measures, such as housing assistance.

7.5 MICRO-LEVEL ECONOMIC AND SOCIAL FACTORS DRIVING CHANGE

It is through the micro-level interactions of work, income generation, support systems, family life and policy that macro-economic changes are transmitted and have an impact on family morphologies (for a New

Zealand review see Callister 2000b). It is important also to recognise that interactions between family life and the economy are not just uni-directional. For example, the family structures, reproductive and work histories, and incomes of the family affect the capacity of women to save for retirement (Marsault 1999).

In the late 1960s and early 1970s two very important sets of change came about which began to empower women economically: increased participation in higher education, and a growth in participation in the paid labour force. For example, the NZW:FEE shows that

> The rates for completion of a first degree-cycle before 25 years went through their most rapid increase for the cohorts attending university in the 1970s. Related to this was a rapid increase in female labour-force participation occurring in the 1970s. It was only in the 1970s 'the distinctly bi-modal pattern of age-specific activity emerged, when returning to the labour force after childbearing became more common' (Pool *et al.* 2000, citing Davies 1993: 70).

By the mid-1970s, however, there were darker clouds gathering that were to end this post-war period of prosperity as measured by increasing purchasing power and growing income equality. A long-term analysis of incomes across the entire post-war period indicates that

> New Zealand has undergone two contrasting periods in the level and distribution of income: a period of gradual equalisation, and of income rising in real value, followed [from 1976] by a period of relatively rapid but also fluctuating dis-equalisation, and with incomes static or declining in real value (Martin 1998: 269).

This set the scene for the changes in family income levels and inequalities described earlier. Policy played a major role in this in terms of the economic restructuring and the redefining of welfare measures. Above all, the macro-economic restructuring introduced in the late 1980s had a major impact on the labour market, notably through high levels of unemployment especially among the young, with rates reaching their nadir around 1990. These labour market changes had a very negative effect on the flow of resources to individuals and families. If we take the entire period 1986 to 1996 (and not just from 1991–96, as is often done), across ages, industries and occupations the number of jobs in 1996 barely exceeded those in 1986. Only Pakeha women benefited from increases in available jobs, but

> . . . [of] the new jobs far more were likely to be part-time rather than full-time, and job creation fell well below the rate of change in demographic

supply, that is the percentage growth in the numbers at working ages. Then discrepancies were particularly marked for the young, for those [Maori, Pasifika and Pakeha] in jobs such as manufacturing, and for Maori and Pacific Islanders . . . to make the situation worse the 1991 budget simultaneously changed the rules under which unemployment benefits could be sought (Pool 1998: 323, citing Pool and Bedford 1997 and Honey and Lindop 1997).

As noted earlier the 1991 Budget also increased the obligations of families to look after the unemployed and in terms of educational support of their young, taking this up to age 24, and for pregnant dependent teenagers (Jackson 1994b).

Even when the analysis is extended to 2001, the results show that the situation seen around 1990 had barely improved, particularly in terms of income. There were also significant increases in inter- and intra-regional inequalities for most factors of human capital and both personal and household incomes (Pool *et al.* 2005c, d; Cochrane *et al.* 2007).

This took place in a period dominated by the macro-economic restructuring driven by neo-liberal ideologies that were focused on the market as the most efficient way not only to deliver economic growth but to deliver social services. The instruments by which these projected efficiencies were to be delivered in the public social sectors were what is termed 'new public management' that would see traditional public administration supplanted by management practices drawn from the business sectors – by definition, neo-liberal ideologues see the private sector as infinitely more efficient than the public. Efficiency is narrowly defined in terms of costs and profits and equals effectiveness in this paradigm; ethical issues can be dealt with simply by seeing the sole responsibility of management as to the shareholders, even when investors are remote (e.g. a pension fund in distant country); and the prime goal of the society is to enhance economic production not reproduction and social well-being.

Translated across to the public sector this took the form of putting aside effectiveness, as it is normally measured by positive impacts on the wider public or on service clients, and replacing it with cost-efficiency and 'public sector accountability' (e.g. see Beckmann and Cooper 2004, whose synthesis draws on work by numerous other authors). Public sector managers were no longer in permanent positions gained after working their way up the ranks but were on contracts, subject to performance reviews and bonuses that were based on outputs rather than outcomes. These ideologies are often cloaked in terminology that may seem logical, but that may have unidentified and possibly perverse consequences. For example, the calls to move from zoning systems to educational vouchers are couched in terms of 'parental choice', a sentiment with which most people would agree – that parents, rather than officials or educationalists, should play a role in determining their children's progress through the education system. But such an approach may increase inequalities by generating multi-tier systems or involve a shift to the marketisation of the delivery of this public good, although not the funding of it. The vouchers in education notion is a central plank in the neo-liberal response to work–life balance issues.

The recommendations of an OECD team that visited New Zealand in late 2003 on 'reconciling work and family life' provide some interesting illustrations of new public management perspectives on this question. For example, they argue that the state should 'redirect "bulk funding" for pre-primary school education from providers to parents [through voucher systems] . . . . Linking such payments to families' working hours could strengthen financial incentives for parents (second earners) seeking work . . . . Modify [the] Domestic Purposes benefit so as to make work pay . . . . Enhance the family-friendly nature of workplaces . . . through subsidies to employers' (OECD 2004: 12). As these examples suggest, the focus is on manipulating the family, particularly the sole-parent household, to meet the needs of the economy in two ways: by coercing or encouraging family members to be in the paid workforce, and additionally by cutting the fiscal costs of welfare. The Canadian demographer Roderic Beaujot reflects on this point, saying 'A commentator on my *Earning Power and Caring in Canadian Families* has proposed that I should switch the title to say 'caring and earning' forcing more thinking on how production should be made to accommodate reproduction, rather than always giving priority to economic production' (Beaujot 2006: 124).

Along with new public sector management went radical and often brutal restructuring of public sector agencies, sometimes, as in the health and social welfare sectors, several times over a few short years; evaluations of these changes typically were centred on processes not real improvements in effectiveness. Health agencies, from the primary to the tertiary level, were totally restructured at least five times in the period 1984 to 2005, each restructuring involving new geographical and sub-sector realignments. Each restructuring brought in new management teams dedicated to making greater efficiencies than their predecessors.

These last paragraphs may seem to have made a rather abstract digression from the theme of our book, yet they are immediately relevant: they impinge, typically in a negative fashion, on the daily lives of many if not most New Zealand families. One way or another, whether for work or family needs or health-related benefits and services or for pensions, a high proportion of New Zealand families have direct (themselves) or indirect (acting on behalf of a relative or friend) contact with the social sector providers, public, non-profit and voluntary, and, increasingly, with market providers of welfare (e.g. retirement homes). For many families, tracking the radical shifts in personnel, their case-manager, their eligibility for benefits and even the structures and names of the agency they must deal with has become an endeavour worthy of Kafka.

One has only to think of the many permutations since the 1980s of the organisation called the Ministry of Social Development (MSD) at the time this book was going to press. This organisation was once known as the Department of Social Welfare, then it spawned various agencies.* But these fragmented and frequently reconstituted structures deal with those policy questions, often sensitive, that are closest to the family: social security, welfare and sometimes aspects of disability. The justice and labour sectors, which similarly deal with questions related to family well-being, have also been subject to restructuring and fragmentation, while the health sector has been massively restructured, including the reassignment of some of the functions at its margins, notably disability, that are no longer part of its 'core business'. Moreover, these agencies, churned in this way through different 'reforms', are not merely dealing with family and other events and crises, but often multiple crises, that are real, immediate and unfolding over individuals', work and family life-cycles. All of these interact with each other, as will be discussed in the next section of the chapter, but also with the policy environment, the agencies implementing policy and the way in which services are provided.

WORK–LIFE BALANCE AND LABOUR MARKET FLEXIBILITY

In any review of the economic factors affecting the family, or on policy, the interrelationship between work and the family is a critical factor; obviously there is the fundamental question of the flow of income and material resources to the household, but there are also the effects of imbalances in the allocation of time between the job and the family, to say nothing of leisure and participation in community and voluntary organisations. During the recent restructuring of the welfare state noted in the last section of this chapter, the reforms in New Zealand and elsewhere in the ESCs involved a shift in policies aimed at producing what is called 'labour market flexibility'.† These policies are often offered as an explanation of the higher fertility of the ESCs, including New Zealand, especially by advocates of neo-liberal economic policies. In the academic literature a more neutral phrase is likely to be used, such as 'labour market arrangements/institutions' or simply 'employment' (see Adsera 2002; McDowell 2001). In reviewing this

---

* For example, the Social Policy Agency; Children and Young Persons; and Work and Industry NZ, which involved a brief marriage with sections of the Department of Labour, now partially dissolved, and with WINZ remarried to MSD.
† We wish to thank Bill Cochrane of the Population Studies Centre, University of Waikato, for his insights on this issue.

important issue there is a lack of New Zealand data, and thus there is a need to turn to the overseas literature, although, as will be seen below, some micro-level New Zealand insights are available.*

The case for flexibility seems to rest on one set of assumptions, built on others:

> Research on the type of jobs women hold sometimes assumes that 'female' jobs have characteristics that make them more compatible with motherhood and that 'flexible' jobs are predominantly held by women, so that they can shape their employment around their work for the family and home . . . .
> Others have argued that predominantly female occupations require less effort ([citing Gary] Becker 1985 [*J. Labor Econ.*]) and are more flexible than other occupations, making it easier for employed women to combine jobs with home responsibilities (Rosenfeld 1996: 199, 212).

Empirical analyses, especially those that might be the bases for modelling fertility–employment interrelationships, encounter major problems with these assumptions, as their focus is essentially on enhancing the role of women only in one part of their lives: the labour market. Their role in family life is more or less ignored or taken as a given. Leisure and community or voluntary service are rarely considered.

Not the least of the problems is that the term 'labour market flexibility' is itself inexact (Deakin and Reed 2000: 4). At a micro-level it is often seen as the availability of part-time work and casualisation, plus strategies by firms allowing labour inputs to vary according to the level of external demand for the firms' output. Moreover, at this level three basic assumptions seem unsustainable: '[I]t does not seem that flexitime is a response to women's needs to combine domestic work with labour market work; [in 1991 in the United States] a greater proportion of men than women had flexible work schedules . . . . To the extent that flexible jobs are also jobs with long and irregular hours, increases in this kind of work would be expected to be associated with lower fertility . . . [and] women's jobs are not easier or more accommodating' (Rosenfeld 1996: 210, 211, 212).

When the other side of women's lives is studied qualitatively at a micro-level, the effects of flexibility on families become clearer. A cross-national

---

* We are mainly drawing here on the extensive qualitative research of Janet Sceats, which has been also embedded in the 2001 quantitative survey (FFS), first reported in Sceats 2003, Sceats *et al.* 2003, Pool and Sceats 2003, Sceats and Kukutai 2005. At the time of writing results are starting to appear from surveys conducted by government agencies, notably the Ministry of Social Development and the Department of Labour (e.g. presented at the seminar, 'Reconciling Work and Family', Institute of Policy Studies, Victoria Uuniversity, Wellington, 21 April 2006). The results publicised to date essentially reinforce the findings of Sceats *et al.* 2003.

analysis in Australia, Britain and New Zealand raised some major questions. Micro-level flexibility definitely has some advantages for less well-off families where both parents need jobs, are prepared to share child-minding and household duties and to work different shifts. Casual and part-time jobs that frequently involve shift work may also be the only feasible sources of jobs both for the working poor, especially sole-parent families, and even for better-off well-educated families. But flexibility, casualisation, shift and part-time work may be extremely disruptive of normal family life (Cairns *et al.* 2002; Johnstone 2002; Sceats 2002).

At a macro-level, flexibility is a strategy aiming to remove some effects of labour supply on demand by firms and the economy in general, in ways that seem to privilege employers rather than workers. That work demands may also grossly disrupt the day-to-day dynamics and material well-being of households is an issue that is not central to that model.

> The argument is that with expansion of the service sector, global competition, and rapidly changing technology, employers need the freedom to bring workers in, to arrange their work schedules – with possibly irregular days and hours – and to dismiss them as needed. Temporary contracts, subcontracting, part-time work, and work outside the regular workday schedule are some of the ways employers enact this flexibility (Rosenfeld 1996: 208).

In policy discourses the notion of flexibility has been taken a step further. It has become associated with the reorientation of social welfare as this affects the relationship between capital and labour, and the costs of benefit systems. In short, it has become coupled with the shift to neo-liberal macro-level economic policy perspectives noted earlier. Theoretically, flexibility should allow more labour market participation coupled with higher fertility. A recent cross-comparative empirical study by Adsera (2002) gives no clear support for arguments favouring or against flexibility. In the United States, where markets are deemed to be flexible, the opportunity costs of childbearing seem lower because women appear to be able to re-enter jobs soon after the birth of their child, a finding that seems to correspond to data from a recent New Zealand study, which found more than half of respondents had gone back to work before their baby was six months old (Sceats 2003). In other jurisdictions, notably in the Nordic countries, the weight of policy is towards funding parents to take leave for months or even years (Gornick and Meyers 2003).

Cross-comparative data on WDCs for 1994 presented by David Coleman do indeed show high positive links between female employment and fertility, but these relationships relate to countries with 'labour market arrangements' that vary significantly. Thus on his graph, the Nordic countries, often seen as having inflexible markets, but also the United Kingdom

and the United States, often cited, especially the latter, as models for flexibility, all have relatively high fertility and levels of participation; Italy and
Spain, whose arrangements also differ, have almost equally low levels of
participation and fertility (Coleman 2005: Fig. 12, 436–40).

This leaves unanswered other questions (the macro-level implications
of these are elaborated for Britain in McDowell 2001). First, there is a fundamental question: why must both partners work when they have a young
child, even when conditions are less than ideal? For example, there may
be difficulties with childcare arrangements that typically in the ESCs will
be *ad hoc* and not necessarily of high quality in terms of the safety and the
social-emotional development of the child (Sceats *et al.* 2003; cf. Letablier
2002); or there may be impacts of shift work on family life. Obviously, however, this is the only way some families are able to survive economically.

Secondly, there is the further simple but fundamental question of
whether or not there are jobs. In many parts of Britain, for example, there
is a job deficit (McDowell 2001: 453), and this is true for some regions in
New Zealand (Pool *et al.* 2005d). Susan Singley and Paul Callister (2003a,
b) show for New Zealand not only that in a rising proportion of households
one or both members of a couple lack an adequate job, but that this falls
heavily on families that are at a childrearing phase when such work may
be essential to make ends meet. This again differs from region to region
(Cochrane *et al.* 2007).

Arguments based on low rates of unemployment as gauged through
labour-force surveys are likely to be spurious, as the definitions used in
these instruments are extremely restrictive: they define out of the labour
force anyone who was not working or actively seeking a job in the reference
period (normally the previous week or month). Where job deficits occur a
large pool of potential workers will often not even try their hand at seeking
work only to risk rejection, even where they have the resources to do so,
such as transport and access to job agencies and proactive programmes
may not really address this issue. British workfare 'schemes [called "New
Deal"] concentrate on improving the quality of the labour supply through
training in the main with little attention given to job creation' (McDowell
2001: 452). Research on New Zealand regions (Pool *et al.* 2005d) shows the
impact on the labour force of discouraged workers,[*] and major differences
in levels of unemployment and rates of part-time work. These continue
despite low levels of unemployment as conventionally measured.

---

[*] These rely on estimates based on projections forward from 1986 to give expected numbers of jobs,
and these results are then compared with observed numbers enumerated in censuses in more
recent years. Circumstantial evidence comes from data on changes in the numbers of persons at
workforce ages on sickness and other benefits.

Thirdly, many couples, and especially women in New Zealand, England and Australia, need to secure and maintain status and advancement in careers, to prepare for which they have invested heavily and typically have postponed childbearing (Sceats *et al.* 2003). This reinforces other labour market patterns, notably gender trends in participation in the 'high tech' as against 'high touch' service occupations 'that increasingly dominate advanced industrial economies'. But associated with these shifts are the growing income inequalities and status gaps between full- and part-time work. In Britain, 'Full-time work for women is astonishingly strongly class differentiated . . . women who work continuously in full-time jobs not only tend themselves to hold higher status jobs than other women [and thus, if parents, to have an income allowing them to purchase quality childcare] but also to be partnered by men in high status employment' (McDowell 2001: 450, 451, 455). Thus part-time and casual workers seldom maintain the job statuses (e.g. promotion prospects) of their full-time peers. Essentially, then, a product of this form of flexibility is a further segmentation of the labour force into full-time workers, who have higher status, and part-time ones, who have lower status and fewer prospects.

The need to work after childbearing often reinforces this segmentation, and thus risks increasing distinctions and inequalities. The cross-national study noted above states that in all three countries there is 'little indication that women have the full range of choice in terms of employment options when they have children . . . . Women in all countries commented on the frustration of being employed part time and a sense of not being taken seriously' (Sceats *et al.* 2003).

Fourthly, some larger employers, especially the public sector where female participation rates are high, can provide better flexibility in work conditions, as in the Nordic countries. This also occurs in those ESCs (notably the United Kingdom) where this is backed up by state intervention in the form of prescribed durations of maternity leave (Sceats *et al.* 2003). But as Gauthier (2002) shows, the ESCs are at the bottom end of the WDCs for these measures. In New Zealand it is probably in the public sector that these conditions are most widely available. In smaller enterprises, particularly outside major urban centres, conditions may be far more dependent on individual goodwill rather than policy.

Ultimately, however, in Australia, England and New Zealand even under the most favourable conditions, and for all except the small minority of women with high-paying jobs and superior back-up arrangements, the satisfactory functioning of flexible conditions is dependent on individual situations, for example:

a supportive boss, supportive husband, or a handy grandmother nearby. If these are present then the lack of policy support is mitigated, and conversely if they are absent it can be difficult, even in an organisation that is 'family friendly'. An unsympathetic boss or supervisor, for instance can make or break the situation for a working mother (Sceats *et al.* 2003).

7.6 THE IMPACT OF CHANGES IN STRUCTURES AND FORMS ON THE FUNCTIONING OF FAMILIES

The family changes outlined in Chapter Six and the drivers of these changes described in this chapter have had the effect of limiting the way families carry out their prime social functions. These roles can be identified here as replacement, nurture and socialisation, or what Kingsley Davis (1970) referred to as 'reproduction, maintenance, placement and socialisation of the young'. Today, with the ageing of the population, one would have also to add the function of support for other adult family members, especially the elderly.

The capacity of families to carry out these functions is determined by both endogenous factors (the way the family structures itself) and exogenous factors (external forces that limit capacity, see Jackson 1994b). Earlier in this chapter it was shown that exogenous factors in general had a major and negative effect on families over this period, and particularly over the ten-year period 1985 to 1995. As a result the impacts of the material and policy props on which families depend were diminished. Above all the need for, and difficulties encountered in, generating incomes required a great deal of reordering of both unpaid work, which is the manifest side of the fulfilment of some major family responsibilities, and paid work (Callister 1998), which financially underpins familial capacities to carry out these functions.

Turning now to the endogenous factors, earlier in Chapter Six it was shown how the family size, age, status and living-arrangement dimensions had changed. Each of these has implications for the carrying out of key functions. Each of these also determines props, support systems coming from within the family itself, that are necessary for the successful fulfilment of many dimensions of family life.

Family size is absolutely fundamental for societal replacement and even for its very survival. This is an issue of great public concern in Europe (Lutz and Scherbov 2000), North America and even Australia (McDonald and Kippen 2000) yet has had a relatively low profile in New Zealand except in the context of ageing.*

---

* Some commentators see an increase in fertility as an antidote to ageing and a way of increasing family support systems. In reality this is not a simple or appropriate solution (see Pool 1997).

Beyond this is a factor with long-term implications for families themselves: a decline in the number of siblings (Johnstone and Pool 1996c: 72; see also Dayal and Lovell 1994). Support within the family, particularly in old age, often depends on the care afforded by a sibling (McPherson 1992).

As the demographer Natalie Jackson reminds us, the age dimension has another highly deterministic effect. The fact, for example, that the Maori population or labour force is younger than the Pakeha has disparate impacts on many social behaviours and structures. A younger average age of childbearing for Maori means that they are less likely than are their Pakeha peers to be able to gain the qualifications that would allow them to work at higher-paying jobs and build up savings or equity. Axiomatically, the younger one becomes a parent the younger one will be likely to become a sole parent (Jackson 2000a; 2005).

The age dimension is linked to the size of families. The later the timing of the first birth, and the greater the force of reproduction at older childbearing ages, then the lower the probability that fertility will reach replacement. In 1912, when timing first became delayed and when fertility at ages 30 years and over exceeded that at 29 years and younger, family sizes were still running at 3.3 births per woman because age-specific rates at 30 years and over were significantly higher than at any other time in the twentieth century. In contrast, rates at ages below 30 years were much lower then than they were to become at the time of the Baby Boom (Jackson and Pool 1994: 21). By 1999, when family size was down to 1.9 births per woman despite increases over the 1980s in rates at older ages, the births to women over 30 years of age were insufficient to counteract what were the lowest rates on record at ages 20–29 years. To return to exact replacement-level fertility but retain the current delayed childbearing model would require rates at ages 30–34 and 35–39 years each to be approximately 25% higher than they are today. In this computation, rates for ages 40 years and over could remain at their present level.

The same factor, age, has a different impact on the functioning of families. Early timing of parenting means that parents often do not have the financial and material resources to devote to nurture and socialisation (Howard 1999). Late childbearing also has its own difficulties, not the least being that caring responsibilities will continue until the parents reach pre-retirement ages or beyond. This effect has been exacerbated by the policy shifts, particularly the responsibilities arising from the 1991 Budget.

In New Zealand public concern around these issues is muted, whereas the link between changes in the status and living-arrangements dimension and the meeting of familial responsibilities are widely discussed. The issues raised most commonly relate to the effects of conjugal stability and associated living arrangements on the upbringing and quality of children's lives. The questions revolve around two points:

1. The socialisation of and access to material assets and affection by the children of divorced and/or sole parents, as against two-parent couples; and

2. The stability of cohabiting unions as against legal marital status, and the effects this might have on childrearing.

In reality, in the period covered in the chapter, most children in New Zealand in all major ethnic groups lived in two-parent households (Johnstone and Pool 1996c; Pool and Jackson 1994: Chapt. 8; Dickson *et al.* 1997: 40; Davey 1999: 235, who also observes that 'most adults 20–59 years continue to live in "couple with children" households'). Nevertheless, there were important ethnic differences, with Pakeha children more likely to live in two-parent households. Twenty-five per cent of Maori and 35% of Pasifika children were in extended families, normally 'two parent plus others'. Overall in 1991, only 13% of Pakeha, 26% of Maori and 15% of Pasifika children were in sole-parent households.[*] Sole-parent families have fewer children on average than others, while two-parent families are likely to be larger. Children were most likely to be in households in which the occupier is aged 30–44 years. In 1991, this was true for 73% of Pakeha, 55% of Maori and 61% of Pasifika families, and in 2001 for 71%, 59% and 59% respectively. The NZW:FEE showed that the vast majority of children are the biological offspring of the parent(s) they live with, although this is slightly less likely for Maori than for Pakeha (Pool 1998: 323). The father of a child was still likely, in the majority of cases, to be there at the fifteenth birthday of their offspring (Hutton 2001). The roles of fathers were, however, undergoing major changes, an issue that will be examined in further detail in later chapters.

By the 1990s fewer and fewer parenting families were large; an increasing proportion had only one or two children. Larger families were disadvantaged because 'on average a lower disposable income is recorded in households where children are present, and the lowest incomes are found among families with the highest average number of dependent children' (Johnstone and Pool 1996c).

7.7 CONCLUSION

Chapters Six and Seven have documented the family demographic changes of the Baby Bust and the Baby Blip and their co-variants. In many ways

---

[*] Data quoted in the press at the time of writing suggest that these percentages are higher today, particularly for Maori.

these trends constituted a reprise of what had appeared as early as the late nineteenth century and had unfolded in the first two-fifths of the twentieth century. These were, for Pakeha, the long-term shift to very low fertility and late childbearing that was temporarily interrupted by the Baby Boom. But there were new elements: first, that the mechanism for the achievement of low fertility was efficient contraception, whereas in the pre-Baby Boom phase it had been age of marriage and the proportions remaining single; and, secondly, that Maori family sizes, which had remained high throughout the period before the Baby Boom and through it, declined for the only time on historical record.

In the Baby Bust and the Baby Blip documented in the last two chapters, marriage trends followed this same pattern, but marriage in recent decades has been only one strategy for the formation of a reproductive union. Depending on how one looks at it, the Baby Boom can be seen as a continuation of early twentieth-century patterns, certainly for Pakeha in terms of the links between formal marriage and reproduction, and for Maori in terms of the continuing high levels of fertility, as just noted. Alternatively, the Baby Boom could be viewed as a deviation in the family transition path, representing a return, in part, to what had occurred in early colonial Pakeha families.

Equally, the Baby Bust that followed the Boom can be seen as a return to pre-Baby Boom patterns, for structures such as delayed childbearing, or viewed as a radically different era, for forms such as the shift to cohabitation. The Baby Blip saw a continuation of the more demographic factors operating in the Baby Bust: delayed childbearing did not preclude parenting altogether, it just postponed it. Parenting occurred eventually, pushing up age-specific rates at ages 25–39 years and the TFR (modestly) almost to replacement, but because of the coincidental arrival of large cohorts at the delayed parenting ages (25–39 years) the number of couples having children was inflated and so too were birth cohort sizes.

In the period to be covered in Chapters Eight and Nine the trends identified in Chapters Six and Seven intensify to produce historically unique family patterns, thereby raising the spectre that the prognosis made by Kingsley Davis long ago (1938) was essentially accurate: reproduction and modern life are difficult to reconcile (for New Zealand, see Sinclair 1944: 122). Indeed, in keeping with the appellations employed in Chapters Five to Seven, Baby Boom, Baby Bust and Baby Blip, Chapters Eight and Nine might be seen to be dealing with an incipient Baby Deficit. The intensification of trends to be analysed in the next two chapters was often a result of policy changes that interacted with social and economic restructuring in ways that had an impact, mainly negative, on the family. Some of the changes over the Baby Bust, Baby Blip and Baby Deficit periods were endogenous to family life itself as it had unfolded over the last few decades, but some were due to exogenous factors.

The period reviewed here, then, saw the intersection of significant changes endogenous to family formation and their structures, and alongside those radical transformations in family forms. This all occurred in a context of unprecedented and extremely rapid economic restructuring and policy reformation that was to produce a totally different societal morphology that was the source for many of the exogenous factors affecting family life.

In one sense the policy changes in this period also represent a shift of direction with the past and a voyage into uncharted waters. Yet a number of the new measures and certainly some of the political commentaries also have an air of *déjà vu* about them. There is almost a return, at least ideationally, to elements of the British Poor Laws and their New Zealand counterparts first introduced in 1846, reformed from the 1890s and gradually to be totally replaced in successive years in the mid-twentieth century as New Zealand moved to a comprehensive welfare state, only to abandon it in the period covered in this chapter and the previous one.

Finally, the Baby Bust was not a uniquely New Zealand phenomenon. In one form or another it occurred more or less simultaneously – give or take a few years here and there – across not only the other WDCs, but in the former Soviet states of Eastern Europe. Indeed the 1990s saw the onset of Baby Deficits across much of East Asia, plus Singapore and South India (Caldwell 2005: 399). This is another empirical example, at least for the WDCs and especially the ESCs, of a mega-trend occurring co-terminously across a number of societies.

CHAPTER EIGHT

The Family in Uncharted Waters: Factors of Reproduction in the Baby Blip and Beyond

8.1 AN ERA OF UNPRECEDENTED PATTERNS AND TRENDS: THE 1990S AND EARLY 2000S

SETTING THE PARAMETERS

This chapter and the next relate to major issues carried across in a relatively seamless way from the period covered in the last two chapters. Most of the family changes to be noted here had their genesis in the two decades from the early 1970s to the early 1990s. But where the last two chapters focused on the analysis of trends, the present one and the next are primarily a stocktaking of the New Zealand family at the dawn of the twenty-first century. There will be a focus on reproduction, because the most fundamental changes to New Zealand households were coming from historically unique patterns of family formation. This present chapter emphasises these trends, while the next chapter looks at how these have come about and why we may have entered a new era for population replacement. The next chapter also documents the family morphologies that flow on from these patterns of family formation and from other changes in society.

These two chapters, then, deal with an intensification of trends that have already been identified and analysed. Yet equally, as will be seen below, this intensification has taken the New Zealand family in new directions to meet unprecedented challenges for which it may not be adequately prepared. Many of the contextual factors seen in the rest of the post-war period appear to have been swept away and adequate substitutes for them not yet developed. Moreover, even when trends seem more a continuation of the Baby Bust patterns than a break from them, the analyses reported in this chapter have revealed that mutations are appearing which, although sometimes nuanced, may presage significant future trends.

It is difficult to set reference years for the start of these two chapters. From a family policy standpoint, particularly if one takes a wider perspective, the commencement might be seen as the restructuring at the end of the 1980s and early 1990s, with the 1991 Budget the most refined marker.

Income inequalities were already starting to grow in the late 1970s and early 1980s, but in the late 1980s differences between families and groups become accentuated. The 1991 Budget reinforced this trend: in the name of reducing dependence on the state, it essentially kicked away some of the key family welfare props, the perverse outcome of which was not a decrease in demand for benefits, but an increase. By 2004–05, however, some of the policy changes introduced in the 1990s were being modified. These points will be picked up in the next chapter.

If levels of reproduction,[*] the subject matter of the present chapter, were to be the criterion, then the late 1970s would be the beginning, for since then and until and including 2004, and with the sole exceptions of the years 1987 to 1992 (if we do Swedish rounding to one place of decimals) when exact replacement was briefly achieved, we have witnessed continuous sub-replacement fertility. This is by far the longest spell for this phenomenon in New Zealand's recorded history. But if we impose a stricter definition on the term sub-replacement (<2.1 births per woman), then 1993 would be the starting point. Sub-replacement fertility has persisted systematically since then in spite of a seeming rise in Maori rates – perhaps real, perhaps an artefact of definitional changes in vital registration in 1995[†] – to an average of 2.6 births per woman in the years 1996 to 2002. This trend followed a period since about 1983 when Maori rates had been barely above replacement. Non-Maori rates (encompassing Pakeha, Pasifika and Asian) have driven the total figure, averaging around 1.8 over the same period, 1996–2003, after having been at exact replacement (2.1) in every year in the Baby Blip (1988–93), then dropping to 2.0 in 1994–95.

EMERGING REPRODUCTIVE REGIMES

Thus the 1990s and early years of the twenty-first century have seen the New Zealand family enter uncharted waters, particularly in the area of reproduction. Most notable have been the unprecedented levels of sub-replacement fertility, a function primarily of delayed primiparous childbearing (first

---

[*] As we noted earlier, in an era of low fertility seemingly minor data errors or rate differences (say 0.2 births per woman) assume relatively significant proportions (Billari 2004). The vital data referred to in this chapter are the official numbers and rates, for the total population and by ethnicity, kindly provided by Statistics New Zealand. Bill Boddington very generously also wrote a carefully thought-out and documented comment on their statistical veracity, particularly for the data by ethnicity. We are deeply indebted to him. While we do not necessarily endorse the ethnic categorisation system developed by Statistics New Zealand, it is important that we cite their figures whose legitimacy derives from the fact that they come from an official agency. We would also thank Robert Didham of Statistics New Zealand for his many useful comments.

[†] And therefore affecting the balance between numbers of Maori and non-Maori births, but not the overall figure.

births). This has resulted in a Baby Deficit, which has had profound and multi-dimensional cultural and social flow-on effects to be described here. Simultaneously, the parity and age structures of the nuclear family were changing. The period from the mid-1990s to the middle of the first decade of the twenty-first century is also notable for the fact that older parenting seemed to be an almost permanent and entrenched pattern, one that has provoked major debates internationally. This trend has not yet lasted as long as the New Zealand Baby Boom but has endured as long as the Baby Boom did in Europe. In contrast, the duration over which we have had fertility very close to or below replacement, since the late 1970s, equals the length of the Baby Boom, even if one uses its most extreme poles, 1943 and 1973, for the definition, and very decidedly if the parameters 1946 and 1973 are used.

In the international literature, as in New Zealand, analyses of trends have focused on changes in rates, typically the TFR.[*] But a Baby Deficit, on which this chapter centres, is as much, perhaps even more, about the products of these rates, the numbers of births, rather than about the rates *per se*. From a policy perspective the interest is less about how birth cohort sizes have been determined than about their quantum effects, for it is that factor that is going to bring pressures on resources and services as these cohorts proceed through various life-cycle stages. While the analysis of rates is indispensable and will be pursued here, the sizes of birth cohorts will also be discussed where appropriate.

The somewhat higher fertility of New Zealand by comparison with the other WDCs is often attributed to ethnic minorities, Maori and Pacific peoples, who have higher rates (this view ignores the counteracting effects of lower rates for Asians, a population about the same size as the Pasifika population). But higher Maori fertility rates (however the births have been allocated by ethnicity in the registration process) have not been the major factor that kept the total population figure close to or at replacement. This parallels the experience of the United States, the other neo-European ESC with higher fertility, where minority reproduction has only a 6–7% effect on overall rates (Frejka 2004 for the US; also see Pool and Sceats 2003, and Chandola *et al.* 2002 for all ESCs). Moreover, as Maori rates have gone through a gentle shift-share to older ages of reproduction over the last few years, their patterns may start to entrench the national sub-replacement fertility.

The TFR for 1999 and all subsequent years has nudged up above 1.9 births per woman, and to 2.01 in 2004, but is still not at replacement: in

---

[*] This is because of an interest in the proximate determinants of fertility (Morgan 2003a: 73).

the year ended March 2006 it was at 2.0. But a detailed review of age-specific rates shows that this was a product of a long-standing trend to later and later childbearing. Rates at younger ages actually declined, whereas for women in their thirties, where degrees of freedom for extra fertility are limited for biological reasons, there were further rate increases. In the longer run even this slight increase may well be unsustainable.

There are other indications, as yet embryonic, that New Zealand's fertility trajectory may join those of Australia, Canada and the United Kingdom (which are well below replacement although not at the extremely low levels seen in countries like Italy) but not the United States (at least in rates, as the US is still around replacement). There is increasing reproductive polarisation, not only between and within age- and social groups, but also between and within regions and socio-economic groupings, along with a marked long-running shift of childbearing to later ages.

Delay is the factor that has driven down levels of reproduction in Europe, for example in the Netherlands, producing sub-replacement completed fertility for cohorts reaching the end of their reproductive spans. What is critical is the displacement of the modal age for childbearing from 25–29 years to 30–34 years, as we are seeing in New Zealand, which will produce a long-term decline in fertility (van Nimwegen *et al.* 2002). In the year ended March 2006 the highest age-specific rate (122 per 1000 women at that age-group)* was at 30–34 years. Moreover, the new low-fertility groups in New Zealand could well be the very couples who might be seen as socio-cultural trend-setters, a point to be picked up later in this chapter. As is true in the United States, the near-replacement fertility belies marked regional differences, again with the lowest rates occurring in the central areas of metropolitan regions in which are concentrated the rapidly growing legions who drive the new economy, and who happen to be at the younger parenting ages of today (say 25–34 years).

Another related trend is becoming apparent: a rapid increase in the proportion of couples and even single women turning to a variety of reproductive and parenting strategies, including not only biomedical interventions (e.g. in-vitro fertilisation) but also adoption and surrogate childbearing. This is to overcome sub-fecundity often due to attempting to conceive at ages at the very end of the reproductive span:

> Unwanted conception is still an issue for many New Zealand women . . . .
> Despite improvements to contraception to avoid pregnancy, we have [. . .]

---

* While this rate is high by comparison with what we have observed for age-specific rates at 30–34 years over recent decades, it is not exceptionally high even by New Zealand standards: at the height of the first peak of the Baby Boom (1962) the rate was 152, and for Maori that year it was 225.

not yet overcome the inverse factor: the desire to conceive on the part of women or couples who seem naturally infertile or who experience sub-fertility (particularly at older ages). This is an issue discussed often in the popular media, mainly because, although the technology exists for assisted reproduction, it is very expensive and thus not [readily] available to all couples, and in any case does not guarantee certain success (Pool *et al.* 1999: 153).

By the 1990s the problem of reproductive choice, long the focus of family planning agencies concerned with early and unwanted childbearing, had now reappeared in a different guise.

The data used in this chapter are essentially the same as those discussed in Chapter Six. The major difference is that analyses of aspects of family life are more widely available, particularly for the co-variates of forms and structures, than was the case for earlier decades. Another change is that the official statistics agency radically reformulated the coding for ethnic classifications of both vital and census data – thus both numerators and denominators for rates – thereby decreasing the possibility of making valid comparisons over time. One other important development is the grow-ing availability of detailed analyses based on management data sets of the Ministry of Social Development and other government agencies (e.g. Ball and Wilson 2002; Barrett *et al.* 2003; Jensen *et al.* 2003) These studies can throw new light on particular populations (typically beneficiaries).

8.2 TRENDS AND DIFFERENTIALS IN FAMILY FORMATION AND THEIR IMPLICATIONS

REPRODUCTION AND POPULATION REPLACEMENT

For all ethnic groups, family sizes were small by the turn of the twentieth century. Nevertheless, complex patterns of reproductive polarisation had appeared, despite the fact that inter-ethnic ranges were narrower than in the past. At the peak of the Baby Boom, say in 1956, the absolute difference between Maori and non-Maori rates had been massive, 3.1 births per woman (6.9 births per Maori woman compared to 3.8 per non-Maori woman). In 2001, the gap (rounded to one decimal place) between two extreme rates, Pakeha and Pasifika, was only about 1.3 births, between Maori and Pakeha 0.9, and between Pakeha and Asians only 0.1, as is shown in Table 8.1. There were, however, more significant differences between the various ethnic groups for the age patterns of childbearing across the reproductive span. For the total, and for all populations except Maori, the force of childbear-ing is now later in the reproductive span. But for Pacific peoples this is in part because their family sizes are larger and thus their childbearing occurs not just at younger ages, but across the parenting ages. They are the only large population group who in the twenty-first century still have the type of family building and structural profile reminiscent of the model common among married Pakeha in the early to mid-Baby Boom before the revolution that was ushered in by the contraceptive revolution of that time.

Table 8.1: Fertility Indicators for Major Ethnic Groups, 2001

	Maori	Pasifika	Asian	Other	Pakeha	Total	Non-Maori
Total fertility rate	2.63	2.97	1.59	2.35	1.71	1.96	1.80
Percentage of total fertility rate falling below 25 years	42	31	13	21	20	26	21
Percentage of total fertility rate at 30 years and over	32	41	55	50	51	45	50

Note: The fertility data here and quoted elsewhere in this chapter were made available to the authors by Statistics New Zealand (see 310n). These are total response rates and thus are not directly comparable with other data quoted earlier in this book. The year 2001 is selected because it is a census year, and thus there is more chance of reconciling numerators and denominators.

For Maori the force of fertility is still weighted towards younger ages; in 2004 the Maori rate at 20–24 years (152 per 1000 women aged 20–24 years) was almost three times the non-Maori (54, and this latter rate also included Pasifika data). Yet if a longer perspective is taken, between 1986 and 2004, a gradual shift is taking place, as shown in Table 8.2 – the peculiar division by calendar years is necessitated by definitional changes (see note to table). The gains to Maori fertility are at the older ages. These data suggest that Maori may be embarking on a new phase in their family transition, the first being the radical decline in family sizes in the 1970s (Chapters Six and Seven), and the present one a move upwards in age in the patterns of family building, quite possibly a gradual convergence towards Pakeha patterns. In 2004 at 30–34 years the Maori rate was almost twice as high as it had been in 1986, when the non-Maori level at that age had been 49% higher than the Maori; by 2004 the non-Maori rate at this age was only 18% higher than the Maori. In the early years shown on the table there is a shift upwards into all ages 25 years and over, but in the second part of the period rates have increased only at 30 years and over. The question arises, then, whether the increases in Maori fertility in the late 1990s, normally attributed to definitional changes, were not due in part, or instead, to changes in the rhythm of Maori childbearing.

The trend for the population as a whole (all ethnicities) was a shift towards and continuing levels of sub-replacement fertility. Accompanying this has been the delaying of childbearing to increasingly older ages.

Both trends are more deeply entrenched than they were during the only other two periods of low fertility, in the early 1930s and early 1980s (Fig. 2.1; Dharmalingam *et al.*: Table 5.1).

Table 8.2: Changes in Maori Age-specific Fertility Rates (per 1000 Women), 1986–1995 and 1996–2004

Age-group	1986	1995	Diff. % points	1996	2004	Diff. % points
Less than 20 years	80	82	+2	79	69	-10
20–24 years	151	150	-1	162	152	-10
25–29 years	109	117	+8	148	133	-15
30–34 years	59	82	+23	94	104	+10
35–39 years	24	35	+11	46	54	+8
40–44 years	7	8	+1	11	14	+3
Percentage of TFR at ages <25 years	54	49	-5	45	42	-2

Note: For source, see footnote 1 on page 310. Coding both for ethnicity and what constitutes the 'resident population' changed between 1995 and 1996.

In Europe, the long duration of time for which sub-replacement fertility and delayed childbearing has been observed is causing concern – as noted above, for most countries this has been for a longer period than the duration of the Baby Boom. In New Zealand this trend is far less entrenched as rates are still significantly higher – 50% higher – than those seen in Mediterranean Europe (Livi Bacci 2004; Salvini 2004; Zuanna 2004; Cabre 2002). But it is the continuation of this trend for an historically unique duration, almost 30 years, except for briefly almost touching replacement around 1990, that is of interest here, particularly when coupled with the emergence of marked polarisation (see below).

The issue of sub-replacement fertility is a question of major concern beyond the Mediterranean. A paper by John Caldwell and Thomas Schindlmayr (2003) in *Population Studies*, referred to earlier, has provoked a major debate (see *Population Studies* March 2004, especially critiques by John Hobcraft and Dirk van de Kaa). The presidential address to the Population Association of America in 2003 was devoted to this issue, putting forward a more optimistic view than is often the case in Europe (Morgan 2003b; cf. van Nimwegen *et al.* 2002; the special issue of *Genus*, 2004; *Vienna Yearbook of Population Research* 2006; McDonald 2001a, b).

The decreases in fertility across the WDCs have been severe both in relative and absolute terms. In 1995–2000, only Australia, Eire, Iceland, New Zealand, Norway and the United States had TFRs above 1.7 births per woman; France, which had dipped a little, was to go back to reach around 1.9 by the 2000s. It was not that the Baby Boom TFRs were so extraordinarily high – in Europe, Eire, the Netherlands and Portugal were the only countries whose TFRs in 1955–60 and 1960–65 exceeded 3.0 (United Nations, *Population Prospects* 2002), and Japan's was already down to replacement. In contrast, all the neo-Europes, Canada, Australia, New Zealand and the United States, were above 3.0. Eire, whose trajectory, for historically unique circumstances, was in the opposite direction to those of other WDCs, reached 4.0; New Zealand exceeded it. The majority of WDCs had Baby Boom rates (Dharmalingam *et al.* 2007: Table 8.1, using data from the Observatoire Démographique Européenne, the United Nations and Statistics New Zealand) about or more typically below the levels seen today in New Zealand for Maori and Pacific peoples (TFR < 3.0).

Australia and Eire were the only WDCs in which the number of births for the most recent year (2002–04) in the data-base of the Observatoire Démographique Européenne was above the number in 1960, the year that saw the peak of the Baby Boom in many countries.* In most cases the number of births in the most recent year fell far below that for 1960, and even Eire and Australia, the population of the latter having almost doubled in size over those four decades, were barely above their Baby Boom total (2% and 11% higher). Recalling that the total populations of all these countries increased in the period, then it is even more surprising that the absolute falls were so extreme. The number of births in some countries was less than 70% of their 1960 levels. These included Austria, Canada, England and Wales, Germany (combining West and East for both years), Greece, Italy, Northern Ireland, Portugal, Scotland and Spain. Only France, New Zealand, Norway and the United States were above 90% of their 1960 size (Dharmalingam *et al.* 2007: Table 8.1).

The key point is the advent of sub-replacement fertility; most WDCs have now been at sub-replacement for a prolonged period. Into this mix needs to be added the fact that this pattern had been preceded by a Baby Boom that was itself very modest – most Western European countries had TFRs only around 2.3–2.7. Outside New Zealand, especially in Japan and Western Europe, this has raised questions about societal survival. In New Zealand there has been far less discussion of this issue, but a more pessimistic position has been put by Pool (e.g. 1999, 2006), while a more optimistic view has also been put forward (e.g. see Bryant 2003).

As was noted in earlier chapters, late childbearing and lower family sizes were not because of declines in exposure to intercourse – on the contrary, over 85% of women in every cohort interviewed in the NZW:FEE had been in at least one partnership before age 25 years, about the norm for WDCs except in Southern Europe, where the rates are lower (Pool and Sceats 2003:

* We wish to thank Jean-Paul Sardon of the Institut National d'Études Démographiques for making these data available to us.

Table 6). By the end of the twentieth century the status of these unions had changed in New Zealand. For those turning 25 in the late 1980s and early 1990s, only 20–25% had been in a first marriage (as against 89% in any first union) before their twenty-fifth birthday. In contrast, for the cohort of women born 1936–45, the Baby Boom parents, three-quarters of their first unions had been marriages, as was still true for more than half of those women born 1946–55. This situation changed in the Baby Bust, the focus of the previous two chapters, so that it held for only 38% of women born 1956–60 turning 25 before 1985 (Johnstone *et al.* 2001). Across the WDCs, by the 1990s, delayed childbearing had not only become the major proximate determinant of family sizes, but this situation held for all women, no matter what form of union they were living in (van Nimwegen *et al.* 2002). The new trend was historically unique, for in the past delayed childbearing had been due to putting off registered marriage to older ages, after which a first child would be born.

This is one of the more important factors among those producing the absolute declines noted above. It is typically determined by prior life events such as school-leaving age, as we have noted. But regardless of its cause, delayed timing is a factor with major policy implications for low-fertility countries. Moreover, the tempo dimension of childbearing has multiple effects: if delaying occurs, then there will be a sort of demographic hiatus – those people who would have had children do not, thereby reducing the fertility rates at younger ages, then causing a shift-share to older ages when couples, with varying degrees of success, attempt to 'recuperate' the births that have been delayed. A WDC-wide study by Tomas Frejka and Jean-Paul Sardon presented at the 2006 Population Association of America meeting reported that 'only rarely were all delayed births recuperated later in life' (see Frejka and Sardon 2006, citation from *Program Abstracts*: 246).

Another demographic phenomenon is possible and will be investigated for New Zealand a little later in this chapter. This effect is posited in the 'low-fertility trap' hypothesis, caused by

> negative population momentum. The dynamics of age-structure of a
> population imply that as a result of low fertility in past years, fewer and fewer
> women (potential mothers) will enter the reproductive ages in the future.
> The decline in this population sub-group will then exert downward pressure
> on the absolute number of births and the crude birth rate (Lutz and Skirbekk
> 2005: 701; elaborated in Lutz, Skirbekk & Testa 2006).

This may seem an unremittingly negative scenario, but there is a tiny bit of light. It appears that, through a factor we call 'compression of maternity', by speeding up the timing of their second and later births late starters might be able to catch up, to a degree, very much as the late-marrying Irish did in the nineteenth century. Such compression has been reported for recent Dutch cohorts (Lutz, Testa & Skirbekk 2006, in a presentation at the Population Association of America). This is highly relevant for New Zealand, for Janet Sceats's research, using survey data, has shown that New Zealanders have a high potential for the compression of maternity, with shorter inter-birth intervals than other WDC populations (Sceats 1981, 2002; Morgan *et al.* 2001). In all the studies emerging in WDCs, the most critical factors that are identified relate to differentials in parity, timing and spacing.

Unfortunately, as has been lamented earlier in this book, parity progression cannot be readily studied from official data sources. The New Zealand vital data on parity, that is, on the number of previous live births a woman has had when a current birth is registered, are notably deficient. They relate to 'previous issue of this union' (a phrase containing two undefined words), 'confinements' (i.e. multiple births are counted only once) and nuptial births only, not ex-nuptial. We thus have no data on the issue of previous unions, whether or not these 'issue' include stillbirths and what the mother's nuptial status was for previous issue. Consequently, New Zealand researchers do not know whether the reference is only to that part of the union when she was legally married to her present partner. The information might well exclude issue from prior cohabitation with the same person (i.e. ex-nuptial births fathered by the same man, in the case of a woman who has converted cohabitation into legal marriage); or whether she had earlier births (or issue) in a previous separate cohabiting union or marriage.

Nevertheless, for what they are worth, parity data show an interesting trend. In 1962 and 1972 around half of all first births were to women aged 20–24 years, but by 1992 the modal age was 25–29 years (43%) and the next highest 30–34 years (26%). In 2002, 32% of nuptial first births were born to women aged 25–29 years, but 38% to women aged 30–34 years. Mean ages increased from 23.0 years in 1972 to 29.9 in 2002, and medians from 22 years in 1962 to 30 in 2002. For married New Zealand women at least, levels of delay in starting a family seem as high as the Netherlands, which by comparison with other European countries has notably late primiparous childbearing (van Nimwegen *et al.* 2002: Fig. 1). The New Zealand mean of 29.9 years appears to be above that of 29.1 cited for the Netherlands, but the New Zealand data on age at first childbearing are subject to upward biases: as there are no data for significant aspects of any prior reproductive history, the 'first' issue may in fact be of a second or higher order. Fortunately, we have the surveys NZW:FEE and NZFFS, which shed some light on these questions, and they show that the medians cited above, computed from vital data, exaggerate the ages at which women have their first birth. However, these surveys are sample- not population-based and therefore subject to random statistical error. To minimise sampling error effects so as to analyse the changes in family formation strategies using a more robust data-base, the two samples NZW:FEE (1995) and NZFFS (2001) were pooled and weighted. This allowed us to increase the sample size of NZW:FEE by more than 50%, and thus the power of the study. We could now turn to cohorts born over five-year periods (e.g. 1965–69), as against the ten-year spans we have been using in most of the foregoing analyses. Perhaps more importantly this strategy permits the family formation patterns of each cohort to be extended for a further five calendar years, to the end of 2000.

The trends and differentials that are seen in these data are very systematic (Dharmalingam *et al.* 2007: Table 8.2). Over the period from 1975–79 to 1990–95 to 1996–2001, the life-table mean age at first birth increased for both Maori and non-Maori: by 4.4 years, from 19.6 years of age to 22.7 to 24.0, for Maori; and 3.5 years, from 23.8 to 25.6 to 27.3, for non-Maori. Pakeha average ages fell into the mid-range for Western European countries, similar to countries like Sweden or Ireland but younger than for the United Kingdom, and well below the Netherlands. In contrast, Maori ages were below even countries like Portugal; and the means for the total population were in the lower range of Western European countries (see van Nimwegen *et al.* 2000: Fig. 1). Interestingly, a gap between Maori and Pakeha has remained, even as Maori ages have gone up, but there has been a modest convergence: 4.2 years in 1975–79; 3.3 years in 1996–2001.

These results also show that delayed childbearing became more and more entrenched as each cohort passed through the last years of the twentieth century, 1996–2000. For the birth cohort 1970–75, this was an even more important result for a rather unusual reason. This cohort was born at the peak period for Pakeha adolescent fertility, around 1970, and then, as reported elsewhere in this book, had a modestly increased probability of becoming teenage mothers themselves by comparison with the five-year cohorts on either side of them, 1965–69 and 1976–1981 (Dharmalingam *et al.* 2007: Table 8.3).

These results support the general argument that the changes recorded up until the 1990s continued at least until the end of that decade. For example, patterns of contraception went through a change in the late 1990s that was resonant with the hypothesis that sexual activities associated with childbearing (as against as a part of relationships of one sort or another) were being delayed – there was increased use of condoms and less of the Pill and sterilisation, suggesting a trend towards less frequent and perhaps more informal exposure to intercourse, but under circumstances when there was still protection against conception. The data for Maori also reinforce the point that they were going through a very gradual shift upwards in ages of childbearing.

The vital data presented in Table 8.1 show that 50% or more of all births in 2001 were occurring to women at later reproductive ages, a trend that was most extreme among Asians. But against this, a residual effect of the norms of the Baby Boom, early childbearing, lingered on. It may be that this dying gasp of Baby Boom norms among Pakeha, rather than fertility rates among minorities, keeps New Zealand and other ESC levels of reproduction at levels above those of other WDCs, at just below replacement (as was argued by Chandola *et al.* 2002). One might add here that early childbearing is not the sole determinant of relatively higher fertility. France, where the force of early childbearing is well below those of ESCs, has maintained high sub-replacement fertility levels consistently since the late 1970s, when its TFR had paralleled that of the United Kingdom, whereas the UK has seen its rates decrease. This is despite the fact that the UK today has teenage birth rates and a force of early childbearing that now exceeds that of New Zealand (Pool and Sceats 2003). This question of the distribution of childbearing across the reproductive ages will be returned to later when reproductive polarisation is discussed.

CONTRACEPTION, STERILISATION AND ABORTION

By the mid- to late 1990s contraceptive use was both highly efficient and, except for a small minority, accepted across society (Pool *et al.* 1999). Depending on a woman's age and to a lesser degree her ethnicity, the Pill and sterilisation continued to be the dominant methods, as had become true in the 1970s, but since then condom use has also become an important element (Dharmalingam *et al.* 2007: Tables 7.1 and 7.2; except for 1995, the data used there have been specially tabulated for this book). The interesting issue instead was the shift-share between various methods, which was driven by two factors. The first was the increasing age at parenting that meant delays to older ages and with this a decline in the prevalence of sterilisation, and the second was concern over STDs plus increases in the numbers and range of partners a woman might have. The younger the cohort, the higher the proportion of women who will have had more than one partner by ages 20 or 25 years (Pool *et al.* 1999: 21–22). Increases in the frequency of repartnering (Dharmalingam *et al.* 2004: Chapt. 3) also meant, inevitably, that women across the reproductive span, even at older ages, were more likely to be exposed to intercourse infrequently and informally, and thus to turn to condom use. Some women combined this with the Pill to have protection from both conception and the possible risk of infection.

In 1976 Pill use at ages 25–29 years had outrun sterilisation by four to one; but by 2001 this had increased dramatically to ten to one, and even at older ages the Pill became increasingly preferred over sterilisation. But use of both these methods declined, the slack being taken up, especially at younger ages, by the condom or the condom plus the Pill, and, especially at older ages, by women using no method at all. This latter trend does not indicate a failure to use efficient methods when appropriate, but instead was a function of delayed childbearing. In the 1970s, women aged 30 years and over were typically trying to avoid pregnancy and had turned to the Pill or sterilisation, but by 2001 women in this age-group were frequently trying to become pregnant and thus not using any method.

The data presented here relate only to women who were currently exposed to intercourse and not pregnant, and who were using one or more methods of contraception and sterilisation (in Dharmalingam *et al.* 2007: Table 7.1); or to all women currently exposed to intercourse and risk of conception (Dharmalingam *et al.* 2007: Table 7.2). These tables show a rapid and significant shift-share away from the Pill between 1976 and 1986 (a ten-year span), then between 1986 and 1995 (nine-year span), and, even more rapidly at the younger reproductive ages, between 1995 and 2001 (only a five-year span) to the condom and other methods. For example, at 20–24 years Pill use decreased from 77% (1976) and 76% (1986) to 71% (1995), then plummeted to 53% (2001); conversely, condom use went from 6% (1976), 12% (1986) and 21% (1995) to 36% (2001). The fourth contraceptive revolution was truly under way, especially at the end of the 1990s; this was the mechanism that produced patterns of family formation that had not been experienced previously.

Back in the 1970s and 1980s relationships, whether involving marriage or cohabitation, had typically been long term and intense and thus the newly available efficient technologies of fertility regulation were entirely apposite. They were employed as a means of freeing women from fears of pregnancy to pursue advanced education or a career, both of which were opening up rapidly to women at that time. But in their twenties today in the new millennium many women are likely to be in higher education, living at home, in a LAT, or between relationships. This means that many women may be exposed to intercourse more irregularly than was true in the recent past. Pill use demands a level of motivation and pre-meditation that does not always fit well with the partnerships engaged in by some young people today. Moreover, there is evidence from Canada, and probably the same thing occurred in New Zealand, that in the 1970s if anything women were over-protected – using the Pill when exposure to intercourse was not likely or irregular (Sceats and Pool 1978: Conclusion). A further factor seen in New Zealand today but not operating in the 1970s and 1980s is the presence in New Zealand of a large group of young overseas students, tens of thousands in some years, most of whom are in their teens or early twenties and who are away from home and from their normal support systems.

Given the patterns of exposure to intercourse just described, it is not entirely surprising that abortion rates actually increased in this period, from a TAR in 1991 the equivalent of 0.41 abortions per woman over the reproductive span, to 0.65 in 2003. Except at 40–44 years, where abortion rates were low and often occurring for biomedical reasons, the highest increases were seen at 20–24 years. Around 2000 the general abortion rate (GAR) for New Zealand, 20 per 1000 women aged 15–44 years, was above the level for most comparable WDCs, but below those for Australia and the United States (*Demographic Trends* 2003: Table 7.02; see also Table 7.1, 7.2 and 7.3 in the present study). This is a major change from the 1980s when the New Zealand rate was among the lowest (Sceats 1988b).

Abortion is an intervention of last recourse, not lightly undertaken and frequently turned to in desperation under extreme circumstances. But these circumstances hold whether it is carried out as a legal or illegal procedure. In fact, as the experience of Italy showed, if the procedure is legalised and access to contraception liberalised, the likelihood of women needing an abortion will probably decline (Sceats 1988b: Chapt. 2, 51 compares Réunion and Mauritius, two relatively similar societies but whose history of fertility control was very different). Against that, abortion rates may remain steady even when conditions that should reduce them are operating. Of course today in societies where abortion has been legalised we can measure this; if it is illegal and thus clandestine the only indicator available on possible levels is indirect: the incidence of post-abortal septicaemia (the Italian data, directly collected secretly prior to liberalisation, are an exception).

Another factor seems to have operated in New Zealand over the 1990s: there was a rapid increase in the size of the Asian population. By 2002 Asians were contributing 16% of all abortions, and 18% by 2003. Their contribution in both years greatly exceeded their proportions in the population, but this impression is confounded by two factors. First, Asians represented a higher proportion of the resident population at the youth ages (about 12% of youth) than in the total population (7% of the population at all ages). Secondly, there were large numbers of Asian visitors at these ages, typically students on short-term courses, as noted above. While their numbers may not have been included in the denominator for abortion rates, they may well have been included in the numerator, simply because clinics would not have been able to distinguish the true place of residence of patients, a protection of confidentiality built into the Contraception, Sterilisation and Abortion Act 1977 (see Sceats 1988b: Chapt. 4, which discusses that Act, and prior and subsequent legislation). One must add that this is further confounded by the way in which Statistics New Zealand now codes ethnicity (see abortion data in *Demographic Trends* 2002: Table Notes).

Nor do abortion ratios (abortions to known conceptions) help determine the incidence of terminations among Asians not normally resident. This is because the births in the denominator would typically be to residents, whereas the numerator would include both those on study/visitors' visas and resident women. These ratios were very high, well above (54%) those for the population as a whole (*Demographic Trends* 2002: Table 7.02).[*]

Meanwhile, and particularly for the Pakeha population with its regime of delayed fertility, something else was occurring: a slight increase in the number of abortions carried out for medical reasons (e.g. indications of severe fetal abnormality; risk of fetal abnormalities increases with age of mother after age 30 years) after the first trimester. In 1983, 1.8% of abortions had been from sixteen weeks on; by 2003 the level overall was 2.7%, but at ages 35 years and over the proportions were around 4%. Later and very young childbearing are both subject to higher risks than at other ages.

REPRODUCTIVE CHOICE AND DELAYED CHILDBEARING: MICRO-LEVEL IMPLICATIONS

The regimes of contraception, sterilisation and abortion just discussed mean that reproductive choice in terms of avoiding pregnancy is now almost assured at young ages for all but a minority of couples. In contrast, at older ages a new problem of choice (when and how to conceive) has emerged. The determinants at young ages are bio-social and/or socio-psychological (e.g. whether or not they are risk-takers), while at older ages the determinants are biomedical and/or socio-economic, particularly the work–life balance to be discussed below (also covered in Chapter Seven). In the last two decades technological responses to problems of conception have focused on the issues more pertinent to women and couples at older reproductive ages, although improvements have been made to both technical aspects and social marketing for contraception directed to younger people, in part because of the threats associated with HIV/AIDS and other STDs.

The delay in parenting and the development of new assisted reproductive technologies (ARTs) signalled another very significant change both bio-socially and in the value system: growing acceptance and public acknowledgement of the problems of sub-fecundity,[†] and an associated increase in the proportion of births that were assisted by hormonal methods, in-vitro fertilisation or egg or sperm donation. In Europe between one and 3.7% of all children born in 2000 were conceived by these means.

---

[*]   As noted in Tables 7.1 and 7.2, TARs and GARs are computed in exactly the same way as TFRs and GFRs, except the numerators are abortions not births. They can be interpreted in the same way. The alternative indices, abortion ratios, are used widely but are a less robust measure as they are subject to trend effects of a different sort in each of the demoninator and numerator. Thus they do not measure trends in abortions *per se*, but the relationships between abortion and fertility.

[†]   Demographic terminology is used here (Grebenik and Hill 1974, drawn on for Pool 1991: Glossary). See also Chapter One, 3n.

In New Zealand it is estimated that 1.6% of births were through IVF or sperm/egg donation.

Not surprisingly, there were major age differences in resort to ARTs. Age-specific rates cannot be calculated because of a lack of nationwide data, but the age distribution for a leading practice shows that 16% of IVF- and donor-conceived pregnancies were at ages younger than 30 years, 77% for women in their thirties, 41% of the total in the first five-year age-group and 36% into the second, and the rest at 40 years and over. By 35–39 years, natural fecundability levels would be significantly lower (personal communication, John Peek, Fertility Associates, to whom grateful acknowledgement is made).

The delay in childbearing and the application of reproductive technologies has actually had a minor but noticeable bio-social impact on the structures of New Zealand families – an increase in the incidence of multiple births. Fairly consistently from the early 1880s until 1991, about nine to eleven per 1000 confinements (0.9–1.1%) comprised twins or triplets with one or both or all three being live born. The exceptions were around the two world wars. For example, just after World War I, in 1920, after the troops had got home and the 'flu pandemic, the level increased to twelve per 1000. In 1941, just after the first large-scale movement of troops overseas, the rate reached thirteen per 1000. But the real shift occurred after 1991, when the rate went up to twelve per 1000. By 2001 it was sixteen per 1000, as it was in 2003.*

Sixteen per 1000, or 1.6%, may not seem high, but it actually exceeds the figure for France in 2000, the highest on record there, and their data allow them insights as far back as the eighteenth century. In contrast, the long-standing New Zealand norm of nine to eleven multiple births per 1000 confinements was similar to that of France. The trend followed there since 1700 has been described as a 'fork-like shape', with highs at two extreme dates, the 1700s and today, and also in 1919 just after troops had been demobilised *en masse*. Levels in 2000 in France were, however, above the highs seen in the eighteenth century, and both of these were above the 1919 peak (Pison and Couvert 2004: Fig. 1).

French demographers Gilles Pison and Nadege Couvert explain the peaks by referring to delayed childbearing (the probability of twinning increases for older mothers). This occurred both in the earlier period and over the last three decades: delayed marriage and parenting in the absence

---

* The published data for recent years do not permit disaggregation by ethnicity – until 1962 Maori births had been on a separate register and thus Pakeha rates are quoted here for all years up till 1961. It is probable that, given an older average age of childbearing and quite possibly a higher resort to ARTs, that Pakeha levels may be higher than the rates quoted here for the total population.

of contraception in the first case, but controlled fertility and delayed child-bearing in the early twenty-first century. As noted above, the New Zealand rate in the early 2000s is marginally higher than the French, but given the high force of reproduction at older ages here (see below in this chapter) this is easily explained. Overall, one-third of the recent rise in twinning in France comes from the increase in delayed childbearing. But there is another factor: in France ARTs account for two-thirds of the recent rise in rates of multiple birthing (Pison and Couvert 2004).

Pison and Couvert also investigate two historical factors that help explain why rates are higher today. First, the peaks around periods of extreme demographic change, in this case war, is because with the troops returning or leaving there was a surge of marriages and pregnancies, selective in the latter case for the more fecund women. As they note,

> The phenomenon of selectivity becomes apparent in certain circumstances, as during the First World War when many couples were reunited only briefly during short leave periods and only the most fecund could conceive. At the end of the war and the return of the soldiers selectivity once again played a role, producing in the first months following demobilisation a temporary rise in twinning rates (Pison and Couvert 2004: 903).

The first factor would have affected New Zealand in the early period of World War II, being more marked because of leave before the embarkation of the Second New Zealand Expeditionary Force in 1940. In contrast with France, the effects of the return from World War I were more drawn out and staged because of shipping and the impact of the 'flu epidemic (return-ees were quarantined in Narrow Neck Camp), and thus more muted.

A second factor emerges from Pison and Couvert's analysis of the Baby Boom (2004). Over the course of the twentieth century, family limitation had become increasingly efficient, particularly to control family size. But in the early Baby Boom fertility regulation was not as efficient, nor was it as systematically employed as in later years of the twentieth century. In New Zealand's case, once the post-war early Baby Boom was passed, parity and family-size-limitation norms were relaxed and parents went on to have a third or fourth child (the TFR exceeded 4.0 around 1960). Thus, curiously, in a period of earlier childbearing there was also a return to later, higher-parity parenting and thus a modest increase in twinning by comparison with the late nineteenth century. By 1970, early childbearing followed by efficient family limitation had become the overwhelming norm and thus the very low late nineteenth-century rates were resumed, only to be abandoned with the Baby Blip around 1990. This illustrates the point that factors such as twinning, once determined strongly by age at first exposure to intercourse and thus conception, are today a function not only of ARTs

.such as hormonal methods or in-vitro fertilisation, but also of the other side of reproductive technology, modern contraception.

The net result is that the structure of the New Zealand family is changing in yet another way that has no historical antecedents. Not only are the parents likely to be older by the standards of most of the second half of the twentieth century and, in the case of primiparous mothers, even of the first half, but they are also more likely to be parents of twins or triplets (still a very few cases). In 1971, in the peak years for Pakeha teenage childbearing, 19% of births were to women aged 30 years or more, as were 29% of multiple births. In 2003, 50% of births were to these older women, and this applied to 63% of twins and triplets. Among older couples subject to the selectivity noted just above, fifteen per 1000 of those in the late Baby Boom (1971) had multiple births, a figure approximating the earlier and most recent peaks in France. But by 2003, 21 per 1000 of women aged 30 years and over would expect to give birth to twins.

DELAYED CHILDBEARING: MACRO-LEVEL IMPLICATIONS

The effects on fertility of timing and delayed childbearing, and other life-events were raised earlier in this chapter and the hypothesis of a low-fertility trap was introduced. But 'delayed life transitions', to use the term employed by Canadian demographer Roderic Beaujot, have other major implications both for the families concerned and for the wider society (2006). Some of these derive from a factor largely exogenous to family formation – prolonged education – and others such as delayed childbearing are endogenous to the family itself. Among the transitions Beaujot lists are: leaving home, union formation, first childbirth, the completion of formal education and entry into the labour force. For older parents in their thirties and forties, there may be a severe strain from looking after young children and balancing this with the need to protect their job status, essential if the family is to maintain its standard of living.

At a societal level the highest-profile effect of delayed childbearing and low fertility is population ageing. The spectre of 60–70 year olds working at the supermarket checkout counter or stacking shelves is actually starting to occur in retirement zones in the United States, and is now seen in New Zealand in places like Thames. But there is also an age-structural transition, a momentum effect, that precedes structural ageing (the percentage at older ages, as against the growth in the numbers of the elderly, or numerical ageing), and which is working its way through the reproductive ages.

Momentum effects do not produce just one wave and its attendant trough; for New Zealand, because of the dynamics of fertility and specifically the Depression, Baby Boom, Baby Bust and Baby Blip, there have been several waves. These were produced by major recent fluctuations in fertility and thus in the sizes of birth cohorts born since the 1930s: the lows of the Depression, gradually increasing to a peak in the Baby Boom around 1960, then a shallow trough in the 1960s, followed by another peak around 1970 at the end of the Baby Boom, then a deep trough with the Baby Bust, shifting back to a third low peak in the Baby Blip around 1990, and the slow decline since (see Figures 5.1 and 5.2). These peaks and troughs are of major significance for policy in New Zealand (Pool 2003). Among many other impacts they also have a feedback effect on reproduction itself by the way they change the sizes of the parenting cohorts.

This factor is picked up in Table 8.3. The upper panel, using census data and projections to 2011 (to see the effect of the Baby Blip about 1990 on reproductive potential about 2015), shows how the age structure has changed, and will change further, at reproductive ages. The severe fluctuations shown there have contributed along with the age-specific fertility rates to both inflated and deflated numbers of births at these ages, and also to an incipient low-fertility-trap effect. Even if rates remained unchanged, birth numbers would vary because of the age-structural changes, but rates are also changing, dropping at young ages and increasing at ages 30 years and over, as is shown in the lower panel of Table 8.3, drawing on vital data. The combined effect of these two trends is an increase in the contribution to national natality by women at older reproductive ages, involving a net change from 42% of the births occurring to women aged 30 years or over to 52%. As the total birth numbers are relatively unchanged, this shift is because of a tempo effect that conflates with birth numbers to change the entire reproductive regime in complex ways, and which could have much longer implications.

The elderly of the early twenty-first century, say around 70–79 years of age, generally had their children when they were relatively young, typically when they were in their twenties. The parents of today, by contrast, are increasingly having children when they are at ages 30–34 years. In 1974 the total population rate per 1000 at 20–24 years had been 175, whereas in 2004 it was only 71. In 1984 at 25–29 years it was 147, but by 1994 it had dropped to 126, and went down further to 110 (2004). In contrast, at 30–34 years the rate has increased from 77 per 1000 (1984), to 105 (1994) and to 120 (2004); and at 35–39 the changes have been from 22 to 40 to 61. Even at the upper reaches, at 40–44 years, rates had gone up from four to seven to twelve. The lower panel of Table 8.3 looks at these patterns of reproduction for the end of the twentieth and the start of the twenty-first centuries.

Today parents may have a first child in their thirties and a second, occasionally a third, child thereafter, even in their forties. Thus they will almost certainly be responsible for dependent offspring until they are at, even into, retirement. This is more than a familial or moral obligation, for it will be recalled that the welfare reforms of the early 1990s made parents legally responsible for unmarried children until those young adults were aged 25 years. Add to this the trends towards prolonged education, leaving home when an adult (in the thirties for Italian men), to say nothing of phenomena such as boomerang kids and cluttered nests (discussed later in the chapter) and one is positing a heady brew that will produce major demographically driven shifts in family dynamics.

Table 8.3: Age Structures at Reproductive Ages and Shifting Reproductive Patterns at the Dawn of the Twenty-first Century

Panel A: Age distribution of women at reproductive ages, 1991 and 2001 (000s)

Year	Age-group					
	15–19	20–24	25–29	30–34	35–39	40–44
1991	139.9	135.1	139.3	138.6	124.9	118.2
2001	130.3	121.0	128.9	147.1	154.8	147.2
2011	152.9	139.0	126.7	144.2	159.7	163.3

Panel B: Numbers of births and rates (per 1000), 1996 and 2004

	Age-group					
	15–19	20–24	25–29	30–34	35–39	40–44
1996						
No.	4379	11,399	17,397	16,253	6705	1066
Rate	33	81	119	105	44	8
2004						
No.	4008	9960	14,071	18,290	9602	2016
Rate	27	71	110	120	61	12

Sources: Census; official projections 2004-base series 2; vital statistics.

In sum, the data shown in Table 8.3 have implications both for policy and for family dynamics. While overall birth numbers are' such that we have not yet entered a low-fertility trap these shifts may well have that effect in the longer term. This point will be returned to and illustrated in the conclusion to the present chapter.

REPRODUCTIVE POLARISATION: SOCIO-CULTURAL AND SOCIO-ECONOMIC DIMENSIONS

Earlier in the twentieth century there had been reproductive polarisation, as already discussed. This reappeared in the last decades of the twentieth century, taking a number of forms that were unprecedented, particularly demonstrating differences by labour-force status (whether full time, part time or not currently employed).

Over the period from 1981 to 1996, and then through to 2001, the rhythm of childbearing changed very significantly for both Maori and

non-Maori, and for the total population. This was reflected in the cumulative number of births by ages 30–34 years. This age-group is used here
because it is a pivotal one analytically. It provides a summary measure of
the fertility achieved during the peak ages for reproduction, in a bio-social
sense, 20–29 years. Equally, and for bio-social reasons, those women who
are childless at this stage in their reproductive span can be expected to end
with a reduced family size by comparison with women who have started at
younger ages.

Table 8.4 gives data on children ever born to women aged 30–34 years,
drawn from the two most recent censuses for which this information was
collected, 1981 and 1996. Data from the NZFFS (2001) are also referred to in
the table note, providing the most recent information on this. These latter
figures come from survey data and are thus subject to sampling errors. The
absence of this information at the most recent census available at time of
writing (2001) is a severe lacuna, but at least the survey throws some light
on possible changes since 1996.

In 1981, the major fertility differential was between non-Maori and
Maori, constituting a simple dichotomisation between low- and high-
fertility populations. Pacific peoples also had high rates at that time, but
because of the migration process, which often caused separations between
spouses, their levels were not as high as for Maori. Asian rates at 30–34
years were low (Khawaja 1985, esp. Table 85). A key factor distinguishing
Maori and non-Maori was the cumulative fertility to 30–34 years, itself a
function mainly of patterns of birth limitation – as was shown in earlier
chapters. At that time Pakeha had their births early, then abruptly terminated childbearing, often, for those aged 30–34 years in 1981, by resorting
to sterilisation. Thus the percentage of women childless at these ages was
low and similar to Maori, whereas the proportion with four or more children differed significantly and was higher for Maori.

By 1996, not only had the average number ever born alive dropped,
so too had the percentage going on to four or more children. The absolute difference between the two ethnic groups had declined, although the
Maori figure was still three times that of Pakeha. The NZFFS data (2001)
suggest that this trend became further entrenched. The percentage childless increased for both, but so too did the absolute and relative differences
between Maori and Pakeha. What was now starting to show up were new
sorts of differentials, occurring, however, within quite limited parameters
of low fertility. The key feature was now no longer the wide spread in fertility
levels between high- and low-fertility societies living in the same country, for size differences were declining even for minority ethnic groups (a
detailed analysis of 1996 census data on fertility by ethnicity is in Statistics
New Zealand 2004). Instead the main difference was whether or not the
nuclear family unit was childless (see Statistics New Zealand 2001: Chapt.

5 and Conclusion). The total absence of children, or of grandchildren, was now starting to redefine family structures in a way that was historically unique, and along with this the one-child family was becoming far more common.

Table 8.4: Women Aged 30–34 Years, Average Number of Children Born Alive, Percentage Childless, Percentage with Four or More Children, 1981 and 1996

	1981			1996		
	Number of children	Percentage of women with:		Number of children	Percentage of women with:	
	Average	Zero	4+ children	Average	Zero	4+ children
Maori	3.15	10	40	2.36	17	23
Non-Maori	2.14	14	12	1.55	30	7
Total*	2.21	14	14	1.66	28	9
Pasifika†	–	–	–	2.22	20	20
Asian†	–	–	–	1.22	31	2

Source: Census.
* By 2001 the rates for the total population for zero births had increased to 29%; by the 2006 census this had risen to 34%, increasing for all ethnic groups (Robert Didham, personal communication).
† As the constituent populations, by volume, by ethnicity and by birthplaces, changed significantly for these two groups between 1981 and 1996, only data for the latter date are given here.

Differential fertility is not new. Malthus's famous theory of population grew out of his observation that the poor had a greater tendency to have large families than the rich (Malthus 1798). What is new, however, is the existence of differentials in timing, spacing and completed fertility when the overall fertility is at sub-replacement level (or spread around replacement, as in New Zealand). This new form of differential is termed reproductive polarisation. Schulze and Tyrell argue that polarisation in reproduction has mutually reinforcing cumulative impacts on other dimensions of life, such as education, income, lifestyle and demographic behaviours. It is a more powerful construct by which to interpret current patterns of childbearing than individualisation and deinstitutionalisation (of the conventional family), the two concepts that had underpinned the arguments around the second demographic transition in the WDCs (Schulze and Tyrell 2002; see also Eckert-Jaffe *et al.* 2002; Pool and Sceats 2003).

Whatever the analytical power of the construct, certainly a new feature of patterns of reproduction at the end of the twentieth century was the way that fertility levels were polarising along the lines just summarised above. Of course, it will be recalled from earlier chapters that this was not an entirely new phenomenon. But the form it has taken is novel, although even so there were some echoes of the past. Notable among these was a tension between the capacity to participate fully in the labour force, and the demands of parenting. This tension, however, did necessarily take an entirely new form. Before, and even during the Baby Boom, the choice was between working (and not marrying, and thus not being at risk of conception) and parenting.

Table 8.5: Reproductive Polarisation, Percentage of Women Aged 30–34 Years who were Childless

Workforce status	NZW:FEE 1995	Census 1996	NZFFS 2001
Full time			
Professional-managerial	59	65	67
Other occupations	32	47	40
Part time			
Professional-managerial	13	13	13
Other occupations	8	11	7
Unemployed	24	21	*
Not in the labour force	5	10	9

Sources: 1995 NZW:FEE; 1996 census; 2001 NZFFS.
Note: The NZW:FEE and NZFFS probably are over-representative of women who were at home during the day (Marsault *et al.* 1997). In the surveys 'full time' and 'part time' were by self declaration, whereas in the census they are by hours worked (30 hours and over is full time). While this latter statistic is widely used its veracity is difficult to check.
* Only four cases in cell.

By the 1990s polarisation revolved around workforce status, whether or not a woman was in the labour force, and if so whether full time or part time, as is shown in Table 8.5. Significant was the type of occupation she was in, professional or managerial as against other jobs, but this factor was far less important than the effects of full-time work, as against any other workforce status. NZFFS data are subject to statistical error but there is some indication of increasing childlessness between 1995/96 and 2001 among the full-time professional-managerial workers at ages 30–34 years. At both dates part-time workers, whatever their occupations, had levels of childlessness close to women outside the labour force. Unemployed women are somewhere in between, as some will have been full-time, others part-time workers. The 2006 census saw these trends maintained, especially for full-time workers in 'other' occupations (53% childless, cf. 47% 1996) (Robert Didham, personal communication).

Associated with occupation was level of education, for prolonged education is typically followed by full-time pursuit of career goals. In the NZW:FEE only 5% of women in their early thirties with no qualification were childless, as were 19% of those with secondary education, 26% with non-university tertiary education, but 56% with university training. Data from across the WDCs show that the gaps in cumulative fertility between women of all educational categories combined and the *least well educated* are relatively narrow. In contrast, the gaps between all women and the *most qualified* have widened for recent cohorts, and this tendency is most marked in the ESCs, including New Zealand (Pool and Sceats 2003: Table 2).

Thus these results show that higher education and pursuit of a career increasingly are key factors determining childlessness, and that this association is becoming more and more important. To date in New Zealand this has not shown up in significant differences in completed family size, but has manifested itself in marked differences in patterns of family formation, as was noted in Chapter Six, for age at marriage and, above all, age at first birth. These will definitely have flow-on effects for cumulative fertility by age, those who are childless at given ages and completed family size (see also Statistics New Zealand 2001: esp. Conclusion).

These patterns are not restricted to New Zealand. A comparative analysis of Britain and France showed that polarisation related to labour-force status is more of a phenomenon and more marked in 'liberal' Britain than in 'conservative' France: 'social polarizations are crystallized in France by the third child, whereas they are evident in England beginning with the first child'. This is because the family policies of France allow greater reconciliation of career and motherhood compared to the family policies of Britain (Ekert-Jaffe *et al.* 2002: 502; see also Gauthier 2002; Pool and Sceats 2003). In another comparative study on polarisation in ten European countries it was shown that 'demographic polarisation [families with children versus without children] is negatively correlated with the degree of services that are provided to young families' (Schulze and Tyrell 2002). Of the ten countries studied, Britain, the ESC in this sample, stood out for its high level of reproductive polarisation.

The empirical results presented here show that reproductive polarisation in New Zealand resembles that observed for Britain. This is probably not surprising given the historical, cultural, economic and political connections between the two countries, noted earlier. The paradigm for family policies enacted in New Zealand over the last two decades is also Thatcherite and neo-liberal (Pool and Sceats 2003). The result of this is for childbearing polarisation to parallel inequalities in work, education, income and the receipt of welfare benefits. As the comparative research on the European countries showed, social and public policies that minimise the incompatibility between working life and family life have the potential to reduce and even halt the process of reproductive polarisation, and consequently the social polarisation related to this (Pool *et al.* 2007).

In the past, by its gatekeeping function for exposure to intercourse, marital status had a significant impact on fertility. Today its role is far more subtle, but is still linked to a degree to the probability of having or not having children. In the NZW:FEE, only 12% of those aged 30–34 who were currently married were childless, whereas levels for women cohabiting, for those in no partnership, and those living apart were much higher, ranging between 31% and 45%. That is, being outside formal marriage did not totally preclude the possibility of childbearing, it merely reduced that probability, while marriage made it more likely. This association is not unexpected, for marital unions are now often entered into, by converting an existing cohabiting union into a marriage and thus formalising it, because a couple already have one or more children and marry to show publicly their commitment to each other. Others move from a consensual union into marriage for the same reason, but in order to have any future children born within the marriage.

Between 1981 and 1996, overall levels of childlessness by age increased, as did the proportions of families with one child, although this pattern was rather less systematic or as radical. Conversely, families with two or three children decreased across most ages. These trends held true when controls were introduced for all socio-economic characteristics of women and, as has been shown above, for socio-cultural factors as well. But within each socio-economic or socio-cultural group the rank differences between various marital statuses remained more or less consistent over time (Dharmalingam *et al.* 2003).

Reproductive polarisation occurs in other ways. A regional analysis shows that there are now increasing sub-national differentials in fertility in New Zealand. To a degree these cross-cut factors such as ethnicity, in that low TFRs are found in central Auckland and central Wellington urban areas, both of which contain significant Maori and Pasifika minorities. But across the entire country regions with high percentages of Maori have higher fertility rates. For Maori the lowest levels are found in central Auckland and the North Shore, yet among the highest rates are those in neighbouring urban South Auckland (Pool 1991). For New Zealand as a whole for all ethnicities, there is a north–south gradient, with the lowest regional levels seen in Otago and Canterbury, the very provinces, incidentally, from which the Pakeha fertility decline of the late nineteenth century spread. But mediating this is the factor noted above of very low fertility rates, which in places like central Auckland and central Wellington resemble those of parts of Western Europe (Pool *et al.* 2005a; Pool 1999).

In 1971, because of the maintenance of high fertility in regions in which Maori were found in large numbers (e.g. Tongariro, the East Coast, using the appellations employed then), the inter-regional span in the TFR had been relatively high in absolute terms (1.04 live births between the highest and lowest regions), but low in relative terms (37%). Relative ranges then increased to 49%, but absolute differences declined (0.84, 1981) (Khawaja 1985: Table 86). By 1991 both absolute and relative differences were opening up (0.93 live births; 52%), and by 2001 they were the widest ever for over the last three decades for those years for which there are data. The absolute span was 1.05 births in a period in which the national TFR was below replacement, and the relative inter-regional range was 67%.

REPRODUCTIVE POLARISATION: THE AGE-STRUCTURAL DIMENSION
There is another very important dimension to reproductive polarisation: the way in which reproduction is distributed across the reproductive span, the 'force of reproduction', as this has been called here. In New Zealand today reproduction is increasingly concentrated in the later years of the childbearing span. Against this there is the continuing tradition of early childbearing, albeit one that has declined over the years. But neither of these trends are normal for other WDCs, except for other ESCs. In the ESCs, and above all in New Zealand, relative to the WDCs as a whole, fertility levels are higher at younger and older ages, but lower over the middle range. This is shown in Figure 8.1 and modeled schematically in Figure 8.2. There the ESCs have patterns of reproduction that, by comparison with the WDCs as a whole, polarise into the younger and older parts of the childbearing span. Most importantly, the ESCs have lower levels at 25–34 years.

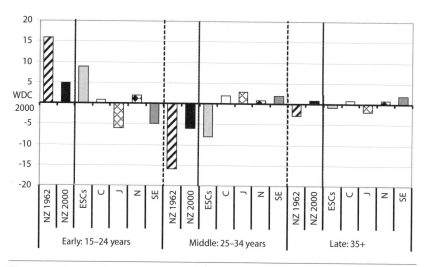

Figure 8.1: Force of Reproduction in the Early, Middle and Late Parts of the Reproductive Span in the 1990s: Percentage-point Difference (+/-) between Country Groupings and the WDCs as a Whole

Source: Figures 8.1 and 8.2 adapted from Pool and Sceats (2003).
Note: ESCs: English-speaking countries; C: Continental Europe; J: Japan; N: Nordic countries; SE: Southern Europe.

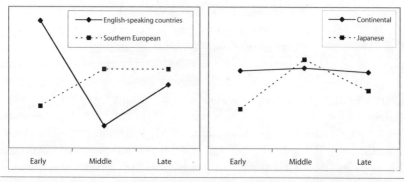

Figure 8. 2: Schematic Diagrams of Four Different Patterns of Reproduction

Note: In this figure, 'Continental' includes Central and North-western Europe and the Nordic countries.

There are clearly now marked patterns of this sort of reproductive polarisation in New Zealand. But this is not systematically the case across the WDCs. France, for example, referred to earlier in the chapter for sustaining higher levels of sub-replacement, has lower levels of age-structural polarisation than does the United Kingdom.

This moves the analysis over to less proximate determinants of the patterns of reproduction, an issue that will be held over until the next chapter. But two more questions specifically relevant to reproductive regimes must be raised: what do couples want in terms of family building? and how close are their intentions to their actual childbearing?

REPRODUCTIVE INTENTIONS

The issue of reproductive intentions prompts many questions. Will delayed childbearing and the associated patterns of polarisation mean diminished childbearing? Do women at these ages intend eventually to have children? If so, will the constraints couples face outweigh their desire to have children and leave them with fewer children than they might have wished to have? Peter McDonald, an Australian demographer,

> proposes that there is a considerable desire for children, as seen through childbearing intentions, but the risks and uncertainties of a globalising world make people hesitate to have children. A globalising world probably produces more risks that are partly handled through stronger investment in one's own human capital leaving less time for reproduction . . . . [Moreover] as women gained status in families they had fewer children, which in turn promoted women's status in non-familial institutions (Beaujot and Muhammad 2006: 15–16, quoting paper of McDonald to the Population Association of America).

Attitudinal data are notoriously difficult to interpret as they reflect views held at the moment of the interview, and also they may represent ideals or desires affected by societal norms rather than the reality for the respondent given their particular situation. In demography there is a long tradition, going back at least to World War II, of attempting to tease out these different interpretations. Summarising these studies, Kellie Hagewen and Philip Morgan use recent data to show that there is a systematic set of differences in European countries between 'ideal' and 'expected' (given the respondents' circumstances) family sizes, and between them and the actual TFRs. In most countries the gradient is steep between ideals (highest) and TFRs (lowest): in Spain, for example, the ideal is about 2.0, the expected about 1.75 and the TFR about 1.2. In contrast, for the United States the ideal is somewhat higher (2.4), but the expected very close to the TFR (2.1). Moreover, in a fascinating analysis they demonstrate that the differences between the intended and current number of births decrease by age and virtually converge, and that this relationship has been remarkably stable across time (Hagewen and Morgan 2005: Figs 1, 3, 4). For us the interest is whether New Zealand follows the American or the European pattern.

We do not have data on ideal or expected family sizes, but from the NZW: FEE and NZFFS we do have some on intentions among childless women. These data are presented in Table 8.6 and indicate that most women intend to have children. Indeed, Janet Sceats argues that New Zealand family life may be underpinned by relatively powerful pro-natalist norms going back to the early colonial period, reinforced by what happened in the Baby Boom and by the social infrastructure that came in to support family building. But these norms are today constantly being tested against a reality that is far less family friendly than was the case in the Baby Boom, or at least as the Baby Boom has been carried down to us through nostalgia (Sceats 2006; 1988: Chapt. 12). Thus the data on cumulative fertility in the NZW: FEE show that, historically, most women who delayed childbearing went on to have a child in their thirties, but today with increasing proportions delaying first births into their late thirties, bio-social factors will mean that growing numbers will be at risk of being infertile.

The proportion in each age-group who are still childless decreases with age, but is higher at each age-group in 2001 than it was in 1995, reflecting the increasing delay in childbearing. Thus 22% of women in their early thirties in 1995 had no children; this had risen to almost 30% for this age group in 2001, while, among women in their late thirties, the proportion childless increased from 11% to 18%.

Arguably these intentions are the 'hardest' of the attitudinal variables as they relate to a group who have delayed first childbearing, but are faced with decisions about whether or not to commence parenting. This is particularly true at older ages when the decision to delay is no longer an option, and where few wanting children are likely to have more than one. Moreover, if women in their thirties in New Zealand are following the United States pattern of an increasing convergence by age with other family size attitudes then these data will throw indirect light on desired family sizes (Sceats 2006).

Table 8.6: Proportion Intending to Have Children Among those Women Childless at the Time of Each Survey, 1995 and 2001

	Yes	No	Don't know	Number of childless women	Total number of women	Expected proportions childless	
Age-group	(1)	(2)(N)	(3) (N)	(4)	(5)	(6)*	(7)†
NZW:FEE, 1995							
20–24	81.4	10.3(30)	8.2(24)	291	403	7.4	13.4
25–29	70.2	21.6(37)	8.2(14)	171	420	8.8	12.1
30–34	54.5	31.3(31)	14.1(14)	99	454	6.8	9.9
35–39	32.0	50.0(25)	18.0(9)	50	440	5.7	7.7
NZFFS, 2001							
20–24	84.3	6.4(11)	9.3(16)	172	233	4.7	11.6
25–29	81.2	11.1(13)	7.7(9)	117	240	5.4	9.2
30–34	58.7	17.3(13)	24.0(18)	75	257	5.1	12.1
35–39	25.0	61.4(27)	13.6(6)	44	249	10.8	13.2

* $\dfrac{\text{Number of women who do not intend to have children (column 2)}}{\text{Total number of women (column 5)}} = \text{column (6)}$

† $\dfrac{\text{Number of women who do not intend (column 2) plus don't know (column 3)}}{\text{Total number of women (column 5)}} = \text{column (7)}$

Although over 50% of women aged 20–29 were childless in 1995, a vast majority of them (over 80%) intended to become parents in the future. This was also the case, although not to the same extent (55%), among childless women in their early thirties. As the last columns in Table 8.6 indicate, if women's stated intentions to have children in the future were to become true, between 5% and 13% intend to remain childless by the end of their reproductive span. At the population level, it is estimated that at least 11% of women intend to remain childless in their late thirties, an age-group that for most women is a proxy for the onset of an increasing frequency of anovulatory cycles and thus declining fecundability. This can be compared with actual births: at age-group 35–39 years 6% of women in 1995 and 11% in 2001 were childless voluntarily or involuntarily.

The shift upwards in the age of childbearing is reflected in the higher proportions in 2001 of childless women aged 25–34 years who intend to have children, compared with 1995. But by their late thirties the likelihood of parenting is diminishing and thus the proportion of these childless women intending to have a child drops off. Significantly this drop-off was higher in 2001 than in 1995. For women 35–39 years who had no children in 1995 one in three intended to have a child, but by 2001 this had fallen to one in four. The dual effects of childlessness and the intention to have no children increased. This would equate to between 6% (1995) and 13% (2001) of all women in this age-group remaining childless.

Of course, as we have noted, intentions do not signify final behaviours, but in this case New Zealand seems to have moved towards the American pattern. In 1995, 6–8% expected to be childless in their late thirties, but by 2001 this had increased to 11–13% (columns 6 and 7). The only comparable data on actual fertility come from the 1996 census, showing that 12% of women aged 40–44 years were indeed childless, a level closer to the 2001 intentions than those expressed in 1995; by contrast, for women belonging to the maternal cohorts finishing childbearing at the end of the Baby Boom and the start of the Baby Bust, aged 55–59 and 60–64 years at the 1996 census, the levels of childlessness were lower, around 9%.

Given the caveats listed above, too great a store should not be put on the predictive power of these data. Nevertheless, if we were to take them at their face value they raise some disconcerting questions. The 1995 data may reflect a lag effect, whereby norms reflect earlier expectations and actual behaviours, the nostalgia enduring from the Baby Boom to which we have made reference earlier. But by 2001, it seems that women were becoming more realistic, pitching their intentions towards what might be the reality. Hagewen and Morgan see the convergence of expectations and actual rates as indicating that 'continued replacement-level fertility is a reasonable forecast in the United States' (2005: 523). The variables we have had to employ are qualitatively different from theirs – the intention to have at least one child, as against their variable, expected family size. But what seems to be an emerging reasonable fit between intentions and actual behaviours may signify that a similar forecast would apply to New Zealand.

New Zealand women may well have realistic assessments of their reproductive options: of the conditions necessary for meeting 'Mr Right' and settling down to have children, of work and cost constraints and of the biosocial limitations imposed by late childbearing. For example, cost factors, such as housing and student debt, are even being noted among better-off urban professionals in New Zealand who are 35 years and over and childless (Sceats 2006).

Further light is thrown on the factor of student loans by the New Zealand University Students Association Income and Expenditure Survey carried out in 2004 on tertiary-level students of all categories of study, a survey which allowed us to collect data about younger adults, most under 30 years of age.* This survey provided information on the co-variates of

---

* A grant from the Foundation for Research, Science and Technology allowed the authors to commission several questions in this survey. We wish to thank the New Zealand University Students Association for allowing us to have access to the survey.

reproductive intentions, notably whether or not the respondent had a student loan. The survey was carried out by a market research company TNS Research and covered 3969 students in universities, colleges of education and polytechnics.

These data show that a vast majority of the students, irrespective of whether they had student loans or not, reported that student loans would have an impact on their decision to have children. While three in four students felt that a student loan would have at least some impact on their decision to have children, about one in five (21%) considered the impact would be 'high'. Interestingly, more among those with no student loans felt that student loans would impact on decisions to have children than among those who had student loans. In another study of medical interns, the student loan was cited as a major constraint to their saving for the future and likely to have an impact on their decisions about having children (Sceats 2006, citing Moore *et al.* 2006).

The question that arises is whether such groups will remain small outliers or spearhead a major shift that might extend to other non-metropolitan regions and the less well-off. Perhaps mediating this is fragmentary evidence of relatively well-off families, sometimes professionally trained women, who have two or even three children and remain outside the workforce for a prolonged period while their children are young. Sometimes they are conservative in attitude, prescribing the place of the mother as being in the home and not at work. At other times they may be in a family that has sufficient income that they can afford to quit the labour force, even though this might mean that they lose seniority, or fail to keep up their skill base and thus have difficulties re-entering the workforce. Increasingly, however, the option of one parent staying at home caring for children and the other in the workforce earning enough to support the family unit is becoming a privilege of the wealthier, where once it had been the norm (Sceats and Kukutai 2005).

Qualitative data show that New Zealand women often hold as an ideal not only having children, but having a family of two to three. Most see a one-child family as undesirable. In the qualitative study such views were expressed particularly by Maori women, who often reported considerable family expectations for them to have children. Although many Pakeha women felt there was greater acceptance of childlessness and the one-child family, social expectations seemed to produce a lingering ambivalence about the desirability of such a situation: 'It is acceptable today, but you don't create a family with an only child . . . . People expect you to have two . . . having one child is often frowned on'. There is concern among some about low fertility in New Zealand, and a regret for the loss of larger families and the values these were seen to represent. Yet others see New Zealand as a great place to have children, in spite of concerns about growing costs and the lack of family-friendly policies. Some respondents returned from overseas with this objective in mind (Sceats 2003, 2005). In this way they were very different from their counterparts living in London, who were interviewed in a directly comparable survey (Cairns *et al.* 2003), but similar to respondents in the Australian arm of this study (Johnstone 2003). Among the attractions of coming home was the presence of family networks, a point we will return to below.

The data in Table 8.6 refer only to childless women. A separate analysis, not reproduced here, of the intention to have additional children among those with one or two children showed the proportion decreases with age and parity. For instance, among those aged 30–34 and with one child, 64% intend to have another child; but this was only 22% among those aged 35–39 years. Similarly, among those aged 30–34 and with two children, about 20% intend to have another child, but this decreases to 9% among those aged 35–39 years.

There are indications in the data in Table 8.6 that levels of childlessness were increasing in the five-year period 1996–2001, and that there was also a growth in negative intentions. However, the data presented here, with all the caveats that we have expressed, reflect anecdotal evidence.

8.3 CONCLUSION

The final chapter will synthesise the major themes raised in this book by looking at continuity and change. But by the early 2000s another issue had emerged: there was increasing evidence of a rupture with the past. The New Zealand family was definitely entering a new era, with historically unique characteristics, as has been noted for particular elements of family life in this chapter. Above all, the unfolding story seemed to be centred on the *raison d'être* for family life, societal replacement, and thus the focus in these last chapters on issues of reproduction. This is a major concern in Europe but as yet has very limited traction in New Zealand.

Just how far the Pakeha population has moved away from the family life, and particularly the family formation patterns, of the society of yesteryear is seen in Figures 8.3 and 8.4. They bring forward to 2001 the figures for the period 1874 to 1961 based on Coale Indices first presented in Figures 4.1 and 4.2, the results of which are incorporated here. In earlier chapters we expressed our caveats about these methods and these same comments, of course, also apply here. But they allow us to contrast New Zealand with other populations, and in the present chapter we compare back over most of the time-span of Pakeha in New Zealand. Because the relevant data are available for Maori for only a short period, the same exercise cannot usefully be carried out for Maori or for the total population.

In Figure 8.3, the period up to 1961 shows a society maintaining its levels of replacement by marital fertility and, by 1961, through very high proportions marrying. Moreover, for the first time in Pakeha recorded history levels of ex-nuptial fertility had also increased (Figure 8.4), thus bringing Pakeha society towards the model seen in early nineteenth-century England. In those years, in the period 1801–25, ex-nuptial fertility rates increased in consonance with high rates of nuptiality and of marital fertility, thus deviating from an hypotheised pattern (set out in Figure 4.2).

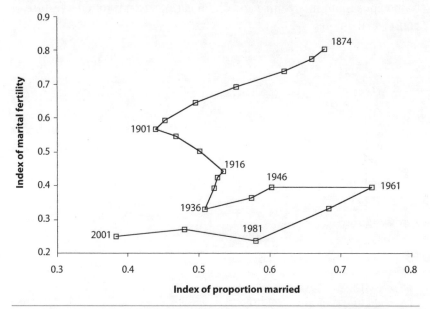

Figure 8.3: Timepath for Change in Marital Fertility (*Ig*) and Nuptiality (*Im*), Proportion Married, Pakeha 1874–2001

Note: For details of methods (the so-called Coale indices) and sources for this and Figure 8.4, see Figures 4.1 and 4.2.

Figures 8.3 and 8.4 show that from 1961 to the present Pakeha went through a linear shift to low levels of nuptiality and to very low levels of marital fertility, yet to high levels of ex-nuptial fertility. The trough running from 1971 to 2001 in Figure 8.3 is noteworthy and unprecedented, for it falls significantly below what was experienced in the Depression in 1936, and far below what had been seen historically. But in this figure the relationships in 2001 are a more extreme version of what had been seen in 1936 – lower proportions marrying and low levels of marital fertility. In terms of the proportions married, these are even more extreme than for the values seen in 1901 at the end of a decline in rates of reproduction manipulated, essentially, by changes in proportions marrying. Nevertheless, in 1901 and 1936 ex-nuptial childbearing was of little consequence at all.

By 1991 and 2001, by contrast, Pakeha had changed direction in terms of the relationships between ex-nuptial fertility and marriage patterns. There was simply no precedent for this in their observed historical trends of family formation. Moreover, for the first time ever there is a correlation with the hypothetical model incorporated in Figure 4.2. On the line A–B set out in Figure 4.2, Pakeha fit the situation denoted by B, where 'the weakly enforced or non-existent taboo on pre-marital sexual intercourse will give rise to higher levels of illegitimate fertility' (Woods 2000: 101). Of course, both exposure to intercourse and childbearing are now often a feature of consensual unions.

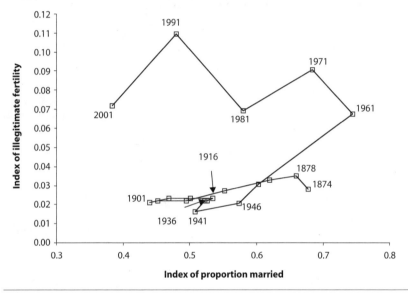

Figure 8.4: Timepath for Change in Illegitimate (Ex-Nuptial) Fertility (*Ih*) and Nuptiality (*Im*), Pakeha 1874–2001

In Figure 8.4, 1991 seems to be a pivotal year, signalling the start of a downturn in ex-nuptial fertility, yet paradoxically a decrease in the proportion married. Paralleling this are inflections in the trends for other statistics that have been quoted in this and other chapters – for example, the slowing down of the increases in divorce and of sole parenting. Does 1991, then, represent the turning point in the revolution that we have followed in other chapters, and with it the achievement of a sort of equilibrium? Until late in the Baby Boom delayed marriage signified, essentially, very low levels of exposure to intercourse. But the Baby Bust, and the way that it occurred (delayed childbearing and then recuperated births), mutated this totally, while the Baby Blip and then the Baby Deficit have reinforced but have stabilised the trends emerging in the Baby Bust, and in doing so seem to have ushered in a new regime.

If this scenario is correct, then the new regime of the early twenty-first century will see delayed first childbearing, but, along with this, perhaps increasing numbers of couples marrying only for reasons of social commitment and, perhaps if it proves to be bio-socially and financially possible, sealing that with a pregnancy or having a ceremony attended by their children. Conception would thus no longer be the reason for becoming married – or marriage being the reason for becoming pregnant – but instead would be primarily a demonstration of the commitment of a mature couple, who probably have experienced other relationships. This might well be a central element in the new systems of mores, norms and values that seem to be emerging in the early twenty-first century. We are not judging them as better or worse than the existing ones, but recognising that they are different (see the reflective paper by Victor Piché and Celine Le Bourdais on the demographic future of Quebec, 2003).

In sum, Figures 8.3 and 8.4 substantiate the argument that we are now in a different and historically unprecedented era, at least for the majority Pakeha population. In all probability similar data for Maori would show a more extreme situation. What cannot be forecast is whether the current pattern will become entrenched and perhaps more marked, even perhaps navigating New Zealand into other uncharted waters, or whether instead there will be a reprise of the past.

The analysis in this chapter does point in one of these directions: the trends, at least for family formation, seem to be developing their own endogenous demographic momenta generated by a mix of fertility rates and parenting cohort sizes. But the latter quantum effect is essentially a function of fluctuations in birth numbers in the past, which in turn has often been a result of shifts in the tempo of childbearing. In their most extreme form today they could produce a low-fertility trap, in accord with the hypothesis put forward by Lutz *et al.* (2006). A return to much higher fertility would be possible only if two of its elements – high rates of fertility and a return to the force of reproduction centring on young ages, either of which is highly unlikely in the foreseeable future – were operating simultaneously and together counterbalancing the effects of smaller cohorts reaching parenting ages.

The interactions of these various factors can be illustrated by positing some scenarios, then projecting fertility until 2016, showing the sizes of the birth cohorts that the different models imply. Table 8.7 sets these out.

These are not forecasts but merely scenarios posited to allow an argument to be developed. That said, every one of the scenarios shows a systematic decline in the numbers of births, the key factor for policy. Thus they may indicate that New Zealand faces an incipient low-fertility trap, although not yet in the league of Italy or Spain. But in thinking about this, we should remember that it took some 30 years for those populations to get to the situation they are in today, following a Baby Boom that produced TFRs only in the middle of the range 2.0 to 3.0; 2016 is 20 years or so on from when we last saw above-replacement fertility in New Zealand, 30 years from when replacement fertility was a consistent trend. According to most scenarios for most years, the births will be to older mothers: the sole exception is in 2016 when, if 2004 patterns were to prevail, the arrival of the Baby Blip at young parenting ages – when in their twenties – will have a significant impact. This goes back to the impacts of tempo, for example relatively early childbearing, on fertility patterns. What about the maintenance of high levels of sub-replacement fertility?[*] New Zealand has behind it a period of recent higher fertility when TFRs were far higher than those in most of Europe. Moreover, current rates are just below replacement. But we should remember that not long ago this latter argument was being put forward by European analysts, who have since seen their TFRs drop by a third. Thus it would be foolhardy to posit the argument that New Zealand will maintain a fertility regime around replacement.

Table 8.7: Age-specific Patterns of Fertility and the Birth Cohort Sizes they Generate: Scenarios to 2016

Births	Assumptions			
	No changes to 2004 rates	Assuming 10% increase at 30+ years	Assuming 10% decrease at <30 years, 10% increase at 30+ years	Assuming 10% decrease at <30 years, no change at 30+ years
2006				
% <30	48	46	44	46
% 30+	52	54	56	54
# of births	57,900	60,900	58,600	55,600
2011				
% <30	49	47	44	46
% 30+	51	53	56	54
# of births	57,000	59,900	57,100	54,200
2016				
% <30	52	49	47	49
% 30+	48	51	53	51
# of births	55,600	58,200	55,300	52,700

Note: The third and fourth assumptions are most in accord with what has been happening to fertility patterns over the last decade or so.

---

[*] This would have the advantage that replacement migration would have a greater chance of operating than would be true for a population such as Japan with very low levels of sub-replacement fertility (Pool 2006). This is an argument advanced by Peter McDonald, but it presupposes that migration inflows can replenish not only for quantum but also for demographic characteristics (e.g. age-groups). To add to this, the inflows would also have to replace the quantum and characteristics of the population of the diaspora, which in New Zealand's case is very large.

Finally, it is the instability of the results that is among their more interesting features. It is the fact that, depending on the demographic scenario, the numbers of births may vary significantly.

This exercise provides a useful summation of this chapter. On the one hand we have entered into such uncharted waters that we cannot predict with any degree of certainty what the future of the New Zealand family might be, at least in that aspect which relates to its most important feature and function, family building. But, on the other hand, unless there are dramatic and, from present perspectives, unimaginable changes, rates of reproduction will continue to dwindle, at least in terms of their most important characteristic: the number of babies born. Unless the Baby Blip cohort that reaches key reproductive ages over the next decade, and thus produces a booster to the population at parenting ages, has children younger and at higher rates than has been the case for the cohorts before them, then we are destined to slide towards European models of sub-replacement fertility.

In the next chapter we will review the implications of the changes in family formation and other societal changes, such as ageing and ethnic diversification, for household morphologies. We will then turn to look at the factors that might have determined the patterns of family formation discussed in the present chapter and other morphologies discussed in the next.

CHAPTER NINE

The Family in Uncharted Waters: Morphologies and their Determinants

9.1 SHIFTS IN MORPHOLOGIES: THEIR SOCIAL, ECONOMIC AND POLICY CONTEXTS

If we turn now to aspects of family life other than reproduction, the focus of the last chapter, and look particularly at family forms, the dawn of the twenty-first century saw the reinforcement of trends already outlined for the Baby Bust period. An example was the case of cohabitation, which had become the modal form of first union in the Baby Bust. But now through civil unions legislation cohabiting heterosexual and homosexual couples could formalise and register their relationship, and thereby signal publicly their commitment to one another. The *de factos* of the Baby Bust could choose to be the *de jures* of the new twenty-first-century world.

Other aspects of household morphology were changing, but their analysis in this chapter requires in the main a simple book-keeping exercise, using as a checklist the detailed review that was made in Chapters Six and Seven, and then identifying any new features. Some other shifts were in partial response to changes in the patterns of family formation discussed last chapter, in partial response to previous changes in forms (e.g. divorce and sole parenting) and in partial response to wider demographic changes in the society – for example, ageing, the diaspora of New Zealanders and increasing ethnic diversity at home.

The overall effect was that, in this most recent period, the structures (family sizes, but particularly household age structures, and especially for parenting cohorts) that had evolved in the Baby Bust and Baby Blip became a more marked feature of New Zealand households. By contrast, the most significant changes in forms (statuses, living arrangements) had been more or less played out by the end of the last period covered in Chapters Six and Seven. Yet, paradoxically, at the beginning of the twenty-first century there was an outpouring of concern among conservative groups over family forms, whereas these same commentators expressed far less anxiety about changing structures. The one structural element on which they did focus, declining family sizes, was attributed to changes in family forms, especially the decreasing role of registered marriage. Undoubtedly, the legislative changes noted above provoked this panic even though the real, as against symbolic, import has so far been limited. The floodgates were not opened and followed by the formalisation of huge volumes of civil unions because for most *de facto* couples, heterosexual or same sex, this did not seem to be a major concern. But in the lead-up to the passage of this bill, the very specific issue of civil unions became confounded with more widespread public concerns about family life in general. Sometimes this debate became further conflated with anxieties about issues such as the prevalence of child abuse and dysfunctional families, generated by some high-profile cases. This upsurge in concern found political voice through a minority political party that emphasised 'family values' in its 2002 election manifesto. Their pressure led the government in 2003 to establish a commission to review issues relating to family life.

In the policy domain at the start of the twenty-first century there were also subtle but important changes. By the late 1990s, the neo-liberal revolution had successfully swept in marketisation and had attempted to minimise the role of the state. Seemingly it had triumphed by achieving much of the goal of targeted and parsimonious social policy regimes. These features of New Zealand's social policy environment laid down during the Baby Bust and Baby Blip were not unique. Across the WDCs there were 'new uncertainties in the lives of young people arising from economic deregulation and social liberalisation' (McDonald 2006: 213–14). But now the focus of attention was turning away from the macro-level state-directed elements of public policy, where, instead, by the end of the 1990s doctrines and actions associated with managerialism, underpinned by neo-liberal ideologies, were increasingly the *modus operandi* at a micro-level. That is, enterprises and employers, in the names of economic efficiency and labour-force productivity, were introducing practices that had a significant impact on individuals' workplace and private lives, through such factors as longer working hours. An important factor was employment legislation introduced in the early 1990s with the intention of eliminating collective bargaining both for wages and work conditions. These policies attempted to make all employer–employee relationships dependent on individual contracts. These policies were reformulated to a degree in the early 2000s, but even so this did not fully rewrite all aspects of the earlier legislation.

In the Baby Boom and Baby Bust the aim of policy, based on the principle of a social wage, to which reference was made in earlier chapters, had been to ensure that any negative events that happened at the workplace had a minimal effect on the family and vice versa. Under the new policy regimes and with the implementation of micro-level managerialist workplace processes, the mediating role of policy had been diminished and thus, through workplace obligations for its employed members, the family was now more exposed to what happened on the job. For example, work hours that might seriously disrupt family routines could be prescribed at the whim of the employer or manager.

There was an additional dimension: not only had the policy instruments changed, as is implicit in the last few paragraphs, but policy had to meet new social needs, some driven by the emerging reproductive regimes and their attendant effects on family structures, and others by the now prevalent family forms. The net result was that, over the 1990s and the early twenty-first century, the public policy props discussed earlier, those that in the Baby Boom and until the 1980s had maintained an environment conducive to replacement fertility, were further eroded. An increasingly important factor was that, in the sphere most critical to an individual employee, the dynamics governing work and its interface with family life seem to have increased in intensity, for many people affecting work–life balances, especially those surrounding job–family interactions, but also leisure and other non-remunerated pastimes. The insecurity that many women feel as they juggle the dual roles of mother and worker is eloquently described by respondents in Janet Sceats's qualitative studies (2003, 2005, 2006).

Legislation attempting to harmonise these different dimensions of social life, such as a parental leave bill in 2002 or legislation in 2004 on annual leave, both of which were subject to high levels of opposition, seem to have turned New Zealand back a little towards the policies seen in other WDCs (outlined in Gornick and Meyers 2003). Nevertheless, in 2006 the gaps between us, and Nordic and northern Continental Europe were still marked.

In combination, the social, economic and policy environments affect the way in which New Zealanders form their families and shape the evolving household morphologies. Thus much of the analysis of these contextual factors must centre on their implications for family formation and household morphologies. But this is not to lose sight of the fact that there were other co-terminous, but not necessarily co-varying, changes in family patterns coming from other major societal transitions. Most notable were transformations in family structures and forms resulting from the increasing ethnic diversity of New Zealand society. This saw a decrease in the proportion of the population having traditional Anglo-Celtic roots, and whose family types had been the overwhelmingly dominant form for roughly a century and a quarter. Increasing cultural diversity also took another form, as there was also growth in the numbers of multi-ethnic households. Over and beyond these factors was that of population ageing, which has an immediate impact on the morphologies of households. In this case, however, the society-wide trend is largely a result of past patterns of family formation: the sizes of families and the tempo of childbearing.

Another important factor affecting the dynamics of an increasing number of New Zealand families was the diaspora of New Zealanders. More than 10%, perhaps even 20% of New Zealanders, most commonly young people, were living overseas at any time.* About 10% of Maori were living in Australia in the 'newest Maori migration' (Bedford and Pool 2003).

9.2 HOUSEHOLD MORPHOLOGIES IN 2001: THEIR TYPES AND STRUCTURAL FEATURES

HOUSEHOLDERS: AGES, TYPE OF HOUSEHOLD IN WHICH THEY LIVE AND THEIR ETHNICITY

The recent patterns of family formation, especially delayed childbearing and the demographic squeeze discussed in earlier chapters, have had an impact on household structures. The effects have been further reinforced by more general population changes, especially overall population ageing, the growth of the Maori population and the Pasifika and Asian migratory inflows. In this section of the chapter, as a form of stocktaking, summary tables on these changes will be presented (drawn from Dharmalingam *et al.* 2007: Tables 5.9, 5.10 and 5.11, which also provides further age-structural details).

The combination of delayed childbearing plus the more generic age-structural transition is clear in Table 9.1. The large decrease in the number of occupiers aged younger than 30 years is offset by increases in the later parenting ages. A slight decrease at the older middle ages is compensated for by increases at old ages.

Table 9.1: Percentage Distribution of Households by Occupier's Age, Total Population, 1976 and 2001

Occupier age	1976	2001
<30 years	20	14
30–44 years	29	33
45–64 years	34	33
65+ years	18	20
Total	100	100

Note: The data in this table and the tables following on structures are drawn from the census.

* Personal communication, Jacques Poot, co-principal researcher, 'Circulation and Settlement of New Zealanders in Australia' (Marsden Fund project).

In the shift-shares in household types, the one whose proportionate contribution has changed the most is the two-parent family, as is shown in Table 9.2. Countering this is the growth, most importantly, in the single-person family, and to a lesser degree in sole-parent households and couple-only families. What is interesting is that there are almost as many parents-plus-other households as sole-parent households, yet the former type has a far lower profile. Below more detail will be supplied on some of these household types.

Table 9.2: Percentage of Households by Type, Total Population, 1976 and 2001

Household type	1976	2001
Non-related	7	5
Single person	14	23
Couple only	20	25
Parents plus others	10	9
Sole parent	5	10
Two parents	43	28
Total	99	100

This table also demonstrates a point discussed in earlier chapters. Households are conventionally analysed under two broad headings: family, which includes parenting units of various sorts as well as couples without children, and non-family, which includes households formed by non-related people, classically the student flat, but also single-person households, the most rapidly growing category. In a philosophical sense, for many such units it is a misnomer to categorise one-person households as 'non-family', as most often they house older persons who are widows or widowers, frequently living in the house in which they raised their children and which is often viewed by the grown-up offspring and their children as the family home. Indeed, as the geographer Brian Heenan notes, 'Married or unmarried, the vast majority of elderly New Zealanders . . . lived in private homes' (1993: 49).

Few elderly lived in institutions in 2001: 7% of the population aged 65 years and over, but 9% of the women at that age, as against only 5% of older men. Of course, the older the age-group the higher the proportion in institutions: 2% at 65–74 years, 7% at 75–84 years, 28% at 85–94, and a majority, but only a bare majority (53%) at 95 years and over. But while the percentages living in hospitals or retirement homes was much higher among the oldest of the old, only 11% of all elderly were at ages at which institutionalisation was more prevalent, that is, 85 years and over.

In line with the broader demographic changes noted earlier, there were ethnic shifts, as is seen in Table 9.3, which relates to the 'occupier', the reference person in the census enumeration (see also Dharmalingam *et al.*

2007: Table 9.1). Declines in the proportion Pakeha were counterbalanced by increases in the percentage of households whose occupier belonged to minority ethnic groups. Nevertheless, in 2001 four-fifths of households still had an occupier who was Pakeha.*

Table 9.3: Percentage of Households by Ethnicity of Occupier, 1976 and 2001

Ethnicity	1976	2001
Pakeha	88	80
Maori	7	11
Asian/Other	3	5
Pasifika	2	4

Intermarriage has long been a feature of New Zealand social life (Pool 1991), and rates remained high in the 1990s (Callister 2003). Not surprisingly, over the period 1991–2001 there was also an increase in the number of households that were multi-ethnic (Dharmalingam *et al.* 2007: Table 9.2). In 1991, 91% of households were composed of members who were of the same ethnicity, but by 2001 this had dropped to 88%. Thus the proportionate distribution of households by ethnicity is changing, but so too are ethnic structures within households.

FAMILY HOUSEHOLDS AT THE DAWN OF THE TWENTY-FIRST CENTURY: AN OVERVIEW

The category 'family households' includes a wide range of sub-types. Most are parenting families of one sort or another, but couple-only households typically include persons who could/might become parents, or who have been and are now at an empty-nest phase. Because of the demographic factors and changing patterns of family formation noted above there is a shift-share unfolding within this broad category, particularly for Pakeha, plus a move to single-person households. For Pakeha, these purely normative processes are producing a decrease in the two-parent category, not so much by a shift into sole-parent families, but by the growth of the couple-only unit.

In 2001, the size of the Pakeha couple-only category exceeded that for two-parent households; in 1976, it had been half (Dharmalingam *et al.*

* A major problem with these data is that the occupier's ethnicity may not be representative of the other members of the household. Dharmalingam *et al.* 2007: Table 9.1, using unprioritised data, looks at individuals, household 'occupiers', both those persons who gave only one ethnic response and those who reported that they were 'mixed'. In Dharmalingam *et al.* 2007: Table 9.2, in contrast, where the unit of reference is the household, one is studying the ethnicity of all household members, and thus the only practical strategy was to use prioritised responses.

2007: Table 5.11). For other ethnic groups two-parent families still greatly outnumber couple-only families. Thus recognition has to be given to the main causes of the upsurge in couple-only households: the factors of family formation noted earlier; and now the delays in childbearing, coupled with a decrease in family sizes. This is a norm for WDCs and, in Europe at least, is a matter of major policy concern, affecting the capacity of societies to replace themselves. As already noted, in New Zealand this concern has barely surfaced in policy circles, despite the significance of this trend.

Overall, that is, in the total population, parenting households (two parent + sole parent + parents plus) do in fact constitute a majority of families. But they are a declining category, significantly so in the case of Pakeha, to a lesser degree for Maori and very slightly for Pacific peoples. In contrast, parenting households comprise an increasing proportion of Asian/Other households, as is shown in Table 9.4. Shifts within the category of parenting households will be discussed below.

Table 9.4: Parenting Households as a Percentage of Family Households, 1976 and 2001

Ethnicity	1976	2001
Pakeha	73	59
Maori	90	84
Pasifika	93	92
Asian/Other	75	86
Total	74	65

Table 9.5: Children in Parenting Households: Percentage by Ethnicity of Occupier, 1976 and 2001, and Changes, 1976–2001

Ethnicity	Percentage distribution		Change 1976–2001	
	1976	2001	N (000s)	%
Pakeha	81	67	-205,635	-26
Maori	14	18	+22,818	+17
Pasifika	3	8	+40,365	+147
Asian and Other	2	7	+33,790	+150
TOTAL	100	100	-99,291	-10

Notes: The totals do not exactly tally because of the 9360 children with ethnicity unspecified in 2001. Of the Asian and Other group in 2001, 12% of the children in 2001 were in the 'Other' category, and almost none in 1976. The growth of the Asian-alone category was rather slower, 121%.

Between 1976 and 2001, because of the decreases in fertility discussed earlier, there was a net loss in the number of children living in parenting households of all categories combined (sole + two parent + parents plus).

In 2001 there were 99,000 fewer than there had been in 1976, despite the fact that the population as a whole had increased in size from 3.1 million to almost four million in that time, and despite the fact that the total number of households had grown by 384,000, or 42%. Along with this, there had also been a shift-share in the ethnic distribution of the dependent child population living in parenting households, as is shown in Table 9.5. The percentage Pakeha decreased not only because the growth in the numbers belonging to other ethnic groups was more rapid than that for Pakeha, but also because the numbers of Pakeha dependent children dropped very significantly. That said, the distribution in 2001 was more or less in line with the overall population distribution, but very different from the ethnic distribution of households (compare with Table 9.3). While only two-thirds of children lived in Pakeha families, four-fifths of all households were still Pakeha, a function of the number of Pakeha couple-only and single-person units.

FAMILY HOUSEHOLDS THAT COMPRISE TWO OR THREE GENERATIONS

'Family households' include sole-parent households, two-parent households, two-parents-plus-others households and couple-only households. All family households that are not couple only are, by definition, parenting households, comprising two or more generations.

As shown in Table 9.6, according to the 2001 census, about half of all family households were estimated to have at least two generations, that is, to fit the mould of a 'conventional' nuclear parenting household. This prevalence varies by the ethnicity of the occupier. Levels were higher among the Pasifika and Asian populations, moderately so for Maori, but low for Pakeha.

Table 9.6: Estimated Percentage of Households that are Family Households Comprising at Least Two Generations, 2001

Ethnicity	Percentage
Pakeha	41.4
Maori	65.6
Pasifika	79.8
Asian	71.3
Other	64.8
Total	46.3

An interesting trend has been the growth in the number of multi-generational households, but only limited information on these is directly available. Moreover, the transactions and exchanges between generations are not only complex and multi-directional, but may be intense regardless of living arrangements (e.g. co-residency as against the generations living separately) (Hillcoat-Nalletamby and Dharmalingam 2004).

Table 9.7: Percentage of Family Households with Children Under Sixteen Years and Members 65+ Years in 1991 and 2001, by Ethnicity of Occupier

Ethnicity	1991	2001
Pakeha	0.7	0.9
Maori	2.6	2.9
Pasifika	5.7	8.0
Asian	3.5	6.0
Other	1.5	3.0
Total	1.2	1.6

Nevertheless, a crude estimate of the number of co-resident families of three or more generations is attempted here. It was obtained by looking at households with children under sixteen years and one or more members aged 65 years and over (assuming that such people are unlikely to be the parents of the young children). The data in Table 9.7 show that this type of household is most prevalent for Pasifika and Asian families and is increasing.

FAMILY HOUSEHOLDS THAT CONTAIN MORE THAN ONE ADULT COUPLE (EXTENDED-FAMILY TYPE)

We have loosely applied the term 'extended' to one census category, proscribed as it is by co-residence and thus not covering other links with the wider family or whanau. Our classification is thus far less refined than McPherson's (2000), to be discussed below.

Overall, between 1976 and 2001 there were no significant changes in this category, but there were major shift-shares between ethnic groups. Using the census data on 'parents-plus' households, the only category that provides data on such families, results by ethnicity are shown in Table 9.8.

Table 9.8: Percentage of Family Households that are Extended (Parents plus Others, or Two or More Parenting Couples, Living in the Same Dwelling)

	1976	2001
Pakeha	11	9
Maori	26	25
Pasifika	40	36
Asian	12	27
Total	13	13

Pakeha and Maori percentages in this category have declined modestly as family age-composition has changed. The decline in the Pasifika level was greater, a function of migration and settlement processes. Earlier migrants were often housed with relatives, but today higher and higher proportions of Pacific peoples are New Zealand born and moving into neolocal nuclear families (though the proportion living with extended family members remains high compared to the total population).* In contrast, the Asian level has increased significantly. This is because through migration and family reunion the Asian population of 2001 was structurally very different from that of 1976. Back then the proportion of Asians who were New Zealand born was much higher.

The census merely provides a snapshot at various points. More information on structures and dynamics of extended families comes from recent research by Mervyl McPherson. She shows that the size of this family type is not normally large, and is typically based around genealogical proximity. Support is, therefore, normally afforded to closer relatives – first degree – although for a minority this will extend to more distant kin. Pakeha tend to have loose informal and selective networks. Generally in the extended families she studied there was a sense of family obligation (McPherson 2000: 170–71; see also Hope 1997). A recent French study has shown that such networks are a critical factor in helping the elderly to maintain independence, with those older persons institutionalised having much smaller networks on average (Desesquelles and Brouard 2003).

SOLE-PARENT HOUSEHOLDS

In many commentaries on family policy, the poster-child for assertions that the family is in dire straits is the sole-parent household. As was noted earlier, they are also the group of mothers, for most are mothers, who are being coerced into employment by policy measures of one sort and another. They often suffer opprobrium, more than most, for the difficulties they face in contributing to economic production and the fiscal burden they are seen to represent. Moreover, the sole-parent family is seen as a unit in need of constant monitoring, yet, in contrast, these parents receive little approbation for the way in which they have assisted in building the national fertility. The focus on the solo parent – on 'getting them back to work' regardless of the costs to quality childraising – detracts attention from the very critical point that the children in such families are a potential asset as future citizens, workers and contributors to an economy that may well have future labour deficits. A recent OECD report on New Zealand calls on the need for 'enhanced case management for clients of Domestic Purposes

---

* There is the possibility that there may be undercounts of this category, particularly for Pasifika households hosting immigration overstayers or other persons who avoid census enumeration.

Benefit, and enforced mutual obligations (requiring sole parents to seek work actively) if reform [that 'directly links working hours with financial support to parents'] does not lead to a significant increase of employment among sole parents'. There is little consideration of the inequalities their children may face, and there are no recommendations about meeting children's needs as the parents are forced into work, except for the provision of 'out-of-school-hours care capacity' and 'pre-primary school education'. But even this is seen entirely in the context of 'linking such payments [by 'paying childcare subsidies directly to users'] to families' working hours' (OECD 2004: 12).

In this context, it is a truism, but one worth remembering, that re-production is a pre-requisite for sole parenting, and is often the determinant of the separation that has led to sole parenting. For this category of household the balancing of work and family is the most difficult and many are forced on to welfare however hard they try to avoid this situation.

The proportions of family households in this category have increased over the last two and a half decades, particularly among minority ethnic groups, as is shown in Table 9.9. In 2001, while only about one in ten family households were sole parent among the Pakeha population, it was about one in four family households for Maori, and about one in seven family households among the Pasifika population. The proportion of parenting households involved was also increasing, and with this an increment in the numbers of dependent children that were being raised in these families.

Table 9.9: Percentage of Family Households that are Sole Parent, 1976 and 2001

Ethnicity of occupier	1976			2001		
	Percentage of all households	Percentage of all family households	Percentage of parenting households	Percentage of all households	Percentage of all family households	Percentage of parenting households
Pakeha	5	6	9	8	12	20
Maori	7	9	10	19	24	29
Pasifika	5	5	6	14	16	18
Asian	5	6	*	10	12	14
Total	5	7	0	10	13	21

* Very few cases; thus included with Pakeha in 1976.

However, the rate of growth of this type of household has actually been slowing. As was discussed in Chapters Six and Seven, of parenting households the sole-parent category went from 9% in 1976 to 19% in 1991, and then in the 1990s up very slightly to 21%. The growth in the number of such households was 32% (for the years 1976–81), 74% (for the decade

1981–91), and then increased by only 15% (the next decade, 1991–2001). The decreases in teenage pregnancy, of pre-nuptial conception then marital birth but later divorce and the recent slow increase or plateauing of rates of divorce clearly were having an impact on the prevalence of sole parenting.

Not only is this household category not growing rapidly, despite the widespread moral panic of recent years, but sole parenting is also a misunderstood phenomenon. To summarise what was noted in earlier chapters, sole-parenting households are more likely to be female headed. Sole parenting is a fluid situation not a fixed status, as separated women typically remarry or enter another union: close to three-quarters of those separated from first marriage re-partner within ten years (Dharmalingam *et al.* 2004; Pool and Moore 1986). Sole parents cluster in the age-range 30–44 years. As a result of earlier childbearing Maori and Pacific peoples are likely to become sole parents at a younger age than are Pakeha. Beyond this, sole-parent families of all ethnicities and ages are often embedded into a wider household, frequently of two parents (that is the parents of the sole parent), and others for Maori and Pacific peoples, among whom embedding is most prevalent (Jackson and Pool 1996). Finally, the proportions of all women or men who are sole parents are very low: less than 10% for most age-groups of women.

TWO-PARENT HOUSEHOLDS
The prototypical household of the Baby Boom comprised two parents and their dependent young children. But except among Asians, two-parent and parent-plus families have declined as a percentage of all households; yet these two categories still constitute 80% of parenting families. Moreover, their 'dependent' children are now far more likely than in the Baby Boom to be young adults than little children.

The decline is not because of a major shift into other forms of parenting families. Instead, the drivers are mainly the decreases in fertility noted earlier, and a squeeze on parenting as young couples delay childbearing and live in couple-only households. But ahead of the couples who are delaying and ahead of the couples at the modal ages for parenting, are today older cohorts, who had their births at much younger ages than is the norm today, whose children have left and who are thus couple-only households. The results for Asians are a little different and are a function of their migration patterns.

It must be noted that the most important contribution to the decreases in the proportion of the total family households has been the compensating growth in the proportions of couple-only families, not sole-parent families. Thus the results in Table 9.10 are in part the inverse of trends to be seen in Table 9.11.

Table 9.10: Two-parent Family Households as a Percentage of Family Households

Ethnicity of Occupier	1976	2001
Pakeha	55	38
Maori	56	34
Pasifika	48	39
Asian	36	47
Total	55	38

COUPLE-ONLY HOUSEHOLDS

Because of the squeeze noted in earlier chapters, coming mainly from a major shift in Pakeha family formation patterns to smaller families and later childbearing, there has been a radical increase in couple-only households, as is shown in Table 9.11. Young Pakeha are delaying childbearing and older Pakeha who had their children at much younger ages are now empty-nesters. The couple-only category is about to undergo a further shift as couples with delayed births, a pattern that is the norm today, remain parenting households with dependent children when the occupier is older and even retired. The data on Asians reflect the 1990s migration wave which brought in couples with children (compare Table 9.10).

Table 9.11: Couple-only Households as a Percentage of Family Households

Ethnicity of occupier	1976	2001
Pakeha	27	41
Maori	10	16
Pasifika	7	8
Asian	25	14
Total	26	35

NON-FAMILY HOUSEHOLDS

The last category of household is the group termed 'non-family' that comprises two sub-categories, non-related persons (e.g. student flats) and single-person households. We are interested here primarily in the latter groups, as they represent a family life-cycle stage – typically dissolution through widow(er)hood – and because changes in this sub-category have altered the entire distribution of household types.

Except among Asians, there has been an increase in the number and proportion of households comprising persons living alone, as is shown in Table 9.12. This is a reflection in part of the growth of the elderly population, but also a shift in the preferred living patterns of the elderly. In 1976, 40% of households with older persons were one person; in 2001 this was

50%. Along with the elderly one-person households, there has also been an increase in the number of young persons choosing to live alone, in part because of declines in fertility. In 1976, 50% of one-person households housed older persons; by 2001 this was down to 43%.

The person living alone today is more likely to be a woman, but historically it was usually a male, the old 'codger' eking out an existence on his own. This was particularly true while there were still cohorts containing the survivors of the goldfield and Vogel migration inflows, and which as a result had high masculinity ratios (Fairburn 1989: Chapt. VII). Again in the Depression of the 1930s there was an upsurge in this phenomenon, often driven by 'swaggies' looking for work. But there was little of this in the Baby Boom, which was not only a period in which the nuclear-parenting household reigned supreme, but also one when the prosperity of that era ensured that some of the economic factors (notably unemployment) likely to produce sole-person households had been minimised. In remote areas there were still vestigial 'man alone' sole-person households, and undoubtedly this holds true today, but they are a small minority of the total.

Table 9.12: Percentage of Households Lived in by One Person Only

Ethnicity of occupier	1976	2001
Pakeha	15	25
Maori	7	16
Pasifika	4	8
Asian	22	10
Total	14	23

POLARISATION IN FAMILY MORPHOLOGIES: THE REGIONAL DIMENSION

The previous chapter raised the issue of reproductive polarisation. But this is not the only form of differentiation occurring in New Zealand families at the turn of the twenty-first century. There are also economic factors affecting family well-being: income polarisation and its co-variate, family access to remunerated work. But even looking at family organisation *per se*, it is clear from the analysis above that family structures vary in many different ways. The morphologies represented in the preceding section of the chapter were for the nation as a whole; they will now be analysed by taking as an example regional differences in household structural distributions and household incomes. The most important point is that household structures (age-standardised by occupier's age) differ significantly by region, reflecting the underlying factor of geographic variations in age structures, ethnic composition, labour-force participation and related factors of human capital. As these differences have been analysed in detail elsewhere, there is no need here to do more than briefly summarise the major trends.

Sole parenting is more frequent in the north of the country, outside Auckland. In contrast, Auckland, along with Wellington and the South Island regions, has low levels. To a significant degree the percentage of the population who are Maori determine these differences, but in turn they are mediated by factors such as the level of urbanisation. In contrast, the frequency of couple-only households is higher in low-fertility areas of the South Island. Two-parent families are more common in the rural areas that have high fertility. Parent-plus families are most typically found in the regions from Hawke's Bay and Waikato north, especially the Auckland region, where the concentrations of Asians and Pacific peoples play a major role. Non-family households are a significant category in urban areas with large student populations. Finally, single-person households reach high proportions from Taranaki-Manawatu-Wanganui southwards, in the regions with higher proportions at older ages (Pool *et al.* 2005a).

The regional differentials in household structures seem to parallel spatial differentials in individual and household incomes. Between 1986 and 2001, the average incomes (median) for New Zealand as a whole remained stable. There had been a marked decline between 1986 and 1991 that reversed over the 1990s for both individuals and households. But income levels in some regions never regained parity with those seen in 1986 (all values cited here are inflation adjusted). Essentially, it is Auckland, Wellington and, to a lesser degree, Canterbury that made up the losses sustained nationally as a result of the restructuring carried out in the late 1980s and early 1990s.

The gap between the lowest regional income and the highest increased by over 20% between 1986 and 2001. Moreover, within each region household income inequalities appear to have worsened. The individual regions show marked heterogeneity in terms of changes in median household incomes between 1986 and 2001. Gisborne, Northland, the West Coast and, to a lesser extent, Manawatu-Wanganui suffered major declines in household incomes, while Auckland and Marlborough experienced large increases (Pool *et al.* 2005b; Cochrane *et al.* forthcoming).

This often accompanied regional differentials in rates of household joblessness. These were higher in marginal, isolated regions, such as Northland, Gisborne and the West Coast. Inter-regional ranges more than doubled in the period of restructuring in the late 1980s and early 1990s, then decreased slightly but in 2001 were still twice what they had been in 1986 (Cochrane 2003).

EMERGING HOUSEHOLD MORPHOLOGIES: A SUMMARY

The above brief analysis shows that by 2001 household forms were distributed differently from their Baby Boom profile. To reiterate an important point made earlier, this book is dealing with the percentage distributions of family types, not with individual families, and in this sense one can argue that there was more diversity proportionately at the beginning of the twenty-first century than there had been earlier. While all the forms seen in 2001 were present in 1976, or 1956, it was the share of the total that varied.

In 1976 the two-parent family had been the modal form of family household, but this is no longer the case. The shifts have not come from the very modest increases in the share of families that are sole parent – in fact growth in that category has slowed – but in couple-only families. For all households it is the single-person unit that has increased its contribution to the total. A key factor in this has been the delay of major life transitions (Beaujot 2006).

Thus the period under review here saw increases in household types that were less common at the end of the Baby Boom: for example, single-person, multi-generational and cluttered-nest households. Some of the changes represent shifts in social attitudes towards family structures (e.g. cluttered nests), but others (increases in single-person and couple-only households) were a result of demographic trends, not just ageing but also patterns of family formation such as delayed childbearing. Alongside these socio-demographic factors there were economic changes, notably a shift towards more and more inequality between households, as measured by both inter- and intra-regional trends. Thus family structural polarisation was a trend paralleling reproductive polarisation.

The profile for other aspects of family forms at the end of the 1990s was very similar to what had existed in the preceding two decades. In particular, the trend towards establishing cohabiting unions intensified and the increase in divorce slowed in the late 1990s. The 2001 NZFFS survey data did not provide the rich bank of retrospective data of the 1995 survey. Thus it was not possible to analyse the changes in the 1990s rigorously and in detail. However, the 2001 data do provide some interesting results. In 2001, among respondents aged 20–24, 37% were cohabiting, 12% were married and 12% were LAT. The corresponding figures in 1995 had been 27%, 14% and 20%. Thus between 1995 and 2001, it appears that the percentage who were LATs declined, but that the prevalence of cohabiting unions went up. Marital status data by age and education for 2001 showed that LAT relationships were more common among those with a first-level university degree and aged 25–29. For instance, among those in this category aged 25–29, 41% were cohabiting, while 6% were LAT. The corresponding figures among those with no educational qualifications were 50% and 0%.

9.3 FAMILY DYNAMICS IN THE NEW MILLENNIUM

We are faced with a conundrum at this point. On the one hand, shifts in family formation, family forms and family structures have produced a set of family dynamics that in combination may well be historically unique. The cluttered nest, to be described below, was probably common traditionally; whether this also involved boomerang kids is another question. Certainly some of the dynamics described below represent marked departures from what occurred in the Baby Boom. On the other hand, some of today's dynamics do seem to have precedents, but dating from far further back, before the Baby Boom. Perhaps the most radical recent change is in the roles played by fathers, to be discussed below.

Another example is the LAT phenomenon, involving unmarried children co-residing in the most intimate of ways under their parents' roof. At first glance this may seem to be historically unique, and would have shocked Baby Boom parents. Yet, historically, in parts of Europe, the Amish country of Pennsylvania and even in the prim and proper colonies of early New England, a courting ritual of 'bundling' occurred, where young married couples were encouraged to share the same bed in their parents' homes, albeit fully clothed. This serves to remind us that seemingly unprecedented phenomena may in fact have occurred in the past in other guises.

One further caveat must be given. In the main we are dealing here with aggregate data. These give us information on groups of family types or people, not the dynamics of individual families. As has been stressed in earlier chapters, New Zealand studies that might throw further light on micro-level dynamics are thin on the ground.

EMPTY NESTS, CLUTTERED NESTS AND BOOMERANG KIDS

Turning to family formation *per se*, there is another dimension to the ways in which families dissolve and morphologies develop and then erode: children leaving home. This is a function more of changes in the social, economic and policy environment than of proximate factors, and as such will be referred to in the next section of the chapter. But one point should be made here. The recent declines in cohabitation at the youngest ages are due in part to teenagers and young adults delaying their departure from the family home, or even returning to what, by the 1980s, Canadian researchers were calling the 'cluttered nest' (Boyd and Pryor 1989). These trends were precipitated, in part, by socio-economic contextual factors (e.g. prolonged education, especially of women; costs associated with independent living). Furthermore, the emergence of the LAT phenomenon means that co-residence is no longer a pre-requisite for a consensual union.

A sociologically important trend internationally is for increasing numbers of youths and adults to stay at home with their parents, or for those who have fled the nest to return to clutter it. In Japan young women in this category are called 'parasite singles'; elsewhere they are termed 'boomerang kids'. Living with a parent or parents may go far beyond the mere continuation of residence as a dependant – for example, young men or women may be couples in every sense except co-residence.

New Zealand has a tradition of children leaving home quite young, often boarding or flatting in non-related households. In the Baby Boom this went as far as the establishment of neolocal residence by couples in their late teens or early adulthood. While this latter trend has declined, flatting has continued and intensified in the 1990s. It is most marked in metropolitan regions for reasons that have to do with the attraction of larger centres, especially those with tertiary educational institutions, for students and workers, especially the more skilled (Pool *et al.* 2005b).

In contrast, there has been an increase in genuine cluttered-nest households. This involves increases in the percentage of households, especially in larger urban areas, which are composed of parents and their young-adult offspring aged 25 years and over. Both the growth in this phenomenon and the proportion of households involved are highest in Auckland and Wellington. Levels were also high in peripheral regions, notably Gisborne, which had been subject to the return migration of discouraged workers from the larger urban areas (Pool *et al.* 2005b). The comments here refer of course to adults rather than the dependent children (i.e. below sixteen years), discussed elsewhere in the chapter. But this issue will be returned to below when dependent children in households are examined.

LOOKING AFTER CHILDREN

Families, therefore, face the possibility of cluttered nests inhabited by adult offspring, perhaps as well as their 'partners' and even grandchildren. But the capacity of any given family to nurture dependent infants and non-adult children also varies, as measured by factors such as household income. Because of income inequalities the environments in which children are being raised differ, with polarisation evident between the advantaged and disadvantaged. Indeed, the income and other data presented earlier (also see below) show that these disparities are increasing, as in the United States (McLanahan 2004; see also Gornick and Meyers 2003: 9). Whether or not both parents are present, particularly whether or not they are both in remunerated work, at least gaining incomes around the average level, is an important factor of differentiation and a major cause of inequalities between households.

The living arrangements for children have shifted significantly since the 1950s. According to the 1995 NZW:FEE survey results, the proportion of children who live with a sole parent at some point in their life has been increasing since the early 1950s birth cohorts. Although this has occurred for both Maori and non-Maori children, the rates for Maori children are above those for non-Maori (Dharmalingam *et al.* 2004: Chapt. 5; Hutton 2001; McPherson 1996).

Beneath these figures lies a less manifest trend that is linked to the delayed childbearing that increasingly features as a factor of New Zealand family life: 'children born to older women are [likely to experience] lower levels of sole parenting than those of younger mothers' (Hutton 2001: 11). Moreover, one must add here another qualification noted earlier: that many sole-parent families, especially Maori and Pasifika, are embedded in extended families of one sort and another. That said, the growth of this sort of household certainly means that there is a concomitant increase in the numbers of disadvantaged households.

American researchers have long been able to analyse the ages at which children leave home, but until the advent of the NZW:FEE this could not be done by their New Zealand counterparts (Pool *et al.* 2007: Chapt. 3). With the NZW:FEE some interesting preliminary results can now be presented. The typical New Zealand child is dependent on their parents into their late teens or early adulthood. One in five will leave home before age seventeen, and about three in five by 20 years, more frequently female than male offspring, and most frequently Maori. The type of union the mother was in is a key factor, with higher levels of propensity to leave home earlier for children living with a sole mother, and highest of all for those living with their biological mother and a stepfather (Dharmalingam *et al.* 2004: Chapt. 7).

Interestingly, the propensity to leave home has declined over time. Among children born before 1970, 23% had left home by seventeen years; for those born in the 1970s the proportion was only 15% (Dharmalingam *et al.* 2004: Chapt. 7). Once again this suggests that the cluttered nest is replacing the empty nest, both for youth and the adult offspring aged 25 years and over discussed earlier.

This change in the roles of families is apparent in another way that seems to be an emerging feature of modern family life: time-use surveys across the WDCs show that parents are spending more time with their children (Gauthier *et al.* 2004). Unfortunately, New Zealand data were not included in their analysis, but the limited evidence suggests that these conclusions apply here (Callister 1999; Hillcoat-Nalletamby and Dharmalingam 1999; Ministry of Women's Affairs and Department of Statistics 2001). Certainly the qualitative in-depth research of Janet Sceats showed that New Zealand fathers as well as mothers do, in fact, interact with their children in activities such as play, reading, feeding and bathing, in spite of the long hours many were working (Sceats 2002, 2005). One interesting dimension, not noted by the respondents, is that within the home the time spent on each domestic task may be shorter today because of labour-saving devices, so that, ironically, some working parent(s) may be able to spare more time with children than was the case with the stay-at-home, full-time mother of the Baby Boom. Most importantly

> paid work does not appear to impinge directly on the investment that parents make in their children. Employed parents devote slightly less time to their children than non-employed parents, but the difference is small compared to the difference by employment status in time devoted to paid work . . . .
> [A]ctivities that involve a higher degree of parent-child interaction, such as playing appear to have been responsible (Gauthier *et al.* 2004: 664).

Two points can be drawn from this brief review. First, the data presented suggest that family life may be more interactive and children more dependent for a longer duration than in the past. This does not fit with some of the commentaries heard in public debates about family dynamics. Secondly, these more intense internal dynamics must be set alongside growing external pressures, especially work (see below), to which we will turn a little later in this chapter.

FATHERS' ROLES IN FAMILIES

In the public debate on families another significant issue is the perception that fathers have a declining role in families. This takes two dimensions: (i) that fathers are absent because of travel or family dissolution; or (ii) that, although co-resident, they are distant from their children. Are these widespread perceptions that families are increasingly 'fatherless' justified? Underlying this is a second issue that we will briefly explore but cannot develop far as we lack the relevant data: the redefinition of the roles of men in terms of their relationships with their children (see Marcil-Gratton *et al.* 2003).

Taking the first question, the NZW:FEE gains us some fragmentary insights. This survey of women included a battery of questions on children they had borne or adopted, stepchildren or minors for whom they were in some way responsible. By examining the data on the experience children had of sole parenting, 'defined by whether the child's mother is living with a partner or not' (Hutton 2001: 4), it is possible to compute indirectly the number of children who, by a given age, were likely not to have a co-resident father.

By one year of age, the level varied by birth cohort from 4% for Baby Boom children born 1953–60 to 8% for those born 1981–85. The rate then jumped to 11%, perhaps because of the divorce law changes described earlier that were introduced just before this, but then subsequently rose only very slightly. Interestingly, the inflection at this time paralleled the experience with divorce trends. The result for birth cohorts that had reached fifteen years is different and rather surprising: relatively less inter-cohort change. Nineteen per cent of the birth cohort of 1953–60 had experienced life in a sole-parent family one or more times by fifteen years, whereas for the cohort of 1976–80 the rate was not much higher, at 25% (Hutton 2001: 5).

This also suggests that 75% of children have fathers who will still be part of the co-resident family when they are teenagers. The detailed shifts by age documented by Deborah Hutton (2001: Table 1) suggest, however, that there has been a recent shift downwards in the age by which children's fathers may no longer be a part of the household. But there is no commensurate growth in the proportions gone by the time the child is older. In other words, the overall cumulative probability that a family will lose a co-resident father is rising only slowly, but the marital break is now likely to have occurred when the children are younger.

The second issue, the redefinition of the role of fathers, comes about through the changes in family forms, in work patterns and in their interface described in detail in Chapters Six and Seven. The demographers Nicole Marcil-Gratton, Celine le Bourdais and Heather Juby argue that this role has changed because of 'important modifications that touch family life as this affects children, women and men . . . [but that it is men] who have had to face if not the most spectacular of challenges, perhaps the most difficult to contend with' (Marcil-Gratton *et al.* 2003: 145). These Quebec authors commence their analysis with a discussion of what they call 'The apogee of the *pater familias* (1945–70)', noting that

> yesterday the definition of a 'good father to his family' could be summarised for men as the exercise of paternal authority, on the one hand, and the taking in charge, on the other hand, of the economic welfare of the family. The Second World War and political imperatives imposed a break in this model: the absence of fathers forced the transfer of paternal authority to wives . . . [who also] took in charge family responsibilities . . . . The 30 years which followed . . . were . . . characterised by the return of paternal authority to the traditional incumbents, [and] the rights and duties of each [person] in the family were clearly defined once again.
>
> From 1945 until the beginning of the 1970s one saw the 'traditional' model of the family, based on the complementarity of roles, reaffirmed, indeed consecrated (Marcil-Gratton *et al.* 2003: 145–46; translation by Ian Pool).

This picture they paint certainly applied as much to New Zealand as to Quebec and Canada in general. In Chapter Five we described the Baby Boom in detail; after that the family landscape changed in complex and confusing ways. Above all, fathers' roles became more ambiguous and also, in many cases, links with their families were diminished. Yet equally for many families there has been an increase in fathers' interactions with their children and the removal of emotional barriers between the authority figure, the *pater familias*, and the remaining family members.

Numerous factors produced the 'transformation of masculine and feminine roles between 1990 and 2000'. Marcil-Gratton *et al.* give a list that probably also applies in New Zealand. Thus there is 'mastery over fertility' (through more efficient contraception), the shift from 'mothers' work to mothers at work', 'access of both sexes to higher education' and the complex patterns of LATs, cohabitation and marriage, all factors that we have described earlier. They also list ways in which the role of 'paternity [*per se* has been] redefined'. Biological paternity can now be documented definitively (through DNA). Despite the pressures coming from work–family imbalances, there are increases in interactions with children for fathers as well as mothers, and particularly for resident fathers (Marcil-Gratton *et al.* 2003: *passim*).

There is another side to this, produced by the 'growth in conjugal instability that sets in train for a growing number of families ruptures in daily co-existence between non-custodial ['*non gardiens*'] parents and their children'. This is most likely to be faced by fathers who have separated from their spouses. In Canada, as in New Zealand, most commonly it is the fathers who live apart under these circumstances and who find it difficult 'to recreate satisfactory linkages with their children, which [often] leads to a progressive disinterest in them'. Then there is the problem of serial paternity, when reconstitution and blending (see below) confronts men (more often than women) with the exigencies of being a distant father to their biological children while playing a daily role as stepfather to the children of their new partner, or, if the children are older, being a 'stepfather-in-law' or a 'step-grandfather'. In some cases this is further confounded by the fact that the blended family may also contain the couple's own biological children, and that the mother involved may also be separated from biological children of a previous union. There are further permutations if and when reconstituted unions break down, and so on. Much of this is the stuff of the popular media and need not be developed further here. But we do need to mention that, beyond these situations, there are what Marcil-Gratton *et al.* term the 'dismissed fathers', a high-profile minority in New Zealand and elsewhere who have had their links with their children severed legally or extremely limited and proscribed, who sometimes are excluded altogether yet often must provide child support (Marcil-Gratton *et al.* 2003: *passim*).

BLENDED FAMILY HOUSEHOLDS

In the last two chapters there was a discussion of trends in divorce and in remarriage. This produces what are termed reconstituted or 'blended' families, consisting of the couple, *his* and/or *her* children, and *their* children. There are few data at a national level on this phenomenon, but the NZW:FEE permitted inferences to be made (Dharmalingam *et al.* 2004: Chapt. 6).

The prevalence rate (women aged 20–59 years who had ever been in a blended family/those who had ever had children) for this type of family structure and form appears to have increased over time. 'Full' blending, where both partners' children from previous unions are involved, is far less common (2.5%) than 'partial' blending (children from the union(s) of one only partner, (15.9%). Overall, 18% of NZW:FEE women respondents had been in a blended union, and this was higher for Maori (25%). There was also an educational difference with levels higher among the less well educated (Dharmalingam *et al.* 2004: Chapt. 6).

Life-table data allow a more precise estimate of the incidence of the blending than the figures just quoted. Here, though, the results relate only to biological offspring. The cumulative probability that a woman will have been a partner in a blended family before she reaches 50 years of age is 28% (42% for Maori; 26% for non-Maori). By age 30 years, 31% of Maori will have experienced such a union, as against 12% of non-Maori, but for the latter by 40 years the probabilities jump to 21% and for Maori they also increase, to 41%. The earlier exposure to blending by Maori is, of course, a disparate impact coming from their much younger childbearing; entering a blended family requires prior childbearing. Conversely, prolonged education and avoidance of childbearing also delays this: at 30 years a woman with no education is four times as likely to be in a blended family than a university-educated woman (Dharmalingam *et al.* 2004: Chapt. 6).

Turning to the children in blended families, one in five of all children were likely to have been in such a household before they reached seventeen years of age (i.e. were no longer dependent). But this rate is increasing, as is shown by the analysis of data on children's birth cohorts. There are no differences by gender of child, but there are by the child's ethnicity and the education of the mother (Dharmalingam *et al.* 2004: Chapt. 6).

Finally, how does the stability or its lack in blended family life affect the children? The duration of time spent in blended families is generally short. One-quarter of such children, overall, had left such a family situation for whatever reason (our data do not allow us to give more precision to this) within two years, 43% by five years. Differentials in this case revolved around two demographic factors: not unexpectedly, how old the child was when blending occurred, and the birth cohort of the child. For children born prior to 1970, cumulative life-table probabilities show that 11% spent less than one year in a blended family; for the children born 1990–95 the level was three times this, indicating, perhaps, that such family types were becoming more stable.

9.4 LESS DIRECT DETERMINANTS OF CHANGES IN FAMILY MORPHOLOGIES

Less direct determinants of changes in family formation, structures and forms were also going through shifts at this time. Clearly, something significant happened contextually in the underlying value systems, policy and the political-economic environment to propel New Zealand families demographically into new territory. This takes us back to an earlier point: as a net result the family may be facing major problems meeting its most basic societal responsibility: replacement of the adult population. Growing polarisation in terms of factors such as income, childcare and access to work also affects the capacities of many families to carry out nurturing and socialisation. To conclude the empirical analyses in this book, we turn to the social and economic contexts of this recent phase of the family transition. Many aspects are continuations of what has been reported for the last few decades but, as the preceding analysis of trends has shown, there has been sufficient and widespread change to raise the questions: is New Zealand at a point of inflection? Is the country entering or has it already entered a new phase?

VALUE SYSTEMS AND THE POLICY ENVIRONMENT

We have argued that in the hundred or so years from the 1870s to the 1970s the New Zealand value system was essentially Pakeha, which seems to have had its roots in the norms of pre-Victorian rather than Victorian Britain. But in the Baby Bust this changed significantly in two ways. First, the Pakeha demographic hegemony was challenged by rapidly expanding ethnic diversity and thus New Zealand saw competing value systems. High and increasing levels of inter-marriage meant that even within one family different cultural traditions could be operating simultaneously, particularly if one goes out beyond the nuclear household and looks at wider families. Secondly, in common with other European-origin societies in the WDCs, Pakeha family norms and values were themselves going through a revolution. In part this had been engendered by the effects of the Pill, not as a simple contraceptive but as the driver of public and private discourse, attitudes and behaviours in the domain of reproduction, sexuality and family structures.

Understanding values and norms is largely dependent on the observation of women and couples who are at family-building ages. Despite
teenagers' high profile in the media, there are far fewer robust data relating
to the reproductive values and behaviours of these young adults: will they
follow the reproductive regimes of those persons currently at parenting
ages or will they go back to the reproductive behaviours of their mothers
or grandmothers, particularly in terms of the timing of first births? Ultimately, this is an unsolvable problem, because, even if we had data on their
attitudes, the one sure rule about reproductive intentions is that they are
poor predictors (e.g. Henripin and Lapierre-Adamcyk 1974).

Beyond this there are other contextual factors involved, many of which
have been discussed already in Chapter Seven, but two points of which jus-
tify brief elaboration. First, European research has shown that the stronger
role for values favouring individualisation and de-institutionalisation, key
elements of the second demographic transition, accompanied and may
have provided the bases for other normative shifts (Lesthaeghe and Moors
1995). These were the changes in attitudes that opened the way for major
assaults on the welfare state, and also built up a value system that minimised
collective and community responsibility and support for families. There
were inter-cohort differences in these shifts in values, with the young, that
is, those at early parenting ages who were to delay childbearing, not unexpectedly more likely to adopt the new attitudes.

In New Zealand, this change in ideology can be found in a wide range
of areas, for example, from an emphasis on family self-reliance (Shipley *et
al.* 1991) to critiques that the state fostered welfare dependency and calls to
pressure beneficiaries, particularly sole parents, into work schemes (OECD
2004: 1–2). Related arguments include the push for vouchers for education so that 'parents [will] have the authority to select their child's school'.
Coupled with this are arguments favouring, for example, decentralisation
of the governance of schools (e.g. www.maxim.org.nz, Media Release, 10
October 2003).

Secondly, in New Zealand's case, after the radical fiscal and financial
restructuring in the late 1980s, central government in the early 1990s introduced far-reaching bodies of social policy that affected almost every aspect
of family life. This occurred most severely in the 1991 Budget (Shipley *et al.*
1991). Ideologically driven policies that were largely theoretical constructs
in Europe, even in Margaret Thatcher's Britain, were turned into actual
policy in New Zealand around 1990. The interest this attracted from afar
constituted a replay, in an opposite direction, of what had happened about
a century earlier, when the dreams of European Fabian socialists were
actually being legislated by the Seddon Liberals in New Zealand.

The 1991 Budget, presented and passed through all legislative steps
under urgency on one day, is thus the most outstanding milestone for this

discussion, as it represented the apotheosis of a revolution that had run the most extreme section of its course by the early 1990s. In a sense the reforms were a standard-bearer in developed countries for an entire philosophy and operational approach that *Guardian* journalist Richard Drayton has characterised as 'Shock, Awe and Hobbes' (2006). The New Zealand neo-liberal programme was restricted to the internal economy, but the measures employed were similar to, although not as severe as (because we were a wealthier country), the structural adjustment programmes forced on the developing world by the IMF and the World Bank. The key point for the well-being of New Zealand families was not just that restructuring of the policy environment occurred, but that unprecedented changes were imposed by extreme policy initiatives that lacked an evidence base beyond ideology. While these extremes are less evident today than they were in the 1990s, significant vestiges of this attitude still persist and are aired in the public discourse.

For this chapter, it is necessary to note that the present welfare and family policy system of the new millennium exists in a framework that comes from our recent past – the restructuring from 1986 to about 1993. This framework, moreover, is not just in the area of family policy *qua* family policy, but extends into numerous adjunct areas that impinge directly on the family, with housing and the student loan schemes as two obvious examples. In the latter case an educational policy becomes a family policy, *par excellence*, because legally families are responsible for their unmarried offspring until they reach 25 years of age (Jackson 1994b, c). Since the end of the most turbulent period of restructuring, from the early 1990s on, the system has been both reinforced and amended. As a result, some of the extremes have been modified to a degree, as in both housing policy and the student loans system. A wide range of other measures and counter-measures have been introduced since 1991 (and its immediate aftermath), but often they relate less to the meta-policy principles that underlay and were clearly spelt out in some of the documents supporting the 1991 Budget, and more to implementation and service delivery. Typically they involve a shuffling of bureaucratic processes and structures rather than really fundamental changes in policy, and often produce agencies or administrative units that have a short shelf-life.

The churning of agencies during the restructuring period and the probable impact of this on the access of families to services was raised earlier when discussing the Baby Bust and Baby Blip. But at the end of the 1990s came yet another bureaucratic reorganisation in an area that was most central to family policy. This was the creation of Work and Income New Zealand (WINZ) from two ministeries, Labour and Social Welfare. This example is instructive as it highlights both the philosophical and operational paradigms that underlie much of the social policy domain affecting families even today. This restructuring attempted to force links between two different spheres of life, work and the family, by addressing unemployment, sole-parent benefits (DPB) and other forms of income support for families, even national superannuation for retirees. But, after major problems of establishment and implementation, WINZ in its original form soon had to be re-restructured. To add to the general confusion, other related functions such as the monitoring of children at risk were also spun-off to different agencies, often accompanied by a total restructuring of tasks, personnel and management.

Finally, as a part of this movement, through the 1990s various changes had been made to the family support measures, most notably in 1996. A feature of these was that they were targeted and minimalist, whereas the old family benefit had been universal. A new initiative in 2004, incorporated into the budget, attempted to cater for families by increasing support, although the measures introduced were not without criticisms (St John and Craig 2004).

ECONOMIC AND SOCIAL FACTORS: HOUSING

In comparison to the Baby Boom, it appears that in the late 1990s and early twenty-first century families, in particular those that are economically disadvantaged, face many problems that limit their capacities to carry out their basic functions for the wider society. Their constraints are both *endogenous* to the family itself, a result of the changes in forms and structures that have occurred over recent decades, and *exogenous*, as a result both of policy changes and the way that the economy has been managed over the last years of the twentieth century. In the latter regard, this discussion is not on economic growth, *per se*, which would be beyond the brief of this study, but more on the effects of the distributional aspects of the economy on family life.

Access to housing is an economic factor that has an immediate effect on family life, but a somewhat anomalous one. It is a social sector issue because quality of housing is a fundamental element of family well-being. For the homeless or those living in temporary or very poor housing, whether owned or rented, it is a 'basic need', as that term is used in the development literature. Need is represented in regions such as the East Coast or parts of Northland where a lot of the housing stock is substandard but owned, while in urban areas some of the substandard stock is rented.

A dwelling is also, however, a market good, a physical capital asset. This attribute puts it in a very different light, shifting the emphasis from social policy needs to meeting the laws of supply and demand. Families approach the housing market, or the rental market, not just to gain minimal shelter, but according to their requirements across a wide range of features including design and location. Unrequited demand, however, can mean that families are placed in a situation where they have unmet social needs. This can arise when the market fails, for example, when the focus in construction is on the building of up-market dwellings for the well-off thus diverting tradespeople away from building ordinary family homes. The market might cater disproportionately to second-home buyers or those seeking property as rental investments, making it difficult for first-home buyers to enter the market. Both these situations appear to have occurred in the 1990s and early twenty-first century, exacerbated for many young couples by the need to service student loans. As one childless woman in Sceats's study (2005) noted, 'It's really uncomfortable to have a mortgage and a student loan. You need to have a house [if you have a baby]'.

Housing is also a key element in the fiscal and financial sectors. It is the average family's major investment and capital asset, and its most common form of savings. It is the basis for local-body rates and, if a rental property, will attract business and personal taxes. In New Zealand, as discussed in earlier chapters, the owned, one-household dwelling situated on a separate section (lot) is the preferred form of dwelling for most New Zealand parenting and post-parenting families. Despite the prescriptions of some economists who would have New Zealanders rent accommodation and invest in equities and assets other than housing, in reality no other significant stock of dwellings exists in New Zealand, and not the higher-density housing such as apartments or the row houses one might find on Coronation Street or even parts of Sydney.

It follows that housing policy must deal with need, which traditionally has been met in New Zealand by public-sector rental housing. But policy also has an impact on many other aspects of housing. In the past there was state support to help young couples achieve ownership, but more recently policy interventions have instead attempted to privilege market aspects, on the grounds that the market was a more efficient provider of housing than the public sector, and this has often had negative effects for families. For example, the de-regulation of the construction industry has had perverse consequences on the quality and even safety of buildings, and the elimination of state-sponsored training and apprenticeship schemes has seen a severe shortage of skilled workers.

Until recently it was a given, almost a rite of passage, for couples wishing to start a family to set up neolocal residence in a house they owned, typically purchased with a mortgage to the bank and often with family assistance. But there has been a decline in home ownership: at the key family-building age-group, for occupiers aged 30–49 years 77% of houses were owner occupied in 1986, but by 2001 this had dropped to 65%. For some types of families, typically the most vulnerable, the declines were even greater: couple-only households saw a decrease in the same period from 77% down to 74%; two-parent (and today typically two-income) households from 80% to 78%; but extended families from 67% to 57% and sole-parent households from 63% to 49% (Pool *et al.* 2005b: 24 and Appendix Table 8).

ECONOMIC AND SOCIAL FACTORS: INCOMES

Growing income disparities by and through the 1990s have had a differential impact on financial resources available to families. Parenthetically, it can be noted that the census data for personal and household (see below) incomes cover all sources, market and non-market, which is very useful for the exercise that we are engaged in here – it allows the researcher to see what is coming into the household each year, although it does not reveal anything about capital assets (e.g. house ownership) that might contribute to wealth. In 1986 the income (inflation adjusted to the 1996 dollar, and age-standardised) at the lower quartile for individuals was $9,753, but by 2001 it was down to $8,164. By contrast the upper quartile had grown from $30,469 to $32,010; and the inter-quartile range had widened from $ 20,716 to $23,846 (Pool *et al.* 2005c).

It is outside the scope of the present book to look at the underlying causes of these growing disparities. But the economic literature does provide some pointers. In their study of trends in income inequalities in New Zealand, Podder and Chatterjee have used sources we have not drawn on here (the Household Expenditure and Income Surveys, HEIS; Household Economic Surveys, HES).* Their conclusion is extremely sobering: 'the bottom *80%* of New Zealand income recipients suffered a reduction in their share of the total incomes paid out, while the top *5%* enjoyed a 25% gain after 12 years of painful restructuring' (Podder and Chatterjee 1998: 26).

They also look at causes and conclude that, 'While it is difficult to connect directly the economic reform measures used in New Zealand with the observed deterioration in [equality], the possible channels through which policy-induced changes in the economy might have been transmitted to the "national cake" can be, and have been identified'. They note three causal factors: first, the 'sharp increase in unemployment'; secondly, the 'distortions of the financial markets, which saw the nominal interest rates soar to unprecedented levels in the later 1980s'; and, thirdly and '[m]ore significantly,

---

* The HEIS and HES are based on samples and therefore subject to sampling-error problems, which censuses avoid, and they are not systematic in coverage. But for economists they have an advantage over censuses in that they separate sources of income. Our interest is far less in this than in the economic impact on the living conditions of individuals and households. Thus we have drawn primarily on studies that employ the census data that are available continuously over much of the post-war period.

perhaps, the drastic cuts in welfare benefits put in place in 1991 [that] despite being directed towards the poor somewhat better, failed to stem the tide of rising overall inequality because of the inadequacy of the transfers'. They also point to a factor exogenous to New Zealand, and thus outside its domestic control, that served to reinforce the endogenously induced trends coming from restructuring: the demand for highly skilled labour coming at that time from a global industrial labour-force transformation towards information technologies and other factors of the 'new economy' (Podder and Chatterjee 1998: 25; and Chatterjee and Podder 2002).

The trends and differentials for household incomes have been marked. Essentially, as we will show, the parenting households have been disadvantaged and the gaps have increased since 1986 for the most vulnerable (sole-parent) families. Even worse, these are the families that, disproportionately, are likely to be bringing up the national stock of children.

Household-income computations are more complex than those for personal incomes, involving not just inflation adjustments and age-standardisation (based on the age of the occupier to take account of factors such as the disproportionate presence of, for example, superannuitants' households), but also what is termed equivalisation. This is a calculation which allows the household structure, adult and child, to be taken into account.[*] These computations do not take account of the way income is shared in reality within New Zealand households (see Fleming with others 1997).

For New Zealand, between 1986 and 2001 median household incomes as a whole actually fell, albeit by only $91, and there were increasing inequalities between regions and types of families. The inter-regional range had been $12,975 in 1986, but had risen to $15,722 by 2001, between Wellington ($41,181, just above Auckland) and the West Coast ($25,459, just below Northland). Over the fifteen-year period 1986–2001, equivalised, age-standardised and inflation-adjusted household incomes rose in six regions, modestly in most (below $404) but very significantly in two of these, Auckland (by $4,119) and Marlborough (by $3,290). In the latter case this was from a low base, so that in 2001 they were still $1,600 below the national figure ($33,557 in 1996 dollars). Moreover, three regions saw extreme declines: Northland (-$5,591), Gisborne (-$4,226) and the West Coast (-$3,129). In seven other regions modest declines were recorded (less than $384). Finally, in 2001 there were only two regions in which household incomes exceeded the national level: Auckland and Wellington. Waikato was the only region that had a level that was less than $1,000 below, but its household income still fell $7,566 below Auckland. Thus by 2001 there was

---

[*]   We use here a formula for equivalising designed by John Jensen of the Ministry of Social Development.

marked polarisation between regions (Cochrane *et al.* 2007; also Mowbray 2001, who uses survey sources, see 374n).

There were also major differences between incomes for different household types, by age of occupier. In 1986 sole parents at the key childrearing ages (25–54 years) had incomes that were about half of the figure for all households headed by an occupier of this age. But in real dollar terms by 2001 these had fallen by 16% (25–34 years), 16% (35–44 years) and 13% (45–54 years), and were thus even more disadvantaged by comparison with households as a whole.

Among so-called family households at family-building ages, couple-only households were the best off in 1986, being in receipt of a median income, for example, of $57,931 at ages 25–34, and saw increases in their median incomes over the fifteen years, for example by $2,529 at ages 25–34 years. At 25–34 years in 1986, two-parent households started off well below the figure for all households at this age-group (-$4,028), improved their real income by 2001, but the gap had widened (-$7,530) by comparison with the overall figure at this age ($40,104). At ages 35–44 and 45–54 years they were far below the level for their ages for all households in 1986 and, though the gap narrowed, significantly so at 45–54 years, they had still not caught up. The attempt at catch-up in financial well-being during the years 1986 to 2001 could only be achieved by major increases in the proportions of parenting households that brought in two incomes. Obviously, this is an impossibility for the sole-parent family, but these financial gains were being achieved by childrearing couples at a cost in terms of quality of life, as families struggled to manage work–life imbalances (Cochrane *et al.* 2007).

It is when the data on quartiles are considered that the negative impacts of economic restructuring on the family are most clearly seen. As is very clear in Table 9.13, the most advantaged are couple-only households, most of which will be dual earner with no responsibilities for children, and the most disadvantaged are sole parents. For all age and household-type categories, the 25th-percentile levels barely changed, whereas for the 75th percentile they went up very significantly for couple-only households, both absolutely and relatively, and relatively speaking also for two-parent households. In their case this was not so much because personal incomes increased – as shown above there were only modest gains even for the upper-quartile incomes – but because the two-adult households became two-earner households, often by force of circumstances. The sole-earner household would have to struggle to make ends meet.

The sheer advantage of being a childless household stands out here. At each age-group the growth alone in the household income of couple-only families at the 75th percentile equals or exceeds the *total income* (all sources) for sole parents at the 25th percentile. Even at the 75th percentile, sole-parent incomes are half those of other parenting families, and only a quarter to a third of those of couple-only households. Moreover the gaps between sole-parent and all other family household types have been growing in real dollar terms.

Table 9.13: Family Households at Key Parenting Ages, Income Quartiles, 1986 and 2001 (in 1996 dollars)

	1986			2001		
Age-groups	25–34	35–44	45–54	25–34	35–44	45–54
Non-parenting families:						
Couple only						
25th percentile	42,949	37,289	32,199	44,609	38,151	34,602
75th percentile	73,163	74,442	64,630	85,140	85,669	78,315
Parenting families:						
Sole parent						
25th percentile	8278	12,150	12,549	9805	**11,327**	**11,774**
75th percentile	20,488	27,239	34,487	**19,126**	**25,105**	**31,253**
Two parent						
25th percentile	22,044	25,880	25,046	22,874	26,904	26,522
75th percentile	38,498	47,609	49,174	45,099	58,805	64,578
Extended (3+ adults, plus children)						
25th percentile	24,916	29,665	31,717	**23,055**	**25,462**	**28,661**
75th percentile	43,610	55,210	63,851	49,581	**54,526**	67,620

Source: Cochrane *et al.* 2007. Values for 2001 that fall below those for 1986 are in bold. Medians and detailed data are in Dharmalingam *et al.* 2007: Table 9.3.

The two-parent and extended-family households have similar low 25th-percentile levels, but sole-parent households fall far below them and couple-only far above. In the case of sole parents the inter-quartile ranges dropped – in fact at most ages and for both quartiles, their real incomes dropped over the period. For the other categories the 25th quartiles remained almost unchanged, but the 75th quartile grew very significantly, and thus inter-quartile gaps increased.

Thus the message to families in the early twenty-first century is clear: if a couple wants to maintain their financially advantageous situation, they should remain childless. Even the two-parent household, the classical nuclear family, kept its head above water simply by ensuring that both partners worked, something that had not been as necessary in the 1980s.

ECONOMIC AND SOCIAL FACTORS: THE IMPACTS ON THE HOUSEHOLD AND ON CHILDCARE

A related issue is the way in which the economy has been managed at a micro-level, in terms of human resources (as against human capital). Today in the ESCs the trend is not just for childbearing polarisation, but also for increasing differentials in access to and quality of childcare. In turn this often parallels a dichotomisation into 'work rich' and 'work poor' households (McDowell 2001: 452), an issue alluded to earlier. Typically, polarisation is between the high- and low-income families. The former are frequently late-starting parents, who have the means for 'suburban', or quasi-suburban inner city (say a large owner-occupied row house) childrearing, as well as the capacity to buy quality childcare. The latter households, particularly if subsidised or free childcare is not available, may have to spend a considerable proportion of their earnings on childcare, choice of which may be determined more by cost and location than by quality (Sceats 2002). Family incomes also play a role: 'In the United States, women's childcare choices are circumscribed by their economic resources' (Rindfuss and Brewster 1996: 282). Obtaining quality childcare in ESCs such as New Zealand, where there is limited state support (compare France), is most easily achieved by women in full-time employment in high-status jobs.

Moreover, those who opt to combine parenting and work may need to limit the time at home spent caring for a very young child. In the surveys conducted by Janet Sceats, those respondents who returned to work early typically had some misgivings. The reasons they gave are complex and manifold: they include financial need, job insecurity, the need to retain skills and career progression – there was little evidence that rampant consumerism, the charge often levelled at working parents, was a key driver. Two of Sceats's respondents repudiate that charge (2003):

> I think there is an attitude that you are only working for selfish reasons rather than because you have to, and I don't think people realise that you are really forced to go to work if you want to feed your children properly and clothe them properly.

> It hurts. It cuts pretty deep when people say you should be at home with your kids . . . I don't actually have a choice. Well I could choose to be at home, but the pressure that that would put on the family financially, it's not worth it. It's actually better that I carry the stress and not the whole family.

For some women a number of reasons apply but, while most wanted to return to work for whatever reason, the return to the job early created tensions for them. One woman expressed poignantly a view that was commonly held. Referring to putting her son in childcare, she said 'It broke my heart to leave him'.

Thus, in New Zealand, there has been a steady increase in the proportion of women whose youngest child is under the age of two being in the workforce, from about a quarter in 1976 to almost half of such women in

2001. There is a growing trend in several ESCs, including New Zealand, for women to return to the workforce when their children are very young, often under one year of age, and who are being placed in the charge of non-family care-givers, either in their own homes or in various types of childcare facilities (Sceats 2002, 2003; Sceats *et al.* 2003).

If older cohorts represent some type of norm, then the return to work was occurring much more rapidly than in the past, as is very clear in Table 9.14. By the time the cohort born between 1972 and 1981 were having their children (in the late 1990s), one-quarter who went back to work or to study had done so before their baby had reached three months of age, almost half did so within six months of parturition and more than half before twelve months had passed. For some this was by choice, but for many it was because of economic and career pressures.

Table 9.14: Cumulative Percentage (Life-table Values) of Women from Various Cohorts Returning to Work/Study, by Age of Youngest Child at that Time (of All Women who Returned to Work/Study)

Mothers' birth cohort	Duration after parturition			
	<3 months	<6 months	<12 months	<2 years
1937–51	11	15	19	22
1952–61	11	20	32	36
1962–71	20	29	42	50
1972–81	25	41	58	64

Source: Sceats 2003: Table 5, drawing on NZFFS data.

This table reflects the situation before the introduction of the recent paid parental leave provisions. But even with these reforms the choices New Zealand couples have available to them are far less generous than those of which many North-west European parents can avail themselves (Gornick and Meyers 2003: Table 5.1).

In New Zealand since the early 1990s such care, including that of infants, has been considered to be part of the early-childhood education system and controlled by the Ministry of Education, in contrast to the situation in the Nordic countries and France, where emphasis is more upon the welfare, security and socialisation of the child than his or her education. At a workshop on low fertility in Tokyo in November 2002 (National Institute for Population and Social Security) debate on this issue split participants into two distinct camps: an American participant favouring vouchers and arguing about educational goals for childcare; the Europeans emphasising safety, security and socialisation in state-funded, universal pre-school centres.

Women who have the financial and other means for childrearing, including the capacity to buy quality childcare, will often have achieved these by delaying childbearing to pursue their education and establish a career. As a result, many among them may end up childless even though they may have wished to have a family or with a completed family size smaller than they might have desired. On the other hand there are the less well-off who start childbearing earlier and end up having larger families. Their childbearing pattern prevents them from gaining the better qualifications that would afford them a comparable family environment or quality childcare for their children. They are faced with a struggle on welfare benefits or low incomes gained by whosoever of the couple has a job. Some, however, go to heroic lengths to change their situation, undertaking retraining and upskilling when their children are very young so that they may re-enter the labour force at a better level when their children are less dependent (Sceats 2003).

With targeting, couples ineligible for benefits may find it especially difficult to provide for their children and both parents may need to work. This is further complicated when males face unemployment, low-paid jobs or when they are self-employed, a very common situation in New Zealand. The overall changes in labour-force participation over the last two decades saw increases in levels for women, both in areas where they had not been represented historically (e.g. some business sectors) and in those where they had been clustered (e.g. public sector service jobs such as teaching, nursing and welfare). But it also saw decreases in employment opportunities for men, particularly in those sectors in which, traditionally, they had been concentrated, for example manufacturing. The household income effects of this phenomenon are reported for the United States: 'At low levels of [male relative income], young people learn to look at the income-producing power of female earnings: the income effects on fertility of a woman's earnings increases at such times' (Macunovich 1996: 251).

A net result of these shifts in workforce participation in the ESCs is that there is now not only demographic (reproductive) but also benefit polarisation (see also Eckert-Jaffe *et al.* 2002), between those families that need and seek welfare and those who do not seek it, even when they may need it. It is this dichotomisation that undoubtedly drives the moral panic prevalent in the ESCs, expressed often in terms that have strong eugenics overtones: the 'wrong people' having children (for New Zealand, see Bassett 2003a, b). That the higher-profile early-childbearing groups are also often the more visible minorities, adds to polarisation in public discourses. The policy response has not been to formulate family-friendly policies relating to work and childcare that might bolster reproduction and aid families to socialise and nurture their children, but to argue for rather punitive measures that aim at pressuring the unmarried poor not to have children (*Contract with America* 1994; for New Zealand, see Richardson 1995: 213–14).

PROPS AND SUPPORTS ENDOGENOUS TO THE FAMILY: NETWORKS, GRANDPARENTS

Some support systems and props are endogenous to the family itself. Clearly family networks are the instruments through which support can be garnered for members who face problems. These include not only assistance with childrearing and childcare, but also looking after older members of the family, financial support for actions such as house purchase, and so on. It must also be recognised that these transactions may be multi-directional – a grandmother may help with childcare while her children help meet her own needs. Numerous transactions in different directions may be occurring simultaneously.

This again raises issues, first discussed in Chapter Two, around the definition of the word family: the difference between a kinship approach, as in anthropology, and the use of co-residence as the conceptual basis, as is the statistical norm. As was noted, both approaches are flawed; neither captures adequately the exact morphology and dynamics of the family, of its kin and of its affines. The net result is that this area is extraordinarily difficult to research, yet remains fundamental to all of social life.

At a population level there are few data on the parameters of support, either the networks involved or the prevalence, directions and forms it takes. Nevertheless, three recent studies have thrown some light on these. From the NZW:FEE Maggie Hope looked at networks for both Maori and Pakeha. As might be expected Maori support networks were both more *extensive* and, to the degree that this could be assessed from the NZW:FEE, more *intensive*. But once size of family of orientation was controlled for the differences diminished. There were major interactions between the timing of family formation and the life-cycle stage (Hope 1997).

McPherson's recent (2000) study explores this further. Her results are sobering: 'the potential supply of family members to provide support does not exceed the demand for support, and then there is still a need for state-provided services. This is particularly so for the cohort born 1972–76 in New Zealand, currently in their 20s'. Nevertheless, 'some New Zealand policies which attempt to involve families are doing it in a top-down way which still denies families the choice *not* to be involved . . . [having a] negative impact . . . [that] often leaves them unable to cope' (McPherson 2000: 174–76).

The Mid-life Transactions Programme looked at the links between family members aged 40–54 years, their own generation, and those above and below. A major finding is that mid-lifers provide support to both the generation below (children) and the generation (above). However, the nature of support differed. While support given to children was material in nature, the support given to parents was both emotional and material (Koopman-Boyden *et al.* 2000, esp. the chapter by Hillcoat-Nalletamby; also Hillcoat-Nalletamby and Dharmalingam 2001).

A re-emerging issue is the role of grandparents in direct involvement in childraising and other family issues. Because of declines in family sizes and delayed childbearing, many persons entering retirement may never be able to assume a grandparent role as they may not have any grandchildren. Paradoxically, increases in extended longevity should have privileged this opportunity.

The analysis of the roles and functions associated with becoming a grandparent is not a highly developed research field, possibly because most family researchers are at middle ages or younger and, as with much of the economic literature on ageing, have a generation-centric approach which leads them to see the elderly in terms of a familial or fiscal burden. Thus, in contrast, say, to marriage and divorce, there is little on achieving grandparenthood, which is often associated with, and as important in its way as, reaching retirement. For many older people it is one of the more positive aspects of the ageing process. While we cannot report empirical studies on this issue, anecdotally, among both Maori and Pakeha, for older parenting-age women and couples, and their parents, there is some *angst* about the creeping growth of infertility.* At grandparenting ages, there is a not unrealistic fear that their generation might be the first in recent memory in which a significant minority will never be grandparents. The discourse relating to this is often entered into hesitantly and in sorrow, and even sometimes as a confidential comment, that there are 'no signs of any grandchildren'.

For persons and couples leaving middle age, there is a common pre-sumption that grandparenting will occur when they are in their fifties or early sixties. For the parents who are delaying conception today, however, grandparenthood may not occur until they are in their late sixties or seventies, if their offspring follow the pattern of very late childbearing that the current parenting generation has pursued.

From the fragments of information available, it seems that, historically, by sheer dint of circumstances grandparents were often co-resident and directly involved in the daily lives of families. For their part families frequently had to look after these elderly members, but in return may have inherited material or other assets, or received other benefits. But the neolocal residence of young couples that reached its apogee in the Baby Boom limited this exchange, and thus relationships became less frequent and more ritualised. The nurturing role was vested in the mother, who in that

* This is a comment frequently made when more general research findings on declines in fertility are presented in public; for example, as at a seminar on low fertility in New Zealand at the Institute of Policy Studies, VUW, on 26 October 2006, where the issue of grandparenting was raised repeatedly by participants.

gender-segmented society stayed at home to look after the house and family. In the Baby Bust and Baby Blip the separate spheres for grandparental and parental roles were enhanced by the fact that grandparents were sometimes still quite young and still working, or if retired had shifted to retirement zones away from their children and grandchildren. Furthermore, at the same time more and more young New Zealand couples were living overseas and carrying out their childrearing there (cf. Short *et al.* 2006).

By the 1990s and the period leading to the Baby Deficit, however, inter-generational relations had started to change in significant but subtle ways. With higher and higher rates of female labour-force participation, even very soon after a baby is born (see Table 9.14), the availability of a grandparent, most often a grandmother, has become a sometimes crucial element in the nurturing of children of working parents. One of the respondents of Janet Sceats's survey (2003) put it this way: 'I had my Mum . . . . She is like the rock in our family because she will be there for us in a heartbeat'.

Ironically, then, in this era of Baby Deficit, the function of grandparenting is becoming critical in a new sense: the difficulties of reconciling work and family life noted below mean that many parents have major problems with childcare, in its many different manifestations. While childcare services have increased both in quality and quantity in recent years in New Zealand, the cost of quality care remains an issue, as does the lack of such care in or near workplaces, particularly outside major urban areas. Safety, cost and back-up care in emergencies are the concerns of many working mothers, many of whom increasingly are turning to grandparents to take on the role of child care-giver. This may span a wide gamut of tasks, from limited involvement, such as picking up children from nursery or primary school and looking after them until the parents get home from work, to school holiday care, to total care of children whose parents are absent or unable to provide this.

The grandparent is so important a backup that among working-age respondents in the surveys directed by Janet Sceats there were a number who had given up high-paying jobs overseas and returned to New Zealand specifically to avail themselves of family or whanau support (Sceats 2002; Sceats *et al.* 2003; Sceats 2003; Sceats and Kukutai 2005). Nevertheless, the chances of having grandparents residing near at hand to provide such sup-port are becoming more limited today. This is not just because of decreases in geographical propinquity, the clustering of the young into Auckland and Wellington (Pool *et al.* 2005a) or the New Zealand diaspora, or because the available time of grandparents may be restricted by competing demands, but also because of the age-structural transitions New Zealand populations are going through (Pool 2003). There is polarisation in this as in many other aspects of family life. Some couples who have delayed their child-bearing may have parents who are still relatively young but with decreasing work and other obligations, and thus likely to be able to care for grand-children. Alternatively, others who have delayed childbearing may have older parents who are well into retirement and not only unable to play a central role in caring for grandchildren but in increasing need of support themselves. Lastly, of course, there are families that face physical separa-tion between grandparents and their children and grandchildren. Even in this case grandparents may be recruited to help in emergencies or to allow the parents a break from the burdens of parenting.

Pool and Sceats (2003: Table 9) attempted to give a crude estimate of the role of grandparenting generations, terming it the 'potential for grand-mother support', by computing a ratio between infants and toddlers and women at ages at which they could be expected still to be physically very active and thus possibly available for care-giving. For this they used the measure $P_{0-4}/P_{\text{female, 50-64}}$. In New Zealand's case in 1995, as the Baby Blip had occurred, thereby increasing, as it were, the 'stock' of babies, the ratio was the highest in the WDCs and was, in fact, above the levels seen in numerous other WDCs at the height of their Baby Boom eras (1955). In short, relative to possible demand New Zealand actually has a shortage of potential grandmothers by comparison with other WDCs. This is espe-cially significant because in New Zealand, unlike other WDCs, the state furnishes young parents with minimal supports which might substitute for grandparents or 'co-residential female support' (Short *et al.* 2006).

PROPS AND SUPPORTS ENDOGENOUS TO THE FAMILY: EFFECTS OF MOBILITY

These sorts of family transactions, including grandparents working as carers, or the inverse case of middle-aged couples looking after ageing par-ents, are limited by increasingly complex patterns of mobility. These may involve geographic movements, what is termed 'conjugal mobility' and even cultural shifts (Koopman-Boyden *et al.* 2000). Moreover, the support is not just from parents at retirement ages to their offspring at childrearing ages. The availability of support for elderly relatives is determined by the size of networks, geographical proximity and other factors. Most of the constraints are in fact demographic in form and were mentioned above (see Heenan and Wither 1985: 25–27; and various chapters in Koopman-Boyden ed. 1978).

It is clear that New Zealanders, as individuals and thus probably as families, are highly mobile. Census data are available on the percentage of people who moved between 1991 and 1996, and from 1996 to 2001, but they do not include those who have moved offshore. This caveat aside, the likeli-hood of moving from one place to another within New Zealand increased marginally between the first half and the later half of the 1990s: 52% of the population aged over fifteen had moved during the 1991–96 period compared to 56% during the 1996–2001 period. While movement within New Zealand increased by three percentage points, the increase in movement from overseas was only one percentage point. In terms of age, people aged 15–44 years are most likely to move, followed by the older adult population (45–64 years) and then the older population (65 years and over).

The 2001 census data on ethnicity and mobility show that there are substantial ethnic differentials, with Maori more likely than non-Maori to have moved within New Zealand. But, as might be expected, proportionately fewer Maori moved from overseas between 1996 and 2001 than was true for the non-Maori population – Maori immigrants can come only from Maori resident or born overseas. As noted earlier, though, 10% of all Maori live in Australia.

The inter-regional migration within New Zealand showed that there are five regions which had net inflows for the total population during the 1980s and 1990s: Auckland, the Bay of Plenty, Nelson–Tasman, Marlborough and Canterbury. Auckland had consistently high increases across all three periods, 1986–91, 1991–96 and 1996–2001. All the other regions suffered outflows during the last fifteen to twenty years. The three regions with the largest losses are Southland, Gisborne and the West Coast (these last few paragraphs are drawn from Pool *et al.* 2005a).

Adding to geographical mobility is also conjugal mobility, coming from the shifts in family morphologies outlined earlier. It introduces another set of complex factors into the equation and the networks, props and supports for families become complex and risk being diluted. One common example of this was highlighted in a weekend magazine article published just before Christmas in 2005, when journalist Janet McAllister painted a vivid, and probably rather accurate, picture of the 'seasonal minefield for blended families' as they try to sort out and implement the comings and goings and dynamics on Christmas Day (2005; for the demographic dimensions of this see Villeneuve-Gokalp 1999). The complications because of reconstitution and blending must be seen alongside the possibility of a general decline in the sizes of networks coming from decreases in family sizes.

Nevertheless, from careful, micro-simulation studies overseas a somewhat surprising finding has emerged. Because of reconstitution and blending there is actually an increase in the range and size of the 'family network' (Wachter 1997). This does not address the quality of these networks, but logically speaking there is no reason why support from step-family members should be any stronger or weaker than from affines, or even kin. A study in the United Kingdom showed, however, that this logic does not always prevail. There, grandparents differentiated between those grandchildren who were their direct descendants and those that had entered the family though remarriage or re-partnering in the parental generation. This affected not just major issues such as inheritance but extended to recognition of birthdays and other occasions (Lynda Clark, personal communication, 2001).

In a multi-cultural society it is important also to recognise the impacts of inter-ethnic mobility accompanying inter-marriage, discussed earlier. Its importance here lies in its effects on family life, where cultural norms may affect the quantum and quality of support. Traditionally, movement was between Maori and Pakeha and vice versa (Pool 1991; Kukutai 2003). But, recently, this has become more complex, not just because immigration streams have become more varied, but also with the high mobility of New Zealanders travelling and living overseas and, with it, a higher propensity for New Zealanders to meet and marry non-New Zealanders. Thus the New Zealand family is not just likely to be bi-ethnic, Maori–Pakeha, but also to include members from a very wide range of cultural backgrounds. This is the real diversifying of New Zealand at the society's most intimate level (see Archie 2005).

PROPS AND SUPPORTS EXOGENOUS TO THE FAMILY: THE 'NEW ECONOMY'

The policy factors noted above have continued to play a role in shaping at least the contexts of family life, and even perhaps families themselves. This becomes critical in the area of household incomes, where the trend has been for inequalities to grow. Some observers think this can be largely explained by demographic factors (Hyslop and Maré 2001), while an opposite view is that policy changes have been the key factor (Podder and Chatterjee 2002).

In part, these different interpretations result from the fact that changes producing inequalities and other effects have been extremely complex. They comprise work, family and leisure pursuits of people. But, as was raised last chapter, they are especially dependent on the way in which the economy is organised and managed, in particular whether or not family members have jobs, the ways in which they are employed (e.g. casually or on a more permanent basis; full time or part time), the capacities of families to meet basic needs and to be consumers. In responding to the many demands of the 'New Economy' families are, in fact, facing stresses that are historically unique.

Recently the ESCs, especially the United States, have played a major role in developing and branding the so-called 'New Economy'. According to the reviewer of a recent book by Robert Reich, its growth

> encourages a division between the talented few and the routine many: it also
> results in greater insecurity for everyone, leading them to work harder, [and]

promote themselves more relentlessly . . . the traditional job for life provided not just security but structure . . . [although] over the course of history, structure has been of negligible importance in the world of work . . . work has been about survival, and structure has come, if at all, from other sources, for the most part feudal or religious (Seabright 2002).

The higher levels of skill, and the costs involved in achieving these, as demanded by the 'flexible economy' (discussed in the last chapter), create further insecurities between aspirations for structure and progression in the labour force, and the realities of the job market (see also McDowell 2001). For the less skilled, a lack of qualifications produces further tensions (Seabright 2002).

Childbearing and -rearing add further stress: taking time off to look after children may threaten tenure, job status and career development. In Sceats's study of women trying to balance, often because of financial pressures, work and family, a significant number expressed fears about their workplace security, saying that they lacked 'job safety', in spite of policies designed to protect jobs through parental leave provisions (Sceats 2005). Such concerns can be a significant deterrent to having children, as one young woman in this study noted: 'It's not at all secure. I wouldn't get my job back – no way they'd keep it open for 12 months, so I'd be moved aside or I wouldn't get back in. I couldn't do this job if I had kids. It's not fair on kids'. Even those in privileged positions as highly trained professionals are not immune to fears that their careers are vulnerable once they have children, particularly if they opt to work part time when their children are young:

> There are no opportunities to nurture my career, it's barely ticking over. I'm holding back the waters and keeping myself barely employable. What am I missing – full inclusion at work, I need to foster contacts in my profession, exposure in conferences, speaking, keeping abreast. I'm barely able to do update reading unless driven by work (Barrister working for a government agency).

Tensions and even severe hardship have also come from the decimation of traditional manufacturing in countries across the WDCs, and the resultant job losses there, against the growth of financial and information industries increasingly concentrated in major metropolitan areas. In New Zealand this change was particularly rapid and brutal, with job losses far exceeding demographic changes in labour supply. The most extreme impacts fell on manufacturing and other production and processing jobs. As we noted above, it was typically men in manufacturing and some clerical industries who most keenly felt the impacts of this restructuring (Honey and Lindop 1997), and this has had an effect on family life.

In the 1980s and early 1990s, New Zealand and other ESCs had entered enthusiastically into restructuring, emphasising flexible labour markets (discussed in detail earlier), contracting, out-sourcing and similar management strategies. Accompanying this have been major shifts in ESC family policy environments, taking away many of the mechanisms for reconciling family life and the workplace (OECD 2004: esp. Recommendations; see also Department of Labour 2004). These changes produced unforeseen consequences, not just in the way the work schedule impinges on the family's time together, but in the well-being of the children and even the propensity of families to be 'dysfunctional': a family in which the parents' job schedules force them to be at work at overlapping or simultaneous times may not be able to provide adequate parenting for their children.

In contrast, familialism in Southern Europe or the public policy frameworks of the Nordic countries may be better adapted to achieve a higher degree of harmonisation between work and family life, but as yet countries like New Zealand have not created viable, alternative props and structures to meet the effects of changes in work–life balances. This sets us alongside the United States and also makes us different from Western Europe. In European WDCs, for example, few parents work non-standard hours – a pre-requisite for real labour market flexibility. Moreover, 'families headed by employed parents are less likely to be poor', and 'children in every one of these [European countries] are also doing better [than America] on dimensions ranging from infant birth weight to adolescent childbearing' (Gornick and Meyers 2003: 9–10).[*]

Another almost contradictory feature has emerged. Some members of the workforce are working very long hours – in fact, New Zealand workers work longer hours than employees in most WDCs. For some, working 50 hours or more a week, these levels increased between 1986 and 1996 and then 'plateaued out' through to 2001. But there was also a polarisation of work hours between those working long weeks and those who by choice or because of job availability had a short work week. Levels of part-time employment have grown rapidly, especially for the young (Callister 2004; see also Honey 2001).

These changes may have affected family structures in New Zealand in two ways. As already noted, most frequently it is skilled women who will have delayed pregnancy in order to train and to gain significant career experience. This shows in the data on education and cumulative fertility in earlier chapters, and those on reproductive polarisation presented earlier in this chapter. A recent paper, cited earlier in this chapter, comparing the

---

[*] Their conclusions are based on the most powerful cross-national data source available in this area, the Luxembourg Income Study, covering most WDCs but unfortunately not New Zealand.

United Kingdom and France, pinpoints the effects of this and of the tensions that this produces. In Britain

> State intervention is minimal, while France practised a generous family
> policy. The net result is that social polarisation of fertility is significant in
> Britain but not in France. Becoming a mother or moving to higher parities
> is more difficult for better educated British women than for their French
> counterparts (Eckert-Jaffe *et al.* 2002: 491 and 507).

These factors must be among those that explain why France has maintained a consistent and relatively high level of fertility by WDC standards (Letablier 2002). Three qualitative studies, for example, carried out in the ESCs, in England, New Zealand and Australia (Cairns *et al.* 2002; Johnstone 2002; Sceats 2002 and 2003), show that highly qualified, career-oriented women often have the financial means to purchase private-sector childcare when they have only one child, but that it becomes increasingly difficult to sustain full-time work once they have a second child. The relationship between education and fertility is thus two-way: not only is it those women who avoided early childbearing who have the qualifications referred to here, but across these studies covering three ESCs a significant proportion of respondents reported that they were working more to retain their job skills than for the income left after childcare costs had been met.

The focus of this book is the family, but we need to acknowledge its reciprocal: the workplace. It needs mentioning because it affects the self-esteem of women as employees, as individuals and within families. While there are stresses on the family life side of the equation, there are often also tensions at the work end. Many women feel that they have difficulty in meeting their employment obligations. In Sceats's surveys (2003, 2005) this issue came up time and time again. For example, on balancing work and family: 'It impedes your feeling of satisfaction in everything you do because you can never be the best mother that you want to be, and you can never be the best employee you would like to be' (2003). Another, reflecting the contemporary workplace environment in which many parents find themselves, lamented: 'I don't feel like I'm giving everything. I used to work till six or seven. I need 60–70 hours to do this job, and I have to do it in 40, and I can't do it. I get by, but I am never on top of it' (2005).

THE IMPLICATIONS FOR NEW ZEALAND FAMILIES

For all women, pregnancy and childbirth involve spells outside the labour force, requiring complex coping strategies that vary enormously (Hillcoat-Nalletamby and Baxendine 2005). For some women, for example, the length of time before they return to work after parturition may be very short indeed (Sceats 2002, 2003). The net result of spells in and out of work to meet the demands of childbearing and -rearing is that some life goals, such as saving for retirement, are difficult to achieve (Marsault 1999).

As noted earlier, job loss among men, especially in less skilled and manual occupations, has often meant that women enter the labour market as the principal breadwinner, on whom the family, in the absence of comprehensive benefits, becomes dependent. This was shown for East Germany, where the fall of the Berlin Wall saw many industries unable to compete with those in the West. Similar pressures exist for sole parents whose households on average have the lowest incomes (Konietzka and Kreyenfeld 2002; for New Zealand, see Johnstone and Pool 1996). These tensions have been increased by the 'Workfare' and related schemes introduced by public policy agencies in numerous ESC jurisdictions, aimed at getting women, in particular sole mothers, back into the labour force. For example, Britain 'has bought into the workfare ideal . . . Mothers of dependent children are now expected to work' (McDowell 2001: 452). There are calls for cutting welfare, and these are linked to fertility, but such links are retrospective, applying to those who have children already. It is the early starters and women from minorities who are disproportionately affected by these policies.

Families not on welfare may also face pressures coming from the economic costs of childrearing, increasing expectations and values surrounding quality of childcare, including regulations relating to equipment that is legally deemed 'safe'. An example in automobile-dependent New Zealand, a country that lacks adequate public transport, is the regulation relating to toddler car seats that meet prescribed safety standards. They are costly, while their use has the effect of limiting the number of children able to be carried in a typical family car, a contrast with the Baby Boom when three to four would be transported unrestrained. The costs of education are also an issue, even where children attend public schools but families are required to fund extras. Health care is also a cost that families are increasingly expected to carry (Sceats 2003, 2005).

For an increasing proportion of families, financial survival depends on both partners working full time. The costs of housing, basic needs and the demands noted above place pressures on them. In many families these are often met only by spouses working complicated shifts, including midnight to early morning, that allow one parent to be on hand for the children while the other is working, and then to change roles.

The reality for many families is worse than this. The burden of economic restructuring in the mid-1980s to early 1990s was borne disproportionably by families with younger parents and those already on low incomes (Pool and Johnstone 1996). Perhaps most disturbing is a series of seemingly interconnected changes, most affecting ages 30–44 years, showing up in national and regional data. Data on this age-group provide the most sensitive indicators of the vulnerabilities of families, their capacities to bear, socialise and nurture children and also their job participation rates and thus their capacities to contribute to economic productivity. At these ages, male labour-force participation rates dropped very significantly in the late 1980s, and the inter-regional ranges that had been low in 1986 grew by 1991 and remained high. Female rates dropped in the late 1980s and then increased, but more than a third of women were working part time. Male part-time work also increased. Full-time equivalent levels of participation for men had increased by the late 1990s, but this failed to meet the demographic supply: that is, there was more rapid growth in the numbers of persons likely to be family breadwinners and available for jobs than in the work at their disposal. Moreover, at this time many men in this age-group were among the discouraged worker population (Pool *et al.* 2005d).*

By the early 1990s many families were in a vulnerable situation. Many male employment avenues had been gutted by restructuring, whereas women frequently could step into the breach for their households by entering the expanding part-time service industries, or the areas of the economy that were growing rapidly (Sceats and Kukutai 2005). This was composed of the seemingly more highly skilled managerial and professional occupations, but many of which were really upgraded or repackaged jobs of the type in which women had always been over-represented: teaching, nursing and clerical jobs, now often rated as managerial, in finance, banking, retailing and real estate. To step aside from this employment in order to focus on the bearing, socialisation or nurturing of children would deplete the family of a significant, perhaps the major or only, source of earnings and thus render it more vulnerable.

In addition this period saw a marked rise in the number of households with no adult member in paid employment, the so called work-poor households (Singley and Callister 2003a and b). Such households increased in number from around 13% of all households in 1986 to over 20% in 1993, before returning to close to 1986 levels in 2002 (Singley and Callister 2004: 17). Despite this, the overall proportion of children living in work-poor households remains some five percentage points higher (14%) in 2002 than in 1986 (9%). At the same time the proportion of childrearing households amongst all work-poor households has risen from around a third in 1986 to close to 45% in 2002.

---

* Official statistical estimates of discouraged workers are limited by the way questions are referenced in labour-force surveys, but a different approach was taken for the estimates cited here: they are based on projections forward of the data on jobs at the 1986 census to give expected jobs. These were then compared with those enumerated at any subsequent census.

It should also be noted that while the work-poor households as a proportion of all households has fallen from its peak in the early 1990s the
absolute number of work-poor households was around 50,000 higher in
2002 than in 1986. About half of this growth occurred amongst one of the
lowest income groups, solo parents (Singley and Callister 2004: 21).

9.5 CONCLUSION: 'THE SHOCK OF THE NEW' OR THE ENTRENCHMENT OF BABY BUST TRENDS?

It could well be that the family forms and structures at the turn of the
twenty-first century are really a function of a period-bound set of unique
determinants. These latter factors comprise the cluster of economic, policy
and social factors discussed above, such as the 'New Economy', the features
of which Will Hutton or Robert Reich have so passionately expostulated.
They are time bound because they result from the dominance of a particular
value system relating to how the political economy should be driven
and managed. This has implications both at the macro-level, in the way
values drive social and fiscal policy, above all the role of the state in family
support and in regulating labour markets, and also at the micro-level as
managerialism affects the work–life balance.

It must be stressed that these same exogenous factors have made the
New Zealand family vulnerable, and this is disturbing. This vulnerability,
particularly in terms of its capacity to meet its societal obligation of
replacement, is more extreme, at least for Pakeha, than at any time in its
history. The period of land loss in the late nineteenth century had a similar
effect on Maori. In their case, replacement and the very survival of the
population at that time had been threatened by low rates of infant and
childhood survivorship. Ironically for Pakeha, anxiety about the family at
the dawn of the twenty-first century is a reprise of fears expressed at the
beginning of the twentieth over the rapid declines in Pakeha fertility levels
that had just taken place.

In the early twenty-first century, observers also see the family as under
threat, but some commentators have attributed this not to family formation
and fertility declines but to family dynamics *per se*, as reflected in shifts in
family forms. These are often seen as eroding familial capacities. The data
presented here on aspects of family form do not by any means negate such
arguments: a number of aspects of forms have been subject to rapid and
quite possibly destabilising change over the recent past. But, as we have
shown here, more frequently factors exogenous to the family have made it
vulnerable, and this is a disturbing situation, for the family is the linchpin
of society. Demographically driven structural changes have not only

played a major role, but, in many cases, are inexorable, with long-lasting momentum effects that are equally deterministic. Yet these changes to the family appear to take a secondary place in public debate than factors that are perhaps more dramatic but also more ephemeral.

It may be that the changes of the last few years cannot be reversed; that New Zealand has crossed the Rubicon. This would mean that we face family change without precedence and which really would shake the very foundations of social organisation. Again, replacement is the function most under challenge. This leads to another conclusion: that the twin factors of viability and vulnerability may induce severe and unprecedented tensions within families, revolving around their capacities and thus their perceived failures to meet social responsibilities of bearing and rearing the new generation. This might be reinforced by society-wide concerns that the family is no longer the cornerstone of social organisation and orderly change.

Unfortunately, there are quite simply few reliable time-series data available allowing the scholar or commentator to evaluate the different conundrums posed in the last few paragraphs, or on which to base conclusions that the family is more capable or less capable of meeting its obligations or more functional or less functional than it was in the past. Instead the knowledge gap tends to be filled with ideology, prejudice and assumptions about the past.

One set of data, the fertility data on which this and the previous chapter have focused, do, however, provide reasonably firm and valid comparisons over time, and even between societies. They relate in particular to one family function – replacement, and its consequences. Family form was shown to be an important factor in earlier years, as marriage patterns determined levels of replacement, yet this is far less important today when union formation is not intimately linked to reproduction. Turning to reproduction, the previous chapter pointed to later and later childbearing on average, and more childlessness, a trend confirmed, it seems, by early 2006 census results (Robert Didham, personal communication). This is a rhythm of reproduction that has no historical precedents in New Zealand.

Turning now to the contextual data reviewed in this chapter, it appears that, increasingly, the props necessary for the maintenance of this prime function of replacement are being pulled away. The stress on couples to meet their social responsibility of reproduction in the absence of these props is likely to create severe problems for families, tensions that again are probably without precedence.

The demographic data reviewed last chapter showed that the national natality will continue to creep downwards unless something is done to reverse the trend. The key seems to rest with changing the tempo of childbearing to exploit the larger Baby Blip cohorts that will be reaching younger reproductive ages from 2010 on. This will need to happen in a way that allows reproductive choice, that allows both women and men to reach their full potential, and that allows both to contribute to production and reproduction, and also to participate fully in the workplace and in the life of their families. The present chapter identified the constraints on the present generation of parents that limit this contribution.

The final chapter contextualises the present chapter's discussion of the near future and the recent past by synthesising the major themes analysed in this and earlier chapters. This allows an assessment of the inheritance on which the New Zealand family of the twenty-first century can draw.

PART THREE: TOWARDS A SYNTHESIS

CHAPTER TEN

Conclusion: Continuity and Change, Parallelism and Polarisation

10.1 TRENDS: DOES FORM FOLLOW FUNCTION?

TRENDS IN FAMILY FORMATION, STRUCTURES AND FORMS

The earlier chapters have described the evolution of the New Zealand family through a transition. Each period covered has not only seen its passage through a different phase, but the playing out of changes, typically with long-term, major social consequences. In the main these consequences relate to the role and functions that the family performs for the wider society. In this regard the mantra of designers that 'form follows function' does not apply. Instead, over the long term the functioning of the family has been most significantly affected by endogenous structural changes, such as size and other aspects of its architecture; its forms have also changed, dramatically and in high-profile ways, over the last few decades. Yet the shifts in forms seem to have had less impact on functions than have structural changes or, at various times (e.g. 1930s Depression; post-Baby Boom), exogenous factors. Over the last few decades in particular, all four dimensions of the family – family formation, forms, structures and exogenous factors – have interacted as its way of life has entered uncharted waters.

The fulfilment of family functions has been put at risk. The main reasons, especially as regards the replacement function, seem to have been, on the one hand, internal structural factors, most notably trends in family formation, and, on the other, the policy and economic environment exogenous to the family. In contrast, the high-profile shifts in forms seem more symptomatic than causal: a bit like the appearance of rashes when the highest fevers and greatest chances of cross-infection have passed.

Both Pakeha and Maori shared the same family tradition, starting at a point when there were high levels of fertility, with those for Pakeha being close to biological maxima. These can be set by reference to populations such as that of eighteenth-century Quebec, whose patterns of family formation were almost replicated by mid- to late nineteenth-century Pakeha, though not quite reaching the extremely high rates observed in Quebec. Such trends were made possible only by early and universal marriage, including widow remarriage.

Maori followed essentially the same model, nearly universal entry into unions at early ages, but in their case the bio-social determinants of reproduction, such as high levels of fetal loss and maternal deprivation, were less favourable in the nineteenth century than was the case for Pakeha. The initial phase of the Maori family transition came not through fertility but because they went through the first of two major periods of improvement in childhood survivorship (occurring in 1895–1910 and 1945–61, Pool 1991: Chapts 5, 6 and 7). Once fetal, infant and childhood mortality declined in significance, Maori attained the same high reproductive rates that Pakeha had achieved in the pioneer period, but for Maori this trend continued until the mid-twentieth century. For Pakeha these levels were never seen again, although a limited reprise to medium levels was to occur in the Baby Boom.

Until recently, for both cultural groups, family formation and fertility unfolded within formal marriage, although the exact forms of this varied. Pakeha weddings were legitimised by civil registration as well as in a church; Maori by customary procedures incorporating community sanctions, although they could also have civil or church weddings. In the Victorian era the involvement of the state as the agency legitimising and recording unions (marriages) was a relatively recent innovation, having replaced the church only at the outset of Victoria's reign. This procedure not only fitted the requirements of Victorian middle-class morality, but also defined contractual needs, such as those relating to marital property, the legitimacy of offspring and rights of inheritance. The governments of the era also used this form of registration as a means of verifying and rationing access to other aspects of civil society, such as benefits and schooling. As the welfare state was instituted and expanded, these links became more and more formalised and routine.

This point has been emphasised here because it raises a very important issue for the rest of the chapter. In reality, as in popular memory, the links between registered marriage, the form of formal union imported by Pakeha colonists as one of the keystones for societal governance, administration and the access to services came from these early days, along with many of the features of family life around which the value system has been built. In fact, as we showed earlier, the value system may go back even further than those of Victorian England: there are indications that some features of Pakeha family life had their roots in the behaviour patterns seen in late eighteenth- and early nineteenth-century England. So embedded were these values that when family sizes began to fall in the neighbouring New South Wales colony in the late nineteenth century, as in New Zealand, there was concern about the viability of the family, a 'panic' that was repeated in later years and yet again, it seems, in the early twenty-first century.

There is an interesting aspect to each episode of panic in New Zealand: typically they were triggered by evidence of some significant demographic structural change: rapid fertility declines in the late nineteenth century; low fertility in the Depression; the high profile of adolescents coming from a cohort that had an inflated size because of the clustering of families of a similar age in the Hutt Valley (Mazengarb Report, 1954); and low and delayed childbearing, along with reproductive polarisation, at the dawn of the twenty-first century. Thus the story told here starts from a foundation of large families and of reproduction within marriage. For Pakeha, because of migration and other reasons, such a pioneer family was nuclear to a degree and neolocal. For Maori, in contrast, residence of the more extended family form, the whanau, was typically in a marae setting that privileged whanaungatanga.

These were the characteristics of the family of yesteryear, and they were relayed, more or less intact in terms of the broader aspects of their forms, until the end of the Baby Boom. For Pakeha – not for Maori – structures changed very significantly over the century from 1870 to 1970, mainly in terms of only two attributes: timing of first birth and family size. Sizes first declined rapidly, then at a gentler pace, only to rise again in the Baby Boom. Changes in forms did occur, but slowly and gently, not radically. Marriage remained the route to parenthood: it was the proportion marrying and the age when this occurred that changed.

For both Maori and Pakeha structural changes in terms of place of residence also occurred. For Pakeha this was suburbanisation and the forming of a nuclear family in an owner-occupied house. This was a sufficiently dramatic phenomenon to have left a record in the annals of social history, literature and popular culture. But its impact on Pakeha society was to be far less dramatic than the wrenching apart of many Maori whanau, a challenge to the very roots of whanaungatanga, that the Maori rural exodus after World War II provoked.

By 1970, for both Maori and Pakeha, a nuclear, suburban family lifestyle prevailed. Maori were struggling to come to terms with this, while Pakeha, in the dying gasp of the Baby Boom, were following patterns of family formation, early marriage and conception, often pre-nuptial, that were to have flow-on effects on family forms over the next two decades or so, mainly through trends in divorce.

LOOKING AT THE LAST THREE DECADES

In the 1970s Maori family sizes declined dramatically, one of several severe demographic shocks this population has sustained since World War II.

One was a good shock in the form of rapid improvements in infant and childhood survivorship between 1945 and 1961, but this had ramifications for family sizes for it significantly increased the proportions of the total population at ages from birth to fourteen years. The other shocks they faced at this time – the rural exodus, the sectoral transformation of the Maori industrial labour force, and the decline in fertility – often had favourable effects, but all carried with them implications that were problematic. Urbanisation produced the 'torn whariki' noted in earlier chapters; Maori family sizes plummeted over just one generation; and the new urban jobs into which Maori had moved were often to be those eliminated a decade or two later when radical economic restructuring occurred.

The 1970s also saw Pakeha family sizes decline, but more modestly. Accompanying this decrease, however, was the shift to later childbearing, the family formation regime that was to become dominant.

Overshadowing the structural changes since 1970, at least in terms of public discourse, for both Maori and Pakeha, were shifts in family forms. In retrospect such a focus seems somewhat counter-intuitive. Certainly this is so in the case of Maori, for the rural exodus and the fertility decline involved far more fundamental and disruptive shifts in family life than the changes in form occurring from 1970 to the present. Be this as it may, popular perceptions of family changes over the 1970s to 1990s for both Maori and Pakeha, and for Pacific peoples who became a significant presence in the 1970s, revolved around shifts in forms, such as the replacement of marriage by cohabitation for first union, divorce and remarriage. These changes in forms often did, of course, translate into structural changes. The growth in the proportion of families that were sole parent or that were blended are just two examples discussed in earlier chapters.

It could be argued that the depth of moral panic about the family witnessed today is because the forms, at least their public faces (for who knows what occurred to the internal dynamics of the families of the days of yore – historians and genealogists may throw some light on these), remained relatively unchanged until the 1970s, even in the face of massive fluctuations in structures. But this comfortable conclusion is dashed by the fact that panics have occurred as much in the past as at present. Moral panic is almost a *sine qua non* of public discourse on the family.

By the late 1990s, the more radical changes in forms seemed to have run their course. But by then more latent and historically unique structural changes were becoming evident, although still accorded less attention than that given to forms. Sub-replacement fertility, late childbearing except for a minority and reproductive polarisation are now the prevalent patterns of family formation and have a major impact on family structures, especially age patterns and the rise of the couple-only household. Other broader changes in the society, notably influxes of Asian migrants and an age-structural transition, are also reinforcing family structural shifts.

In the past there had been polarisation for factors such as patterns of reproduction. But one of the unique features of early twenty-first-century family life is the polarisation across many family dimensions, to name three examples: reproduction, income and access to jobs. Within the limits imposed by low fertility rates on average, levels of reproductive polarisation seemed rather marked.

TRENDS IN REPRODUCTION RATES AND REPRODUCTIVE POLARISATION

An important general conclusion that emerges from the study of family formation in this book is the way in which, over the long span of the history, fertility levels have interacted with reproductive polarisation. This synthesis is supported by the evidence presented in the following two figures (10.1 and 10.2), which show that when fertility levels are higher, reproductive polarisation is much less marked; when fertility rates fall, differentials not just in rates but in the tempo of childbearing open up.

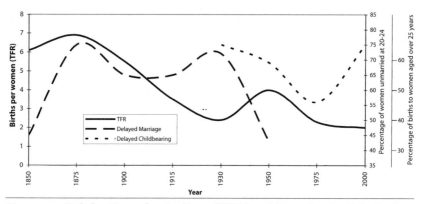

Figure 10.1: Pakeha, Reproductive Rates (TFRs) and Reproductive Polarisation by Age

Figure 10.1 compares trends in fertility, measured by TFRs, with two indices of the age-related type of polarisation, early/late marriage and early/late childbearing, used here because they are easily recorded indicators. High percentages never married at ages 20–24 years, or the percentage of births occurring to women aged over 25 years,[*] signify polarisation into

---

[*] Strictly speaking, the age-specific fertility rate as a percentage of the TFR – see Dharmalingam *et al.* 2007: Table 3.7.

early and late starters of families. But the effect of delayed marriage and childbearing on the age-profile of fertility is merely one sort of polarisation and thus simply a proxy for the other types that have been examined earlier: regional, income, religious, workforce status, socio-economic and so on. The second figure extrapolates from Figure 10.1 to provide a schematic diagram.

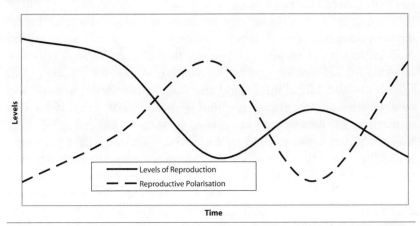

Figure 10.2: Schematic Diagram, Reproduction and Reproductive Polarisation

The percentages never married constitute a reasonably reliable, albeit indirect, indicator of the tempo of childbearing (and thus evidence of age-related polarisation) until the end of the Baby Boom: until then, for most women, childbirth was closely associated with marriage. In this period the so-called nuptiality valve operated efficiently. The data are available for the period since then, but the series is cut off here at 1966 simply because after that cohabitation replaced marriage as the preferred first union and because fertility became dissociated from formal unions, and the nuptiality valve was no longer a controlling factor leading to polarisation. There is an interesting and expected lag effect between marriage and birth trends, and a flow-on from these to the TFR, especially in the 1960s.

Maori data are not included on these graphs simply because their transition was very abrupt, from high age-specific rates in the 1960s to a marked concentration of childbearing at the youngest ages in the 1970s. Their fertility decline was primarily because of limitation at ages 25 years and over, and this strategy not only concentrated births at younger ages but also increased the tempo of childbearing. It is only recently that the tempo has started to change and a gradual shift to delayed childbearing becomes evident.

When fertility rates were extremely high, as was the case for Pakeha in the 1870s or Maori in the 1950s, then clearly the possibilities for polarisation were also minimised (almost every woman in the reproductive span would marry and have babies). But, in the Baby Boom, Pakeha did not have hyper-fertility and thus there was room for differentiation; yet it did not occur on any significant scale: differences were between individuals, not between socially defined groups of mothers.

It is interesting that the overall rates for some parts of the Baby Boom resemble those of Pakeha at the dawn of the twentieth century; yet within these parameters the period around 1900 saw marked polarisation, whereas the Baby Boom did not – at its peak childbearing was almost universal and most births were to women aged younger than 30 years. In 1966, only 24% of births were to women aged 30 years and over; 19% in 1971; and 17% in 1976. It was also only in this second phase of the Baby Boom that effective contraception became available to most women, including those who were unmarried. The data we have just quoted show that it was employed effectively only after family size intentions had been achieved. Thus the tempo of childbearing at that time was highly compressed into the earliest part of the reproductive span, allowing little room for differentiation (Dharmalingam *et al.* 2007: Tables 3.7 and 3.8; see also Sceats 1988, 1999; and Morgan *et al.* 2001). The lack of age differentiation, and near universality drove the lack of social differentials in fertility. In 2001, in contrast, 54% of births were to women over 30 years, and major socio-economic differentials are also evident, particularly by employment status (full time, part time or unemployed).

FROM TRENDS TO FORECASTING

For the family to meet its function of replacement and for the population size to be maintained or to grow slightly, family sizes need to remain around 2.0–2.1 live births per woman. The alternative, replacement migration, is not a systematically viable alternative (Pool 2006). While New Zealand is currently only just below this level the portents, presented earlier, are for the level to go down as it has over recent years. But what if this forecast were wrong, if another baby boom did occur? After all, in the late 1930s similar gloomy prognoses were being made; yet the low fertility of the Depression was followed by the unpredicted Baby Boom.

This leads to one of the most fundamental questions of demographic cosmology: could a baby boom occur again?[*] Or, more realistically, could a baby boom of a modified sort occur again? And, if so, what might be

---

[*] It sits alongside meta-questions such as the limits of human longevity, the impacts of AIDS and the future growth of the planet's population. All these issues have profound and immediate policy implications; none is purely of academic interest.

the modified circumstances? A real baby boom would require a social revolution, involving a return to very early ages at marriage, and, by implication, a radical turnaround in all aspects of work–life balances, and quite probably gender relations and female labour-force participation rates. This seems an unlikely scenario, but there could be others. For example, one might involve a return to the reproductive polarisation of the early twentieth century between those women who had babies (and did not work) and those who worked, were unmarried and childless. Or, if childbearing continued to be delayed, the Irish strategy of the early twentieth century might be adopted: very high marital fertility rates for married women once marriage had occurred (by implication this would necessitate their leaving paid employment). Another alternative could be the introduction of a wide range of extremely expensive pro-natalist policies, which probably would not work.* In the May 2004 Budget speech in Australia, Treasurer Peter Costello saw it this way: 'One for Mum, one for Dad and one for the Country'.

More subtle measures that attempt to speed up the tempo for factors, such as the age of entry into education and career, that affect childbearing are being seriously looked at in Western Europe. But they involve quantum changes in the value system, and significant changes in work–life balance and the policy environment. They might have the effect of raising birth numbers and rates to women aged, say, 25–29 years, and perhaps of systematically pushing the levels of replacement above 2.1 births per woman. To work, such measures would need to be universally accessible and not targeted benefits; one side issue is to reduce factors of polarisation that engender eugenicist attitudes. They would have to ensure, also, that recent gains in levels of attainment of tertiary education and in access to the labour market by young women were not lost, again requiring quantum changes in behaviours and attitudes (Pool 2006; Sceats 2006; discussion at the seminar at which these papers were presented).

These scenarios may seem a little far-fetched, especially if they involve major shifts in norms. But it is equally clear that were a real baby boom to occur, say to raise TFRs to above 3.0 births per woman, its social effects could be extremely profound; forewarned is forearmed. But this does not mean that every time a minor blip in the birth rate or more typically a surge in births at a few hospitals occurs a baby boom is under way, despite the fris-

---

* In seeking measures by which Quebec could succeed in its desire for a 'revenge of the cradles (*la revanche des berceaux*)' by which the French-speaking population would survive and grow, the provincial government funded a carefully designed research study on what might be needed to get Québécoises to reproduce. Despite putting to survey respondents a hypothetical range of extremely costly and politically unrealistic measures across housing, welfare, baby bonuses, parental leave, scholarships and other areas, the simulations showed that the net effect on the birth rate would be microscopic (Henripin and Lapierre-Adamcyk 1974).

sons that typically, and momentarily, sweep the media. Crying wolf like that risks creating issue fatigue and scepticism and trivialising the importance of the issue. Instead, one might applaud the careful monitoring of indicative trends such as that done by the late Gerard Calot and his successor Jean-Paul Sardon at the Observatoire Démographique Européenne, which includes most WDCs, including New Zealand, in its brief. They keep a wary eye month by month on rates in the developed countries, a little like the way experts watch for outbreaks of avian 'flu and other diseases.

10.2 CONTINUITY AND CHANGE

A striking feature of New Zealand family life is the fact that, in the face of often quite dramatic external changes, there has been continuity for some patterns of family formation and structures, or the reprise of reproductive and structural shifts that have occurred in earlier periods. This pattern has been less marked, however, for forms, as these remained more or less unchanged until the end of the Baby Boom. But underlying the value system and the behaviours we see as Pakeha may be cultural patterns imported from pre-Victorian British society.

Restricting our comments to New Zealand itself, the higher fertility and early childbearing of the pioneer period was an antecedent to the Baby Boom. Similarly, the rapid declines in fertility of the late nineteenth century were repeated in the Baby Bust a century later. There had been low fertility in the inter-war period, and even sub-replacement rates in the Depression of the 1930s, but this constituted a gradual change and thus does not qualify as a bust. There are no data permitting an analysis of whether the Baby Blip also had a precedent at the start of the twentieth century, but it is an empirical fact that the late nineteenth-century transition was followed by four decades of low to very low fertility. If the notion of continuity has any validity, then the most recent era of low fertility following the Baby Bust may be expected to last a long time yet.

Obviously the argument of history repeating itself cannot be pushed too far. The Baby Boom peak reached only a TFR of just over 4.0 births per woman, whereas pioneer rates were around 7.0; the first baby bust of the late nineteenth century saw a drop from 7.0 to a TFR of 3.5 and then down to 3.0; the second bust, of the 1970s and 1980s, went to 1.8 from above 4.0 at the peak of the Baby Boom. Nevertheless, in both cases the bust produced rates that were about 40% to 45% of those at the start of the decline – a remarkably similar level of relative change.

In the last few chapters a question raised is whether the changes seen in the 1990s have been so marked and produced such an historically unique situation – above all, the decade-long Baby Deficit – that continuities will be broken and the New Zealand family will never be the same again. If family sizes continue to be small or smaller, down, say, to the 1.5 births per woman or fewer seen in much of Europe, and if childbearing contin- ues to be delayed, or becomes later and later, then this historically unique situation could become the norm. Such a trend would bring with it the age-structural and other societal changes faced by countries such as Italy.

The long-term pattern of very low fertility, also historically unique, seen today in parts of Europe means that this scenario for New Zealand is not without precedents. In this context, it must be stressed that one is dealing with the most fundamental aspect of family structure – the very replacement of society itself. As we noted earlier, this is placing families in a situation of tension, as couples in their thirties struggle to meet not only replacement but additionally the nurturing and social-emotional obligations society expects from them, and also attempt simultaneously to respond to a frequently unsympathetic work environment. Perhaps New Zealand is reaching a point where it encounters fully the paradox posed by Kingsley Davis (quoted earlier): that in an era when many families in WDCs have material conditions at their disposal unavailable to past gen- erations, the family and modern lifestyles co-exist with difficulty. This spectre had briefly appeared in the Depression of the 1930s but was swept to one side in the Baby Boom, that prototypical era of the suburban, neolo- cal nuclear family in its stand-apart house on its quarter-acre lot, only to reappear in the 1990s. At that stage the lack of fit between modern life, even the suburban lifestyle when it could be sustained, and the family seems to have been exacerbated by policies pursued in New Zealand and other ESCs, and by managerialism, the bell-hop of neo-liberal economics.

However, the collective memory of past family life becomes important in this regard, for it not only shapes value systems but also clearly affects the perceptions of policy-makers and political lobby groups. This study has shown that such a memory is sometimes selective. Moreover, any past period is a collection of complex factors never repeated in exactly the same way subsequently.

We have argued that in New Zealand there is still a collective memory of the Baby Boom and this may fashion norms and aspirations of couples. But as a reference period for nostalgia the Baby Boom represents an aberrant era. Not only were fertility rates exceptionally high by twentieth-century standards, it saw a level of homogeneity in Pakeha patterns of family for- mation seen only once before – in the 1870s. Moreover, earlier chapters have shown that many of the key props for family well-being operating in the Baby Boom (e.g. housing support, family benefits) have been removed, so that material realities may increasingly conflict with the aspirations of families.

The selective memory becomes particularly important when looking at the links between marriage, as against union formation, and social cohesion. The family of the past is seen by some commentators as providing a better model than that which is prevalent at present, and for the present that past is typically seen to be the Baby Boom. A lobby group of the early twenty-first century, the Maxim Institute, is explicit about this and its implications: 'For a quarter century we have seen the foundation of our society weakened and the keystone for future generations, the family unit, is now in disarray' (www.maxim.org.nz). Without wishing to denigrate observers who feel this way, it is instructive to note that this is not an historically unique situation: such views have been expressed in the past, even in so-called golden eras. *Guardian* book reviewer Nicholas Lezard muses on a similar phenomenon in Britain: 'A falling birthrate, a decline in the institution of marriage. The 1960s (boo, hiss)? No the 1890s and earlier. Looks like the rot set in earlier than we thought' (1996).

It is true that in the recent past, during the Baby Boom, married families predominated and fertility was high. But on detailed analysis this period looks far from idyllic: the married family was often formed after pre-marital conception had occurred and often dissolved in the quarter century since then – that is, the marital break-up will be attributed to recent events and not to its root causes in the Baby Boom, a symptomatic rather than a causal diagnosis. This is not to argue that the family of today is any better or worse than that of the Baby Boom; it is simply to make the point that it is different, not just in its structures and forms, but also in its policy and economic contexts. As earlier chapters show, in the last two regards – in terms of access to family income support, household incomes, capacity to purchase a house – the family of today is certainly disadvantaged by comparison with those of the Baby Boom.

Even if they preferred to be one income, married and suburban, akin to the modal group in the Baby Boom, families today – except for the small minority who are very well-off or extraordinarily frugal – would be unable to achieve this. Moreover, the oft-stated argument of conservative commentators that the young family of today is financially vulnerable because it is driven by consumerism is only partly true. In reality households also have non-discretionary transaction costs unknown to past generations, or at least to Baby Boom couples: childcare, school 'donations' in public schools, some health costs, unavoidable commuting expenses, regulation compliance costs (e.g. for children's car seats) and few spare hours at their disposal to lay down the family veggie garden, to cite just a few examples. And, in any case, growing household consumption is the motor of the very economic growth so lauded by neo-liberal economists.

This then is to recognise that recent change in the New Zealand family may be a more powerful factor than continuity or replication. Whether the changes in structures and forms are for the better or for the worse is clearly a matter of opinion, although almost all observers would agree that those that interfere with family functions, for example, those impinging on the capacities of many households to meet the needs of their children because of increases in household income inequalities, would be undesirable.

The entire architecture of the New Zealand nuclear family of a parent or parents and their child(ren) in the early twenty-first century is very different in form and structure from its predecessors. It is small; it is neolocal; it may well be reconstituted or blended; and it may comprise only one parent. Some of these factors are new, some repeat past experience.

Today, however, a 'family' is also far more likely than in the past to constitute a couple only or a person living alone, typically a widow(er). Other contingencies, such as mobility, and family formation and reconstitution strategies also mean that, whether a parenting or non-parenting family, it may well be geographically separated from the extended family but paradoxically its potential network may be wider. If one adds this to the economic and policy factors noted earlier, such as student debt, which leads many young adults to remain in or return to the family home at ages when previous generations would have fled the family nest, then it becomes a very different structure from that of the past. Add in the propensity to cohabit and shifts in other aspects of family form and one could argue that change rather than continuity is the norm.

Different though the family may be, this does not necessarily presage its disappearance, disarray or disintegration. One of America's leading family demographers, Larry Bumpass, has argued:

> Asking whether or not the family is disappearing misses the point. What is at issue is not the persistence of the institution of the family but, rather, the nature of family patterns . . . Understanding the long-term character of institutional change should direct social policy towards the amelioration of consequences, rather than an attempt to stem the tide (1990).

10.3 THE FAMILY TRANSITION: KEY FINDINGS AND THEIR THEORETICAL IMPLICATIONS

These findings are of substantive interest for those researchers involved in New Zealand social life. But the transition analysed over the last few chapters may have broader theoretical implications. The notion of a transition was first raised in Chapter Two, where this model was set out to provide a framework for the later empirical chapters. The patterns of family life during pivotal periods in the transition are summarised below for selected decades representing different transitional phases. Figure 2.1, which graphed Maori and Pakeha TFRs from 1840 to 2002, is used to organise this review of some possible theoretical questions. This review produces a finding of wider interest: that changes in the 'props' available to the family assume a major role as drivers of transition phases.

THE 1870S AND 1880S

In the 1880s and previous decades, the material determinants of family organisation and change or the props for family formation, and for the structures and forms observed at that time, revolved for the average Pakeha household around what by contemporary British standards was a rather advantaged life. Above all, the chance to own land or a house was something beyond the dreams of many British Victorian family heads. This was coupled with an adequate diet, based on year-round production in most regions and an over-abundance of meat. The government through its land settlement programmes, public works and assisted-passage migration aided young workers and their families. Those unfortunate enough to become destitute, however, had to turn for help to a parsimonious, chaotic and somewhat punitive welfare system. But for the overwhelming majority, conditions provided a relatively favourable environment in which families could replace themselves.

In part this was a function of the process of economic modernisation to which the colony and then the young Dominion was subject. New Zealand Pakeha benefited from early modernisation, of the type seen in other ESCs, that led to urbanisation of a rather peculiar type before it had occurred in many other WDCs. By dint of good luck, by the introduction of technology and through emerging land tenure systems, modernisation also led to the application of advanced capital-intensive but labour-extensive farming that formed the base of the export economy. New Zealand 'recolonised' itself (to paraphrase James Belich) to remain for six to eight decades in a comfortable, almost uterine, dependent political-economic relationship with its metropole, before facing a brutal parturition in 1967.

Underlying the props was a value system that, at least as far as norms were manifested in fertility behaviours, had been imported from the mother country; underpinning the peculiar process of modernisation was, again in Belich's words, an ideology that New Zealand was a 'Better Britain in the South Seas'. That is, it would adopt and embellish Britishness. But the British norms seemed to hark back to an England and Wales of the period 1801–25 rather than the 1860s or 1870s; Scottish antecedents for high fertility seem even further back – one can cite the Highlands of the 1790s, whereas by the period in which New Zealand was being settled rates there were much lower. But the north and west of Scotland were the areas most depleted by migration, and perhaps Highland emigrants who eventually ended up in New Zealand carried with them the value systems of the late eighteenth century. But the analysis here can only be speculative. It requires in-depth research either resorting to expository or genealogical techniques to confirm our postulates or to modify them.

The favoured situation of Pakeha contrasted markedly with the conditions under which Maori were living at this time. In the 1850s, Maori enterprises were playing an important role in national development, including in the processing and export industries. But by 1901 they were a poor, marginalised population largely dependent on subsistence, deprived of their key resources, land, forest, lakes, rivers and even ocean fishing grounds. The instrument for this had been war and land confiscation in some areas in the 1860s, and, to the end of the century and beyond, by the Native Land Court and other so-called legal processes. This deprived Maori of the props, adequate food resources and other basic needs, for replacement but also for infant and childhood survivorship.

These props were transmitted by proximate factors that were different for Maori and Pakeha. For the latter these were facilitated by early marriage, probable widow remarriage and thus high levels of childbearing. For Maori, bio-social factors, fetal and post-natal, affected survivorship and thus threatened replacement.

THE 1920S AND 1930S
By the 1920s some of the socio-economic props of the pioneer period were still operating efficiently – despite being a highly urbanised population Pakeha were not tenement or even apartment dwellers but lived in owner-occupied houses. But economic conditions were not always buoyant and became very unfavourable in the 1930s Depression, which was long and deep in New Zealand. But the value system which had emphasised family forms, notably nuptial childbearing, also focused on the separation of career and family for women: almost all women had to choose one or the other. For Pakeha women, late marriage or celibacy had also become the key proximate factor – most sex was within marriage, and an ex-nuptial conception would be followed by a precipitated marriage and a marital birth, a behavioural pattern seemingly inherited from pre-Victorian Britain. Thus childbearing was contained within marriage.

For Maori this was also true. But they were going through a slow process of recuperation, with a modest acceleration in the early 1900s, coming from very successful primary health-care campaigns run by Maori physicians such as Drs Maui Pomare (later Sir) and Te Rangihiroa (Sir Peter Buck) that visibly lifted Maori infant and childhood survivorship. The bio-social constraints to reproduction were gradually diminishing in impact, while a more settled existence, albeit generally isolated from mainstream New Zealand, had come to prevail.

The net result was a crossover effect. Pakeha fertility declined, marriage and parenting were at older ages and there were high levels of celibacy. Accompanying this was the appearance of significant levels of polarisation, mainly in the replacement function of family life. Meantime, in the virtual absence of contraception, Maori fertility was high at young ages. Soon Maori rates were double those of Pakeha, and by the end of World War II Maori TFRs equalled those achieved by Pakeha in the 1870s, and thus were at levels close to biological maxima.

In the 1930s the occurrence of an ethnic fertility differential in New Zealand was sufficiently evident for it to come to the attention of the late British demographer David Glass, who wrote a classical paper on Maori demography (1945). This was published in the *Eugenics Review*, and used net reproduction rates, a methodology that was very popular in the later inter-war years but which drove eugenics concerns and racist fears (the 'white races' were seen as declining); David Glass was certainly not in this camp but was a great liberal pioneer of social demography. At home, however, the differential provoked the eugenicist polemic of H. Sinclair (1944). These eugenicist concerns were not to wholly disappear; they reappeared at the dawn of the twenty-first century.

THE BABY BOOM: THE 1950S AND 1960S

We jump now to the 1950s, to the Baby Boom, a period for Pakeha and even for Maori when the socio-economic props favoured family formation, quite possibly for the last time, at least in the history presented here. Above all, family formation could have its locus in the family home, owner occupied by the vast majority, or in detached houses subject to low non-market rents for the less fortunate. Surrounding this was a welfare state apparatus, and a generally buoyant economy, benefiting Pakeha and Maori, imperfectly in the latter case. But in both cases family life took place in households that were increasingly urban. Contextualising this seems to have been a value system that was centred on childbearing within the neolocal nuclear family. Parenthood, especially motherhood was a vocation to be entered into at a young age; it was a life path that was gender-segregated from the parallel career of the husband. Parenting was by definition within marriage; the minority of young Pakeha women who fell outside this model either righted their situation by a hasty marriage – a popular option – or were shunted off out of sight to single mothers' homes and their babies quickly adopted out. Maori did not necessarily fit this model, but in those years they were a small minority even though their presence in urban areas was now felt. Above all this was played out in the new housing estates where their lifestyle seemed, at least from the outside, to parallel that of the majority Pakeha. Generally obscured was the wrenching apart of Maori society that had been caused by rapid urbanisation.

The replacement function of the family was the primary one, so that it could be argued that the others were seen to be ancillary to reproduction. If that could be achieved – within marriage of course – then all the others would necessarily fall into step.

The events preceding the report of the Mazengarb Commission (1954) shocked this cosy society, a shock magnified by the extraordinary, panic-driven follow-up of sending the report to every dwelling and family in the country. In retrospect this whole episode seems very curious. The clustering of adolescents in the Hutt Valley was a chance outcome of the housing estates being peopled by families of similar ages, producing a youth wave of persons actually born before the Baby Boom, a phenomenon, however, that was repeated at this time in similar suburban areas across the neo-Europes. The behaviours of these adolescents – congregating in milk bars (or soda bars, as they were called in North America) to drink milk shakes, and getting up to all sorts of activities down by the Hutt River – seem incredibly mild today. But those activities of Hutt Valley youth were certainly seen as an affront to the morals of post-war New Zealand society.

More importantly, as Belich has noted, they were symptomatic of the underbelly of Baby Boom life, 'a sexual revolution ten or twenty years before it was supposed to have happened' (Belich 2001: 505–6). In the rush to judgement similar panics about 'larrikins' in the past were forgotten; but, more importantly, the incident was a preview of the onset of 'youth culture' that became more prominent across the WDCs in the late 1950s, and especially in the 1960s and 1970s (Belich 2001: 504–11; King 2004: 430–31; Kurlansky 2005: 178–80). The significance of this incident is, therefore, not so much that it represents a major social upheaval akin to the events that were soon to follow – it should have been a minor footnote in New Zealand's social history – but that it is a marker post for far more fundamental changes in family and related lifestyles.

Without the pre-condition of surplus males, Baby Boom marriage was consummated and childbearing occurred, both at historically unprecedentedly young ages. Fertility rose to levels not seen since the 1890s. Maori, despite now mainly living in urban households, continued to have high fertility with minimal differentials between rural and urban. Indeed, apart from a 215 children difference in TFRs between Maori and Pakeha, the Baby Boom could be seen as a period in which reproductive polarisation was minimised.

By the end of the Baby Boom a new factor entered the equation: the introduction of new contraceptive technologies meant that control over reproduction was now more efficient than ever before. With care, reproductive choice could be extended down to protected first intercourse. That said, the Baby Boom ended not with a whimper but a bang, as around 1970 Pakeha had levels of teenage pregnancy not seen either before or since. The rest of the 1970s saw rapid changes occur in every aspect of family life: formation, structures and forms, aided and abetted by the new contraceptive technology and sterilisation. At a technical level it seemed to answer an age-old problem: the unpredictability of conception for women.

THE END OF THE AFFAIR OR THE START OF UNPRECEDENTED TRENDS? THE 1990S AND BEYOND

To finish this story, let us now turn to the most recent decade. The differences from the Baby Boom are huge. Moreover, earlier chapters in this book have demonstrated that the recent past represents a period without precedents in the history of the New Zealand family.

The props for the central function of reproduction have been eroded; many would say kicked away rather brutally in the years just before and after 1990. An owner-occupied house has become a distant dream for many young couples about to start their family; the welfare system has been re-jigged completely from being universalistic and relatively munificent to targeted and parsimonious; survival for most families demands two incomes; and the job market in which the couple or sole parent is operating has been severely managerialised.

The career had been a demanding mistress for many Baby Boom fathers, often to the detriment of their family life, but by the new millennium it frequently became a dominatrix for both husbands and wives. The much vaunted move to deregulated labour markets and workplace flexibility has for many resulted in working long hours, for low wages, with job insecurity and a decrease in the quality of working conditions (e.g. holidays, pension schemes, overtime) that once were the norm. Technology which could have been anticipated to lighten work loads, may have actually increased them; the freeing up of time for family life seems not to have materialised. At the same time, and perhaps as a consequence of these changes to the job side of the work–life balance equation, household and personal income inequalities grew very significantly. For the privileged minority on high incomes, living conditions had never been better, but even then there was a catch for all but the very rich: the maintenance of this lifestyle still demanded dual incomes and thus either avoidance of childbearing altogether, significant expenditure on childcare or a drop in their standard of living. In short the clearly delineated alternatives of the 1920s – do not marry and continue to be in the labour market, or marry and have children, and remain outside the labour force – had given way to a far more complex set of alternatives in the 1990s and 2000s. The tensions engendered by the well-off in responding to these were major problems, but so too were the tensions felt by the less well-off, not just in order to maintain a high quality lifestyle, but often in attempting to provide their basic needs.

The context to all this, the value system, also underwent mutations. The women's movement of the 1970s and 1980s had fought for equal access to education and employment, and had achieved a great deal in this regard. But it had not really addressed gender equality in the interface between the job and the family; career equality is a reality for a minority of women, equality in the household for others, but not both for all women. Essentially work and income generation and their concomitants (e.g. the drive for success given the investment put into education, training, career mobility) came to be a priority for women during the key family-building ages of 25–34 years, and family life had to fit in around them. Reproductive choice took on a new meaning, but it was a choice that young men were still not reqired to make.

In the Baby Boom, especially around 1970, reproductive choice had referred to young women's choices that were determined by individual behaviours and above all access to efficient contraception which would bring predictability in women's lives – fighting for the latter was a major goal of the feminist and family-planning movements in the 1970s, a target that had been largely achieved by the 1980s. Canadian data quoted earlier show that by the early 1970s, in fact, individual social psychological traits, such as achievement motivation, were playing an increasing role and access to knowledge and services was a factor of diminishing importance. In New Zealand, there was a further factor, an ethnic differential: Maori viewed reproductive choice in terms of family limitation; for Pakeha, timing of first birth was a key issue. The quality and the range of family-planning methods available to couples and women was also an issue of public discourse, including in the 1970s a heated debate around abortion.

By the end of the 1990s reproductive choice for women or couples typically revolved around the prolongation of education and the related need to meet career goals, and/or the financial and material situation of families. The high proportions having their first babies in their thirties, shows that choice frequently had closed in around couples, leaving limited options: delaying childbearing or not becoming parents at all. The former again placed severe constraints on choice for women once the bio-social limits of fecundability were reached.

The consequences of these tensions and the associated difficulties involved in achieving a work–life balance, along with delays in parenting, produced reproductive and familial polarisation never before seen in New Zealand. With this came moral panics and the emergence of neo-eugenicist views. In turn these were often wrapped up in neo-liberal ideology and incorporated into more general attacks on the welfare state, indeed some critics even questioned the existence of the state itself; markets and morality somehow became conflated in complex ways.

Value systems relating to family dynamics *per se* changed radically and perhaps inexorably. Nowhere was this more evident than in those relating to family forms. The deterministic association between exposure to intercourse, marriage and childbearing now no longer held; a correlate of this was that entering a union could involve short-term relationships, cohabitation or, decreasingly, marriage. Parenting became something apart, typically entered into as a life-cycle phase consciously and in its own right, and not as a consequence of pre-marital indiscretions or something following hard on the heels of a wedding. But as these links diminished in social significance so too did nuptial childbearing; a significant minority of babies were now being born outside marriage. By the end of the period discussed here the legal system was catching up with these social changes and new codes governing unions were legislated.

For a range of reasons divorce rates increased in the period. Not least among the determinants were the effects of early marriage, particularly if precipitated by or quickly followed by pregnancy, quintessential features of the Baby Boom. As it passed into history, its effects lingered on in divorce and solo parenting.

Not surprisingly, among more conservative commentators these shifts in forms were viewed as transformations threatening the capacity of families to meet their broader social responsibilities, and even as determinants of the decay of social order. Concern about these changes in forms overshadowed rapid shifts in structures that in the long run may be of more fundamental importance than shifts in forms. The changes in forms are symptoms of changes in values; but the shifts in structures are the result of fundamental transitions in the props and their associated value systems. The shifts in forms – increases in ex-nuptial fertility, solo parenting, divorce and cohabitation – saw their most rapid increases in the 1970s and 1980s, and rates have plateaued since. In contrast, the quantum changes in ages at childbearing have continued and intensified over recent years.

One of these demographic changes, the very significant declines in teenage pregnancy, seems somehow to have been missed in the policy discourse on family life. Instead, the 'adolescent mother' (and, less emblematically, other unmarried mothers), has been reified into the personification of moral and fiscal profligacy, something she had never really been subject to when levels were very high, around 1970. But at that stage she was probably pressured into marriage and nuptial childbearing, only, in many cases, to see her marriage dissolve ten or fifteen or twenty years later, requiring her to seek state support on the DPB.

Alongside these changes were other shifts in rates and patterns of childbearing. Family sizes are much smaller today, and parenting is occurring on average at older and older ages, when reproductive choice is constrained by the twin factors of biology and the negative effects of managerialism on the work–life balance.

IMPLICATIONS: TOWARDS THEORY

The description of the evolution of the New Zealand family presented here is of intrinsic interest because of what it tells us about our society. But beyond this we should ask whether this New Zealand history sheds light on broader theoretical questions. Theory has two major functions: it provides a means of explaining what has been observed empirically and it extrapolates from these observations and explanations to make predictions. But what might be achieved at best here is an explicandum rather than an explanation.

The major reasons for this are simple and have been fully rehearsed in earlier chapters: there is a lack of data on household dynamics, especially on the social-emotional and social-psychological dimensions of family life. Thus analysts are placed in a virtually untenable position. They can observe the broader trends in formation, structures and forms, as was done in the empirical chapters, although only really the first of these factors could be analysed for earlier periods. They can identify those trends that seem significant or systematic, particularly the high-profile events such as marriage and childbearing or the most manifest of structures, such as whether the household is a parenting or non-parenting one. These can then be deemed 'normative', in the sense that large groups or the majority of some population or sub-population follow them. But analysts must then make a leap of faith when they interpret these norms by drawing on the fragments of information that we have on the social, cultural and psychological contexts. Of course, the analysis here was aided and abetted by the fact that we could appeal to cross-comparative data from overseas studies and to the wide number of different theories relating to the family (elaborated more in Pool *et al.* 2007). But, ultimately, this research has to impute rather than simply describe the latent structures and value systems that might have produced the observed trends. This is what we are doing here. We cannot claim that formal hypothesis testing or even direct explanation of these factors could be turned to – but, to use present-day policy-studies and organisational jargon, we wish to make the rationale behind our processes of interpretation more 'transparent'.

What emerges from this history is the importance for family life of material props, factors that in a narrow sense are exogenous to the household. These include basic needs for family well-being, such as housing, income or access to the labour market, and, as for Maori in early years, child survivorship. They also comprise measures, both those specific to the family or to social welfare and those which are directed to other seemingly unrelated public policy goals but have consequences for social processes and behaviours and family life. For example, macro-economic restructuring, structural adjustments, to use the international terminology, directed to resolving problems in national accounts such as high levels of government debt, can affect the labour market and social welfare and through them the family. These same determinants may play a role in encouraging or discouraging family formation and its attendant structures; but, less definitively, they can also be cited as variables affecting the way some structures emerge (e.g. the parent-plus household may be formed as much for meeting basic needs such as shelter as for some underlying cultural value favouring multi-generational and/or multi-family households); and even less certain is the impact of these props on family forms. But what is important for the present discussion is that these props *have* been documented over time, and thus some reasonably valid comments can be made.

At first the props seem to have created conditions favourable to replacement, which can be measured; little can be said about whether or not they advantaged other family functions. This is because the quantum and quality of familial inputs to socialisation or societal cohesion in the past cannot be systematically documented – hopefully, historians and sociologists will gradually reduce these knowledge gaps. The documentation of the formal aspects of socialisation, for example, are being recorded by experts in the history of education and tell a lot about the broader society, but not an equivalent amount about the family.

In the Baby Boom the props appear to have been maximised by the interventions of the welfare state and by general prosperity, and seem to have provided a reasonably secure environment for families. This contrasted with the Depression years, in which replacement suffered in the absence of a modern welfare state and in the face of economic hardship. This merely postponed the impact of the spectre about which Kingsley Davis was musing at the end of the Depression, before the last World War and before the onset of the Baby Boom: the incompatibility of modern life and the lifestyles necessary to sustain a family of reproduction.

But the Baby Boom seems to have provided only a temporary reprise in a long-term trend that could well see Davis's gloomy prognosis fulfilled. Since then the props have been demonstrably eroded or eliminated, a process accelerated by the aggressive entry into the policy domain of ideologies legitimised by neo-classical economics. The self-imposed structural adjustments effected in New Zealand in the late 1980s and early 1990s had very clear impacts on family well-being and on driving up inequalities. The attendant ideologies relating to efficiency and productivity have played a significant role in increasing reproductive polarisation, and probably in a long-term reduction in levels of replacement. That the structural adjustments were co-terminous with an increase in fertility around 1990 was, however, purely demographic chance, as documented earlier.

Thus a first more theoretical point is the importance of props for the processes of family formation, and some aspects of family structure. The research here has provided reasonable, but imperfect, evidence in support of this argument. It certainly presents an explicandum for, and may even explain some of the reasons for, the shifts in family formation, and attendant changes in structures (e.g. family sizes; age structures of households). Perhaps this extends to other family functions. One could argue, for example, that the tensions noted here engendered by the work–family imbalance or the growing inequalities in well-being make many families vulnerable and, through that, susceptible to behaviour patterns that might be seen by some observers to be 'dysfunctional'.

The role of the value system is more difficult to pin down, but, not unexpectedly, it does seem to have played a major part. Its role may be even more fundamental because norms and values also help to shape the type and forms that props might take. And there are some manifest pointers to their possible features. It should also be noted that it is not just the value systems endogenous to family life that play a role here, but also those which are exogenous to family life yet which shape ideas that are extant in both the market and policy sectors, and among decision-makers.

The colonial period saw values favouring early childbearing imported from pre-Victorian England and Wales, perhaps partially enhanced by the spirit of rapid economic development. The latter values were not sufficient in themselves to drive replacement, and soon must have withered, because, as has been shown, fertility dropped rapidly in the late nineteenth century.

Around World War I, much of society had become urban and dependent on industries relying on waged employees rather than the family labour force still typifying rural New Zealand (especially dairying areas). The opposition in Taranaki to the 1877 Education Act because of what it would do to the family workforce was witness to that; in the 1950s the tired pupils bussed in from farms to small-town New Zealand high schools and falling asleep at their desks indicated how long this reliance on unpaid family labour took to die. The rules governing urban labour, dependent on underlying values manifest, for example, in the Employment of Females Act 1873 introduced to protect women and children against exploitation, had another less desirable impact not only on gender segmentation within the labour force itself but on reproductive choice for women. This early manifestation of the importance of the value system had echoes at the end of the twentieth century, after the Baby Boom, when the work–life balance became highly distorted in complex ways, placing further constraints on reproductive choice, especially for older women.

Thus it can be argued, albeit with less confidence than for the material props, that an appeal to the importance of value structures provides at least an explicandum of the changes observed in many aspects of family formation over the periods covered in this book. It seems, for example, that at present the more dominant social and economic value systems may be antithetical to norms favouring the replacement function.

Turning now to the other dimension of theory, prediction, it is useful to go back to Kingsley Davis's argument. The analyses here seem to confirm that the New Zealand family is at least on the cusp of, if not already fully exposed to, two sets of forces that maximise the incompatibility of modern life and replacement. These come from both the material props to family formation and structures, and the value system that determines and contextualises the material structures. To reverse these would require a return to something like what was seen in the Baby Boom, but that could mean also a return to many other factors that were dominant then and that in retrospect seem undesirable, such as gender segmentation of both the work and family spheres of life. Perhaps, however, there are models that would be acceptable, such as some of the welfare regimes seen in North-western Europe. But their adoption would require changes in values – in particular the rights and wrongs and fiscal implications – relating to much higher levels of state intervention.

Even were policies from these regimes to be initiated, the ultimate question of gender equity could not be solved: it will always be women who bear babies. Moreover, they are probably more likely than men to play key roles in rearing children. What is needed is again a huge change in the value system. While accepting that women must bear children, full equality demands that men's work regimes and career paths are changed so that they too can play a greater part in childrearing.

This is an appropriate point at which to look at the future.

10.4 THE FUTURE

Possibly the New Zealand family has changed forever. Some of its historical structures and forms may be replicated in the future, but the social, economic and policy contexts will almost certainly be different – the need for strategies to care for an ageing population will be one major foreseeable contextual difference, and already this is starting to produce intergenerational competition for resources, both within the family and across the wider society. But contextual factors in turn will have major implications for families. Families themselves will be ageing, facing familial burdens, but will also have familial capacities for caring. Beyond this, unless work–

life, job–family balances are resolved, then the capacities of all adult family members to be involved in the factors of both 'production and reproduction' – nurturing the new generation, caring for older family members and pursuing a career – will be severely jeopardised, to the detriment of social and economic development. Clearly all adults must have the choice to work if future dependency burdens are to be reduced, but they must also have the choice to become parents, again a family function that was never more important than it is now if the population is to replace itself.

At present the likelihood of another baby boom, even were it desirable, is very low indeed, and even the chances of another baby blip seem to be fading. The props of reproduction are no longer evident and for many who are childless or have only one child the managerialist work ethos, and constraints emanating from the perceived direct and indirect costs of having children, described in earlier chapters, do not seem to be relenting. This essentially limits their reproductive choice in order for them to pursue careers in which they have made considerable educational and economic investment, or simply to ensure their family's basic needs and well-being are met.

To a significant degree the future of the New Zealand family rests on resolving factors exogenous to the family itself which impinge on family structures and their capabilities to carry out societal functions. Yet much of the focus in public debate is on family forms and on seeing changes in these as endogenous to the family itself, rather like blaming the victim.

Until there is a more comprehensive and reasoned discourse, then the family may fail New Zealand because in many ways New Zealand has failed its families. This book has shown that as an institution the family is undergoing change, sometimes radical in nature, but that family policy instruments and the socio-economic environment, rather than coming to the aid of the family, may be exacerbating the situation and putting undue pressures on households.

Against that, this book has also demonstrated that, over time and repeatedly, this most important of social institutions has been resilient, reappearing in a new and often vigorous form, regardless of the ways in which it has been rendered vulnerable by circumstances often beyond its immediate control. The family systems of all major New Zealand ethnic groups share this common experience of assaults on their viability, as we have documented here: the tearing apart of the Pakeha emigrant family that left the mother country on a long and arduous journey; the appalling levels of infant and childhood mortality among their Maori contemporaries at that time; or the hostile ways in which the early Chinese colonists were treated, segregated from other settlers and from their families back home in China. More recently, we can point to the effects on whanau of the post-war Maori urban migration; or on aiga as Samoans and other Pacific peoples moved to New Zealand at the end of the Baby Boom period, only to be hunted in dawn raids for overstayers a few years later; to the difficulties the modern Asian migrant 'astronaut' family has in keeping together its strands in Asia and New Zealand; or the severing of support systems in the families of the New Zealand diaspora.

A better knowledge base about New Zealand family life should provide the foundations for fundamental and sympathetic changes to policy and to the way that outside institutions, such as work, have an impact on families and the functions they perform. It is to be hoped that this study will contribute to such an understanding.

BIBLIOGRAPHY

ABBREVIATIONS

AJS	*American Journal of Sociology*
ANU	Australian National University
AUP	Auckland University Press
CUP	Cambridge University Press
ECE/FFS	Economic Commission for Europe/Family and Fertility Study
ESCAP	Economic and Social Commission for Asia and the Pacific
IPS	Institute of Policy Studies
JAPA	*Journal of the Australian Population Association*
JMF	*Journal of Marriage and the Family*
NZPR	*New Zealand Population Review*
OUP	Oxford University Press
PAA	Population Association of America
PANZ	Population Association of New Zealand
PDR	*Population and Development Review*
PS	*Population Studies*
PSC	Population Studies Centre
SPJNZ	*Social Policy Journal of New Zealand*
VUP	Victoria University Press

The references here are works consulted and cited in the text and/or cited in the web appendix, authored by Pool, Dharmalingam, Sceats and Susan Singley, (2007).

Adair, V. and Dixon, R. (eds) (1998) *The Family in Aotearoa New Zealand*, Addison Wesley Longman, Auckland.
Adsera, A. (2002) 'Changing Fertility Rates in Developing Countries: The Impact of Labour Market Institutions', unpublished paper drawing on presentation to Population Association of America (PAA), 2002, Atlanta.
AJHR (various years) *Appendices to the House of Representatives*, Govt Printer, Wellington.
Allison, P. D. (1984) *Event History Analysis: Regression for Longitudinal Event Data*, Sage University Paper Series on Quantitative Applications in the Social Sciences, Sage, Beverly Hills, CA.
Anderson, Michael (1998) 'Fertility Decline in Scotland, England and Wales, and Ireland: Comparisons from the 1911 Census of Fertility', *Population Studies (PS)* 52: 177–99.
Anderson, Morton (1906, reprinted 2006) 'Declining Birthrate in "the Britain of the South Seas"', *New Zealand Medical Journal* 119, 1229, February (reprinting 5,19: 1–8).
Archey, C. (2005) *Skin to Skin*, Penguin, Auckland.
Arnold, R. (1980) *The Farthest Promised Land*, Victoria University Press (VUP) with Price Milburn, Wellington.
Arunachalam, D., *see* Dharmalingam, A.
Australian Bureau of Statistics (1984) *Australian Families 1982*, Catalogue No. 4408.0, Canberra.
Australian Bureau of Statistics (1988) *Family Formation Survey, Australia, September 1986*, Catalogue No. 3223.0, Canberra.
Axinn, W. G. and Thornton, A. (1993) 'Mothers, Children, and Cohabitation; The Intergenerational Effects of Attitudes and Behaviors', *American Sociological Review* 58: 233–46.
Bajos, N., Moreau, C., Leridon, H. and Ferrand, M. (2004) 'Pourquoi le nombre d'avortements n'a-t-il baissé en France depuis 30 ans?' *Population et Sociétés* 407, December.
Baker, M. (2001) *Families, Labour and Love: Family Diversity in a Changing World*, Allen and Union; Crows Nest, NSW.
Baker, M. and Phipps, S. (1997) 'Canada', in Kamerman, S. and Kahn, A., *Family Change and Family Policy in Great Britain, Canada, New Zealand and the United States*,

Clarendon, Oxford: 103–206.

Ball, D. (1999a) 'Delayed Childbearing in New Zealand', M.Soc.Sci. thesis, University of Waikato, Hamilton.

Ball, D. (1999b) 'A Trend to Later Parenthood: A Brief Overview', in Pool, I. and Johnstone, K. (eds), *The Life Courses of New Zealand Women: Fertility, Family Formation and Structure, Fertility Regulation, Education, Work and Economic Wellbeing*, papers presented to Ministry of Women's Affairs seminar, 8 June 1999, Wellington, Population Studies Centre (PSC), University of Waikato, Hamilton: 41–44.

Ball, D. and Wilson, M. (2002) 'The Prevalence and Persistence of Low Income Among New Zealand Children: Indicative Measures from Benefit Dynamics Data', *Social Policy Journal of New Zealand (SPJNZ)* 18: 92–117.

Ball, D., Baxendine, S., Pool, I. and Dharmalingam, A. (1999) 'Family Building Patterns among New Zealand Women of Pacific Island Origin', paper presented at the Pacific Vision Conference, 27 July 1999, Auckland.

Barber, J. and Axinn, W. (1998) 'The Impact of Parental Pressure for Grandchildren in Young People's Entry into Cohabitation and Marriage', *PS* 52: 129–44.

Barlow, J. and Duncan, S. (1994) *Success and Failure in Housing Provision*, Pergammon, Elsevier Science, Oxford.

Barrett, G., Krsinic, F. and Wilson, M. (2002) 'Young Children Supported by Benefits in New Zealand: A Duration Analysis', *New Zealand Population Review (NZPR)* 29, 1: 131–53.

Bassett, M. (2003a) 'Poor Should Stop Breeding', *Dominion Post*, 30 September.

Bassett, M. (2003b) 'Money Won't Cure Cycle of Child Abuse', *New Zealand Herald*, 17 November.

Bathgate, M., Alexander, D., Mitikulena, A., Borman, B., Roberts, A. and Grigg, M. (1994) *The Health of Pacific Islands People in New Zealand*, Analysis and Monitoring Report 2, Public Health Commission, Wellington.

Beaujot, R. (2006) 'Delayed Life Transitions: Trends and Implications', in McQuillan, K. and Revanera, Z. (eds) *Canada's Changing Families*, University of Toronto Press: 105–32.

Beaujot, R. and Muhammad, A. (2006) 'Transformed Families and the Basis for Childbearing', in McQuillan and Revanera (eds) *op cit*: 15–48.

Becker, G. A. (1981) *A Treatise on the Family*, Harvard University Press, Cambridge, MA.

Beckman, A. and Cooper, C. (2004) 'Globalisation, the New Managerialism and Education: Rethinking the Purpose of Education in Britain', *Journal for Critical Education Policy Studies* 2, 2: www.jceps.com.

Bedford, R. and Pool, I. (1985) 'Cultural Demography: Ethnicity', in Economic Commission for Asia and the Pacific (ESCAP), *The Population of New Zealand: Country Monograph Series No. 12*, 2 vols, United Nations, NY: vol. 2, 1–30.

Bedford, R. and Pool, I. (2004) 'Flirting with Zelinksy in Aotearoa/New Zealand: A Maori Mobility Transition', in Taylor, J. and Bell, M. (eds) *Population Mobility of Indigenous Peoples in Australasia and North America*, Routledge, London: 44–76.

Bedford, R., Ho, E., Lidgard, J. and Goodwin, J. (1997) 'International Migration in the Asia Pacific Region: Perspectives on Theory and Method', PSC Discussion Paper No. 23, University of Waikato, Hamilton.

Bélanger, A. and Turcotte, P. (1999) 'L'influence des caractéristiques sociodémographiques sur le début de la vie conjugale des Québécoises', *Cahiers Québécois de Démographie* 28, 1–2: 173–97.

Belich, J. (1996) *Making People*, Allen Lane, Penguin, Auckland.

Belich, J. (2001) *Paradise Reforged*, Allen Lane, Penguin, Auckland.

Bennet, N., Blanc, A. and Bloom, D. (1988) 'Commitment and the Modern Union: Assessing the link between premarital cohabitation and subsequent marital stability', *American Sociological Review* 53: 127–38.

Bennett, N. G., Bloom, D. E. and Craig, P. H. (1989) 'The Divergence of Black and White Marriage Patterns', *American Journal of Sociology (AJS)* 95: 692–722.

Bernhardt, E. M. (2000) 'Repartnering among Swedish Men and Women: A Case Study of Emerging Patterns in the Second Demographic Transition', paper presented to FFS Flagship Conference, United Nations, Economic Commission for Europe (ECE), Population Activities Unit/Population and Family Studies Unit, Flemish Scientific Institute/United Nations Fund for Population, 29–31 May, Brussels, Belgium.

Berrington, A. and Diamond, I. (1999) 'Marital Disruption among the 1958 British Birth Cohort: the Role of Cohabitation', *PS* 53(1): 39–48.

Billari, F. (2004) 'Synthetic Fertility Measures and the Search for Commonalities: Discusssion of Paper "Explanations of the Fertility Crisis in Modern Societies: a Search for Commonalities", by Caldwell and Schindlmayr 2003 [*op cit* in the present bibliography]', *PS* 58, 1: 84–85.

Birks, S. and Callister, P. (eds) (1999) *Perspectives on Fathering*, Issue Paper Number 4, Centre for Policy Evaluation, Massey University, Palmerston North.

Birrel, B. and Rapson, V. (1998) *A Not So Perfect Match: The Growing Male/Female Divide, 1986–1996*, Centre for Population and Urban Research, Monash University, Melbourne.

Black, D., Gates, G., Sanders, S. and Taylor, L. (2000) 'Demographics of the Gay and Lesbian Population in the United States: Evidence from Available Systematic Data Sources', *Demography* 37(2): 139–54.

Blaikie, A. (1994) *Illegitimacy, Sex and Society: North East-Scotland, 1750–1900*, Clarendon, Oxford.

Blom, Svein (1994) 'Marriage and Cohabitation in a Changing Society: Experience of Norwegian Men and Women Born in 1945 and 1960', *European Journal of Population* 9: 143–73.

Blum, A. (1984) 'Fécondité, solidarité intergenerationelle, isolement', in AIDELF (eds) *Les Familles d'Aujourd'hui*, Colloque de Genève 1984, AIDELF, Paris: 583–600.

Bongaarts, J. (1982) 'Proximate Determinants [of Fertility]', in Ross, J. (ed.) *International Encyclopaedia of Population*, 2 vols, Free Press, NY: vol. 1, 275–79.

Booth, A. and Crouter, A. C. (eds) (2000) *Does It Take a Village? Community Effects on Children, Adolescents and Families*, Lawrence Erlbaum, Mahwah, NJ.

Borrie, W. (1970) *The Growth and Control of World Population*, Weidenfeld and Nicolson, London.

Borrie, W. (1994) *The European Peopling of Australasia: A Demographic History, 1788–1988*, Demography Program, Australian National University (ANU), Canberra.

Boyd, M. and Pryor, E. (1989) 'The Cluttered Nest: The Living Arrangements of Young Canadian Adults', *Canadian Journal of Sociology* 14, 4: 461–77.

Bracher, M. (1987) 'The Australian Family Project', *Journal of the Australian Population Association (JAPA)* 4: 106–22.

Bracher, M. (1990) 'Explaining First Marriage Trends in Australia', *JAPA* 7: 128–50.

Bracher, M. and Santow, G. (1990) 'The Family Histories of Australian Women', *European Journal of Population* 6: 227–56.

Bracher, M. and Santow, G. (1998) 'Economic Independence and Union Formation in Sweden', *PS* 52(3): 275–94.

Bracher, M., Santow, G., Morgan, S. P. and Trussell, J. (1993) 'Marriage Dissolution in Australia: Models and Explanations', *PS* 47: 403–25.

Brahim, A. B. (2004) 'Transition des structures par âge et vieillissement en Tunisie', paper presented at CICRED seminar, Age-Structural Transitions: Demographic Bonuses, but Emerging Challenges for Population and Sustainable Development, Paris, February.

Brewster, K. L. (1994) 'Racial Differences in Sexual Activity among Adolescent Women: The Role of Neighborhood Characteristics', *American Sociological Review* 59: 408–24.

Brookes, B. (ed.) (2000) *At Home in New Zealand: History, Houses, People*, Bridget Williams Books, Wellington.

Bryant, J. (2003) 'Growth-Friendly Demography of New Zealand', *NZPR* 29, 2: 35–62.

Bulcroft, R. A. and Bulcroft, K. A. (1993) 'Race Differences in Attitudinal Factors in the Decision to Marry', *Journal of Marriage and the Family (JMF)* 55: 338–56.

Bumpass, L. L. (1990) 'What is Happening to the Family', *Demography* 27, 4: 483–98.

Bumpass, L. L. and Lu, H.-H. (2000) 'Trends in Cohabitation and Implications for Children's Family Contexts in the United States', *PS* 54, 1: 29–42.

Bumpass, L. L. and Raley, R. K. (1995) 'Redefining Single-Parent Families: Cohabitation and Changing Family Reality', *Demography* 32: 97–110.

Bumpass, L. L., Raley, R. K. and Sweet, J. A. (1995) 'The Changing Character of Stepfamilies: Implications of Cohabitation and Nonmarital Childbearing', *Demography* 32: 425–36.

Bumpass, L. L. and Sweet, J. A. (1989) 'National Estimates of Cohabitation', *Demography*

26(4): 615–25.

Bumpass, L. L., Sweet, J. A. and Cherlin, A. (1991) 'The Role of Cohabitation in Declining Rates of Marriage', *JMF* 53, 4: 913–27.

Burch, T. and Bélanger, D. (1999) 'L'étude des unions en démographie: des catégories aux processus', *Cahiers Québécois de Démographie* 28, 1–2: 23–52.

Burch, T. and Madon, A. K. (1986) *Union Formation and Dissolution: Results from the 1984 Family Survey*, Statistics Canada, Catalogue No. 99–963, Ottawa.

Burgess, E., Locke, H. and Thomes, M. (1971) *The Family: From Traditional to Companionship*, Van Nostrand Reinhold, NY.

Cabre, A. (2002) 'Facts and Factors on Low Fertility in Southern Europe: The Case of Spain', International Workshop on Low Fertility, Tokyo, 20–22 November.

Cabre, A. and Esteve, A. (2004) 'Marriage Squeeze and Changes in Family Foundation: Historical Comparative Evidence in Spain, France and United States in the XXth Century', paper presented at PAA annual meeting, Boston, April.

Cairns, H., Harris, S. and Clarke, L. (2002) 'Mothers, Work and Childcare [in England]', unpublished report prepared for National Institute of Population and Social Security, Tokyo.

Caldwell, J. (1982) *Theory of Fertility Decline*, Arnold, London.

Caldwell, J. C. and Schindlmayr, T. (2003) 'Explanation of the Fertility Crises in Modern Societies: A Search for Commonalities', *PS* 57, 3: 241–64.

Callister, P. (1998) '"Work-rich" and "Work-poor" Individuals and Families', *SPJNZ* 10: 101–21.

Callister, P. (1999) 'The Early Childhood Education and Care Arrangements of Pre-school Children of Work-rich and Work-poor Couples', paper prepared for the Dept of Labour, presented at the Childcare, Families and Work seminar, organised by the National Advisory Council on the Employment of Women, Wellington, December.

Callister, P. (2000a) 'A Not So Perfect Match: The New Zealand Experience', *NZPR* 26(1): 1–21.

Callister, P. (2000b) *Living and Working in New Zealand*, Institute of Policy Studies (IPS), Victoria University, Wellington.

Callister, P. (2001) *A Polarisation into Work-rich and Work-poor Households in New Zealand? Trends from 1986 to 2000*, Dept of Labour, Wellington.

Callister, P. (2002) 'Ageing Population and Social Policy in New Zealand: Could "Family Friendly" Policies increase both Fertility and Women's Employment?', *NZPR* 28, 2: 221–52.

Callister, P. (2003) 'Maori/Non-Maori Intermarriage', *NZPR* 29, 2: 89–106.

Callister, P. (2005) 'Overworked Families? Changes in the Paid Working Hours of Families with Young Children', unpublished paper, summarising papers prepared for Dept of Labour (Future of Work Programme).

Cameron, J. (1985a) 'Conceptualizing "Family": An Epistemological Concern for Family Researchers', *NZPR*, April: 7–18.

Cameron, J. (1985b) 'Families, Households and Housing', in ESCAP *op cit*, vol. 2: 139–69.

Cameron, J. (1990) *Why have Children?* Canterbury University Press, Christchurch.

Cameron, J. (1997) *Without Issue: New Zealanders Who Choose Not to Have Children*, Canterbury University Press, Christchurch.

Cameron, J. (with Pool, I. and Douglas, E. M. K.) (1981) 'ESCAP Portability Study', unpublished report to ESCAP/UN, PSC, University of Waikato, Hamilton.

Campbell, R. and Devine, T. (1990) 'The Rural Experience [in Scotland]', in Fraser, W. and Morris, R. (eds) *op cit*: 46–72.

Carmichael, G. (1982) 'Aspects of Ex-Nuptiality in New Zealand: Toward a Social Demography of Marriage and the Family Since the Second World War', unpublished PhD thesis, ANU, Canberra.

Carmichael, G. (1984) 'Living Together in New Zealand: Data on Co-Residence at Marriage and on de facto Unions', *NZPR* 10, 3: 41–54.

Carmichael, G. (1985) 'Remarriage among Divorced Persons in New Zealand', *Australian Journal of Social Issues* 20, 2: 87–104.

Carmichael, G. (1988a) *With This Ring: First Marriage Patterns, Trends and Prospects in Australia*, Australian Family Formation Project Monograph No. 11, Australian Institute of Family Studies, Melbourne.

Carmichael, G. (1988b) 'Socio-demographic Correlates of Divorce in New Zealand', *JAPA* 5(1): 58–81.

Carmichael, G. (ed.) (1993) *Trans-Tasman Migration: Trends, Causes and Consequences*, Bureau of Immigration Research, Melbourne.

Carmichael, G. (1996) 'Consensual Partnering in New Zealand: Evidence from Three Censuses', *NZPR* 22: 1–44.

Carmichael, G. (2000) 'Taking Stock at the Millennium: Fertility and Family Formation in Australia', in Carmichael and Dharmalingam, A. (eds) *Populations of New Zealand and Australia at the Millennium*, a joint special issue of the *Journal of Population Research*, Aust., and the *Population Review*, NZ, Canberra and Wellington: 91–104.

Cartwright, S. (1985) 'Law and Population', in ESCAP (eds) *op cit*: vol. 2, 187–94.

Casterline, J., Lee, R. and Foote, K. (eds) (1996) *Fertility in the United States*, Population Council, NY.

Castles, F. (1993a) 'Introduction', in Castles (ed.) *op cit, Families of Nations: Patterns of Public Policy in Western Democracies*, Dartmouth Publishing, Aldershot, Hants: xiii–xxiii.

Castles, F. (1993b) 'Changing Courses in Economic Policy: The English Speaking Nations in the 1980s', in Castles (ed.) *op cit*: 3–34.

Castles, F. (1998) *Comparative Public Policy: Patterns of Post-War Transformation*, Edward Elgar, Cheltenham.

Castles, F. and Mitchell, D. (1993) 'Worlds of Welfare and Families of Nations', in Castles, F. (ed.) *op cit*: 93–128.

Castles, F., Gerritsen, R. and Vowles, J. (1996) *The Great Experiment: Labour Parties and Public Policy Transformation in Australia and New Zealand*, Allen and Unwin, St Leonards, NSW.

Castles, I. (1993) *Australia's Families – Selected Findings from the Survey of Families in Australia March 1992 to May 1992*, Australian Bureau of Statistics, Catalogue No. 4418.0, Canberra.

Castles, I. (1994) *Focus on Families: Demographics and Family Formation*, Australian Bureau of Statistics, Catalogue No. 4420.0, Canberra.

Castro Martin, T. and Bumpass, L. L. (1989) 'Recent Trends in Marital Disruption', *Demography* 26: 37–51.

Census of England and Wales (1871), Eyre and Spottiswoode for Her Majesty's Stationery Office, London.

Census of Scotland (1871) Murray and Gibb for Her Majesty's Stationery Office, Edinburgh.

Chandola, T., Coleman, D. and Hiorns, R. (2002) 'Distinctive Features of Age-Specific Fertility Profiles in the English Speaking World: Common Patterns in Australia, Canada, New Zealand and the United States, 1970–98', *PS* 56: 181–200.

Charbonneau, H. (1975) *Vie et mort de nos ancêtres: étude démographique*, Les Presses de l'Université de Montreal.

Chase-Dunn, C. and Hall, T. (1994) 'The Historical Evolution of World-Systems', *Sociological Inquiry* 64(3): 257–80.

Chatterjee, S. and Podder, N. (2002) 'Economic Inequality in Colour: Some Ethnic Dimensions of Income Distributions in New Zealand 1984–1998', Discussion Paper 02–06, Dept of Applied and International Economics, Massey University, Palmerston North.

Cherlin, A. (1980) 'Postponing Marriage: The Influence of Young Women's Work Expectations', *JMF* 42: 355–65.

Cherlin, A. (1981) *Marriage, Divorce and Remarriage*, Harvard University Press, Cambridge, MA.

Cherlin, A. (1990) 'Recent Changes in American Fertility, Marriage and Divorce', *Annals of the American Academy of Political and Social Science* 510, July: 145–54.

Cherlin, A. (1992) *Marriage, Divorce, and Remarriage*, Harvard University Press, Cambridge, MA.

Chesnais, J.-C. (1996) 'Fertility, Family and Social Policy in Contemporary Western Europe', *Population and Development Review* (PDR) 22, 4: 729–39.

Cochrane, B. (2003) 'Workless Households in New Zealand: A Regional Overview, 1986–2001', paper presented to Population Association of New Zealand (PANZ) Conference, Christchurch, July.

Cochrane, B., Pool, I. and Baxendine, S. (forthcoming 2007) 'New Zealand Regions,

1986–2001: Household Incomes, Joblessness and Parenting', PSC Discussion Paper, University of Waikato, Hamilton.

Coghlan, T. A. (1903) *The Decline in the Birth Rate of New South Wales and Other Phenomena of Child-Birth: An Essay in Statistics*, Government Printer, Sydney.

Coleman, D. (1999) 'Demographic Data for Europe – a Review of Sources', *Population Trends*, Winter, Office for National Statistics, London.

Coleman, D. (2005) 'Population Prospects and Problems in Europe', proceedings of the International Conference, Trends and Problems of the World Population in the XXI Century: 50 Years since Rome 1954, *Genus* LXI, 3–4: 413–64.

Coleman, D. and Salt, J. (1992) *The British Population*, OUP.

Coleman, J. S. (1988) 'Social Capital in the Creation of Human Capital', *AJS* 94(supp.): S95–S120.

Condliffe, J. B. (1959) *New Zealand in the Making*, Allen and Unwin, London.

Connell, K. (1975) *The Population of Ireland, 1750–1845*, Greenwood Press, Westport, CT.

Contract with America (1994), Republican Party (USA).

Cooney, T. M. and Hogan, D. P. (1991) 'Marriage in an Institutionalized Life Course: First Marriages among American Men in the Twentieth Century', *JMF* 53: 178–90.

Corman, D. (2000) 'Family Policies, Working Life and the Third Child: France and Sweden', FFS Flagship Conference *op cit.*

Courel, A. and Pool, I. (1973) 'Haute-Volta', in Caldwell, J. *et al.* (eds), *Croissance démographique et évolution socio-économique en Afrique de l'ouest*, Paris and NY, Population Council 1992–2016: version in English published by Columbia University Press (1975).

Courgeau, D. (2000) 'New Approaches and Methodological Innovations in the Study of Partnership and Fertility Behavior', FFS Flagship Conference *op cit.*

Crowther, M. (1990) 'Poverty, Health and Welfare [Scotland]', in Fraser, W. and Morris, R. (eds) *op cit*: 265–89.

Dalla Zuanna *et al. see* Zuanna *et al.*

Dankossou, I. *et al.* (1973) 'Niger', in Caldwell, J. *et al.* (eds) *Croissance démographique . . . op cit*: 917–36.

DaVanzo, J. and Goldscheider, F. K. (1990) 'Coming Home Again: Return to the Parental Home of Young Adults', *PS* 44: 241–55.

Davey, J. (1993) *Birth to Death III*, IPS, Victoria University, Wellington.

Davey, J. (1998) *Birth to Death IV*, IPS, Victoria University, Wellington.

Davey, J. (1999) 'Living Alone: One-Person Households in New Zealand', *NZPR* 25, 1 and 2: 81–96.

Davey, J. (2003) *Two Decades of Change in New Zealand: From Birth to Death*, IPS, Victoria University, Wellington.

Davies, L. (with Jackson, N.) (1993) *Women's Labour Force Participation: The Past 100 Years*, A Women's Suffrage Centenary Project, Social Policy Agency, Wellington.

Davis, K. (1937) 'Reproductive Institutions and the Pressure for Population', *Sociological Review*, July: 289–306; reprinted in Archives, *PDR* 23, 3: 611–24.

Davis, K. (1970) *Human Society* (24th edn), Macmillan, NY.

Davis, K. (1986) 'Low Fertility in Evolutionary Perspective', in Davis, K., Bernstam, M. and Ricardo-Campbell, R. (eds) *Below Replacement Fertility in Industrial Societies: Causes, Consequences, Policies*, supplement to *PDR* 12, 2: 48–65.

Davis, K. and Blake, J. (1956): Social Structure and Fertility: An Analytical Framework', *Economic Development and Cultural Change* 4: 211–35.

Davis, P. and Lay-Yee, R. (1999) 'Early Sex and its Behavioural Consequences in New Zealand', *Journal of Sex Research* 36: 135–44.

Day, L. (1992) *The Future of Low Birthrate Populations*, Routledge, London.

Dayal, N. and Lovell, R. (1994) 'The New Zealand Family', *SPJNZ* 2: 12–20.

Deakin, S. and Reed, M. (2000) *The Contextual Meaning of Labour Market Flexibility, Economic Theory and the Discourse of European Integration*, ESRC Centre for Business Research, Cambridge.

Demeny, P. (1997) 'Replacement-Level Fertility: The Implausible End Point of the Demographic Transition', in Jones, G., Douglas, R., Caldwell, J. and D'Souza, R., *The Continuing Demographic Transition*, Clarendon, Oxford: 94–110.

Demeny, P. (2005) 'Chapter 1: Policy Challenges of Europe's Demographic Changes: From Past Perspectives to Future Prospects', in Macura, M., MacDonald, A. L. and Haug, W. (eds) *The New Demographic Regime: Population Challenges and Policy Responses*, United Nations (ECE), NY and Geneva: 1–9.

Department of Labour (2004) *Achieving Balanced Lives and Employment: What New Zealanders are Saying about Work-Life Balance*, Dept of Labour, Wellington.

Department of Statistics, *see* Statistics New Zealand; also Hockey, Khawaja.

Désesquelles, A. and Brouard, N. (2003) 'Le Réseau familial des personnes âgées de 60 ans ou plus vivant à domicile ou en institution', *Population* 58, 2: 201–27.

Desrosiers, H. and Le Bourdais, C. (1993) 'Les Unions libres chez les femmes canadiennes: Étude des processus de formation et de dissolution', in Cordell, D. D., Gauvreau, D., Gervais, R. R. and Le Bourdais, C. (eds) *Population, Reproduction, Sociétés: Perspectives et Enjeux de Démographie Sociale*, Les Presses de l'Université de Montreal: 197–214.

Dharmalingam, A. (1999) 'Marriage, Cohabitation and Divorce', in Pool, I. and Johnstone, K. (eds) *op cit.*

Dharmalingam, A., Hillcoat-Nalletamby, S., Pool, I. (1997) 'First Sexual Intercourse and Teenage Pregnancy in New Zealand', paper presented to PAA Conference, Washington, DC, April.

Dharmalingam, A., Pool, I., Dickson, J. (2000) 'Bio-Social Determinants of Hysterectomy in New Zealand', *American Journal of Public Health* 90(9): 1455–58.

Dharmalingam, A., Pool, I. and Johnstone, K. (1998b) 'Work and the Timing of First Live Births in New Zealand', *Proceedings of the 7th Conference on Labour, Employment, and Work*, Victoria University, Wellington, November: 113–40.

Dharmalingam, A., Pool, I. and Sceats, J. (2007) *A Demographic History of the New Zealand Family From 1840: Tables*, Auckland University Press (AUP): www.auckland.ac.nz/uoa/aup/nzfamily/tables.cfm.

Dharmalingam, A., Baxendine, S., Pool, I., Sceats, J. (2000) 'Pill Discontinuation in New Zealand', FFS Flagship Conference *op cit.*

Dharmalingam, A., Pool, I., Hillcoat-Nalletamby, S. and McLuskey, N. (1998a) 'Divorce in New Zealand', paper presented to PAA Conference, Chicago, April.

Dharmalingam, A., Pool, I., Sceats, J. and Baxendine, S. (2003) 'Reproductive Polarisation in New Zealand', paper presented to PAA Conference, Minneapolis, May.

Dharmalingam, A., Pool, I., Sceats, J., Mackay, R. (2004) *Patterns of Family Formation in New Zealand*, Ministry of Social Development, Wellington.

Dickson, J. (1997) 'Sterilisation in New Zealand: The Third Contraceptive Revolution', M.Soc.Sci. thesis, University of Waikato, Hamilton.

Dickson, J., Ball, D., Edmeades, J., Hanson, S. and Pool, I. (1997) 'Recent Trends in Reproduction and Family Structures', briefing paper prepared for the participants at the Population Conference, 12–14 November, Wellington, PSC, University of Waikato, Hamilton (also online under Dept of Labour).

Dickson, N., Sporle, A., Rimene, C. and Paul, C. (2000) 'Pregnancies among New Zealand Teenagers: Trends, Current Status and International Comparisons', *New Zealand Medical Journal* 23, June: 241–45.

Dixon, S. (2000) 'Pay Inequality between Men and Women in New Zealand', *Occasional Paper Series 2000/1*, Labour Market Policy Group, Dept of Labour, Wellington.

Douglas, E. M. K. (1977) 'The New Net Goes Fishing', in Caldwell, J. (ed.) *The Persistence of High Fertility*, ANU, Canberra: 267–79.

Douglas, E. M. K. (with Cameron, J., Pool, I., Tumata, J.) (1981) 'Maori Fertility and Family Structure', unpublished report to ESCAP/UN, PSC, University of Waikato. Hamilton.

Douglas, T. (1994) 'Demographic Changes and their Social Consequences for Maori', in Kia Pumau, *Tonu Proceedings of the Hui Whaka Pumau*, Maori Development Conference, Massey University

Drayton, R. (2006) 'Shock, Awe and Hobbes', *Guardian Weekly*, 6–12 January: 13.

DTZ New Zealand (2005) 'Housing Tenure Aspirations and Attainment', for Centre for Housing Research Aotearoa/NZ and Building Research, www.DTZ.com.

Duncan, G., Young, J. and Rodgers, W. (1994) 'Les familles monoparentales aux Etats-Unis: Dynamique, Niveau de Vie etc., Conséquences sur le Développement d'Enfant', *Population* 49, 6: 1419–36.

Durie, M. Fitzgerald E., Kingi, T. K. *et al.* (2003) 'Monitoring Maori Progress Te Ngahuru: A Maori Outcome Framework', in Pool, I., Dharmalingam, A., Bedford, R., Pole, N. and Sceats, J. (eds) *Population and Social Policy*, special issue of *NZPR* 29(1), PANZ, Wellington.

Easting, S. K. (1992) 'A Theoretical Understanding of Women's Work', in Armstrong, N. *et al.* (eds) *Proceedings, Women and Work Conference: Direction and Strategies*, Social Policy Centre, Massey University, Palmerston North.

Easton, B. (1977) 'The Economic Life-Cycle of the Family', *Australian and New Zealand Journal of Sociology* 13, 1: 85–89.

Easton, B. (1978) 'Income and Fertility in New Zealand: A Cross-Sectional Study', *Proceedings, New Zealand Demographic Society Conference* (collected papers, not paginated, but deposited in major libraries).

Easton, B. (1979) 'The Family Costs of Children', *Proceedings, New Zealand Demographic Society Conference op cit.*

Easton, B. (1980) *Social Policy and the Welfare State in New Zealand*, Allen and Unwin, Auckland.

Easton, B. (1981) *Pragmatism and Progress: Social Security in the Seventies*, University of Canterbury, Christchurch.

Eaton, J. and Meyer, A. (1954) *Man's Capacity to Reproduce: The Demography of a Unique Population*, Free Press, Glencoe, IL.

Eckert-Jaffe, O., Joshi, H., Lynch, K., Mougiz, R., Rendall, M. (2002) 'Timing of Births and Socio-Economic Status in France and Britain: Social Policies and Occupational Polarisation', *Population* (English edition) 57, 3: 475–508.

Eckert-Jaffe, O. and Solaz, A. (2000) 'Does Unemployment bother the Young Couple? French Fertility Survey 1994', FFS Flagship Conference *op cit.*

Economic Commission for Europe/Family and Fertility Study (ECE/FFS) (various authors, various dates, each country outlined) *Fertility and Family Surveys in Countries in the ECE Region: Standard Country Report*, NY and Geneva, United Nations (ECE and UNFPA).
ENGLISH-SPEAKING COUNTRIES
Canada: Wu, Z. (1999).
New Zealand: Johnstone, K., Baxendine, S., Dharmalingam, A., Hillcoat-Nalletamby, S., Pool, I. and Paki Paki, N. (2001).
FRENCH-SPEAKING
France: Toulemon, L. and de Guibert-Lantoine, C. (1998).
DUTCH/GERMAN-SPEAKING
Austria: Prinz, C., Lutz, W. and Nowak, V. (1998).
Belgium: Lodewijckx, E. (1999).
The Netherlands: Latten, J. and de Graaf, A. (1997).
Switzerland: Gabadinho, A. and Wanner, P. (1999).
NORDIC
Denmark: Carnerio, I. and Knudsen, L. (2001).
Finland: Nikander, T. (1998).
Norway: Noack, T. and Ostby, L. (1996).
Sweden: Granström, F. (1997).
SOUTHERN EUROPEAN
Greece: Symenonidou, H. (2002).
Italy: de Sandre, P., Ongaro, F., Rettaroli, R. and Salvini, S. (2000).
Portugal: Carrilho, M. and Magalhaes, G. (2000).
Spain: Delgado, M. and Martin, T. (1999).

Economic and Social Commission for Asia and the Pacific (first draft written by Pool, I. and Khan, M.) (1986) *The Family Fertility and Contraception in Asia and the Pacific: A Review of Seven Cross-Comparative Micro-demographic Country Studies*, Asian Population Studies No. 65, Population Division, ESCAP, United Nations, Bangkok.

Edin, K. (2000) 'What Do Low-Income Single Mothers Say about Marriage?' *Social Problems* 47(1): 112–33.

Edmeades, J. (1999) 'Family Formation and Contraception in New Zealand', M.Soc.Sci.

thesis, University of Waikato, Hamilton.

Eldred-Grigg, S. (1980) *A Southern Gentry: New Zealanders Who Inherited the Earth*, Reed, Wellington.

Eldred-Grigg, S. (1984) *Pleasures of the Flesh: Sex and Drugs in Colonial New Zealand, 1840–1915*, Reed, Wellington.

Ellwood, D. T. and Crane, J. (1990) 'Family Change among Black Americans: What Do We Know?' *Journal of Economic Perspectives* 4: 65–84.

Engelen, T. and Kok, J. (2003) 'Permanent Celibacy and Late Marriage in the Netherlands, 1890–1960', *Population* (English edition) 58, 1: 67–96.

Ermisch, J. (1994) 'Economie, Politique et Changement Familial', *Population* 49, 6: 1377–88.

ESCAP (Population Division) (1985) *Country Monograph Series No. 12: The Population of New Zealand*, 2 vols, United Nations, Bangkok and NY.

Esping-Andersen, G. (1990) *The Three Worlds of Welfare Capitalism*, Polity Press, Cambridge.

Esping-Andersen, G. (1999) *Social Foundations of Post-Industrial Economies*, OUP, NY.

Fairburn, M. (1989) *The Ideal Society and its Enemies*, AUP.

Farmer, R. (1985) 'International Migration', in ESCAP (1985) *op cit*: vol. 1, 54–89.

Fedreci, N. K., Mason, K. and Soner, S. (eds) (1993) *Women's Position and Demographic Change*, Clarendon Press, Oxford.

Fergusson, D. (1987) 'Family formation, dissolution and reformation', in *New Zealand Families in the Eighties and Nineties*, proceedings of the SSRFC symposium, Canterbury University, November: 15–30.

Fergusson, D. (1998) 'The Christchurch Health and Development Study: An Overview and Some Key Findings', *SPJNZ* 10: 154–75.

Fernandez-Kelly, M. P. (1994) 'Towanda's Triumph: Social and Cultural Capital in the Transition to Adulthood in the Urban Ghetto', *Journal of Urban and Regional Research* 18: 88–111.

Festy, P. (1979) *Fécondité des pays occidentaux de 1870 à 1970*, Institut National d'Études Démographiques, Paris.

Festy, P. (1994) 'L'enfant dans la famille: Vingt ans dans l'environnement familial des enfants', *Population* 49, 6: 1245–96.

Fitzgerald, E. and Durie, M. (2000) 'Assessing and Addressing Maori Outcomes: Preliminary Findings from Te Hoe Nuku Roa Maori Household research', *NZPR* 26, 1: 115–21.

Fleming, R. (with Taiapa, J., Pasikale, A. and Easting, S.) (1997) *The Common Purse: Income Sharing in New Zealand Families*, AUP and Bridget Williams Books, Auckland.

Fleming, R. (1999) 'Families of a Different Kind: Patterns of Kinship Support and Obligation in Remarriage Families and Implications for Public Policy', *SPJNZ* 12: 91–105.

Fleming, R. and Easting, S. (1994) *The Intra Family Income Study*, Ministry of Women's Affairs and Massey University Social Policy Research Centre, Wellington.

Fletcher, I. (1979) 'The Effect of World War II on Marriages and Fertility among the Non-Maori Population of New Zealand', *New Zealand Population Newsletter*, December: 14–20.

Flinn, M., Gillespie, J., Hill, N., Maxwell, A., Mitchison, R., Smout, C., with Adamson, D. and Lobban, R. (1976) *Scottish Population History, the 17th Century to the 1930s*, Cambridge University Press (CUP).

Forster, R. and Tienda, M. (1996) 'What's Behind Racial and Ethnic Differentials?' *PDR* 22(supp.): 109–33.

Fossett, M. A. and Kiecolt, K. J. (1993) 'Mate Availability and Family Structure among African Americans in U.S. Metropolitan Areas', *JMF* 55: 288–301.

Fraser, W. H. and Morris, R. (eds) *People and Society in Scotland: Vol. II 1830–1914*, 3 vols, John Donald Publishers Ltd., Edinburgh.

Freedman, R. (1982) 'Fertility Decline: Theories', in Ross (ed.) *op cit*: vol. 1, 258–66.

Freedman R., Whelpton, P. K. and Campbell, A. A. (1959) *Family Planning, Sterility and Population Growth*, McGraw-Hill Book Company, NY.

Frejka, T. (1983) 'Induced Abortion and Fertility: A Quarter Century of Experiences in Eastern Europe', *PDR*, 9, 3: 494–520.

Frejka, T. (1990) (with Atkin, L.) *Seminar on the Fertility Transition in Latin America*, Buenos Aires, 1990, IUSSP, Liège: 179–91.

Frejka, T. (2004) 'The Curiously High Fertility of the USA: Discusssion of Paper "Explanations of the Fertility Crisis in Modern Societies: a Search for Commonalities", by Caldwell and Schindlmayr 2003 [*op cit*]', *PS* 58, 1: 88–92.

Frejka, T. and Sardon, J.-P. (2006) 'The Impact of First Birth Trends on Fertility in Developed Countries: A Cohort Analysis', paper presented to PAA Conference, Los Angeles, March.

Friedman, D., Hechter, M. and Kanazawa, S. (1994) 'A Theory of the Value of Children', *Demography* 31, 3: 375–401.

Fukuda, N. (2005) 'Education, Gender Equity and the Entry into Motherhood in Japan', *Journal Musashi Sociological Society* 7: 1–30.

Garasky, S. and Meyer, D. R. (1996) 'Reconsidering the Increase in Father-Only Families', *Demography* 33(3): 385–93.

Garret, E., Reid, A., Schurer, K. and Szreter, S. (2001) *Changing Family Size in England and Wales: Place, Class and Demography 1891–1911*, CUP.

Gauthier, A. (1996) *The State and the Family: A Comparative Analysis of Family Policies in Industrialized Countries*, Clarendon Press, Oxford.

Gauthier, A. (2002) 'Family Policies in Industrialized Countries', *Population* (English edition) 57, 3, May–June: 447–74.

Gauthier, A. and Hatzius, J. (1997) 'Family Benefits and Fertility: An Econometric Analysis', *PS* 51, 3: 295–306.

Gauthier A., Smeeding, T. and Furstenberg, F. (2004) 'Are Parents in Industrialised Counties Investing Less Time in Children?', *PDR* 30, 4: 6, 47–72.

Gendall, K. (1999) 'Parental Employment and Childcare Use', in Dept of Labour seminar, Childcare, Families and Work, National Advisory Council on the Employment of Women, Wellington, December.

Genus (2004) Special Issue.

Gibson, A. C. (1971) 'Demographic History of New Zealand', PhD thesis, University of California, Berkeley.

Gibson, A. C. (1973) 'Urbanisation in New Zealand', *Demography*, 10 February: 71–84.

Gierveld, J. de Jong (2005) 'Longevity and the Care of Children: The Relationship Between Older Parents and Adult Children', address, Waikato Branch, New Zealand Gerontological Association, 17 May.

Gierveld, J. de Jong, Tilburg, T. and Leecchini, L. (1997) 'Socio-economic Resources, Household Composition, and the Social Network as Determinants of Well-being among Dutch and Tuscan Older Adults', *Genus* LIII, 3–4: 75–100.

Gill, T., Koopman-Boyden, P., Parr, A. and Willmott, W. (1976) *The Rural Women of New Zealand: A National Survey (1975)*, Sociology Dept, University of Canterbury, Christchurch.

Glass, D. (1945) 'The Maori Population', *Eugenics Review* XXXVII, April 1945–January 1946: 67–70.

Goldscheider, F., Turcotte, P. and Kopp, A. (1999) 'The Changing Determinants of Women's First Union Formation in Industrialised Countries', paper presented to European Population Conference, The Hague, September.

Goldscheider, F. K. and Waite, L. J. (1986) 'Sex Differences in the Entry into Marriage', *AJS* 92(1): 91–109.

Goldstein, J. (1999) 'The Leveling of Divorce in the United States', *Demography* 36(3): 409–14.

Goode, W. (1965) *The Family*, Foundations of Modern Sociology Series, Prentice Hall, Englewood Cliffs, NJ.

Goodger, K. (1998) 'Maintaining Sole Parent Families in New Zealand: An Historical Review', *SPJNZ* 10: 122–53.

Gornick, J. and Meyers, M. (2003) *Families that Work*, Russell Sage Foundation, NY.

Granstrom, F. (1997) *Standard Country Report: Sweden*, FFS Countries of the ECE Region, ECE, United Nations, NY and Geneva.

Grebenik, E. and Hill, A. (1974) *International Demographic Terminology: Fertility, Family Planning and Nuptiality*, IUSSP, Liege.

Grebenik, E., Hohn, C. and Mackensen, R. (eds) (1989) *Later Phases of the Family Life Cycle*, Clarendon, Oxford.

Grigsby, J. and McGowan, J. B. (1986) 'Still in the Nest: Adult Children Living with Their Parents', *Sociology and Social Research* 70: 146–48.

Grossbard-Schectman, S. and Granger (1998) 'Travail des femmes et marriage du baby-boom au baby-bust', *Population* 4: 731–52.

Hagewegen, K. and Morgan, P. (2005) 'Intended and Ideal Family Size in the US, 1970–2002', *PDR* 31, 3: 507–27.

Hajnal, H. (1965) 'European Marriage Patterns in Perspective', in Glass, D. V. and Eversley, D. (eds) *Population in History*, Arnold, London: 101–43.

Harloe, M. (1995) *The People's Home? Social Rented Housing in Europe and America*, Oxford, Blackwell.

Harre, J. (1966) *Maori and Pakeha: A Study of Mixed Marriage in New Zealand*, Frederick A. Praeger, NY.

Harre, J. (1972) 'Maori–Pakeha Intermarriage', in Schwimmer, E. (ed.) *The Maori People in the 1960s*, Blackwood and Janet Paul, Auckland: 118–31.

Hawke, G. (1985) *The Making of New Zealand*, CUP.

Heenan, L. D. B. (1977) 'A Note on Area-Based Fertility Data from the Census, 1971', *New Zealand Population Newsletter* 2, 3: 1–3.

Heenan, L. B. D. (1993) 'Older New Zealanders: Population Patterns and Trends', in Koopman-Boyden, P. (ed.) *New Zealand's Ageing Society*, Daphne Brasell Associates Press, Wellington: 29–54.

Heenan, L. B. D. and Wither, A. (1985) *On the Geographical Distribution and Migration of Older New Zealanders: A Review of the Literature*, Social Science Research Funding Committee, Wellington.

Heer, D. M., Hodge, R. W. and Felson, M. (1985) 'The Cluttered Nest: Evidence that Young Adults are More Likely to Live at Home Now than in the Recent Past', *Sociology and Social Research* 69: 436–41.

Henripin, J. (1968) *Tendances et facteurs de la fécondité au Canada*, Govt Printer, Ottawa.

Henripin, J. and Lapierre-Adamcyk, É. (1974) *La fin de la revanche des berceaux: qu'en pensent les Québécoises?* Les Presses de l'Université de Montreal.

Hillcoat-Nalletamby, S. (1999) 'The Interface between Work and Family Formation', in Pool and Johnstone (eds) *op cit*: 55–69.

Hillcoat-Nalletamby, S. (2000) 'Households and Generations', in Koopman-Boyden, P., Dharmalingam, A., Grant, B., Hendy, V., Hillcoat-Nalletamby, S., Mitchell, D., O'Driscoll, M. and Thompson, S., *Transactions in Mid-Life Families*, Monograph Series No. 1, PANZ, Wellington: 37–52.

Hillcoat-Nalletamby, S. and Baxendine, S. (2005) 'The "Ins and Outs" of Work: Diversity or Homogeneity in New Zealand Women's Employment Patterns?' PSC Discussion Paper No. 49, University of Waikato, Hamilton.

Hillcoat-Nalletamby, S. and Dharmalingam, A. (1999) 'Parents' Work Arrangements and Informal Care Use: Multivariate Analysis of Factors Associated with Mothers' Employment Status', paper prepared for the Dept of Labour, presented at Childcare, Families and Work seminar, National Advisory Council on the Employment of Women, Wellington, December.

Hillcoat-Nalletamby, S. and Dharmalingam, A. (2001) 'Inter-generational Solidarity in New Zealand: Exchanges of Assistance Between Mid-Life Individuals and their Families', paper presented at the IUSSP General Population Conference, Changing Family Networks, 18–24 August.

Hillcoat-Nalletamby, S. and Dharmalingam, A. (2003): 'Midlife Parental Support for Adult Children in New Zealand', *Journal of Sociology* (Australia) 39, 3: 271–90.

Hillcoat-Nalletamby, S. and Dharmalingam, A. (2004) 'Solidarity across Generations in New Zealand: Factors influencing Parental Support for Children within a Three-generational Context', PSC Discussion Paper No. 46, University of Waikato, Hamilton.

Hillcoat-Nalletamby, S., Dharmalingam, A., Pool, I. (1999) 'Family Formation, Support Resources and Women's Economic Activity: A New Zealand Case Study', in Tabutin, D. *et al.*, Institut de Démographie de l'Université Catholique de Louvain, *Théories, Paradigmes et Courants Explicatifs en Démographie*, Chaire Quetelet, 1997, Academia

Bruylant/L'Harmattan, Louvain-la-Neuve: 577–600.

Ho, E., Bedford, R. and Bedford, C. (2000) 'Migrants in their Family Context: Application of a Methodology', PSC Discussion Paper No. 34, University of Waikato, Hamilton.

Hobcraft, J. (2000) 'Moving beyond Elaborate Description: Towards Understanding Choices about Parenthood', FFS Flagship Conference *op cit.*

Hobcraft, J. (2004) 'Method, Theory and Substance in Understanding Choices about Becoming a Parent, Progress or Regress: Discussion of Paper "Explanations of the Fertility Crisis in Modern Societies: a Search for Commonalities", by Caldwell and Schindlmayr 2003 [*op cit*]', *PS* 58, 1: 81–84.

Hockey, R. and Khawaja, M. (1982): 'Sub-National Differentials in Fertility: Regression Analysis', *Demographic Bulletin* 5, 1: 5–30.

Hogan, D. P. and Kitagawa, E. M. (1985) 'The Impact of Social Status, Family Structure, and Neighborhood on the Fertility of Black Adolescents', *AJS* 90: 825–52.

Honey, J. (2001) 'New Zealand Jobs: A Demographic Accounting', PSC Discussion Paper No. 40, University of Waikato, Hamilton.

Honey, J. and Lindop, J. (1997) 'The Changing Structures of the New Zealand Labour Force', briefing paper, Population Conference, see Dickson *et al. op cit.*

Hooper, A. (1958) 'Social Relations among Cook Islanders in Auckland', unpublished MA thesis, University of Auckland.

Hopa, N. (1996) 'The Torn Whariki', in Smith, A. B. and Taylor, N. J. (eds) *Supporting Children and Parents through Family Change*, University of Otago Press, Dunedin: 53–60.

Hope, M. (1997) 'Who Cares? Informal Family Support Networks for Maori and Pakeha Women', M.Soc.Sci dissertation, University of Waikato, Hamilton.

Howard, S. (1999a) 'Adolescent Fertility: A Discussion of its Determinants and Consequences within New Zealand', M.Soc.Sci. thesis, University of Waikato, Hamilton.

Howard, S. (1999b) 'Adolescent Birth in New Zealand', in Pool, I. and Johnstone, K. (eds) *op cit*: 35–40.

Huber, J. (ed.) (1991) *Macro-micro Linkages in Sociology*, Sage, Newbury Park, CA.

Hunn, J. (1961) *Report on the Department of Maori Affairs*, Govt Printer, Wellington.

Hutton, D. (2001) 'Solo Parenting in New Zealand: Who are the Children?' PSC Discussion Paper No. 39, University of Waikato, Hamilton.

Hutton, W. (2002) *The World We're In*, Little Brown, London.

Hyslop, D. and Maré, D. (2001). *Understanding Changes in the Distribution of Household Incomes in New Zealand Between 1983–86 and 1995–98*, Working Paper (vol. 01/21), The Treasury, Wellington.

Ip, M. (1990) *Home Away from Home: The Stories of Chinese Women in New Zealand*, New Women's Press, Auckland.

Jackson, N. (1994a) 'Youth Unemployment and the "Core Family": Population Policy and Political Economy', M.Soc.Sci. thesis, University of Waikato, Hamilton.

Jackson, N. (1994b) 'Familial Capacity: The Demographic Components of Caring Capacity', New Zealand Family Rights and Responsibilities Symposium: International Year of the Family, October, Wellington, International Year of the Family Committee, Wellington.

Jackson, N. (1994c) 'Youth Unemployment and the "Invisible Hand": A Case for a Social Measure of Unemployment', in Morrison, P. S. (ed.) *Labour, Employment and Work in New Zealand*, proceedings of the 6th conference, 24–25 November, Victoria University, Wellington: 177–88.

Jackson, N. (2000a) 'The Double Structural Nature of Indigenous Disadvantage: A Case of Disparate Impacts', *NZPR* 26, 1: 55–68.

Jackson, N. (2000b) 'Higher Education Contribution Scheme – A HECS on the Family?' in Carmichael and Dharmalingam (eds) *op cit*: 105–20.

Jackson, N. (2005) 'Disparate Demography, Disparate Impact and Indigenous Disadvantage', paper presented at IUSSP, XXVth International Population Conference, Tours, July.

Jackson, N. and Pool, I. (1994) *Fertility and Family Formation in the 'Second Demographic Transition': New Zealand Patterns and Trends*, Research Report No. 2, New Zealand Institute for Social Research and Development, Christchurch.

Jackson, N. and Pool, I. (1996) 'Will the Real New Zealand Family Please Stand Up?

Substantive and Methodological Factors affecting Research and Policy on Families and Households', *SPJNZ* 6: 148–82.

Jackson, N., Cheung, J. and Pool, I. (1994) 'Maori and Non-Maori Fertility: Convergence, Divergence or Parallel Trends?' PSC Discussion Paper No. 3. University of Waikato, Hamilton.

Jacoby, E. (1958) 'A Fertility Analysis of New Zealand Marriage Cohorts', *PS* 12: 18–39.

Jacoby, E. (1961) 'Some Demographic Observations on First-Order Births in the Light of the Cohort Approach', *Economic Record* 26, 2: 308–19.

Jain, S. K. (1972) *Source Book of Population Data: New Zealand Non-Maori Population 1921–67*, 3 vols, Dept of Demography, ANU, Canberra.

Jensen, J., Krishnan, V., Spitta, M. and Sathyandra, S. (2003) 'Living Standards and Demographic Characteristics: An Analysis Using the NZELSI Scale', *NZPR* 29, 1: 199–228.

Johnstone, K. (1996) 'Aspects of Induced Abortion in New Zealand', paper tabled by Abortion Supervisory Committee, in Inquiry into the Abortion Supervisory Committee, *Report of the Justice and Law Reform Committee, New Zealand House of Representatives*, Wellington.

Johnstone, K. (2002) 'The Qualitative Study of Children, Childrearing, Work and the Family in Australia', unpublished report prepared for National Institute of Population and Social Security, Tokyo.

Johnstone, K. and Pool, I. (1996a) 'Family Demographic Change: 1: Two-Parent Families', *Butterworths Family Law Journal* 2, 1: 298–301.

Johnstone, K. and Pool, I. (1996b) 'New Zealand Families: Size, Income and Labour Force Participation', *New Zealand Journal of Social Policy* 7: 143–73.

Johnstone, K. and Pool, I. (1996c) 'Family Demographic Change: 3: Stocktaking the Nation's Children', *Butterworths Family Law Journal* 2, 3: 72–74.

Johnstone, K., Baxendine, S., Dharmalingam, A., Hillcoat-Nalletamby, S., Pool, I. (2001) *Standard Country Report: New Zealand*, ECE/FFS *op cit.*

Jones, E. (1971) 'Fertility Decline in Australia and New Zealand, 1981–1936', *Population Index* 37, 4: 301–38.

Jones, G. (1982) 'Sociological and Economic Theories [of Fertility]', in Ross (ed.) *op cit*: vol. 1, 279–85.

Jones, G. and Douglas, R. (1997) 'Introduction', in Jones *et al.* (eds) *op cit.*

Jones, G., Douglas, R., Caldwell, J. and D'Souza, R. (1997) *The Continuing Demographic Transition*, Clarendon, Oxford: 1–12.

Kaa, van de, *see* van de Kaa.

Kamerman, S. B. and Kahn, A. J. (1997a) 'Introduction', in Kamerman and Kahn (eds) *op cit*: 1–28.

Kamerman, S. and Kahn, A. (1997b) 'United States', in Kamerman and Kahn (eds) *op cit*: 305–418.

Kamerman, S. and Kahn, A. (eds) (1997c) *Family Change and Family Policies in Great Britain, Canada, New Zealand and the United States*, Clarendon, Oxford.

Keilman, N. (1988) 'Dynamic Household Models', in Keilman, N., Kuijsten, A. and Vossen, A. (eds) *Modelling Household Formation and Dissolution*, Clarendon, Oxford.

Kelsey, J. (1999) *Reclaiming the Future: New Zealand and the Global Economy*, Bridget Williams Books, Wellington.

Kennedy, R. (1975) *The Irish: Emigration, Marriage and Fertility*, University of California Press, Berkeley and LA.

Keys, C. L. (1969) 'Some Aspects of Marital Fertility in the Auckland Urban Area', unpublished MA thesis, University of Auckland.

Khawaja, M. (1985) 'Trends and Differentials in Fertility', in ESCAP *op cit*: vol. 1, 152–77.

Khawaja, M. (1986) *Trends and Patterns in New Zealand Fertility 1912–1983*, Dept of Statistics, Wellington (authorship not attributed).

Khawaja, M. and Hockey, R. (1979) 'Sub-National Differentials in New Zealand Fertility, 1971–76', *Quarterly Demographic Bulletin* 3, 2: 4–17.

Khoo, S.-E. (1985) *Family Formation and Ethnicity*, Working Paper No. 9, Institute of Family Studies, June, Melbourne.

Khoo, S.-E. (1986) *Living Together: Young Couples in de facto Relationships*, Working Paper No. 10, Institute of Family Studies, June, Melbourne.

Khoo, S.-E. (1987) 'Living together as Married: A Profile of de facto Couples in Australia', *JMF* 49: 185–191.

Kiernan, K. and Cherlin, A. (1999) 'Parental Divorce and Partnership Dissolution in Adulthood: Evidence from a British Cohort Study', *PS* 53: 49–63.

Kilmartin, L. and Thorns, D. (1978) *Cities Unlimited*, George Allen and Unwin Ltd, Sydney.

King, M. (2003) *The Penguin History of New Zealand*, Penguin, Auckland.

Kirk, D. (1968) *Europe's Population in the Inter-War Years*, Gordon and Breach Science Publishers, NY.

Klijzing, E. and Macura, M. (1997) 'Cohabitation and Extra-marital Childbearing: Early FFS Evidence', Procceedings International Population Conference, Beijing, 1997, IUSSP, Liege: vol. 2, 885–902.

Koball, H. (1998) 'Have African-American Men Become Less Committed to Marriage? Explaining the Twentieth Century Racial Cross-Over in Men's Marriage Timing', *Demography* 35(2): 251–58.

Konietzka, D. and Kreyenfeld, M. (2002) 'Women's Employment and Non-Marital Chilbearing: A Comparison between East and West Germany in the 1990s', *Population* (English edition) No. 2: 331–58.

Koopman-Boyden, P. (ed.) (1978) *Families in New Zealand Society*, Methuen, Wellington.

Koopman-Boyden, P. (1978) 'The Elderly in the Family', in Koopman-Boyden (ed) *op cit*: 57–70.

Koopman-Boyden, P. and Hillcoat-Nalletamby, S. (2000) 'Conceptual Models of the Family and Family Relationships', in Koopman-Boyden *et al. op cit*: 7–22.

Kramarow, E. (1995) 'Living Alone Among the Elderly in the United States: Historical Perspectives on Household Change', *Demography* 32: 335–52.

Kravdal, O. (1999) 'Does Marriage Require a Stronger Economic Underpinning than Informal Cohabitation?' *PS* 53: 63–80.

Krishnan, V., Schoeffel, P. and Warren, J. (1994) *The Challenge of Change: Pacific Island Communities in New Zealand, 1986–1993*, New Zealand Institute for Social Research and Development, Wellington.

Kukutai, T. (2003) *The Dynamics of Ethnicity Reporting: Maori in New Zealand*, discussion paper prepared for Te Puni Kokiri, Ministry of Maori Development, Wellington.

Kukutai, T., Pool, I. and Sceats, J. (Portal Consulting and Associates) (2002) 'Central North Island Iwi: Population Patterns and Trends', Wai 791, #A-97, Research Report for the Waitangi Tribunal (commissioned by the Crown Forestry Rental Trust, April), Wellington.

Kurlansky, M. (2004) *1968: The Year that Rocked the World*, Vintage Books, London.

Labrum, B. (2004) 'Negotiating an Increased Range of Functions: Families and the Welfare State', in Dalley, B. and Tennant, M. (eds) *Past Judgement: Social Policy in New Zealand History*, University of Otago Press, Dunedin: 157–74.

Lampard, E. (1967) 'Historical Aspects of Urbanisation', in Hauser, P. and Schnore, L. (eds) *The Study of Urbanisation*, John Wiley, NY: 514–54.

Landale, N. S. and Hauan, S. M. (1996) 'Migration and Premarital Childbearing among Puerto Rican Women', *Demography* 33(4): 429–42.

Lapierre-Adamcyk, É., Le Bourdais, C. and Marcil-Gratton, N. (1999) 'Vivre en couple pour la première fois: La signification du choix de l'union libre au Québec et en Ontario', *Cahiers Québécois de Démographie* 28, 1–2: 199–227.

Lapierre-Adamcyk, É. and Charvet, C. (1999) 'L'Union libre et le marriage: un bilan des travaux en démographie', *Cahiers Québécois de Démographie* 28, 1–2: 1–21.

Lapierre-Adamcyk, É., Pool, I. and Dharmalingam, A. (1997) 'New Forms of Reproductive and Family Behaviour in the Neo-Europes: Findings from the "European Fertility and Family Survey" on Canada and New Zealand', paper presented to IUSSP, International Population Conference, Beijing, October.

Latten, B. and de Graaf, A. (1997) *Standard Country Report: The Netherlands*, ECE/FFS *op cit*.

Legare, J. (2003) 'Un siècle de vieillissement démographique', in Piché, V. and Le Bourdais, C. (eds) *La Démographie Québécoise: Enjeux du XXI Siècle*, Les Presses de l'Université de Montreal: 176–92.

Lepina, M.-C. and Pool, I. (2000) 'Social and Spatial Differentials in Age-Structural

Transitions: Implications for Policies on Ageing', *Espace, Population et Sociétés*: 399–410.

Lerman, R. I. (1989) 'Employment Opportunities of Young Men and Family Formation', *American Economic Review* 79: 62–66.

Lesthaeghe, R. (1983) 'A Century of Demographic Change in Western Europe', *PDR* 9, 3: 411–35.

Lesthaeghe, R. (1991) 'The Second Demographic Transition in Western Countries: An Interpretation', InterUniversity Programme in Demography, Working Papers, Brussels.

Lesthaeghe, R. and Moors, G. (1995) 'Is There a New Conservativism that Will Bring Back the Old Family? Ideational Trends and the Stages of Family Formation in Germany, France, Belgium and the Netherlands', InterUniversity Programme in Demography, Working Papers, Brussels.

Letablier, M. T. (2002) 'Fertility and Family Policies in France', presentation to International Workshop/Seminar on Low Fertility and Social Policies, National Institute of Population and Social Security, November, Tokyo.

Levesque, A. (1986) 'Prescribers and Rebels: Attitudes to European Women's Sexuality in New Zealand 1860–1916', in Brookes, B., Macdonald, C. and Tennant, M., *Women in History: Essays on European Women in New Zealand*, Allen and Unwin Wellington: 1–12.

Levine, B. (1982) 'Contraceptive Use: United States Overview', in Ross, J. (ed.) *International Encyclopedia of Population*, Free Press, NY: vol. 1, 120–22.

Lichter, D. T., LeClere, F. B. and McLaughlin, D. K. (1991) 'Local Marriage Market Conditions and the Marital Behavior of Black and White Women', *AJS* 96: 843–67.

Lichter, D. T., McLaughlin, D. K., Kephart, G. and Landry, D. J. (1992) 'Race and the Retreat from Marriage: A Shortage of Marriageable Men?' *American Sociological Review* 57: 781–99.

Lichter, D. T., McLaughlin, D. K. and Ribar, D. C. (1997) 'Welfare and the Rise in Female Headed Families', *AJS* 103, 1: 112–43.

Livi Bacci, M. (2004a) 'Preface', *Genus* LX, 1: 15–17.

Livi Bacci, M. (2004b) 'The Narrow Path of Policies', *Genus* LX, 1: 207–32.

Livi Bacci, M. and Salvini, S. (2000) 'Trop de famille et trop peu d'enfants: la fécondité en Italie depuis 1960', *Cahiers Québécois de Démographie* 29, 2: 231–54.

London, R. A. (1999) 'Trends in Single Mothers' Living Arrangements from 1970 to 195: Correcting the Current Population Survey', *Demography* 35, 1: 125–131.

Lutz, W., Sanderson, W. and Scherbov, S. (2001) 'The End of World Population Growth', *Nature* 412: 543–45.

Lutz, W. and Scherbov, S. (2000) 'What do we know about the Future Changes in the Proportions of Children and Elderly in Europe?', Reprint Research Report Series, International Institute for Applied Systems Analysis, Laxenburg, Austria.

Lutz, W. and Skirbekk, V. (2005) 'Policies addressing the Tempo Effect in Low-fertility Countries', *PDR* 31, 4: 699–720.

Lutz, W., Skirbekk, V. and Testa, M. (2006) 'The Low-fertility Trap Hypothesis: Forces that may Lead to Further Postponement and Fewer Births', *Vienna Yearbook of Population 2006*, Austrian Academy of Sciences: 167–92.

Lutz, W., Testa, M. and Skirbekk, V. (2006) 'The Low-fertility Trap Hypothesis', paper presented to PAA Conference, Los Angeles, March.

McAloon, J. (2002) *No Idle Rich: The Wealthy of Canterbury and Otago, 1840–1914*, University of Otago Press, Dunedin.

Macdonald, C. (1990) *A Woman of Good Character*, Allen and Unwin, Historical Branch, Dept of International Affairs, Wellington.

Maclennan, W. (1981) 'Variations in Fertility in New Zealand, and their Significance', unpublished MA thesis, University of Auckland.

Macpherson, C. (1978) 'The Polynesian Migrant Family: A Samoan Case Study', in Koopman-Boyden, P. (ed.) *op cit*: 120–37.

Macunovich, D. (1996) 'Fertility and Female Labor Force Participation', in Casterline, J., Lee, R. and Foote, K. (eds) *Fertility in the United States*, Population Council, NY: 223–57.

Malpas, N. (1999) 'Les couples européens: qui sont-ils?' *Cahiers Québécois de Démographie* 28, 1–2: 117–49.

Malthus, T. R. (1798) 'An Essay on the Principle of Population', in Flew, A. (ed.) *Malthus: An Essay on the Principle of Population*, Penguin, Harmondsworth (1970): 61–217.

Manning, W. D. (1995) 'Cohabitation, Marriage, and Entry Into Motherhood', *JMF* 57: 191–200.

Manning, W. D. and Smock, P. J. (1995) 'Why Marry? Race and the Transition to Marriage among Cohabitors', *Demography* 32, 4: 509–20.

Marcil-Gratton, N., Le Bourdais, C. and Juby, H. (2003) 'Être père au xxi siècle: vers une rédefinition du rôle des hommes auprès des enfants', in Piché, V. and Le Bourdais, C. (eds) *La Démographie Québécoise: Enjeux du XXI Siècle*, Les Presses de l'Université de Montreal: 145–75.

Marr, W. and McCready, D. (1997) 'Housing Quality and Affordability among Female Householders in Canada', *Genus* LIII 3–4: 215–41.

Marsault, A. (1999) 'Retirement Provision for New Zealand Women: The Role of Demographic Influences', PSC Discussion Paper No. 38. University of Waikato, Hamilton.

Marsault, A., Pool, I., Dharmalingam, A., Hillcoat-Nalletamby, S., Johnstone, K., Smith, C. and George, M. (1997) *Technical and Methodological Report, NZW:FEE*, Technical Report Series, PSC, University of Waikato, Hamilton.

Martin, B. (1999) 'Incomes of Individuals and Families in New Zealand, 1951–1996', unpublished PhD thesis, University of Waikato, Hamilton.

Maxim Institute (various dates) 'Media Releases', www.maxim.org.nz.

May, H. (1992) *Minding Children, Managing Men: Conflict and Compromise in the Lives of Post War Pakeha Women*, Bridget Williams Books, Wellington.

Mazumdar, P. (2003) 'Eugenics', in Demeny, P. and McNicoll, G. (eds) *Encyclopedia of Population*, 2 vols, Mamillan Reference Books, Thompson Gale, NY: vol. 1, 319–22.

McAllister, J. (2005) 'Spending Christmas Day as a Family Can Be Impossible After a Bitter Break-up and There's a Fight Over Who Gets the Children', *Weekend Herald: Canvas*, 17 December: 18–20.

McCreary, J. (1966) *Housing and Welfare Needs of Islanders in Auckland: Report to the Minister of Island Territories*, Govt Printer, Wellington.

McDonald, P. (1974) *Marriage in Australia: Age at First Marriage and Proportions Marrying, 1860–1971*, Australian Family Formation Monograph No. 2, ANU Demography Programme, Canberra.

McDonald, P. (2000a) 'Gender Equity, Social Institutions and the Future of Fertility', *Journal of Population Research* 17(1): 1–16.

McDonald, P. (2000b) 'Gender Equity in Theories of Fertility Transition', *PDR* 26, 3: 427–39.

McDonald, P. (2001a) 'Low Fertility not Politically Sustainable', *Population Today* 29, 6: 3–8.

McDonald, P. (2001b) 'Work-family Policies are the Right Approach to the Prevention of Low Fertility', *People and Place* 9, 3: 17–27.

McDonald, P. (2002) 'Sustaining Fertility through Public Policy: the Range of Options', *Population* (English edition) 57, 3: 417–46.

McDonald, P. (2006) 'An Assessment of Policies that Support Having Children from the Perspectives of Equity, Efficiency and Efficacy', *Vienna Yearbook of Population, 2006*, Austrian Academy of Sciences: 214–34.

McDonald, P. and Kippen, R. (2000) 'Population Futures for Australia and New Zealand: An Analysis of Options', *NZPR* 25(2): 45–65.

McDowell, L. (2001) 'Father and Ford revisited: Gender, Class and Employment Change in the New Millennium', *Transactions Inst. of British Geographers*, NS 26: 448–64.

McIlraith, J. (1911) *The Course of Prices in New Zealand*, Govt Printer, Wellington.

McLanahan, S. (2004) 'Diverging Destinies: How Children are Faring Under the Second Demographic Transition', *Demography* 41, 4: 607–27.

McLean, R. (199) 'Scottish Emigrants to New Zealand: Motives, Means and Backgrounds', unpublished PhD thesis, University of Edinburgh.

McLuskey, N. (1999) 'Marital Disruption: A Demographic Analysis of Separation in New Zealand', unpublished M.Soc.Sci. thesis, University of Waikato, Hamilton.

McNeish, J. (2003) *Dance of the Peacocks*, Vintage, Auckland.

McPherson, M. (1992) 'Cohort Vulnerability to Lack of Support in Old Age', unpublished M.Soc.Sci. thesis, University of Waikato, Hamilton.

McPherson, M. (1995) *Divorce in New Zealand*, Social Policy Research Centre, Massey University, Palmerston North.

McPherson, M. (2003) *The Nature and Role of the Extended Family in New Zealand*

and Its Relationship with the State, Social Policy Research Centre, Massey University, Palmerston North.

Mehryar, A. H. and Ahmad-Nia, S. (2004) 'Age-structural Transition in Iran: Short- and Long-term Consequences of Drastic Fertility Swings during the Final Decades of the Twentieth Century', in Pool and Wong (eds) *op cit* (2006).

Mein Smith, *see* Smith.

Menken, J. (1985) 'Age and Fertility: How Long Can you Wait?' *Demography* 22, 4: 469–83.

Metge, J. (1964) *A New Maori Migration: Rural and Urban Relations in Northern New Zealand*, Athlone and Melbourne University Presses, London and Melbourne.

Metge, J. (1976) *The Maoris of New Zealand: Rautahi*, Routledge and Kegan Paul, London.

Metge, J. (1995) *New Growth From Old: The Whanau in the Modern World*, VUP, Wellington.

Michael, R. T., Fuchs, V. R. and Scott, S. R. (1980) 'Changes in the Propensity to Live Alone, 1950–1976', *Demography* 17: 39–53.

Midland Health (1997) *Sexual and Reproductive Health in the Midland Health Region*, vol. 2, part 3, Health and Disability Analysis Unit, Midland Health, Hamilton.

Ministry of Social Policy (1999) 'Draft Tender Brief for a Study of Changes in Family Form in New Zealand', 24 December, Wellington.

Ministry of Social Policy (2000) 'Departmental Contestable Research Pool: Bid for Extension of Family Dynamics/Effectiveness Funding', paper presented to Ministry of Science and Technology, February, Wellington.

Ministry of Women's Affairs and Statistics New Zealand (2001) *Around the Clock: Findings from the New Zealand Time-Use Survey, 1988–89*, Wellington.

Moffitt, R. (1992) 'Incentive Effects of the U.S. Welfare System: A Review', *Journal of Economic Literature* 30(1): 1–61.

Moore, J., Gale, J., Dew, K. and Davie, G. (2006) 'Student Debt among Junior Doctors in New Zealand; Part 1: Quantity, Distribution, and Psycho-social Impact', *NZ Medical Journal* 119, 1229, February: www.nzma.org.nz/journal/index.shtml.

Morgan, P. (2004) *Family Matters: Family Breakdown and its Consequences*, New Zealand Business Roundtable, Wellington.

Morgan, S. Phil (2003a) 'Baby Boom, Post-World War II', in Demeny, P. and McNicoll, G. (eds) *Encyclopaedia of Population*, Macmillan Reference Books, Thompson Gale, NY: vol. 2, 73–77.

Morgan, S. Phil (2003b) 'Low Fertility in the 21st Century', *Demography* 40, 4: 589–603.

Morgan, S. Phil, Pool, I., Sceats, J. and Dharmalingam, A. (2001) 'The Link of Early Childbearing to Marriage and to Subsequent Fertility in New Zealand', *NZPR* 27, 1 and 2: 49–76.

Morris, R. (1990) 'Urbanisation and Scotland', in Fraser, W. and Morris, R. (eds) *op cit*: 73–102.

Mowbray, M. (2001) *Distributions and Disparity: New Zealand Household Incomes*, Ministry of Social Policy, Wellington.

Mowbray, M. and Khan, A. (1984) 'One and Two Parents from the Census', *NZPR* 10, 3: 27–40.

Munoz-Perez, F. and Prioux, F. (1999) 'Les Enfants nés hors mariage et leurs parents', *Population* 54, 3: 481–508.

Murphy, M. (1993) 'The Contraceptive Pill and Women's Employment as Factors in Fertility Change in Britain, 1963–80', *PS* 47, 2: 221–44.

Murphy, M. (1996) 'Household and Family Structures among Ethnic Minority Groups in Britain', in Coleman, D. and Salt, J. (eds) *Ethnic Minorities in Britain: Census Vol. I*, HMSO, London.

Murphy, M. (2000) 'The Evolution of Cohabitation in Britain 1960–95', *PS* 54, 1: 43–56.

Murphy, M. and Wang, D. (1998) 'Family and Socio-demographic Influences on Patterns of Leaving Home in Postwar Britain', *Demography* 35(3): 293–305.

Murray, C. (1984) *Losing Ground: American Social Policy, 1950–1980*, Basic Books, NY.

Murray, M. (2004) 'Primogeniture, Patrilineage and the Displacement of Women', in Wright, N., Ferguson, M. and Buck, A., *Women, Property, and the Letter of the Law in Early Modern England*, Toronto University Press: 121–36.

Myles, J. (1996) 'When Markets Fail: Social Welfare in Canada and the US', in Esping-Andersen, G. (ed.) *Welfare States in Transition*, Sage, London: 116–40.

National Center for Health Statistics (1994*) Monthly Vital Statistics Report: Advance Report of Final Natality Statistics, 1992*, Public Health Service, Government Printing Office, Washington, DC.

Neville, R. J. W. (1985) 'Trends and Differentials in the Age-Sex Structure', in ESCAP *op cit* (eds): 29–53.

Newman, A. (1881) 'A Study of the Causes Leading to the Extinction of the Maori', *Transactions and Proceedings, NZ Institute*, 14: 58–77.

Newton, K. (2001) 'Social Capital, Civil Society, and Democracy', *International Political Science Review* 22(2): 201–14.

New Zealand Historical Atlas (1997), McKinnon, M. (ed.), David Bateman Ltd/Dept of Internal Affairs, Auckland.

NZOYB, *New Zealand Official Yearbook* (various years) Statistics New Zealand, Wellington.

Nimwegen, van, *see* van Nimwegen.

Noack, T. and Ostby, L. (1996) *Standard Country Report: Norway*, ECE/FFS *op cit.*

Nolan, M. (2000) *Breadwinning: New Zealand Women and the State*, Canterbury University Press, Christchurch.

OECD (2004) *Babies and Bosses: Reconciling Work and Family Life, Vol. 3, New Zealand Portugal and Switzerland*, OECD, Paris.

Oláh, Livia Sz. (2001) 'Gender and family stability: Dissolution of the first parental union in Sweden and Hungary', paper presented at the Flagship conference, FFS *op cit*, published 19 February, www.demographic-research.org/volumes/vol4/2/4-2.pdf.

Oliver, W. H. (1988) 'Social Policy in New Zealand: An Historical Overview', in Royal Commission of Social Policy, *The April Report: Vol. 1, New Zealand Today*, Govt Printer, Wellington: 3–45.

Olssen, E. and Levesque, A. (1978) 'Towards a History of the European Family in New Zealand', in Koopman-Boyden (ed.) *op cit*: 1–25.

O'Neill, C. J. (1979) 'Fertility: Past, Present and Future', in Neville, R. J. W. and O'Neill (eds) *The Population of New Zealand: Interdisciplinary Perspectives*, Longman Paul, Auckland: 125–49.

O'Neill, C. J. (1985) 'Nuptiality and Marital Status', in ESCAP *op cit:* vol. 1, 193–208.

O'Neill, D. P., Hudson, R., Boren, R., O'Connell, B. M. and Donnell, A. A. (1976) *Ex-Nuptial Children and the Parents*, Dept of Social Welfare, Govt Printer, Wellington.

Oppenheimer, V. K., Kalmjhn, M. and Lim, N. (1997) 'Men's Career Development and Marriage Timing during a Period of Rising Inequality', *Demography* 34, 3: 311–30.

Oppenheimer, V. K. and Lew, V. (1995) 'American Marriage Formation in the Eighties: How Important Was Women's Economic Independence?' in Mason, K. and Jenssen, A. (eds) *Gender and Family Change in Industrialized Countries*, Clarendon Press, Oxford.

Oxford Companion to Music (1978) (12th edn) OUP, London.

Pagnini, D. L. and Morgan, S. P. (1996) 'Racial Differences in Marriage and Childbearing: Oral History Evidence from the South in the Early Twentieth Century', *AJS* 101, 6: 1694–718.

Papastergiadis, N. (2000) *The Turbulence of Migration: Globalization, Deterritorialization and Hybridity*, Policy Press, Cambridge.

Papps, T. O'H. (1985a) 'Sources of Demographic Data', in ESCAP *op cit:* vol. 2, 200–23.

Papps, T. O'H. (1985b) 'The Growth and Distribution of Population: Historical Trends', in ESCAP *op cit:* vol. 1, 10–28.

Patterson, S. (1976) *Divorce in New Zealand: A Statistical Study*, Research Section, Dept of Justice, Wellington, New Zealand.

Pennec, S. (1996) 'La Place des familles à quatre générations en France', *Population* 51, 1: 31–60.

Peron, Y. (2003) 'Du mariage obligatoire au mariage facultatif', in Piché and Le Bourdais (eds) *op cit*: 110–43.

Phillips, R. (1981) *Divorce in New Zealand: A Social History*, OUP, Auckland and NY.

Piché, V. and Le Bourdais, C. (2003) 'La démographie québécoise au xxième siècle: d'autres révolutions à venir?' in Piché and Le Bourdais (eds) *op cit*: 300–13.

Pickens, K. (1980) 'Marriage Patterns in a 19th Century British Colonial Population', *Journal of Family History*, Summer: 180–96.

Pinelli, A., de Rose, A., del Giulo, P. and Rossina, A. (2000) 'Interrelationships between Partnership and Fertility Behaviour', FFS Flagship Conference *op cit.*

Pison, G. and Couvert, N. (2004) 'La fréquence des accouchements gémellaires en France. La triple influence de la biologie, de la médicine et des comportements familiaux', *Population* 59, 6: 877–908.

Podder, N. and Chatterjee, S. (2002) 'Sharing the "National Cake" in Post Reform New Zealand: Income Inequality Trends in Terms of Income Sources', unpublished paper, Massey University, Dept of Applied and International Economics, published in (2002) *Journal of Public Economics* 86, 1: 1–27.

Pool, I. (1959a) 'A Social Geography of Auckland', 2 vols, unpublished MA thesis, University of Auckland.

Pool, I. (1959b) 'State Housing in Auckland', *Geographic Society Newsletter*: 1–2.

Pool, I. (1961) 'Maoris in Auckland', *Journal of the Polynesian Society*, vol. 70: 43–66.

Pool, I. (1970) 'Ghana: Male Attitudes to Family Limitation and Family Size', *Studies in Family Planning*, December: 1–3.

Pool, I. (1977) *The Maori Population of New Zealand*, AUP.

Pool, I. (1985) 'Mortality Trends and Differentials', in ESCAP *op cit*: vol. 1, 209–42.

Pool, I. (1986) *Population and Social Trends: Implications for New Zealand Housing*, Research Paper 86/3 National Housing Commission, Wellington.

Pool, I. (1991) *Te Iwi Maori*, AUP.

Pool, I. (1992) 'The New Zealand Family: Structural Changes in the Context of Shifts in Societal Values', *NZPR* 18, 1 and 2: 69–86.

Pool, I. (1994) 'Cross-Comparative Perspectives on New Zealand Health', in Spicer, J., Trlin, A. and Walton, J. (eds) *Social Dimensions of Health and Disease: New Zealand Perspectives*, Dunmore, Palmerston North: 16–50.

Pool, I. (1996) 'Family Demographic Changes: Good News or Bad News?', in Smith, A. and Taylor, N. *op cit*: 11–34.

Pool, I. (1997) 'Ageing and Other Competing Dependencies', *Public Sector* 3, 2 (abridged from 'Technical and Policy Aspects of Ageing in New Zealand', PSC Discussion Paper No. 21).

Pool, I. (1998) 'The Family Court in 2015: The Socio-demographic Context', paper in New Zealand Law Society (eds) *NZLS Family Law Conference, 31 August–2 September, Christchurch*, Butterworths, Wellington.

Pool, I. (1999) 'People (=Population) and Public Policy in New Zealand', *NZPR* 25: 57–79.

Pool, I. (2000a) 'New Zealand Population Then, Now, Hereafter', in Carmichael and Dharmalingam (eds) *op cit*: 23–58.

Pool, I. (2000b) 'Vers un modèle de la transition-age structurelle: une conséquence, mais aussi une composante de la transition démographique', Conferencier invité, Congrès de l'Association Canadienne-française pour l'avancement de science, Montreal, May.

Pool, I. (2000c) '"Political Arithmetick" and Constitutional Concerns: How New Zealand Society will Change', in James, C. (ed.) *Building the Constitution*, Institute of Public Policy, Victoria University, Wellington: 221–31.

Pool, I. (2002) 'Transfers of Capital and Shifts in New Zealand's Regional Population Distribution, 1840–1996', PSC Discussion Paper No. 42, University of Waikato, Hamilton.

Pool, I. (2003) 'Ageing, Population Waves, Disordered Cohorts and Policy', *NZPR*, Special Issue 29(1): 19–39.

Pool, I. (2004) 'Human Capacity, or Fiscal Capacity in Support of the Aged? A Demographic Perspective', paper presented to 'Expanding Horizons: The Art and Science of Ageing', New Zealand Association of Gerontology Conference, Christchurch, April.

Pool, I. (2005) 'Family Vulnerability: Effects of Changes to Dynamics, Forms and Structures on Functions', *Family Law: The New Era – Professionalism in the Family Court*, proceedings of the Family Law Conference, October, Continuing Legal Education, New Zealand Law Society, Wellington: 355–75.

Pool, I. (2006) 'Fertility and Reproductive Polarisation: The Current Situation in New Zealand in Cross-national and Historical Perspective', paper presented to Sub-Replacement Fertility: Is this an Issue for New Zealand Seminar, IPS, Victoria University, Wellington, October: www.ips.ac.nz.

Pool, I. (with Cameron, J., Douglas, E. M. K., Tumata, J.) (1985) 'The ESCAP Family and Fertility Study Pre-Test', unpublished report for ESCAP/UN PSC, University of Waikato, Hamilton.

Pool, I. and Bedford, R. (1997) 'Population Change: From Dynamics and Structures to Policies', Plenary Session Paper, Population Conference, Wellington, November, PSC, University of Waikato, Hamilton.

Pool, I. and Cheung, J. (2004) 'A Cohort History of Mortality in New Zealand', *NZPR* 29, 2: 107–37.

Pool, I. and Cheung, J. (2005) 'Why Were New Zealand Levels of Life-expectation so High at the Dawn of the Twentieth Century?' *Genus*, LXI, 2: 9–33.

Pool, I. and Crawford, C. (1979) 'The Life-cycle as a Tool for Research on Children and the Family in New Zealand', *Proceedings, New Zealand Demographic Society Conference*, Demographic Society, Wellington.

Pool, I. and Crawford, C. R. (1980) 'Adolescent Ex-Nuptial Births and Ex-Nuptial conceptions in New Zealand', *NZPR* 6, 2: 20–28.

Pool, I. and Hillcoat-Nalletamby, S. (1999) 'Fathers, Families, Futures: A Population Perspective', in Birks, S. and Callister, P. (eds) *Perspectives on Fathering*, Issue Paper No. 4, Centre for Policy Evaluation, Massey University, Palmerston North: 12–22.

Pool, I. and Johnstone, K. (1996) 'Family Demographic Change: 2, Sole-parent families', *Butterworths Family Law Journal* 2, 2: 41–44.

Pool, I. and Moore, M. (1986) *Lone Parenting in Canada: Characteristics and Determinants*, Statistics Canada, Ottawa.

Pool, I. and Sceats, J. (1981) *Fertility and Family Formation in New Zealand*, Ministry of Works, Wellington.

Pool, I. and Sceats, J. (2003) 'Low Fertility of the English-Speaking Countries', proceedings of the National Institute for Population and Social Security, International Workshop/Seminar on Low Fertility and Family Policies, Tokyo, November 2002, *Journal of Population and Social Security (Population)*, supplement to vol. 1: www.ipss.go.jp/webj/WebJournal.files/population/ps03_6.html.

Pool, I. and Tiong, F. (1991) 'Sub-National Differences in the Pakeha Fertility Decline', *NZPR* 17, 2: 46–64.

Pool, I. and Wong, L. (Rodriguez) (2006) 'Age-structural Changes and policy: An Emerging Issue', *Age-Structural Transitions: Demographic Bonuses, but Emerging Challenges for Population and Sustainable Development*, CICRED, Paris.

Pool, I., Dharmalingam, A. and Sceats, J. (2000) 'What Happened in the Seventies Mummy? Periodicity in New Zealand Family Formation', FFS Flagship Conference *op cit.*

Pool, I., Jackson, N. and Dickson, J. (1998) 'Family formation and Structure: The Implications of Cradle Conservatism and Reproductive Reprise', in Adair and Dixon *op cit*: 88–129.

Pool, I., Prachuabmoh, V. and Tuljapurkar, S. (2005) 'Age-structural Transitions, Population Waves and "Political Arithmetick"', in Tuljapurkar, Pool and Prachuabmoh (eds) *Riding the Age Waves: Population, Resources and Development*, Springer, Dordrecht: 3–10.

Pool, I., Sceats, J. and Cheung, J. (2002) 'Vivre plus longtemps peut-être en santé, mais avoir peu de descendants? Quelques implications pour la société néo-zélandaise', *Vivre plus longtemps, avoir moins d'enfants, Quelles Implications*, Actes, Colloque international de Byblos-Jbeil, Association international des démographes de langue française, October 2000, Presses Universitaires de France, Paris: 603–13.

Pool, I., Baxendine, S., Cochrane, B. and Lindop, J. (2005a) 'New Zealand Regions 1986–2001: Population Dynamics', PSC Discussion Paper, University of Waikato, Hamilton.

Pool, I., Baxendine, S., Cochrane, B. and Lindop, J. (2005b) 'New Zealand Regions 1986–2001: Households and Families, and Their Dwellings', PSC Discussion Paper, University of Waikato, Hamilton.

Pool, I., Baxendine, S., Cochrane, B. and Lindop, J. (2005c) 'New Zealand Regions 1986–2001: Incomes', PSC Discussion Paper, University of Waikato, Hamilton.

Pool, I., Baxendine, S., Cochrane, B. and Lindop, J. (2005d) 'New Zealand Regions 1986–2001: Labour Market Aspects of Human Capital', PSC Discussion Paper, University of Waikato, Hamilton.

Pool, I., Baxendine, S., Cochrane, B. and Lindop, J. (2005e) 'New Zealand Regions 1986–2001: Population Structures', PSC Discussion Paper, University of Waikato, Hamilton.

Pool, I., Dharmalingam, A., Sceats, J. and Singley, S. (2007) *Studying the New Zealand Family: Analytical Frameworks, Concepts, Methodologies, Data-bases and Knowledge Bases*, AUP: www.auckland.ac.nz/uoa/aup/nzfamily/studyingthenzfamily.cfm

Pool, I., Dickson, J., Dharmalingam, A., Hillcoat-Nalletamby, S., Johnstone, K. and Roberts, H. (1999) *New Zealand's Contraceptive Revolutions*, Social Science Monograph Series, PSC, University of Waikato. Hamilton.

Pool, I., Sceats, J. E., Hooper, A., Huntsman, J., Plummer, E. and Prior, I. (1987). 'Social Change, Migration and Pregnancy Intervals', *Journal of Biosocial Science* 19, 1: 1–15.

Poot, J. and Siegers, J. (2001) 'The Macro-economics of Fertility in Small Open Economies: A Test of the Becker-Barro Model for the Netherlands and New Zealand', *Journal of Population Economics* 14: 1–28.

Population Division (1958) *Multilingual Demographic Dictionary*, United Nations, NY.

Potts, M. *et al.* (1977) *Abortion*, CUP.

Poulsen, M., Rowland, D. and Johnstone, R. (1975) 'Patterns of Maori Migration in New Zealand', in Kosinski, L. and Prothero, M. (eds) *People on the Move*, Methuen, London: 309–24.

Prinz, C., Lutz, W., Nowak, V. and Pfeiffer, C. (1998) *Standard Country Report: Austria*, ECE/FFS *op cit.*

Prinz, C. (1995) *Cohabiting, Married, or Single? Portraying, Analyzing, and Modeling New Living Arrangements in the Changing Societies of Europe*, Ashgate Publishing Company, Brookfield, VA.

Rainwater, L. and Smeeding, T. (1994) 'Le bien-être économique des enfants européens: une perspective comparative', *Population* 49, 6: 1437–50.

Raley, R. K. (1996) 'A Shortage of Marriageable Men? A Note on the Role of Cohabitation in Black-White Differences in Marriage Rates', *American Sociological Review* 61 (6): 973–83.

Registrar-General, England and Wales (various years) *Annual Report of . . . Births, Deaths and Marriages*, Eyre and Spottiswoode for Her Majesty's Stationery Office, London.

Registrar-General, Ireland (various years) *Annual Report of Births, Deaths and Marriages*, Alexander Thom for Her Majesty's Stationery Office, Dublin.

Registrar-General, Scotland (various years) *Births, Deaths and Marriages*, Murray and Gibb for Her Majesty's Stationery Office, Edinburgh.

Reid, A., Worth, H., Hughes, A., Saxton, P., Robinson, E. and Aspin, C. (1998) *Male Call/Waea Mai, Tane Ma Report No. 8: Men Who have Sex with Men and Women*, New Zealand AIDS Foundation, Auckland.

Reinken, J. and Blakey, V. (1976) *Family Growth Study*, Management Services Research Unit, Dept of Health, Wellington.

Rele, J. R. (1967) *Fertility Analysis Through Extension of Stable Population Technique*, Institute of International Studies, University of California, Berkeley.

Rendall, M. S. (1999) 'Entry or Exit? A Transition-Probability Approach to Explaining the Prevalence of Single Motherhood Among Black Women', *Demography* 36, 3: 369–76.

Richardson, R. (1995) *Making a Difference*, Shoal Bay Press, Christchurch.

Rindfuss, R. (1991) 'The Young Adult Years: Diversity, Structural Change and Fertility', *Demography* 28, 4: 493–512.

Rindfuss, R. and Brewster, K. (1996) 'Childrearing and Fertility', in Casterline, Lee and Foote (eds) *op cit*: 258–89.

Rindfuss, R. R. and VandenHeuvel, A. (1990) 'Cohabitation: A Precursor to Marriage or an Alternative to Being Single', *PDR* 16, 4: 703–26.

Ringen, S. (ed.) (1997) 'Great Britain', in Kammeman and Kahn (eds) *op cit*: 29–102.

Rochford, M. (1993) *A Profile of Sole Parents from the 1991 Census*, Research Report Series No. 15, Research Unit, Social Policy Agency, Wellington.

Rochford, M., Pawakapan, N., Martin, S. and Norris, M. (1992) *A Profile of Sole Parents from the 1986 Census*, Research Series 13, Research Section, Dept of Social Welfare, Wellington.

Romaniuc, A. (1984) *Fertility in Canada: From Baby-Boom to Baby-Bust*, Statistics Canada,

Ministry of Supply and Services, Ottawa.

Rosenberg, W. (1958) 'The Relationship between Size of Families and Incomes in New Zealand', *Economic Record* 34: 260–64.

Rosenfeld, R. (1996) 'Women's Work Histories', in Casterline, Lee and Foote (eds) *op cit*: 199–222.

Roth, M. C. (1980) 'New Zealand Family: Cornerstone of Colonisation', unpublished MA thesis, University of Auckland.

Roussel, L. (1993) 'Fertility and the Family' United Nations/Council of Europe (eds) *Proceedings European Population Conference*, UN/ECE, Geneva and NY: 35–110.

Rowland, D. (1971) 'Maori Migration to Auckland', *New Zealand Geographer* 27, 1: 21–37.

Rowland, D. (1973) 'Maoris and Pacific Islanders in Auckland', in Johnstone, R. J. (ed.) *Urbanisation in New Zealand*, Reed Education, Wellington: 253–96.

Royal Commission on the Decline of the Birth-rate and of the Mortality of Infants in New South Wales (Dr C. K. MacKellar, Chairman), New South Wales Parliamentary Papers 1904, Second Session: vol. 4, 791ff.

Ruggles, S. (1994) 'The Origins of African-American Family Structure', *American Sociological Review* 59, 1: 136–151.

Ruzicka, L. and Caldwell, J. (1977) *The End of Demographic Transition in Australia*, Australian Family Formation Project Monograph No. 5, ANU, Canberra.

Ryder, N. (1982) 'Fertility Trends: United States', in Ross (ed.) *op cit*: vol. 1, 286–92.

St John, S. and Craig, D. (2004) *Cut Price Kids: Does the 2004 'Working for Families' Budget Work for Children*, Child Poverty Action Group, Auckland.

Salvini, S. (2004) 'Low Italian Fertility: The Bonaccia (dead calm) of the Antilles', *Genus* LX, 1: 19–38.

Santi, L. (1987) 'Change in the Structure and Size of American Households: 1970 to 1985', *JMF* 49: 833–38.

Santi, L. (1988) 'The Demographic Context of Recent Change in the Structure of American Households', *Demography* 25: 509–19.

Santow, G. (1989) 'A Sequence of Events in Fertility and Family Formation', *International Population Conference*, New Delhi, Liege, International Union for the Scientific Study of Population: vol. 3, 217–29.

Santow, G. (1993) 'Coitus interruptus in the twentieth century', *PDR* 19(4): 767–92.

Santow, G. and Bracher, M. (1994) 'Change and continuity in the formation of first marital unions in Australia', *PS* 48: 475–496.

Santow, G., Bracher, M. and Guoth, N. (1988) *Household Composition in Australia*, Australian Family Project Working Paper No. 5, ANU, Canberra.

Sarantakos, S. (1984) *Living Together in Australia*, Longman Cheshire, Melbourne.

Saxton, P., Dickson, N., Hughes, A. and Paul, C. (2002). *GAPSS 2002: Findings from the Gay Auckland Periodic Sex Survey*, Auckland New Zealand AIDS Foundation.

Scanzoni, J. (1972) *Sexual Bargaining*, Prentice Hall, Englewood Cliffs, NJ.

Sceats (Pool) J. (1978) 'Family Building in a Canadian City: An Analysis of the Timing and Spacing of Pregnancies', *PS* 32, 3: 585–92.

Sceats, J. (1981) 'Family Formation in Canada and New Zealand: An Analysis of the Timing and Spacing of Pregnancies', *NZPR* 7, 3: 28–34.

Sceats, J. (1988a) 'Implications of Changes in New Zealand Family Formation and Household Structure', in Crothers, C. and Bedford, R. (eds) *The Business of Population*, New Zealand Demographic Society, Wellington.

Sceats, J. (1988b) 'Abortion in a Low Fertility Country: New Zealand, a Case Study', unpublished PhD thesis, University of London.

Sceats, J. (1999) 'Cohort Patterns and Trends in the Timing and Spacing of Births', in Pool, I. and Johnstone, K. (eds) *op cit*: 26–34.

Sceats, J. (2002) 'Report on a Qualitative Interview Study of Children, Child-rearing and the Family in New Zealand', prepared for the National Institute of Population and Social Security, Tokyo.

Sceats, J. (2003) 'The Impossible Dream: Motherhood and a Career?' *NZPR*, Special Issue 29, 1: 155–171.

Sceats, J. (2006) 'Fertility and Reproductive Polarisation: The Perspective from within the Family', paper presented to Sub-Replacement Fertility: Is this an Issue for New Zealand

Seminar, IPS, Victoria University, Wellington, October: www.ips.ac.nz.

Sceats, J. and Kukutai, T. (2005) 'The Hand that rocked the Cradle ..', Invited Plenary Paper, Janus Convention, June, Wellington (published 2006 in Williams, D. (ed) *Looking Back: Moving Forward*, Janus Trust/Fraser Books, Masterton).

Sceats, J. and Parr, A. (1995). 'Induced Abortion: National Trends and a Regional Perspective', paper presented to Abortion Providers Conference, Wellington, June, published as a Discussion Paper, Health and Disability Analysis Unit, Midland Health, Hamilton.

Sceats, J. and Pool, I. (1978) *Contraception and Health Care Among Young Canadian Women*, Dept of Sociology and Anthropology, Carleton University, Ottawa.

Sceats, J. and Pool, I. (1985a) 'Fertility Regulation', in ESCAP *op cit*: vol. 1, 178–192.

Sceats, J. and Pool, I. (1985b) 'Perinatal, Infant and Childhood Mortality', in ESCAP *op cit*: vol. 1, 243–68.

Sceats, J., Johnstone, K., Harris, S., Clarke, L. and Kamano, S. (2003) 'Policy and Practice in Balancing Work and Family: Results of a Study of Mothers of Young Children in New Zealand, Australia And Britain', paper presented at the Australian Institute for Family Studies Conference, Melbourne, February.

Schoeni, R. F. (1998) 'Reassessing the Decline in Parent–Child Old-Age Co-residence During the Twentieth Century', *Demography* 35, 3: 307–13.

Schulze, H.-J. and Tyrell, H. (2002) 'What happened to the European Family in the 1980s? The Polarisation between the Family and other Forms of Private Life', in Kaufmann, F.-X. *et al.* (eds) *Family Life and Family Policies in Europe*, 2 vols, OUP: vol. 2, 60–119.

Seabright, P. (2002) 'Who is the Villain? Review of "The Future of Success" by Robert Reich', *London Review of Books*, 22 August: 24–25.

Seuffert, N. (2003) 'Shaping the Modern Nation: Colonial Marriage Law, Polygamy and Concubinage in Aotearoa New Zealand', *Law Text Culture*: 186–223.

Shaw, L. (2000) 'A Woman's Place?' in Brookes (ed.) *op cit*: 165–80.

Shaw-Taylor, L. (2005) 'Family Farms and Capitalist Farms in Mid-19th Century England', *Agricultural History Review* 53, II: 158–91.

Shipley, J. (with Upton, S., Smith, L. and Luxton, J.) (1991) *Social Assistance, Welfare That Works: A Statement of Government Policy on Social Assistance*, Ministry of Social Welfare, Wellington.

Shirley, I., Koopman-Boyden, P., Pool, I. and St John, S. (2000) 'New Zealand', in Kammerman and Kahn *op cit*: 207–304.

Short, S., Goldscheider, F. and Torr, B. (2006) 'Less Help for the Mother: The Decline in Co-residential Female Support for the Mothers of Young Children, 1880–2000', *Demography*, 43, 4: 617–29.

Shyrock, H. and Siegel, J. (with Associates) (1976) *The Methods and Materials of Demography*, Academic Press, NY.

Sinclair, H. (1944) *Population: New Zealand's Problem*, Gordon and Gotch, Dunedin.

Sinclair, K. (1959) *A History of New Zealand*, Penguin, Harmondsworth, Middlesex.

Singley, S. and Callister, P. (2003a) 'Jobless Households in New Zealand, the United States and United Kingdom', *NZPR*, Special Issue 29, 1: 171–98.

Singley, S. and Callister, P. (2003b) 'Work Poor or Working Poor? A Comparative Perspective on New Zealand's Jobless Households', *SPJNZ* 20: 134–55.

Singley, S. G. and Callister, P. (2004) 'Polarisation of employment, 1986–2002: New Zealand in the International Context', Working Paper 06/04, July, Ministry of Social Development, Wellington.

Sissons, J., Wi Hongi, W. and Hohepa, P. (1987) *The Puriri Trees are Laughing: A Political History of the Ngapuhi in the Inland Bay of Islands*, Polynesian Society, Auckland.

Smith, A. and Taylor, N. (eds) (1996) *Supporting Children and Parents through Family Changes*, University of Otago Press, Dunedin.

Smith, H. L., Morgan, S. P. and Koropeckyj-Cox, T. (1996) 'A Decomposition of Trends in the Nonmarital Fertility Ratios of Blacks and Whites in the United States', *Demography* 33, 2: 141–151.

Smith, P. Mein (2002) 'Blood, Birth, Babies, Bodies', *Austalian Feminist Studies*, 17: 305–23.

Smock, P. J. and Manning, W. D. (1997) 'Cohabiting Partners' Economic Circumstances and Marriage', *Demography* 34, 3: 331–41.

Social Monitoring Group (SMG) (1985) *From Birth to Death: First Report of the SMG*, New Zealand Planning Council (NZPC), Wellington.

Social Monitoring Group (1989) *From Birth to Death II: The Second Overview Report*, NZPC, Wellington.

Society for Research on Women (1972) *Urban Women*, SRW, Johnsonville.

Sommestad, L. (1998) 'Welfare State Attitudes to the Male Breadwinning System: The United States and Sweden in Comparative Perspective', in Janssens, A. (ed.) *The Rise and Decline of the Male Breadwinner Family?* International Review of Social History, Supplement 5, CUP: 153–74.

South, S. J. and Crowder, K. D. (1999) 'Neighborhood Effects on Family Formation: Concentrated Poverty and Beyond', *American Sociological Review* 64, 1: 113–32.

Spanier, G. B. (1983) 'Married and Unmarried Cohabitation in the United States, 1980', *JMF* 45, 2: 277–88.

Spanier, G. B. (1985) 'Cohabitation in the 1980s: Recent Changes in the United States', in Davis, K. (ed.), *Contemporary Marriage: Comparative Perspectives on a Changing Institution*, Russell Sage Foundation, NY: 91–111.

Statistics New Zealand, *see also* Hockey, Khawaja.

Statistics New Zealand (1994) *New Zealand Now: Families*, Wellington.

Statistics New Zealand (1995) *New Zealand Then and Now: Asian New Zealanders*, Wellington.

Statistics New Zealand (1998) *1996 Census of Population and Dwellings: Families and Households*, Wellington, New Zealand.

Statistics New Zealand (2001): *Socio-Economic Factors and the Fertility of New Zealand Women: A Study of Data from the 1996 Census*, Wellington.

Statistics New Zealand (2004) *Fertility of New Zealand Women by Ethnicity*, based on the . . . 1996 Census, Wellington.

Statistics New Zealand (2005) *Focusing on Women*, a special report prepared as a background paper to the Janus conference *op cit*, Wellington.

Stenhouse, J. (2005) 'Galileo's Dilemma: Science and Religion', Radio New Zealand Lecture Series, in association with the Royal Society of New Zealand.

Stephens, R. (2000) 'Poverty and Employment: A Comparison of Policy and Outcomes for Single Mothers between the United States and New Zealand', *Institute for Policy Studies Research Papers 00/03*, Johns Hopkins University, Baltimore.

Stephens, R., Waldegrave, C. and Frater, P. (1995) 'Measuring Poverty in New Zealand', *SPJNZ* 5: 88–112.

Sutch, W. (1966) *The Quest for Security in New Zealand, 1840–1966*, OUP, Wellington.

Swain, D. (1985) 'The Transition to Parenthood in New Zealand and a Developmental Conceptual Framework for the Study of Family Change', 2 vols, unpublished PhD thesis, Dept of Sociology, University of Waikato, Hamilton.

Szreter, S. (1999) 'Falling Fertilities and Changing Sexualities in Europe since c. 1850: A Comparative Survey of National Demographic Patterns', in Eder, F. Z., Hall, L. A. and Hekma, G. (eds) *Sexual Cultures in Europe: Themes in Sexuality*, University Press, Manchester: 159–94.

Szreter, S. (2002 edition) *Fertility, Class and Gender in Britain, 1860–1940*, CUP.

Tanfer, K. (1987) 'Patterns of Premarital Cohabitation among Never-Married Women in the United States', *JMF* 49: 483–98.

Teachman, J., Thomas, J. and Paasch, K. (1991) 'Legal Status and the Stability of Coresidential Unions', *Demography* 28: 571–86.

Tennant, M. (2000) 'The Decay of Home Life: The Home in Early Welfare Discourses', in Brookes (ed.) *op cit*: 24–40.

Tepperman, L. and McDaniel, S. (2000) *Close Relations: An Introduction to the Sociology of Families*, Prentice Hall, Toronto.

Testa, M., Astone, N. M., Krogh, M. and Neckerman, K. M. (1989) 'Employment and Marriage among Inner-City Fathers', *Annals of the American Academy of Political and Social Science* 501: 79–91.

Testa, M and Grilli, L (2006) "L'influence des differences de fecondite dans les regions eurpeennes sur la taille ideale de la famille", *Population*, 61,1-2: 107-38

Therborn, G. (2000) 'Globalization: Dimensions, Historical Waves, Regional Effects,

Normative Governance', *International Sociology* 15: 151–79.

Thompson, B. (1985) 'Industrial Structure of the Labour Force', in ESCAP *op cit*: vol. 2, 114–38.

Thomson, D. (1998) *A World Without Welfare: New Zealand's Colonial Experiment*, AUP, with Bridget Williams Books.

Thomson, D. (2006) 'Marriage and Family on the Colonial Frontier', in Ballantyne, T. and Moloughney, B. (eds) *Disputed Histories: Imagining New Zealand's Pasts*, University of Otago Press, Dunedin: 119–41.

Thorns, D. (1992) *Fragmentising Societies*, Routledge, London.

Thornton, A. (1988) 'Cohabitation and Marriage in the 1980s', *Demography* 25: 497–508.

Thornton, A. (1989) 'Changing Attitudes toward Family Issues', *JMF* 51: 873–93.

Thornton, A., Axinn, W. G. and Hill, D. H. (1992) 'Reciprocal Effects of Religiosity, Cohabitation, and Marriage', *AJS* 98: 628–51.

Tienda, M. and Angel, R. (1982) 'Headship and Household Composition Among Blacks, Hispanics, and Other Whites', *Social Forces* 61: 508–31.

Tietze, C. (1981) *Abortion: A World View*, 4th ed., The Population Council, New York.

Tiong, F. (1988) 'Towards a Better Measurement of 19th Century New Zealand Non-Maori Fertility, 1878–1921', unpublished M.Soc.Sci. thesis, University of Waikato.

Toulemon, L. and de Guibert-Lantoine, C. (1998) *Standard Country Report: France*, ECE/FFS *op cit*.

Toynbee, C. (1995) *Her Work and His: Family Kin and Community in New Zealand 1900–1930*, VUP, Wellington.

Toynbee, C. (2000) 'Kinship and Decision to Migrate: The Experience of Scots Migrants to New Zealand', *NZPR* 26, 1: 23–44.

Trlin, A. and Perry, P. (1981) *Manawatu Family Growth Study*, Management Services Research Unit, Dept of Health, Wellington.

Trlin, A. and Ruzicka, L. (1977) 'Non-Marital Pregnancies and Ex-Nuptial Births in New Zealand', *Journal of Bio-Social Science* 9, 2: 163–74.

Turbott, H. B. (1935) *Tuberculosis in the Maori, East Coast, New Zealand*, Govt Printer, Wellington.

Turcotte, P. (1999) 'Recent Family Trends and the Second Demographic Transition in Canada', paper presented at Domestic Partnerships Conference, Kingston, Ontario, October.

United Nations (2001) *Replacement Migration: Is it a Solution to Declining and Ageing Populations?* Dept of Economic and Social Affairs, Population Division, NY.

United Nations (various years) *Population Estimates and Projections*, Economic and Social Affairs, Population Division, NY.

United Nations (various years) *World Population Prospects*, Economic and Social Affairs, Population Division, NY.

United Nations (ECE) and Council of Europe (1994) *European Population Conference, Proceedings*, vol. 2, UN, NY and Geneva.

Vallin, J. (2002) 'The End of the Demographic Transition: Relief or Concern?', *PDR* 28, 1: 105–20.

van de Kaa, D. (1987) 'Europe's Second Demographic Transition', *Population Bulletin* 42, 1, Population Reference Bureau, Washington, DC.

van de Kaa, D. (1988) *The Second Transition Revisited: Theories and Expectations*, Werkstukken Netherlands Institute for Advanced Study in the Social Sciences, Wassenaar.

van de Kaa, D. (2003) 'Second Demographic Transition', in Demeny, P. and McNicoll, G. (eds) *Encyclopaedia of Population*, *op cit*: vol. 2, 872–75.

van de Kaa, D. (2004) 'The True Commonality: In Reflexive Modern Societies Fertility is a Derivative: Discusssion of Paper "Explanations of the Fertility Crisis in Modern Societies: a Search for Commonalities", by Caldwell and Schindlmayr 2003 [*op cit*]', *PS* 58, 1: 77–80.

van Nimwegen, N., Blommesteijn, M., Moors, H. and Beets, J. (2002) 'Late Motherhood in the Netherlands: Current Trends, Attitudes and Policies', *Genus* LVIII, 2: 9–34.

Vasil, R. and Hoon, H.-K. (1996) *New Zealanders of Asian Origin*, IPS, Victoria University, Wellington.

Vienna Yearbook of Population, 2006, Austrian Academy of Sciences.

Villeneuve-Gokalp, C. (1990) 'Du mariage aux unions sans papier: histoire récente des transformations conjugales', *Population* 45, 2: 265–98.

Villeneuve-Gokalp, C. (1997) 'Vivre en couple chacun chez soi', *Population* 52: 1059–82.

Villeneuve-Gokalp, C. (1999) 'La double famille des enfants des parents séparés', *Population* 54, 1: 9–36.

Vosburgh (Gilson), M. (1978) *The New Zealand Family and Social Change: A Trend Analysis*, Occasional Paper in Sociology and Social Welfare, Victoria University, Wellington.

Wachter, K. W. (1997) 'Kinship Resources for the Elderly', *Philosophical Transactions of the Royal Society, London* B., 352: 1811–17.

Waring, M. (1988) *Counting for Nothing: What Men Value and What Women are Worth*, Bridget Williams Books, Wellington.

Watson, M. (1985) 'Urbanization', in ESCAP *op cit*: vol. 1, 118–51.

Weinick, R. M. (1995) 'Sharing a Home: The Experiences of American Women and Their Parents over the Twentieth Century', *Demography* 32(2): 281–97.

Wilson, W. J. (1987) *The Truly Disadvantaged: The Inner City, the Underclass and Public Policy*, University of Chicago Press, IL.

Wilson, W. J. and Neckerman, K. (1987) 'Poverty and Family Structure: The Widening Gap between Evidence and Public Policy Issues', in Wilson (ed.) *op cit*: 63–92.

Winkler, A. E. (1993) 'The Living Arrangements of Single Mothers with Dependent Children: An Added Perspective', *American Journal of Economics and Sociology* 52, 1: 1–18.

Wojkiewicz, R. A., McLanahan, S. S. and Garfinkel, I. (1990) 'The Growth of Families Headed by Women: 1950–1980', *Demography* 27: 19–30.

Woods, R. (1996) 'The Population of Britain in the 19th century', in Anderson, M. (ed.) *British Population History: From the Black Death to the Present Day*, CUP: 281–358.

Woods, R. (2000) *The Demography of Victorian England and Wales*, CUP.

World Bank (1994) *Averting the Old Age Crisis*, Word Bank Policy Research Report, OUP.

Worth, H., Reid, A., Saxton, P., Hughes, A. and Segedin, R. (1997) *Male Call/Waea Mai, Tane Ma Report No. 2: Men in Relationships with Men*, New Zealand AIDS Foundation, Auckland.

Wrigley, E. A., Davies, R., Oeppen, J. and Schofield, R. (1997) *English Population History from Family Reconstitution, 1580–1837*, CUP.

Wrigley, T. (1981) 'Marriage, Fertility and Population Growth in 18th Century England', in Outhwaite, R. B. (ed.) *Studies in the Social History of Marriage*, Europa Publications, London: 137–85.

Wu, Z. (1999) *Standard Country Report: Canada*, ECE/FFS *op cit*.

Young, C. (1987) *Young People Leaving Home in Australia: The Trend Towards Independence*, Australian Family Formation Project Monograph No. 9, Australian Institute of Family Studies, Melbourne.

Young, C. (1991) 'Changes in the Demographic Behaviour of Migrants in Australia and the Transition between Generations', *PS* 45: 67–89.

Young, J. (1997) 'Religious Change in New Zealand: A Population Perspective', unpublished M.Soc.Sci. thesis, University of Waikato, Hamilton.

Zodgekar, A. (1980) 'The Fertility Transition in the Non-Maori Population of New Zealand', *Journal of Biosocial Science* 12: 165–78.

Zuanna, G. dalla (2004) 'Few Children in Strong Families: Values and Low Fertility in Italy', *Genus* LX, 1: 39–70.

Zuanna, G. dalla, Atoh, M., Castiglioni, M. and Kojima, K. (1998) 'Late Marriage among Young People: the Case of Italy and Japan', *Genus* LIV, 3–4: 187–232.

UNPUBLISHED DATA

Canada:	Health Statistics Division, Statistics Canada.
European:	European Demographic Observatory.
Japan:	Nihon University, Population Research Institute (NUPRI).
Netherlands:	Statistics Netherlands, Voorburg/Beerlen 9/16/2002.
United Kingdom:	National Statistics, United Kingdom.
United States:	Centers for Disease Control and Prevention, United States.

INDEX